Lecture Notes in Computer

Commenced Publication in 1973
Founding and Former Series Editors:
Gerhard Goos, Juris Hartmanis, and Jan van Leeuwen

Roberto Giacobazzi (Ed.)

Static Analysis

11th International Symposium, SAS 2004
Verona, Italy, August 26-28, 2004
Proceedings

 Springer

Volume Editor

Roberto Giacobazzi
Università degli Studi di Verona, Dipartimento di Informatica
Strada Le Grazie 15, 37134 Verona, Italy
E-mail: roberto.giacobazzi@univr.it

Library of Congress Control Number: 2004109776

CR Subject Classification (1998): D.3.2-3, F.3.1-2, D.2.8, F.4.2, D.1

ISSN 0302-9743
ISBN 3-540-22791-1 Springer Berlin Heidelberg New York

Springer is a part of Springer Science+Business Media

springeronline.com

© Springer-Verlag Berlin Heidelberg 2004
Printed in Germany

Typesetting: Camera-ready by author, data conversion by Olgun Computergrafik
Printed on acid-free paper   SPIN: 11310426   06/3142   5 4 3 2 1 0

Preface

Static analysis is a research area aimed at developing principles and tools for verification, certification, semantics-based manipulation, and high-performance implementation of programming languages and systems. The series of Static Analysis symposia has served as the primary venue for presentation and discussion of theoretical, practical, and application advances in the area.

This volume contains the papers accepted for presentation at the 11th International Static Analysis Symposium (SAS 2004), which was held August 26–28 in Verona, Italy. In response to the call for papers, 63 contributions were submitted from 20 different countries. Following on-line discussions, the Program Committee met in Verona on May 06, and selected 23 papers, basing this choice on their scientific quality, originality, and relevance to the symposium. Each paper was reviewed by at least 3 PC members or external referees. In addition to the contributed papers, this volume includes contributions by outstanding invited speakers: a full invited paper by Thomas Henzinger (University of Califorina at Berkeley), and abstracts of the talks given by the other invited speakers, Sheila McIlraith (University of Toronto), Ehud Shapiro (Weizmann Institute) and Yannis Smaragdakis (Georgia Institute of Technology).

On the behalf of the Program Committee, the Program Chair would like to thank all the authors who submitted papers and all external referees for their careful work in the reviewing process. The Program Chair would like to thank in particular Samir Genaim, who did an invaluable, excellent job in organizing the Program Committee meeting and the structure of this volume. We would like to express our gratitude to the *Dipartimento di Informatica* and to the *Università degli Studi di Verona*, in particular to Prof. Elio Mosele (president of the university), who handled the logistical arrangements and provided financial support for organizing this event.

SAS 2004 was held concurrently with *LOPSTR 2004, International Symposium on Logic-Based Program Synthesis and Transformation*; *PEPM 2004, ACM SIGPLAN Symposium on Partial Evaluation and Program Manipulation*; and *PPDP 2004, ACM SIGPLAN International Conference on Principles and Practice of Declarative Programming*. There were also several workshops in the area of programming languages. We would like to thank Sandro Etalle (LOPSTR PC Chair), Nevin Heintze and Peter Sestoft (PEPM PC Chairs), Eugenio Moggi (PPDP General Chair), Fausto Spoto (Organizing Chair), and David Warren (PPDP PC Chair) for their help in the organization aspects. Special thanks to all the members of the Organizing Committee who worked with enthusiasm in order to make this event possible and to ENDES, specifically to Anna Chiara Caputo, for the great job she did in the local organization.

Verona, June 2004   Roberto Giacobazzi

Organization

Program Committee

Thomas Ball	Microsoft, USA
Radhia Cousot	Ècole Polytechnique, France
Roberto Giacobazzi (Chair)	Università di Verona, Italy
Chris Hankin	Imperial College London, UK
Thomas Jensen	IRISA, France
Jens Knoop	Technische Universität Wien, Austria
Giorgio Levi	Università di Pisa, Italy
Laurent Mauborgne	École Normale Supérieure, France
Andreas Podelski	Max-Planck-Institut für Informatik, Germany
German Puebla	Technical University of Madrid, Spain
Ganesan Ramalingam	IBM, USA
Francesco Ranzato	Università di Padova, Italy
Martin Rinard	Massachusetts Institute of Technology, USA
Andrei Sabelfeld	Chalmers University of Technology, Sweden
Mary Lou Soffa	University of Pittsburgh, USA
Harald Søndergaard	University of Melbourne, Australia
Reinhard Wilhelm	Universität des Saarlandes, Germany

Steering Committee

Patrick Cousot	École Normale Supérieure, France
Gilberto Filé	Università di Padova, Italy
David Schmidt	Kansas State University, USA

Organizing Committee

Mila Dalla Preda
Samir Genaim
Isabella Mastroeni
Massimo Merro
Giovanni Scardoni
Fausto Spoto
Damiano Zanardini

Referees

Elvira Albert
M. Anton Ertl
Roberto Bagnara
Roberto Barbuti
Joerg Bauer
Michele Bugliesi
V.C. Sreedhar
Paul Caspi
Patrick Cousot
Alexandru D. Salcianu
Mila Dalla Preda
Ferruccio Damiani
Bjorn De Sutter
Bjoern Decker
Pierpaolo Degano
Nurit Dor
Manuel Fahndrich
Jérôme Feret
Gilberto Filé
Steve Fink
Bernd Finkbeiner
Cormac Flanagan
Maurizio Gabbrielli
Samir Genaim
Roberta Gori
David Grove
Daniel Hedin
Dan Hirsch
Charles Hymans
Daniel Kaestner
John Kodumal
Andreas Krall
Viktor Kuncak
Kung-Kiu Lau
Francesca Levi
Donglin Liang
Andrea Maggiolo Schettini
Isabella Mastroeni
Ken McMillan

Massimo Merro
Antoine Miné
Anders Moller
David Monniaux
Carlo Montangero
Damen Mssé
Markus Müller-Olm
Ulrich Neumerkel
Jens Palsberg
Filippo Portera
Franz Puntigam
Xavier Rival
Enric Rodríguez-Carbonell
Sabina Rossi
Salvatore Ruggieri
Andrey Rybalchenko
Rene Rydhof Hansen
Oliver Rüthing
Mooly Sagiv
Giovanni Scardoni
Dave Schmidt
Bernhard Scholz
Markus Schordan
Francesca Scozzari
Clara Segura
Helmut Seidl
Alexander Serebrenik
Vincent Simonet
Fabio Somenzi
Fausto Spoto
Zhendong Su
Francesco Tapparo
Ashish Tiwari
Thomas Wies
Sebastian Winkel
Zhe Yang
Enea Zaffanella
Damiano Zanardini
Andreas Zeller

Table of Contents

Pointer Analysis

Abstract Interpretation and Algorithms

Shape Analysis

Abstract Domain and Data Structures

Shape Analysis and Logic

Termination Analysis

Author Index

Injecting Life with Computers

Ehud Shapiro

Department of Computer Science and Applied Mathematics and
Department of Biological Chemistry
Weizmann Institute of Science, Rehovot 76100, Israel

Abstract. Although electronic computers are the only "computer species" we are accustomed to, the mathematical notion of a programmable computer has nothing to do with wires and logic gates. In fact, Alan Turing's notional computer, which marked in 1936 the birth of modern computer science and still stands at its heart, has greater similarity to natural biomolecular machines such as the ribosome and polymerases than to electronic computers. Recently, a new "computer species" made of biological molecules has emerged. These simple molecular computers inspired by the Turing machine, of which a trillion can fit into a microliter, do not compete with electronic computers in solving complex computational problems; their potential lies elsewhere. Their molecular scale and their ability to interact directly with the biochemical environment in which they operate suggest that in the future they may be the basis of a new kind of "smart drugs": molecular devices equipped with the medical knowledge to perform disease diagnosis and therapy inside the living body. They would detect and diagnose molecular disease symptoms and, when necessary, administer the requisite drug molecules to the cell, tissue or organ in which they operate. In the talk we review this new research direction and report on preliminary steps carried out in our lab towards realizing its vision.

References

1. Benenson Y., Paz-Elitzur T., Adar R., Keinan E, Livneh Z. and Shapiro E. Programmable computing machine made of biomolecules. *Nature*, 414, 430-434, 2001.
2. Benenson Y., Adar R., Paz-Elitzur T., Livneh Z., and Shapiro E. DNA molecule provides a computing machine with both data and fuel. *PNAS*, 100, 2191-2196, 2003.
3. Adar R., Benenson Y., Linshiz G., Rozner A., Tishby N. and Shapiro E. Stochastic computing with biomolecular automata. *PNAS*, in press, 2004.
4. Benenson Y., Gil B., Ben-Dor U., Adar R., and Shapiro E. An autonomous molecular computer for logical control of gene expression *Nature*, 429, 423-429, 2004. Verlag, 2002.

R. Giacobazzi (Ed.): SAS 2004, LNCS 3148, p. 1, 2004.

The BLAST Query Language
for Software Verification[*]

Dirk Beyer[1], Adam J. Chlipala[2], Thomas A. Henzinger[1,2],
Ranjit Jhala[2], and Rupak Majumdar[3]

[1] EPFL, Switzerland
[2] University of California, Berkeley
[3] University of California, Los Angeles

Abstract. BLAST is an automatic verification tool for checking temporal safety properties of C programs. BLAST is based on lazy predicate abstraction driven by interpolation-based predicate discovery. In this paper, we present the BLAST specification language. The language specifies program properties at two levels of precision. At the lower level, monitor automata are used to specify temporal safety properties of program executions (traces). At the higher level, relational reachability queries over program locations are used to combine lower-level trace properties. The two-level specification language can be used to break down a verification task into several independent calls of the model-checking engine. In this way, each call to the model checker may have to analyze only part of the program, or part of the specification, and may thus succeed in a reduction of the number of predicates needed for the analysis. In addition, the two-level specification language provides a means for structuring and maintaining specifications.

1 Introduction

BLAST, the Berkeley Lazy Abstraction Software verification Tool, is a fully automatic engine for software model checking [11]. BLAST uses counterexample-guided predicate abstraction refinement to verify temporal safety properties of C programs. The tool incrementally constructs an abstract reachability tree (ART) whose nodes are labeled with program locations and truth values of predicates. If a path that violates the desired safety property is found in the ART, but is not a feasible path of the program, then new predicate information is added to the ART in order to rule out the spurious error path. The new predicate information is added on-demand and locally, following the twin paradigms of *lazy abstraction* [11] and *interpolation-based predicate discovery* [8]. The procedure stops when either a genuine error path is found, or the current ART represents a proof of program correctness [9].

In this paper we present the BLAST input language for specifying program-verification tasks. The BLAST specification language consists of two levels. On

---

[*] This research was supported in part by the NSF grants CCR-0085949, CCR-0234690, and ITR-0326577.

R. Giacobazzi (Ed.): SAS 2004, LNCS 3148, pp. 2–18, 2004.

the lower level, *observer automata* are defined to monitor the program execution and decide whether a safety property is violated. Observer automata can be infinite-state and can track the program state, including the values of program variables and type-state information associated with individual data objects. On the higher level, *relational queries* over program locations are defined which may specify both structural program properties (e.g., the existence of a syntactic path between two locations) and semantic program properties (e.g., the existence of a feasible path between two locations). The evaluation of a semantic property invokes the BLAST model-checking engine. A semantic property may also refer to an observer automaton, thus combining the two levels of specification.

Consider the following example. If we change the definition of a variable in a program, we have to review all subsequent read accesses to that variable. Using static analysis we can find all statements that use the variable, but the resulting set is often imprecise (e.g., it may include dead code) because of the path-insensitive nature of the analysis. Model checking can avoid this imprecision. In addition, using an observer automaton, we can ensure that we compute only those statements subsequent to the variable definition which (1) use the variable and (2) are not preceded by a redefinition of the variable. The two specification levels allow the natural expression of such a query: on the higher level, we specify the location-based reachability property between definition and use locations, and at the lower level, we specify the desired temporal property by a monitor automaton that watches out for redefinitions of the variable. The resulting query asks the model checker for the set of definition-use pairs of program locations that are connected by feasible paths along which no redefinitions occur.

The BLAST specification language provides a convenient user interface: it keeps specifications separate from the program code and makes the model checker easier to use for non-experts, as no manual program annotations with specification code (such as assertions) are required. On one hand it is useful to orthogonalize concerns by separating program properties from the source code, and keeping them separated during development, in order to make it easier to understand and maintain both the program and the specification [13]. On the other hand it is preferable for the programmer to specify program properties in a language that is similar to the programming language. We therefore use as much as possible C-like syntax in the specification language. The states of observer automata are defined using C type and variable declarations, and the automaton transitions are defined using C code. The query language is an imperative scripting language whose expressions specify first-order relational constraints on program locations.

The two-level specification structure provides two further benefits. First, such structured specifications are easy to read, compose, and revise. The relational query language allows the programmer to treat the program as a database of facts, which can be queried by the analysis engine. Moreover, individual parts of a composite query can be checked incrementally when the program changes, as in regression testing [10]. Second, the high-level query language can be used to break down a verification task into several independent model-checking problems, each checking a low-level trace property. Since the number of predicates in the ART is the main source of complexity for the model-checking procedure, the decomposition of a verification task into several independent subtasks, each involving only a part of the program and/or a part of the specification, can greatly contribute to the scalability of the verification process [14, 17]. A simple instance of this occurs if a specification consists of a conjunction of several properties that can be model checked independently. The relational query engine allows the compact definition of such proof-decomposition strategies.

For a more instructive example, suppose that we wish to check that there is no feasible path from a program location ℓ_0 to a program location ℓ_2, and that all syntactic paths from ℓ_0 to ℓ_2 go through location ℓ_1. Then we may decompose the verification task by guessing an intermediate predicate p_1 and checking, independently, the following two simpler properties: (1) there is no feasible path from ℓ_0 to ℓ_1 such that p_1 is false at the end of the path (at ℓ_1), and (2) there is no feasible path from ℓ_1 to ℓ_2 such that p_1 is true at the beginning of the path (at ℓ_1). Both proof obligations (1) and (2) may be much simpler to model check, with fewer predicates needed, than the original verification task. Moreover, each of the two proof obligations can be specified as a reachability query over locations together with an observer automaton that specifies the final (resp. initial) condition p_1.

The paper is organized as follows. In Section 2, we define the (lower-level) language for specifying trace properties through observer automata. In Section 3, we define the (higher-level) language for specifying location properties through relational queries. In Section 4, we give several sample specifications, and in Section 5, we briefly describe how the query processing is implemented in BLAST.

Related Work. Automata are often used to specify temporal safety properties, because they provide a convenient, succinct notation and are often easier to understand than formulas of temporal logic. For example, SLIC [2] specifications are used in the SLAM project [1] to generate C code for model checking. However, SLIC does not support type-state properties and is limited to the specification of interfaces, because it monitors only function calls and returns. Metal [7] and MOPS [4] allow more general pattern languages, but the (finite) state of the automaton must be explicitly enumerated. Temporal-logic specifications, often enriched with syntactic sugar ("patterns"), are used in Bandera [5] and Feaver [12]. Type-state verification [16] is an important concept for ensuring the reliability of software, but the generally used assumption in this field is to consider all paths of a program as feasible. Relational algebra has been applied to analyze the structure of large programs [3] and in dynamic analysis [6]. Also the decomposition of verification tasks has been recognized as a key issue and strategy-definition languages have been proposed [14, 17]. However, the use of a relational query language to group queries and decompose proof obligations in a model-checking environment seems novel.

2   Trace Properties: Observer Automata

Trace properties are expressed using *observer automata*. These provide a way to specify temporal safety properties of C programs based on syntactic pattern matching of C code. An observer automaton consists of a collection of syntactic patterns that, when matched against the current execution point of the observed program, trigger transitions in the observer. Rather than being limited to a finite number of states, the observer may have global variables of any C type, and it may track type-state information associated with the program variables. The observer transitions are also specified in C syntax; they may read program variables and both read and write observer variables.

2.1   Syntax

The definition of an observer automaton consists of a set of declarations, each defining an observer variable, a type state, an initial condition, a final condition, or an event. Figure 1 gives the grammar for specifying observer automata.

```
Observer:      DeclSeq
DeclSeq:       Declaration | DeclSeq Declaration
Declaration:   'GLOBAL' CVarDef
             | 'SHADOW' CTypeName '{' CFieldSeq '}'
             | 'INITIAL' '{' CExpression '}'
             | 'FINAL' '{' CExpression '}'
             | 'EVENT' '{'
                  Temporal
                  'PATTERN' '{' Pattern '}'
                  Assertion
                  Action
               '}'
Temporal:      'BEFORE' | 'AFTER' | empty
Pattern:       ParamCStmt | ParamCStmt 'AT' LocDesc
Assertion:     'ASSERT' '{' CExpression '}' | empty
Action:        'ACTION' '{' CStatementSeq '}' | empty
```

Fig. 1. The grammar for the observer specification language.

Observer Variables. The control state of an observer automaton consists of a global part and a per-object part. The global part of the observer state is determined by a set of typed, global observer variables. Each observer variable may have any C type, and is declared following the keyword GLOBAL, where the nonterminal CVarDef stands for any C variable declaration. For example, in the case of a specification that restricts the number of calls to a certain function, an observer variable numCalls of type int might be used to track the number of calls made: "GLOBAL int numCalls;".

Type States. The keyword SHADOW allows the programmer to define additional control state of the observer automaton on a per-object basis. For this purpose, each distinct C type CTypeName which occurs in the program may have a type state declared in the specification. The type-state information is declared by the nonterminal CFieldSeq, which stands for any sequence of field definitions for a C structure. These fields are then added as type state to every program variable of type CTypeName. For example, in the case that the program uses a type stack to declare stacks, the following type state may be used to track the size of each program variable of type stack: "SHADOW stack {int size;}". Then, during verification, the type stack is replaced by a new structure type with the additional field size.

Initial and Final Conditions. The initial states of the observer automaton are defined by initial conditions. Each initial condition is declared following the keyword INITIAL as a boolean expression. The nonterminal CExpression is a (side-effect free) C expression that may refer to observer variables, but also to global program variables and associated type-state information. This allows us to encode a precondition when starting the verification process. We call the conjunction of all initial conditions the *precondition* of the observer automaton. If no initial condition is specified, then the precondition is true. Final conditions are just like initial conditions, and their conjunction is called the *postcondition* of the observer automaton. The postcondition is used to check the program and observer states after any finite trace.

Events. The transitions of the observer automaton are defined by events. Each event observes all program steps and, if a match is obtained, specifies how the state of the observer (global variables and type states) changes. The keyword EVENT is followed by up to four parts: a temporal qualifier, a pattern, an assertion, and an action. Intuitively, at each point in the program execution, the observer checks the current program statement (i.e., AST node) being executed against the pattern of each event. If more than one pattern matches, then BLAST declares the specification to be invalid for the given program. If only one pattern matches, then the corresponding assertion is checked. If the assertion is violated, then the observer rejects the trace; otherwise it executes the corresponding action. The Temporal qualifier is either BEFORE or AFTER. It specifies whether the observer transition is executed before or after the source-code AST node that matches the pattern. If a temporal qualifier is omitted, it is assumed to be BEFORE.

The keyword PATTERN is followed by a statement that is matched against the program source code. The pattern is defined by the nonterminal ParamCStmt, followed by an optional program-location descriptor. A pattern is either a C assignment statement or a C function call that involves side-effect free expressions. The pattern may refer to variables named i, for $i \geq 1$, which are matched against arbitrary C expressions in the program. Each such pattern variable may appear at most once in a pattern. There is also a pattern variable named $?, which plays the role of a wild-card. It may occur multiple times in a pattern, and different occurrences may match the empty string, a C expression, or an arbitrary number of actual parameters in a function call. The location descriptor

LocDesc is either a C label, or a string that concatenates the source file name with a line number; e.g., the string "file_19" refers to line number 19 of the source file file. If a location descriptor is specified, then the pattern is matched only against program locations that match the descriptor.

The keyword ASSERT is followed by a program invariant that must hold every time the corresponding pattern matches. Here, CExpression is a boolean condition expressed as a C expression that may refer to global program variables, observer variables, numbered pattern variables $i that occur in the corresponding pattern (which may match local program variables), and type-state information associated with any of these. Numbered pattern variables in an assertion refer to the expressions with which they are unified by the pattern matching that triggers the event. If an assertion is omitted, it is assumed to be always true. If during program execution the pattern of an event matches, but the current state violates the assertion, then the observer is said to *reject* the trace.

The keyword ACTION is followed by a sequence of C statements that are executed every time the corresponding pattern matches. The code in CStatementSeq has the following restrictions. First, as in assertions, the only read variables are global program variables, observer variables, numbered pattern variables, and associated type states. Second, the action code may write only to observer variables and to type-state information. In particular, an observer action must not change the program state. If an action is omitted, it is assumed to be the empty sequence of statements.

Example 1. [**Locking**] Consider the informal specification that a program must acquire and release locks in strict alternation. The observer automaton defined in Figure 2(a) specifies the correct usage of locking functions. An observer variable locked is created to track the status of the (only) global lock. Simple events match calls to the relevant functions. The event for init initializes the observer variable to 0, indicating that the lock is not in use. The other two events ensure that the lock is not in use with each call of the function lock, and is in use with each call of unlock. When these assertions succeed, the observer variable is updated and execution proceeds; when an assertion fails, an error is signaled. The wild-cards $?'s match either a variable to which the result of a function call is assigned, or the absence of such an assignment, thus making the patterns cover all possible calls to the functions lock and unlock.

Figure 2(b) shows the same specification, but now the program contains several locks, and the functions lock and unlock take a lock as a parameter. A lock is assumed to be an object of type lock_t. The observer introduces a type state locked with each lock of the program, and checks and updates the type state whenever one of the functions init, lock, and unlock is called.   □

2.2   Semantics

The semantics of a trace property is given by running the observer automaton in parallel with the program. The automaton accepts a program trace if along the trace, every time an observer event matches, the corresponding assertion is

```
GLOBAL int locked;                    SHADOW lock_t { int locked; }

EVENT {                               EVENT {
  PATTERN { $? = init(); }              PATTERN { init($1); }
  ACTION { locked = 0; }                ACTION { $1->locked = 0; }
}                                     }
EVENT {                               EVENT {
  PATTERN { $? = lock(); }              PATTERN { lock($1); }
  ASSERT { locked == 0 }                ASSERT { $1->locked == 0 }
  ACTION { locked = 1; }                ACTION { $1->locked = 1; }
}                                     }
EVENT {                               EVENT {
  PATTERN { $? = unlock(); }            PATTERN { unlock($1); }
  ASSERT { locked == 1 }                ASSERT { $1->locked == 1 }
  ACTION { locked = 0; }                ACTION { $1->locked = 0; }
}                                     }
```

Fig. 2. (a) Specification for a global lock. (b) Specification for several locks.

true, and moreover, if the trace is finite, then the values of the variables at the end of the trace satisfy the postcondition of the observer automaton. Dually, the automaton rejects the trace if either some assertion or the postcondition fails. We give the semantics of the composition of a program and an observer automaton by instrumenting the program source code with C code for the observer variable, type-state, and event declarations, i.e., the original program is transformed into a new program by a sequence of simple steps. This transformation is performed statically on the program before starting the model-checking engine on the transformed program.

Syntactic pattern matching on literal C code must deal with code structuring issues. BLAST performs pattern matching against a simplified subset of C statements. In our implementation, first a sound transformation from C programs to the simplified statement language is performed by CIL [15]. These simplified statements consist only of variable assignments and function calls involving side-effect free expressions. Second, BLAST's instrumentation of the program with the observer is performed on the simplified language. Third, BLAST performs model checking on the instrumented program, which is represented by a graph whose nodes correspond to program locations and whose edges are labeled with sequences of simplified statements [11]. The model checker takes as input also the pre- and postconditions of the observer automaton, as described in the next section.

Instrumenting Programs. In the following we define the program instrumentation with the observer automaton by describing a transformation rule for each construct of the observer specification.

Observer Variables. Declarations of observer variables are inserted as global declarations in the C program.

Type State. The type-state fields declared by the observer automaton are inserted into the declarations section of the C program by replacing the original declarations of the corresponding types. The actual transformation depends on the "shadowed" type. If the shadowed type is abstract, then the type itself is replaced. In this case, the fields of the original type cannot be analyzed, because their definition is not available. If the shadowed type is not abstract, then the original type becomes one field of the new type, with the other fields holding the type-state information. All type accesses in the program are modified accordingly. For the example in Figure 2(b), first assume that lock_t is an abstract type for the locking data structure. Then the type-state declaration

```
SHADOW lock_t { int locked; }
```

is transformed and inserted as follows in the declarations section of the program:

```
struct __shadow0__ { int locked; };
typedef struct __shadow0__ *lock_t;
```

If, on the other hand, the type lock_t is defined as

```
struct lock_t_struct { int lock_info; }
typedef struct lock_t_struct *lock_t;
```

then the type name is changed to lock_t_orig and the type-state declaration is transformed and inserted as follows:

```
struct __shadow0__ { lock_t_orig shadowed; int locked; };
typedef struct __shadow0__ *lock_t;
```

Additionally, in this case, for every instance mylock of type lock_t, each occurrence of mylock->lock_info is replaced by mylock->shadowed->lock_info.

Events. For every event declaration of the observer automaton an if-statement is generated. The condition of that if-statement is a copy of the assertion, where the pattern variables $i are replaced by the matching C expressions. The then-branch contains a copy of the action code, again with the place holders substituted accordingly. The else-branch contains a transition to the rejecting state of the automaton. Then the original program is traversed to find every matching statement for the pattern of the event. The pattern is matched if the place holders ($i and $?) in the pattern can be replaced by code fragments such that the pattern becomes identical to the examined statement. If two or more patterns match the same statement, then BLAST stops and signals that the specification is invalid (ambiguous) for the given program. As specified by the temporal qualifier BEFORE or AFTER, the generated if-statement is inserted before or after each matching program statement. Consider, for example, the second event declaration from Figure 2(a). For this event, every occurrence of the code fragment lock(); matches the pattern, whether or not the return value is assigned to a variable (because of the wild-card $? on the left-hand side of the pattern). The instrumentation adds the following code before every call to lock in the program:

```
if (locked == 0) {
    locked = 1;
} else {
    { __reject = 1; }    // transition to rejecting state
}
```

Note that the rejecting state of the observer automaton is modeled by the implicitly defined observer variable __reject. This variable must not occur in the program nor in the observer declaration.

Observer Semantics. A state of a program P is a pair (ℓ, v) consisting of a program location ℓ and a memory valuation v. Let ℓ and ℓ' be two program locations, and let p and p' be two predicates over the program variables. The pair (ℓ', p') is *reachable in* P from the pair (ℓ, p) if there exists an executable state sequence (finite trace) of P from a state (ℓ, v) to a state (ℓ', v'), for some memory valuation v that satisfies p and some valuation v' that satisfies p'.

We can now define the semantics of an observer automaton A over a program P in terms of the traces of the instrumented program P_A. Let *pre* be the predicate $pre_A \wedge (\text{\_\_reject} = 0)$, where pre_A is the precondition of A, and let *post* be the predicate $post_A \wedge (\text{\_\_reject} = 0)$, where $post_A$ is the postcondition of A. The location ℓ' is A-*accept-reachable in* P from ℓ if $(\ell', post)$ is reachable in P_A from (ℓ, pre). The location ℓ' is A-*reject-reachable in* P from ℓ if $(\ell', \neg post)$ is reachable in P_A from (ℓ, pre). Note that both accept- and reject-reachability postulate the existence of a feasible path in P from ℓ to ℓ'; the difference depends only on whether the observer automaton accepts or rejects. In particular, it may be that ℓ' is both A-accept- and A-reject-reachable in P from ℓ.

3   Location Properties: Relational Queries

Every observer automaton encodes a trace property. At a higher level, observer automata can be combined by *relational queries*. The queries operate on program locations and specify properties using sets and relations over program locations. The query language is an imperative scripting language that extends the predicate calculus: it provides first-order relational expressions (but no function symbols) as well as statements for variable assignment and control flow.

3.1   Syntax

A simple query is a sequence of statements, where each statement is either an assignment or a print statement. There are three types of variables: string, property, and relation variables. A string variable may express a program location, a function name, or a code fragment. The property variables range over observer automata (i.e., trace properties), as defined in the previous section. The relation variables range over sets of tuples of strings. There is no need to declare the type of a variable; it is determined by the value of the first assignment to the variable. For the convenient and structured expression of more complex queries, the language also has constructs (IF, WHILE, FOR) for the conditional execution and iteration of statements.

```
Statement:  PropVar ':=' '[' Observer ']' ';'
          | RelVar '(' StrExp ',' StrExp ')' ':=' BoolExp ';'
          | 'PRINT' StrExp ';' | 'PRINT' BoolExp ';'

BoolExp:    RelVar '(' StrExp ',' StrExp ')'
          | 'TRUE' '(' StrVar ')' | 'FALSE' '(' StrVar ')'
          | BoolExp '&' BoolExp        // conjunction
          | BoolExp '|' BoolExp        // disjunction
          | '!' BoolExp                // negation
          | 'EXISTS' '(' StrVar ',' BoolExp ')'
          | 'MATCH' '(' RegExp ',' StrVar ')'
          | 'A-REACH' '(' BoolExp ',' BoolExp ',' PropVar ')'
          | 'R-REACH' '(' BoolExp ',' BoolExp ',' PropVar ')'

StrExp:     StrLit | StrVar
```

Fig. 3. Partial syntax of the query language.

The expression language permits first-order quantification over string variables. In the right-hand side expression of an assignment, every variable must either be a relation variable and have been previously assigned a value, or it must be a string variable that is quantified or occurs free. The implemented query language allows relations of arbitrary arity, but for simplicity, let us restrict this discussion to binary relation variables. Also, let us write x and y for the values of the string variables x and y, and R for the set of pairs denoted by the binary relation variable R. Then the boolean expression R(x,y) evaluates to true iff $(x, y) \in R$. To assign a new value to the relation variable R we write "R(x,y) := e" short for "for all x,y let R(x,y) := e," where e is a boolean expression that may contain free occurrences of x and y.

Each print statement has as argument a boolean expression, with possibly some free occurrences of string variables. The result is a print-out of all value assignments to the free variables which make the expression true. For example, "PRINT R(x,y)" outputs the header (x, y) followed by all pairs (x, y) of strings such that $(x, y) \in R$.

The grammar for queries without control-flow constructs is shown in Figure 3. The nonterminals StrVar, PropVar, and RelVar refer to any C identifier; StrLit is a string literal; Observer is a specification of an observer automaton, as defined in Section 2; and RegExp is a Unix regular expression.

3.2 Semantics

The first-order constructs (conjunction, disjunction, negation, existential quantification) as well as the imperative constructs (assignments, control flow, output) have the usual meaning. The boolean expression MATCH(e,x) evaluates to true iff the value of the string variable x matches the regular expression e.

Reachability Queries. Consider an input program P, and a property variable A denoting an observer automaton A. Let *source* and *target* be two boolean expressions each with a single free string variable, say loc_s and loc_t. The boolean expression A-REACH(*source*, *target*, A) evaluates to true for given values ℓ for loc_s and ℓ' for loc_t iff *source* and *target* evaluate to true for ℓ and ℓ', respectively, and ℓ' is A-accept-reachable in P from ℓ. The boolean expression R-REACH(*source*, *target*, A) evaluates to true for given values ℓ for loc_s and ℓ' for loc_t iff *source* and *target* evaluate to true for ℓ and ℓ', respectively, and ℓ' is A-reject-reachable in P from ℓ. These relations are evaluated by invoking the BLAST model checker on the instrumented program.

Syntactic Sugar. Using the above primitives, we can define some other useful queries as follows. The property variable Empty denotes the empty observer automaton, which has no events and pre- and postconditions that are always true. The macro REACH(*source*, *target*) is short-hand for A-REACH(*source*, *target*, Empty); it evaluates to true for given values ℓ for loc_s and ℓ' for loc_t iff both *source* and *target* evaluate to true and there is a feasible path in P from ℓ to ℓ'. The macro SAFE(*source*, A) is short-hand for

$$source \ \& \ !\mathtt{EXISTS}(\mathtt{loc\_t}, \ \mathtt{R\text{-}REACH}(source, \ \mathtt{TRUE}(\mathtt{loc\_t}), \ \mathtt{A}))$$

This boolean expression evaluates to true for a given value ℓ for loc_s iff *source* evaluates to true and there is no feasible path in P from ℓ which makes the observer A enter a rejecting state.

Syntactic Relations. There are a number of useful predefined syntactic relation variables. These are restricted to relations that can be extracted from the AST of the program. The following relations are automatically initialized after starting the query interpreter to access information about the syntactic structure of the program:

- LOC_FUNC(loc,fname) evaluates to true iff the program location loc is contained in the body of the C function fname.
- LOC_FUNC_INIT(loc,fname) evaluates to true iff the program location loc is the initial location of the C function fname.
- LOC_LABEL(loc,lname) evaluates to true iff the location loc contains the C label lname.
- LOC_LHSVAR(loc,vname) evaluates to true iff the location loc contains the variable vname on the left-hand side of an assignment.
- LOC_RHSVAR(loc,vname) evaluates to true iff the location loc contains the variable vname on the right-hand side of an assignment.
- LOC_TEXT(loc,sourcecode) evaluates to true iff the C code at the location loc is identical to sourcecode.
- CALL(fname,funcname_callee) evaluates to true iff the function fname (syntactically) calls the function funcname_callee.

Other relations that reflect the syntactic structure of the program can be added as needed.

Example 2. [**Reachability Analysis**] The following query computes all reachable lines that contain the program code `abort`:

```
source(loc) := LOC_FUNC_INIT(loc,"main");
target(loc) :=
    EXISTS(text, LOC_TEXT(loc,text) & MATCH("abort",text));
result(loc1,loc2) := REACH(source(loc1),target(loc2));
PRINT result(loc1,_);
```

The first statement of the query assigns a set of program locations to the relation variable `source`. The set contains all locations that are contained in the body of function `main`. The second statement constructs the set of program locations that contain the code `abort`. The third statement computes a set of pairs of program locations. A pair of locations is contained in the set `result` iff there is an executable program trace from some location in `source` to some location in `target`. The last statement prints out a list of all source locations with a feasible path to an `abort` statement. The symbol "_" is used as an abbreviation for an existentially quantified string variable which is not used elsewhere.   □

Example 3. [**Dead-Code Analysis**] The following query computes the set of locations of the function `main` that are not reachable by any program execution (the "dead" locations):

```
live(loc1,loc2) :=
    REACH(LOC_FUNC_INIT(loc1,"main"),LOC_FUNC(loc2,_));
reached(loc) := live(_,loc);
PRINT "Following locations within 'main' are not reachable:";
PRINT !reached(loc) & LOC_FUNC(loc,"main");
```

We first compute the set of all program locations that are reachable from the initial location of the function `main`. We print the complement of this set, which represents dead code, restricted to the set of locations of the function `main`.   □

Both of the above examples are simple reachability queries. Examples of more advanced queries, which combine location and trace properties, are presented in the next section.

4   Examples

Impact Analysis. Consider the C program displayed in Figure 4(a). At the label START, the variable j is assigned a value. We wish to find the locations that are affected by this assignment, i.e., the reachable locations that use the variable j before it is redefined. Consider the observer automaton A shown in Figure 4(b). Along a trace, every assignment to j increments the variable gDefined. Thus, gDefined is equal to 1 only when there has been exactly one definition of j. The final condition ensures that along a finite trace, no redefinition of j has occurred. Hence, the desired set of locations is computed by the following query:

```
 1 int j;
 2 void f(int j){};                          GLOBAL int gDefined ;
 3 int compute() {                           INITIAL { gDefined == 0 }
 4    int i;                                  EVENT {
 5    START: j = 1;                               PATTERN { j = $1; }
 6    i = 1;                                       ACTION { gDefined ++ ; }
 7    if (i==0) {                             }
 8       f(j);        // affected if i==0     FINAL  { gDefined == 1 }
 9    }
10    if (i==0) {
11       j = 2;
12    }
13    if (j==2) {  // affected if i==1
14       f(j);        // not affected if i==0
15    }
16    return 0;
17 }
18 int main() {
19    compute();
20    return 0;
21 }
```

Fig. 4. (a) C program. (b) Impact automaton A.

```
GLOBAL int __E;
INITIAL (__E == 0);                  EVENT {
EVENT {                                 PATTERN { $? = system($?); }
  PATTERN { $? = seteuid($1); }         ASSERT { __E != 0 }
  ACTION { __E = $1; }                }
}
```

Fig. 5. (a) Effective UID automaton. (b) Syscall privilege automaton.

```
affected(11,12) :=
    A-REACH(LOC_LABEL(11,"START"), LOC_RHSVAR(12,"j"), A);
PRINT affected(_,12);
```

For our example, BLAST reports that the definition of the variable j at line 5 has impact on line 13. It has no impact on line 8, as that line is not reachable because of line 6. On the other hand, if line 6 is changed to "i=0;", then line 8 is reachable and affected. Now, line 11 is reachable and therefore a redefinition of j takes place. Thus, line 13 is not affected. To compute the effect of each definition of j, we can change the first argument of A-REACH to LOC_LHSVAR(11,"j").

Security Analysis. Consider a simplified specification for the manipulation of privileges in setuid programs [4]. Unix processes can execute at several privilege levels; higher privilege levels may be required to access restricted system resources. Privilege levels are based on user id's. The seteuid system call is used to set the effective user id of a process, and hence its privilege level. The effective user id 0 (or root) allows a process full privileges to access all system resources. The system call runs a program as a new process with the privilege level of the current effective user id. The observer automaton B in Figure 5(a)

tracks the status of the effective user id by maintaining an observer variable
__E, which denotes the current effective user id. Initially, __E is set to 0. The $1
pattern variable in the `seteuid` pattern matches the actual parameter. Every
time `seteuid` is called, the value of __E is updated to be equal to the parameter
passed to `seteuid` in the program.

Suppose we want to check that the function `system` is never called while
holding root privileges. This can be done by adding the event in Figure 5(b)
to the automaton B (call the resulting automaton B') and computing the query
"SAFE(LOC_FUNC_INIT(loc, "main"), B')". The $? wild-card in the `system`
pattern is used to match all remaining parameters. As long as the assertion is
satisfied, the observer does nothing, because the action is empty; however, if the
assertion is not satisfied, the trace is rejected.

Now suppose we want to know which locations of the program can be run
with root privileges, i.e., with __E = 0. This can be accomplished by the following
query:

```
target(loc)  := LOC_FUNC(loc,_);
rootPriv(loc1,loc2) :=
    A-REACH(LOC_FUNC_INIT(loc1, "main"), target(loc2), B");
PRINT rootPriv(_,loc);
```

where automaton B" is automaton B with the final condition "FINAL (__E==0);".

Decomposing Verification Tasks. We now show how the relational query
language and observer automata can be combined to decompose the verification
process [14]. Consider an event e of an observer automaton A with the postcondition $post_A$. We say that e extends A if (1) the assertion of e is always true, and
(2) the action of e writes only to variables not read by A. Let $A.e$ be the observer
automaton obtained by adding to A (1) a fresh observer variable x_e, (2) the
initial condition x_e == 0, and (3) the code x_e = 1 as the first instruction in
the body of the action of e. Define RSplit.$A.e$ to be the pair of observer automata
$(A.e_r^+, A.e_r^-)$ which are $A.e$ with the postconditions changed to $\text{x\_e} = 1 \Rightarrow post_A$
and $\text{x\_e} \neq 1 \Rightarrow post_A$, respectively. Define ASplit.$A.e$ to be the pair of automata
$(A.e_a^+, A.e_a^-)$ which are $A.e$ with the postconditions changed to $\text{x\_e} = 1 \wedge post_A$
and $\text{x}_e \neq 1 \wedge post_A$, respectively.

Lemma 1. *Let P be a program, let A be an observer automaton, and let e be an
event that extends A. Let $(A1, A_2)$ = RSplit.$A.e$ (resp. (A_1, A_2) = ASplit.$A.e$).
A location ℓ' is A-reject-reachable (resp. A-accept-reachable) in P from ℓ iff
either ℓ' is A_1-reject-reachable (resp. A_1-accept-reachable) in P from ℓ, or ℓ' is
A_2-reject-reachable (resp. A_2-accept-reachable) in P from ℓ.*

The split partitions the program traces into those where the event e occurs
and those where it doesn't occur. We can now extend our query language to
allow for boolean macro expressions of the following kind: b SPLIT e, where b is
a boolean expression and e is an event. This macro stands for b with each occurrence of a subexpression of the form R-REACH($\cdot, \cdot, A$), where e extends A, re-
placed by R-REACH($\cdot, \cdot, A_1$) | R-REACH($\cdot, \cdot, A_2$), where (A_1, A_2) = RSplit.$A.e$,

and each occurrence of a subexpression of the form A-REACH($\cdot$, $\cdot$, A) replaced with A-REACH($\cdot$, $\cdot$, A_1) | A-REACH($\cdot$, $\cdot$, A_2), where $(A_1, A_2) = \mathsf{ASplit}.A.e$. By Lemma 1, the boolean expression b SPLIT e is equivalent to b. With a judicious choice of events, we can therefore break down the evaluation of a complex query into multiple simpler queries.

We illustrate this using the example of a Windows device driver for a floppy disk[1], and concentrate the Plug and Play (PNP) manager, which communicates requests to devices via I/O request packets. For example, the request IRP_MN_START_DEVICE instructs the driver to do all necessary hardware and software initialization so that the device can function. Figure 6 shows the code for the PNP manager. The code does some set-up work and then branches to handle each PNP request. We wish to verify a property of the driver that specifies the way I/O request packets must be handled[2]. Let A be the observer automaton for the property.

```
1  NTSTATUS FloppyPnp( IN PDEVICE_OBJECT DeviceObject, IN PIRP Irp) {
2      ...
3      PIO_STACK_LOCATION irpSp = IoGetCurrentIrpStackLocation( Irp );
4      ...
5      switch ( irpSp->MinorFunction ) {
6        L_1: case IRP_MN_START_DEVICE:
7              ntStatus = FloppyStart(DeviceObject, Irp);
8              break;
9        L_2: case IRP_MN_QUERY_STOP_DEVICE:
10             ...
11             break;
12             // several other cases
13       L_k: default:
14             ...
15     }
16     ...
17     return ntStatus;
18 }
```

Fig. 6. A floppy driver.

Intuitively, the verification can be broken into each kind of request sent by the PNP manager, that is, if we can prove the absence of error for each case in the switch statement, we have proved the program correct with respect to the property. Let e_1, ..., e_k be the events that denote the reaching of the program labels L_1, ..., L_k, which correspond to each case in the switch statement. The following relational query encodes the proof decomposition:

(... (SAFE(LOC_FUNC_INIT(loc,"FloppyPnp"), A) SPLIT e_1)

                                    ... SPLIT e_k)

This query breaks the safety property specified by A into several simpler queries, one for each combination of possible branches of the switch statement. While this

---

[1] Available with the Microsoft Windows DDK.

[2] Personal communication with T. Ball and S. Rajamani.

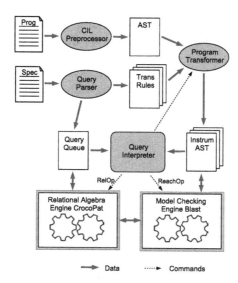

Fig. 7. Architecture of the verification toolkit.

results in exponentially many subqueries, all but k of these subqueries (where more than one, or none of the events happens) are evaluated very efficiently by exploiting the syntactic control-flow structure of the program, by noting that a violation of the subproperty is *syntactically* impossible. The remaining k cases, which are syntactically possible, are then model checked independently, leading to a more efficient check, because independent abstractions can be maintained.

5   Tool Architecture

The overall architecture of the implementation is shown in Figure 7. CIL [15] parses the input program and produces the AST used by the program transformer. The *query parser* parses the specification file and extracts program-transformation rules to later guide the program instrumentation. It also prepares the data structures for the relational computations. The *program transformer* takes as input the representation of the original program and the transformation rules. When required by the query interpreter, it takes one particular set of transformation rules at a time (corresponding to one observer automaton) and performs the instrumentation. The result is the AST of the instrumented code. The *query interpreter* is the central controlling unit in this architecture. It dispatches the current query from the query queue to the relational-algebra engine for execution. If the next statement is a REACH expression, it first requests the instrumented version of the program from the transformer, then requests the relational-manipulation engine to transfer the input relations to the model-checking engine, and then starts the model checker BLAST. When the model checking is completed, the relational-manipulation engine stores the results of the query and gives the control back to the query interpreter.

The *relational-algebra engine* is a calculator for relational expressions. It uses a highly optimized BDD-based library for querying and manipulating relations [3]. This library deals with relations on the level of predicate calculus. There is no need to encode variables and values to bit representations, because the library provides automatic value encoding and efficient high-level operations to abstract from the core BDD algorithms.

References

1. T. Ball and S.K. Rajamani. The SLAM project: Debugging system software via static analysis. In *Proc. POPL*, pages 1–3. ACM, 2002.
2. T. Ball and S.K. Rajamani. SLIC: A specification language for interface checking (of C). Technical Report MSR-TR-2001-21, Microsoft Research, 2002.
3. D. Beyer, A. Noack, and C. Lewerentz. Simple and efficient relational querying of software structures. In *Proc. WCRE*, pages 216–225. IEEE, 2003.
4. H. Chen and D. Wagner. MOPS: An infrastructure for examining security properties of software. In *Proc. CCS*, pages 235–244. ACM, 2002.
5. J.C. Corbett, M.B. Dwyer, J. Hatcliff, and Robby. A language framework for expressing checkable properties of dynamic software. In *Proc. SPIN*, LNCS 1885, pages 205–223. Springer, 2000.
6. S. Goldsmith, R. O'Callahan, and A. Aiken. Lightweight instrumentation from relational queries on program traces. Technical Report CSD-04-1315, UC Berkeley, 2004.
7. S. Hallem, B. Chelf, Y. Xie, and D. Engler. A system and language for building system-specific static analyses. In *Proc. PLDI*, pages 69–82. ACM, 2002.
8. T.A. Henzinger, R. Jhala, R. Majumdar, and K.L. McMillan. Abstractions from proofs. In *Proc. POPL*, pages 232–244. ACM, 2004.
9. T.A. Henzinger, R. Jhala, R. Majumdar, G.C. Necula, G. Sutre, and W. Weimer. Temporal-safety proofs for systems code. In *Proc. CAV*, LNCS 2404, pages 526–538. Springer, 2002.
10. T.A. Henzinger, R. Jhala, R. Majumdar, and M.A.A. Sanvido. Extreme model checking. In *International Symposium on Verification: Theory and Practice*, LNCS 2772, pages 332–358. Springer, 2003.
11. T.A. Henzinger, R. Jhala, R. Majumdar, and G. Sutre. Lazy abstraction. In *Proc. POPL*, pages 58–70. ACM, 2002.
12. G.J. Holzmann. Logic verification of ANSI-C code with SPIN. In *Proc. SPIN*, LNCS 1885, pages 131–147. Springer, 2000.
13. G. Kiczales, J. Lamping, A. Mendhekar, C. Maeda, C.V. Lopes, J.-M. Loingtier, and J. Irwin. Aspect-oriented programming. In *Proc. ECOOP*, LNCS 1241, pages 220–242. Springer, 1997.
14. K.L. McMillan. A methodology for hardware verification using compositional model checking. *Science of Computer Programming*, 37(1–3):279–309, 2000.
15. G.C. Necula, S. McPeak, S.P. Rahul, and W. Weimer. CIL: Intermediate language and tools for analysis and transformation of C programs. In *Proc. CC*, LNCS 2304, pages 213–228. Springer, 2002.
16. R.E. Strom and S. Yemini. Typestate: A programming language concept for enhancing software reliability. *IEEE Trans. Software Engineering*, 12(1):157–171, 1986.
17. E. Yahav and G. Ramalingam. Verifying safety properties using separation and heterogeneous abstractions. In *Proc. PLDI*, pages 25–34. ACM, 2004.

Program Generators and the Tools to Make Them

Yannis Smaragdakis

College of Computing
Georgia Institute of Technology
Atlanta, GA 30332, USA
yannis@cc.gatech.edu

Abstract. Program generation is among the most promising techniques in the effort to increase the automation of programming tasks. In this talk, we discuss the potential impact and research value of program generation, we give examples of our research in the area, and we outline a future work direction that we consider most interesting.

Specifically, we first discuss why program generators have significant applied potential. We believe that program generators can be made easy-to-implement so that they are competitive with traditional software libraries in many software domains. Compared to a common library, a generator implementing a domain-specific language can offer more concise syntax, better static error checking, and better performance through cross-operation optimizations.

Despite the significant applied value of generators, however, we argue that meta-programming tools (i.e., language tools for writing program generators) may be of greater value as a research topic. The reason has to do with the domain-specificity of generators. The value of a program generator is often tied so closely to a software domain that there is little general and reusable knowledge to transmit to other generator researchers. We discuss meta-programming tools as an area with both interesting conceptual problems and great value. A good meta-programming infrastructure can simplify the creation of generators to make them an effective solution for many more domains.

We illustrate our views on generators and meta-programming tools with two artifacts from our latest work: the Meta-AspectJ meta-programming language [6] and the GOTECH generator [5]. Meta-AspectJ enables generating Java and AspectJ programs using code templates, i.e., quote and unquote operators. Meta-AspectJ has two interesting elements. First, we believe that using the AspectJ language as a back-end simplifies the task of writing a generator. The GOTECH generator uses this technique to adapt a Java program for server side execution in a J2EE application server. Second, Meta-AspectJ is a technically mature meta-programming tool – in many respects the most advanced meta-programming tool for Java. For instance, Meta-AspectJ reduces the need to deal with low level syntactic types for quoted entities (e.g., "expression", "statement", "identifier", etc.) through type inference and a context-sensitive parsing algorithm.

R. Giacobazzi (Ed.): SAS 2004, LNCS 3148, pp. 19–20, 2004.
© Springer-Verlag Berlin Heidelberg 2004

Finally, we examine the problem of statically determining the safety of a generator and present its intricacies. We limit our focus to one particular kind of guarantee for generated code: ensuring that the generated program is free of compile-time errors, such as type errors, references to undefined variables, etc. We argue that it is the responsibility of a good meta-programming tool to ensure that the generators written in it will always produce legal programs. Nevertheless, if we do not severely limit the generator, the problem becomes one of arbitrary control- and data-flow analysis. We discuss why the limitations of current meta-programming tools that offer safety guarantees [1, 4] are too strict and we present possible avenues for future research.

For further reading, a full paper accompanying this talk can be found in the PEPM'04 proceedings. The reader may also want to consult one of the good surveys on program generation, examining the topic either from an applied perspective [3] or from a partial evaluation perspective [2].

References

1. C. Calcagno, W. Taha, L. Huang, and X. Leroy. Implementing multi-stage languages using ASTs, gensym, and reflection. In *Generative Programming and Component Engineering (GPCE) Conference*, LNCS 2830, pages 57–76. Springer, 2003.
2. N. D. Jones and A. J. Glenstrup. Program generation, termination, and binding-time analysis. In *Generative Programming and Component Engineering (GPCE) Conference*, LNCS 2487, pages 1–31. Springer, 2002.
3. Y. Smaragdakis and D. Batory. Application generators. *Encyclopedia of Electrical and Electronics Engineering*, 2000. J.G. Webster (ed.), John Wiley and Sons.
4. W. Taha and T. Sheard. Multi-stage programming with explicit annotations. In *Partial Evaluation and Semantics-Based Program Manipulation, Amsterdam, The Netherlands, June 1997*, pages 203–217. New York: ACM, 1997.
5. E. Tilevich, S. Urbanski, Y. Smaragdakis, and M. Fleury. Aspectizing server-side distribution. In *Proceedings of the Automated Software Engineering (ASE) Conference*. IEEE Press, October 2003.
6. D. Zook, S. S. Huang, and Y. Smaragdakis. Generating AspectJ programs with Meta-AspectJ. In *Proceedings of the 2004 Generative Progamming and Component Engineering (GPCE) Conference*. Springer-Verlag, to appear.

Towards Declarative Programming
for Web Services

Sheila McIlraith

Department of Computer Science, University of Toronto
6 King's College Road, Toronto, ON, M4K 2W1, Canada

Abstract. Two trends are emerging in the World Wide Web (WWW). The first is the proliferation of Web Services – self-contained, Web-accessible software applications and associated distributed systems architectures. The second is the emergence of the "Semantic Web," the vision for a next-generation WWW that is computer interpretable. Today's Web was designed primarily for human use. To enable reliable, large-scale automated interoperation of Web services, their properties and capabilities must be understandable to a computer program. In this talk we briefly overview our ongoing work to develop a declarative language for describing Web services on the Semantic Web, contrasting it with emerging industrial Web service and Semantic Web standards. Our declarative representation of Web services enables automation of a wide variety of tasks including discovery, invocation, interoperation, composition, simulation, verification and monitoring.

To address the problem of automated Web service composition, we propose automated reasoning techniques based on the notion of generic procedures and customizing user constraint. To this end, we adapt and extend a logic programming language to enable programs that are generic, customizable and usable in the context of the Web. We combine these with deductive synthesis techniques to generate compositions of Web services. Further, we propose logical criteria for these generic procedures that define when they are knowledge self-sufficient and physically self-sufficient. To support information gathering combined with search, we propose a middle-ground interpreter that operates under an assumption of reasonable persistence of key information. Our implemented prototype system is currently interacting with services on the Web. Parts of this work were done in collaboration with Tran Cao Son, Honglei Zeng and Ronald Fadel.

R. Giacobazzi (Ed.): SAS 2004, LNCS 3148, p. 21, 2004.

Closed and Logical Relations for Over- and Under-Approximation of Powersets

David A. Schmidt[1,2,*]

[1] Kansas State University, Manhattan, Kansas, USA
[2] École Polytechnique, Palaiseau, France
schmidt@cis.ksu.edu

Abstract. We redevelop and extend Dams's results on over- and under-approximation with higher-order Galois connections:

(1) We show how Galois connections are generated from U-GLB-L-LUB-closed binary relations, and we apply them to lower and upper powerset constructions, which are weaker forms of powerdomains appropriate for abstraction studies.

(2) We use the powerset types within a family of logical relations, show when the logical relations preserve U-GLB-L-LUB-closure, and show that simulation is a logical relation. We use the logical relations to rebuild Dams's most-precise simulations, revealing the inner structure of over- and under-approximation.

(3) We extract validation and refutation logics from the logical relations, state their resemblance to Hennessey-Milner logic and description logic, and obtain easy proofs of soundness and best precision.

Almost all Galois-connection-based static analyses are *over-approximating*: For Galois connection, $(\mathcal{P}(C), \subseteq)\langle\alpha_o, \gamma\rangle(A, \sqsubseteq_A)$, an abstract value $a \in A$ proclaims a property of all the outputs of a program. For example, *even* $\in$ *Parity* (see Figure 2 for the abstract domain *Parity*) asserts, "$\forall even$" – all the program's outputs are even numbers, that is, the output is a set from $\{S \in \mathcal{P}(Nat) \mid S \subseteq \gamma(even)\}$.

An *under-approximating* Galois connection, $(\mathcal{P}(C), \supseteq)\langle\alpha_u, \gamma\rangle A^{op}$, where $A^{op} = (A, \sqsupseteq_A)$, is the dual. Here, *even* $\in$ *Parity*^{op} asserts that *all even numbers are included in the program's outputs* – a strong assertion. Also, we may reuse $\gamma : A \to \mathcal{P}(C)$ as the upper adjoint from A^{op} to $\mathcal{P}(C)^{op}$ iff γ preserves joins in $(A, \sqsubseteq_A)$ – another strong demand.

Fortunately, there is an alternative view of under-approximation: $a \in A^{op}$ asserts an *existential property* – there exists an output with property a. For example, *even* $\in$ *Parity*^{op} asserts "$\exists even$" – there is an even number in the program's outputs, which is a set from $\{S \in \mathcal{P}(Nat) \mid S \cap \gamma(even) \neq \emptyset\}$.

Now, we can generalize both over- and under-approximation to multiple properties, e.g., $\forall\{even, odd\} \equiv \forall(even \vee odd)$ – all outputs are even- or odd-valued; and $\exists\{even, odd\} \equiv \exists even \wedge \exists odd$ – the output set includes an even value and an odd value. These examples "lift" A and A^{op} into the *powerset lattices*, $\mathcal{P}_L(A)$ and $\mathcal{P}_U(A)$, respectively, and set the stage for the problem studied in this paper.

* Supported by NSF ITR-0085949 and ITR-0086154.

R. Giacobazzi (Ed.): SAS 2004, LNCS 3148, pp. 22–37, 2004.
© Springer-Verlag Berlin Heidelberg 2004

Concrete transition system:
$$\Sigma = \{c_0, c_1, c_2\}$$
$$R = \{(c_0, c_1), (c_1, c_2)\}$$

$c0 \longrightarrow c1 \longrightarrow c2$

Approximating the state set, Σ, by $A = \{\bot, a_0, a_{12}, \top\}$; $\alpha : \mathcal{P}(\Sigma) \rightarrow A$ is:

$$\alpha\{c_0\} = a_0, \quad \alpha\{c_1\} = a_{12} = \alpha\{c_2\} = \alpha\{c_1, c_2\}, \quad \alpha\{c_1, c_2, c_3\} = \top, \quad \text{etc.}$$

Over-approximating ("may": $\exists\exists$) transition system:

$$A = \{\bot, a_0, a_{12}, \top\}$$
$$R^\sharp = \{(a_0, a_{12}), (a_{12}, a_{12}), (\top, a_{12})\} \qquad a0 \dashrightarrow a12$$

Under-approximating ("must": $\forall\exists$) transition system:

$$A = \{\bot, a_0, a_{12}, \top\}$$
$$R^\flat = \{(a_0, a_{12}), (\bot, \bot)\} \qquad a0 \longrightarrow a12$$

The *mixed transition system* is $(A, R^\flat, R^\sharp)$.

Fig. 1. An example mixed transition system

1   Dams's Mixed-Transition Systems

In his thesis [10] and in subsequent work [11], Dams studied over- and under-approximations of state-transition relations, $R \subseteq C \times C$, for a discretely ordered set, C, of states. Given complete lattice $(A, \sqsubseteq_A)$ and the Galois connection, $(\mathcal{P}(C), \subseteq)\langle\alpha, \gamma\rangle(A, \sqsubseteq_A)$, Dams defined an over-approximating transition relation, $R^\sharp \subseteq A \times A$, and an *under-approximating* transition relation, $R^\flat \subseteq A \times A$, as follows:

$$aR^\sharp a' \text{ iff } a' \in \{\alpha(Y) \mid Y \in min\{S' \mid R^{\exists\exists}(\gamma(a), S')\}\}$$
$$aR^\flat a' \text{ iff } a' \in \{\alpha(Y) \mid Y \in min\{S' \mid R^{\forall\exists}(\gamma(a), S')\}\}\ {}^{1}$$

such that $R^\sharp$ ρ-*simulates* R (that is, all R-transitions are mimicked by $R^\sharp$, modulo $\rho \subseteq C \times A$, where $c\,\rho\,a$ iff $c \in \gamma(a)$), and R ρ^{-1}-*simulates* $R^\flat$. See Figure 1 for an example of R and its *mixed transition system*, $R^\flat$, $R^\sharp$.

For the branching-time modalities $\Box$ ($\forall R$) and $\Diamond$ ($\exists R$),

$$a \models \Box\phi \text{ iff for all } a',\ aR^\sharp a' \text{ implies } a' \models \phi$$
$$a \models \Diamond\phi \text{ iff there exists } a' \text{ such that } aR^\flat a' \text{ and } a' \models \phi$$

Dams proved soundness: $a \models \phi$ and $c\,\rho\,a$ imply $c \models \phi$. With impressive work, Dams also proved "best precision" [11]: For all ρ- (and ρ^{-1}-) simulations, $R^\sharp$ and $R^\flat$ preserve the most $\Box\Diamond$-(*mu-calculus* [20, 21]) properties.

---

^{1} $R^{\exists\exists}$, $R^{\forall\exists}$, and the definitions themselves are explained later in the paper.

1.1 Can We Derive Dams's Results Within Galois-Connection Theory?

Given that Dams begins with a Galois connection, it should be possible to reconstruct his results entirely within a theory of higher-order Galois connections and gain new insights in the process. We do so in this paper.

First, we treat $R \subseteq C \times C$ as $R : C \to \mathcal{P}(C)$. This makes $R^\sharp : A \to \mathcal{P}_L(A)$, where $\mathcal{P}_L(\cdot)$ is a *lower* ($\subseteq$-*ordered*) *powerset constructor*[2].

Given the Galois connection, $\mathcal{P}(C)\langle\alpha_\tau, \gamma_\tau\rangle A$, on states, we "lift" it to a Galois connection on powersets, $F[\mathcal{P}(C)]\langle\alpha_{F[\tau]}, \gamma_{F[\tau]}\rangle\mathcal{P}_L(A)$,   so that

1. $R^\sharp$ ρ-*simulates* R iff $ext_{F[\tau]}(R) \circ \gamma_\tau \sqsubseteq_{A\to F[\mathcal{P}(C)]} \gamma_{F[\tau]} \circ R^\sharp$
2. *the soundness of* $a \models \Box\phi$ *follows from Item 1*
3. $R^\sharp_{best} = \alpha_{F[\tau]} \circ ext_{F[\tau]}(R) \circ \gamma_\tau$

We do similar work for $R^\sharp_{best} : A \to \mathcal{P}_U(A)$ and $\Diamond\phi$, where $\mathcal{P}_U(\cdot)$ is an *upper* ($\supseteq$-*ordered*) *powerset constructor*[3].

The crucial question is: *What is* $F[\mathcal{P}(C)]$? That is, *how should we concretize a set* $T \in \mathcal{P}_L(A)$? First, we write $c\,\rho_\tau\,a$ to assert that $c \in C$ is approximated by $a \in A$. (For example, for Galois connection, $\mathcal{P}(C)\langle\alpha_\tau, \gamma_\tau\rangle A$, define $c\,\rho_\tau\,a$ iff $c \in \gamma_\tau(a)$.) Then, $S \in \mathcal{P}(C)$ is approximated by $T \in \mathcal{P}_L(A)$ iff $S\,\rho_{\mathcal{P}_L(\tau)}\,T$, where

$$S\,\rho_{\mathcal{P}_L(\tau)}\,T \text{ iff for every } c \in S, \text{ there exists } a \in T \text{ such that } c\,\rho_\tau\,a \quad [4]$$

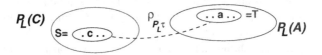

This might suggest that $F[\mathcal{P}(C)]$ is just $\mathcal{P}(C)$, and the concretization, $\gamma_{\mathcal{P}(\rho_\tau)} : \mathcal{P}_L(A) \to \mathcal{P}(C)$, is $\gamma_{\mathcal{P}(\rho_\tau)}(T) = \cup\{S \mid S\,\rho_{\mathcal{P}_L(\tau)}\,T\}$, which concretizes T to the largest set that is approximated by T.

But, as suggested by this paper's prelude, an alternative is to define $F[\mathcal{P}(C)]$ as $\mathcal{P}_L(\mathcal{P}(C))$, because if an abstract state $a \in A$ concretizes to a *set of states*, $\gamma_\tau(a) \subseteq C$, then set $T \in \mathcal{P}_L(A)$ should concretize to a *set of sets of states*:

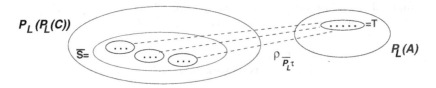

---

[2] Think of the elements of $\mathcal{P}_L(A)$ as sets of properties, like $\forall\{even, odd\}$, as described in the prelude to Section 1.

[3] Think of the elements of $\mathcal{P}_U(A)$ as sets of properties, like $\exists\{even, odd\}$.

[4] This is the lower half of the Egli-Milner ordering, such that when $\rho_\tau \subseteq C \times C$ equals $\sqsubseteq_\tau$, freely generates the lower ("Hoare") powerdomain.

Let Nat be the discretely ordered set of natural numbers, and let complete lattice

$$Parity = \begin{array}{c} any \\ even \quad odd \\ none \end{array}$$

We have the obvious Galois connection, $\mathcal{P}(Nat)\langle \alpha_{Par}, \gamma_{Par}\rangle Parity$, where $\gamma_{Par}(even) = \{2n \mid n \in Nat\}$, $\gamma_{Par}(any) = Nat$, etc. We can lift this to:

$$\gamma_{\bar{\mathcal{P}}_U(Par)} : \mathcal{P}_{\Box}(Parity) \rightarrow \mathcal{P}_{\Box}(\mathcal{P}(Nat)^{op})$$

where $\mathcal{P}_{\Box}(Parity)$ are the superset-ordered, up-closed subsets of $Parity$, and $\mathcal{P}_{\Box}(\mathcal{P}(Nat)^{op})$ are the subset-ordered, superset-closed subsets of $\mathcal{P}(Nat)$. $\gamma_{\bar{\mathcal{P}}_U(Par)}$ is defined as follows:

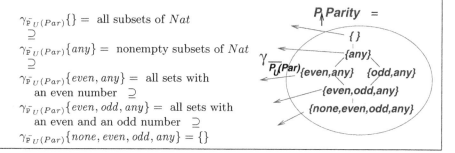

$\gamma_{\bar{\mathcal{P}}_U(Par)}\{\} = $ all subsets of Nat
$\supseteq$

$\gamma_{\bar{\mathcal{P}}_U(Par)}\{any\} = $ nonempty subsets of Nat
$\supseteq$

$\gamma_{\bar{\mathcal{P}}_U(Par)}\{even, any\} = $ all sets with
an even number $\supseteq$

$\gamma_{\bar{\mathcal{P}}_U(Par)}\{even, odd, any\} = $ all sets with
an even and an odd number $\supseteq$

$\gamma_{\bar{\mathcal{P}}_U(Par)}\{none, even, odd, any\} = \{\}$

Fig. 2. An under-approximation of sets of natural numbers by sets of parities

That is, $\bar{S} \in \mathcal{P}_L(\mathcal{P}(C))$ is approximated by $T \in \mathcal{P}_L(A_\tau)$ iff for every set $S \in \bar{S}$, $S\,\rho_{\mathcal{P}_L(\tau)}\,T$. This makes $\gamma_{\bar{\mathcal{P}}_L(\tau)}(T) = \{S \mid S\,\rho_{\mathcal{P}_L(\tau)}\,T\}$, which concretizes T to the set of all sets approximated by T.

For over-approximation, both approaches yield the *same* definition of $R^\#_{best}$: $A \rightarrow \mathcal{P}_L(A)$, but a sound under-approximation *utilizes the second approach*:

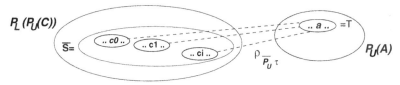

$\bar{S}$ is under-approximated by T iff for every set $S \in \bar{S}$, $S\,\rho_{\mathcal{P}_U(\tau)}\,T$, where

$$S\,\rho_{\mathcal{P}_U(\tau)}\,T \text{ iff for every } a \in T, \text{ there exists some } c \in S \text{ such that } c\,\rho_\tau\,a \text{ }^5.$$

Thus, $\gamma_{\bar{\mathcal{P}}_U(\tau)} : \mathcal{P}_U(A) \rightarrow \mathcal{P}_L(\mathcal{P}(C)^{op})$, and $\gamma_{\bar{\mathcal{P}}_U(\tau)}(T) = \{S \mid S\,\rho_{\mathcal{P}_U(\tau)}\,T\}$, which is crucial to Dams's results. Figure 2 gives an example of the construction.

---

[5] This is the upper half of the Egli-Milner ordering, and when $\rho_\tau \subseteq C \times C$ is $\sqsubseteq_\tau$, freely generates the upper ("Smyth") powerdomain.

1.2   Outline of Results

Applying the just-stated approach, we redevelop and extend Dams's results [10, 11] within a higher-order Galois-connection framework [9]:

1. We show how Galois connections are generated from U-GLB-L-LUB-closed binary relations (cf. [8, 23, 28]).
2. We define lower and upper powerset constructions, which are weaker forms of powerdomains appropriate for abstraction studies [9, 15, 25].
3. We use the powerset types within a family of logical relations, show when the logical relations preserve the closure properties in Item 1., and show that simulation can be proved via logical relations. We incrementally rebuild Dams's most-precise simulations with the logical relations, revealing the inner structure of under- and over-approximation on powersets.
4. We extract validation and refutation logics from the logical relations (cf. [2]), state their resemblance to Hennessey-Milner logic [17] and description logic [3, 6], and obtain easy proofs of soundness and best precision.

2   Closed Binary Relations Generate Galois Connections

The following results are assembled from [4, 8, 14, 23, 24, 28]: Let C and A be complete lattices, and let $\rho \subseteq C \times A$, where $c \rho a$ means c is approximated by a.

Definition 1. *For all $c, c' \in C$, for $a, a' \in A$, for $\rho \subseteq C \times A$, ρ is*

1. *L-closed iff $c \rho a$ and $c' \sqsubseteq c$ imply $c' \rho a$*
2. *LUB-closed iff $\sqcup\{c \mid c \rho a\} \rho a$*
3. *U-closed iff $c \rho a$ and $a \sqsubseteq a'$ imply $c \rho a'$*
4. *GLB-closed iff $c \rho \sqcap\{a \mid c \rho a\}$*

Proposition 2. *For L-U-LUB-GLB-closed $\rho \subseteq C \times A$, $C \langle \alpha_\rho, \gamma_\rho \rangle A$ is a Galois connection, where $\alpha_\rho(c) = \sqcap\{a \mid c \rho a\}$ and $\gamma_\rho(a) = \sqcup\{c \mid c \rho a\}$.*

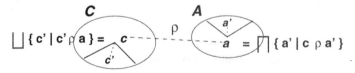

As the diagram above suggests, U- and L-closure make γ_ρ and α_ρ monotonic, and LUB- and GLB- closure make the functions select the most precise answers. Note that $c \rho a$ iff $c \sqsubseteq_C \gamma_\rho(a)$ iff $\alpha_\rho(c) \sqsubseteq_A a$.

Proposition 3. *For Galois connection, $C \langle \alpha, \gamma \rangle A$, define $\rho_{\alpha\gamma} \subseteq C \times A$ as $\{(c, a) \mid \alpha c \sqsubseteq a\}$. Then, $\rho_{\alpha\gamma}$ is L-U-LUB-GLB-closed and $\langle \alpha_{\rho_{\alpha\gamma}}, \gamma_{\rho_{\alpha\gamma}} \rangle = \langle \alpha, \gamma \rangle$.*

2.1   Completing a U-GLB-Closed $\rho \subseteq C \times A$

Often one has a discretely ordered set, C, a complete lattice, A, and an obvious approximation relation, $\rho \subseteq C \times A$. But there is no Galois connection between C and A, because ρ lacks LUB-closure. We complete C to a powerset:

Proposition 4. *For set C, complete lattice A, and $\rho \subseteq C \times A$, define $\bar{\rho} \subseteq \mathcal{P}(C) \times A$ as $S \bar{\rho} a$ iff for all $c \in S$, $c \rho a$. If ρ is U-GLB-closed, then $\bar{\rho}$ is U-GLB-L-LUB-closed and $\gamma_{\bar{\rho}} : A \to \mathcal{P}(C)$ is $\gamma_{\bar{\rho}}(a) = \{c \mid c \rho a\}$.*

Figure 3 shows an application. There is no implementation penalty in applying Proposition 4, because the abstract domain retains its existing cardinality.

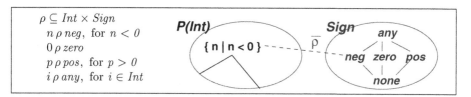

$\rho \subseteq Int \times Sign$
$n \rho neg$, for $n < 0$
$0 \rho zero$
$p \rho pos$, for $p > 0$
$i \rho any$, for $i \in Int$

Fig. 3. Completing $\rho \subseteq Int \times Sign$ to $\bar{\rho} \subseteq \mathcal{P}(Int) \times Sign$

3   Powersets

Definition 5. *For complete lattice, D, a powerset of D is $PD = (E, \sqsubseteq_E, \{\!| \cdot |\!\} : D \to E, \uplus : E \times E \to E)$, such that*

- *$(E, \sqsubseteq_E)$ is a complete lattice*
- *$\{\!| \cdot |\!\}$, the singleton operation, is monotone*
- *$\uplus$, union operation, is monotone, absorptive, commutative, and associative*
- *For every monotone $f : D \to L$, there is a monotone $ext(f) : E \to L$ such that $ext(f)\{\!|d|\!\} = f(d)$, for all $d \in D$.*

Here are examples of powersets from Cousot and Cousot [9]:
Down-Set (Order-Ideal) Completion: For $d \in D$, $S \subseteq D$, define $\downarrow d = \{e \in D \mid e \sqsubseteq d\}$ and $\downarrow S = \cup \{\downarrow d \mid d \in S\}$. Define $\mathcal{P}_\downarrow(D) = (\{\downarrow S \mid S \subseteq D\}, \subseteq, \downarrow, \cup)$.
Join Completion (Subsets of $\mathcal{P}_\downarrow(D)$): $(\mathcal{M}, \subseteq, \downarrow, \sqcup_\mathcal{M})$, where $\mathcal{M} \subseteq \{\downarrow S \mid S \subseteq D\}$ is a *Moore family* (that is, closed under intersections)[6].
Figure 4 presents an example. For monotone $f : D \to L$, let $ext(f) : \mathcal{P}_\downarrow(D) \to L$ be $ext(f)(S) = \sqcup_{d \in S} f(d)$.
Up-Set (Filter) Completion: For $d \in D$ and $S \subseteq D$, define $\uparrow d = \{e \in D \mid d \sqsubseteq e\}$ and $\uparrow S = \cup \{\uparrow d \mid d \in S\}$. Define $\mathcal{P}_\uparrow(D) = (\{\uparrow S \mid S \subseteq D\}, \supseteq, \uparrow, \cup)$.
Dual-Join Completion: Subsets of $\mathcal{P}_\uparrow(D)$: $(\mathcal{M}, \supseteq, \uparrow, \sqcap_\mathcal{M})$, where $\mathcal{M} \subseteq \{\uparrow S \mid S \subseteq D\}$ is a Moore family.
For monotone $f : D \to L$, let $ext(f) : \mathcal{P}_\uparrow(D) \to L$ be $ext(f)(S) = \sqcap_{d \in S} f(d)$.

---

[6] Join completions "add new joins" to D; the trivial join completion is $(\{\downarrow d \mid d \in D\}, \subseteq, \downarrow, \downarrow \circ \sqcup_D)$, which is isomorphic to D, and the most detailed join completion is $\mathcal{P}_\downarrow(D)$.

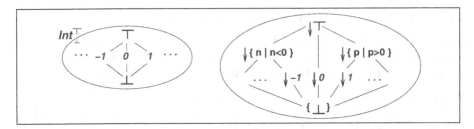

Fig. 4. Complete lattice $Int_0^\sqcap$ and one possible join completion

3.1   Lower and Strongly Lower Powersets

For powerset PD, for $d \in D$ and $S \in PD$, define $d \, \tilde{\in} \, S$ iff $\{|d|\} \uplus S = S$.

Definition 6. *Powerset* $\mathcal{P}_L(D) = (E, \sqsubseteq_E, \{| \cdot |\}, \uplus)$ *is*

1. *a lower powerset iff ((for all $x \, \tilde{\in} \, S_1$, there exists $y \, \tilde{\in} \, S_2$ such that $x \sqsubseteq_D y$) implies $S_1 \sqsubseteq_E S_2$).*
2. *a strongly lower powerset iff ((for all $x \, \tilde{\in} \, S_1$, there exists $y \, \tilde{\in} \, S_2$ such that $x \sqsubseteq_D y$) iff $S_1 \sqsubseteq_E S_2$).*

Although lower powersets are the starting point for powerdomain theory [15, 25][7], we work with strongly lower powersets[8], because

Proposition 7. *For every strongly lower powerset,* $\mathcal{P}_L(D) = (E, \sqsubseteq_E, \{| \cdot |\}, \uplus)$,
(i) $\uplus = \sqcup_E$*; and*
(ii) $\mathcal{P}_L(D)$ *is order-isomorphic to a join-completion of* D, *where* $\tilde{\in}$ *is* $\in$.

Strongly lower powersets let us generalize Proposition 4:

Theorem 8. *For complete lattices C and A, let $\rho \subseteq C \times A$ and let $\mathcal{P}_L(C) = (E, \subseteq, \{| \cdot |\}, \uplus)$ be a join completion (strongly lower powerset). Recall that $\bar{\rho} \subseteq \mathcal{P}_L(C) \times A$ is defined $S \, \bar{\rho} \, a$ iff for all $c \in S$, $c \, \rho \, a$.*

If (i) ρ is U-L-GLB-closed, and (ii) for all $a \in A$, $\{c \mid c \, \rho \, a\} \in E$, then $\bar{\rho}$ is U-L-GLB-LUB-closed and $\gamma_{\bar{\rho}}(a) = \{c \mid c \, \rho \, a\}$.

Thus, $\mathcal{P}_L(C)\langle \alpha_{\bar{\rho}}, \gamma_{\bar{\rho}} \rangle A$ is always a Galois connection for U-L-GLB-closed $\rho \subseteq C \times A$, but the *minimal* join completion of sets $\{c \mid c \, \rho \, a\}$, $a \in A$, also suffices to generate a Galois connection.

For example, say that Int and ρ in Figure 3 are replaced by $Int_\perp^\top$ from Figure 4 and by $\rho \subseteq Int_\perp^\top \times Sign$, which is defined to be ρ augmented by $\top \, \rho \, any$ and $\perp \, \rho \, a$, for all $a \in Sign$. Figure 4 shows ρ's minimal join completion.

3.2   Upper Powersets

As Plotkin [25] notes, the upper and strongly upper powersets coincide, so

Definition 9. *Powerset* $\mathcal{P}_U(D) = (E, \sqsubseteq_E, \{| \cdot |\}, \uplus)$ *is an upper powerset iff* $(S_1 \sqsubseteq_E S_2$ *iff for all* $y \, \tilde{\in} \, S_2$, *there exists* $x \, \tilde{\in} \, S_1$ *such that* $x \sqsubseteq_\top y)$.

For an upper powerset, $\uplus = \sqcap$, and every upper powerset is isomorphic to a dual-join completion.

---

[7] Which requires functions to be Scott-continuous.
[8] Which allows non-Scott-continuous, monotone functions.

4   Logical Relations

We attach these typings to the relations introduced in Section 2:

$$\tau ::= b \mid \tau_1 \rightarrow \tau_2 \mid \mathcal{P}_L(\tau) \mid \mathcal{P}_U(\tau) \mid \bar{\tau}$$

Only typing $\bar{\tau}$ is nonstandard; it is a special case of $\mathcal{P}_L(\tau)$ that we retain for convenience, because it appears so often in the practice of generating Galois connections.

We attach the typings to concrete and abstract domains, D, as follows:

D_b is given, for base type b

$D_{\tau_1 \rightarrow \tau_2}$ are the monotone functions from D_{τ_1} to D_{τ_2}, ordered pointwise

$D_{\mathcal{P}_L(\tau)}$ is a strongly lower powerset generated from D_τ

$D_{\mathcal{P}_U(\tau)}$ is an upper powerset generated from D_τ

Since $\bar{\rho} \subseteq \mathcal{P}_L(C) \times A$ is the completion of $\rho \subseteq C \times A$ (cf. Theorem 8), we define

$$C_{\bar{\tau}} \text{ is } C_{\mathcal{P}_L(\tau)}, \text{ for concrete domain } C_\tau$$
$$A_{\bar{\tau}} \text{ is } A_\tau, \text{ for abstract domain } A_\tau$$

Now, we can define this family of logical relations, $\rho_\tau \subseteq C_\tau \times A_\tau$:

ρ_b is given, for base type b

$f \, \rho_{\tau_1 \rightarrow \tau_2} \, f^\sharp$ iff for all $c \in C_{\tau_1}, a \in A_{\tau_1}, c\,\rho_{\tau_1}\,a$ implies $f(c)\,\rho_{\tau_2}\,f^\sharp(a)$

$S \, \rho_{\mathcal{P}_L(\tau)} \, T$ iff for all $c \tilde{\in} S$, there exists $a \tilde{\in} T$ such that $c\,\rho_\tau\,a$

$S \, \rho_{\mathcal{P}_U(\tau)} \, T$ iff for all $a \tilde{\in} T$, there exists $c \tilde{\in} S$ such that $c\,\rho_\tau\,a$

$S \, \rho_{\bar{\tau}} \, a$ iff for all $c \in S, c\,\rho_\tau\,a$

Again, note that $\rho_{\bar{\tau}} \subseteq C_{\mathcal{P}_L(\tau)} \times A_\tau$ is an instance of $\rho_{\mathcal{P}_L(\tau)} \subseteq C_{\mathcal{P}_L(\tau)} \times A_{\mathcal{P}_L(\tau)}$, where $C_{\mathcal{P}_L(\tau)}$ is treated as a join completion and $A_{\mathcal{P}_L(\tau)}$ is restricted to the trivial join completion, $(\{\downarrow a \mid a \in A_\tau\}, \subseteq, \downarrow, \downarrow \circ \sqcup_{A_\tau})$, which is isomorphic to A_τ.

4.1   Simulations Are Logical Relations

The standard definition of simulation goes as follows:

Definition 10. *For $\rho \subseteq C \times A$ and transition relations, $R \subseteq C \times C$, $R^\sharp \subseteq A \times A$, $R^\sharp$ ρ-simulates R, written $R \lhd_\rho R^\sharp$, iff for all $c, c' \in C, a \in A$,*

$$c\,\rho\,a \text{ and } c\,R\,c' \text{ imply there exists } a' \in A \text{ such that } a\,R^\sharp\,a' \text{ and } c'\,\rho\,a'.$$

When we represent R and $R^\sharp$ as $R : C \rightarrow \mathcal{P}_L(C)$ and $R^\sharp : A \rightarrow \mathcal{P}_L(A)$, respectively, we have

Theorem 11. $R \lhd_{\rho_b} R^\sharp$ *iff* $R\,\rho_{b \rightarrow \mathcal{P}_L(b)}\,R^\sharp$ [9].

A dual simulation, $R^\flat \lhd_{\rho_b^{-1}} R$, is beautifully characterized as $R\,\rho_{b \rightarrow \mathcal{P}_U(b)}\,R^\flat$. We employ these characterizations of simulation and dual-simulation to construct optimal over- and under-approximating transition relations from Galois connections generated from closed, logical relations [10].

---

[9] The proof assumes that R and $R^\sharp$ behave monotonically.

[10] Please see Section 8 for a summary of Loiseaux, et al. [22], which also characterizes simulations as Galois connections.

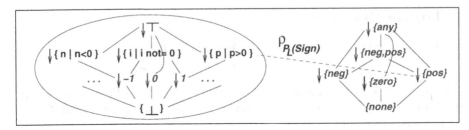

Fig. 5. An L-LUB-closed relation between strongly lower powersets

5 Closure Properties of Logical Relations

Proposition 12. *For* $\rho_\tau \subseteq C_\tau \times A_\tau$ *and for* $F[\tau] \in \{\tau' \to \tau, \ \mathcal{P}_L(\tau), \ \mathcal{P}_U(\tau), \ \bar{\tau}\}$,

If ρ_τ *is L-closed, then so is* $\rho_{F[\tau]}$.
If ρ_τ *is U-closed, then so is* $\rho_{F[\tau]}$.
If ρ_τ *is U-GLB-closed, then so are* $\rho_{\tau' \to \tau}$, $\rho_{\bar{\tau}}$, *and* $\rho_{\mathcal{P}_L(\tau)}$.
If ρ_τ *is L-LUB-closed, then so are* $\rho_{\tau' \to \tau}$ *and* $\rho_{\mathcal{P}_U(\tau)}$.

Preservation of LUB-closure for $\rho_{\mathcal{P}_L(\tau)}$ and GLB-closure for $\rho_{\mathcal{P}_U(\tau)}$ depend on the specific powersets used (cf. Backhouse and Backhouse [4]).

Here are some additional useful properties:

Proposition 13. *Let* $\rho_{\tau_i} \subseteq C_{\tau_i} \times A_{\tau_i}$, *for* $i \in 1..2$, *be U-GLB-L-LUB-closed. For* $f : C_{\tau_1} \to C_{\tau_2}$, $f^\sharp : A_{\tau_1} \to A_{\tau_2}$,

$$f \ \rho_{\tau_1 \to \tau_2} \ f^\sharp \ \textit{iff} \ \alpha_{\rho_{\tau_2}} \circ f \sqsubseteq_{A_1 \to A_2} f^\sharp \circ \alpha_{\rho_{\tau_1}}.$$

In particular, $f \ \rho_{\tau_1 \to \tau_2} \ f^\sharp_{best}$, *where* $f^\sharp_{best}(a) = \alpha_{\rho_{\tau_2}} \circ f \circ \gamma_{\rho_{\tau_1}}$.

If $\rho_\tau \subseteq C_\tau \times A_\tau$ *is L-LUB-closed, then so is* $\rho_{\mathcal{P}_L(\tau)} \subseteq \mathcal{P}_\downarrow(C_\tau) \times \mathcal{P}_L(A_\tau)$, *for any choice of* $\mathcal{P}_L(A_\tau)$; *this follows from*

Proposition 14. *For all* $T \in \mathcal{P}_L(A_\tau)$, *let* $\mathcal{L}_T = \{S \in \mathcal{P}_L(C_\tau) \mid S \ \rho_{\mathcal{P}_L(\tau)} \ T\}$. *If*

1. ρ_τ *is L-LUB-closed; and*
2. *for all* $c \,\tilde{\in}\, \sqcup \mathcal{L}_T$, *there exists* $a \,\tilde{\in}\, T$ *such that* $c = \sqcup S_a$, *where* $S_a \subseteq \{c' \,\tilde{\in}\, S \in \mathcal{L}_T \mid c' \ \rho_\tau \ a\}$

then $\rho_{\mathcal{P}_L(\tau)} \subseteq \mathcal{P}_L(C_\tau) \times \mathcal{P}_L(A_\tau)$ *is LUB-closed.*

That is, given the lower powerset $\mathcal{P}_L(C_\tau)$, we require $\sqcup \mathcal{L}_T \ \rho_{\mathcal{P}_L(\tau)} \ T$, for all $T \,\tilde{\in}\, A_{\mathcal{P}_L(\tau)}$. Item 2 says that every element, $c \,\tilde{\in}\, \sqcup \mathcal{L}_T$, is a join of elements that are all related to some $a \,\tilde{\in}\, T$. By L-LUB closure of ρ_τ, we have $c \ \rho_\tau \ a$, giving LUB-closure for $\rho_{\mathcal{P}_L(\tau)}$.

Often we can use a coarser join completion than $\mathcal{P}_\downarrow(C_\tau)$ to get LUB-closure. For example, for $C_{Int} = Int_\bot^\top$ from Figure 4 and $A_{Int} = Sign$ from Figure 3, the version of $\mathcal{P}_L(Sign)$ in Figure 5(*right*), requires merely the $\mathcal{P}_L(Int_\bot^\top)$ in Figure 5(*left*), for LUB-closure of $\rho_{\mathcal{P}_L(Sign)} \subseteq \mathcal{P}_L(Int_\bot^\top) \times \mathcal{P}_L(Sign)$ [11].

---

[11] Of course, for $\mathcal{P}_L(C_\tau)$ to be useful for giving the semantics of transition relation $R \subseteq C_\tau \times C_\tau$, we require that $\downarrow\{c^\partial \mid cRc^\partial\} \in \mathcal{P}_L(C_\tau)$, for all $c \in C_\tau$.

Proposition 15. *For all $S \in \mathcal{P}_U(C_\tau)$, let $\mathcal{G}_S = \{T \in \mathcal{P}_U(A) \mid S \, \rho_{\mathcal{P}_U(\tau)} \, T\}$. If*

1. *ρ_τ is U-GLB-closed, and*
2. *for all $a \,\tilde{\in}\, \sqcap_{\mathcal{P}_U(A)} \mathcal{G}_S$, there exists $c \,\tilde{\in}\, S$ such that $a = \sqcap_A T_c$, where $T_c \subseteq \{a' \,\tilde{\in}\, T \in \mathcal{G}_S \mid c \, \rho_\tau \, a'\}$,*

then $\rho_{\mathcal{P}_U(\tau)} \subseteq \mathcal{P}_U(C_\tau) \times \mathcal{P}_U(rA_\tau)$ is GLB-closed.

For all choices of $\mathcal{P}_U(C_\tau)$, Proposition 15 successfully applies to $\mathcal{P}_\uparrow(A_\tau)$, the filter completion of A_τ. But often a coarser, dual-join completion of A_τ will do: When giving semantics to transition relation $R \subseteq C_\tau \times C_\tau$, we require only that R's image lies in $\mathcal{P}_U(C_\tau)$: $\uparrow\{c' \mid cRc'\} \in \mathcal{P}_U(C_\tau)$, for all $c \in C_\tau$. This coarser domain for $\mathcal{P}_U(C_\tau)$ lets us use a coarser $\mathcal{P}_U(A_\tau)$ with Proposition 15.

6   Synthesizing a Most-Precise Simulation

Dams [10, 11] proves, for Galois connection $\mathcal{P}(C)\langle\alpha, \gamma\rangle A$ and relation $R \subseteq C \times C$, that the most precise, sound, abstract transition relation $R_0^\sharp \subseteq A \times A$ is

$$R_0^\sharp(a, a') \text{ iff } a' \in \{\alpha(Y) \mid Y \in min\{S' \mid R^{\exists\exists}(\gamma(a), S')\}\}$$

where $R^{\exists\exists}(M, N)$ *holds iff there exist $m \in M$ and $n \in N$ such that mRn.* Recoded as a function, $R_0^\sharp : A \to \mathcal{P}_L(A)$, and simplified, this reads

$$R_0^\sharp(a) = \{\alpha(s') \mid \exists s \in \gamma(a), s' \in R(s)\}$$

Our machinery gives us the same result: Given U-GLB-closed $\rho_b \subseteq C \times A$ and transition function $R : C \to \mathcal{P}(C)$, we generate the Galois connections, $\mathcal{P}(C)\langle\alpha_{\rho_{\bar{b}}}, \gamma_{\rho_{\bar{b}}}\rangle A$ and $\mathcal{P}(C)\langle\alpha_{\rho_{\mathcal{P}_L}(b)}, \gamma_{\rho_{\mathcal{P}_L}(b)}\rangle \mathcal{P}_L(A)$, and synthesize the most precise, sound abstract transition function, $R_{best}^\sharp : A \to \mathcal{P}_L(A)$,

$$R_{best}^\sharp(a) = (\alpha_{\rho_{\mathcal{P}_L}(b)} \circ ext_{\bar{b}}(R) \circ \gamma_{\rho_{\bar{b}}})(a) = \sqcup\{\{\alpha_{\rho_{\bar{b}}}\{s'\}\} \mid \exists s \in \gamma_{\rho_{\bar{b}}}(a), s' \in R(s)\}$$

which is Dams's definition, when $\mathcal{P}_L(A)$ is $\mathcal{P}_\downarrow(A)$. We have $R \, \rho_{\bar{b} \to \mathcal{P}_L(b)} \, R_{best}^\sharp$.

As suggested in Section 1.1, we might also derive an abstract transition relation that is sound with respect to *sets of sets*: We generate the Galois connection, $\mathcal{P}_\downarrow(\mathcal{P}(C))\langle\alpha_{\rho_{\bar{\mathcal{P}}_L}(b)}, \gamma_{\rho_{\bar{\mathcal{P}}_L}(b)}\rangle\mathcal{P}_L(A)$, and for $R : C \to \mathcal{P}(C)$, we generate $R_{best}^\sharp : A \to \mathcal{P}_L(A)$,

$$R_{best}^\sharp = \alpha_{\rho_{\bar{\mathcal{P}}_L}(b)} \circ ext_{\bar{b}}(\{\!|\cdot|\!\}_{\mathcal{P}_\downarrow(\mathcal{P}(C))} \circ R) \circ \gamma_{\rho_{\bar{b}}}$$

where $ext_{\bar{b}}(\{\!|\cdot|\!\}_{\mathcal{P}_\downarrow(\mathcal{P}(C))} \circ R)(S) = \downarrow\{R(c) \mid c \in S\}$, and $\alpha_{\rho_{\bar{\mathcal{P}}_L}(b)}(\bar{S}) = \sqcap\{T \mid$ for all $S \in \bar{S}, S \, \rho_{\mathcal{P}_L(b)} \, T\}$. That is, $ext_{\bar{b}}(\{\!|\cdot|\!\}_{\mathcal{P}_\downarrow(\mathcal{P}(C))} \circ R)$ maps a set of arguments to the set of R-successor sets, and $\alpha_{\rho_{\bar{\mathcal{P}}_L}(b)}$ produces the smallest abstract set that over-approximates each of the successor sets. We have $R \, \rho_{\bar{b} \to \bar{\mathcal{P}}_L(b)} \, R_{best}^\sharp$, and $R_{best}^\sharp$ equals the definition seen earlier.

This development is notational overkill, but there is an important point: *Simulation equivalence is preserved when a concrete transition function is lifted to a function that maps a set of arguments to a set of sets of answers:*

Theorem 16. $R \lhd_\rho R^\sharp$ iff $R\,\rho_{b \to \mathcal{P}_L(b)}\,R^\sharp$ iff $ext_{\bar{b}}(R)\,\rho_{\bar{b} \to \mathcal{P}_L(b)}\,R^\sharp$ iff $ext_{\bar{b}}(\{\!|\cdot|\!\}_{\bar{\mathcal{P}}_L(b)} \circ R)\,\rho_{\bar{b} \to \mathcal{P}_L(b)}\,R^\sharp$.

This idea will prove crucial when working with under-approximations.

6.1   Synthesizing a Most-Precise Dual Simulation

There is a good use for $\rho_{\mathcal{P}_U(\tau)}$: defining a *sound, over-approximation analysis of under-approximations*.

Consider $\rho_{\bar{\mathcal{P}}_U(\tau)} \subseteq \mathcal{P}_\downarrow(\mathcal{P}_U(C)) \times \mathcal{P}_U(A)$; it says that $\bar{S}\,\rho_{\bar{\mathcal{P}}_U(\tau)}\,T$ iff for each set $S \in \bar{S}$, $S\,\rho_{\mathcal{P}_U(\tau)}\,T$, that is, T under-approximates each $S \in \bar{S}$:

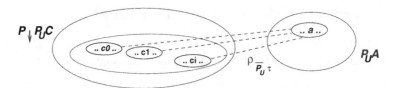

We can readily construct $\rho_{\bar{\mathcal{P}}_U(\tau)}$:

1. Begin with a U-GLB-closed $\rho_\tau \subseteq C \times A$;
2. lift it to a U-L-GLB-closed $\rho_{\mathcal{P}_U(\tau)} \subseteq \mathcal{P}_U(C) \times \mathcal{P}_U(A)$;
3. complete it to a U-GLB-L-LUB-closed $\rho_{\bar{\mathcal{P}}_U(\tau)} \subseteq \mathcal{P}_\downarrow(\mathcal{P}_U(C)) \times \mathcal{P}_U(A)$.

The resulting Galois connection, $\mathcal{P}_\downarrow(\mathcal{P}_U(C))\langle\alpha_{\rho_{\bar{\mathcal{P}}_U(\tau)}}, \gamma_{\rho_{\bar{\mathcal{P}}_U(\tau)}}\rangle \mathcal{P}_U(A)$, is

$$\gamma_{\rho_{\bar{\mathcal{P}}_U(\tau)}} T = \{S \mid S\,\rho_{\mathcal{P}_U(\tau)}\,T\}$$
$$\alpha_{\rho_{\bar{\mathcal{P}}_U(\tau)}} \bar{S} = \sqcap\{T \in \mathcal{P}_U(A) \mid \text{ for all } S \in \bar{S}, S\,\rho_{\mathcal{P}_U(\tau)}\,T\}$$

Figure 2 presents an example.

Dams proves, for Galois connection $\mathcal{P}(C)\langle\alpha,\gamma\rangle A$ and transition relation $R \subseteq C \times C$, that the most precise, sound, underapproximating abstract transition relation, $R_0^\flat \subseteq A \times A$ is

$$R_0^\flat(a, a') \text{ iff } a' \in \{\alpha(Y) \mid Y \in min\{S' \mid R^{\forall\exists}(\gamma(a), S')\}\}$$

where $R^{\forall\exists}(M, N)$ *holds iff for all* $m \in M$, *there exists* $n \in N$ *such that* mRn. Recoded as a function and simplified, this reads

$$R_0^\flat(a) = \{\alpha(Y) \mid Y \in min\{S' \mid \text{ for all } s \in \gamma(a), R(s) \cap S' \neq \{\}\}\}$$

Our machinery gives us the same result: We generate the Galois connection, $\mathcal{P}_\downarrow((\mathcal{P}(C)^{op}))\langle\alpha_{\rho_{\bar{\mathcal{P}}_U(b)}}, \gamma_{\rho_{\bar{\mathcal{P}}_U(b)}}\rangle \mathcal{P}_\uparrow(A)$. Note that C is a set, so $\mathcal{P}(C)^{op}$ is an upper powerset. For transition function, $R : C \to \mathcal{P}(C)$, we generate this most precise, sound under-approximating abstract transition function, $R_{best}^\flat : A \to \mathcal{P}_\uparrow(A)$,

$$R_{best}^\flat = \alpha_{\rho_{\bar{\mathcal{P}}_U(b)}} \circ ext(\{\!|\cdot|\!\} \circ R^{op}) \circ \gamma_{\rho_{\bar{b}}}$$

where $\{\!\vert \cdot \vert\!\} \circ R^{op} : C \to \mathcal{P}_{\downarrow}(\mathcal{P}(C)^{op})$ is $(\{\!\vert \cdot \vert\!\} \circ R^{op})(c) = \uparrow R(c) = R(c)$, and $ext(\{\!\vert \cdot \vert\!\} \circ R^{op}) : \mathcal{P}(C) \to \mathcal{P}_{\downarrow}(\mathcal{P}(C)^{op})$ is $ext(\{\!\vert \cdot \vert\!\} \circ R^{op})(S) = \downarrow_{\mathcal{P}(C)^{op}} \{R(c) \mid c \in S\} = \{S \supseteq R(c) \mid c \in S\}$, and $\alpha_{\rho_{\mathcal{P}_U(b)}}(\bar{S}) = \sqcap\{T \mid \text{for all } S \in \bar{S}, S \rho_{\mathcal{P}_U(b)} T\}$.

That is, $ext(\{\!\vert \cdot \vert\!\} \circ R^{op})$ maps a set of arguments to the set of sets of R-successors, and $\alpha_{\bar{\rho}_{\mathcal{P}_U(b)}}$ produces the largest abstract set that under-approximates each successor set $R(c)$, for $c \in \gamma_{\bar{\rho}_b}(a)$. We simplify and obtain

$$R^{\flat}_{best}(a) = \sqcap\{T \in \mathcal{P}_{\uparrow}(A) \mid \text{for all } a' \in T, \text{for all } s \in \gamma_{\rho_{\bar{b}}}(a), R(s) \cap \gamma_{\rho_{\bar{b}}}(a') \neq \{\}\}$$

which is provably equal to Dams's definition[12].

Finally, dual simulation lifts to sets of arguments:

Theorem 17. $R^{\flat} \lhd_{\rho^{-1}} R$ iff $R \rho_{b \to \mathcal{P}_U(b)} R^{\flat}$ iff $ext(\{\!\vert \cdot \vert\!\} \circ R^{op}) \rho_{\bar{b} \to \bar{\mathcal{P}}_U(b)} R^{\flat}$.

It is a good exercise to attempt to define a Galois connection from a $\rho_{\mathcal{P}_U(b)}$; the result is usually degenerate because LUB-closure is over-constraining[13].

7   Validation and Refutation Logics

Hennessey and Milner proved that $\square\Diamond$-propositions (*Hennessey-Milner logic*) characterize transition relations up to bisimilarity [17]. Loiseaux, et al. [22], proved that all $\square$-properties true of an over-approximating transition relation are preserved in the corresponding concrete transition relation and that when one over-approximating transition relation is more precise than another, then the first preserves all the $\square$-properties of the second. Dams extended this result to under-approximations and $\Diamond$-properties and proved that his definitions of $R^{\sharp}_{best}$ and $R^{\flat}_{best}$ possess the most $\square\Diamond$-propositions of any sound, mixed transition system.

In this section, we manufacture Hennessey-Milner logic from our family of logical relations (cf. [2]) and obtain the above results as corollaries of Galois-connection theory. Recall that these are the typings of the logical relations,

$$\tau ::= b \mid \tau_1 \to \tau_2 \mid \mathcal{P}_L(\tau) \mid \mathcal{P}_U(\tau) \mid \bar{\tau}$$

where $\bar{\tau}$ is an instance of $\mathcal{P}_L(\tau)$. For each of the first four typings, we define a corresponding assertion form, producing this assertion language,

$$\phi ::= p_b \mid f.\phi \mid \forall\phi \mid \exists\phi$$

and the following semantics of typed judgements (let D_τ be either C_τ or A_τ):

$d \models_b p$ is given, for $d \in D_b$
$d \models_{\tau_1 \to \tau_2} f.\phi$ if $f(d) \models_{\tau_2} \phi$, for $d \in D_{\tau_1}$ and $f \in D_{\tau_1 \to \tau_2}$
$S \models_{\mathcal{P}_L(\tau)} \forall\phi$ if for all $d \bar{\in} S, d \models_\tau \phi$, for $S \in D_{\mathcal{P}_L(\tau)}$
$S \models_{\mathcal{P}_U(\tau)} \exists\phi$ if there exists $d \bar{\in} S$ such that $d \models_\tau \phi$, for $S \in D_{\mathcal{P}_U(\tau)}$

---

[12] $R^{\flat}_0(a)$ belongs to and is $\sqsubseteq$ all elements in $R^{\flat}_{best}(a)$.

[13] Consider Figure 2 and $\rho_{\mathcal{P}_U(Parity)} \subseteq \mathcal{P}(Nat)^{op} \times \mathcal{P}_{\mathbb{U}}(Parity)$: What is the least set of natural numbers that "witnesses" $\{even, any\}$? $\{0\}$? $\{2\}$? LUB-closure fails.

Since $\bar{\tau}$ is an instance of $\mathcal{P}_L(\tau)$, we define its judgements for abstract values as

$$a \models_{\bar{\tau}} \phi \;\; \text{if } a \models_\tau \phi, \text{ for } a \in A_\tau.$$

and for concrete values as

$$S \models_{\bar{\tau}} \phi \;\; \text{if } c \models_\tau \phi, \text{ for all } c \in S, \; S \in \mathcal{P}_L(C_\tau)$$

We might abbreviate $d \models_{\tau \to \mathcal{P}_L(\tau)} R.\forall\phi$ by $d \models \forall R\phi$ (as in *description logic* [3]) or by $[R]\phi$ (*Hennessey-Milner logic* [17]) or by $\Box\phi$ when the system studied has only one transition relation, $R \subseteq D_\tau \times D_\tau$ (*CTL* [7]). This hides the reasoning on sets. Similarly, $d \models_{\tau \to \mathcal{P}_U(\tau)} R.\exists\phi$ can be abbreviated by $d \models \exists R\phi$ or $\langle R \rangle \phi$ or $\Diamond\phi$.

The judgements for $\forall\phi$ and $\exists\phi$ employ $R^\sharp$ and $R^\flat$, respectively, to validate the assertions, motivating Dams's mixed transition systems[14].

7.1   Soundness of Judgements

Assume for all types, τ, that the logical relations, $\rho_\tau \subseteq C_\tau \times A_\tau$, are defined. Assume also, for all function symbols, f, typed $\tau_1 \to \tau_2$, that there are interpretations $f : C_{\tau_1} \to C_{\tau_2}$, and $f^\sharp : A_{\tau_1} \to A_{\tau_2}$, such that $f \, \rho_{\tau_1 \to \tau_2} \, f^\sharp$. (Functions f and $f^\sharp$ are used in the semantics of $\models_{\tau_1 \to \tau_2} f.\phi$.)

Definition 18. *Judgement form $\models_{\tau'} \phi$ is sound iff for all $c \in C_\tau$, $a \in A_\tau$, $(a \models_{\tau'} \phi$ holds true and $c \, \rho_\tau \, a)$ imply that $c \models_{\tau'} \phi$ holds true*[15].

Assume that $\models_b p$ is sound for the choice of $\rho_b \subseteq C_b \times A_b$.

Theorem 19. *For all types, τ, all judgement forms, $\models_\tau \phi$, are sound.*

The proof is an easy induction on the structure of τ.

We can add the logical connectives,

$$d \models_\tau \phi_1 \wedge \phi_2 \text{ if } d \models_\tau \phi_1 \text{ and } d \models_\tau \phi_2$$
$$d \models_\tau \phi_1 \vee \phi_2 \text{ if } d \models_\tau \phi_1 \text{ or } d \models_\tau \phi_2$$

and prove these sound, but we will require a dual logic, a *refutation logic*, to define a sound semantics for $\neg\phi$; we do so momentarily.

7.2   Best Precision of Judgements

Say that a judgement form, $\models_{\tau'} \phi$, is *monotone* if $a \models_{\tau'} \phi$ and $a' \sqsubseteq_\tau a$ imply $a' \models_{\tau'} \phi$, for all $a, a' \in A_\tau$ [16]. We assume that all base-type judgements, $\models_b p_b$, are monotone, and from this it follows that all judgement forms are monotone. As a consequence, we have immediately Dams's best-precision result:

Theorem 20. *For Galois connection, $\mathcal{P}(C)\langle\alpha,\gamma\rangle A$, and every $R : C \to \mathcal{P}(C)$, $R^\sharp_{best} : A \to \mathcal{P}_L(A)$ and $R^\flat_{best} : A \to \mathcal{P}_U(A)$ soundly prove the most typed judgements, $a \models_\tau \phi$, for all $a \in A$ and choices of $\mathcal{P}_L(A)$ and $\mathcal{P}_U(A)$.*

---

[14] For set, C_τ, $\mathcal{P}(C_\tau)$ is a strongly lower powerset and $\mathcal{P}(C_\tau)^{op}$ is an upper powerset, so we can readily validate $\forall\phi$ and $\exists\phi$-properties on concrete sets, also.

[15] The judgement form, $\models_{\tau_1^0 \; \tau_2} f.\phi$, shows that τ^0 need not be τ.

[16] The intuition is that $\gamma_{\rho_\tau}(a^0) \subseteq \gamma_{\rho_\tau}(a) \subseteq [\![\phi]\!] \subseteq C_\tau$.

7.3   Validating ¬φ Requires a *Refutation Logic*

For $c \in C$, we *define* $c \models_\tau \neg\phi$ *iff* $c \not\models_\tau \phi$.

The logic in Section 7 validates properties, so we might have also a logic that *refutes* them: Read $a \models_{\tau'}^{\neg pos} \phi$ as "it is not possible that any value modelled by $a \in A_\tau$ has property ϕ."

$$a \models_b^{\neg pos} p \quad \text{is given, for } a \in A_b$$
$$a \models_{\tau_1 \to \tau_2}^{\neg pos} f.\phi \quad \text{if } f^\sharp(a) \models_{\tau_2}^{\neg pos} \phi, \text{ for } a \in A_{\tau_1}, f^\sharp \in A_{\tau_1 \to \tau_2}$$
$$T \models_{\mathcal{P}_U(\tau)}^{\neg pos} \forall\phi \quad \text{if exists } a \tilde{\in} T, a \models_\tau^{\neg pos} \phi, \text{ for } T \in A_{\mathcal{P}_U(\tau)}$$
$$T \models_{\mathcal{P}_L(\tau)}^{\neg pos} \exists\phi \quad \text{if for all } a \tilde{\in} T, a \models_\tau^{\neg pos} \phi, \text{ for } T \in A_{\mathcal{P}_L(\tau)}$$
$$a \models_\tau^{\neg pos} \phi \quad \text{if } a \models_\tau^{\neg pos} \phi, \text{ for } a \in A_\tau$$

In the refutation logic, the roles of $\mathcal{P}_L(\tau)$ and $\mathcal{P}_U(\tau)$ are exchanged.

Definition 21. $\models_{\tau'}^{\neg pos} \phi$ *is sound iff for all* $c \in C_\tau$, $a \in A$, $c \rho_\tau a$ *and* $a \models_{\tau'}^{\neg pos} \phi$ *imply* $c \not\models_{\tau'} \phi$.

Proposition 22. *For all types,* τ, $\models_\tau^{\neg pos} \phi$ *are sound and monotone, assuming that the base-type judgements,* $\models_b^{\neg pos} p_b$, *are*[17].

Corollary 23. *The judgement definitions,*
$$a \models_\tau \neg\phi \quad \text{if } a \models_\tau^{\neg pos} \phi$$
$$a \models_\tau^{\neg pos} \neg\phi \quad \text{if } a \models_\tau \phi$$
are both sound and monotone.

The Sagiv-Reps-Wilhelm TVLA system simultaneously calculates validation and refutation logics[27]. Indeed, we might *combine* $\rho_{\mathcal{P}_L(\tau)}$ and $\rho_{\mathcal{P}_U(\tau)}$ into $\rho_{P_\tau} \subseteq \mathcal{P}(C) \times (\mathcal{P}_L(A) \times \mathcal{P}_U(A))$. This motivates sandwich- and mixed-powerdomains in a theory of over-under-approximation of sets [5, 13, 16, 18, 19].

8   Related Work

In addition to Dams's work [10, 11], three other lines of research deserve mention:
Loiseaux, et al. [22] showed an equivalence between simulations and Galois connections: For *sets* C and A, and $\rho \subseteq C \times A$, they note that $\mathcal{P}(C)\langle post[\rho], \tilde{pre}[\rho]\rangle\mathcal{P}(A)$ is always a Galois connection[18].

For $R \subseteq C \times C$ and $R^\sharp \subseteq A \times A$, simulation is equivalently defined as R *is* ρ-*simulated by* $R^\sharp$ *iff* $R^{-1} \cdot \rho \subseteq \rho \cdot (R^\sharp)^{-1}$ Treating R^{-1} and $(R^\sharp)^{-1}$ as functions, we can define Galois-connection soundness as

$(R^\sharp)^{-1}$ *is a sound over-approximation for* R^{-1} *with respect to* γ *iff*
$$pre[R] \circ \gamma \sqsubseteq_{\mathcal{P}(A) \to \mathcal{P}(C)} \gamma \circ pre[R^\sharp]$$

---

[17] The intuition is that $a \models_{\tau'}^{\neg pos} \phi$ implies $\gamma_{\rho_\tau}(a) \cap [\![\phi]\!] = \{\}$.

[18] $\tilde{pre}[\rho] = \lambda T.\{c \mid \{a \mid c \rho a\} \subseteq T\}$ is ρ "reduced" to an under-approximation function, and $post[\rho] = \lambda S.\{a \mid \text{exists } c \in S, c \rho a\}$. A's partial ordering, if any, is forgotten.

For ρ, R, $R^\sharp$, Loiseaux, et al. prove

1. R is ρ-simulated by $R^\sharp$ iff $(R^\sharp)^{-1}$ is sound for R^{-1} w.r.t. $\tilde{pre}[\rho]$.
2. $a \models \phi \in ACTL$ [7] implies $c \models \phi$, for $c\,\rho\,a$.

Backhouse and Backhouse [4] saw that Galois connections can be characterized within relational algebra, and they reformulated key results of Abramsky [1]: $\rho \subseteq C \times A$ is a *pair algebra* iff there exist $\alpha : C \to A$ and $\gamma : A \to C$ such that $\{(c,a) \mid \alpha c \sqsubseteq_A a\} = \rho = \{(c,a) \mid c \sqsubseteq_C \gamma a\}$.

For the category, $\mathcal{C}$, of partially ordered sets *(objects)* and binary relations *(morphisms)*, *if* an endofunctor, $\sigma : \mathcal{C} \Rightarrow \mathcal{C}$, is also

1. *monotonic*: for relations, $R, S \subseteq C \times C'$, $R \subseteq S$ implies $\sigma R \subseteq \sigma S$
2. *invertible*: for all relations, $R \subseteq C \times C'$, $(\sigma R)^{-1} = \sigma(R^{-1})$,

then σ maps pair algebras to pair algebras, that is, σ is a unary type constructor that lifts a Galois connection between C and A to one between σC and σA.

The result generalizes to n-ary functors and applies to the standard functors, $\tau \times \tau$, $\tau \to \tau$, $List(\tau)$, etc. But the result does not apply to $\mathcal{P}_L(\tau)$ nor $\mathcal{P}_U(\tau)$ – *invertibility* (2) *fails*.

Ranzato and Tapparo [26] studied the completion of upper closure maps, $\mu : \mathcal{P}(C) \to \mathcal{P}(C)$ [19]. Given a logic, $\mathcal{L}$, of form, $\phi ::= op_i(\phi_j)_{0 < j < |op_i|}$, its semantics, $\llbracket \cdot \rrbracket \subseteq \mathcal{P}(C)$, has format

$$\llbracket op_i(\phi_j) \rrbracket = \mathbf{f_i}(\llbracket \phi_j \rrbracket)_{0 < j < |op_i|}$$

where each $\mathbf{f_i} : \mathcal{P}(C)^{|op_i|} \to \mathcal{P}(C)$ gives the semantics of connector op_i. The abstract semantics has form, $\llbracket op_i(\phi_j) \rrbracket^\mu = (\mu \circ \mathbf{f_i})(\llbracket \phi_j \rrbracket^\mu)$, and $\llbracket \phi \rrbracket^\mu \in \mu[\mathcal{P}(C)]$.

Upper closure μ is *$\mathcal{L}$-preserving* if, for all $S \subseteq C$, $\mu S \subseteq \llbracket \phi \rrbracket^\mu$ implies $S \subseteq \llbracket \phi \rrbracket$, and it is *$\mathcal{L}$-strongly preserving* if the *implies* is replaced by *iff*.

Given an $\mathcal{L}$-preserving μ, Ranzato and Tapparo apply the domain-completion technique of Giacobazzi and Quintarelli [12] to complete μ to its coarsest, strongly preserving form: $complete(\mu) = gfp(\lambda\rho.\mu \sqcap \mathcal{M}(R_{\{\mathbf{f_i}\}}(\rho)))$,
where $\sqcap$ operates in the complete lattice of upper closures, $\mathcal{M}$ is the Moore completion, and $R_F(\mu) = \{f(\bar{x}) \mid f \in F, \bar{x} \in \mu[\mathcal{P}(C)]^{|f|}\}$ adds the image points of the logical operations, $\mathbf{f_i}$, to the domain.

This technique can be applied to the present paper to generate strongly preserving, over- and under-approximating Galois connections.

Acknowledgments

Michael Huth and Radha Jagadeesen provided valuable advice within earlier collaborations. Radhia Cousot provided a supportive environment at École Polytechnique. Tino Cortesi, Patrick Cousot, Dennis Dams, and the referees made useful comments.

References

1. S. Abramsky. Abstract interpretation, logical relations, and Kan extensions. *J. Logic and Computation*, 1:5–41, 1990.

---

[19] An upper closure map, $\mu : \mathcal{P}(C) \to \mathcal{P}(C)$, is monotone, extensive, and idempotent, and induces the Galois connection, $\mathcal{P}(C)\langle\mu, id\rangle\mu[\mathcal{P}(C)]$.

2. S. Abramsky. Domain theory in logical form. *Ann.Pure Appl.Logic*, 51:1–77, 1991.
3. F. Baader, et al. *The Description Logic Handbook*. Cambridge Univ. Press, 2003.
4. K. Backhouse and R. Backhouse. Galois connections and logical relations. In *Mathematics of Program Construction*, LNCS 2386. Springer Verlag, 2002.
5. P. Buneman, S. Davidson, and A. Watters. A semantics for complex objects and approximate queries. In *7th ACM Symp. Principles of Database Systems*, 1988.
6. M. Ciocoiu. *Ontology-based translation*. PhD thesis, University of Maryland, 2001.
7. E.M. Clarke, O. Grumberg, and D.A. Peled. *Model Checking*. MIT Press, 2000.
8. P. Cousot and R. Cousot. Abstract interpretation frameworks. *J. Logic and Computation*, 2:511–547, 1992.
9. P. Cousot and R. Cousot. Higher-order abstract interpretation. In *Proceedings IEEE Int. Conf. Computer Lang.*, 1994.
10. D. Dams. *Abstract interpretation and partition refinement for model checking*. PhD thesis, Technische Universiteit Eindhoven, The Netherlands, 1996.
11. D. Dams, R. Gerth, and O. Grumberg. Abstract interpretation of reactive systems. *ACM Trans. Prog. Lang. Systems*, 19:253–291, 1997.
12. R. Giacobazzi and E. Quintarelli. Incompleteness, counterexamples, and refinements in abstract model checking. In *Static Analysis Symposium*, LNCS 2126, pages 356–373. Springer Verlag, 2001.
13. C. Gunter. The mixed power domain. *Theoretical Comp. Sci.*, 103:311–334, 1992.
14. J. Hartmanis and R.E. Stearns. Pair algebras and their application to automata theory. *J. Information and Control*, 7:485–507, 1964.
15. R. Heckmann. *Power domain constructions*. PhD thesis, Univ. Saarbrücken, 1990.
16. R. Heckmann. Set domains. In *Proc. European Symp. Programming*, LNCS, pages 177–196. Springer Verlag, 1990.
17. M.C.B. Hennessy and Robin Milner. Algebraic laws for non-determinism and concurrency. *JACM*, 32:137–161, 1985.
18. M. Huth, R. Jagadeesan, and D.A. Schmidt. Modal transition systems: a foundation for three-valued program analysis. In *Proc. European Symp. Programming*, LNCS, pages 155–169. Springer Verlag, 2001.
19. M. Huth, R. Jagadeesan, and D.A. Schmidt. A domain equation for refinement of partial systems. *Mathematical Structures in Computer Science*, 2004. In press.
20. D. Kozen. Results on the propositional mu-calculus. *Theoretical Computer Science*, 27:333–354, 1983.
21. K.G. Larsen. Modal Specifications. In *Automatic Verification Methods for Finite State Systems*, LNCS 407, pages 232–246. Springer Verlag, 1989.
22. C. Loiseaux, S. Graf, J. Sifakis, A. Bouajjani, and S. Bensalem. Property preserving abstractions for verification of concurrent systems. *Formal Methods in System Design*, 6:1–36, 1995.
23. A. Mycroft and N.D. Jones. A relational framework for abstract interpretation. In *Programs as Data Objects*, LNCS 217, pages 156–171. Springer Verlag, 1985.
24. F. Nielson. Two-level semantics and abstract interpretation. *Theoretical Comp. Sci.*, 69:117–242, 1989.
25. G. Plotkin. Domains. Lecture notes, Univ. Pisa/Edinburgh, 1983.
26. F. Ranzato and F. Tapparo. Strong preservation as completeness in abstract interpretation. In *Proc. European Symp. Programming*, LNCS 2986, pages 18–32. Springer Verlag, 2004.
27. M. Sagiv, T. Reps, and R. Wilhelm. Parametric shape analysis via 3-valued logic. In *Proceedings 28th ACM POPL*, 1999.
28. D.A. Schmidt. Structure-preserving binary relations for program abstraction. In *The Essence of Computation*, LNCS 2566, pages 246–266. Springer Verlag, 2002.

Completeness Refinement
in Abstract Symbolic Trajectory Evaluation

Mila Dalla Preda

Dipartimento di Informatica, Università di Verona
Strada Le Grazie 15, 37134 Verona, Italy
dallapre@sci.univr.it

Abstract. In this paper we study the relation between the lack of completeness in abstract symbolic trajectory evaluation and the structure of the counterexamples that can be derived in case of property failure. We characterize the presence of false negatives as a loss of completeness of the underlying abstraction. We prove how standard completeness refinement in abstract interpretation provides a systematic way for refining abstract symbolic trajectory evaluation in order to gain completeness for the properties of interest.

Keywords: Abstract Interpretation, Completeness, Domain Refinement, Symbolic Trajectory Evaluation, Verification, Model-checking, Data Flow Analysis.

1 Introduction

Symbolic trajectory evaluation (STE) provides a means to formally verify properties over sequential systems [1, 10, 14]. STE is usually presented as one of the main alternative to symbolic model checking (SMC). One advantage of STE compared with SMC is that STE is capable of dealing with larger circuits, thanks to the complexity of the verification algorithm, which is determined largely by the property to be verified. As a drawback, STE is limited in the kind of properties it can handle. In recent years, several efforts have been made to extend the expressiveness of STE to the one of SMC, while preserving the benefits of STE. It has been proposed a generalized version of STE, called generalized symbolic trajectory evaluation (GSTE), that extends STE to all ω-regular properties, making GSTE as powerful as traditional SMC for linear time logic [15–17].

In this paper we consider the earlier STE introduced by [10, 14], and not its generalized, and computationally more expensive, version. An STE property represents a set of constraints (pre and post conditions) that has to be satisfied along any computational path of the system. In STE is the property that drives the algorithm in simulating the computational flow of the system to be verified. Pre and post conditions are expressed as predicates on states. When the number of states increases, this may lead to a phenomenon similar to the state explosion problem in SMC [2, 6], making some sort of abstraction mandatory. Once abstraction is introduced, it is important to check if the results of the approximate

R. Giacobazzi (Ed.): SAS 2004, LNCS 3148, pp. 38–52, 2004.

analysis still hold in the concrete system. Since the relationship between abstract and concrete models is traditionally formalized and studied by abstract interpretation [4], it is natural to observe how abstract symbolic trajectory evaluation (ASTE) and STE can be properly related in abstract interpretation theory [1]. Abstract interpretation provides here the right framework for proving correctness of ASTE with respect to STE.

The Problem

The idea of ASTE is that of verifying temporal properties against an approximated model, which is systematically derived from the concrete semantics of the system we want to analyze. This is always achieved by approximating the information contained in its states. Such approximation, formalized in the abstract interpretation framework, is proved to be correct but not complete [1], meaning that, while the satisfaction of a property on the abstract model implies the satisfaction of the same property on the concrete one, it is not possible to draw any information on the behavior of the real system when a property does not hold in the approximate model. In fact it could happen that the abstract model does not satisfy the property while the real one does, due to the loss of information implicit in the abstraction phase. In this case we say that the abstract analysis returns a false negative. The notion of completeness in abstract interpretation formalizes the fact that no loss of precision is accumulated in abstract computation [5, 8]. This means that the approximation of a semantic function, computed on abstract objects, is equivalent to the approximation of the same computation on concrete objects. Giacobazzi et al. [8] observed that completeness is a domain property, namely that completeness of an abstract interpretation only depends upon the structure of the underlying abstract domain, and that it is always possible to minimally refine or simplify abstract domains to make them complete.

In this paper we are interested in applying abstract domain transformers to refine ASTE in order to make it complete (i.e., no false negatives are possible) for the verification of the properties of interest. In order to avoid to re-introduce the state explosion phenomenon, the size of the refined domain has to be kept as small as possible. Therefore, we are interested in minimally transforming abstractions to make them complete for ASTE. In [7] a similar idea has been applied to make the abstract model checking algorithm strong preserving with respect to the fragment ∀CTL* of the branching time temporal logic CTL*. More recent results [13] have proved that the problem of minimally refining an abstract model in order to get strong preservation for some specification language $\mathcal{L}$, corresponds precisely to the problem of minimally refining the underlying abstract interpretation in order to get completeness with respect to the (adjoint of the) logical/temporal operators in $\mathcal{L}$. As far as we know, no applications of these techniques are known in the field of STE.

Main Results

In ASTE, soundness means that the satisfaction of a property in the abstract model implies the satisfaction of the same property in the concrete one. However, the approximation may not be complete, later called strong preserving as in SMC. In fact, if the property of interest is false in the abstract model, this failure may be caused by some particular computations in the approximated model, which do not arise in the concrete one. Similarly to the abstract model checking case [3, 6, 12] the traces of states corresponding to these computations are called *spurious*. A property in STE is expressed by defining preconditions and postconditions that have to hold along every computation trace. The verification of a property is then performed by checking that, for every possible trace, as long as it satisfies the preconditions it also satisfies the corresponding postconditions. Therefore, when the property is not satisfied, this means that it has been reached a state that does not satisfy the corresponding postcondition. In this case the STE algorithm does not explicitly return a counterexample, even thought this can be derived if it is known the point of the computation where the postcondition fails. Hence, as well as in SMC, strong preservation in STE will correspond to the absence of spurious counterexamples. We prove that spurious counterexamples can be removed in ASTE by refining abstractions. Since the logic used by STE is far less expressive than $\forall CTL^*$, it turns out that the completeness requirement for the abstraction is weaker than the one in [7, 13] making abstract model checking strong preserving. This means that we only need to be precise for a smaller set of logical operators than $\forall CTL^*$, making the refined abstraction weaker, and therefore more efficient when applied to ASTE algorithms.

Structure of the Paper

The paper is organized as follows: in Section 2 we recall the main notions concerning abstract interpretation theory and standard completeness as a domain property, showing a constructive method to minimally modify domains in order to achieve completeness. In Section 3 we present STE in its standard and abstract version, which is sound but not complete. Then we show how both STE and ASTE can be expressed by classical data flow analysis (DFA). In Section 4 we define a systematic method, derived from the standard completeness refinement of the abstract interpretation, for refining the STE abstract model of the system in order to gain strong preservation. We conclude in Section 5 with related works and a discussion of possible further investigations in this field.

2   Abstract Interpretation and Completeness

In the standard Cousot and Cousot's abstract interpretation theory, abstract domains can be specified either by Galois Connections (GCs), i.e. adjunctions, or by upper closure operators (uco) [4]. A complete lattice, denoted $\langle D, \leq, \vee, \wedge, \top, \bot \rangle$, is a set D equipped with an ordering relation $\leq$, where for any $S \subseteq D$: $\vee S$ is the *lub of* S, $\wedge S$ is the *glb of* S, $\top$ is the greatest element and $\bot$ is the least element. A *Galois connection* is given by (C, α, A, γ), where the concrete and abstract domain C and A are complete lattices related by a pair of adjoint maps. The functions $\alpha : A \to C$ and $\gamma : C \to A$ form an adjunction when for all $a \in A, c \in C$: $\alpha(c) \leq_A a \Leftrightarrow c \leq_C \gamma(a)$. In this case α and γ are the monotone abstraction and concretization maps [4]. When each value of the abstract domain A is useful in representing C, namely when $\forall a \in A$. $\alpha(\gamma(a)) = a$, then (C, α, A, γ) is a Galois insertion (GI). An *upper closure operator* on a poset C is an operator $\rho : C \to C$ which is monotone, idempotent, and extensive ($\forall x \in C$. $x \leq \rho(x)$). The set of all upper closure operators on C is denoted by $uco(C)$. Given a complete lattice C, it is well known that $\langle uco(C), \sqsubseteq, \sqcup, \sqcap, \lambda x. \top, \lambda x.x \rangle$ is a complete lattice. The ordering on $uco(C)$ corresponds precisely to the standard order used in abstract interpretation to compare abstract domains with regard to their precision: A is more precise (or concrete) than B iff $A \sqsubseteq B$ in $uco(C)$. Each closure is uniquely determined by the set of its fix-points $\rho(C)$, in particular $X \subseteq C$ is the set of fix-points of an upper closure ρ on C iff X is a *Moore-family* of C, i.e., $X = \mathcal{M}(X) \stackrel{\text{def}}{=} \{\wedge S \mid S \subseteq X\}$ — where $\wedge \emptyset = \top \in \mathcal{M}(X)$, iff X is isomorphic to an abstract domain A in a GI (C, α, A, γ), i.e. $A \cong \rho(C)$ with $\iota : \rho(C) \to A$ and $\iota^{-1} : A \to \rho(C)$ being an isomorphism. In this case $(C, \iota \circ \rho, A, \iota^{-1})$ is a GI where $\rho = \gamma \circ \alpha$. Therefore $uco(C)$ is isomorphic to the so called *lattice of abstract interpretations of C* [5]. In this case $A \sqsubseteq B$ iff $B \subseteq A$ as Moore families of C, iff A is more concrete than B. Recall that given a complete lattice C, the downward closure of $S \subseteq C$ is defined as $\downarrow S \stackrel{\text{def}}{=} \{x \in C \mid \exists y \in S. x \leq y\}$, and $\downarrow x$ is a shorthand for $\downarrow \{x\}$. Recall that a function $f \in C \to D$ is continuous (additive) if f preserves *lub*'s of nonempty chains (arbitrary sets).

Let (C, α, A, γ) be a GI, $f : C \to C$ be a continuous function and $f^\sharp : A \to A$ be a corresponding abstract function on the abstract domain A. Then (C, α, A, γ) and $f^\sharp$ provide a *sound* abstraction of f if $\alpha \circ f \leq f^\sharp \circ \alpha$. Completeness is guaranteed when such condition is satisfied with equality, namely (C, α, A, γ) and $f^\sharp$ are *complete* for f if $\alpha \circ f = f^\sharp \circ \alpha$ [8]. It as been proved that completeness is a property of abstract domains [8]. In particular there exists $f^\sharp : A \to A$ such that (C, α, A, γ) and $f^\sharp$ are complete for f iff $\alpha \circ f = \alpha \circ f \circ \gamma \circ \alpha$ [8]. This result constructively characterizes the structure of complete abstract domains for continuous functions. Recall that, if $f : C \to C$ is a unary function, then $f^{-1}(y) = \{x \mid f(x) = y\}$.

Theorem 1 ([8]). *Let $f : C \to C$ be continuous and $\rho \in uco(C)$. Then ρ is complete for f iff $\bigcup_{y \in \rho(C)} max(f^{-1}(\downarrow y)) \subseteq \rho(C)$.*

By closure under (maximal) inverse image of f we get the most abstract domain which is complete and includes the given domain [8]. Let $\mathcal{R}_f : uco(C) \to uco(C)$, be defined as $\mathcal{R}_f = \lambda X \in uco(C)$. $\mathcal{M}(\bigcup_{y \in X} max(f^{-1}(\downarrow y)))$. It has been proved in [8] that if $f : C \to C$ is a continuous function and $A \in uco(C)$ then:

$$X \text{ is complete for } f \text{ and } X \sqsubseteq A \text{ iff } X = A \sqcap \mathcal{R}_f(X)$$

Therefore, the greatest (viz, most abstract) domain which includes A and which is complete for f is $\mathcal{S}_f(A) = gfp(\lambda X. A \sqcap \mathcal{R}_f(X))$. This domain is called the *complete shell* of A with respect to f.

3   STE and Abstract-STE

In this section we present STE through the formalization adopted by Chou in [1], where this technique was defined both in its concrete and abstract version by abstract interpretation. Chou proved that it is possible to express the STE algorithm as a DFA problem, making the use of abstract interpretation in modeling STE problems the most natural.

Symbolic Trajectory Evaluation

Given a system M, let Σ denote the set of all its states, which is nonempty and finite. A state is an assignment of values to variables (signals) and it can be represented as a boolean vector, where each element corresponds to a particular system signal that can assume either the value 0 or 1. Let $R \subseteq \Sigma \times \Sigma$ be the transition relation on M, where $(s, s') \in R$ means that M can in one step move from state s to state s'. The function $post[R] : \wp(\Sigma) \to \wp(\Sigma)$ is the forward predicate transformer associated with R, where $post[R](X) = \{s \in \Sigma | R(x, s) \wedge x \in X\}$. Dually, we can define the backward predicate transformer associated with R as $\widetilde{pre}[R] : \wp(\Sigma) \to \wp(\Sigma)$, where $\widetilde{pre}[R](X) = \{s \in \Sigma | \forall x \in \Sigma.R(s, x) \Rightarrow x \in X\}$. It is well known that these two predicate transformers form an adjunction, namely that $(\wp(\Sigma), post[R], \wp(\Sigma), \widetilde{pre}[R])$ is a GC [11]. Let $\langle \wp(\Sigma), \subseteq \rangle$ be the complete lattice of all possible predicates over states. A system in STE is modeled by a function $M : \wp(\Sigma) \to \wp(\Sigma)$ defined as: $M(p) = post[R](p)$. Note that M is an additive function that, given a state $s \in \Sigma$, returns the least specified predicate the system can evolve to. Given a sequence of elements s, we denote with $s[i]$ the i-th element of such sequence. A *trajectory* in M is a nonempty sequence of states, $\tau \in \Sigma^+$, such that $\forall i \in \mathbb{N} : 0 < i < |\tau| \Rightarrow \tau[i] \in M(\{\tau[i-1]\})$. The set of trajectories of M is denoted by $Traj(M)$. It is possible to define a partial order on the trajectories of a system, extending the existing order on $\wp(\Sigma)$. Given two trajectories τ and τ' of the same length:

$$\tau \sqsubseteq \tau' \Leftrightarrow \forall i \in \mathbb{N} : 0 < i < |\tau| \quad \tau[i] \subseteq \tau'[i]$$

The properties of the system are expressed through a particular labeled graph, called *assertion graph* or *trajectory assertion* [1, 10]. A trajectory assertion for M is a quintuple $G = (V, v_0, R_G, \pi_a, \pi_b)$, where V is a finite set of vertexes, $v_0 \in V$ is the initial vertex, $R_G \subseteq V \times V$ is a transition relation, and $\pi_a : V \to \wp(\Sigma)$ and $\pi_c : V \to \wp(\Sigma)$ label each vertex v respectively with an antecedent $\pi_a(v)$, also called precondition, and a consequent $\pi_c(v)$, also called postcondition. A *path* of G is a nonempty sequence of vertexes, $\mu \in V^+$, such that $\mu[0] = v_0$ and $\forall i \in \mathbb{N} : 0 < i \leq |\mu| \Rightarrow (\mu[i-1], \mu[i]) \in R_G$. The set of paths of G is denoted by $Paths(G)$. The circuit M *satisfies* the trajectory assertion G, when for every trajectory τ in $Traj(M)$ and for every path μ in $Paths(G)$, as long as τ satisfies the antecedents in μ, τ satisfies the consequents in μ. Formally the circuit M satisfies the assertion graph G, denoted by $M \models G$, if and only if [1]:

$$\forall \tau \in Traj(M) : \forall \mu \in Paths(G) : |\tau| = |\mu| \Rightarrow (\tau \models_a \mu \Rightarrow \tau \models_c \mu) \qquad (1)$$

Where τ a-satisfies (resp., c-satisfies) μ, denoted by $\tau \models_a \mu$ (resp., $\tau \models_c \mu$), iff $\tau[i] \in \pi_a(\mu[i])$ (resp., $\tau[i] \in \pi_c(\mu[i])$) for each $i < |\tau| = |\mu|$.

STE as a DFA Problem

The STE algorithm can be formulated as a DFA problem, namely it is possible to investigate the validity of a property on a circuit by solving a standard data flow equation [1]. Let $\mathcal{F} : (V \to \wp(\Sigma)) \to (V \to \wp(\Sigma))$ be defined as:

$$\mathcal{F}(\Phi)(v) = \begin{cases} C & \text{if } v = v_0 \\ \cup\{F(v')(\Phi(v'))|(v',v) \in R_G\} & \text{otherwise} \end{cases}$$

where $F : V \to (\wp(\Sigma) \to \wp(\Sigma))$ is $F(v)(p) = M(\pi_a(v) \cap p)$ for each vertex $v \in V$ and for all predicates $p \in \wp(\Sigma)$. The fix-point equation $\Phi = \mathcal{F}(\Phi)$ has a least solution $\Phi_* : V \to \wp(\Sigma)$, which is computed as the limit of the following sequence $\langle \Phi_n : V \to \wp(\Sigma) \mid n \in \mathbb{N} \rangle$, where:

$$\Phi_n = \begin{cases} \lambda v \in V. \; \emptyset & \text{if } n = 0 \\ \mathcal{F}(\Phi_{n-1}) & \text{otherwise} \end{cases}$$

The circuit M satisfies the assertion graph G, denoted $M \models_C G$, iff [1]:

$$\forall v \in V : \Phi_*(v) \cap \pi_a(v) \subseteq \pi_c(v) \tag{2}$$

The following theorem proves the equivalence between STE and a DFA problem.

Theorem 2 ([1]). $M \models G \Leftrightarrow M \models_C G$

Abstract Symbolic Trajectory Evaluation

The state explosion problem limits the efficiency of STE, in fact the STE algorithm on boolean vector is practical only for small systems [1]. When the system becomes large the likelihood for the STE algorithm to encounter the state explosion problem increases. To overcome this problem some sort of abstraction must be applied to the system. Let $\langle \hat{P}, \leq \rangle$ be a *complete lattice* of *abstract predicates* such that there is a GC $(\wp(\Sigma), \alpha, \hat{P}, \gamma)$, where $\alpha : \wp(\Sigma) \to \hat{P}$ and $\gamma : \hat{P} \to \wp(\Sigma)$ are respectively the abstraction and concretization maps. The abstract interpretation of M over $\hat{P}$, namely the *abstract model*, is given by the function $\hat{M} : \hat{P} \to \hat{P}$, defined as the best correct approximation of M in $\hat{P}$ [1]:

$$\hat{M}(\hat{p}) = \gamma \circ \alpha(post[R](\gamma(\hat{p})))$$

In the following $\rho = \gamma \circ \alpha$. Note that $\hat{M}$ does not distribute over arbitrary union, i.e., it is not additive. An *abstract trajectory assertion* for the abstract system $\hat{M}$ is therefore a quintuple $\hat{G} = (V, v_0, R_G, \hat{\pi}_a, \hat{\pi}_c)$, where the antecedent and consequent labeling functions are now given by $\hat{\pi}_a, \hat{\pi}_c : V \to \hat{P}$. Let us define $\gamma(\hat{G}) = (V, v_0, R_G, \gamma(\hat{\pi}_a), \gamma(\hat{\pi}_c))$, where $\gamma(\hat{\pi}_a) = \lambda v \in V : \gamma(\hat{\pi}_a(v))$ and $\gamma(\hat{\pi}_c) = \lambda v \in V : \gamma(\hat{\pi}_c(v))$ [1]. Note that $\gamma(\hat{G})$ is a trajectory assertion for M.

The typical abstraction used in STE is the one that approximates sets of boolean vectors with *ternary vectors*. The possible values of the elements of a ternary vector are 0, 1 and X, where X denotes the unknown value, i.e., either 0 or 1.

ASTE as a DFA Problem

In order to formalize ASTE as a DFA problem we only need to compute the fix-point solution, of the recursive equation defined earlier, on the abstract domain $\hat{P}$ instead of $\wp(\Sigma)$. Formally [1] we have $\hat{\mathcal{F}} : (V \to \hat{P}) \to (V \to \hat{P})$:

$$\hat{\mathcal{F}}(\hat{\Phi})(v) = \begin{cases} \hat{\top} & \text{if } v = v_0 \\ \vee\{\hat{F}(v')(\hat{\Phi}(v'))|(v',v) \in R_G\} & \text{otherwise} \end{cases}$$

where $\hat{F} : V \to (\hat{P} \to \hat{P})$ is defined as $\hat{F}(v)(\hat{p}) = \hat{M}(\hat{\pi}_a(v) \wedge \hat{p})$ for each vertex $v \in V$ and for all abstract predicates $\hat{p} \in \hat{P}$. The fix-point equation $\hat{\Phi} = \hat{\mathcal{F}}(\hat{\Phi})$ has a least solution $\hat{\Phi}_* : V \to \hat{P}$, which is computed as the limit of the following sequence $\langle \hat{\Phi}_n : V \to \hat{P} \mid n \in \mathbb{N} \rangle$, where:

$$\hat{\Phi}_n = \begin{cases} \lambda v \in V. \ \hat{\bot} & \text{if } n = 0 \\ \hat{\mathcal{F}}(\hat{\Phi}_{n-1}) & \text{otherwise} \end{cases}$$

The abstract circuit $\hat{M}$ satisfies the abstract trajectory assertion $\hat{G}$, denoted by $\hat{M} \models_A \hat{G}$, if and only if:

$$\forall v \in V : \hat{\Phi}_*(v) \wedge \hat{\pi}_a(v) \leq \hat{\pi}_c(v) \tag{3}$$

It has been proved that ASTE is preserving but not strong preserving for the STE algorithm [1]. Namely if the abstract assertion $\hat{G}$ is satisfied by the abstract model $\hat{M}$, then the concretization of the assertion, $\gamma(\hat{G})$, is satisfied by the concrete model M, but in general the converse does not hold. This means that it can happen that $\hat{M} \not\models_A \hat{G}$, while $M \models_C \gamma(\hat{G})$.

Theorem 3 ([1]). $\hat{M} \models_A \hat{G} \Rightarrow M \models_C \gamma(\hat{G})$

The following is an example showing that strong preservation in general does not hold in ASTE.

Example 1. Consider the circuit M in Figure 1 with five signals x_1, x_2, y_1, y_2, o, where x_1 and x_2 are the input signals, y_1 and y_2 are the results of, respectively, the inverter applied to x_1 and x_2, and o is the output signal computed as the AND of y_1 and y_2. Suppose that the abstract circuit approximates the concrete one by ternary vectors. We want to check if $\hat{M} \models_A \hat{G}$, where $\hat{G}$ is the trajectory assertion on the right side of Figure 1. In the graphical representation of $\hat{G}$ we only specify the labels different from XXXXX: these labels are $\hat{\pi}_a(v_1) = 01XXX$, $\hat{\pi}_a(v_2) = 10XXX$ and $\hat{\pi}_c(v_4) = XXXX0$. $\hat{G}$ specifies that when one of the two inputs is 0 then the output is 0. It is easy to verify that in this case $M \models_C \gamma(\hat{G})$ while $\hat{M} \not\models_A \hat{G}$, because of the loss of information implicit in the ternary abstraction. In fact when computing the abstract fix-point we have that:

$$\hat{\Phi}_3(v_3) = 1001X \vee 0110X = XXXXX$$

while in the concrete computation:

$$\Phi_3(v_3) = \{1001X\} \cup \{0110X\} = \{1001X, 0110X\}$$

it is clear how the abstract case loses information.

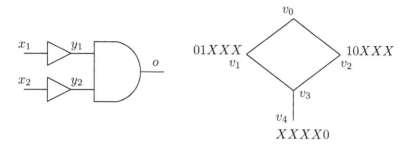

Fig. 1. The circuit and the trajectory assertion $\hat{G}$

4 Completeness in STE

A model satisfies a trajectory assertion when every state sequence of the model satisfying the preconditions satisfies also the postconditions. The checking algorithm verifies this by generating a simulation sequence that satisfies the antecedent (i.e, $\subseteq \Phi_*(v) \cap \pi_a(v)$), and by testing whether the resulting state sequence satisfies the consequent (i.e., $\subseteq \pi_c(v)$). Notice that if a precondition does not hold then the property is trivially true (i.e., $\emptyset \subseteq \hat{\pi}_c(v)$). This suggested us that in order to be precise for this kind of properties it is enough to be precise for the postconditions. Strong preservation holds if the domain contains all those set of states (viz., predicates), that ensure precision for the postconditions along the computations. A sequence of abstract predicates is precise for a given postcondition in a vertex v, if all the states associated with v and reachable from any abstract predicates in the sequence leading to v satisfies the postcondition. This is the idea of what we are going to prove.

We want to investigate the converse of Theorem 3, namely we want to check if $M \models_C \gamma(\hat{G}) = (V, v_0, R_G, \gamma(\hat{\pi}_a), \gamma(\hat{\pi}_c))$, knowing that $\hat{M} \models_A \hat{G}$, where the function $\gamma : \hat{P} \to \wp(\Sigma)$ is the concretization map. From the abstract interpretation theory, we know that there is no loss of information in the concretization phase, namely for each vertex $v \in V$ the set of states represented by $\hat{\pi}_a(v)$ is exactly the same set given by $\gamma(\hat{\pi}_a)$ (the same holds for $\hat{\pi}_c$). Therefore, while checking $M \models_C \gamma(\hat{G})$, we have that: $F(v)(p) = post[R](\hat{\pi}_a(v) \cap p) = post[R](\gamma(\hat{\pi}_a(v)) \cap p)$. For this reason, in the following, with $\hat{\pi}_a$ and $\hat{\pi}_c$ we indicate also $\gamma(\hat{\pi}_a)$ and $\gamma(\hat{\pi}_c)$ respectively.

Counterexamples in STE

When $\hat{M} \not\models_A \hat{G}$, it means that there is at least one vertex that does not satisfy condition (3). Let the *failure vertex* v_n be a vertex reachable from the initial vertex v_0, which does not satisfy (3), i.e., $\hat{\Phi}_*(v_n) \wedge \hat{\pi}_a(v_n) \not\subseteq \hat{\pi}_c(v_n)$. This means that there are some states associated with $\hat{\Phi}_*(v_n)$ that satisfy the precondition but not the postcondition on v_n. The *abstract counterexamples* are therefore the sequences of abstract predicates from $\hat{\Phi}_*(v_0) \wedge \hat{\pi}_a(v_0)$ to $(\hat{\Phi}_*(v_n) \wedge \hat{\pi}_a(v_n)) \setminus \hat{\pi}_c(v_n)$ (see Figure 2). These sequences provide a proof of the failure of the trajectory assertion in the abstract model. The problem now is to ensure that at least one

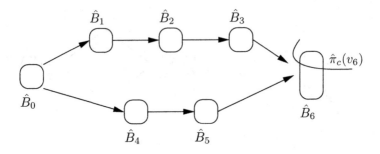

Fig. 2. Counterexamples

of these sequences corresponds to a possible behavior of the concrete system. This happens when there is a *concrete counterexample* corresponding to the abstract one. A concrete counterexample is therefore a sequence of states from $\Phi_*(v_0) \cap \hat{\pi}(v_0)$ to $(\Phi_*(v_n) \cap \hat{\pi}_a(v_n)) \setminus \hat{\pi}_c(v_n)$, where the fix-point Φ_* is computed on the concrete domain, i.e. it is computed in STE.

Definition 1. *Assume $\hat{M} \not\models_A \hat{G}$ and let v_n be the failure vertex. An abstract counterexample for v_n is a sequence of abstract predicates associated with each vertex v_i, for $i = 0 \ldots n$, having the following structure: $\hat{B}_0 \ldots (\hat{B}_n \setminus \hat{\pi}_c(v_n))$, where $\hat{B}_i = \hat{\Phi}_*(v_i) \wedge \hat{\pi}_a(v_i)$ and $(v_i, v_{i+1}) \in R_G$. A concrete counterexample that corresponds to the abstract counterexample $\hat{B}_0 \ldots (\hat{B}_n \setminus \hat{\pi}_c(v_n))$, is any trajectory $x_0 \ldots x_n$, where $x_i \in B_i$ with $B_i = \Phi_*(v_i) \cap \hat{\pi}_a(v_i)$.*

Observe that, by definition, $B_i \subseteq \hat{B}_i$. An abstract counterexample $\hat{T}$ for a property $\hat{G}$ is *spurious* if there is no concrete counterexample corresponding to it. If there is a concrete trajectory from a state associated to the initial vertex v_0 to a state associated to the failure vertex v_n that does not satisfy the postcondition, then also the concrete model does not satisfy $\gamma(\hat{G})$, i.e., $\hat{M} \not\models_A \hat{G} \Rightarrow M \not\models_C \gamma(\hat{G})$. Otherwise we loose strong preservation, since the states of the abstract predicate associated to v_n that cause the property failure are not reachable in the concrete model, where the trajectory assertion turns out to hold. This happens when all the abstract counterexamples are spurious.

Figure 2 shows how abstract counterexamples are typically derived. Assume that v_6 is the failure vertex. The abstract counterexamples are then given by the following sequences $\hat{B}_0, \hat{B}_1, \hat{B}_2, \hat{B}_3, (\hat{B}_6 \setminus \hat{\pi}_c(v_6))$ and $\hat{B}_0, \hat{B}_4, \hat{B}_5, (\hat{B}_6 \setminus \hat{\pi}_c(v_6))$. Strong preservation is guaranteed if at least one of them corresponds a concrete computation.

Identification of Spurious Counterexamples

In this section we characterize the spuriousness of an abstract counterexample. Let $\hat{T} = \hat{B}_0 \ldots (\hat{B}_n \setminus \hat{\pi}_c(v_n))$ be an abstract counterexample and let v_n be the corresponding failure vertex. Let us define the following sequence of predicates:

- $X_n = \hat{B}_n \setminus \hat{\pi}_c(v_n)$
- $X_{n-i} = pre[R](X_{n-i+1}) \cap \hat{B}_{n-i}$

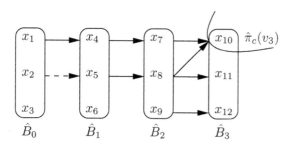

Fig. 3. Counterexample

By construction $X_{n-i} \subseteq \hat{B}_{n-i}$ is the largest subset of states, associated to v_{n-i}, from which there is a concrete computation to a state in $\hat{B}_n \setminus \hat{\pi}_c(v_n)$. It is clear that $X_{n-i} \subseteq \overline{\overline{pre}^i[R](\hat{\pi}_c(v_n))}$, where the over line stands for set complementation. The idea is that $\hat{T}$ is not spurious iff all the set X_{n-i} are not empty, as the following lemma proves.

Lemma 1. *The following are equivalent:*

(i) $\hat{T} = \hat{B}_0 \ldots (\hat{B}_n \setminus \hat{\pi}_c(v_n))$ *is not spurious;*
(ii) for all $0 \le i \le n$ then $X_{n-i} \neq \emptyset$.

The assumption that all sets X_{n-i} are not empty trivially implies that X_0 is not empty. This means that there is a concrete computation from the states associated to the initial vertex to the ones in X_n, and this trajectory is the concrete counterexample we were looking for. On the other hand, let X_{n-j} be the first set to be empty in the above sequence. By definition this means that the states in X_{n-j+1} are not reachable from $\hat{B}_{n-j}$, namely the states leading to the failure of the property are introduced by the abstraction.

Example 2. Consider the abstract counterexample $\hat{T} = \hat{B}_0, \hat{B}_1, \hat{B}_2, (\hat{B}_3 \setminus \hat{\pi}_c(v_3))$ in Figure 3, where $\hat{B}_i = \hat{\Phi}_*(v_i) \cap \hat{\pi}_a(v_i)$ and $x_i \in \Sigma$. If the concrete system includes the transition (x_2, x_5), then $\hat{T}$ is not spurious. In fact, all the sets X_j are not empty: $X_3 = \{x_{11}, x_{12}\}$, $X_2 = \{x_8, x_9\}$, $X_1 = \{x_5\}$ and $X_0 = \{x_2\}$, and there is a concrete trajectory x_2, x_5, x_8, x_{11} that corresponds to this abstract counterexample. Otherwise, by not considering (x_2, x_5), it is clear that $\hat{T}$ becomes spurious. In fact $X_0 = \emptyset$.

From Lemma 1, we derive the algorithm **Check-Spurious** that, given an abstract counterexample, checks whether it is spurious or not.

Check-Spurious$(M, \hat{T})$
$X := \hat{B}_n \setminus (\hat{\pi}_c(v_n))$
$j := n$
while $(X \neq \emptyset$ and $j > 0)$ do
    $j := j - 1$
    $X := pre[R](X) \cap \hat{B}_j$

if $(X \neq \emptyset)$
      then return *true*
      else return *false*

The complexity of the algorithm clearly depends on the length of the abstract counterexample considered and on the number of the transitions in the concrete model.

Completeness and Counterexamples

We are interested to force strong preservation by refining abstractions. This means that we have to refine the abstractions so that if there is an abstract predicate associated to a vertex that does not satisfy the postcondition, then there is at least one concrete state associated to that vertex that does not satisfy the postcondition and is reachable from the states associated to the initial vertex. Recall from [9] that, given two elements a and b of a complete lattice L, by definition $a \to b = \bigvee\{s | a \wedge s \leq b\}$. When L is *relatively pseudo-complemented* (or equivalently a *complete Heyting algebra*), if for any $a, b \in L$: $a \to b \in L$, such that $a \wedge c \leq b \Leftrightarrow c \leq a \to b$. It is well known that if L is of the form $\wp(S)$ then $a \to b = \neg a \cup b$.

Lemma 2. *Let* $\rho \in uco(\wp(S))$, $c \in \rho$, *and* $x \in \wp(S)$. *If* $c \to x \in \rho$ *then* $\rho(c \cap x) = \rho(c \cap \rho(x))$.

The following lemma gives a way to systematically refine the abstraction in order to avoid all the spurious counterexamples relatively to the failure vertex v_n, with respect to a trajectory assertion $\hat{G}$.

Lemma 3. *Given a trajectory assertion* $\hat{G}$, *if for all* $v_i, v_{i+1} \in V$ *such that* $(v_i, v_{i+1}) \in R_G$ *we have that the element* $\hat{\pi}_a(v_{i+1}) \to post[R](\hat{B}_i) \in \rho$ *and that* $\mathcal{R}_{post[R]}(\{\hat{\pi}_c(v_n), \hat{\top}\}) \subseteq \rho$, *then every abstract counterexample of the form* $\hat{B}_0 \ldots (\hat{B}_n \setminus \hat{\pi}_c(v_n))$ *is not spurious.*

Example 3. This example refers to Example 2 and shows that, when strong preservation does not hold, namely when we do not consider the transition (x_2, x_5) in Figure 3, then we contradict the hypothesis of Lemma 3. We have: $X_3 = \{x_{11}, x_{12}\}$, $X_2 = \{x_8, x_9\}$, $X_1 = \{x_5\}$, and $X_0 = \emptyset$. Observe that $\widetilde{pre}[R](\hat{\pi}_c(v_3)) = \{x_7\}$, $\widetilde{pre}^2[R](\hat{\pi}_c(v_3)) = \{x_4\}$, $\widetilde{pre}^3[R](\hat{\pi}_c(v_3)) = \{x_1\}$. By definition computing $\hat{B}_1$ we have:

$$\begin{aligned}
\hat{B}_1 &= \hat{\Phi}_*(v_1) \wedge \hat{\pi}_a(v_1) \\
&= \rho(post[R](\hat{\Phi}_*(v_0) \wedge \hat{\pi}_a(v_0))) \cap \hat{\pi}_a(v_1) \\
&= \rho(post[R](\hat{B}_0)) \cap \hat{\pi}_a(v_1) \\
&= \{x_4, x_5, x_6\}
\end{aligned}$$

Moreover note that $post[R](\hat{B}_0) \cap \hat{\pi}_a(v_1) = \{x_4\}$ and $\{x_4\} \subseteq \widetilde{pre}^2[R](\hat{\pi}_c(v_3))$. The abstraction ρ is monotone therefore: $\rho(post[R](\hat{B}_0) \cap \hat{\pi}_a(v_1)) \subseteq \rho(\widetilde{pre}^2[R](\hat{\pi}_c(v_3)))$.

The fact that $\hat{B}_1 = \rho(post[R](\hat{B}_0)) \cap \hat{\pi}_a(v_1) \not\subseteq \widetilde{pre}^2[R](\hat{\pi}_c(v_3))$, contradicts the hypothesis $\hat{\pi}_a(v_1) \to post[R](\hat{B}_0) \in \rho$ and $\widetilde{pre}^2[R](\hat{\pi}_c(v_3)) \in \rho$. This because, from Lemma 2, when $\hat{\pi}_a(v_1) \to post[R](\hat{B}_0)$ then $\rho(post[R](\hat{B}_0) \cap \hat{\pi}_a(v_1)) = \rho(post[R](\hat{B}_0)) \cap \hat{\pi}_a(v_1)$, therefore $\rho(post[R](\hat{B}_0)) \cap \hat{\pi}_a(v_1) \subseteq \rho(\widetilde{pre}^2[R](\hat{\pi}_c(v_3)))$. This means that $\rho(post[R](\hat{B}_0)) \cap \hat{\pi}_a(v_1) \subseteq \widetilde{pre}^2[R](\hat{\pi}_c(v_3))$, since for hypothesis $\widetilde{pre}^2[R](\hat{\pi}_c(v_3)) \in \rho$. So applying Lemma 3 we have: $\hat{B}_1 = \{x_4\}$, $\hat{B}_2 = \{x_7\}$, and $\hat{B}_3 = \{x_{10}\}$. In this situation $\hat{M} \models_A \hat{G}$.

The algorithm **Refine** is derived from Lemma 3. This algorithm, given an abstract spurious counterexample $\hat{T}$, refines the abstraction in order to make all the counterexamples, leading to the final vertex v_n of $\hat{T}$, not spurious.

> **Refine**$(\hat{T}, M, \hat{G}, \rho)$
> $S := \hat{\pi}_c(v_n)$
> for $j = n$ downto 1 do
> $\rho := \mathcal{M}(\rho \cup \widetilde{pre}[R](S))$
> $S := \widetilde{pre}[R](S)$
> for each $(v_i, v_{i+1}) \in R_G$ do
> $\rho := \mathcal{M}(\rho \cup (\hat{\pi}_a(v_{i+1}) \to post[R](\hat{B}_i)))$

Thanks to Lemma 3 we have that by adding to the abstract domain all the elements in $\mathcal{R}_{post[R]}(\{\hat{\pi}_c(v), \hat{\top}\})$ and $\hat{\pi}_a(v_{i+1}) \to post[R](\hat{B}_i)$ for all the vertexes, we gain strong preservation for all possible counterexamples for $\hat{G}$.

Theorem 4. *If* $\{\mathcal{R}_{post[R]}(\{\hat{\pi}_c(v), \hat{\top}\}) | v \in V\} \subseteq \rho$ *and for each* $(v_i, v_{i+1}) \in R_G$ *we have that* $\hat{\pi}_a(v_{i+1}) \to post[R](\hat{B}_i) \in \rho$, *then:*

$$M \models_C \gamma(\hat{G}) \quad \Rightarrow \quad \hat{M} \models_A \hat{G}$$

In other words, by adding to the abstract domain all the elements $\widetilde{pre}^j[R](\hat{\pi}_c(v))$ for each $v \in V$, where the index j stands for the iteration of the operator $\widetilde{pre}[R]$, together with all the elements $\neg\hat{\pi}_a(v_{i+1}) \cup post[R](\hat{B}_i)$, where $(v_i, v_{i+1}) \in R_G$, we gain strong preservation with respect to the property $\hat{G}$. This corresponds to refine the abstraction with respect to a restricted form of Heyting completion (see [9]) and complete shell with respect to $post[R]$ (see [8]).

From Theorem 4 we can derive the algorithm **PropertyCompl**, which refines the abstract domain with respect to a given property, making ASTE complete with respect to $\hat{G}$.

> **PropertyCompl**$(M, \hat{G}, \rho)$
> for $i = 1$ to $|V|$ do
> $S := \hat{\pi}_c(v_i)$
>   while $(\widetilde{pre}[R](S) \neq \emptyset)$
> $\rho := \mathcal{M}(\rho \cup \widetilde{pre}[R](S))$
> $S := \widetilde{pre}[R](S)$
>   for $j = 1$ to $|V|$ do
>   if $(v_i, v_j) \in R_G$
>   then $\rho := \mathcal{M}(\rho \cup (\hat{\pi}_a(v_j) \to post[R](\hat{B}_i)))$

In the following example we consider the circuit of Example 1, and apply Theorem 4 to the underlying abstract domain in order to reach strong preservation.

Example 4. Consider the circuit and the trajectory assertion of Example 1. By computing the abstract fix-point solution $\hat{\Phi}_*$, we obtain at the fourth iteration step that the fix-point is reached and for all $v \in V$ then $\hat{\Phi}_*(v) = XXXXX$. It results that $\hat{\Phi}_*(v_4) \wedge \hat{\pi}_a(v_4) \not\subseteq \hat{\pi}_c(v_4)$, therefore, by definition, $\hat{M} \not\models_A \hat{G}$. In this case we have two abstract counterexamples, $\hat{T}_1 = \hat{B}_0, \hat{B}_1, \hat{B}_3, (\hat{B}_4 \setminus \hat{\pi}_c(v_4))$ and $\hat{T}_2 = \hat{B}_0, \hat{B}_2, \hat{B}_3, (\hat{B}_4 \setminus \hat{\pi}_c(v_4))$. Also the solution to the concrete data flow equation Φ_* is reached at the fourth iteration step, where $\Phi_4(v_0) = \Phi_4(v_1) = \Phi_4(v_2) = XXXXX$, while $\Phi_4(v_3) = \{1001X, 0110X\}$ and $\Phi_4(v_4) = \{10010, 01100\}$. In this case $\Phi_*(v) \cap \hat{\pi}_a(v) \subseteq \hat{\pi}_c(v)$ holds for each vertex $v \in V$, and in particular $\Phi_*(v_4) \cap \hat{\pi}_a(v_4) \subseteq \hat{\pi}_c(v_4)$, therefore $M \models_C \gamma(\hat{G})$. The problem here is that $\hat{T}_1$ and $\hat{T}_2$ are both spurious, in fact the states in $\hat{B}_3 = \hat{\Phi}_*(v_3) \wedge \hat{\pi}_a(v_3)$ that lead to a state that does not satisfy $\hat{\pi}_c(v_4)$, are not reachable in the concrete system, but they are introduced by the abstraction when computing $\hat{\Phi}_*(v_3)$. Here $\widetilde{pre}[R](\hat{\pi}_c(v_4)) = \{0000X, 0110X, 1001X\}$ is not an element of the abstract domain, in fact the ternary vector that abstracts this set of states is XXXXX. We can observe that by adding this element to the abstract domain we gain strong preservation.

$$\hat{\Phi}_3(v_3) = \rho(\rho(post[R](\hat{\pi}_a(v_1) \wedge \hat{\Phi}_2(v_1)))) \vee$$
$$\rho(post[R](\hat{\pi}_a(v_2) \wedge \hat{\Phi}_2(v_2)))$$
$$= \rho(\rho(post[R](10XXX \wedge XXXXX)) \vee$$
$$\rho(post[R](01XXX \wedge XXXXX)))$$
$$= \rho(1001X \vee 0110X) = \{1001X, 0110X, 0000X\}$$

$$\hat{\Phi}_4(v_4) = \rho(post[R](\hat{\pi}_a(v_3) \wedge \hat{\Phi}_3(v_3)))$$
$$= \rho(post[R](XXXXX \wedge \{1001X, 0110X, 0000X\}))$$
$$= \rho(\{10010, 01100, 00000\}) = XXXX0$$

Now we have $\hat{\Phi}_*(v_4) \wedge \hat{\pi}_a(v_4) = XXXX0 = \hat{\pi}_c(v_4)$, and therefore $\hat{M} \models_A \hat{G}$.

The following example shows that the converse of Theorem 4 is not true. In particular we show that, even thought all the elements $\hat{\pi}_a(v_{i+1}) \rightarrow post[R](\hat{B}_i)$ are included in the domain, the lack of completeness for $post[R]$ does not affect the strong preservation for the given property.

Example 5. Let us consider the same circuit used earlier in Example 1 but a different trajectory assertion $\hat{G}$, where the set of vertexes $V = \{v_0, v_1, v_2, v_2, v_3\}$ and the transition relation $R_G = \{(v_0, v_1), (v_0, v_2), (v_1, v_3), (v_2, v_3), (v_3, v_4)\}$, are the same of the previous example, while the labels different from XXXXX are: $\hat{\pi}_a(v_1) = 10XXX$, $\hat{\pi}_a(v_2) = 00XXX$ and $\hat{\pi}_c(v_4) = XXXX0$. It is easy to verify that here $\hat{M} \models_C \hat{G}$ and $M \models_A \gamma(\hat{G})$. At the fourth iteration step, the fix-point of $\hat{\Phi}_*$ is reached and $\hat{\Phi}_4(v_0) = \hat{\Phi}_4(v_1) = \hat{\Phi}_4(v_2) = XXXXX$, while $\hat{\Phi}_4(v_3) = X00XX$ and $\hat{\Phi}_4(v_4) = X00X0$. For all $v \in V$ the satisfaction condition holds: $\hat{\Phi}_*(v) \wedge \hat{\pi}_a(v) \leq \hat{\pi}_c(v)$, i.e., $\hat{M} \models_A \hat{G}$. In this case we have strong preservation even though $\widetilde{pre}[R](\hat{\pi}_c(v_4))$ is not an element of the abstract domain.

5 Related Works and Conclusions

In this paper we have studied the impact of the standard notion of completeness in abstract interpretation based STE. It turns out that through domain refinements it is possible to achieve strong preservation for ASTE. In particular Lemma 3 gives a systematic way for refining the abstract domain in order to achieve strong preservation with respect to a particular failure vertex v_n of a trajectory assertion $\hat{G}$. The idea here is to refine the abstract domain when it is necessary for the property of interest. When the STE algorithm returns a negative answer, we check if all the corresponding counterexamples are spurious, and only in this case we refine. An alternative solution is the one proposed by Theorem 4, where a larger amount of information is added to the domain at once, in order to make it complete for every possible abstract counterexample for $\hat{G}$. The converse of Theorem 4 does not hold in general. In fact the proposed conditions for strong preservation in ASTE with respect to a property $\hat{G}$ are too strong: ASTE can be complete for a trajectory assertion $\hat{G}$, even when the hypothesis of Theorem 4 do not hold, as shown in Example 5. As future works it would be interesting to verify if the restricted completeness for $post[R]$ together with the Heyting completion are necessary conditions for strong preservation with respect to every possible property expressed as a trajectory assertion. This would agree with the observation in [13], where the authors proved that an abstraction is strong preserving relatively to a given temporal logic fragment $\mathcal{L}$ of the μ-calculus, if and only if the underlying abstract domain is complete with respect to the adjoint of the operators in $\mathcal{L}$. This means that completeness refinement minimally transforms the abstract domain in order to make it strong preserving for a given logic. In this case we could have an in depth comprehension on the structure of the STE underlying logic. In fact, in view of [13], it seems that the logic of STE, with basic operations given by conjunction ($\cap$), next (X), and domain restriction ($\rightarrow$), is strictly weaker than μ-calculus.

A result analogous to the one obtained here for ASTE with respect to trajectory assertions, is the one obtained in [7] for abstract model checking (AMC) with respect to the fragment $\forall CTL^*$ of the branching time temporal logic CTL^*. It is well known that strong preservation in AMC is achieved when there are no spurious counterexamples [2, 6]. In [7] the authors studied the relation between standard completeness and strong preservation in AMC, and it turns out that the latter one is guaranteed by making the underlying abstract domain complete with respect to $post[R]$.

In this paper we have considered STE and not its generalized version GSTE, which is known to handle all ω-regular properties. It is reasonable to guess that strong preservation for GSTE, with respect to ω-regular properties, is related to the standard notion of completeness of abstract interpretation. In order to better understand the relation between GSTE and STE, it would be interesting to study the conditions making their abstractions strong preserving.

References

1. C.T. Chou. The mathematical foundation of symbolic trajectory evaluation. pages 196–207, 1999.
2. E. M. Clarke, O. Grumberg, and D. E. Long. Model checking and abstraction. *ACM Trans. Program. Lang. Syst.*, 16(5):1512–1542, 1994.
3. E.M. Clarke, O. Grumberg, S. Jha, Y. Lu, and H. Veith. Counterexample-guided abstraction refinement. In *Proc. of the 12th Internat. Conf. on Computer Aided Verification (CAV '00)*, volume 1855 of *Lecture Notes in Computer Science*, pages 154–169. Springer-Verlag, Berlin, 2000.
4. P. Cousot and R. Cousot. Abstract interpretation: A unified lattice model for static analysis of programs by construction or approximation of fixpoints. In *Conference Record of the 4th ACM Symp. on Principles of Programming Languages (POPL '77)*, pages 238–252. ACM Press, New York, 1977.
5. P. Cousot and R. Cousot. Systematic design of program analysis frameworks. In *Conference Record of the 6th ACM Symp. on Principles of Programming Languages (POPL '79)*, pages 269–282. ACM Press, New York, 1979.
6. O. Grumberg E. M. Clarke and D. A. Peled. *Medel Checking*. MIT Press, 1999.
7. R. Giacobazzi and E. Quintarelli. Incompleteness, counterexamples and refinements in abstract model-checking. In P. Cousot, editor, *Proc. of The 8th International Static Analysis Symposium, SAS'01*, volume 2126 of *Lecture Notes in Computer Science*, pages 356–373. Springer-Verlag, 2001.
8. R. Giacobazzi, F. Ranzato, and F. Scozzari. Making abstract interpretations complete. *J. of the ACM.*, 47(2):361–416, 2000.
9. R. Giacobazzi and F. Scozzari. A logical model for relational abstract domains. *ACM Trans. Program. Lang. Syst.*, 20(5):1067–1109, 1998.
10. A. Jain. *Formal Hardware Verification by Symbolic Trajectory Evauation*. PhD thesis, Carnegie-Mellon University, July 1997.
11. C. Loiseaux, S. Graf, J. Sifakis, A. Bouajjani, and S. Bensalem. Property preserving abstractions for the verification of concurrent systems. *Formal Methods Syst. Des.*, 6:11–44, 1995.
12. Y. Lu. *Automatic Abstract in Model Checking*. PhD thesis, Department of Electrical and Computer Engineering, Carnegie Institute of Technology, Carnegie Mellon University, Pittsburgh, 2000.
13. F. Ranzato and F. Tapparo. Strong preservation as completeness in abstract interpretation. In D. Schmidt, editor, *Proc. of the 13th European Symp. on Programming (ESOP '04)*, volume 2986 of *Lecture Notes in Computer Science*, pages 18–32. Springer-Verlag, 2004.
14. C.J.H. Seger and R.E. Bryant. Formal verification by symbolic evaluation of partially-ordered trajectories. *Formal Methods in System Designs*, 6(2):147–189, 1995.
15. J. Yang and A. Goel. Gste through a case of study. In *International conference on Computer-Aided Design*, pages 534–541. IEEE/ACM, 2002.
16. J. Yang and C. J. H. Seger. Introduction to generalized symbolic trajectory evaluation. In *International conference on Computer Design*, pages 360–365. IEEE, 2001.
17. J. Yang and C. J. H. Seger. Generalized symbolic trajectory evaluation - abstraction in action. In *Formal Methods in Computer-Aided Design: Fourth Internetional Conference*, volume 2517 of *Lecture Notes in Computer Science*, pages 70–87. Springer, 2002.

Constraint-Based Linear-Relations Analysis

Sriram Sankaranarayanan, Henny B. Sipma, and Zohar Manna*

Computer Science Department
Stanford University
Stanford, CA 94305-9045
{srirams,sipma,zm}@theory.stanford.edu

Abstract. Linear-relations analysis of transition systems discovers linear invariant relationships among the variables of the system. These relationships help establish important safety and liveness properties. Efficient techniques for the analysis of systems using polyhedra have been explored, leading to the development of successful tools like HyTech. However, existing techniques rely on the use of approximations such as widening and extrapolation in order to ensure termination. In an earlier paper, we demonstrated the use of Farkas Lemma to provide a translation from the linear-relations analysis problem into a system of constraints on the unknown coefficients of a candidate invariant. However, since the constraints in question are non-linear, a naive application of the method does not scale. In this paper, we show that by some efficient simplifications and approximations to the quantifier elimination procedure, not only does the method scale to higher dimensions, but also enjoys performance advantages for some larger examples.

1 Introduction

Linear-relations analysis discovers linear relationships among the variables of a program, that hold in all the reachable program states. Such relationships are called *linear invariants*. Invariants are useful in the verification of both safety and liveness properties. Many existing techniques rely on the presence of these invariants to prove properties of interest. Some types of analysis, e.g., *variable-bounds* analysis, can be viewed as specializations of linear-relations analysis. Traditionally, this analysis is framed as an abstract interpretation in the domain of polyhedra [7, 8]. The analysis is carried out using a *propagation-based* technique, wherein polyhedral iterates that converge towards the final result, are computed. This convergence is ensured through the use of *widening*, or *extrapolation*, operators. Such techniques are popular in the domains of discrete and hybrid programs, motivating tools like HyTech [12] and improved widening operators over polyhedra [11, 1].

* This research was supported in part by NSF grants CCR-01-21403, CCR-02-20134 and CCR-02-09237, by ARO grant DAAD19-01-1-0723, by ARPA/AF contracts F33615-00-C-1693 and F33615-99-C-3014, and by NAVY/ONR contract N00014-03-1-0939.

R. Giacobazzi (Ed.): SAS 2004, LNCS 3148, pp. 53–68, 2004.

Alternatively, the fixpoint equations arising from abstract interpretation may be posed explicitly, and solved without relying directly on iteration or widening. This is achieved through applications of *Farkas Lemma* in our earlier work [6]. Given a *template inequality* with unknown coefficients, our technique computes constraints on the values of the coefficients, such that substituting any solution back into the template yields a valid invariant relationship. However, the constraints themselves are non-linear with existentially quantified parameters. Nevertheless, an exact elimination is possible in theory through quantifier elimination techniques for the theory of reals [16, 5, 17]. In practice, however, the technique using exact quantifier elimination does not scale to systems with more than five variables.

Fortunately, the constraints obtained in this process, though non-linear, exhibit many structural properties that can be exploited to simplify and solve them. In many cases, a series of simplifications resolves the constraints into a linear system. For instance, whenever the underlying transition system is a Petri net, the system of constraints resolves into a linear system [14]. This has led us to verify transition systems derived from Petri Nets with as many as 40 dimensions and 50 transitions. The use of quantifier elimination is clearly inefficient in such situations. In this paper, we provide a set of exact and heuristic rules for simplifying and solving the constraints for general linear transition systems. Most of our rules are exact, but their application may not resolve the constraints. Therefore, some heuristics are used instead of an exact elimination as a last resort.

At lower dimensions, our technique performs poorly in terms of time and space, relative to the propagation-based approach. When the dimension is increased, our technique not only scales but in some cases, outperforms the propagation-based techniques. Furthermore, our technique enjoys several advantages over related approaches that are very useful for analyzing larger systems, as presented in Section 4. The remainder of this paper consists of Section 2 on preliminaries, Section 3 on the constraint structure and solving rules, and Section 4 on some experimental results.

2 Preliminaries

We recount some standard results on polyhedra, and then define linear transition systems, followed by a description of *propagation-based* analysis techniques. We then demonstrate an alternative approach called *constraint-based* analysis.

2.1 Linear Assertions

Through this discussion, let $\{x_1, \ldots, x_n\}$ be a set of real-valued variables. Constant reals are denoted by a, b with subscripts, and unknown coefficients by c, d with subscripts. Further details about linear assertions can be obtained from standard texts [15].

Definition 1 (Linear Assertions) A *linear expression* is of the form $a_1 x_1 + \cdots + a_n x_n + b$. The expression is *homogeneous* iff $b = 0$, or else it is *inhomogeneous*. A *linear inequality* is of the form $\alpha \bowtie 0$, where $\bowtie \in \{\geq, =, >\}$. The inequality is *strict* if $\bowtie \in \{>\}$. A *linear assertion* is a finite conjunction of linear inequalities. Linear assertions can be homogeneous or otherwise, depending on the underlying linear expressions. The set of points in $\mathcal{R}^n$ satisfying a linear assertion (homogeneous assertion) is called a *polyhedron* (*polyhedral cone*).

We shall assume that linear assertions do not contain any strict inequalities. It is well-known that any polyhedron is representable by a set of constraints (as a linear assertion), or by its *vertices*, and *rays* (infinite directions), collectively called its *generators*. The problem of computing the generators, given the assertion, and vice-versa have been well-studied with efficient algorithms [9]. However, the number of generators of a polyhedron can be worst-case exponential in the number of constraints (the n-dimensional hypercube is an example). Basic operations on these assertions are computed thus:

Intersection Combine the inequalities in both the polyhedra.
Convex Union Combine the generators of the two polyhedra.
Projection Project the generators of the polyhedron.
Containment Test every generator of φ_1 for subsumption by φ_2.
Emptiness A polyhedron is empty iff it has no generators.

We now state *Farkas Lemma*, which describes the linear consequences of a linear assertion. A proof is available from the standard references [15].

Theorem 1 (Farkas Lemma). *Consider a linear assertion S over real-valued variables $x_1, \ldots, x_n$,*

$$
S: \quad
\begin{array}{c}
a_{11} x_1 + \cdots + a_{1n} x_n + b_1 \geq 0 \\
\vdots \qquad\qquad \vdots \quad\; \vdots \\
a_{m1} x_1 + \cdots + a_{mn} x_n + b_m \geq 0
\end{array}
$$

When S is satisfiable, it implies a given linear inequality ψ : $a_1 x_1 + \cdots + a_n x_n + b \geq 0$, i.e, $S \models \psi$, if and only if there exist non-negative real numbers $\lambda_0, \lambda_1, \ldots, \lambda_m$ such that $a_p = \sum_{i=1}^{m} \lambda_i a_{ip}$, $p \in [1, n]$, and $b = (\sum_{i=1}^{m} \lambda_i b_i) + \lambda_0$ Furthermore, S is unsatisfiable if and only if the inequality $-1 \geq 0$ can be derived as shown above.

In the rest of the paper we represent applications of this lemma by a table as shown below:

$$
\begin{array}{c|ccccc}
\lambda_0 & & & & & 1 \geq 0 \\
\lambda_1 & a_{11} x_1 + \cdots + & a_{1n} x_n + & b_1 \geq 0 \\
\vdots & \vdots & & \vdots & \vdots \\
\lambda_m & a_{m1} x_1 + \cdots + & a_{mn} x_n + & b_m \geq 0 \\
\hline
& c_1 x_1 + \cdots + & c_n x_n + & d \geq 0 \leftarrow \psi, \text{ or} \\
& & & -1 \geq 0 \leftarrow \text{ false}
\end{array}
\left. \phantom{\begin{array}{c}1\\1\\1\\1\end{array}} \right\} S
$$

The table shows the antecedents above the line and the consequences below. For each column, the sum of the column entries above the line, with appropriate multipliers, must be equal to the entry below the line. If a row corresponds to an equality rather than an inequality, we drop the requirement that the multiplier corresponding to it be non-negative.

2.2   Transition Systems and Invariants

In this section, we define linear transition systems and linear invariants. Our presentation concentrates only on linear systems. The reader is referred to standard textbooks for a more general presentation [13].

Definition 2 (Linear Transition Systems) Let $V = \{x_1, \ldots, x_n\}$ be a set of *system variables*. A *linear transition system* over V is a tuple $\langle L, \mathcal{T}, \ell_0, \Theta \rangle$, where L is a set of *locations*, $\mathcal{T}$ is a set of *transitions*, each transition $\tau \in \mathcal{T}$ is a tuple $\langle \ell_i, \ell_j, \rho_\tau \rangle$, such that $\ell_i, \ell_j \in L$ are the *pre-* and the *post-* locations, respectively, and ρ_τ is a linear assertion over $V \cup V'$, where V denotes the current-state variables, and V' the next-state variables. Location $\ell_0 \in L$ is the *initial location*, and Θ is a linear assertion over V specifying the initial condition.

Example 1. Let $V = \{x, y\}$ and $L = \{\ell_0\}$. Consider the transition system shown below. Each transition models a concurrent process, that updates the variables x, y atomically.

$$\Theta = (x = 0 \ \wedge \ y = 0)$$
$$\mathcal{T} = \{\tau_1, \tau_2\}$$
$$\tau_1 = \left\langle \ell_0, \ell_0, \left[x' = x + 2y \ \wedge \ y' = 1 - y \right] \right\rangle$$
$$\tau_2 = \left\langle \ell_0, \ell_0, \left[x' = x + 1 \ \wedge \ y' = y + 2 \right] \right\rangle$$

A given linear assertion ψ is a *linear invariant* of a linear transition system (LTS) at a location ℓ iff it is satisfied by every state reaching ℓ. An *assertion map* maps each location of a LTS to a linear assertion. An assertion map η is an *invariant map* if $\eta(\ell)$ is an invariant at ℓ, for each $\ell \in L$. In order to prove a given assertion map invariant, we use the theory of inductive assertions due to Floyd and Hoare [13].

Definition 3 (Inductive Assertion Maps) An assertion map η is inductive iff it satisfies the following conditions:

Initiation: $\Theta \models \eta(\ell_0)$,
Consecution: For each transition $\tau : \langle \ell_i, \ell_j, \rho_\tau \rangle$, $\eta(\ell_i) \ \wedge \ \rho_\tau \models \eta(\ell_j)'$.

It can be shown by mathematical induction that any inductive assertion map is also an invariant map. It is well known that the converse need not be true in general. The standard technique for proving an assertion invariant is to find an inductive assertion that strengthens it. For example, the assertion $x + y \geq 0$ is an invariant for the LTS in Example 1.

Iteration #	$\eta(\ell_0)$	Iteration Type
0	$x = y = 0$	Init
1	$y - 2x \geq 0,\ x - y + 1 \geq 0,\ x \geq 0$	Propagation
2	$5x + 3y \leq 22,\ x - y + 2 \geq 0,\ x \geq 0$ $x + 5y \geq 0,\ 2x - y + 1 \geq 0$	Propagation
3	$x \geq 0,\ 2x - y + 1 \geq 0$	Widening
4	$true$	Widening

Fig. 1. Sequence of Propagation and Widening Steps for LTS in Example 1.

Propagation-Based Analysis. These techniques are based on the *abstract-inter-pretation* framework formalized by Cousot and Cousot [7], and specialized for linear relations by Cousot and Halbwachs [8]. The technique starts from an inital assertion map, and weakens it iteratively using the *Post* and the *Widening* operators. When the iteration converges, the resulting map is guaranteed to be inductive, and hence invariant. Termination is guaranteed by the design of the widening operator. Often widening is not used, or replaced by an *Extrapolation* operator, and the termination guarantee is traded-off against accuracy.

Definition 4 (Post-condition and Widening Operators) The *post-condition* operator takes an assertion φ, and a transition relation ρ_τ.

$$post(\varphi, \tau) = (\exists V_0)(\varphi(V_0) \wedge \rho_\tau(V_0, V))$$

Intersection, followed by quantifier elimination using projection computes post. However, more efficient strategies for computing post exist when ρ_τ has a special structure.

   Given assertions $\varphi_{\{1,2\}}$ such that $\varphi_1 \models \varphi_2$, the *standard widening* $\varphi_1 \nabla \varphi_2$ is an assertion φ that contains (roughly) all the inequalities in φ_1 that are satisfied by φ_2. The details along with key mathematical properties of widening are described in [8, 7], and enhanced versions appear in [11, 4, 1].

As mentioned earlier the analysis begins with an initial assertion map defined by $\eta_0(\ell_0) = \Theta$, and $\eta_0(\ell) = \emptyset$ for $\ell \neq \ell_0$. At each *step*, the map η_i is updated to map η_{i+1} as follows:

$$\eta_{i+1}(\ell) = \eta_i(\ell) \ \langle \text{OP} \rangle \ \left[\eta_i(\ell) \bigsqcup_{\tau_j \equiv \langle \ell_j, \ell, \rho \rangle} (post(\eta_i(\ell_j), \tau_j)) \right]$$

where OP is the convex hull ($\sqcup$) operator for a propagation step, and the widening (∇) operator for a widening step. The overall algorithm requires a predefined *iteration strategy*. A typical strategy carries out a predefined sequence of initial propagation steps, followed by widening steps until termination. The choice of a strategy is of the utmost importance for minimizing the number of propagation and widening steps, in general.

   The method described above was applied to the LTS in Example 1. Using the standard widening [8], we obtain the sequence of iterates shown in Figure 1.

The result does not change even when the number of initial propagation steps k, is increased to 4. Using the widening operator by Bagnara et al., implemented in the PPL library [1], and $k = 4$ does not change the result, even if the number of propagation steps is increased. Surprisingly, when the number of initial propagation steps is reduced to $k = 3$, it yields the invariant $11x+10y \geq 0$, $11x+12y \geq 0$, for $k = 2$, the invariant $7x + 6y \geq 0$, $7x + 8y \geq 0$. $k = 0, 1$ also produce the trivial invariant (*true*). This demonstrates that an increase in the number of initial propagation steps does not necessarily increase the accuracy of the result.

Constraint-Based Analysis. The framework of abstract interpretation [7] shows that any semantic analysis can be expressed as a fixpoint equation in an abstract domain. Consequently, linear-relations analysis is a fixed point computation in the domain of polyhedra. This computation is done by iteration in the propagation-based analysis of Cousot and Halbwachs [8]. We propose to use Farkas Lemma to generate constraints from the LTS description, directly describing the relevant fixed-point. The resulting constraints are solved using non-linear quantifier elimination.

Let C be a set of template variables. A *template* is an inequality of the form $c_1 x_1 + \cdots + c_n x_n + d \geq 0$, where $c_{1,\ldots,n}, d \in C$. A *template map*, associates each location with a template. We shall use $\eta(\ell)$ to denote both the inequality, and the template expression at ℓ, disambiguated by context. We reduce the inductive assertion generation problem to one of computing those variables for which a given template map η is inductive. The answer consists of encoding initiation and consecution using Farkas Lemma.

Initiation: The implication $\Theta \models \eta(\ell_0)$ is encoded.

Consecution: For each $\tau : \langle \ell_i, \ell_j, \rho_\tau \rangle$, the implication $\eta(\ell_i) \wedge \rho_\tau \models \eta(\ell_j)'$ is encoded. We shall explore the structure of the resulting constraints in detail through the remainder of the paper.

The definition of consecution can be *relaxed* into two stronger forms:

Local Consecution: For transition $\tau : \langle \ell_i, \ell_j, \rho \rangle$, $\rho \models \eta(\ell_j)' \geq 0$,
Increasing Value: For transition $\tau : \langle \ell_i, \ell_j, \rho \rangle$, $\rho \models \eta(\ell_j)' \geq \eta(\ell_i)$.

Both these conditions imply consecution. Any map in which some transitions satisfy these stronger conditions continues to remain an inductive assertion map.

Example 2. Consider the LTS in Example 1. We fix a template map $\eta(\ell_0) = c_1 x + c_2 y + d$, $C = \{c_1, c_2, d\}$ being unknown quantities. Initiation is encoded using Farkas Lemma,

$$
\begin{array}{c|ccc}
\lambda_1 & x & & = 0 \\
\lambda_2 & & y & = 0 \\
\hline
& c_1 x + c_2 y + d \geq 0 & \leftarrow \eta(\ell_0)
\end{array} \left.\right\} \Theta
$$

resulting in the constraints

$$(\exists \lambda_1, \lambda_2)\, [c_1 = \lambda_1 \ \wedge \ c_2 = \lambda_2 \ \wedge \ d \geq 0]$$

After eliminating the multipliers, we obtain $d \geq 0$ for the initiation constraint. Consecution is encoded using Farkas Lemma as

$$
\begin{array}{r|l}
\mu_1 & c_1 x + c_2 y \qquad\qquad\qquad + d \geq 0 \leftarrow \eta(\ell_0) \\
\lambda_1 & x + 2y - \quad x' \qquad\qquad = 0 \\
\lambda_2 & \qquad y \qquad + \quad y' - 1 = 0 \\
\hline
& c_1 x' + c_2 y' + d \geq 0 \leftarrow \eta'(\ell_0)
\end{array}
\;\Big\}\; \rho_{\tau_1}
$$

which produces the constraints

$$
(\exists \mu_1)\,[\mu_1 c_1 - c_1 = 0 \,\wedge\, \mu_1 c_2 + c_2 - 2c_1 = 0 \,\wedge\, \mu_1 d - d - c_2 \leq 0]
$$

After eliminating $\lambda_1, \lambda_2, \mu_1$, the resulting constraint simplifies to $c_2 = c_1 \geq 0$. Similarly, the constraint obtained for τ_2 simplifies to $c_1 + 2c_2 \geq 0$. The overall constraint is the conjunction of the initiation and consecution constraints, which reduces to $c_1 = c_2 \geq 0$, $d \geq 0$. Solutions are generated by $c_1 = 1$, $c_2 = 1$, $d = 0$, corresponding to the inductive assertion $x + y \geq 0$ at ℓ_0.

3   The Constraint System and Its Solution

In this section, we study the constraint structure arising from the encoding discussed briefly in Section 2, and in detail elsewhere [6].

We fix a linear transition system Π with variables $\{x_1, \ldots, x_n\}$, collectively referred to as $\boldsymbol{x}$. The system is assumed to have a single location ℓ to simplify the presentation. The template assertion at location ℓ, is $\alpha(\boldsymbol{c}) = c_1 x_1 + \cdots + c_n x_n + d \geq 0$. The coefficient variables $\{c_1, \ldots, c_n, d\}$ are collectively referred to as $\boldsymbol{c}$. The system's transitions are $\{\tau_1, \ldots, \tau_m\}$, where $\tau_i : \langle \ell, \ell, \rho_i \rangle$. The initial condition is denoted by Θ. The system in Example 1 will be used as a running example to illustrate the presented ideas.

3.1   Deriving Constraints

We use Farkas Lemma (Theorem 1) in order to derive constraints for initiation and consecution, as shown in Example 2.

Initiation. The case for initiation is relatively straightforward. We encode initiation by encoding $\Theta \models \alpha(\boldsymbol{c}) \geq 0$. The conditions on $\boldsymbol{c}$ are obtained from the application of Farkas Lemma after eliminating the multipliers. In practice, the constraints are derived using Farkas' Lemma. The result is a linear assertion over the unknowns $\boldsymbol{c}$, and the multipliers $\boldsymbol{\lambda}$. The multipliers are eliminated using polyhedral projection. Let $\Theta = (x = 0 \,\wedge\, y = 0)$, and $c_1 x + c_2 y + d \geq 0$. The initiation constraint, obtained by using Farkas Lemma is $d \geq 0$, as shown in Example 2.

Consecution. Consecution for a transition τ_i encodes the assertion

$$(\alpha(c) \geq 0) \wedge \rho_i \models (\alpha(c)' \geq 0)$$

Using Farkas Lemma, the constraints obtained are homogeneous, and involve an existentially quantified non-linear parameter μ_i. We shall term the class of constraints thus obtained *parametric linear assertions*.

Definition 5 (Parametric Linear Assertion) Let c be a set of variables and $\mu_1, \ldots, \mu_m$ be *parameters*. A *parametric linear expression* (PL expression) is of the form $\alpha_1 + \mu_i \alpha_2$, where $\alpha_{\{1,2\}}$ are (homogeneous) linear expressions over c. A parametric linear (in)equality is of the form $\beta \bowtie 0$, β being a PL expression. A PL assertion is a finite conjunction of PL equalities and inequalities.

For a transition τ_i, and template $\alpha(c)$, the consecution constraints obtained through Farkas Lemma form a parametric linear assertion over a single parameter μ_i.

Example 3. We encode consecution for transition τ_2 from Example 1.

$$
\begin{array}{r|llll}
\mu_2 & c_1 x + c_2 y & & + d \geq 0 & \leftarrow \eta(\ell_0) \\
\lambda_1 & x & - x' & + 1 = 0 & \\
\lambda_2 & y & & - y' + 2 = 0 & \left.\right\} \rho_{\tau_2} \\
\hline
 & & c_1 x' + c_2 y' & + d \geq 0 & \leftarrow \eta'(\ell_0)
\end{array}
$$

which yields the constraints

$$\exists(\mu_2, \lambda_1, \lambda_2) \begin{bmatrix} \mu_2 c_1 + \lambda_1 = 0 \\ \mu_2 c_2 + \lambda_2 = 0 \\ -\lambda_1 = c_1 \\ -\lambda_2 = c_2 \\ \mu_2 d - d + \lambda_1 + 2\lambda_2 \leq 0 \end{bmatrix}$$

Eliminating λ_1, λ_2 yields $\mu_2 c_1 - c_1 = 0 \wedge \mu_2 c_2 - c_2 = 0 \wedge \mu_2 d - d - c_1 - 2c_2 \leq 0$.

These constraints are parametric linear. Local and increasing consecutions can be enforced by setting $\mu_2 = 0, 1$, respectively.

The Overall Constraint. The overall constraint obtained is the conjunction of the constraints obtained from initiation and consecution for each transition. This constraint is a combination of several types of constraints. Initiation results in a linear assertion, whereas each consecution condition results in PL assertions over parameters $M = \{\mu_1, \ldots, \mu_m\}$, the parameter μ_i arising from τ_i. Each of these parameters is required to be nonnegative, and is existentially quantified. In order to compute the actual constraint over c, the parameters in M need to be eliminated.

Example 4. The overall constraint for the system in Example 1 is now

$$
\exists(\mu_1, \mu_2) \left(
\underbrace{d \geq 0}_{\text{Initation}} \wedge
\underbrace{\left[
\begin{array}{c}
\mu_1 c_1 - c_1 = 0 \\
\mu_1 c_2 + c_2 - 2c_1 = 0 \\
\mu_1 d - d - c_2 \leq 0 \\
\mu_1 \geq 0
\end{array}
\right]}_{\tau_1} \wedge
\underbrace{\left[
\begin{array}{c}
\mu_2 c_1 - c_1 = 0 \\
\mu_2 c_2 - c_2 = 0 \\
\mu_2 d - d - c_1 - 2c_2 \leq 0 \\
\mu_2 \geq 0
\end{array}
\right]}_{\tau_2}
\right)
$$

3.2   Exact Elimination

The constraints in Example 4 are non-linear and existentially quantified. However, the theory of non-linear assertions over reals admits computable quantifier elimination, as shown by Tarski [16]. Many others have improved the algorithm [5, 17]. Packages like REDLOG and QEPCAD can handle small/medium
sized examples. In our earlier work, we used these techniques to handle the constraints derived from elimination. However, there are many drawbacks to using
these tools.

1. The technique does not scale to systems of more than five variables.
2. The technique yields large formulas with many non-linear constraints that
   cancel in the final result, leading to much redundant effort.
3. The structure in the constraints is not fully utilized. The constraints are of
   low degree, and exhibit a uniform structure. This is lost as soon as some of
   the parameters are eliminated.
4. In case the underlying LTS has some special structure, the use of elimination
   may be completely unnecessary, as demonstrated for the case of Petri Net
   transitions in [14]. The result can be extended to cases where a subset of the
   transitions have a *Petri-net like* structure, as is the case with many systems.

Of course, the *completeness* of quantifier elimination, and Farkas Lemma lead to
theoretical claims of completeness (see [6] for details). We are not aware of any
alternative exact procedure for solving these constraints precisely. Therefore, we
shall concentrate on under-approximate elimination.

3.3   Under-Approximate Elimination Technique

Any under-approximate elimination technique is sound.

Lemma 1. *Let $\psi(c, \mu)$ be the overall constraints obtained from encoding induc-
tiveness. Let $\varphi(c)$ be an assertion such that*

$$
\varphi(c) \models (\exists \, \mu \geq 0) \, \psi(c, \mu)
$$

Any solution to φ is an inductive assertion.

Proof. Let $c = a$ be a solution to φ. Then, there exist positive parameters μ
such that $\psi(a, \mu)$ holds. The rest follows by the soundness of our constraint
generation process. See [6] for a proof.

We first split the overall constraints $\psi(c, \mu)$ into different groups: $\varphi_{\{eq,in\}}$, $\gamma_{\{eq,in\}}$, and ψ_μ:

- φ_{eq} and φ_{in} contain the equalities and inequalities, respectively, on c. We assume $\varphi_{eq} \models \varphi_{in}$.
- γ_{eq} and γ_{in} contain the PL equalities and inequalities, respectively, over c and μ.
- ψ_μ contains the constraints on μ, conjunctions of linear inequalities, equalities, and disequalities, where the disequalities are produced by our constraint solving rules.

Example 5. The constraints from Example 4 are classified as follows:

$$
\underbrace{d \geq 0}_{\varphi_{in}} \wedge \underbrace{\begin{bmatrix} \mu_1 c_1 - c_1 = 0 \\ \mu_1 c_2 + c_2 - 2c_1 = 0 \\ \mu_2 c_1 - c_1 = 0 \\ \mu_2 c_2 - c_2 = 0 \end{bmatrix}}_{\gamma_{eq}} \wedge \underbrace{\begin{bmatrix} \mu_1 d - d - c_2 \leq 0 \\ \mu_2 d - d - c_1 - 2c_2 \leq 0 \end{bmatrix}}_{\gamma_{in}} \wedge \underbrace{\begin{bmatrix} \mu_1 \geq 0 \\ \mu_2 \geq 0 \end{bmatrix}}_{\psi_\mu}
$$

The *linear part* of a system of constraints is defined as the constraint $\varphi_{in} \wedge \varphi_{eq}$. The system is unsatisfiable if $\varphi_{\{in,eq\}}$ or ψ_μ are, and *trivial* if φ_{eq} is of the form $c_1 = \ldots = c_n = 0$. The only inductive assertion that a trivial system can possibly yield is $1 \geq 0$.

Constraint Simplification. The simplifications involving equalities in φ_{eq}, ψ_μ, are the following:

1. Every equality expression in φ_{eq} of the form $a_1 c_1 + \cdots + a_n c_n + a_{n+1} d = 0$ forms a *rewrite rule* of the form $c_i \rightarrow -\frac{a_{i+1}}{a_i} c_{i+1} - \cdots - \frac{a_{n+1}}{a_i} d$, where i is the smallest index with $a_i \neq 0$.
2. Apply this rule to eliminate c_i over the linear and PL parts. Simplify, and repeat until all the equalities have been converted.

Similarly, a constraint of the form $\mu = a$ in ψ_μ is used to rewrite μ in $\gamma_{\{eq,in\}}$. The constraints added to $\varphi_{\{eq,in\}}$ can trigger further simplifications and similarly, constraints in γ_{eq} can be used as rewrite rules in order to simplify constraints in γ_{in}.

Factorization and Splitting. A PL expression is *factorizable* iff it can be written in the form $(\mu - a)\alpha$, where α is a linear expression over c. Deciding if an expression is factorizable is linear time in the expression size. A PL equality $(\mu - a)\alpha = 0$ factorizes into two factors $\mu - a = 0 \vee \alpha = 0$. Similarly a PL inequality $(\mu - a)\alpha \geq 0$ factorizes into $(\mu - a \geq 0 \wedge \alpha \geq 0) \vee (\mu - a \leq 0 \wedge \alpha \leq 0)$. Since our system of constraints is a conjunction of (in)equalities, factorization splits a constraint system into a *disjunction* of two systems. The following is a factorization strategy, for equalities:

1. Choose a factorizable expression $(\mu - a)\alpha = 0$, and remove it from the constraints,
2. Create two constraint systems, each containing all the remaining constraints. Add $\mu = a$ to one system, rewriting all occurrences of μ by a. Add $\alpha = 0 \land \mu \neq a$ to the other system, and simplify.

Example 6. The constraint system in Example 4 has a factorizable equality $\mu_2 c_i - c_i = 0$, for $i \in \{1, 2\}$. We add $\mu_2 = 1$ to one child, and $c_1 = 0 \land c_2 = 0$ to the other, yielding

$$
\begin{bmatrix}
\left.\begin{array}{r} d \geq 0 \\ -c_1 - 2c_2 \leq 0 \end{array}\right\} \varphi_{in} \\
\left.\begin{array}{r} \mu_1 c_1 - c_1 = 0 \\ \mu_1 c_2 + c_2 - 2c_1 = 0 \end{array}\right\} \gamma_{eq} \\
\mu_1 d - d - c_2 \leq 0 \leftarrow \gamma_{in} \\
\left.\begin{array}{r} \mu_1 \geq 0 \\ \mu_2 = 1 \end{array}\right\} \psi_\mu
\end{bmatrix}
\lor
\begin{bmatrix}
\left.\begin{array}{r} c_1 = 0 \\ c_2 = 0 \end{array}\right\} \varphi_{eq} \\
d \geq 0 \leftarrow \varphi_{in} \\
\left.\begin{array}{r} \mu_1 d - d \leq 0 \\ \mu_2 d - d \leq 0 \end{array}\right\} \gamma_{in} \\
\left.\begin{array}{r} \mu_1 \geq 0 \\ \mu_2 \neq 1 \end{array}\right\} \psi_\mu
\end{bmatrix}
$$

The constraints on the right are *trivial*. The system on the left can be factorized using the equality $\mu_1 c_1 - c_1 = 0$. We obtain:

$$
\begin{bmatrix}
2c_2 - 2c_1 = 0 \leftarrow \varphi_{eq} \\
\left.\begin{array}{r} d \geq 0 \\ -c_1 - 2c_2 \leq 0 \\ -c_2 \leq 0 \end{array}\right\} \varphi_{in} \\
\left.\begin{array}{r} \mu_1 = 1 \\ \mu_2 = 1 \end{array}\right\} \psi_\mu
\end{bmatrix}
\lor
\begin{bmatrix}
c_1 = 0 \leftarrow \varphi_{eq} \\
\left.\begin{array}{r} d \geq 0 \\ -c_1 - 2c_2 \leq 0 \end{array}\right\} \varphi_{in} \\
\mu_1 c_2 + c_2 = 0 \leftarrow \gamma_{eq} \\
\mu_1 d - d - c_2 \leq 0 \leftarrow \gamma_{in} \\
\left.\begin{array}{r} \mu_1 \geq 0 \\ \mu_2 = 1 \\ \mu_1 \neq 1 \end{array}\right\} \psi_\mu
\end{bmatrix}
$$

The system on the left (unsimplified) has been completely linearized. The system on the right can be further factored using $\mu_1 c_2 + c_2 = 0$, yielding $\mu_1 = -1$ on one side, and $c_2 = 0$ on the other. Setting $\mu_1 = -1$ contradicts $\mu_1 \geq 0$, while setting $c_2 = 0$ makes the system trivial. Therefore, repeated factorization and simplification yields the linear assertion $c_1 = c_2 \land c_1 \geq 0 \land d \geq 0$, which is equivalent to the result of the exact elimination.

Simplification and factorization can be repeatedly applied to split the initial constraints into a tree of constraints, such that each leaf has no more rules applicable. Each node in the tree is equivalent to the disjunction of its children. Therefore, the root is equivalent to the disjunction of all the leaves. The leaves can be either completely resolved (linear), unsatisfiable, trivial, or *terminal*. A terminal leaf is satisfiable and non-trivial, but contains unresolved non-linearities, which cannot be further split or simplified.

Handling Terminal Constraints. There are many ways of handling these constraints, some exact and some under-approximate.

#	name	description
1	Simplification	Substitute equalities into Expressions
2	Factorization	Choose a factorizable expression, and split disjuncts
3	Subsumption	Test containment of linear part w.r.t fully-resolved nodes
4	Split	Use lemmas 2,3 to split
5	Instantiate	Set $\mu_i = 0, 1$, split and proceed

Fig. 2. Constraint-simplification rules.

Subsumption. If a terminal (or even a non-terminal branch) has its linear part subsumed by another fully linear leaf, we can ignore it without loss of accuracy. Checking subsumption allows us to eliminate non-terminal nodes too. Even though polyhedral containment is expensive for higher-dimensions, we find that a significant fraction of the nodes explored are eliminated this way.

Split In some special cases, it is possible to simplify a terminal system further. The following lemmas are inspired by our work on Petri Net Transitions [14].

Lemma 2. *Let α_1, α_2 be linear expressions, and μ be a parameter not occurring in $\alpha_{\{1,2\}}$. Then*

$$- (\exists \mu \geq 0) \, (\alpha_1 + \mu\alpha_2 = 0) \equiv \left[\begin{array}{c} (\alpha_1 = \alpha_2 = 0) \, \vee \\ (\alpha_1 \leq 0 \, \wedge \, \alpha_2 > 0) \, \vee \, (\alpha_1 \geq 0 \, \wedge \, \alpha_2 < 0) \end{array} \right],$$
$$- (\exists \mu \geq 0) \, (\alpha_1 + \mu\alpha_2 \geq 0) \equiv (\alpha_1 \geq 0) \, \vee \, (\alpha_2 > 0).$$

These lemmas can be extended to systematically handle more complicated constraints on μ. They can also be modified to apply when more than one constraint exists, with loss of completeness.

Lemma 3. $(Ac \geq 0) \, \vee \, (Bc > 0) \models (\exists \mu \geq 0) \, Ac + \mu Bc \geq 0$

Instantiate Finally, instantiating some parameter μ to $\{0, 1\}$ lets us resolve it. Other values of μ are also possible. However, using $\{0, 1\}$ restricts the template assertion $\alpha \geq 0$ to satisfy local or increasing-value consecution, respectively, as defined in Section 2. The advantage of this strategy is that it is efficient and simple, especially if some invariants are to be generated in as short a time as possible.

4   Experimental Results

We have implemented our method and evaluated it on several programs. Our prototype implementation uses the library PPL for manipulating polyhedra [2] supplemented with our own implementation of some of the rules in Figure 2, discussed below. We compared our method against forward propagation with two different widenings provided by PPL: the standard CH79 widening [8] and BHRZ03 widening [1]. The BHRZ03 operator is provably more accurate, but less efficient than the CH79 widening. Since we implemented the post-condition ourselves, we present separately the time spent computing post-conditions and the time spent on PPL-provided widening.

Experimenting with a few strategies, we converged on a strategy that scaled to larger examples. Some of the salient features of the strategy are the following:

- For multi-location systems, the transitions are classified as *intra*-location and *inter*-location. The constraints for the intra-location transitions at each location are resolved by a subset of the rules described previously. Specifically, factorization is performed only over equalities, and Lemmas 2 and 3 are not used. Handling factors over inequalities requires more polyhedral reasoning at every simplification while the use of the two lemmas requires sophisticated reasoning involving equalites, inequalities and disequalities. Our disequality constraint solver uses heuristic rules whose completeness remains unresolved.
- Local and increasing consecution are used for each inter-location transition. This strategy can be proven exact for many situations.
- The constraints for each location and the inter-location transitions are combined conjunctively. Converting this CNF expression to DNF is a significant bottleneck, requiring aggressive subsumption tests.
- Constraints are solved *depth-first* as much as possible, favouring branches that can be resolved faster. The collection of linear constraints from resolved branches enable aggressive subsumption testing. The CNF to DNF conversion is also performed in a depth-first fashion to enable invariants to be computed eagerly.

As an added benefit, the execution can be interrupted after a reasonable amount of time, and still yield many non-trivial invariants. In several cases our invariants are disjoint with the results of forward propagation, because propagation-based techniques can compute invariants $\varphi_1 \wedge \varphi_2$ that are *mutually inductive*, that is, neither φ_1 nor φ_2 are inductive by themselves, while our technique only discovers single inequalities that are inductive by themselves. However, repeating the procedure with the computed invariants added to the guards of the transition system usually provides the stronger invariants.

4.1   Low Dimensional Systems

Figure 3 shows the experimental results for some small to medium sized examples from the related work and some benchmarks from analysis tools such as FAST [3]. The number of variables for each program is shown in the second column. The table shows for each program the time (in seconds) of our (constraint-based) approach, and the time taken by the CH79 and BHRZ03 approach. All computation times were measured on an Intel Xeon 1.7 GHz CPU with 2 Gb RAM. The last two columns show the strength of the invariants computed by our method compared with those computed by CH79 and BHRZ03, respectively. A + indicates that our invariants are strictly stronger, or no invariants were obtained by the other method within 1 hour. The $+^3$ = indicates that our invariants were stronger for three locations, while they were the same for the other locations. An =, $\neq$ and − indicate that our invariants are equal, incomparable, and strictly weaker, respectively. The suffix N indicates that all the variables in the system were constrained to be positive to increase the number of invariants discovered

Program		Constraint-based method			CH79 time (secs)			BHRZ03 time (secs)			C-B Invariants versus	
Name	vars	time	# br	# sub	total	post	widen	total	post	widen	CH79	BHRZ03
SEE-SAW	2	0.03	13	8	0	0	0	0	0	0	+	+
ROBOT	3	0.02	2	1	0.01	0	0.01	0.01	0.01	0	=	=
TRAIN-HPR97	3	0.86	25	5	0.02	0.02	0	0.02	0.02	0	$+^3 =$	$+^3 =$
RAND	4	0.02	3	2	0.01	0	0	0	0	0	=	=
BERKELEY	4	0.06	11	8	0.01	0	0.01	0.01	0	0.01	≠	≠
BERKELEY-N	4	0.04	9	4	0.01	0.01	0	0.01	0	0.01	+	+
HEAPSORT	5	0.1	21	12	0.02	0.01	0.01	0.02	0.02	0	≠	≠
TRAIN-RM03	6	1.16	193	99	0.06	0.05	0.01	0.07	0.05	0.02	+	=
EFM	6	0.36	57	23	0	0	0	0.01	0.01	0	−	−
EFM1	6	0.32	57	27	0	0	0	0.01	0.01	0	−	−
LIFO	7	0.88	58	51	0.29	0.27	0.02	0.32	0.29	0.03	≠	≠
LIFO-N	7	10.13	1191	593	0.27	0.25	0.02	0.32	0.27	0.04	+	+
CARS-MIDPT	7	0.1	17	8	32.8	5	27.8	> 3600			+	+
BARBER	8	1.68	125	84	0.18	0.17	0.01	20.41	0.18	20.23	+	+
SWIM	9	0.42	36	22	0.08	0.06	0.02	0.61	0.06	0.55	−	−
SWIM1	9	0.88	65	32	0.07	0.06	0.01	0.59	0.06	0.53	=	=

Fig. 3. Experimental results for some low-dimensional systems. #br is the number of branches, #sub is the number pruned by subsumption tests.

in one run. The programs SWIM1, EFM1 were obtained by adding the previously computed invariants as guards to the transition relations.

The figure shows that for the programs tested our invariants are mostly superior or comparable, but at a significant extra cost in computation time for the smaller dimensions. However, the situation changes when the dimensionality of the systems is increased beyond ten variables, as shown in the next section.

4.2 Higher-Dimensional Systems

To evaluate our method for systems with more variables we compared its performance on instances of two parameterized systems.

Pre-emptive Scheduler: The first system is an n process pre-emptive scheduler inspired by the two-process example in Halbwachs et. al. [11]. Two arrivals of process p_i are separated by at least c_i time units, for a fixed c_i. Process p_i preempts process p_j for $j < i$. The system has n locations, where location ℓ_i denotes that process p_i is executing and that there are no waiting processes p_j for $j > i$.

Convoy of Cars: The second system consists of n cars on a straight road whose accelerations are controlled (as in real life), determining their velocity. The lead car non-deterministically chooses an acceleration. The controller for each car detects when the lead car is too close or too far, and, after a bounded reaction time, adjusts acceleration. Time was discretized in order to linearize the resulting transition system.

Program		Constraint-based method			CH79 time (secs)			BHRZ03 time (secs)			C-B Invariants versus	
Name	vars	time	# br	# sub	total	post	widen	total	post	widen	CH79	BHRZ03
SCHEDULER												
2 proc.	7	0.54	23	10	0.15	0.12	0.02	0.19	0.12	0.07	$\neq -$	$\neq -$
3 proc.	10	8.21	36	16	39.5	26.9	12.8	2232	27.5	2204	$+^3$	$\neq^3$
4 proc.	13	284	55	26	> 3600			> 3600			$+^4$	$+^4$
5 proc.	16	> 3600	81	41	> 3600			> 3600			?	?
CARS												
2 proc.	10	3.54	93	44	5.22	4.23	0.97	443	200	243	+	$\neq$
3 proc.	14	20.5	468	239	> 3600			> 3600			+	+
4 proc.	18	1006	3722	1897	> 3600			> 3600			+	+

Fig. 4. Performance Comparison on parameterized examples SCHEDULER and CARS.

Figure 4 shows the performance comparison In all cases above 10 variables, our technique out-performs the other two techniques. The propagation-based techniques ran out of time for these systems. Our method ran out of time for the 5-process scheduler. It did so while converting a large CNF formula into a DNF formula. In fact, two different timeouts, 700s and 3600s, yielded the same (non-trivial) invariants. A total of 19 disjuncts in the normal form conversion were found to be relevant within the first 700 seconds, while all the 75791 disjuncts computed in the next 2900 seconds were found to be subsumed by the original 19. This suggests that a vast majority of disjuncts in the computed DNF form yield the same invariant, which was confirmed by other examples.

5   Conclusion

Linear programming, as a discipline has seen tremendous advances in the past century. Our research demonstrates that some ideas from linear programming can be used to provide alternative techniques for linear-relations analysis. Analysis carried out this way has some powerful advantages. It provides the ability to adjust the complexity and the accuracy in numerous ways. The constraint-based perspective for linear relations analysis can be powerful, both in theory and in practice.

Future work needs to concentrate on increasing the dimensionality and the complexity of the application examples for this analysis. Numerous mathematical tools remain to be explored for this domain. The use of numerical, and interval-numerical techniques for handling robustness in polyhedral computations has remained largely unexplored. Manipulation techniques for compressed representations along the lines of Halbwachs et al. [10] has also shown promise. Further investigations into the geometry of these constraints will yield a precise and faster analysis.

Acknowledgements

The authors are grateful to the people behind PPL [2] for making this study possible, and the anonymous reviewers for their detailed comments.

References

1. Bagnara, R., Hill, P. M., Ricci, E., and Zaffanella, E. Precise widening operators for convex polyhedra. In *Static Analysis Symposium* (2003), vol. 2694 of *LNCS*, Springer-Verlag, pp. 337–354.

2. Bagnara, R., Ricci, E., Zaffanella, E., and Hill, P. M. Possibly not closed convex polyhedra and the Parma Polyhedra Library. In *Static Analysis Symposium* (2002), vol. 2477 of *LNCS*, Springer-Verlag, pp. 213–229.

3. Bardin, S., Finkel, A., Leroux, J., and Petrucci, L. Fast: Fast accelereation of symbolic transition systems. In *Computer-aided Verification* (July 2003), vol. 2725 of *LNCS*, Springer-Verlag.

4. Besson, F., Jensen, T., and Talpin, J.-P. Polyhedral analysis of synchronous languages. In *Static Analysis Symposium* (1999), vol. 1694 of *LNCS*, pp. 51–69.

5. Collins, G. Quantifier elimination for real closed fields by cylindrical algebraic decomposition. In *Automata Theory and Formal Languages* (1975), H.Brakhage, Ed., vol. 33 of *LNCS*, Springer-Verlag, pp. 134–183.

6. Colón, M., Sankaranarayanan, S., and Sipma, H. Linear invariant generation using non-linear constraint solving. In *Computer Aided Verification* (July 2003), vol. 2725 of *LNCS*, Springer-Verlag, pp. 420–433.

7. Cousot, P., and Cousot, R. Abstract Interpretation: A unified lattice model for static analysis of programs by construction or approximation of fixpoints. In *ACM Principles of Programming Languages* (1977), pp. 238–252.

8. Cousot, P., and Halbwachs, N. Automatic discovery of linear restraints among the variables of a program. In *ACM Principles of Programming Languages* (Jan. 1978), pp. 84–97.

9. Fukuda, K., and Prodon, A. Double description method revisited. In *Combinatorics and Computer Science*, vol. 1120 of *LNCS*. Springer-Verlag, 1996, pp. 91–111.

10. Halbwachs, N., Merchat, D., and Parent-Vigouroux, C. Cartesian factoring of polyhedra for linear relation analysis. In *Static Analysis Symposium* (2003), vol. 2694 of *LNCS*, Springer-Verlag, pp. 355–365.

11. Halbwachs, N., Proy, Y., and Roumanoff, P. Verification of real-time systems using linear relation analysis. *Formal Methods in System Design 11*, 2 (1997), 157–185.

12. Henzinger, T. A., and Ho, P. HYTECH: The Cornell hybrid technology tool. In *Hybrid Systems II* (1995), vol. 999 of *LNCS*, Springer-Verlag, pp. 265–293.

13. Manna, Z., and Pnueli, A. *Temporal Verification of Reactive Systems: Safety.* Springer-Verlag, New York, 1995.

14. Sankaranarayanan, S., Sipma, H. B., and Manna, Z. Petri net analysis using invariant generation. In *Verification: Theory and Practice* (2003), vol. 2772 of *LNCS*, Springer-Verlag, pp. 682–701.

15. Schrijver, A. *Theory of Linear and Integer Programming.* Wiley, 1986.

16. Tarski, A. A decision method for elementary algebra and geometry. *Univ. of California Press, Berkeley 5* (1951).

17. Weispfenning, V. The complexity of linear problems in fields. *Journal of Symbolic Computation 5*, 1-2 (April 1988), 3–27.

Spatial Analysis of BioAmbients[*]

Hanne Riis Nielson, Flemming Nielson, and Henrik Pilegaard

Technical University of Denmark
{riis,nielson,hepi}@imm.dtu.dk

Abstract. Programming language technology can contribute to the development and understanding of Systems Biology by providing formal calculi for specifying and analysing the dynamic behaviour of biological systems. Our focus is on BioAmbients, a variation of the ambient calculi developed for modelling mobility in computer systems. We present a static analysis for capturing the spatial structure of biological systems and we illustrate it on a few examples.

1   Introduction and Motivation

Systems biology is an approach to studying biological phenomena that is based on a *high level* view of biological systems. The main focus is not the *structure* of biological components but rather the *dynamics* of these components. This poses a challenge for computer science: can programming language technology be used to model and analyse not only the structure of biological processes but also their evolution?

Pioneering work by Shapiro et al [15] demonstrated how biological processes could be specified in the π-calculus [7]; the formalism showed its strength at the molecular and biochemical level but it was less successful at the higher abstraction levels where compartments play a central role. Here, on the other hand, a version of the Ambient Calculus [3], called BioAmbients [13, 14], shows promise as the hierarchical structure of the ambients is very similar to that of compartments; the main difference between the two calculi is in the choice of the primitives for modelling the interaction between ambients or compartments. Surely biological systems are very complex and the scope for developing calculi of computation that capture various aspects of these systems is endless; recent work includes [2, 5, 8, 12].

The main goal, of course, is to capture the behaviour of biological systems in a faithful manner. Over the years biologists have collected observations about biological systems in large databases and it is important to investigate to what extent our models can explain these data in a satisfactory way. It turns out that many of the observations collected by the biologists concern *spatial properties* (as opposed to temporal properties) and this is where static analysis – and the present paper – gets into the picture.

[*] This research has been supported by the LoST project (number 21-02-0507) funded the Danish Natural Science Research Council.

R. Giacobazzi (Ed.): SAS 2004, LNCS 3148, pp. 69–83, 2004.

Overview of the Paper. In Section 2 we present the syntax and semantics of BioAmbients. The spatial analysis is developed in two stages: First a *compatibility analysis* is developed in Section 3; it computes an over-approximation of the possible interactions within the system of interest. This information is then used in the *spatial analysis* presented in Section 4; this analysis contains a novel treatment of recursion and a new technique for reducing the space complexity of the analysis. Finally, Section 5 illustrates our approach on a few examples and contains our concluding remarks.

2   BioAmbients

BioAmbients [13, 14] differ from Mobile Ambients [3] and its siblings Safe Ambients [6], Boxed Ambients [1] and Discretionary Ambients [11] in a number of ways. The most important difference is that the names (or identities) of the ambients do not control the interaction between ambients, but rather names (of channels) serve that purpose. BioAmbients follow the approach of safe and discretionary ambients and specify interactions by matching capabilities and co-capabilities; the communication primitives have some reminiscents of boxed ambients in that communication can occur across ambient boundaries but it is based on channels as in the π-calculus.

BioAmbients deviate from the other ambient calculi in having a non-deterministic choice operation in addition to the construct for parallelism (just as the π-calculus [7]). The pioneering development presented in [13, 14] observes the need to use a general recursion construct in order to faithfully model biological systems but the theoretical development is only performed for the classical replication construct. To be able to analyse such examples we shall therefore study a version of BioAmbients with a general recursion operator and, as we shall see in later sections, this poses some interesting technical challenges for the theoretical properties of the analysis.

The syntax of BioAmbients is given in Table 1; here we write P for processes and M for capabilities. Each ambient has an *identity* $\mu \in$ **Ambient** and each capability has a *label* $\ell \in$ **Lab**; these annotations have no semantic significance but are useful as "pointers" into the process and also serve a rôle in the analysis. (We shall not require that identities or labels are unique.) Furthermore, each name has a *canonical name* $\lfloor n \rfloor \in$ **Name** and we shall demand that alpha-renaming preserves the canonical name; consequently it will be the canonical name rather than the name that will be recorded in the analysis. For the sake of simplicity, we shall assume that a subset $\mathbf{C} \subseteq$ **Name** of the canonical names is reserved for constants and below we shall require that names introduced by $(n)P$ satisfy $\lfloor n \rfloor \in \mathbf{C}$. The capabilities M are based on names and hence we shall write $\lfloor M \rfloor \in$ **Cap** for the corresponding *canonical capability* obtained by replacing the names with the corresponding canonical names. The input capabilities $(n?\{p\}$, etc.) introduce new names p acting as placeholders (or variables); below we shall require that $\lfloor p \rfloor \in \mathbf{V}$ where $\mathbf{V} = $ **Name** $\setminus \mathbf{C}$. Finally, processes may be recursively defined using the construct $\mathsf{rec}\, X.\, P$ and to simplify the development

Table 1. Syntax of processes P and capabilities M.

$P ::= 0$		inactive process
$\mid (n)P$		binding box for the name n
$\mid [P]^{\mu}$		ambient P with the identity μ
$\mid M^{\ell}.P$		prefixing with the capability M labelled ℓ
$\mid P \mid P^{\partial}$		parallel processes
$\mid P + P^{\partial}$		non-deterministic (external) choice
$\mid \text{rec}\, X.\, P$		recursive process $(X = P)$
$\mid X$		process identifier
$M ::= \text{enter}\ n$	$\mid \text{accept}\ n$	enter movement
$\mid \text{exit}\ n$	$\mid \text{expel}\ n$	exit movement
$\mid \text{merge}-\ n$	$\mid \text{merge}+\ n$	merge movement
$\mid n!\{m\}$	$\mid n?\{p\}$	local communication
$\mid n\_!\{m\}$	$\mid n\hat{\ }?\{p\}$	communication to child
$\mid n\hat{\ }!\{m\}$	$\mid n\_?\{p\}$	communication to parent
$\mid n\#!\{m\}$	$\mid n\#?\{p\}$	communication between siblings

we shall require that X indeed occurs inside P; obviously the usual replication operation $!\,P$ can be obtained as $\text{rec}\,X.\,(P \mid X)$ (assuming X does not occur free in P). Analogously to the treatment of names we shall require that each process identifier X has a canonical identity $\lfloor X \rfloor$ that is preserved by alpha-renaming.

Programs will be processes $P_{\star}$ satisfying the predicate $\mathsf{PRG}_{\mathbf{C}}(P_{\star})$ defined as the conjunction of the following conditions (explained below):

- $P_{\star}$ has no free process identifiers; formally $\mathsf{fpi}(P_{\star}) = \emptyset$.
- $P_{\star}$ only has free names from $\mathbf{C}$; formally $\lfloor \mathsf{fn}(P_{\star}) \rfloor \subseteq \mathbf{C}$.
- $P_{\star}$ is well-formed wrt. $\mathbf{C}$; formally $\mathbf{C} \vdash P_{\star}$.

Here we write $\mathsf{fpi}(P)$ for the set of *free process identifiers* of P and $\mathsf{fn}(P)$ for the *free names* of P; the canonicity operation $\lfloor \cdot \rfloor$ is extended in a pointwise manner to sets of names. The *well-formedness predicate* $\mathbf{C} \vdash P$ serves two purposes: first, it enforces the implicit typing requirements imposed by the division of **Name** into the two disjoint subsets $\mathbf{C}$ and $\mathbf{V}$; secondly, it imposes the condition that process identifiers are actually used recursively in the processes they define. The predicate is formally defined in Table 2 and uses $\mathsf{bn}(M)$ to denote the *bound names* of the capability M. Note that the condition will reject processes like $(n)\,[\text{enter}\ n^{\ell_1} \mid m?\{n\}^{\ell_2}.\,\text{enter}\ n^{\ell_3}]^{\mu}$ where the same name n is introduced as a constant and also introduced in an input capability; a simple alpha-renaming will, of course, solve the problem.

We shall write $P[m/n]$ for the process that is as P except that all free occurrences of the name n are replaced by the name m. Similarly, we shall write $P[Q/X]$ for the process that is as P except that all free occurrences of the process identifier X are replaced by the process Q. In both cases we take care to perform the necessary alpha-renamings (preserving canonicity) to avoid capturing free names or process identifiers.

Table 2. Well-formedness of processes with respect to $\mathbf{C}$: $\mathbf{C} \vdash P$.

$$\mathbf{C} \vdash 0 \qquad \frac{\mathbf{C} \vdash P}{\mathbf{C} \vdash (n)P} \; \text{if } \lfloor n \rfloor \in \mathbf{C} \qquad \frac{\mathbf{C} \vdash P}{\mathbf{C} \vdash [P]^{\mu}} \qquad \frac{\mathbf{C} \vdash P}{\mathbf{C} \vdash M^{\ell}.P} \; \text{if } \lfloor \mathsf{bn}(M) \rfloor \cap \mathbf{C} = \emptyset$$

$$\frac{\mathbf{C} \vdash P \quad \mathbf{C} \vdash P^{\Game}}{\mathbf{C} \vdash P \mid P^{\Game}} \qquad \frac{\mathbf{C} \vdash P \quad \mathbf{C} \vdash P^{\Game}}{\mathbf{C} \vdash P + P^{\Game}} \qquad \frac{\mathbf{C} \vdash P}{\mathbf{C} \vdash \mathsf{rec}\,X.\,P} \; \text{if } X \in \mathsf{fpi}(P) \qquad \mathbf{C} \vdash X$$

Table 3. Structural congruence: $P \equiv Q$ is the least congruence defined by the above.

Alpha-renaming of bound names and bound process identifiers:

$\quad P \equiv Q \qquad$ if P may be alpha-renamed to Q (preserving canonicity)

Reordering of parallel processes: Reordering of choice processes:

$$P \mid P^{\Game} \equiv P^{\Game} \mid P \qquad\qquad\qquad P + P^{\Game} \equiv P^{\Game} + P$$
$$(P \mid P^{\Game}) \mid P^{\Game\Game} \equiv P \mid (P^{\Game} \mid P^{\Game\Game}) \qquad (P + P^{\Game}) + P^{\Game\Game} \equiv P + (P^{\Game} + P^{\Game\Game})$$
$$P \mid 0 \equiv P \qquad\qquad\qquad\qquad P + 0 \equiv P$$

Scope rules for name bindings:

$$(n)0 \equiv 0$$
$$(n)(m)P \equiv (m)(n)P$$
$$(n)([P]^{\mu}) \equiv [(n)P]^{\mu}$$

$$(n)(P \mid P^{\Game}) \equiv ((n)P) \mid P^{\Game} \quad \text{if } n \notin \mathsf{fn}(P^{\Game})$$
$$(n)(P + P^{\Game}) \equiv ((n)P) + P^{\Game} \quad \text{if } n \notin \mathsf{fn}(P^{\Game})$$

Recursion:

$$\mathsf{rec}\,X.\,P \equiv P[\mathsf{rec}\,X.\,P/X]$$

Example 1. To illustrate the development we consider the following program P_{virus}; as we shall see shortly it models how the gene of a virus may infect a cell:

$$\begin{aligned}
[\; &\mathsf{rec}\,X.\; \mathsf{enter}\; n_1^{\ell_1}.\; X + \mathsf{exit}\; n_2^{\ell_2}.\; X + c^{\hat{}}?\{x\}^{\ell_3}.\; \mathsf{expel}\; x^{\ell_4}.\; X \\
&|\; [\, \mathsf{exit}\; n_3^{\ell_5}.\; 0\,]^{gene}\,]^{virus} \\
&|\; [\, \mathsf{rec}\,Y.\; \mathsf{accept}\; n_1^{\ell_6}.\; Y + \mathsf{expel}\; n_2^{\ell_7}.\; Y + c_-!\{n_3\}^{\ell_8}.\; Y\,]^{cell}
\end{aligned}$$

It is trivial to check that the well-formedness condition is fulfilled for $\mathbf{C} = \{\lfloor c \rfloor, \lfloor n_1 \rfloor, \lfloor n_2 \rfloor, \lfloor n_3 \rfloor\}$.   □

Semantics. The semantics follows the standard approach and is specified by the *structural congruence relation* $P \equiv Q$ in Table 3 and the *transition relation* $P \rightarrow Q$ in Table 4. The congruence relation uses a disciplined notion of alpha-renaming that preserves canonicity. The movement interactions merely give rise to a rearrangement of the ambient structure where some potential continuations are excluded (due to the presence of the non-deterministic choice operation). The communication interactions also exclude some potential continuations but they

Table 4. Transition relation: $P \to Q$.

Movement of ambients:

$$[(\text{enter } n^{\ell_1}. P + P^{\square}) \mid P^{\square\square}]^{\mu_1} \mid [(\text{accept } n^{\ell_2}. Q + Q^{\square}) \mid Q^{\square\square}]^{\mu_2} \to [[P \mid P^{\square\square}]^{\mu_1} \mid Q \mid Q^{\square\square}]^{\mu_2}$$

$$[[(\text{exit } n^{\ell_1}. P + P^{\square}) \mid P^{\square\square}]^{\mu_1} \mid (\text{expel } n^{\ell_2}. Q + Q^{\square}) \mid Q^{\square\square}]^{\mu_2} \to [P \mid P^{\square\square}]^{\mu_1} \mid [Q \mid Q^{\square\square}]^{\mu_2}$$

$$[(\text{merge- } n^{\ell_1}. P + P^{\square}) \mid P^{\square\square}]^{\mu_1} \mid [(\text{merge+ } n^{\ell_2}. Q + Q^{\square}) \mid Q^{\square\square}]^{\mu_2} \to [P \mid P^{\square\square} \mid Q \mid Q^{\square\square}]^{\mu_2}$$

Communication between ambients:

$$(n!\{m\}^{\ell_1}. P + P^{\square}) \mid (n?\{p\}^{\ell_2}. Q + Q^{\square}) \to P \mid Q[m/p]$$

$$(n\_!\{m\}^{\ell_1}. P + P^{\square}) \mid [(n\hat{\ }?\{p\}^{\ell_2}. Q + Q^{\square}) \mid Q^{\square\square}]^{\mu} \to P \mid [Q[m/p] \mid Q^{\square\square}]^{\mu}$$

$$[(n\hat{\ }!\{m\}^{\ell_1}. P + P^{\square}) \mid P^{\square\square}]^{\mu} \mid (n\_?\{p\}^{\ell_2}. Q + Q^{\square}) \to [P \mid P^{\square\square}]^{\mu} \mid Q[m/p]$$

$$[(n\#!\{m\}^{\ell_1}. P + P^{\square}) \mid P^{\square\square}]^{\mu_1} \mid [(n\#?\{p\}^{\ell_2}. Q + Q^{\square}) \mid Q^{\square\square}]^{\mu_2} \to [P \mid P^{\square\square}]^{\mu_1} \mid [Q[m/p] \mid Q^{\square\square}]^{\mu_2}$$

Execution in context:

$$\frac{P \to Q}{(n)P \to (n)Q} \qquad \frac{P \to Q}{[P]^{\mu} \to [Q]^{\mu}} \qquad \frac{P \to Q}{P \mid R \to Q \mid R} \qquad \frac{P \equiv P^{\square} \quad P^{\square} \to Q^{\square} \quad Q^{\square} \equiv Q}{P \to Q}$$

do not modify the overall ambient structure; however, some of the processes are modified in order to reflect the new binding of names. The semantics of recursion amounts to a straightforward unfolding in the congruence relation; this is more general than the overly restrictive semantics used in [9].

Example 2. The semantics of the program P_{virus} of Example 1 is illustrated on Figure 1. The initial configuration is shown in the upper leftmost frame where the tree structure reflects that *cell* and *virus* are siblings (with a common father denoted $\top$) and *gene* is a subambient of *virus*. The first step of the semantics will be for *virus* to move into *cell* using the pair (enter $n_1^{\ell_1}$, accept $n_1^{\ell_6}$) of capabilities and we obtain the configuration depicted in the bottom leftmost frame of the figure. Now there are two possibilities: either *virus* moves out of *cell* using the pair (exit $n_2^{\ell_2}$, expel $n_2^{\ell_7}$) of capabilities and we are back in the initial configuration at the top or, alternatively, there is a communication from *cell* to *virus* over the name c using the pair $(c\_!\{n_3\}^{\ell_8}, c\hat{\ }?\{x\}^{\ell_3})$ of capabilities during which x is bound to n_3 as indicated in the corresponding frame of the figure. The pair (exit $n_3^{\ell_5}$, expel $n_3^{\ell_4}$) of capabilities will now move *gene* out of *virus* and we reach a configuration where *virus* can exit and enter *cell* any number of times or the communication over c may happen again after which the system ends in a stuck configuration (shown in the top rightmost frame of the figure). □

3   Compatibility Analysis

The aim of the spatial analysis is to extract an over-approximation of the possible hierarchial structures of the ambients. For this we need to approximate the potential interactions between the ambients and motivated by [4] we shall

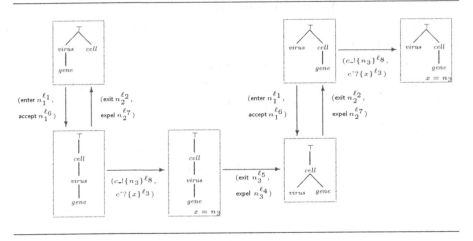

Fig. 1. Illustration of the semantics of the running example.

develop a compatibility analysis. Given a process P, the aim of the compatibility analysis is to identify pairs of labelled capabilities that, from a syntactic point of view, *may* engage in a transition. Intuitively, this means that the two capabilities must match and that it must be possible for them to occur in parallel processes. As an example, in $[\text{enter } n^{\ell_1}]^{\mu_1} \mid [\text{accept } m^{\ell_2}]^{\mu_2}$ the capabilities labelled ℓ_1 and ℓ_2 may interact because from a syntactic point of view we cannot preclude that n and m may turn out to be equal; however, if we replace the parallel composition with a non-deterministic choice then they will never be able to interact.

The matching condition will ignore the actual names occurring in the capabilities (because even the canonical names are not preserved under reduction) and to formalise this we shall introduce the notion of a *skeleton capability*: $\lceil M \rceil$ is simply obtained from M by replacing all names in M with the token " · ". The *matching condition* on skeleton capabilities can now be expressed by the predicate

$$\text{match}(\lceil M_1 \rceil, \lceil M_2 \rceil)$$

that holds if and only if

$$(\lceil M_1 \rceil, \lceil M_2 \rceil) \in \{ \ (\text{enter } \cdot, \text{accept } \cdot), \ (\text{exit } \cdot, \text{expel } \cdot), \ (\text{merge}- \cdot, \text{merge}+ \cdot),$$
$$(\cdot?\{\cdot\}, \cdot!\{\cdot\}), \ (\cdot\,\widehat{\ }?\{\cdot\}, \cdot\,\widehat{\ }!\{\cdot\}), \ (\cdot\_?\{\cdot\}, \cdot\,\widehat{\ }!\{\cdot\}), \ (\cdot\#?\{\cdot\}, \cdot\#!\{\cdot\}) \}$$

In order to define the compatibility information we shall first need to extract the set of *labelled skeleton capabilities* occurring within a process. This is done using the function $\text{caps}_\Gamma(P)$ of Table 5; here Γ is a mapping that to each process identifier associates a set of labelled skeleton capabilities. The mapping Γ is useful later (in the definition of comp) when we encounter subprocesses with free process identifiers.

The *compatibility information* is then obtained using the function $\text{comp}_{\Gamma\Delta}(P)$ of Table 5. Here Γ is as above whereas Δ is a mapping that to each process

Table 5. Capabilities, $\text{caps}_\Gamma(P)$, and compatible pairs of capabilities, $\text{comp}_{\Gamma\Delta}(P)$.

$$\text{caps}_\Gamma(0) = \emptyset \qquad\qquad \text{caps}_\Gamma((n)P) = \text{caps}_\Gamma(P)$$
$$\text{caps}_\Gamma([P]^\mu) = \text{caps}_\Gamma(P) \qquad\qquad \text{caps}_\Gamma(M^\ell.P) = \{\lceil M \rceil^\ell\} \cup \text{caps}_\Gamma(P)$$
$$\text{caps}_\Gamma(P \mid P^\square) = \text{caps}_\Gamma(P) \cup \text{caps}_\Gamma(P^\square) \qquad \text{caps}_\Gamma(P + P^\square) = \text{caps}_\Gamma(P) \cup \text{caps}_\Gamma(P^\square)$$
$$\text{caps}_\Gamma(\text{rec } X. P) = \text{caps}_{\Gamma[X\square\ \square]}(P) \qquad\qquad \text{caps}_\Gamma(X) = \Gamma(X)$$

$$\text{comp}_{\Gamma\Delta}(0) = \emptyset \qquad\qquad \text{comp}_{\Gamma\Delta}((n)P) = \text{comp}_{\Gamma\Delta}(P)$$
$$\text{comp}_{\Gamma\Delta}([P]^\mu) = \text{comp}_{\Gamma\Delta}(P) \qquad\qquad \text{comp}_{\Gamma\Delta}(M^\ell.P) = \text{comp}_{\Gamma\Delta}(P)$$
$$\text{comp}_{\Gamma\Delta}(P \mid P^\square) = \text{comp}_{\Gamma\Delta}(P) \qquad\qquad \text{comp}_{\Gamma\Delta}(P + P^\square) = \text{comp}_{\Gamma\Delta}(P)$$
$$\cup\ \text{comp}_{\Gamma\Delta}(P^\square) \qquad\qquad\qquad \cup\ \text{comp}_{\Gamma\Delta}(P^\square)$$
$$\cup\ \text{cross}_\Gamma(P, P^\square)$$
$$\text{comp}_{\Gamma\Delta}(\text{rec } X. P) = \text{comp}_{\Gamma'\Delta[X\square\ \square]}(P) \qquad \text{comp}_{\Gamma\Delta}(X) = \Delta(X)$$
$$\text{where } \Gamma^\square = \Gamma[X \mapsto \text{caps}_{\Gamma[X\square\ \square]}(P)]$$

$$\text{cross}_\Gamma(P, P^\square) = \{(\lceil M_1 \rceil^{\ell_1}, \lceil M_2 \rceil^{\ell_2}) \in (\text{caps}_\Gamma(P) \times \text{caps}_\Gamma(P^\square)) \cup (\text{caps}_\Gamma(P^\square) \times \text{caps}_\Gamma(P))$$
$$\mid \text{match}(\lceil M_1 \rceil, \lceil M_2 \rceil)\}$$

identifier associates a set of pairs of labelled skeleton capabilities; again we are parametric on Γ and Δ so that we can handle processes with free process identifiers. In the case of parallel composition the definition of comp uses the auxiliary operation cross to record that capabilities in the two branches may interact with one another and the caps function is used in order to specify this. This is in contrast to the definition provided for non-deterministic choice where it is known that capabilities from the two branches never will interact.

Example 3. For the running example P_{virus} of Examples 1 and 2 we get:

$$\text{CP}_{\text{virus}} = \{\ (\text{enter } \cdot^{\ell_1}, \text{accept } \cdot^{\ell_6}),$$
$$(\text{exit } \cdot^{\ell_2}, \text{expel } \cdot^{\ell_7}),\ (\text{exit } \cdot^{\ell_5}, \text{expel } \cdot^{\ell_4}),\ (\text{exit } \cdot^{\ell_5}, \text{expel } \cdot^{\ell_7}),$$
$$(\cdot\_!\{\cdot\}^{\ell_8}, \cdot^{\wedge}?\{\cdot\}^{\ell_3})\ \}$$

Comparing with Figure 1 we see that this is indeed an over-approximation of the actual interactions that can take place: the pair $(\text{exit } \cdot^{\ell_5}, \text{expel } \cdot^{\ell_7}) \in \text{CP}_{\text{virus}}$ has no analogue in Figure 1. □

Example 4. Consider the artificial variant P'_{virus} of the process of Example 1 where the virus exists in two variants, one with a gene much as before and one with a harmless gene:

$$[\,\text{rec } X. \text{ enter } n_1^{\ell_1}. X + \text{exit } n_2^{\ell_2}. X + c^{\wedge}?\{x\}^{\ell_3}. \text{ expel } x^{\ell_4}. X$$
$$\mid (\,[\text{exit } n_3^{\ell_5}. 0 + \text{accept } n_4^{\ell_6}. 0\,]^{gene_1} + [\text{enter } n_4^{\ell_7}. 0\,]^{gene_2}\,)\,]^{virus}$$
$$\mid [\text{rec } Y. \text{ accept } n_1^{\ell_8}. Y + \text{expel } n_2^{\ell_9}. Y + c\_!\{n_3\}^{\ell_{10}}. Y\,]^{cell}$$

The compatibility analysis will compute the following information:

$$\text{CP}'_{\text{virus}} = \{\ (\text{enter } \cdot^{\ell_1}, \text{accept } \cdot^{\ell_6}),\ (\text{enter } \cdot^{\ell_1}, \text{accept } \cdot^{\ell_8}),\ (\text{enter } \cdot^{\ell_7}, \text{accept } \cdot^{\ell_8}),$$
$$(\text{exit } \cdot^{\ell_2}, \text{expel } \cdot^{\ell_9}),\ (\text{exit } \cdot^{\ell_5}, \text{expel } \cdot^{\ell_4}),\ (\text{exit } \cdot^{\ell_5}, \text{expel } \cdot^{\ell_9}),$$
$$(\cdot\_!\{\cdot\}^{\ell_{10}}, \cdot^{\wedge}?\{\cdot\}^{\ell_3})\ \}$$

Note that despite the over-approximation this correctly captures that for example the capabilities labelled ℓ_7 and ℓ_6 of the two genes never will be able to interact.   □

The correctness of the compatibility analysis follows from:

Lemma 1. *If $P \equiv Q$ and $\mathbf{C} \vdash P$ then $\mathrm{comp}_{\Gamma\Delta}(P) = \mathrm{comp}_{\Gamma\Delta}(Q)$. If $P \rightarrow Q$ and $\mathbf{C} \vdash P$ then $\mathrm{comp}_{\Gamma\Delta}(Q) \subseteq \mathrm{comp}_{\Gamma\Delta}(P)$.*

In the subsequent analyses we shall make use of the compatibility relation for the overall program $P_\star$ of interest. Writing $[]$ for the empty mapping we shall use the abbreviation $\mathsf{CP}_\star$ for $\mathrm{comp}_{[][]}(P_\star)$ thereby exploiting that $P_\star$ has no free process identifiers. Thus it follows from Lemma 1 that if $\mathsf{PRG}_{\mathbf{C}}(P_\star)$ and $P_\star \rightarrow^* Q$ then $\mathrm{comp}_{[][]}(Q) \subseteq \mathsf{CP}_\star$ so $\mathsf{CP}_\star$ remains a correct over-approximation.

4   Spatial Analysis

We are now ready to embark on the spatial analysis: for a program $P_\star$ we want to approximate what ambients may turn up inside what other ambients. To extract this information we shall develop an analysis extracting the following information:

- An approximation of the contents of ambients:

$$\mathcal{I} \subseteq \mathbf{Ambient} \times (\mathbf{Ambient} \cup (\mathbf{Cap} \times \mathbf{Lab}))$$

  Here $\mu' \in \mathcal{I}(\mu)$ means that μ' may be a subambient of the ambient μ and $\lfloor M \rfloor^\ell \in \mathcal{I}(\mu)$ means that the labelled *canonical* capability $\lfloor M \rfloor^\ell$ may be within the ambient μ.
- An approximation of the relevant name bindings:

$$\mathcal{R} \subseteq \mathbf{V} \times \mathbf{C} \qquad (\subseteq \mathbf{Name} \times \mathbf{Name})$$

  Here $\nu' \in \mathcal{R}(\nu)$ means that the constant (canonical) name ν' may be bound to the variable (canonical) name ν.

The judgements of the analysis take the form

$$(\mathcal{I}, \mathcal{R}) \models^\mu P$$

and express that when the subprocess P (of $P_\star$) is enclosed within an ambient with the identity $\mu \in \mathbf{Ambient}$ then $\mathcal{I}$ and $\mathcal{R}$ correctly capture the behaviour of P – meaning that $\mathcal{I}$ will reflect the contents of the ambients as P evolves inside $P_\star$ and $\mathcal{R}$ will contain all the bindings of names that take place. The analysis is specified in Table 6 and refers to Table 7 for auxiliary information about the recursion construct and to Table 8 for a specification of the closure conditions $\mathrm{closure}_{\lceil M \rceil}$. Below we comment on the clauses.

Table 6. Analysis specification: $(\mathcal{I}, \mathcal{R}) \models^\mu P$.

$(\mathcal{I}, \mathcal{R}) \models^\mu 0$	iff	true
$(\mathcal{I}, \mathcal{R}) \models^\mu (n)P$	iff	$(\mathcal{I}, \mathcal{R}) \models^\mu P$
$(\mathcal{I}, \mathcal{R}) \models^\mu [P]^{\mu'}$	iff	$\mu^\square \in \mathcal{I}(\mu) \wedge (\mathcal{I}, \mathcal{R}) \models^{\mu'} P$
$(\mathcal{I}, \mathcal{R}) \models^\mu M^\ell.P$	iff	$\lfloor M \rfloor^\ell \in \mathcal{I}(\mu) \wedge (\mathcal{I}, \mathcal{R}) \models^\mu P \wedge \mathsf{closure}_{\square M \square}$
$(\mathcal{I}, \mathcal{R}) \models^\mu P \mid P^\square$	iff	$(\mathcal{I}, \mathcal{R}) \models^\mu P \wedge (\mathcal{I}, \mathcal{R}) \models^\mu P^\square$
$(\mathcal{I}, \mathcal{R}) \models^\mu P + P^\square$	iff	$(\mathcal{I}, \mathcal{R}) \models^\mu P \wedge (\mathcal{I}, \mathcal{R}) \models^\mu P^\square$
$(\mathcal{I}, \mathcal{R}) \models^\mu \mathsf{rec}\, X.\, P$	iff	$\forall \mu^\square : \mu^\square \in \mathcal{L}_{\square X \square}(\mathsf{G}^\mu(\mathsf{rec}\, X.\, P)) \Rightarrow (\mathcal{I}, \mathcal{R}) \models^{\mu'} P$
$(\mathcal{I}, \mathcal{R}) \models^\mu X$	iff	true

Table 7. Auxiliary analysis information for recursion: $\mathsf{G}^\delta(P)$.

$\mathsf{G}^\delta(0) = \emptyset$	$\mathsf{G}^\delta((n)P) = \mathsf{G}^\delta(P)$
$\mathsf{G}^\delta([P]^\mu) = \mathsf{G}^\mu(P)$	$\mathsf{G}^\delta(M^\ell.P) = \mathsf{G}^\delta(P)$
$\mathsf{G}^\delta(P \mid P^\square) = \mathsf{G}^\delta(P) \cup \mathsf{G}^\delta(P^\square)$	$\mathsf{G}^\delta(P + P^\square) = \mathsf{G}^\delta(P) \cup \mathsf{G}^\delta(P^\square)$
$\mathsf{G}^\delta(\mathsf{rec}\, X.\, P) = \mathsf{G}^{\square X \square}(P) \cup \{\lfloor X \rfloor \to \delta\}$	$\mathsf{G}^\delta(X) = \{\lfloor X \rfloor \to \delta\}$

Table 6 specifies a simple syntax directed traversal of the process with the clauses for ambients and capabilities being two of the more interesting ones as they check that $\mathcal{I}$ contains the correct initial information. The clause for $(n)P$ is very simple since n is a constant (in contrast to a variable); in particular there is no need to impose any requirements on $\mathcal{R}$. The clauses for the parallel and the choice constructs look exactly the same; however, the use of the compatibility information in the closure conditions of Table 8 ensures that they are indeed handled differently.

The clause for recursion ensures that the analysis result is valid in *all* the contexts in which the recursion construct $\mathsf{rec}\, X.\, P$ may be encountered including those arising from its unfolding. These contexts are provided by the auxiliary operation $\mathsf{G}^\delta(P)$ (see Table 7) that constructs a simple *regular grammar* for the potential contexts of the process identifiers. The non-terminals of the grammar are the canonical process identifiers, the terminal symbols are the ambient identities and the right hand side of the productions will contain exactly one (non-terminal or terminal) symbol. The language generated by the grammar $\mathsf{G}^\mu(\mathsf{rec}\, X.\, P)$ when $\lfloor X \rfloor$ is the start symbol is written $\mathcal{L}_{\lfloor X \rfloor}(\mathsf{G}^\mu(\mathsf{rec}\, X.\, P))$ and it approximates the contexts in which the recursion construct may be encountered. This language is clearly finite. As an example, for the process $[\mathsf{rec}\, X.\, \mathsf{rec}\, Y.\, (X \mid [Y]^{\mu_2})]^{\mu_1}$ we obtain a grammar with the productions $\{\lfloor X \rfloor \to \mu_1, \lfloor Y \rfloor \to \lfloor X \rfloor, \lfloor X \rfloor \to \lfloor Y \rfloor, \lfloor Y \rfloor \to \mu_2\}$. The language generated by this grammar by the non-terminal $\lfloor X \rfloor$ is $\{\mu_1, \mu_2\}$ reflecting that the outermost recursion may occur in both contexts as can be seen by unfolding both X and Y once.

Turning to the *closure conditions* of Table 8 we first observe that there are two clauses for each matching pair of skeleton capabilities and one of these is trivial. In each case the pre-condition of the non-trivial clause checks whether

Table 8. Closure condition on $\mathcal{I}$ and $\mathcal{R}$.

$\mathsf{closure}_{\mathsf{enter}\,\cdot}$	$= \forall \mu, \mu_1, \mu_2, \nu_1, \nu_2, \ell_1, \ell_2 :$
	$\quad \mathsf{enter}\ \nu_1^{\ell_1} \in \mathcal{I}(\mu_1) \wedge \mu_1 \in \mathcal{I}(\mu) \wedge \mathsf{accept}\ \nu_2^{\ell_2} \in \mathcal{I}(\mu_2) \wedge \mu_2 \in \mathcal{I}(\mu) \wedge$
	$\quad \langle \mathcal{R} \rangle(\nu_1) \cap \langle \mathcal{R} \rangle(\nu_2) \neq \emptyset \wedge \mathsf{CP}_\star(\mathsf{enter}\ \cdot^{\ell_1}, \mathsf{accept}\ \cdot^{\ell_2})$
	$\quad \Rightarrow \quad \mu_1 \in \mathcal{I}(\mu_2)$
$\mathsf{closure}_{\mathsf{accept}\,\cdot}$	$= \mathsf{true}$
$\mathsf{closure}_{\mathsf{exit}\,\cdot}$	$= \forall \mu, \mu_1, \mu_2, \nu_1, \nu_2, \ell_1, \ell_2 :$
	$\quad \mathsf{exit}\ \nu_1^{\ell_1} \in \mathcal{I}(\mu_1) \wedge \mu_1 \in \mathcal{I}(\mu_2) \wedge \mathsf{expel}\ \nu_2^{\ell_2} \in \mathcal{I}(\mu_2) \wedge \mu_2 \in \mathcal{I}(\mu) \wedge$
	$\quad \langle \mathcal{R} \rangle(\nu_1) \cap \langle \mathcal{R} \rangle(\nu_2) \neq \emptyset \wedge \mathsf{CP}_\star(\mathsf{exit}\ \cdot^{\ell_1}, \mathsf{expel}\ \cdot^{\ell_2})$
	$\quad \Rightarrow \quad \mu_1 \in \mathcal{I}(\mu)$
$\mathsf{closure}_{\mathsf{expel}\,\cdot}$	$= \mathsf{true}$
$\mathsf{closure}_{\mathsf{merge}-\,\cdot}$	$= \forall \mu, \mu_1, \mu_2, \nu_1, \nu_2, \ell_1, \ell_2 :$
	$\quad \mathsf{merge}-\ \nu_1^{\ell_1} \in \mathcal{I}(\mu_1) \wedge \mu_1 \in \mathcal{I}(\mu) \wedge \mathsf{merge}+\ \nu_2^{\ell_2} \in \mathcal{I}(\mu_2) \wedge \mu_2 \in \mathcal{I}(\mu) \wedge$
	$\quad \langle \mathcal{R} \rangle(\nu_1) \cap \langle \mathcal{R} \rangle(\nu_2) \neq \emptyset \wedge \mathsf{CP}_\star(\mathsf{merge}-\ \cdot^{\ell_1}, \mathsf{merge}+\ \cdot^{\ell_2})$
	$\quad \Rightarrow \quad \mathcal{I}(\mu_1) \subseteq \mathcal{I}(\mu_2)$
$\mathsf{closure}_{\mathsf{merge}+\,\cdot}$	$= \mathsf{true}$
$\mathsf{closure}_{\cdot!\{\cdot\}}$	$= \forall \mu, \nu_m, \nu_p, \nu_1, \nu_2, \ell_1, \ell_2 :$
	$\quad \nu_1!\{\nu_m\}^{\ell_1} \in \mathcal{I}(\mu) \wedge \nu_2?\{\nu_p\}^{\ell_2} \in \mathcal{I}(\mu) \wedge$
	$\quad \langle \mathcal{R} \rangle(\nu_1) \cap \langle \mathcal{R} \rangle(\nu_2) \neq \emptyset \wedge \mathsf{CP}_\star(\cdot!\{\cdot\}^{\ell_1}, \cdot?\{\cdot\}^{\ell_2})$
	$\quad \Rightarrow \quad \langle \mathcal{R} \rangle(\nu_m) \subseteq \mathcal{R}(\nu_p)$
$\mathsf{closure}_{\cdot?\{\cdot\}}$	$= \mathsf{true}$
$\mathsf{closure}_{\ldots\_!\{\ldots\}}$	$= \forall \mu, \mu_c, \nu_m, \nu_p, \nu_1, \nu_2, \ell_1, \ell_2 :$
	$\quad \nu_1\_!\{\nu_m\}^{\ell_1} \in \mathcal{I}(\mu) \wedge \nu_2\hat{\ }?\{\nu_p\}^{\ell_2} \in \mathcal{I}(\mu_c) \wedge \mu_c \in \mathcal{I}(\mu) \wedge$
	$\quad \langle \mathcal{R} \rangle(\nu_1) \cap \langle \mathcal{R} \rangle(\nu_2) \neq \emptyset \wedge \mathsf{CP}_\star(\cdot\_!\{\cdot\}^{\ell_1}, \cdot\hat{\ }?\{\cdot\}^{\ell_2})$
	$\quad \Rightarrow \quad \langle \mathcal{R} \rangle(\nu_m) \subseteq \mathcal{R}(\nu_p)$
$\mathsf{closure}_{\cdot\hat{\ }?\{\cdot\}}$	$= \mathsf{true}$
$\mathsf{closure}_{\cdot\hat{\ }!\{\cdot\}}$	$= \forall \mu, \mu_c, \nu_m, \nu_p, \nu_1, \nu_2, \ell_1, \ell_2 :$
	$\quad \nu_1\hat{\ }!\{\nu_m\}^{\ell_1} \in \mathcal{I}(\mu_c) \wedge \mu_c \in \mathcal{I}(\mu) \wedge \nu_2\_?\{\nu_p\}^{\ell_2} \in \mathcal{I}(\mu) \wedge$
	$\quad \langle \mathcal{R} \rangle(\nu_1) \cap \langle \mathcal{R} \rangle(\nu_2) \neq \emptyset \wedge \mathsf{CP}_\star(\cdot\hat{\ }!\{\cdot\}^{\ell_1}, \cdot\_?\{\cdot\}^{\ell_2})$
	$\quad \Rightarrow \quad \langle \mathcal{R} \rangle(\nu_m) \subseteq \mathcal{R}(\nu_p)$
$\mathsf{closure}_{\cdot\_?\{\cdot\}}$	$= \mathsf{true}$
$\mathsf{closure}_{\cdot\#!\{\cdot\}}$	$= \forall \mu, \mu_1, \mu_2, \nu_m, \nu_p, \nu_1, \nu_2, \ell_1, \ell_2 :$
	$\quad \nu_1\#!\{\nu_m\}^{\ell_1} \in \mathcal{I}(\mu_1) \wedge \mu_1 \in \mathcal{I}(\mu) \wedge \nu_2\#?\{\nu_p\}^{\ell_2} \in \mathcal{I}(\mu_2) \wedge \mu_2 \in \mathcal{I}(\mu) \wedge$
	$\quad \langle \mathcal{R} \rangle(\nu_1) \cap \langle \mathcal{R} \rangle(\nu_2) \neq \emptyset \wedge \mathsf{CP}_\star(\cdot\#!\{\cdot\}^{\ell_1}, \cdot\#?\{\cdot\}^{\ell_2})$
	$\quad \Rightarrow \quad \langle \mathcal{R} \rangle(m) \subseteq \mathcal{R}(\nu_p)$
$\mathsf{closure}_{\cdot\#?\{\cdot\}}$	$= \mathsf{true}$

an abstract version of the firing conditions of the corresponding transition rule is fulfilled and the conclusion then records an abstract version of the resulting configuration. The $\mathcal{I}$ relation is used to check the spatial conditions, the $\mathcal{R}$ relation is used to check the potential agreement of names, and the compatibility information of $\mathsf{CP}_\star$ is used to check whether the current pairs of canonical capabilities may interact at all. Since the relation $\mathcal{R}$ is only concerned with the names that act as variables we shall use a slightly modified version of $\mathcal{R}$ namely

Table 9. Three BioAmbient example processes from [14].

Membranal pore :

$[\mathrm{rec}\, X_1.\ \mathrm{enter}\ cell_1^{\ell_1}.\ X_1 + \mathrm{exit}\ cell_2^{\ell_2}.\ X_1]^{mol_1}$
$|\ [\mathrm{rec}\, X_2.\ \mathrm{enter}\ cell_1^{\ell_3}.\ X_2 + \mathrm{exit}\ cell_2^{\ell_4}.\ X_2]^{mol_2}$
$|\ [\mathrm{rec}\, X_3.\ \mathrm{accept}\ cell_1^{\ell_5}.\ X_3 + \mathrm{expel}\ cell_2^{\ell_6}.\ X_3]^{cell}$

Single substrate enzymatic reaction :

$[\mathrm{rec}\, X.\ \mathrm{accept}\ esbind^{\ell_1}.\ (\mathrm{expel}\ unbind^{\ell_2}.\ X + \mathrm{expel}\ react^{\ell_3}.\ X)$
$\qquad +\mathrm{accept}\ epbind^{\ell_4}.\ (\mathrm{expel}\ unbind^{\ell_5}.\ X + \mathrm{expel}\ react^{\ell_6}.\ X)]^{enzyme}$
$|\ [\mathrm{rec}\, X_1.\ \mathrm{enter}\ esbind^{\ell_7}.\ \mathrm{rec}\, X_2.\ (\mathrm{exit}\ unbind^{\ell_8}.\ X_1$
$\qquad\qquad +\mathrm{exit}\ react^{\ell_9}.\ \mathrm{enter}\ epbind^{\ell_{10}}.\ X_2)]^{mol}$

Two-protein complex :

$[\mathrm{rec}\, X_1.\ \mathrm{merge-}\ cplx^{\ell_1}.\ brk?\{u\}^{\ell_2}.\ \mathrm{expel}\ brk^{\ell_3}.\ X_1]^{mol_1}$
$|\ [(bb)\ \mathrm{rec}\, X_2.\ \mathrm{merge+}\ cplx^{\ell_4}.\ brk!\{d\}^{\ell_5}.\ bb!\{d\}^{\ell_6}.\ [\mathrm{merge+}\ bb^{\ell_7}.\ \mathrm{exit}\ brk^{\ell_8}.\ X_2]^{mol_1}$
$\qquad |\ \mathrm{rec}\, X_3.\ bb?\{v\}^{\ell_9}.\ [\mathrm{merge-}\ bb^{\ell_{10}}.\ X_3]^{mol_2}]^{mol_2}$

$$\langle \mathcal{R} \rangle \subseteq (\mathbf{V} \cup \mathbf{C}) \times \mathbf{C}$$

that takes care of variables as well as constants; it is defined by:

$$(\forall n : n \in \mathbf{C} \Rightarrow \langle \mathcal{R}\rangle(n, n)) \quad \wedge \quad (\forall n, m : \mathcal{R}(n, m) \Rightarrow \langle \mathcal{R}\rangle(n, m))$$

The analysis result for the program $P_\star$ is then the minimal $\mathcal{I}$ and $\mathcal{R}$ such that $(\mathcal{I}, \mathcal{R}) \models^\top P_\star$ where $\top$ is the identity of an artificial top-level ambient.

Example 5. The analysis of the running example P_{virus} gives rise to the following minimal $\mathcal{I}$ and $\mathcal{R}$:

μ	$\mathcal{I}(\mu)$
cell	$gene, virus, c\_!\{n_3\}^{\ell_8}, \mathrm{expel}\ n_2^{\ell_7}, \mathrm{accept}\ n_1^{\ell_6}$
gene	$\mathrm{exit}\ n_3^{\ell_5}$
virus	$gene, \mathrm{expel}\ x^{\ell_4}, c\hat{\ }?\{x\}^{\ell_3}, \mathrm{exit}\ n_2^{\ell_2}, \mathrm{enter}\ n_1^{\ell_1}$
$\top$	$gene, cell, virus$

n	$\mathcal{R}(n)$
x	n_3

Figure 2 (a) gives a graphical representation of the ambient part of the relation $\mathcal{I}$. There is one node for each of the ambient identities and an edge from the node representing μ_1 to the one representing μ_2 if and only if $(\mu_1, \mu_2) \in \mathcal{I}$. The edge is *solid* if (μ_1, μ_2) is introduced into $\mathcal{I}$ by the initialisation rules of Table 6 and it is *dotted* if it is introduced by the closure conditions of Table 8. Note that the trees of the individual frames of Figure 1 are all subgraphs of this figure (as should be expected from the semantic correctness result to be presented below). The example also shows that the analysis is indeed an over-approximation: although it is reported that the gene may occur at the top-level, it will never happen. □

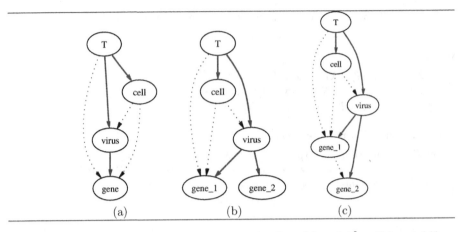

Fig. 2. Spatial analysis of the running examples P_{virus} (a) and P^{0}_{virus} ((b) and (c)).

Example 6. To illustrate the importance of the comp relation consider the artificial variant of the virus process of Example 4. Figure 2 (b) gives a graphical representation of the $\mathcal{I}$ component of the analysis result and as expected we observe that the harmless gene does not change its position within the ambient hierarchy.

If we were to remove the tests on the compatibility relation in the closure condition of Table 8 then we would obtain a more imprecise result as illustrated on Figure 2 (c): it now seems that one of the genes may move into the other. The reason for this is, of course, that without the compatibility test the analysis does not observe that the two genes will never be present at the same time. □

Turning to the correctness of the analysis we shall state that the analysis result is invariant under the structural congruence:

Lemma 2. *If $P \equiv Q$ and $\mathbf{C} \vdash P$ then $(\mathcal{I}, \mathcal{R}) \models^{\mu} P$ if and only if $(\mathcal{I}, \mathcal{R}) \models^{\mu} Q$.*

To express the correctness of the analysis result under reduction we shall first introduce a new operation that expands the $\mathcal{I}$ component of the analysis to take the bindings of the variables into account as specified by the $\mathcal{R}$ component. Thus if enter $\nu^{\ell} \in \mathcal{I}(\mu)$ then ν may be the canonical name of a variable and we shall construct the relation $\mathcal{I}@\mathcal{R}$ such that enter $\nu'^{\ell} \in \mathcal{I}@\mathcal{R}(\mu)$ for all possible constants ν' that can be bound to ν, that is, for all $\nu' \in \langle \mathcal{R} \rangle(\nu)$. More generally, we define $\mathcal{I}@\mathcal{R}$ as follows:

If $\lfloor M \rfloor^{\ell} \in \mathcal{I}(\mu)$, $\nu \in \mathsf{fn}(\lfloor M \rfloor)$ and $\nu' \in \langle \mathcal{R} \rangle(\nu)$ then $\lfloor M \rfloor^{\ell}[\nu'/\nu] \in \mathcal{I}@\mathcal{R}(\mu)$.

We can now express that the analysis result is preserved under reduction in the following sense:

Lemma 3. *Assume $\mathsf{PRG}_{\mathbf{C}}(P)$ and $\mathsf{comp}_{\lfloor\ \rfloor\lfloor\ \rfloor}(P) \subseteq \mathsf{CP}_{\star}$; if furthermore $P \to Q$ and $(\mathcal{I}, \mathcal{R}) \models^{\top} P$ then $(\mathcal{I}@\mathcal{R}, \mathcal{R}) \models^{\top} Q$.*

It is immediate to show that $\mathcal{I}@\mathcal{R} = (\mathcal{I}@\mathcal{R})@\mathcal{R}$ and hence we can state the overall correctness result as follows:

Theorem 1. *If* $\mathsf{PRG_C}(P_\star)$, $(\mathcal{I}, \mathcal{R}) \models^\top P_\star$ *and* $P_\star \rightarrow^* Q$ *then* $(\mathcal{I}@\mathcal{R}, \mathcal{R}) \models^\top Q$.

5 Concluding Remarks

We have presented a spatial analysis for a version of BioAmbients with a general recursion construct that allows us to express mutual recursion as seems to be required in order to model biological systems. The analysis has been implemented using the Succinct Solver [10] and has subsequently been applied to a number of examples including three small examples from [13, 14] presented below. We conclude with a comparison with related work – indicating those techniques that are new to this paper.

Three Examples. The first example of Table 9 is a *membranal pore* allowing molecules to pass through a membrane. The example is specialised to the case of a single cell and two molecules and when executed the two membranes may enter and leave the cell any number of times and independently of one another. This is clearly captured by the analysis result of Figure 3. Also the analysis tells us that the cell will never enter one of the molecules and that the molecules will never enter one another; while this may be easy to see for a small example it may not be so obvious for a larger system.

The second example of Table 9 models a *single-substrate enzymatic process* and compared with the previous example its control structure is more complex in that it uses a double recursion and a number of names to control the interaction between the ambients. The analysis result depicted in Figure 3 exhibits the underlying spatial structure.

The final example of Table 9 models the formation and breakage of a *two-protein complex*. Initially the system consists of two molecules and the complex is formed by the merge operation. The breakage is initiated by a communication followed by a communication over a private name and finally the complex is separated into two molecules with the same structure as in the initial configuration. The rather complex control structure is reflected in the analysis result presented in Figure 3 showing that both molecules can be inside one another and that they both have the ability to reconstruct themselves.

Comparison with Related Work. The work presented in this paper is one of the first static analyses of calculi for modelling biological systems; to the best of our knowledge, the only preceeding work is that of [9] and the present work comprises a number of improvements and novelties.

One important difference is the way names are handled. In [9] we follow the traditional approach of control flow analysis and use an environment $\mathcal{R}$ that corresponds more closely to the auxiliary environment $\langle\mathcal{R}\rangle$ used here. Hence, in [9] we make an entry into $\mathcal{R}$ whenever a name is introduced (and in the case of a constant it is mapped to itself) and when we make an entry with a

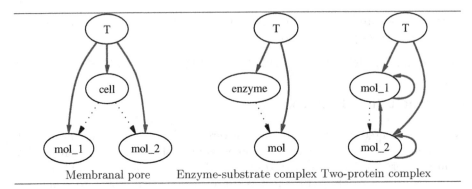

Membranal pore   Enzyme-substrate complex   Two-protein complex

Fig. 3. Spatial analysis of examples in Table 9.

free name into $\mathcal{I}$ we make sure to make entries corresponding to all bindings of the free name as recorded in the environment (i.e. $\mathcal{R}$). While this leads to a rather natural formulation of the clauses and straighforward formulations of the semantic correctness result, the relations become overly large. Hence in the interest of obtaining more manageable implementations we have chosen *not* to add constants into environments and only to make *representative* entries into $\mathcal{I}$ that are then expanded "on the fly" during look-up. Essentially we are trading space for time which generally is a good strategy when using the Succinct Solver. To formulate the semantic correctness of the analysis we therefore need to make a similar expansion and this is achieved using $\mathcal{I}@\mathcal{R}$.

Another important difference is our treatment of recursion which is technically much more complex than the traditional treatment of replication (as in $!P$). The treatment of recursion in [9] was unsatisfactory in that the unfolding of the recursion construct was part of the transition relation rather than the congruence as in the present paper, and hence [9] misses some of the interactions correctly captured here. (To the best of our knowledge the analysis in [9] is correct with respect to the semantics.) For a correct treatment of this general way of unfolding recursion we have had to ensure that the body of the recursion is analysed in all contexts that may arise dynamically. While this may sound like just another component that could be added to the analysis (e.g. tracking occurrences of process identifiers in $\mathcal{I}$) it actually turns out to be important *not* to include this information into the analysis in order for the analysis to be semantically correct. Hence we have defined an operation G^δ for constructing a simple *regular grammar* deriving the possible contexts; it is essential for semantic correctness of the analysis that this information is not stored in components like $\mathcal{I}$ and $\mathcal{R}$ but rather computed "on the fly". This technique is likely to be useful for other calculi also outside the realm of biological systems.

Acknowledgements

The authors would like to thank Corrado Priami and Debora Schuch da Rosa for fruitful discussions.

References

1. M. Bugliesi, G. Castagna, and S. Crafa. Boxed Ambients. In *Theoretical Aspects in Computer Science (TACS 2001)*, volume 2215 of *Lecture Notes in Computer Science*, pages 37–63. Springer, 2001.
2. L. Cardelli. Brane calculi. 2003. Available from `http://www.luca.demon.co.uk`.
3. L. Cardelli and A. D. Gordon. Mobile Ambients. In *Foundations of Software Science and Computation Structures (FoSSaCS 1998)*, volume 1378 of *Lecture Notes in Computer Science*, pages 140–155. Springer, 1998.
4. C.Bodei, P.Degano, C. Priami, and N. Zannone. An enhanced cfa for security policies. In *Proceedings of the Workshop on Issues on the Theory of Security (WITS'03) (co-located with ETAPS'03)*, 2003.
5. V. Danos and C. Laneve. Core formal molecular biology. In *European Symposium on Programming (ESOP03)*, volume 2618. Springer Lecture Notes in Computer Science, 2004.
6. F. Levi and D. Sangiorgi. Controlling interference in ambients. In *Proceedings of the 27th ACM SIGPLAN-SIGACT Symposium on Principles of Programming Languages (POPL 2000)*, pages 352–364. ACM Press, 2000.
7. R. Milner. *Communicating and Mobile Systems: The pi-Calculus*. Cambridge University Press, 1999.
8. M. Nagasaki, S. Onami, S. Miyano, and Kitano H. Bio-calculus: Its concept and molecular interaction. *Genome Informatics*, 10:133–143, 1999.
9. F. Nielson, H. Riis Nielson, C.Priami, and D. Schuch da Rosa. Control Flow Analysis for BioAmbients. *Proceedings of BioConcur, to appear in ENTCS*, 2004.
10. F. Nielson, H. Riis Nielson, and H. Seidl. A succinct solver for ALFP. *Nordic Journal of Computing*, 9:335–372, 2002.
11. Hanne Riis Nielson, Flemming Nielson, and Mikael Buchholtz. Security for Mobility. In *Foundations of Security Analysis and Design II*, volume 2946. Springer Lecture Notes in Computer Science, 2004.
12. C. Priami, A. Regev, W. Silverman, and E. Shapiro. Application of a stochastic passing-name calculus to representation and simulation of molecular processes. *Information Processing Letters*, 80:25–31, 2001.
13. A. Regev. *Computational system biology: A calculus for biomolecular knowledge*. PhD thesis, Tel Aviv University, 2003.
14. A. Regev, E. M. Panina, W. Silverman, L. Cardelli, and E. Shapiro. BioAmbients: An abstraction for biological compartments. *Theoretical Computer Science, to appear*, 2004.
15. A. Regev, W. Silverman, and E. Shapiro. Representation and simulation of biochemical processes using the π-calculus process algebra. In *Pacific Symposium of Biocomputing (PSB2001)*, pages 459–470, 2001.

Modular and Constraint-Based Information Flow Inference for an Object-Oriented Language

Qi Sun[1,*], Anindya Banerjee[2,**], and David A. Naumann[1,***]

[1] Stevens Institute of Technology, USA
{sunq,naumann}@cs.stevens-tech.edu
[2] Kansas State University, USA
ab@cis.ksu.edu

Abstract. This paper addresses the problem of checking programs written in an object-oriented language to ensure that they satisfy the information flow policies, confidentiality and integrity. Policy is specified using security types. An algorithm that infers such security types in a modular manner is presented. The specification of the algorithm involves inference for libraries. Library classes and methods maybe parameterized by security levels. It is shown how modular inference is achieved in the presence of method inheritance and override. Soundness and completeness theorems for the inference algorithm are given.

1 Introduction

This paper addresses the problem of checking programs to ensure that they satisfy the information flow policies, confidentiality and integrity. Confidentiality, for example, is an important requirement in several security applications – by itself, or as a component of other security policies (e.g., authentication), or as a desirable property to enforce in security protocols [1]. In the last decade, impressive advances have been made in specifying static analyses for confidentiality for a variety of languages [14]. Information flow policy is expressed by labeling of input and output channels with levels, e.g., low, or public, (L) and high, or secret, (H) in a security lattice $(L \leq H)$. Many of these analyses are given in the style of a security type system that is shown to enforce a *noninterference* property [6]: a well-typed program does not leak secrets.

Previous work of Banerjee and Naumann provides a security type system and noninterference result for a class based object-oriented language with features including method inheritance/overriding, dynamic binding, dynamically allocated mutable objects, type casts and recursive types [3]. It is shown how several object-oriented features can be exploited as covert channels to leak secrets. Type checking in Banerjee and Naumann's security type system requires manually annotating all fields, method parameters and method signatures with security types.

* Supported in part by NSF grant CCR-0208984 and NJCST.
** Supported in part by NSF grants CCR-0296182 and CCR-0209205.
*** Supported in part by NSF grant CCR-0208984 and NJCST.

R. Giacobazzi (Ed.): SAS 2004, LNCS 3148, pp. 84–99, 2004.
© Springer-Verlag Berlin Heidelberg 2004

The primary focus of this paper is the *automatic inference* of security type annotations of well-typed programs. In this paper, we are not interested in full type inference, and assume that a well-typed program is given. There are several issues to confront. First, we demand inference of some, possibly all, security levels of *fields* in a class. This means that security types of fields will involve *level variables* and the same is true for method types where level variables will appear in types of method parameters and in the result type.

The second issue, a critical challenge for scalability, is achieving *modular* security type inference for class-based languages. A non-modular, whole-program inference, say, for the language in [3], would perform inference in the context of the entire class table; if method m in class A is called in the body of method n declared in class B, then the analysis of $B.n$ would also involve the analysis of $A.m$. Moreover, every use of $A.m$ in a method body would necessitate its analysis. Our insistence on modular inference led us to the following choices: code is split into library classes (for which inference has already been performed) and the current analysis unit (for which inference is currently taking place). Inference naturally produces polymorphic types; so it seemed appropriate to go beyond previous work [3] and make libraries polymorphic. To track information flow, e.g., via field updates, *constraints* on level variables are imposed in the method signature; thus library method signatures appear as constrained polymorphic types. To avoid undecidability of inference due to polymorphic recursion [8, 7], mutually recursive classes and methods in the current analysis unit are analyzed monomorphically[1].

Because we are analyzing an object-oriented language, the third issue we confront is achieving modular inference in the presence of method inheritance and override. The current analysis unit can contain subclasses of a library class with some library methods overridden or inherited. To achieve modularity, we require that the signature of a library method is *invariant* with respect to subclassing. Getting the technical details correct is a formidable challenge and one which we have met. We provide some intuition on the problem presently.

The research reported in this paper is being carried out in the context of a tool, currently under development, that handles the above issues. The tool helps the programmer design a library interactively by inferring the signatures of new classes, together with a constraint set showing the constraints that level variables in the signature must obey. The security types of the new classes are inferred in the context of the existing library. The new code may inherit library methods – this causes the polymorphic signature of a library method to be instantiated at every use of the method, and the instantiated constraints will apply to the current context.

Handling method override is more subtle; modularity requires that the polymorphic type inferred for a library method must be satisfied by all its overriding methods. For an overriding method in a subclass, if the inference algorithm generates constraints that are not implied by the constraints of the superclass method, then the unit must be rejected.

---

[1] It is possible that because we are not doing full type inference, polymorphic recursion in this setting is decidable. But we do not yet have results either way.

To cope with such a situation, there are a couple of approaches one may adopt. Because changing library code makes the inference process non-modular, one can change the code in the subclass, by relabeling field and parameter levels with ground constants in a sensible way, and re-run the tool to deliver the relaxed signatures. (This will be illustrated by an example in section 4.2). A more practical approach is that during library design, the designer may want to consider anticipated uses of those library methods that are expected to be overridden in subclasses. The inferred signature of such library methods – an extreme example being abstract methods with no implementation – may be too general; hence, the designer may want to make some of the field types and method signatures more specific. Then, there would be more of a possibility that the constraints in the method signatures of library methods will imply those in the signatures of the overriding methods. Thus the security type signature we assume for library methods is allowed to be an arbitrary one.

Contributions and Overview. This paper tackles all of the issues above. Our previous work [3] did not cope with libraries. Here, we do; thus we provide a new security type system for the language with polymorphic classes and methods that guarantees noninterference. We provide an inference algorithm that, in the context of a polymorphic library, infers security type signatures for methods of the current analysis unit. By restricting the current analysis unit to only contain monomorphic types, we can show that the algorithm computes principal monomorphic types, as justified by the completeness of the inference algorithm for such restricted units. Although there have been studies about both type inference and information flow analysis for imperative, functional and object-oriented programs, we have not found any work that addresses security type inference for object-oriented programs in the presence of libraries. We believe that the additional details required to account for modularity in the presence of method inheritance and override are a novel aspect of our work.

After discussing two simple examples in section 2, we describe the language extended with parameterized classes in section 3, explain the inference algorithm in section 4 and give the soundness and completeness theorems in section 5. Related work and a discussion of the paper appear in section 6.

2   Examples

Consider the following classes:

> **class** *TAX* **extends** *Object* {
>   **int** *income;*
>   **int** *tax(***int** *salary){ self.income := salary; result := self.income * 0.20; }}*
> **class** *Inquiry* **extends** *Object*{
>   *TAX employee;* **int** *est;*
>   **bool** *overpay(){***int** *tmp:=employee.tax(1000);result:=(tmp≥self.est);}}*

The type of method *tax* in class *TAX*, written *mtype(tax, TAX)*, is $int \rightarrow int$. Assuming that *income* has security level H, a possible security type for method *tax*, is $L, H \dashv\!\langle H \rangle\!\rightarrow H$: when the level of the current object[2] is L and the level of *salary* is at most H then *tax* returns a result of level at most H and only H fields (the H in the middle) may be updated[3] during method execution. This security type can be verified using security type checking rules for method declaration and commands.

In security type inference, we *infer* security types for the level of field *income* and for method *tax*. We assume that *TAX* is a well-formed class declaration. The inference algorithm is given class *TAX* as input, but with *income*'s type annotated, e.g., as $(\mathbf{int}, \alpha_1)$, where α_1 is a placeholder for the actual level of the field. It is also possible for *income* to be annotated with a constant level (e.g., L or H). Apart from annotating fields, we also annotate the parameter and return types of methods. In the sequel, we will let letters from the beginning of the Greek alphabet range over level variables.

The type, $(\alpha_2, \alpha_5 \dashv\!\langle \alpha_3 \rangle\!\rightarrow \alpha_4) \mid \{\alpha_5 \leq \alpha_1, \alpha_3 \leq \alpha_1, \alpha_2 \leq \alpha_1, \alpha_1 \leq \alpha_4\}$ is inferred for method *tax*; that is, if the level of the *TAX* object is at most α_2 and the level of *salary* is at most α_5, then the level of the return result is at most α_4 and fields of level at most α_3 can be assigned to during execution of *tax*. The first constraint precludes, e.g., assigning H value to L field.

The class *TAX* can now be converted into a library class, parameterized over α_1 and method *tax* given a polymorphic method signature.

> **class** *TAX*<α_1>**extends** *Object* {
> $(\mathbf{int}, \alpha_1)$ *income;*
> $(\mathbf{int}, \alpha_4)$ *tax*(($\mathbf{int}, \alpha_5)$ *salary*){*self.income* := *salary;*
>   *result* := *self.income**0.20;* }}

Library class *TAX*<α_1> can be instantiated in multiple ways in the analysis of another class, for instance, by instantiating α_1 with a ground level, say H. The intention is that for any ground instantiation of $\alpha_1, \ldots, \alpha_5$ that satisfies the constraints, the body of *TAX* should be typable in the security type system.

The inference of class *Inquiry* takes place in the context of the library containing *TAX*. Because *TAX* is parameterized, the type of field *employee* is assumed to be *TAX*<β_1> and the level of *employee* is β_2. We could have chosen the level of *employee* to be H, but by typing rules, this would prevent access to a public field, say *name*, of *employee*. Note that the level of *est* is completely specified. The inferred type of method *overpay* is $(\alpha_6, () \dashv\!\langle \alpha_7 \rangle\!\rightarrow \alpha_8) \mid K$. Some of the constraints in K generated by our inference algorithm are $\alpha_6 \leq \alpha_8$, $\beta_1 \leq \alpha_8$ and $\beta_2 \leq \alpha_8$.

Suppose *Inquiry* is annotated differently, so that the type of the *employee* field is $(TAX<H>, \beta_2)$, i.e., β_1 above has been instantiated to H. Then the level of the result of the call to *tax* (i.e., level α_8) will also be secret – this was predicted by the constraint $\beta_1 \leq \alpha_8$. Suppose Q is an object of type *Inquiry* and suppose that its level is H. Then to prevent implicit information leakage

---

[2] i.e., the level of *self*. This information is used to prevent leaks of the pointer to the current target object to other untrusted sources[3].

[3] This information, called the *heap effect*, is required to prevent leaks due to implicit flow via conditionals and method call [5, 3].

due to the call to *overpay*, the return result should be H [3]. This can be seen from the constraint $\alpha_6 \leq \alpha_8$ with α_6, the level of Q, instantiated to H. Finally, if *employee* itself is H, then the constraint $\beta_2 \leq \alpha_8$ forces the level of the return result to be H as expected.

Section 3 formalizes the annotated language and discuss security typing rules for which noninterference can be shown. Next, section 4 considers a sublanguage of the annotated language with programs annotated with level variables; for this language we specify an algorithm that infers security types. We discuss restrictions of the language to handle undecidability of inference and formalize inference for inheritance and override of library methods in the current analysis unit in a way that maintains modularity. These restrictions and treatments will be illustrated by an example that overrides method *TAX.tax* in section 4.3.

3   Language and Security Typing

We use the sequential class-based language from our previous work [3]. The difference is in the annotated language, where classes and methods may be polymorphic in levels. This allows a library class to be used in more than one way. We make an explicit separation between a library class and a collection of additional classes that are based on the library.

First, some terms: a *unit* is a collection of class declarations. A *closed unit* is a collection of class declarations that is well formed as a complete program, that is, it is a class table. The library is a closed unit from which we need its polymorphic type signature, encoded in some auxiliary functions defined later. A program based on a library can consist of several classes which extend and use library classes and which may be mutually recursive. We use the term *analysis unit* for the classes to which the inference algorithm is applied. Due to mutual recursion, several classes may have to be considered together. An analysis unit must be well formed in the sense that the union of it with the library should form a closed unit.

The Annotated Language. We shall now define the syntax for library units and also adapt the security typing rules from our previous work to the present language. Essentially, a polymorphic library is typable if all of its ground instances are.

The grammar is in Table 1. Although identifiers with overlines indicate lists, some of the formal definitions assume singletons to avoid unilluminating complication.

Since the problem we want to address is secure information flow, all the programs are assumed to be well formed as ordinary code; i.e. when all levels are erased, including class parameters $<\overline{\lambda}>$. Typing rules for our Java-like language are standard and can be found in our previous paper [3]. It suffices to recall that a collection of class declarations, called a *class table*, is treated as a function CT so that $CT(C)$ is the code for class C. Moreover, $field(f, C)$ gives the type of field f in class C and $mtype(m, C)$ gives the parameter and return types for

Table 1. Language grammar

$$
\begin{array}{rll}
T & ::= \texttt{bool} \mid C & \text{(where } C \text{ ranges over } ClassName) \\
\kappa & ::= \texttt{H} \mid \texttt{L} & \text{(level constants)} \\
\lambda & ::= \alpha \mid \kappa & \text{(level variable, constant)} \\
U & ::= T\texttt{<}\overline{\lambda}\texttt{>} & \text{(we also use } W \text{ and } R \text{ for this category)} \\
CL & ::= \texttt{class } C\texttt{<}\overline{\alpha}\texttt{> extends } U\{(\overline{U}, \overline{\lambda})\ \overline{f};\ \overline{M}\} \\
M & ::= U\ m\ (\overline{U}\ \overline{x})\{S\} \\
S & ::= x := e \mid e.f := e \mid x := \texttt{new } U \mid x := e.m(\overline{e}) \mid S; S \mid U\ x := e \texttt{ in } S \mid \\
 & \quad \texttt{if } e \texttt{ then } S \texttt{ else } S \\
e & ::= x \mid \texttt{null} \mid \texttt{true} \mid e.f \mid e == e \mid e \texttt{ is } U \mid (U)e
\end{array}
$$

method m declared or inherited in C. Subtyping is invariant: $D \leq C$ implies $mtype(m, C) = mtype(m, D)$.

We use T to represent an ordinary data type, while U ranges over parameterized class types, which take the form $T\texttt{<}\overline{\lambda}\texttt{>}$. Declaration of a parameterized class binds some variables $\overline{\alpha}$ in the types of the superclass and fields:

$$\texttt{class } C\texttt{<}\overline{\alpha}\texttt{> extends } D\texttt{<}\overline{\lambda}\texttt{>}\{(\overline{U}, \overline{\lambda'})\ \overline{f}; \overline{M}\}$$

All variables appearing in field declarations are bound at the class level. Thus the parameterized class declaration above must satisfy a *well formedness* condition: $\overline{\alpha} \supseteq var(\overline{\lambda}) \cup var(\overline{U}) \cup var(\overline{\lambda'})$. These variables, if appear in method declaration and body, are also bound in class level. The rest free variables are bound in method level for method polymorphism.

Field types, including security label, can be retrieved by a given function $lsfield(f, U)$ which returns the appropriate type of field f in a (possibly instantiated) class U. Thus for the declaration displayed above, $lsfield(f, C\texttt{<}\overline{\alpha}\texttt{>}) = (\overline{U}, \overline{\lambda'})$, and for any $\overline{\lambda''}$ of the right length, $lsfield(f, C\texttt{<}\overline{\lambda''}\texttt{>}) = (\overline{U}, \overline{\lambda'})[\overline{\alpha} \leftarrow \overline{\lambda''}]$. We require that $lsfield(f, U)$ is defined iff $field(f, T)$ is defined, and moreover[4] if $U \preceq U'$ and $lsfield(f, U')$ is defined, then $lsfield(f, U) = lsfield(f, U')$.

Method types, possibly polymorphic, need more delicate treatment. Types for methods are given using a signature function $lsmtype$ so that $lsmtype(m, U)$, for method m declared or inherited in class U returns m's signature and a set K of constraints in the form of inequalities between constants and variables. We require that $lsmtype(m, T\texttt{<}\overline{\lambda}\texttt{>})$ is defined iff $mtype(m, T)$ is, and in that case the signature takes the form $\lambda_0, (\overline{U}, \overline{\lambda_1}) \text{--} \langle\lambda_2\rangle \mapsto (R, \lambda_3)|K$. The signature expresses the following policy: If the information in "self" is at most λ_0 and the information in parameters is at most $\overline{\lambda_1}$ with type $\overline{U}$, then any fields written are at level λ_2 or higher and the result level is at least λ_3, with result type R provided that the constraints K are satisfied.

Following our previous work [3], we also require *invariance under subclassing*: if $U \preceq R$ and m is declared in R, then $lsmtype(m, U) = lsmtype(m, R)$ (regardless of whether m is inherited or overridden in U). Analogous to the sub-

---

[4] The security subtyping relation $\preceq$ is defined in Table 2.

Table 2. Auxiliary definitions

For T, T^0 such that $T \leq T^0$, we define:

$$instance(T<\overline{\kappa}>, T) \quad = \quad T<\overline{\kappa}>$$

$$instance(T<\overline{\kappa}>, T^0) \quad = \quad \text{let class } T<\overline{\alpha}> \text{ extends } T^{00}<\overline{\lambda}> = CT(T)$$
$$\text{in } instance(T^{00}<\overline{\lambda}[\overline{\alpha} \leftarrow \overline{\kappa}]>, T^0)$$

$$T<\overline{\kappa}> \preceq T^0<\overline{\kappa^0}> \quad \Leftrightarrow \quad instance(T<\overline{\kappa}>, T^0) = T^0<\overline{\kappa^0}>$$

$$tcomp(T<\overline{\lambda}>, T^0<\overline{\lambda^0}>) = \quad \text{let } T^0<\overline{\lambda^{00}}> = instance(T<\overline{\lambda}>, T^0)$$
$$\text{in } \cup_i \{\lambda_i^{00} \leq \lambda_i^0; \lambda_i^0 \leq \lambda_i^{00}\}$$

classing requirement on methods in object-oriented languages, this is to ensure information flow security in the context of dynamic method dispatch.

The subtyping relation $\preceq$ must take polymorphism and information flow into account. For built-in type, we define bool $\preceq$ bool. Class subtyping can be checked using the $\preceq$ function defined in Table 2, which propagates instantiation of a class up through the class hierarchy. The definition uses another function, *instance*, that carries out this propagation and constructs a suitable instantiation of a supertype. The auxiliary definition for downcast appears in the appendix. For use in inference, we need to generate a set of constraints such that two types with variables are in the $\preceq$ relation; this is the purpose of function *tcomp*. We assume that if the analysis unit mentions a parameterized class, it provides the right number of parameters.

Security Typing Rules. Although the typing rules work with parameterized class declarations and with polymorphic method signatures, the typing rules for expressions and commands in method bodies only apply to ground judgements. A security type context Δ is a mapping from variable names to security types. We adopt the notation style for typing judgements from [3]. A judgement $\Delta \vdash e : (U, \kappa)$ says that expression e in context Δ has security type (U, κ). A judgement $\Delta \vdash S : \text{com } \kappa_1, \kappa_2$ says that, in the context Δ, command S writes no variables below κ_1, which is in the store and will be gone after the execution of the method, and no fields below κ_2, which will stay in the heap until garbage-collected.

We give the rule for method call, $x := e.m(\overline{e})$, below. It uses the polymorphic signature function of the method m, and requires that there must be some satisfying ground instance compatible with the levels at the call site; this is ensured by requiring satisfiability of a constraint set K' which contains the constraints needed to match security types of parameters and arguments.

$$\frac{\Delta, x : (U, \kappa) \vdash e : (W, \kappa_3) \quad}{\begin{array}{c} \Delta, x : (U, \kappa) \vdash \overline{e} : (\overline{U}, \overline{\kappa_4}) \quad lsmtype(m, W) = \lambda_0, (\overline{U'}, \overline{\lambda}) - \langle \lambda_1 \rangle \rightarrow (U', \lambda_2) | K \\ \kappa_5 \leq \kappa \quad \kappa_3 \leq \kappa \quad K' = K \cup K'' \cup tcomp(U', U) \cup tcomp(\overline{U'}, \overline{U}) \\ K'' = \{\overline{\kappa_4} \leq \overline{\lambda}, \lambda_2 \leq \kappa, \kappa_6 \leq \lambda_1, \kappa_3 \leq \lambda_0, \kappa_3 \leq \lambda_1\} \quad K' \text{ is satisfiable} \end{array}}{\Delta, x : (U, \kappa) \vdash x := e.m(\overline{e}) : \text{com } \kappa_5, \kappa_6}$$

Table 3. Typing rules for method declarations and class declarations

$$lsmtype(m, C<\overline{\kappa^\partial}>) = \lambda_0, (\overline{U}, \overline{\lambda}) \neg \langle \lambda_3 \rangle \mapsto (U, \lambda_4) | K$$
$$V = vars(\lambda_0, (\overline{U}, \overline{\lambda}) \neg \langle \lambda_3 \rangle \mapsto (U, \lambda_4) | K)$$

$$\frac{\text{for all } I \text{ with } ok(K, V, I) : \text{let } \kappa_0, (\overline{U^\partial}, \overline{\kappa}) \neg \langle \kappa_3 \rangle \mapsto (U^\partial, \kappa_4) = I(\lambda_0, (\overline{U}, \overline{\lambda}) \neg \langle \lambda_3 \rangle \mapsto (U, \lambda_4)) \text{ in}}{}$$
$$\frac{\overline{x} : (\overline{U^\partial}, \overline{\kappa}), \text{self} : (C, \kappa_0), \text{result} : (U^\partial, \kappa_4) \vdash S : \text{com } \kappa_1, \kappa_2 \qquad \kappa_3 \leq \kappa_2}{C<\overline{\kappa^\partial}> \text{ extends } R \vdash U \; m(\overline{U} \; \overline{x})\{S\}}$$

$$\frac{\text{for all } M \in \overline{M}, \text{ all } \kappa: \quad C<\overline{\kappa}> \text{ extends } I(R) \vdash I(M) \qquad \text{where } I = [\overline{\alpha} \leftarrow \overline{\kappa}]}{\vdash \text{class } C<\overline{\alpha}> \text{ extends } R\{\overline{U} \; \overline{f}; \overline{M}\}}$$

Table 3 gives the rules for class and method declarations. A class declaration is typable provided that all of its method declarations are. Typing a method declaration requires checking its body with respect to all ground instantiations, I, over the variables V given by $lsmtype$. We define $ok(K, V, I)$ to mean that I satisfies K.

Noninterference. Like FlowCaml [15], our system uses a level-polymorphic language, both for more expressive libraries and because it is the natural result from inference. The noninterference property asserted by a polymorphic type is taken to be ordinary noninterference for all ground instances that satisfying the constraints that are part of the type. By lack of space in this paper, we omit the semantics and thus cannot formally define noninterference. Informally, a command is noninterfering if, for any two initial states that are indistinguishable for L (i.e., if all H fields and variables are removed), if both computations terminate then the resulting states are indistinguishable. Indistinguishability is defined in terms of a ground labeling of fields and variables. A method declaration is noninterfering with respect to a given type if its body is noninterfering, where the method type determines levels for parameters and result. A class table is noninterfering if, for every ground instantiation of every class, every method declaration is noninterfering.

The forthcoming technical report [18] shows that if a class table is typable by the security rules then it is noninterfering.

4   Inference

In this section we give the complete inference process. The algorithm has two steps. In the first step (sections 4.1 and 4.2) it outputs the constraints that ensure the typability of the classes being checked. In the second step (section 4.3), it takes the output from the first step, produces the parameterized signatures, and checks the subclassing invariance of these signatures. Then the new parameterized signatures can be added to the library.

4.1   Input

One input to the inference algorithm is the pair of auxiliary functions giving the polymorphic signatures of a library, namely, $lsfield$ for fields and $lsmtype$ for methods.

The other input is the current analysis unit. Unlike library methods, all methods implemented in the analysis unit are treated monomorphically with respect to each other during the inference, even though they may override polymorphic methods in the library. In particular, although we do not have explicit syntax for mutual recursion[5], mutually recursive classes are put in the same analysis unit and are treated monomorphically. Method bodies can of course instantiate library methods differently at different call sites.

For any set V of variables, we write I^{*V} for some fixed renaming that maps V to distinct variables not in V.

The signature functions, *usfield* and *usmtype*, provide the types of fields and methods for classes in *unit*. We refrain from defining the simpler one, *usfield*. For any set V of level variables, define $usmtype(m, T, V)$ as follows:

1. If T has a declaration of m
   - If T has a superclass U in *unit* that declares m, then $usmtype(m, T, V) = usmtype(m, U, V)$.
   - Otherwise (i.e, any superclass of T that declares m is in the library), $usmtype(m, T, V)$ has parameter types and return type as declared in T; the heap effect and self level are two variables distinct from all level variables in *unit* and the signature has the empty constraint set.
2. If T inherits m from its superclass U
   - If U is in *unit*, $usmtype(m, T, V) = usmtype(m, U, V)$.
   - If U is a library class, $usmtype(m, T, V) = I^{*V} lsmtype(m, U)$.

By definition, *usmtype* may return a type that is either monomorphic or polymorphic, depending on whether there are any declarations of m in *unit* at or above T. If there are none, the method type is polymorphic and a renaming is needed to ensure variable freshness. On the other hand, if there is a declaration of m in *unit* at or above T, *usmtype* returns a fixed monomorphic type for all call sites – even if m has also been defined in the library.

4.2   Inference Rules

The inference algorithm is presented in the form of rules for a judgment that generates constraints and keeps track of variables in use in order to ensure freshness where needed. For expressions, the judgment has the form

$$\Delta, V \vdash e : U \rightsquigarrow \alpha, K, V'$$

where V, V' are sets of level variables, with $V \subseteq V'$. The judgment means that in security type context Δ, expression e has type U and level α provided the constraints in K are satisfied. Each rule also has a condition to ensure freshness of new variables, e.g., $\alpha \notin V$. The constraints K may be expressed using other new variables; V' collects all the new and existing variables. The correctness property is that any ground instantiation I of V' that satisfies K results in an

---

[5] In contrast with explicit syntax for mutual recursion, say, in ML.

Table 4. Inference algorithm: selected command cases

$$\frac{\begin{array}{c}\Delta, x : (U, \lambda_1) \vdash e : U^{\square} \rightsquigarrow \alpha_2, K_1, V_1 \\ K^{\square} = K_1 \cup \{\alpha_2 \leq \lambda_1, \alpha_3 \leq \lambda_1\} \cup tcomp(U^{\square}, U) \qquad \alpha_3, \alpha_4 \notin V_1\end{array}}{\Delta, x : (U, \lambda_1), V \vdash x := e \rightsquigarrow \mathtt{com}\,(\alpha_3, \alpha_4), K^{\square}, \{\alpha_3, \alpha_4\} \cup V_1}$$

$$\frac{\begin{array}{c}(\;\;\begin{array}{c}(\lambda_0, (\overline{U^{\square}}, \overline{\lambda}) - \langle \lambda_1 \rangle \mapsto R, \lambda_2)|K = usmtype(m, W, V_1) \\ \vee \quad (\lambda_0, (\overline{U^{\square}}, \overline{\lambda}) - \langle \lambda_1 \rangle \mapsto R, \lambda_2)|K = I^{\square \, V_1}(lsmtype(m, W))\end{array}\;\;) \\ \Delta, x : (U, \lambda), V \vdash e : W \rightsquigarrow \alpha_3, K_0, V_0 \qquad \Delta, x : (U, \lambda), V_0 \vdash \overline{e} : \overline{U} \rightsquigarrow \overline{\alpha_4}, K_1, V_1 \\ V^{\square} = V_1 \cup var(K) \cup var(R) \cup var(\overline{U^{\square}}) \cup var(\lambda_0, \overline{\lambda}, \lambda_1, \lambda_2) \\ K^{\square} = K \cup K_0 \cup K_1 \cup tcomp(\overline{U}, \overline{U^{\square}}) \cup tcomp(R, U) \cup K^{\square \square} \\ K^{\square \square} = \{\overline{\alpha_4} \leq \overline{\lambda}, \alpha_3 \leq \lambda_0, \alpha_3 \leq \lambda_1, \lambda_2 \leq \lambda, \alpha_5 \leq \lambda, \alpha_6 \leq \lambda_1, \alpha_3 \leq \lambda\} \\ \alpha_5, \alpha_6 \notin V^{\square \square} \qquad V^{\square} = \{\alpha_5, \alpha_6\} \cup V^{\square \square}\end{array}}{\Delta, x : (U, \lambda), V \vdash x := e.m(\overline{e}) \rightsquigarrow \mathtt{com}\,(\alpha_5, \alpha_6), K^{\square}, V^{\square}}$$

expression typable in the security type system, once we instantiate α and the other variables. This is formalized in the soundness theorem.

There is a similar judgment for commands: $\Delta, V \vdash S \rightsquigarrow \mathtt{com}\,(\alpha_1, \alpha_2), K', V'$ where V, V' are level variables with $V \subseteq V'$ means that in security type context Δ, command S writes to variables of level α_1 or higher and to fields of level α_2 or higher.

We refrain from giving the full set of rules, but discussing just a few cases, which are given in Table 4. The first rule in the table is for variable assignment. This may help the reader become familiar with the notation. The inferred type for the assignment is $\mathtt{com}\,(\alpha_3, \alpha_4)$, where α_3, α_4 are fresh. The generated constraint set K' contains the set K_1 obtained during the inference of e; U' is the type of e and α_2 is the inferred level of e. As expected from the typing rule for assignment, K' contains the constraint set $\{\alpha_2 \leq \lambda_1, \alpha_3 \leq \lambda_1\}$ and also the constraints between variables in U' and U generated by $tcomp(U', U)$, which ensures the subtyping relation between U' and U.

The most complicated rule is for method invocation (Table 4). It is developed from the typing rule for method invocation(Table 3). One can see that the conditions in the typing rule evolve to the constraints in the inference rule. There are two cases depending on the static type of the target. If the target is defined in the library, $lsmtype$ will return the polymorphic method type and a renaming I^{*V} is used in the rule for freshness. Otherwise, $usmtype$ returns the appropriate method signature, already renamed if necessary. In both cases, the type will be matched against the calling context and constraints in the returned signature will be integrated. The rule uses $tcomp$ to generate constraints that ensure type compatibility.

The rules apply by structural recursion to a method body, generating constraints for its primitive commands (like assignment and method call) and constraints for combining these constituents (like in if/else). The rule for method declaration, first rule in Table 5, matches a method body with its declared type and checks it, generating an additional constraint.

Table 5. Inference algorithm for method declaration and class declaration

$$\frac{\Delta, V \vdash S \rightsquigarrow \mathtt{com}\ (\alpha_1, \alpha_2), K_1, V_1 \qquad \Delta = [\overline{x} : (\overline{U}, \overline{\lambda}); \mathtt{self} : (U, \lambda_0);\ \mathtt{result} : (R, \lambda_4)]}{C\ \mathtt{extends}\ D, V \vdash R\ m(\overline{U}\ \overline{x})\{S\} \rightsquigarrow K_1 \cup \{\lambda_3 \leq \alpha_2\}, V_1}$$

where $usmtype(m, C, V_1) = (\lambda_0, (\overline{U}, \overline{\lambda})) \!-\! \langle \lambda_3 \rangle \!\rightarrow\! (R, \lambda_4)|\varnothing$

$$\frac{\forall M_i \in \overline{M} \quad C\ \mathtt{extends}\ D, V_{i-1} \vdash M_i \rightsquigarrow K_i, V_i}{V_0 \vdash \mathtt{class}\ C\ \mathtt{extends}\ D\{\overline{U}\ \overline{f}, \overline{M}\} \rightsquigarrow \cup_{1 \leq i \leq n} K_i, V_n}$$

The rule for class declaration, also in Table 5, combines the constraints for all its methods. We refrain from stating a formal rule for the complete analysis unit. The conclusion, written $lsmtype, lsfield, usmtype, usfield \vdash unit \rightsquigarrow K, V$ depends on two hypotheses. First, each class declaration in $unit$ has been checked by the rule in the table, yielding constraints K over variables V. This check is obtained by enumerating the class declarations in $unit$, threading variable sets from one class to the next, and then taking for K the union of the constraints. The initial variable set contains all the fresh variables used in the definition of $usmtype$ and all level variables that occur in $unit$. The second hypothesis is that overriding declarations do not introduce new constraints, which would invalidate the analysis of the library which is assumed in the form of $lsmtype$. If this check fails, the analysis fails. We will address the check at the end of section 4.3.

4.3 Building a New Library

In this subsection we illustrate the manipulation of parameterized classes, resulting in a new library signature. Then we give the definitions. Finally, we outline how subclassing invariance is checked.

Producing New Signatures. Assume we define a class $CreditTAX$ that extends TAX. We have filled in level variables where needed.

```
class CreditTAX extends TAX<γ₁> {
    (int, γ₀) credit;
    (int, γ₂)  tax((int, γ₃) salary){
        self.income:=salary; result:=self.income*0.2-self.credit;}}
```

Assume $usmtype(tax, CreditTAX, \{\gamma_0, \gamma_1, \gamma_2, \gamma_3\})$ returns $(\gamma_s, (int, \gamma_3)) \!-\! \langle \gamma_h \rangle \!\rightarrow\! (int, \gamma_2)|\varnothing$. We run the program on the code, and get the output K, V, where V includes $\gamma_0, \gamma_1, \gamma_2, \gamma_3$ and other temporary level variables generated during the inference.

To put $CreditTAX$ into the library, we need to produce its signature. First we define the list of formal parameters by collecting variables γ_0 from field declarations and γ_1 from the "extends" clause. Second, we attach the generated constraint K to each method in the unit. The converted signature for $Credit$-TAX, in pseudocode, is:

class $CreditTAX<\gamma_0, \gamma_1>$ **extends** $TAX <\gamma_1> \{$
    $credit: (\mathbf{int}, \gamma_0);$
    $tax:$ $(\gamma_s, (\mathbf{int}, \gamma_2))\negthinspace-\negthinspace\langle\gamma_h\rangle\negthinspace\mapsto\negthinspace(\mathbf{int}, \gamma_3) \mid K \ ; \}$

Now we formalize the process of producing new signatures. By the algorithm we can get (K, V) on the classes in the unit. For converting the code, let X be the set of class names declared in $unit$. We study any class $C \in X$. Let V' be all the variables in V that appear in the supertype or field type/label of C. Let $unit'$ be $unit$ but with every C in X replaced by $C<V'>$. The $unit'$ is now a parameterized class with polymorphic methods.

Now we need to combine the signatures from the library and the unit. Based on $unit'$, we will build a new signature function that can access the converted unit and the library uniformly. Assume $unit'(T) = \mathtt{class}\ T<\bar{\alpha}>\{\ldots\}$.

$$
\begin{aligned}
&fieldmerge\ (lsfield, usfield)(f, T<\bar{\lambda}>) = \\
&\quad \mathtt{if}\ T\ \mathrm{in}\ unit\ \mathtt{then}\ \ usfield(f, T)[\bar{\alpha} \leftarrow \bar{\lambda}] \\
&\quad \mathtt{else}\ \ lsfield(f, T<\bar{\lambda}>) \\
&methmerge\ (lsmtype, usmtype, K)(m, T<\bar{\lambda}>) = \\
&\quad \mathtt{if}\ m\ \mathrm{is\ inherited\ from\ class}\ D\ \mathrm{in\ the\ library}\ \mathtt{then} \\
&\qquad\qquad lsmtype(m, instance(T<\bar{\lambda}>, D)) \\
&\quad \mathtt{else}\ \ (fst(usmtype(m, T, \varnothing))|K)[\bar{\alpha} \leftarrow \bar{\lambda}]
\end{aligned}
$$

In $methmerge$, $T.m$ is implemented in the unit. So the third parameter for $usmtype$ is insignificant and the constraint in the return of $usmtype(m, T, \varnothing)$ is empty. We use fst to strip off this empty constraint.

Checking Method Declarations for Proper Override. Rather than delving into algorithmic optimizations, we just specify the check for overriding declarations informally. We want to ensure that $U.m$ properly overrides $U'.m$ where U' is a super class of U. We assume the constraint set has been simplified in that only level constants and variables that are in the formal class parameter list or method type signature are kept. For example, $\{\alpha \leq \beta, \beta \leq \gamma\}$ can be transformed into $\{\alpha \leq \gamma\}$ if β is insignificant.

The condition for proper override can be expressed as: *Every constraint in the overriding method must be entailed [13] by the constraints in the overridden method.* For example, assume $lsmtype(U, m) = (L, ()\negthinspace-\negthinspace\langle\alpha_2\rangle\negthinspace\mapsto\negthinspace\alpha_3)|K$ and $lsmtype(U', m) = (\beta_1, ()\negthinspace-\negthinspace\langle\beta_2\rangle\negthinspace\mapsto\negthinspace\beta_3)|K'$. We want to check if $U.m$ is properly implemented. Since the level of $self$ is L for $U.m$, $\beta_1 = L$ should be entailed by K'. Also, if $\alpha_2 \leq \alpha_3 \in K$, K' should entail it too.

We return to the $CreditTAX$ example. It is not difficult to figure out that K is the same as the constraint set (after the name conversion) in $TAX.tax$ except that there is one more inequality, $\gamma_0 \leq \gamma_3$, in K. This is necessary to ensure the typability of $CreditTAX$, but it makes the method tax more restrictive than declared in TAX. When tax is invoked on a $CreditTAX$ object as an instance of TAX, the caller may assume $\gamma_0 = H, \gamma_3 = L$ as a valid precondition because $TAX.tax$ does not impose any constraint between γ_0 and γ_3. But this constraint is obviously unsatisfiable for *CreditTAX.tax* in the context of dynamic dispatch, and violates the underlying policy. To make *CreditTAX* pass the check $\gamma_0 \leq \gamma_3$, one can relabel field *credit* with *L*.

We only compare constraints for a particular method – it is certainly not the case that the constraints from the library imply all constraints for *unit*, e.g., the unit can have additional methods.

Complexity. The time/space cost for the inference algorithm to generate constraints is low-order polynomial in the size of the program, and independent of the security lattice. We can show that the time to generate the constraint set is $O(mn(s+t)^3 2^{2|P|})$, where m is the number of methods in the unit; n is the length of the unit; s, t are the number of distinct variable in class level and method level, perspectively; $|P|$ is the size of the permission set. The size of the generated constraint set is $O(n(s+t)^3 2^{2|P|})$.

5   Soundness and Completeness of the Inference Algorithm

5.1   Soundness

Theorem 1 (Soundness of inference algorithm).
Assume $sigs \vdash unit \leadsto K, V$ [6]. Let *unit'* be the converted *unit* and *sfield = fieldmerge (lsfield, usfield)* and *smtype = methmerge(lsmtype, usmtype, K)* be the converted signatures, then *sfield, smtype ⊢ unit'*.

5.2   Completeness of Inference Algorithm

In our system, the most general signatures of mutually recursive classes cannot be represented in finite forms. Thus the inference algorithm cannot be complete, since our algorithm will always terminate and produce finite output. We have to restrict the classes in current analysis unit in order to prove completeness.

Define a unit to be *monomorphically typed* if all type references and method invocations for the same class or method in a class body are instantiated exactly in the same way.

Theorem 2 (Completeness).
If $I(unit)$ is monomorphically typed in $I(sigs)$, the constraints produced by the algorithm for *unit* are satisfiable by an extension of I.

In other words, this means that the algorithm yields principal types for a monomorphically typed unit with respect to the polymorphic library. This is analogous to type inference of recursive functions in ML. For example, in the ML term, letrec $f(x) = t_1$ in t_2, all occurrences of f in t_1 are monomorphic. The current unit is comparable to t_1, and t_2 is comparable to classes in other units that can use current unit polymorphically once it has been made part of a library. The theorem relies on lemmas for expressions, commands, method and class declarations. We only list the lemma for expressions and commands.

---

[6] We use *sigs* to abbreviate *lsfield, lsmtype, usfield, usmtype*.

Lemma 1. Assume $I(e)$ is monomorphically typed in $I(sigs)$. If $I(sigs), I(\Delta) \vdash I(e) : U_c, \kappa$ and $sigs, \Delta, V \vdash e : U \rightsquigarrow \alpha, K, V'$ where U_c is a type parameterized over level constants, then $\exists I' \supseteq I . ok(I', K, V') \wedge \kappa = I'(\alpha) \wedge U_c = I'(U)$

Lemma 2. Assume $I(S)$ is monomorphically typed in $I(sigs)$. If $I(sigs), I(\Delta) \vdash I(S) : \mathsf{com}\ \kappa_1, \kappa_2$ and $sig, \Delta, V \vdash S \rightsquigarrow (\mathsf{com}\ \alpha_1, \alpha_2), K', V'$, then
$\exists I' \supseteq I . ok(I', K', V') \wedge \kappa_1 = I'(\alpha_1) \wedge \kappa_2 = I'(\alpha_2)$.

6 Related Work and Discussion

Related Work. Volpano and Smith [19], give a security type system and a constraint-based inference algorithm for a simple procedural language. The type system guarantees noninterference: a well-typed program does not leak sensitive data. The inference algorithm is sound and complete with respect to the type system. However, they do not handle object-oriented features, and their suggestion to handle library polymorphism by duplicating code is impractical.

Myers [9, 10] gives a security type system for full Java, but leaves open the problem of justifying the rules with a noninterference result. Myers, Zdancewic and their students have implemented a secure compiler, Jif[7], that implements the security typing rules. Jif handles several advanced features like constrained method signature, exceptions, declassification, dynamic labels and polymorphism. Jif's inheritance allows overriding methods to be more general than overridden methods, which means that the constraints in the overridden method must be stronger than the overriding method. However, inference in the system is only intraprocedural. Field and method types are added either manually or by default.

Simonet presents a version of ML with security flow labels, termed Flow-Caml[16, 15] which supports polymorphism, exceptions, structural subtyping and the module system. The type system is polymorphic and has been shown to ensure noninterference. Simonet and Pottier[12] give an algorithm to infer security types. They also prove soundness of type inference.

There is a rich literature on type inference for object-oriented programs [20, 11, 2, 4, 21]. However, we are interested in security type inference, rather than full type inference; we assume that a well-typed program is given. We found it difficult to adapt the techniques in these works because they do not consider modular inference in the presence of libraries.

We have a working prototype for a whole program analysis for the language in [3]. It accepts a class declaration that is partly annotated with level constants, generating a constraint set and checking its satisfiability. If the code is typable, the output will be a polymorphic type for the given program in its most general form. The extension of the prototype for the present paper is currently under way.

---

[7] On the web at http://www.cs.cornell.edu/jif/

Deployment Model. For an application developer, the signatures in the library specify security requirements. The developer must annotate additional methods in the current analysis unit with new policies. Running a check on the annotated program can then tell whether it is secure with respect to the library policies.

For library designers, the tool is helpful in that it not only enforces the specified security policies, but also gives designers a chance to revise the result signatures if the signatures appear too *general* and seem likely to prevent subclasses from being implemented because subclasses cannot introduce new flows.

To make the result signatures more general for a collection of classes, it is advisable to make the analysis unit as small as possible. Classes that make mutually recursive references need to be analyzed together. This is the only reason to make units have more than one class.

Conclusion. The main contribution of this paper is the specification of a modular algorithm that infers security types for a sequential, class-based, object-oriented language. This requires the addition of security level variables to the language and moreover, requires classes parameterized with security levels. The inference algorithm constructs a library where each class is parameterized by the levels in its fields. Each method of a parameterized class can be given a polymorphic, constrained signature. This has the additional benefit of being more expressive and flexible for the programmer. We have given soundness and completeness theorems for the algorithm and work is in progress on a prototype. We have not yet experimented with the scalability of our technique to real sized programs. Such an experiment and its results will be reported in the first author's dissertation. Our work would also benefit from a comparison with the HM(X) constraint-based type inference framework [17]. Our suspicion, however, is that to prove soundness and completeness, there might be substantial overhead in the translation of our security types to the HM(X) framework.

References

1. Martin Abadi. Secrecy by typing in security protocols. *Journal of the ACM*, 46(5):749–786, September 1999.
2. Ole Agesen. The cartesian product algorithm: Simple and precise type inference of parametric polymorphism. In *European Conference on Object Oriented Programming (ECOOP)*, pages 2–26, 1995.
3. Anindya Banerjee and David A. Naumann. Secure information flow and pointer confinement in a Java-like language. In *IEEE Computer Security Foundations Workshop (CSFW)*, pages 253–270. IEEE Computer Society Press, 2002.
4. Gilad Bracha, Martin Odersky, David Stoutamire, and Philip Wadler. Making the future safe for the past: Adding genericity to the Java programming language. In Craig Chambers, editor, *ACM Symposium on Object Oriented Programming: Systems, Languages, and Applications (OOPSLA)*, pages 183–200, Vancouver, BC, 1998.
5. Dorothy Denning and Peter Denning. Certification of programs for secure information flow. *Communications of the ACM*, 20(7):504–513, 1977.

6. J. Goguen and J. Meseguer. Security policies and security models. In *Proceedings of the 1982 IEEE Symposium on Security and Privacy*, pages 11–20, 1982.
7. Fritz Henglein. Type inference with polymorphic recursion. *ACM Transactions on Programming Languages and Systems*, 15(2):253–289, April 1993.
8. Alan Mycroft. Polymorphic type schemes and recursive definitions. In *Sixth International Symposium on Programming*, number 166 in Lecture Notes in Computer Science. Springer-Verlag, 1984.
9. Andrew C. Myers. JFlow: Practical mostly-static information flow control. In *ACM Symposium on Principles of Programming Languages (POPL)*, pages 228–241, 1999.
10. Andrew C. Myers. *Mostly-Static Decentralized Information Flow Control*. PhD thesis, Laboratory of Computer Science, MIT, 1999.
11. Jens Palsberg and Michael I. Schwartzbach. Object-oriented type inference. In *ACM Symposium on Object Oriented Programming: Systems, Languages, and Applications (OOPSLA)*. ACM Press, 1991.
12. François Pottier and Vincent Simonet. Information flow inference for ML. In *ACM Symposium on Principles of Programming Languages (POPL)*, pages 319–330, 2002.
13. Jakob Rehof and Fritz Henglein. The complexity of subtype entailment for simple types. In *Proceedings LICS '97, Twelfth Annual IEEE Symposium on Logic in Computer Science, Warsaw, Poland*, June 1997.
14. Andrei Sabelfeld and Andrew C. Myers. Language-based information-flow security. *IEEE J. Selected Areas in Communications*, 21(1):5–19, January 2003.
15. Vincent Simonet. Flow Caml in a nutshell. In Graham Hutton, editor, *Proceedings of the first APPSEM-II workshop*, pages 152–165, March 2003.
16. Vincent Simonet. The Flow Caml System: documentation and user's manual. Technical Report 0282, Institut National de Recherche en Informatique et en Automatique (INRIA), July 2003.
17. Christian Skalka and François Pottier. Syntactic type soundness for HM(X). In *Proceedings of the Workshop on Types in Programming (TIP'02)*, volume 75 of *Electronic Notes in Theoretical Computer Science*, July 2002.
18. Qi Sun, Anindya Banerjee, and David A. Naumann. Constraint-based security flow inferencer for a Java-like language. Technical Report KSU CIS TR-2004-2, Kansas State University, 2004. In preparation.
19. Dennis Volpano and Geoffrey Smith. A type-based approach to program security. In *Proceedings of TAPSOFT'97*, number 1214 in Lecture Notes in Computer Science, pages 607–621. Springer-Verlag, 1997.
20. Mitchell Wand. Complete type inference for simple objects. In *Proc. 2nd IEEE Symposium on Logic in Computer Science*, pages 37–44, 1987.
21. Taejun Wang and Scott Smith. Precise constraint-based type inference for java. In *European Conference on Object Oriented Programming (ECOOP)*, 2001.

Information Flow Analysis in Logical Form

Torben Amtoft and Anindya Banerjee*

Department of Computing and Information Sciences
Kansas State University, Manhattan KS 66506, USA
{tamtoft,ab}@cis.ksu.edu

Abstract. We specify an information flow analysis for a simple imperative language, using a Hoare-like logic. The logic facilitates static checking of a larger class of programs than can be checked by extant type-based
approaches in which a program is deemed insecure when it contains an
insecure subprogram. The logic is based on an abstract interpretation
of program traces that makes independence between program variables
explicit. Unlike other, more precise, approaches based on a Hoare-like
logic, our approach does not require a theorem prover to generate invariants. We demonstrate the modularity of our approach by showing that
a frame rule holds in our logic. Moreover, given an insecure but terminating program, we show how strongest postconditions can be employed
to statically generate failure explanations.

1 Introduction

This paper specifies an information flow analysis using a Hoare-like logic and
considers an application of the logic to explaining insecure flow of information
in simple imperative programs.

Given a system with high, or secret (H), and low, or public (L) inputs and
outputs, where $L \leq H$ is a security lattice, a classic security problem is how to
enforce the following end-to-end *confidentiality* policy: protect secret data, i.e.,
prevent leaks of secrets at public output channels. An information flow analysis
checks if a program satisfies the policy. Denning and Denning were the first to
formulate an information flow analysis for confidentiality[11]. Subsequent advances have been comprehensively summarized in the recent survey by Sabelfeld
and Myers [27]. An oft-used approach for specifying static analyses for information flow is *security type systems* [23, 29]. Security types are ordinary types
of program variables and expressions annotated with security levels. Security
typing rules prevent leaks of secret information to public channels. For example,
the security typing rule for assignment prevents H data from being assigned to
a L variable. A well-typed program "protects secrets", i.e., no information flows
from H to L during program execution.

In the security literature, "protects secrets" is formalized as *noninterference* [13] and is described in terms of an "indistinguishability" relation on states.

---

* Supported by NSF grants CCR-0296182 and CCR-0209205.

R. Giacobazzi (Ed.): SAS 2004, LNCS 3148, pp. 100–115, 2004.
© Springer-Verlag Berlin Heidelberg 2004

Two program states are indistinguishable for L if they agree on values of L variables. The noninterference property says that any two runs of a program starting from two initial states indistinguishable for L, yield two final states that are indistinguishable for L. The two initial states may differ on values of H variables but not on values of L variables; the two final states must agree on the current values of L variables. One reading of the noninterference property is as a form of (in)dependence [7]: L output is independent of H inputs. It is this notion that is made explicit in the information flow analysis specified in this paper.

A shortcoming of usual type-based approaches for information flow [4, 14, 29, 24] is that a type system can be too imprecise. Consider the sequential program $l := h; l := 0$, where l has type L and h has type H. This program is rejected by a security type system on account of the first assignment. But the program obviously satisfies noninterference – final states of any two runs of the program will always have the same value, 0, for l and are thus indistinguishable for L.

How can we admit such programs? Our inspiration comes from abstract interpretation [8], which can be viewed as a method for statically computing approximations of program invariants [9]. A benefit of this view is that the static abstraction of a program invariant can be used to annotate a program with pre- and postconditions and the annotated program can be checked against a Hoare-like logic. In information flow analysis, the invariant of interest is *independence of variables*, for which we use the notation $[x \# w]$ to denote that x is independent of w. The idea is that this holds provided any two runs (hereafter called *traces* and formalized in Section 2) which have the same initial[1] value for all variables *except for w* will at least agree on the current value of x. This is just a convenient restatement of noninterference but we tie it to the static notion of variable independence.

The set of program traces is potentially infinite, but our approach statically computes a finite abstraction, namely a set of independences, $T^{\#}$, that describes a set of traces, T. This is formalized in Section 3. We formulate (in Section 4) a Hoare-like logic for checking independences and show (Section 5) that a checked program satisfies noninterference. The assertion language of the logic is decidable since it is just the language of finite sets of independences with subset inclusion. Specifications in the logic have the form, $\{T^{\#}\}\ C\ \{T_1^{\#}\}$. Given precondition $T^{\#}$, we show in Section 6 how to compute strongest postconditions; for programs with loops, this necessitates a fixpoint computation[2]. We show that the logic deems the program $l := h; l := 0$ secure: the strongest postcondition of the program contains the independence $[l \# h]$.

Our approach falls in between type-based analysis and full verification where verification conditions for loops depend on loop invariants generated by a theorem prover. Instead, we approximate invariants using a fixpoint computation. Our approach is modular and we show that our logic satisfies a frame rule (Section 7). The frame rule permits local reasoning about a program: the relevant

---

[1] The initial value of a variable is its value before execution of the whole program.
[2] The set of independences is a finite lattice, hence the fixpoint computation will terminate.

independences for a program are only those $[x \mathrel{\#} w]$ where x occurs in the program. Moreover, in a larger context, the frame rule allows the following inference (in analogy with [21]): start with a specification $\{T^{\#}\}\ C\ \{T_0^{\#}\}$ describing independences before and after store modifications; then, $\{T^{\#} \cup T_1^{\#}\}\ C\ \{T_0^{\#} \cup T_1^{\#}\}$ holds provided C does not modify any variable y, where $[y \mathrel{\#} w]$ appears in $T_1^{\#}$. The initial specification, $\{T^{\#}\}\ C\ \{T_0^{\#}\}$ can reason with only the slice of store that C touches.

We also show (Section 9) that strongest postconditions can be used to statically generate failure explanations for an insecure but terminating program. If there is a program fragment C whose precondition contains $[l \mathrel{\#} h]$, but whose strongest postcondition does not contain $[l \mathrel{\#} h]$, we know statically that C is an offending fragment. Thus we may expect to find two initial values of h which produce two different values of l. We consider two ways this may happen [11]; we do not consider termination, timing leaks and other covert channels. One reason for failure of $[l \mathrel{\#} h]$ to be in the strongest postcondition, is that C assigns H data to a L variable. The other reason is that C is a conditional or a while loop whose guard depends on a high variable and which updates a low variable in its body. Consider, for example, if h then $l := 1$ else $l := 0$. Our failure explanation for the conditional will be modulo an *interpretation function*, that, for distinct variables h_1 and h_2 map h_1 to *true* and h_2 to *false*. Under this interpretation, the execution of the program produces two different values of l. This explains why l is not independent of h. Because we use a static analysis, false positives may be generated: consider if h then $l := 7$ else $l := 7$, a program that is deemed insecure when it is clearly not. However, such false positives can be ruled out by an instrumented semantics that tracks constant values more precisely.

Contributions. First and foremost, we formulate information flow analysis in a logical form via a Hoare-like logic. The approach deems more programs secure than extant type-based approaches. Secondly, we describe the relationship between information flow and program dependence, explored in [1, 16], in a more direct manner by computing independences between program variables. The independences themselves are static descriptions of the noninterference property. In Section 8, we show how our logic conservatively extends the security type system of Smith and Volpano [29], by showing that any well-typed program in their system satisfies the invariant $[l \mathrel{\#} h]$. Thirdly, when a program is deemed insecure, the annotated derivation facilitates explanations on *why* the program is insecure by statically generating counterexamples. The development in this paper considers *termination-insensitive* noninterference only: we assume that an attacker cannot observe nontermination. Complete proofs of all theorems appear in the companion technical report [2].

2   Language: Syntax, Traces, Semantics

This section gives the syntax of a simple imperative language, formalizes the notion of traces, and gives the language a semantics using sets of traces.

Syntax. We consider a simple imperative language with assignment, sequencing, conditionals and loops as formalized by the following BNF. Commands $C \in$ **Cmd** are given by the syntax

$$C ::= x := E \mid C_1 \; ; C_2 \mid \text{if } E \text{ then } C_1 \text{ else } C_2 \mid \text{while } E \text{ do } C$$

where **Var** is an infinite set of variables, $x, y, z, w \in$ **Var** range over variables and where $E \in$ **Exp** ranges over expressions. Expressions are left unspecified but we shall assume the existence of a function $\text{fv}(E)$ that computes the free variables of expression E. For commands, $\text{fv}(C)$ is defined in the obvious way. We also define a function *modified* : **Cmd** $\rightarrow \mathcal{P}(\textbf{Var})$ that given a command, returns the set of variables potentially assigned to by the command.

Traces. A trace $t \in$ **Trc** associates each variable with its initial value and its current value; here values $v \in$ **Val** are yet unspecified but we assume that there exists a predicate *true?* on **Val**. (For instance, we could have **Val** as the set of integers and let *true?*(v) be defined as $v \neq 0$). We shall use $T \in \mathcal{P}(\textbf{Trc})$ to range over sets of traces. Basic operations on traces include:

- ini-$t(x)$ which returns the initial value of x as recorded by t;
- cur-$t(x)$ which returns the current value of x as recorded by t;
- $t[y \mapsto v]$ which returns a trace t' with the property: for all $x \in$ **Var**, ini-$t'(x) = $ ini-$t(x)$ and if $x \neq y$ then cur-$t'(x) = $ cur-$t(x)$; but cur-$t'(y) = v$.
- The predicate *initial* T on sets of traces T holds iff for all traces $t \in T$, and for all variables x, we have ini-$t(x) = $ cur-$t(x)$.

For instance, we could represent a trace t as a mapping **Var** $\rightarrow$ **Val** $\times$ **Val**; with $t(x) = (v_i, v_c)$ we would then have ini-$t(x) = v_i$ and cur-$t(x) = v_c$.

We shall write $t_1 \stackrel{x}{=} t_2$ to denote that cur-$t_1(x) = $ cur-$t_2(x)$, and we shall write $\neg(t_1 \stackrel{x}{=} t_2)$ to denote that $t_1 \stackrel{x}{=} t_2$ does not hold. Also, we shall write $t_1 =_x t_2$ to denote that for $y \neq x$, ini-$t_1(y) = $ ini-$t_2(y)$ holds. That is, the initial values of all variables, *except for* x, are equal in t_1 and t_2.

Semantics. We assume that there exists a semantic function $\llbracket E \rrbracket : \textbf{Trc} \rightarrow \textbf{Val}$ which satisfies the following property: if for all $x \in \text{fv}(E)$ we have $t_1 \stackrel{x}{=} t_2$, then $\llbracket E \rrbracket(t_1) = \llbracket E \rrbracket(t_2)$. The definition of $\llbracket E \rrbracket$ would contain the clause $\llbracket x \rrbracket(t) = $ cur-$t(x)$. For each T and E we define

$$E\text{-true}(T) = \{t \in T \mid \text{true?}(\llbracket E \rrbracket(t))\}$$
$$E\text{-false}(T) = T \setminus E\text{-true}(T).$$

The semantics of a command has functionality $\llbracket C \rrbracket : \mathcal{P}(\textbf{Trc}) \rightarrow \mathcal{P}(\textbf{Trc})$, and is defined in Fig. 1. To see that the last clause in Fig. 1 is well-defined, notice that $\mathcal{F}^C$ is a monotone function on the complete lattice $\mathcal{P}(\textbf{Trc}) \rightarrow \mathcal{P}(\textbf{Trc})$.

$$[\![x := E]\!] = \lambda T.\{t^0 \mid \exists t \in T : t^0 = t[x \mapsto [\![E]\!](t)]\}$$

$$[\![C_1 ; C_2]\!] = \lambda T.[\![C_2]\!]([\![C_1]\!](T))$$

$$[\![\text{if } E \text{ then } C_1 \text{ else } C_2]\!] = \lambda T.[\![C_1]\!](E\text{-true}(T)) \cup [\![C_2]\!](E\text{-false}(T))$$

$$[\![\text{while } E \text{ do } C_0]\!] = lfp(\mathcal{F}^C) \text{ where } C = \text{while } E \text{ do } C_0 \text{ and}$$
$$\mathcal{F}^C : (\mathcal{P}(\mathbf{Trc}) \to \mathcal{P}(\mathbf{Trc})) \to (\mathcal{P}(\mathbf{Trc}) \to \mathcal{P}(\mathbf{Trc}))$$
$$\mathcal{F}^C(f) = \lambda T.f([\![C_0]\!](E\text{-true}(T))) \cup E\text{-false}(T)$$

Fig. 1. The Trace Semantics.

3   Independences

We are interested in a finite abstraction of a (possibly infinite) set of concrete traces. The abstract values are termed *independences*: an independence $T^\# \in$ **Independ** $= \mathcal{P}(\mathbf{Var} \times \mathbf{Var})$ is a set of pairs of the form $[x \mathbin{\#} w]$, denoting that the *current* value of x is independent of the *initial* value of w. This is formalized by the following definition of when an independence correctly describes a set of traces. The intuition is that x is independent of w iff any two traces which have the same initial values except on w must agree on the current value of x; in other words, the initial value of w does not influence the current value of x at all.

Definition 1. $[x \mathbin{\#} w] \models T$ *holds iff for all* $t_1, t_2 \in T$: $t_1 \underset{w}{=} t_2$ *implies* $t_1 \overset{x}{=} t_2$.
   $T^\# \models T$ *holds iff for all* $[x \mathbin{\#} w] \in T^\#$ *it holds that* $[x \mathbin{\#} w] \models T$.

Definition 2. *The ordering* $T_1^\# \preceq T_2^\#$ *holds iff* $T_2^\# \subseteq T_1^\#$.

This is motivated by the desire for a subtyping rule, stating that if $T_1^\# \preceq T_2^\#$ then $T_1^\#$ can be replaced by $T_2^\#$. Such a rule is sound provided $T_2^\#$ is a subset of $T_1^\#$ and therefore obtainable from $T_1^\#$ by removing information. Clearly, **Independ** forms a complete lattice wrt. the ordering; let $\sqcap_i T^\#_i$ denote the greatest lower bound (which is the set union). We have some expected properties:

- If $T^\# \models T$ and $T_1 \subseteq T$ then $T^\# \models T_1$;
- if $T_1^\# \models T$ and $T_1^\# \preceq T_2^\#$ then $T_2^\# \models T$;
- if for all $i \in I$ it holds that $T_i^\# \models T$, then $\sqcap_{i \in I} T_i^\# \models T$.

Moreover, we can write a concretization function $\gamma :$ **Independ** $\to \mathcal{P}(\mathcal{P}(\mathbf{Trc}))$: $\gamma(T^\#) = \{T \mid T^\# \models T\}$. It is easy to verify that γ is completely multiplicative. Therefore [20, p.237] there exists a Galois connection between $\mathcal{P}(\mathcal{P}(\mathbf{Trc}))$ and **Independ**, with γ the concretization function. Finally, we have the following fact about initial sets of traces.

Fact 1 *For all* T, *if initial* T *then* $[x \mathbin{\#} y] \models T$ *for all* $x \neq y$.

4   Static Checking of Independences

To statically check independences we define, in Fig. 2, a Hoare-like Logic where judgements are of the form $G \vdash \{T_1^{\#}\} \, C \, \{T_2^{\#}\}$. The judgement is interpreted as saying that if the independences in $T_1^{\#}$ hold *before* execution of C then, provided C terminates, the independences in $T_2^{\#}$ will hold *after* execution of C. The context $G \in \textbf{Context} = \mathcal{P}(\textbf{Var})$ is a *control dependence*, denoting (a superset of) the variables that at least one test surrounding C depends on. For example, in if x then $y := 0$ else $z := 1$, the static checking of $y := 0$ takes place in the context that contains all variables that x is dependent on. This is crucial, especially since x may depend on a high variable.

We now explain a few of the rules in Fig. 2. Checking an assignment, $x := E$, in context G, involves checking any $[y \mathbin{\#} w]$ in the postcondition $T^{\#}$. There are two cases. If $x \neq y$, then $[y \mathbin{\#} w]$ must also appear in the precondition $T_0^{\#}$. Otherwise, if $x = y$ then $[x \mathbin{\#} w]$ appears in the postcondition provided all variables referenced in E are independent of w; moreover, w must not appear in G, as otherwise, x would be (control) dependent on w.

Checking a conditional, if E then C_1 else C_2, involves checking C_1 and C_2 in a context G_0 that includes not only the "old" context G but also the variables that E depends on (as variables modified in C_1 or C_2 will be control dependent on such). Equivalently, if w is not in G_0, then all free variables x in E must be independent of w, that is, $[x \mathbin{\#} w]$ must appear in the precondition $T_0^{\#}$.

Checking a while loop is similar to checking a conditional. The only difference is that it requires guessing an "invariant" $T^{\#}$ that is both the precondition and the postcondition of the loop and its body.

In Section 6, when we define *strongest postcondition*, we will select $G_0 = G \cup \{w \mid \exists x \in \text{fv}(E) \bullet [x \mathbin{\#} w] \notin T_0^{\#}\}$ for the conditional and the while loop. Instead of guessing the invariant, we will show how to compute it using fixpoints.

Example 1. We have the derivations

$$\emptyset \vdash \{\{[l \mathbin{\#} h], [h \mathbin{\#} l]\}\} \, l := h \, \{\{[h \mathbin{\#} l], [l \mathbin{\#} l]\}\} \text{ and}$$
$$\emptyset \vdash \{\{[h \mathbin{\#} l], [l \mathbin{\#} l]\}\} \, l := 0 \, \{\{[h \mathbin{\#} l], [l \mathbin{\#} l], [l \mathbin{\#} h]\}\}$$

and therefore also

$$\emptyset \vdash \{\{[l \mathbin{\#} h], [h \mathbin{\#} l]\}\} \, l := h \, ; l := 0 \, \{\{[h \mathbin{\#} l], [l \mathbin{\#} l], [l \mathbin{\#} h]\}\}$$

With the intuition that l stands for "low" or "public" and h stands for "high" or "sensitive", the derivation asserts that if l is independent of h before execution, then provided the program halts, l is independent of h after execution. By Definition 1, any two traces of the program with different initial values for h, agree on the current value for l. Thus the program is secure, although it contains an insecure sub-program.

Example 2. The reader may check that the following informally annotated program gives rise to a derivation in our logic. Initially, G is empty, and all variables are pairwise independent; we write $[x \mathbin{\#} y, z]$ to abbreviate $[x \mathbin{\#} y], [x \mathbin{\#} z]$.

$$[\text{Assign}] \; G \vdash \{T_0^{\#}\} \; x := E \; \{T^{\#}\} \quad \begin{array}{l} \text{if } \forall [y \,\#\, w] \in T^{\#} \bullet \\ \quad x \neq y \Rightarrow [y \,\#\, w] \in T_0^{\#} \\ \quad x = y \Rightarrow w \notin G \land \forall z \in \text{fv}(E) \bullet [z \,\#\, w] \in T_0^{\#} \end{array}$$

$$[\text{Seq}] \quad \dfrac{G \vdash \{T_0^{\#}\} \, C_1 \, \{T_1^{\#}\} \quad G \vdash \{T_1^{\#}\} \, C_2 \, \{T_2^{\#}\}}{G \vdash \{T_0^{\#}\} \, C_1 \,;C_2 \, \{T_2^{\#}\}}$$

$$[\text{If}] \quad \dfrac{G_0 \vdash \{T_0^{\#}\} \, C_1 \, \{T^{\#}\} \quad G_0 \vdash \{T_0^{\#}\} \, C_2 \, \{T^{\#}\}}{G \vdash \{T_0^{\#}\} \, \text{if } E \text{ then } C_1 \text{ else } C_2 \, \{T^{\#}\}} \quad \begin{array}{l} \text{if } \; G \subseteq G_0 \\ \text{and } w \notin G_0 \Rightarrow \forall x \in \text{fv}(E) \bullet [x \,\#\, w] \in T_0^{\#} \end{array}$$

$$[\text{While}] \quad \dfrac{G_0 \vdash \{T^{\#}\} \, C \, \{T^{\#}\}}{G \vdash \{T^{\#}\} \, \text{while } E \text{ do } C \, \{T^{\#}\}} \quad \begin{array}{l} \text{if } \; G \subseteq G_0 \\ \text{and } w \notin G_0 \Rightarrow \forall x \in \text{fv}(E) \bullet [x \,\#\, w] \in T^{\#} \end{array}$$

$$[\text{Sub}] \quad \dfrac{G_1 \vdash \{T_1^{\#}\} \, C \, \{T_2^{\#}\}}{G_0 \vdash \{T_0^{\#}\} \, C \, \{T_3^{\#}\}} \quad \text{if } T_0^{\#} \preceq T_1^{\#} \text{ and } T_2^{\#} \preceq T_3^{\#} \text{ and } G_0 \subseteq G_1$$

Fig. 2. The Hoare Logic.

$$
\begin{array}{ll}
& \{[l \,\#\, h, x], [h \,\#\, l, x], [x \,\#\, l, h]\} \\
x := h & \{[l \,\#\, h, x], [h \,\#\, l, x], [x \,\#\, l, x]\} \\
\text{if } x > 0 & (G \text{ is now } \{h\}) \\
\quad \text{then } l := 7 & \{[l \,\#\, x, l], [h \,\#\, l, x], [x \,\#\, l, x]\} \\
\quad \text{else } x := 0 & \{[l \,\#\, h, x], [h \,\#\, l, x], [x \,\#\, l, x]\} \\
\quad \text{end of if} & \{[l \,\#\, x], [h \,\#\, l, x], [x \,\#\, l, x]\}
\end{array}
$$

A few remarks:

- in the preamble, only x is assigned, so the independences for l and h are carried through, but $[x \,\#\, l, x]$ holds afterwards, as $[h \,\#\, l, x]$ holds beforehand;
- the free variable in the guard is independent of l and x but not of h, implying that h has to be in G.

5   Correctness

We are now in a position to prove the correctness of the Hoare logic with respect to the trace semantics.

Theorem 2. *Assume that*

$$G \vdash \{T_0^{\#}\} \, C \, \{T^{\#}\} \text{ where for all } [x \,\#\, y] \in T_0^{\#}, \text{ it is the case that } x \neq y.$$

Then, initial T implies $T^{\#} \models [\![C]\!](T)$.

That is, if T is an *initial set*, then $T^{\#}$ correctly describes the set of concrete traces obtained by executing command C on T.

The correctness theorem can be seen as the noninterference theorem for information flow. Indeed, with l and h interpreted as "low" and "high" respectively, suppose $[l \mathbin{\#} h]$ appears in $T^{\#}$. Then any two traces in $[\![C]\!](T)$ (the set of traces resulting from the execution of command C from initial set T) that have initial values that differ only on h, must agree on the current value of l.

Note that the correctness result deals with "terminating" traces only. For example, with $P = \texttt{while } h \neq 0 \texttt{ do } h := 7$ and $T^{\#} = \{[l \mathbin{\#} h], [h \mathbin{\#} l]\}$ we have the judgement $\emptyset \vdash \{T^{\#}\} P \{T^{\#}\}$ (since $\{h\} \vdash \{T^{\#}\} h := 7 \{T^{\#}\}$) showing that P is deemed secure by our logic, yet an observer able to observe non-termination can detect whether h was initially 0 or not.

To prove Theorem 2, we claim the following, more general, lemma. Then the theorem follows by the lemma using Fact 1.

Lemma 1. *If $G \vdash \{T_0^{\#}\} C \{T^{\#}\}$ and $T_0^{\#} \models T$ then also $T^{\#} \models [\![C]\!](T)$.*

6   Computing Independences

In Fig. 3 we define a function

$$sp : \mathbf{Context} \times \mathbf{Cmd} \times \mathbf{Independ} \to \mathbf{Independ}$$

with the intuition (formalized below) that given a control dependence G, a command C and a precondition $T^{\#}$, $sp(G, C, T^{\#})$ computes a postcondition $T_1^{\#}$ such that $G \vdash \{T^{\#}\} C \{T_1^{\#}\}$ holds, and $T_1^{\#}$ is the "largest" set (wrt. the subset ordering) that makes the judgement hold. Thus we compute the "strongest provable postcondition", which might differ[3] from the strongest *semantic* postcondition, that is, the largest set $T_1^{\#}$ such that for all T, if $T^{\#} \models T$ then $T_1^{\#} \models [\![C]\!](T)$.

In the companion technical report [2], we show how to also compute "weakest precondition"; we conjecture that the developments in Sections 7 and 9 could also be carried out using weakest precondition instead of strongest postcondition.

We now explain two of the cases in Fig. 3. In an assignment, $x := E$, the postcondition carries over all independences $[y \mathbin{\#} w]$ in the precondition if $y \neq x$; these independences are unaffected by the assignment to x. Suppose that w does not occur in context G. Then x is not control dependent on w. Moreover, if all variables referenced in E are independent of w, then $[x \mathbin{\#} w]$ will be in the postcondition of the assignment.

The case for $\texttt{while}$ is best explained by means of an example.

Example 3. Consider the program

$$C = \texttt{while } y \texttt{ do } l := x \; ; x := y \; ; y := h.$$

Let $T_0^{\#} \ldots T_8^{\#}$ be given by the following table. For example, the entry in the column for $T_4^{\#}$ and in the row for x shows that $[x \mathbin{\#} h] \in T_4^{\#}$ and $[x \mathbin{\#} l] \in T_4^{\#}$.

---

[3] For example, let $C = l := h - h$ and $T^{\#} = \{[l \mathbin{\#} h]\}$. Then $[l \mathbin{\#} h]$ is in the strongest semantic postcondition, since for all T and all $t \in [\![C]\!](T)$ we have cur-$t(l) = 0$ and therefore $[l \mathbin{\#} h] \models [\![C]\!]T$, but not in the strongest provable postcondition.

$sp(G, x := E, T^\#) =$
$$\{[y \# w] \mid y \neq x \wedge [y \# w] \in T^\#\} \cup \{[x \# w] \mid w \notin G \wedge \forall y \in \mathrm{fv}(E) \bullet [y \# w] \in T^\#\}$$

$sp(G, C_1 \, ; C_2, T^\#) = sp(G, C_2, sp(G, C_1, T^\#))$

$sp(G, \text{if } E \text{ then } C_1 \text{ else } C_2, T^\#) =$
$\quad$ let $G_0 = G \cup \{w \mid \exists x \in \mathrm{fv}(E) \bullet [x \# w] \notin T^\#\}$
$\qquad T_1^\# = sp(G_0, C_1, T^\#)$
$\qquad T_2^\# = sp(G_0, C_2, T^\#)$
$\quad$ in $T_1^\# \cap T_2^\#$

$sp(G, \text{while } E \text{ do } C_0, T^\#) =$
$\quad$ let $\mathcal{H}_C^{T^\#, G} : \textbf{Independ} \to \textbf{Independ}$ be given by $(C = \text{while } E \text{ do } C_0)$
$\qquad \mathcal{H}_C^{T^\#, G}(T_0^\#) =$
$\qquad\quad$ let $G_0 = G \cup \{w \mid \exists x \in \mathrm{fv}(E) \bullet [x \# w] \notin T_0^\#\}$
$\qquad\quad$ in $sp(G_0, C_0, T_0^\#) \cap T^\#$
$\quad$ in $lfp(\mathcal{H}_C^{T^\#, G})$

Fig. 3. Strongest Postcondition.

	$T_0^\#$	$T_1^\#$	$T_2^\#$	$T_3^\#$	$T_4^\#$	$T_5^\#$	$T_6^\#$	$T_7^\#$	$T_8^\#$
$h \#$	$\{l, x, y\}$	$\{l, x, y\}$	$\{l, x, y\}$	$\{l, x, y\}$	$\{l, x, y\}$	$\{l, x, y\}$	$\{l, x, y\}$	$\{l, x, y\}$	$\{l, x, y\}$
$l \#$	$\{h, x, y\}$	$\{h, l\}$	$\{h, l\}$	$\{h, l\}$	$\{h\}$	$\{l\}$	$\{l\}$	$\emptyset$	$\{l\}$
$x \#$	$\{h, l, y\}$	$\{h, l, y\}$	$\{h, l, x\}$	$\{h, l, x\}$	$\{h, l\}$	$\{h, l\}$	$\{l, x\}$	$\{l\}$	$\{l\}$
$y \#$	$\{h, l, x\}$	$\{h, l, x\}$	$\{h, l, x\}$	$\{l, x\}$	$\{l, x\}$	$\{l, x\}$	$\{l, x\}$	$\{l, x\}$	$\{l, x\}$

Our goal is to compute $sp(\emptyset, C, T_0^\#)$ and doing so involves the fixed point computation sketched below.

		Iteration	
	first	second	third
while y do	$T_0^\#$	$T_4^\# = T_3^\# \cap T_0^\#$	$T_7^\# = T_6^\# \cap T_0^\#$
G_0 :	$\{y\}$	$\{h, y\}$	$\{h, y\}$
$l := x$	$T_1^\#$	$T_5^\#$	$T_8^\#$
$x := y$	$T_2^\#$	$T_6^\#$	$T_6^\#$
$y := h$	$T_3^\#$	$T_6^\#$	$T_6^\#$

For example, the entry $T_6^\#$ in the column marked "second" and in the second row from the bottom, denotes that $sp(\{h, y\}, x := y, T_5^\#) = T_6^\#$.

Note that after the first iteration, $[l \# h]$ is still present; it takes a second iteration to filter it out and thus detect insecurity. The third iteration affirms that $T_7^\#$ is indeed a fixed point (of the functional $\mathcal{H}_C^{T_0^\#, \emptyset}$ defined in Fig. 3).

Theorem 3 states the correctness of the function sp, that it indeed computes a postcondition. Then, Theorem 4 states that the postcondition computed by sp is the strongest postcondition. We shall rely on the following property:

Lemma 2 (Monotonicity). *For all* C, *the following holds (for all* G, G_1, $T^{\#}, T_1^{\#}$ *):*

1. *if* $G \subseteq G_1$ *then* $sp(G, C, T^{\#}) \preceq sp(G_1, C, T^{\#})$;
2. *if* $T^{\#} \preceq T_1^{\#}$ *then* $sp(G, C, T^{\#}) \preceq sp(G, C, T_1^{\#})$.

Theorem 3. *For all* C, G, $T^{\#}$, *it holds that* $G \vdash \{T^{\#}\} \, C \, \{sp(G, C, T^{\#})\}$.

Theorem 4. *For all judgements* $G \vdash \{T_1^{\#}\} \, C \, \{T^{\#}\}$, $sp(G, C, T_1^{\#}) \preceq T^{\#}$.

The following result is useful for the developments in Sections 7 and 9:

Lemma 3. *Given* y, C *with* $y \notin$ modified(C). *Then for all* $T^{\#}$, G, w: $[y \# w] \in T^{\#}$ *implies* $[y \# w] \in sp(G, C, T^{\#})$.

7 Modularity and the Frame Rule

Define $lhs(T^{\#}) = \{y \mid [y \# w] \in T^{\#}\}$. Then we have

Theorem 5 (Frame rule (I)). *Let* $T_0^{\#}$ *and* C *be given. Then for all* $T^{\#}$, G:

1. *If* $lhs(T_0^{\#}) \cap$ modified$(C) = \emptyset$ *then* $sp(G, C, T^{\#} \cup T_0^{\#}) \supseteq sp(G, C, T^{\#}) \cup T_0^{\#}$.
2. *If* $lhs(T_0^{\#}) \cap$ fv$(C) = \emptyset$ *then* $sp(G, C, T^{\#} \cup T_0^{\#}) = sp(G, C, T^{\#}) \cup T_0^{\#}$.

Note that the weaker premise in 1 does not imply the stronger consequence in 2, since (with $[z \# w]$ playing the role of $T_0^{\#}$)

$$sp(\emptyset, x := y + z, \{[y \# w]\} \cup \{[z \# w]\}) = \{[y \# w], [z \# w], [x \# w]\}$$
$$sp(\emptyset, x := y + z, \{[y \# w]\}) \cup \{[z \# w]\} = \{[y \# w], [z \# w]\}.$$

In separation logic [17, 25], the frame rule is motivated by the desire for local reasoning: if C_1 and C_2 modify disjoint regions of a heap, reasoning about C_1 can be performed independently of the reasoning about C_2. In our setting, a consequence of the frame rule is that when analyzing a command C occurring in a larger context, the relevant independences are the ones whose left hand sides occur in C.

Theorem 5 is proved by observing that part (1) follows from Lemmas 3 and 2; then part (2) follows using the following result:

Lemma 4. *Let* $T_0^{\#}$ *and* C *be given, with* $lhs(T_0^{\#}) \cap$ fv$(C) = \emptyset$. *Then for all* $T^{\#}$ *and* G, $sp(G, C, T^{\#} \cup T_0^{\#}) \subseteq sp(G, C, T^{\#}) \cup T_0^{\#}$.

As a consequence of Theorem 5 we get the following result:

Corollary 1 (Frame rule (II)). *Assume that* $G \vdash \{T_1^{\#}\} \, C \, \{T_2^{\#}\}$ *and that* $lhs(T_0^{\#}) \cap$ modified$(C) = \emptyset$. *Then* $G \vdash \{T_1^{\#} \cup T_0^{\#}\} \, C \, \{T_2^{\#} \cup T_0^{\#}\}$.

Proof. Using Theorems 5 and 4 we get $sp(G, C, T_1^{\#} \cup T_0^{\#}) \supseteq sp(G, C, T_1^{\#}) \cup T_0^{\#} \supseteq T_2^{\#} \cup T_0^{\#}$. Since by Theorem 3 we have $G \vdash \{T_1^{\#} \cup T_0^{\#}\} \, C \, \{sp(G, C, T_1^{\#} \cup T_0^{\#})\}$, the result follows by [Sub].

A traditional view of modularity in the security literature is the "hook-up property" [19]: if two programs are secure then their composition is secure as well. Our logic satisfies the hook-up property for sequential composition; in our context, a secure program is one which has $[l \# h]$ as an invariant (if $[l \# h]$ is in the precondition, it is also in the strongest postcondition). With this interpretation, Sabelfeld and Sands's hook-up theorem holds [28, Theorem 5].

8   The Smith-Volpano Security Type System

In the Smith-Volpano type system [29], variables are labelled by security types; for example, $x : (T, \kappa)$ means that x has type T and security level κ. To handle implicit flows due to conditionals, the technical development requires commands to be typed ($\mathbf{com}\,\kappa$) with the intention that all variables assigned to in such commands have level at least κ. The judgement $\Gamma \vdash C : (\mathbf{com}\,\kappa)$ says that in the security type context Γ, that binds free variables in C to security types, command C has type ($\mathbf{com}\,\kappa$).

We now show a conservative extension: if a command is well-typed in the Smith-Volpano system, then for any two traces, the current values of low variables are independent of the initial values of high variables. For simplicity, we consider a command with only two variables, h with level H and l with level L.

Theorem 6. *Assume that C can be given a security type wrt. environment* $h : (\_, H), l : (\_, L)$. *Then for all $T^\#$, if $[l \# h] \in T^\#$ then $[l \# h] \in sp(\emptyset, C, T^\#)$.*

The upshot of the theorem is that a well-typed program has $[l \# h]$ as *invariant*: if $[l \# h]$ appears in the precondition, then it also appears in the strongest postcondition.

9   Counter-Example Generation

Assume that a program C cannot be deemed secure by our logic, that is, $[l \# h] \notin sp(\emptyset, C, T^\#)$ (where $T^\# \supseteq \{[l \# h]\}$). Then we might expect that we can find a "witness": two different initial values of h that produce two different final values of l. However, below we shall see three examples of false positives: programs which, while deemed insecure by our logic, do not immediately satisfy that property. Ideally, we would like to strengthen our analysis so as to rule out such false positives; this does not seem immediately feasible and instead, in order to arrive at a suitable result, we shall modify our semantics so the false positives become genuine positives. The programs in question are:

$$l := h - h. \tag{1}$$

$$\mathtt{if}\ h\ \mathtt{then}\ l := 7\ \mathtt{else}\ l := 7 \tag{2}$$

$$\mathtt{while}\ h\ \mathtt{do}\ l := 7 \tag{3}$$

To deal with (1), a program where writing a high expression to a low variable does not reveal anything about the high variable, we shall assume that expressions are unevaluated (kept as symbolic trees); formally we demand that if there exists $z \in \mathrm{fv}(E)$ with $\neg(t_1 \stackrel{z}{=} t_2)$, then $[\![E]\!](t_1) \neq [\![E]\!](t_2)$.

To deal with (2), a program where writing to a low variable under high guard does not immediately enable an observer to determine the value of the high variable, we *tag* each assignment statement so that an observer can detect which branch is taken.

Finally, we must deal with (3), a program where there cannot be two different final values of l. There seems to be no simple way to fix this, except to *rule out loops*, thus in effect considering only programs with a fixed bound on run-time (since for such, a loop can be unfolded repeatedly and eventually replaced by a sequence of conditionals; this is how we handle loops with low guard). Remember (cf. Section 5) that a program deemed *secure* by our logic may not be really secure if non-termination can be observed; similarly a program deemed *insecure* may not be really insecure if non-termination cannot be observed.

Even with the above modifications, the existence of a witness is not amenable to a compositional proof. For consider the program $x := E_1(h) \; ; l := E_2(x)$ where E_1 and E_2 are some expressions. Inductively, on the assignment to l, we can find two different values for x, v_1 and v_2, such that the resulting values of l are different. But we then need an extremely strong property concerning the assignment to x: that there exists two different values of h such that evaluating $E_1(h)$ wrt. these values produces v_1, respectively v_2.

Instead, we shall settle for a result which says that *all* pairs of different initial values for h are witnesses, in that the resulting values of l are different. Of course, we need to introduce some extra assumptions to establish this stronger property. For example, consider the program if $h = 0$ then $l := 17$ else $l := 7$ where two different values of h, say 3 and 4, may cause the same branch to be taken. To deal with that, our result must say that for every two values of h there exists an interpretation of *true?* such that wrt. that interpretation, different values of l result. In the above, we might stipulate that $true?(3 = 0)$ but not $true?(4 = 0)$. It turns out to be convenient to let that interpretation depend on the guard in question; hence we shall also tag guards so as to distinguish between different occurrences of the same guard.

We thus end up with a semantics $[\![C]\!]_\mathcal{I}$ parametrized wrt. an interpretation $\mathcal{I}$; the full development is in [2] where the following result is proved:

Theorem 7. *Assume that* $sp(\emptyset, C, T^\#) = T_1^\#$, *with* $[x \,\#\, h] \in T^\#$ *for* $x \neq h$ *and with* $[l \,\#\, h] \notin T_1^\#$. *Further assume that* $\neg(t_1 \overset{h}{=} t_2)$, *with the tags of* t_1 *and* t_2 *being disjoint from the tags in* C.

Then there exists an interpretation $\mathcal{I}$ *such that* $\neg([\![C]\!]_\mathcal{I}(t_1) \overset{l}{=} [\![C]\!]_\mathcal{I}(t_2))$.

10   Discussion

Perspective. This paper specifies an information flow analysis for confidentiality using a Hoare-like logic and considers an application of the logic to explaining *insecurity* in simple imperative programs. Program traces, potentially infinitely many, are abstracted by finite sets of variable independences. These variable independences can be statically computed using strongest postconditions, and can be statically checked against the logic.

Giacobazzi and Mastroeni [12] consider attackers as abstract interpretations and generalize the notion of noninterference by parameterizing it wrt. what an attacker can analyze about the input/output information flow. For instance, assume an attacker can only analyze the *parity* (odd/even) of values. Then

while h do $l := l + 2$; $h := h - 1$

is secure, although it contains an update of a low variable under a high guard. We might try to model this approach in our framework by parameterizing Definition 1 wrt. parity, but it is not clear how to alter the proof rules accordingly. Instead, we envision our logic to be put on top of abstract interpretations. In the above example, the program would be abstracted to while h do $h := h - 1$ which our logic already deems secure.

Related Work. Perhaps the most closely related work is the one of Clark, Hankin, and Hunt [6], who consider a language similar to ours and then extend it to Idealized Algol, requiring distinguishing between identifiers and locations. The analysis for Idealized Algol is split in two stages: the first stage does a control-flow analysis, specified using a flow logic [20]. The second stage specifies what is an acceptable information flow analysis with respect to the control-flow analysis. The precision of the control-flow analysis influences the precision of the information flow analysis. Flow logics usually do not come with a frame rule so it is unclear what modularity properties their analysis satisfies. For each statement S in the program, they compute the set of dependences introduced by S; a pair (x, y) is in that set if different values for y prior to execution of S may result in different values for x after execution of S. For a complete program, they thus, as expected, compute essentially the same information as we do, but the information computed *locally* is different from ours: we estimate if different *initial* values of y, i.e., values of y prior to execution of *the whole program*, may result in different values for x after execution of S. Unlike our approach, their analysis is termination-sensitive.

To make our logic termination-sentitive, we could (analogous in spirit to [6]) define $[\perp \# w]$ to mean that if two tuples of initial values are equal except for on w, then either both tuples give rise to terminating computations, or both tuples give rise to infinite computations. For instance, if

$\vdash \{T_0^\#\}$ while $x > 7$ do $x := x + 1$ $\{T^\#\}$

and $[x \# h]$ does not belong to $T_0^\#$ then $[\perp \# h]$ should not belong to $T^\#$ (neither of any subsequent assertion), since different values of h may result in different values of x and hence of different termination properties. To prove semantic correctness for the revised logic we would need to also revise our semantics, since currently it does not facilitate reasoning about infinite computations.

Joshi and Leino [18] provide an elegant semantic characterization of noninterference that allows handling both termination-sensitive and termination-insensitive noninterference. Their notion of security for a command C is equationally characterized by C ; $HH = HH$; C ; HH, where HH means that an arbitrary value is assigned to a high variable. They show how to express their notion of security in Dijkstra's weakest precondition calculus. Although they do not consider synthesizing loop invariants, this can certainly be done via a fixpoint computation with weakest preconditions. However, their work is not concerned with computing dependences, nor do they consider generating counterexamples.

Darvas, Hähnle and Sands [10] use dynamic logic to express secure information flow in JavaCard. They discuss several ways that noninterference can be expressed in a program logic, one of which is as follows: consider a program with variables l and h. Consider another copy of the program with l, h relabeled to fresh variables l', h' respectively. Then, noninterference holds in the following situation: running the original program and the copy sequentially such that the initial state satisfies $l = l'$ should yield a final state satisfying $l = l'$. Like us, they are interested in showing insecurity by exhibiting distinct initial values for high variables that give distinct current values of low variables; unlike us, they look at actual runtime values. To achieve this accuracy, they need the power of a general purpose theorem prover, which is also helpful in that they can express declassification, as well as treat exceptions (which most approaches based on static analysis cannot easily be extended to deal with).

Barthe, D'Argenio and Rezk [5] use the same idea of self-composition (i.e., composing a program with a copy of itself) as Darvas et alii and investigate "abstract" noninterference [12] for several languages. By parameterizing non-interference with a property, they are able to handle more general information flow policies, including a form of declassification known as delimited information release [26]. They show how self-composition can be formulated in logics describing these languages, namely, Hoare logic, separation logic, linear temporal logic, etc. They also discuss how to use their results for model checking programs with finite state spaces to check satisfaction of their generalized definition of noninterference.

The first work that used a Hoare-style semantics to reason about information flow was by Andrews and Reitman [3]. Their assertions keep track of the security level of variables, and are able to deal even with parallel programs. However, no formal correctness result is stated.

Conclusion. This paper was inspired in part by presentations by Roberto Giacobazzi and Reiner Hähnle at the Dagstuhl Seminar on Language-based Security in October 2003. The reported work is only the first step in our goal to formulate more general definitions of noninterference in terms of program (in)dependence, such that the definitions support modular reasoning. One direction to consider is to repeat the work in this paper for a richer language, with methods, pointers, objects and dynamic memory allocation; an obvious goal here is interprocedural reasoning about variable independences perhaps using a higher-order version of the frame rule [22]. Hähnle's Dagstuhl presentation inspired us to look at explaining insecurity by showing counterexamples. We plan to experiment with model checkers supporting linear arithmetic, for example BLAST [15], to *(i)* establish independences that our logic cannot find (cf. the false positives from Sect. 9); *(ii)* provide "genuine" counterexamples that are counterexamples wrt. the original semantics.

Acknowledgements

We would like to thank Reiner Hähnle, Peter O'Hearn, Tamara Rezk, David Sands, and Hongseok Yang, as well as the participants of the *Open Software Quality* meeting in Santa Cruz, May 2004, and the anonymous reviewers, for useful comments on a draft of this paper.

References

1. Martín Abadi, Anindya Banerjee, Nevin Heintze, and Jon G. Riecke. A core calculus of dependency. In *ACM Symposium on Principles of Programming Languages (POPL)*, pages 147–160, 1999.
2. Torben Amtoft and Anindya Banerjee. Information flow analysis in logical form. Technical Report CIS TR 2004-3, Kansas State University, April 2004.
3. G. R. Andrews and R. P. Reitman. An axiomatic approach to information flow in programs. *ACM Transactions on Programming Languages and Systems*, 2(1):56–75, January 1980.
4. Anindya Banerjee and David A. Naumann. Secure information flow and pointer confinement in a Java-like language. In *IEEE Computer Security Foundations Workshop (CSFW)*, pages 253–270. IEEE Computer Society Press, 2002.
5. Gilles Barthe, Pedro R. D'Argenio, and Tamara Rezk. Secure information flow by self-composition. In *IEEE Computer Security Foundations Workshop (CSFW)*, 2004. To appear.
6. David Clark, Chris Hankin, and Sebastian Hunt. Information flow for Algol-like languages. *Computer Languages*, 28(1):3–28, 2002.
7. Ellis S. Cohen. Information transmission in sequential programs. In Richard A. DeMillo, David P. Dobkin, Anita K. Jones, and Richard J. Lipton, editors, *Foundations of Secure Computation*, pages 297–335. Academic Press, 1978.
8. Patrick Cousot and Radhia Cousot. Abstract interpretation: a unified lattice model for static analysis of programs by construction or approximation of fixpoints. In *ACM Symposium on Principles of Programming Languages (POPL)*, pages 238–252. ACM Press, New York, NY, 1977.
9. Patrick Cousot and Radhia Cousot. Automatic synthesis of optimal invariant assertions: mathematical foundations. In *Proceedings of the ACM Symposium on Artificial Intelligence and Programming Languages, SIGPLAN Notices*, volume 12, pages 1–12. ACM Press, August 1977.
10. Ádám Darvas, Reiner Hähnle, and Dave Sands. A theorem proving approach to analysis of secure information flow. Technical Report 2004-01, Department of Computing Science, Chalmers University of Technology and Göteborg University, 2004. A fuller version of a paper appearing in Workshop on Issues in the Theory of Security, 2003.
11. Dorothy Denning and Peter Denning. Certification of programs for secure information flow. *Communications of the ACM*, 20(7):504–513, 1977.
12. Roberto Giacobazzi and Isabella Mastroeni. Abstract non-interference: Parameterizing non-interference by abstract interpretation. In *ACM Symposium on Principles of Programming Languages (POPL)*, pages 186–197, 2004.
13. J. Goguen and J. Meseguer. Security policies and security models. In *Proc. IEEE Symp. on Security and Privacy*, pages 11–20, 1982.

14. Nevin Heintze and Jon G. Riecke. The SLam calculus: programming with secrecy and integrity. In *ACM Symposium on Principles of Programming Languages (POPL)*, pages 365–377, 1998.
15. Thomas A. Henzinger, Ranjit Jhala, Rupak Majumdar, and Gregoire Sutre. Software verification with Blast. In *Tenth International Workshop on Model Checking of Software (SPIN)*, volume 2648 of *Lecture Notes in Computer Science*, pages 235–239. Springer-Verlag, 2003.
16. Sebastian Hunt and David Sands. Binding time analysis: A new PERspective. In *Partial Evaluation and Semantics-Based Program Manipulation (PEPM '91)*, volume 26 (9) of *Sigplan Notices*, pages 154–165, 1991.
17. Samin Ishtiaq and Peter W. O'Hearn. BI as an assertion language for mutable data structures. In *ACM Symposium on Principles of Programming Languages (POPL)*, pages 14–26, 2001.
18. Rajeev Joshi and K. Rustan M. Leino. A semantic approach to secure information flow. *Science of Computer Programming*, 37:113–138, 2000.
19. Daryl McCullough. Specifications for multi-level security and a hook-up. In *IEEE Symposium on Security and Privacy, April 27-29, 1987*, pages 161–166, 1987.
20. Flemming Nielson, Hanne Riis Nielson, and Chris Hankin. *Principles of Program Analysis*. Springer-Verlag, 1999. Web page at
www.imm.dtu.dk/~riis/PPA/ppa.html.
21. Peter O'Hearn, John Reynolds, and Hongseok Yang. Local reasoning about programs that alter data structures. In *Computer Science Logic*, volume 2142 of *LNCS*, pages 1–19. Springer, 2001.
22. Peter O'Hearn, Hongseok Yang, and John Reynolds. Separation and information hiding. In *ACM Symposium on Principles of Programming Languages (POPL)*, pages 268–280, 2004.
23. Peter Ørbæk and Jens Palsberg. Trust in the λ-calculus. *Journal of Functional Programming*, 7(6):557–591, November 1997.
24. François Pottier and Vincent Simonet. Information flow inference for ML. *ACM Transactions on Programming Languages and Systems*, 25(1):117–158, January 2003.
25. John C. Reynolds. Separation logic: a logic for shared mutable data structures. In *IEEE Symposium on Logic in Computer Science (LICS)*, pages 55–74. IEEE Computer Society Press, 2002.
26. Andrei Sabelfeld and Andrew Myers. A model for delimited information release. In *Proceedings of the International Symposium on Software Security (ISSS'03)*, 2004. To appear.
27. Andrei Sabelfeld and Andrew C. Myers. Language-based information-flow security. *IEEE J. Selected Areas in Communications*, 21(1):5–19, January 2003.
28. Andrei Sabelfeld and David Sands. A Per model of secure information flow in sequential programs. *Higher-order and Symbolic Computation*, 14(1):59–91, 2001.
29. Dennis Volpano and Geoffrey Smith. A type-based approach to program security. In *Proceedings of TAPSOFT'97*, number 1214 in Lecture Notes in Computer Science, pages 607–621. Springer-Verlag, 1997.

Type Inference Against Races[*]

Cormac Flanagan[1] and Stephen N. Freund[2]

[1] Dept. of Computer Science, University of California at Santa Cruz
Santa Cruz, CA 95064
[2] Dept. of Computer Science, Williams College, Williamstown, MA 01267

Abstract. The race condition checker `rccjava` uses a formal type system to statically identify potential race conditions in concurrent Java programs, but it requires programmer-supplied type annotations. This paper describes a type inference algorithm for `rccjava`. Due to the interaction of parameterized classes and dependent types, this type inference problem is NP-complete. This complexity result motivates our new approach to type inference, which is via reduction to propositional satisfiability. This paper describes our type inference algorithm and its performance on programs of up to 30,000 lines of code.

1 Introduction

A race condition occurs when two threads in a concurrent program manipulate a shared data structure simultaneously, without synchronization. Errors caused by race conditions are notoriously hard to catch using testing because they are scheduling dependent and difficult to reproduce. Typically, programmers attempt to avoid race conditions by adopting a programming discipline in which shared variables are protected by locks.

In a previous paper [10], we described a static analysis tool called `rccjava` that enforces this lock-based synchronization discipline. The analysis performed by `rccjava` is formalized as a type system, and it incorporates features such as *dependent types* (where the type of a field describes the lock protecting it) and *parameterized classes* (where fields in different instances of a class can be protected by different locks).

Our previous evaluation of `rccjava` indicates that it is effective for catching race conditions. However, `rccjava` relies on programmer-inserted type annotations that describe the locking discipline, such as which lock protects a particular field. The need for these type annotations limits `rccjava`'s applicability to large, legacy systems. Hence, to achieve practical static race detection for large programs, annotation inference techniques are necessary.

In previous work along these lines, we developed Houdini/rcc [11], a type inference algorithm for `rccjava` that heuristically generates a large set of candidate type annotations and then iteratively removes all invalid annotations. However, this approach could not handle parameterized classes or methods, which limits its ability to handle many of the synchronization idioms of real programs.

---

[*] This work was supported in part by the National Science Foundation under Grants CCR-0341179 and CCR-0341387.

R. Giacobazzi (Ed.): SAS 2004, LNCS 3148, pp. 116–132, 2004.

In the presence of parameterized classes, the type inference problem for rccjava is NP-complete, meaning that any type inference algorithm will have an exponential worst-case behavior. This complexity result motivates our new approach to type inference, which is via reduction to propositional satisfiability. That is, given an unannotated (or partially-annotated) program, we translate this program into a propositional formula that is satisfiable if and only if the original program is typeable. Moreover, after computing a satisfying assignment for the generated formula, we translate this assignment into appropriate annotations for the program, yielding a valid, explicitly-typed program. This approach works well in practice, and we report on its performance on programs of up to 30,000 lines of code.

Producing a small number of meaningful error messages for erroneous or untypeable programs is often challenging. We tackle this aspect of type inference by generating a weighted MAX-SAT problem [4] and producing error messages for the unsatisfied clauses in the optimal solution. Our experience shows that the resulting warnings often correspond to errors in the original program, such as accessing a field without holding the appropriate lock.

We have implemented our algorithm in the *Rcc/Sat* tool for multithreaded Java programs. Experiments on benchmark programs demonstrate that it is effective at inferring valid type annotations for multithreaded code. The algorithm's precision is significantly improved by performing a number of standard analyses, such as control-flow and escape analysis, prior to type checking.

The key contributions of this paper include:

- a type inference algorithm based on reduction to propositional satisfiability;
- a refinement of this approach to generate useful error messages via reduction to weighted MAX-SAT; and
- experimental results that validate the effectiveness of this approach.

The annotations constructed by Rcc/Sat also provide valuable documentation to the programmer; facilitate checking other properties such as atomicity [16, 15, 12]; and can help reduce state explosion in model checkers [24, 25, 14, 9].

2   Types Against Races

2.1   Type Checking

This section introduces RFJ2, an idealized multithreaded subset of Java with a type system that guarantees race freedom for well-typed programs. This type system extends our previous work on the rccjava type system [10], for example with parameterized methods. To clarify our presentation, RFJ2 also simplifies some aspects of rccjava. For example, it does not support inheritance. (Inheritance and other aspects of the full Java programming language are dealt with in our implementation, described in Section 4.)

An RFJ2 program (see Figure 1) is a sequence of class declarations together with an initial expression. Each class declaration associates a class name with a body that consists of a sequence of field and method declarations. The self-reference variable "this" is implicitly bound within the class body.

$$
\begin{array}{lll}
P & ::= defn^{\Box}\ e & \text{(program)} \\
defn & ::= \texttt{class}\ cn\langle \texttt{ghost}\ x^{\Box}\rangle\ \{\ field^{\Box}\ meth^{\Box}\ \} & \text{(class declaration)} \\
field & ::= t\ fn\ \texttt{guarded\_by}\ l & \text{(field declaration)} \\
meth & ::= t\ mn\langle \texttt{ghost}\ x^{\Box}\rangle(arg^{\Box})\ \texttt{requires}\ s\ \{\ e\ \} & \text{(method declaration)} \\
arg & ::= t\ x & \text{(argument declaration)} \\
c,t & ::= cn\langle l^{\Box}\rangle & \text{(type)} \\
l & ::= x\ |\ \alpha\ |\ l\cdot\theta & \text{(lock expression)} \\
s & ::= \emptyset\ |\ \{l\}\ |\ s\cup s\ |\ \beta\ |\ s\cdot\theta & \text{(lock set expression)} \\
\theta & ::= [x_1 := l_1,\ldots,x_n := l_n] & \text{(substitution)}
\end{array}
$$

$$
\begin{array}{ll}
e,f ::= x\ |\ \texttt{null}\ |\ \texttt{new}\ c(e^{\Box})\ |\ e.fn\ |\ e.fn = e\ |\ e.mn\langle l^{\Box}\rangle(e^{\Box}) & \text{(expressions)} \\
\quad\ |\ \texttt{let}\ x = e\ \texttt{in}\ e\ |\ \texttt{synchronized}\ x\ e\ |\ e.\texttt{fork}
\end{array}
$$

$$
\begin{array}{lll}
\alpha \in LockVar & x,y \in Var & fn \in FieldName \\
\beta \in LockSetVar & cn \in ClassName & mn \in MethodName
\end{array}
$$

Fig. 1. The idealized language RFJ2.

The RFJ2 language includes type annotations that specify the locking discipline. For example, the type annotation $\texttt{guarded\_by}\ x$ on a field declaration states that the lock denoted by the variable x must be held whenever that field is accessed (read or written). Similarly, the type annotation $\texttt{requires}\ x_1,\ldots,x_n$ on a method declaration states that these locks are held on method entry; the type system verifies that these locks are indeed held at each call-site of the method, and checks that the method body is race-free given this assumption.

The language provides *parameterized classes*, to allow the fields of a class to be protected by some lock external to the class. A parameterized class declaration

$$
\texttt{class}\ cn\langle \texttt{ghost}\ x_1\ldots x_n\rangle\ \{\ \ldots\ \}
$$

introduces a binding for the *ghost* variables $x_1\ldots x_n$, which can be referred to from type annotations within the class body. The type $cn\langle y_1\ldots y_n\rangle$ refers to an *instantiated version* of cn, where each x_i in the body is replaced by y_i. As an example, the type $\texttt{Hashtable}\langle y_1, y_2\rangle$ may denote a hashtable that is protected by lock y_1, where each element of the hashtable is protected by lock y_2.

The RFJ2 language also supports *parameterized method* declarations, such as

$$
t\ m\langle \texttt{ghost}\ x\rangle(cn\langle x\rangle\ y)\ \texttt{requires}\ x\ \{\ \ldots\ \}
$$

which defines a method m that is parameterized by lock x, and which takes an argument of type $cn\langle x\rangle$. A corresponding invocation $e.m\langle z\rangle(e')$ must supply a ghost argument z and an actual parameter e' of type $cn\langle z\rangle$.

Expressions include object allocation $\texttt{new}\ c(e^*)$, which initializes a new object's fields with its argument values; field read and update; method invocation; and variable binding and reference. The expression $\texttt{synchronized}\ x\ e$ is evaluated in a manner similar to Java's $\texttt{synchronized}$ statement: the lock for object

(a) Example Program **Ref**

```
class Lock⟨⟩ { }                             let lock = new Lock⟨⟩();
class Ref⟨ghost x⟩ {                            r1 = new Ref⟨α3⟩(1);
  int y guarded_by α1                           r2 = new Ref⟨α4⟩(2)
  boolean lessThan(Ref⟨α2⟩ o) requires β {   in synchronized (lock) {
    this.y < o.y ;                               r1.lessThan(r2);
  }                                            }
}
```

(b) Constraints

$$\alpha_1 \in \{ \text{ this, x } \}$$ decl. of y
$$\alpha_2 \in \{ \text{ this, x } \}$$ decl. of lessThan
$$\beta \subseteq \{ \text{ this, x, o } \}$$ decl. of lessThan
$$\alpha_3 \in \{ \text{ lock } \}$$ first new expr.
$$\alpha_4 \in \{ \text{ lock, r1 } \}$$ second new expr.

$$\alpha_1 \in \beta$$ access to this.y
$$\alpha_1[\text{this} := \text{o}, \text{x} := \alpha_2] \in \beta$$ access to o.y
$$\beta[\text{this} := \text{r1}, \text{x} := \alpha_3, \text{o} := \text{r2}] \subseteq \{\text{lock}\}$$ requires for call
$$\alpha_2[\text{this} := \text{r1}, \text{x} := \alpha_3, \text{o} := \text{r2}] = \alpha_4$$ arg. type for call

(c) Conditional Assignment

$$Y(\alpha_1) = (b_1?\text{this} : \text{x})$$ decl. of y
$$Y(\alpha_2) = (b_2?\text{this} : \text{x})$$ decl. of lessThan
$$Y(\beta) = (b_4?\text{this} : \emptyset) \cup (b_5?\text{x} : \emptyset) \cup (b_6?\text{o} : \emptyset)$$ decl. of lessThan
$$Y(\alpha_3) = \text{lock}$$ first new expr.
$$Y(\alpha_4) = (b_3?\text{lock} : \text{r1})$$ second new expr.

(d) Boolean Constraints

$$(b_1?\text{this} : \text{x}) \in (b_4?\text{this} : \emptyset) \cup (b_5?\text{x} : \emptyset) \cup (b_6?\text{o} : \emptyset)$$ access to this.y
$$(b_1?\text{o} : (b_2?\text{this} : \text{x})) \in (b_4?\text{this} : \emptyset) \cup (b_5?\text{x} : \emptyset) \cup (b_6?\text{o} : \emptyset)$$ access to o.y
$$(b_4?\text{r1} : \emptyset) \cup (b_5?\text{lock} : \emptyset) \cup (b_6?\text{r2} : \emptyset) \subseteq \{\text{lock}\}$$ requires for call
$$(b_2?\text{r1} : \text{lock}) = (b_3?\text{lock} : \text{r1})$$ arg. type for call

(e) Boolean Formula

$$[(b_1 \wedge b_4) \vee (\neg b_1 \wedge b_5)]$$ access to this.y
$$\wedge \ [(b_1 \wedge b_6) \vee (\neg b_1 \wedge ((b_2 \wedge b_4) \vee (\neg b_2 \wedge b_5)))]$$ access to o.y
$$\wedge \ [\neg b_4 \wedge \neg b_6]$$ requires for call
$$\wedge \ [(b_2 \wedge \neg b_3) \vee (\neg b_2 \wedge b_3)]$$ arg. type for call

Fig. 2. Example program and type inference constraints.

x is acquired, the subexpression e is then evaluated, and finally the lock is released. The expression $e.\text{fork}$ starts a new thread. Here, e should evaluate to an object that includes a nullary method **run**. The fork operation spawns a new thread that calls that **run** method.

The RFJ2 type system leverages parameterized methods to reason about thread-local data. (This approach replaces the escape by analysis embedded in our earlier type system [10].) Specifically, the **run** method of each forked thread takes a **ghost** parameter tl_lock denoting a *thread-local* lock that is always held by that thread:

$$t \ \text{run}\langle\text{ghost tl\_lock}\rangle() \ \text{requires tl\_lock} \ \{ \ e \ \}$$

Intuitively, the underlying run-time system creates and acquires this thread-local lock when a new thread is created. This lock may be used to guard thread-local data and may be passed as a ghost parameter to other methods that access thread-local data. In a similar fashion, we also introduce an implicit, globally-visible lock called main_lock, which is held by the initial program thread and can be used to protect data exclusively accessed by that thread.

2.2 Type Inference

Our previous evaluation of the race-free type system rccjava indicates that it is effective for catching race conditions [10]. However, the need for programmer-inserted annotations limits its applicability to large, legacy systems, which motivates the development of type inference techniques for race-free type systems.

In this paper we describe a novel type inference system for RFJ2. We introduce *lock variables* α and *lockset variables* β, collectively referred to as *locking variables*. Locking variables may be mentioned in type annotations, as in guarded_by α, requires β, or $cn\langle \alpha_1, \alpha_2 \rangle$. During type inference, each lock variable α is resolved to some specific program variable in scope, and each lock set variable β is resolved to some set of program variables in scope. As an example, Figure 2(a) presents a simple reference cell implementation, written in RFJ2 extended with primitive types and operations, that contains locking variables.

An RFJ2 program is *explicitly-typed* if it contains no locking variables. The *type inference* problem is, given a program with locking variables, to resolve these locking variables so that the resulting explicitly-typed program is well-typed.

Parameterized classes introduce substitutions that complicate the type inference problem. We use the notation $[x_1 := l_1, \ldots, x_n := l_n]$ to denote a substitution θ that replaces each program variable x_i with the lock expression l_i. To illustrate the need for these substitutions, consider the class declaration:

$$\text{class } cn\langle \text{ghost } x \rangle \ \{ \ t \ \textit{fn } \text{guarded\_by } l; \ \}$$

If a variable p has type $cn\langle y \rangle$, then the field $p.fn$ is protected by $\theta(l)$, where the substitution $\theta \equiv [x := y]$ replaces the formal ghost parameter x by the actual parameter y. The application of a substitution to most syntactic entities is straightforward; however, the application of a substitution θ to a lock expression l is delayed until any lock variables α in the lock expression are resolved. We use the syntax $l \cdot \theta$ to represent this *delayed substitution*. Similarly, if the *lock set expression* s denote the set of locks in a method's requires clause, then the application of a substitution θ to s yields the delayed substitution $s \cdot \theta$. The following examples illustrate substitutions on various syntactic entities. (Due to space limitations, we do not present an exhaustive definition.)

$$\theta(x) = l \quad \text{if } \theta \equiv [\ldots, x := l, \ldots]$$
$$\theta(\text{synchronized } x \ e) = \text{synchronized } \theta(x) \ \theta(e)$$
$$\theta(l) = l \cdot \theta$$
$$\theta(s) = s \cdot \theta$$

Since the type rules reason about delayed substitutions, we include these delayed substitutions in the programming language syntax, but we require that substitutions do not appear in source programs.

The type rules for RFJ2 generate a collection of *constraints* that contain delayed substitutions. These constraints include equality constraints between lock expressions and containment constraints between lock set expressions:

$$C ::= s \subseteq s \mid l = l$$

The core of the type system is defined by the judgment:

$$P; E; s \vdash e : t \ \& \ \bar{C}$$

Here, the program P is included to provide access to class declarations; E is an environment providing types for the free variables of the expression e; the lock set s describes the locks held when executing e; t is the type inferred for e; and $\bar{C}$ is the generated set of constraints.

Most of the type rules are straightforward. The complete set of type judgments and rules is contained in Appendix A. Here we briefly explain two of the more crucial rules. The rule for `synchronized` x e checks e with an extended lock set that includes x, since the lock x is held when evaluating e. The rule for $e.fn$ checks that e is a well-typed expression of some class type $cn\langle l_{1..n}\rangle$ and that cn has a field fn of type t, guarded by lock l.

$$\frac{P; E; s \vdash x : t' \ \& \ \bar{C} \qquad P; E; s \cup \{x\} \vdash e : t \ \& \ \bar{C}'}{P; E; s \vdash \mathtt{synchronized} \ x \ e : t \ \& \ (\bar{C} \cup \bar{C}')}$$

$$\frac{\begin{array}{c} P; E; s \vdash e : cn\langle l_{1..n}\rangle \ \& \ \bar{C} \\ \mathtt{class} \ cn\langle \mathtt{ghost} \ x_{1..n}\rangle \ \{\ldots t \ fn \ \mathtt{guarded\_by} \ l \ldots\} \in P \\ \theta = [\mathtt{this} := e, x_j := l_j \ ^{j \in 1..n}] \\ P; E \vdash \theta(t) \ \& \ \bar{C}' \end{array}}{P; E; s \vdash e.fn : \theta(t) \ \& \ (\bar{C} \cup \bar{C}' \cup \{\theta(l) \in s\})}$$

Since the protecting lock expression l (and type t) may refer to the ghost parameters $x_{1..n}$ and the implicitly-bound self-reference `this`, neither of which are in scope at the field access, we introduce the substitution θ which substitutes appropriate expressions for these variables. The constraint $\theta(l) \in s$, an abbreviation for $\{\theta(l)\} \subseteq s$, ensures that the substituted lock expression is in the current lock set. The type of the field dereference is computed by applying the substitution θ to the field type t, which must yield a well-formed type.

The type system defines the top-level judgment $P \vdash \bar{C}$, where $\bar{C}$ is the generated set of constraints for the program P. Applying these type rules to the example program `Ref` of Figure 2(a) yields the constraints shown in Figure 2(b). (We ignore `main_lock` in this example for simplicity).

We next address the question of when the generated constraints over the locking variables are satisfiable. An *assignment*

$$A : (LockVar \rightarrow Var) \cup (LockSetVar \rightarrow 2^{Var})$$

resolves lock and lock set variables to corresponding program variables and sets of program variables, respectively. We extend assignments to lock expressions, lock set expressions, and substitutions. In particular, since an assignment resolves all locking variables, any delayed substitutions can be immediately performed.

$$
\begin{array}{lll}
A : l \rightarrow Var & A : s \rightarrow 2^{Var} & A : \theta \rightarrow \theta \\
A(x) = x & A(\emptyset) = \emptyset & A([x_1 := l_1, \ldots, x_n := l_n]) = \\
A(l \cdot \theta) = A(\theta)(A(l)) & A(\{l\}) = \{A(l)\} & \quad [x_1 := A(l_1), \ldots, x_n := A(l_n)] \\
& A(s_1 \cup s_2) = A(s_1) \cup A(s_2) & \\
& A(s \cdot \theta) = A(\theta)(A(s)) &
\end{array}
$$

We also extend assignments in a compatible manner to other syntactic units, such as constraints, expressions, programs, etc.

An assignment A *satisfies* a constraint C (written $A \models C$) as follows:

$$A \models s_1 \subseteq s_2 \quad \text{iff} \quad A(s_1) \subseteq A(s_2)$$
$$A \models l_1 = l_2 \quad \text{iff} \quad A(l_1) = A(l_2)$$

If $A \models C$ for all $C \in \bar{C}$ then we say A is a *solution* for $\bar{C}$, written $A \models \bar{C}$. A set of constraints $\bar{C}$ is *valid*, written $\models \bar{C}$, if every assignment is a solution for $\bar{C}$. For example, the constraints of Figure 2(b) for the program Ref are satisfied by the assignment: $\alpha_1 = \alpha_2 = \mathtt{x}, \alpha_3 = \alpha_4 = \mathtt{lock}$, and $\beta = \{\mathtt{x}\}$.

We say P is *well-typed* if $P \vdash \bar{C}$ and the constraints $\bar{C}$ are satisfiable. If a solution A for the constraints $\bar{C}$ exists, the following theorem states that the explicitly-typed program $A(P)$ is well-typed. (Proofs for the theorems in this paper appear in an extended report [13].)

Theorem 1. *If $P \vdash \bar{C}$ and $A \models \bar{C}$ then $A(P) \vdash A(\bar{C})$ and $\models A(\bar{C})$.*

For explicitly-typed programs, since the generated constraints $\bar{C}$ do not contain locking variables, checking the satisfiability of $\bar{C}$ is straightforward. In the more general case where P is not explicitly-typed, the type inference problem involves *searching* for a solution A for the generated constraints $\bar{C}$. Due to the interaction between parameterized classes and dependent types, the type inference problem for RFJ2 (and similarly for rccjava) is NP-complete. (The proof is via a reduction from propositional satisfiability.)

Theorem 2. *For an arbitrary program P, the problem of finding an assignment A such that $A(P)$ is explicitly-typed and $A(P) \vdash \bar{C}$ and $\models \bar{C}$ is NP-complete.*

Despite this worst-case complexity result, we demonstrate a technique in the next section that has proven effective in practice.

3   Solving Constraint Systems

3.1   Generating Boolean Constraints

For each lock variable α mentioned in the program, the type rules introduce a *scope constraint* $\alpha \in \{x_1, \ldots, x_n\}$ that constrains α to be one of the variables $x_1, \ldots, x_n$ in scope. A similar constraint $\beta \subseteq \{x_1, \ldots, x_n\}$ is introduced for each lock set variable β. These scope constraints specify the possible choices for each locking variable, and enable us to translate each constraint C over locking variables into a *Boolean constraint* D that uses Boolean variables to encode the possible choices for each locking variable. The notation $b\,?\,X : Y$ denotes X if the Boolean variable b is true, and denotes Y otherwise.

$$
\begin{array}{lll}
D ::= S \subseteq S \mid L = L & \text{(Boolean constraints)} \\
L ::= x \mid b\,?\,L : L & \text{(conditional lock expressions)} \\
S ::= \emptyset \mid \{L\} \mid b\,?\,S : S \mid S \cup S & \text{(conditional lock set expressions)} \\
b \in \mathit{BoolVar} & \text{(Boolean variables)}
\end{array}
$$

From the scope constraints, we generate a *conditional assignment*

$$Y : (LockVar \rightarrow L) \cup (LockSetVar \rightarrow S)$$

that encodes the possible choices for each locking variable. For example, the scope constraints $\alpha \in \{x_1, \ldots, x_n\}$ and $\beta \subseteq \{y_1, \ldots, y_m\}$ yield:

$$Y(\alpha) = b_1?x_1 : (b_2?x_2 : (\ldots b_{n-1}?x_{n-1} : x_n) \ldots)$$
$$Y(\beta) = (b_1^\emptyset?\{y_1\} : \emptyset) \cup \cdots \cup (b_m^\emptyset?\{y_m\} : \emptyset)$$

where each Boolean variable b_i and b_i' is fresh[1].

We extend the conditional assignment to translate each constraint C to a Boolean constraint $D = Y(C)$, and to translate lock expressions, lock set expressions, and substitutions, as follows. Since the conditional assignment (conditionally) resolves locking variables, as part of this translation we immediately apply any delayed substitutions, to yield a substitution-free Boolean constraint:

$$
\begin{array}{rcl}
Y : C & \rightarrow & D \\
Y(s_1 \subseteq s_2) & = & Y(s_1) \subseteq Y(s_2) \\
Y(l_1 = l_2) & = & Y(l_1) = Y(l_2)
\end{array}
\qquad
\begin{array}{rcl}
Y : s & \rightarrow & S \\
Y(\emptyset) & = & \emptyset \\
Y(\{l\}) & = & \{Y(l)\} \\
Y(s_1 \cup s_2) & = & Y(s_1) \cup Y(s_2) \\
Y(s \cdot \theta) & = & Y(\theta)(Y(s))
\end{array}
$$

$$
\begin{array}{rcl}
Y : l & \rightarrow & L \\
Y(x) & = & x \\
Y(l \cdot \theta) & = & Y(\theta)(Y(l))
\end{array}
\qquad
\begin{array}{rcl}
Y([x_1 := l_1, \ldots, x_n := l_n]) & = & \\
{} [x_1 := Y(l_1), \ldots, x_n := Y(l_n)] &&
\end{array}
$$

Figure 2(c) and (d) show the conditional assignment and Boolean constraints for the example program **Ref**.

A *truth assignment* $B : BoolVar \rightharpoonup Boolean$ assigns truth values to Boolean variables. We extend truth assignments to L and S in a straightforward manner:

$$
\begin{array}{rcl}
B : L & \rightarrow & Var \\
B(x) & = & x \\
B(b?\,L_1 : L_2) & = & \begin{cases} B(L_1) \text{ if } B(b) \\ B(L_2) \text{ if } \neg B(b) \end{cases}
\end{array}
\qquad
\begin{array}{rcl}
B : S & \rightarrow & 2^{Var} \\
B(\emptyset) & = & \emptyset \\
B(\{L\}) & = & \{B(L)\} \\
B(b?\,S_1 : S_2) & = & \begin{cases} B(S_1) \text{ if } B(b) \\ B(S_2) \text{ if } \neg B(b) \end{cases} \\
B(S_1 \cup S_2) & = & B(S_1) \cup B(S_2)
\end{array}
$$

A truth assignment B satisfies a set of Boolean constraints $\bar{D}$ if $B \models D$ for each $D \in \bar{D}$, where:

$$
\begin{array}{lll}
B \models S_1 \subseteq S_2 & \text{iff} & B(S_1) \subseteq B(S_2) \\
B \models L_1 = L_2 & \text{iff} & B(L_1) = B(L_2)
\end{array}
$$

For example, the Boolean constraints of Figure 2(d) are satisfied by the following truth assignment: $b_1 = b_2 = b_4 = b_6 = $ **false** and $b_3 = b_5 = $ **true**.

The application of a truth assignment B to a conditional assignment Y yields the (unconditional) assignment $B(Y)$, defined as $B(Y)(x) = B(Y(x))$.

The translation from constraints to Boolean constraints is semantics-preserving, in the sense that if the generated Boolean constraints are satisfiable, then the original constraints are also satisfiable.

---

[1] We could encode the choice for the first constraint as a decision tree with only $\log n$ Boolean variables.

Theorem 3. *Suppose $\bar{D} = Y(\bar{C})$ and let B be a truth assignment. Then $B(Y) \models \bar{C}$ if and only if $B \models \bar{D}$.*

3.2   Solving Boolean Constraints

The final step is to find a truth assignment B satisfying the generated Boolean constraints $\bar{D}$. We accomplish this step by translating $\bar{D}$ into a Boolean formula F, which can then be solved by a standard propositional satisfiability solver such as Chaff [21]. The Boolean formula syntax and this translation are as follows:

$$F \quad ::= \quad \mathbf{true} \mid \mathbf{false} \mid b \mid F \vee F \mid F \wedge F \mid \neg F$$

$$[\![\cdot]\!] : \bar{D} \to F$$
$$[\![\bar{D}]\!] = \wedge_{D \text{ in } \bar{D}} [\![D]\!]$$

$$[\![\cdot]\!] : D \to F$$

$$[\![x = x]\!] = \mathbf{true}$$
$$[\![x = y]\!] = \mathbf{false} \ \text{ if } x \not\equiv y$$
$$[\![L = (b?L_1 : L_2)]\!] = (b \wedge [\![L = L_1]\!])$$
$$\vee(\neg b \wedge [\![L = L_2]\!])$$
$$[\![(b?L_1 : L_2) = L]\!] = [\![L = (b?L_1 : L_2)]\!]$$
$$[\![\emptyset \subseteq S]\!] = \mathbf{true}$$
$$[\![(S_1 \cup S_2) \subseteq S]\!] = [\![S_1 \subseteq S]\!]$$
$$\wedge [\![S_2 \subseteq S]\!]$$

$$[\![(b?S_1 : S_2) \subseteq S]\!] = (b \wedge [\![S_1 \subseteq S]\!])$$
$$\vee(\neg b \wedge [\![S_2 \subseteq S]\!])$$
$$[\![\{L\} \subseteq \emptyset]\!] = \mathbf{false}$$
$$[\![\{L\} \subseteq (b?S_1 : S_2)]\!] = (b \wedge [\![\{L\} \subseteq S_1]\!])$$
$$\vee(\neg b \wedge [\![\{L\} \subseteq S_2]\!])$$
$$[\![\{L\} \subseteq (S_1 \cup S_2)]\!] = [\![\{L\} \subseteq S_1]\!]$$
$$\vee [\![\{L\} \subseteq S_2]\!]$$
$$[\![\{L_1\} \subseteq \{L_2\}]\!] = [\![L_1 = L_2]\!]$$

Figure 2(e) presents the formulas for the four constraints from our example program. This translation is semantics preserving with respect to the standard notion of satisfiability $B \models F$ for Boolean formulas.

Theorem 4. *If $F = [\![\bar{D}]\!]$ then for all B, $B \models F$ if and only if $B \models \bar{D}$.*

In summary, our type inference algorithm proceeds as follows: Given a program P with locking variables, we generate from P a collection of constraints $\bar{C}$ over the locking variables; we extract a conditional assignment Y from $\bar{C}$ and generate Boolean constraints $\bar{D} = Y(\bar{C})$; and we generate a corresponding Boolean formula $F = [\![\bar{D}]\!]$. We use a propositional satisfiability solver to determine a truth assignment B for F, in which case we also have that $B \models \bar{D}$ by Theorem 4 and $(B(Y)) \models \bar{C}$ by Theorem 3, and therefore the explicitly-typed program $(B(Y))(P)$ is well-typed. Conversely, if the generated formula F is unsatisfiable, then there is no assignment A such that $A(P)$ is well-typed.

4   Implementation

We have implemented our inference algorithm in the Rcc/Sat checker, which supports the full Java programming language (although it does not currently detect race conditions on array accesses). Rcc/Sat takes as input an unannotated or partially-annotated program, where any typing annotations are provided in comments starting with "#", as in /*# guarded_by y */.

Rcc/Sat first adds a predetermined number of ghost parameters to all classes and methods lacking user-specified parameters. Next, for each unguarded field, Rcc/Sat adds the annotation guarded_by α, where α is fresh. Rcc/Sat also uses fresh locking variables to add any missing requires annotations and class and method instantiation parameters. Rcc/Sat then performs our type inference algorithm. If the generated constraints are satisfiable, then the satisfying assignment is used to generate an explicitly-typed version of the program. Section 4.2 outlines how we generate meaningful error messages when they are not.

4.1   Java Features

We handle additional features of the Java programming language as follows.

Scope Constraints. Rcc/Sat permits lock expressions to be any *final* object references, including: (1) this; (2) ghost parameters; (3) final variables, static fields, and parameters; and (4) well-typed expressions of the form $e.f$, where e is a constant expression and f is a final field. This set may be infinite, and we heuristically limit it to expressions with at most two field accesses.

Inheritance, Subtyping, and Interfaces. Given the declaration

        class C⟨ghost a₁,...,aₙ⟩ extends D⟨ghost b₁,...,bₖ⟩ { ... }

we consider the type instantiation $C\langle l_{1..n}\rangle$ to be an immediate subtype of $D\langle m_{1..k}\rangle$ provided $m_i \equiv b_i[a_j := l_j{}^{j\in 1..n}]$ for all $i \in 1..k$. The subtyping relation is the reflexive and transitive closure of this rule. The signature of an overriding method must match that of the overridden form, after applying the type parameter substitutions induced by the inheritance hierarchy. Interfaces are handled similarly.

Inner Classes. Non-static inner classes may access the type parameters from the enclosing class and may declare their own parameters. Thus, the complete type for such a class is $Outer\langle l_{1..n}\rangle . Inner\langle m_{1..k}\rangle$.

Static Fields, Methods, and Inner Classes. Static members may not refer to the enclosing class' type parameters since static members are not associated with a specific instantiation of the class.

Thread Objects. To allow Thread objects to store thread-local data in their fields, Rcc/Sat adds an implicit final field tl_lock to each Thread class. This field is analogous to (and replaces) the ghost parameter on the run method in RFJ2. It may guard other fields and is assumed to be held when run is invoked.

Escape Mechanisms. We provide escapes from the RFJ2 type system through a "no_warn" annotation that suppresses the generation of constraints for a line of code. Also, since ghost parameters are erased at run time, the ghost parameters in typecasts of the form (C⟨a⟩)x are not checked dynamically.

4.2   Reporting Errors

We introduce two important improvements that enable the tool to pinpoint likely errors in the program when the generated constraints are unsatisfiable.

First, we change the algorithm to check each field declaration in a program separately, thereby enabling us to distinguish fields with potential races from those that are race-free. To check a single field, we generate the constraints as before, except that we only add field access constraints for accesses to the field of interest. The analysis is compositional in this manner because the presence or absence of races on one field is independence of races on other fields.

There is a possibility that the same locking variable will be assigned different values when checking different fields. If this occurs, we can compose the results of the separate checks together by introducing additional type parameters and renaming locking variables as necessary. For example, if a type instantiation $C\langle\alpha\rangle$ of class $C\langle\text{ghost x}\rangle$ becomes $C\langle\text{l1}\rangle$ when checking one field of C and $C\langle\text{l2}\rangle$ when checking another, we can change the class declaration to $C\langle\text{ghost x1, x2}\rangle$, and instantiate it as $C\langle\text{l1,l2}\rangle$ at the conflicting location.

Second, when there are race conditions on a field, it is often desirable to infer the most likely lock protecting it and then generate errors for locations where that lock is not held. For example, the following program is not well-typed:

```
1:  class C⟨ghost y⟩ {
2:    int c guarded_by α;
3:    void f1() requires y { c = 1; }
4:    void f2() requires y { c = 2; }
5:    void f3() requires this { c = 3; }
6:  }
```

Our tool produces the following diagnostic message at the likely error site:

```
C.java:5: Lock 'y' not held on access to 'c'.  Locks held: { this }.
```

To pinpoint likely error locations in this way, we express type inference as an optimization problem instead of a satisfiability problem. First, we add weights to some of the generated constraints, as follows. A constraint C with weight w is written as the weighted constraint $W = C|_w$.

$\alpha \in \{\text{y}, \text{this}, \text{no\_lock}\}$	Scope constraint for c
$\alpha \in \{\text{y}, \text{this}\}\ \|_2$	Requirement that c is guarded by a valid lock
$\alpha \in \{\text{y}, \text{no\_lock}\}\ \|_1$	Access constraint for c from f1
$\alpha \in \{\text{y}, \text{no\_lock}\}\ \|_1$	Access constraint for c from f2
$\alpha \in \{\text{this}, \text{no\_lock}\}\ \|_1$	Access constraint for c from f3

These five constraints refer to no_lock, a lock name used in the checker to indicate that no reasonable guarding lock can be found for a field. Given constraints $\bar{C}$ and weighted constraints $\bar{W}$, we compute the optimal assignment A such that:

1. $A \models C$ for all $C \in \bar{C}$, and
2. the sum $\sum \{w \mid C|_w \in \bar{W} \ \wedge \ A \models C\}$ is maximized.

Note that we do not require all constraints in $\bar{W}$ be satisfied by A. For the constraints above, A is the assignment $\alpha = \text{y}$, with a value of 4. We then generate error messages for all constraints in $\bar{W}$ that are not satisfied by A. The constraint $\alpha \in \{\text{this}, \text{no\_lock}\}\ \|_1$ is not satisfied by the optimal assignment A, yielding the above error message. Conversely, if the optimal assignment A did not satisfy the constraint $\alpha \in \{\text{y}, \text{this}\}\ \|_2$, then we would generate the error message:

```
C.java:2: No consistent guarding lock for field 'c'.
```

We have found that the heuristic of weighting declaration constraints 2–4 times more than field access constraints works well in practice.

We solve the constraint optimization problem for $\bar{W}$ and $\bar{C}$ by translating the constraints into a weighted MAX-SAT problem and solving it with the PBS tool [4]. The translation is similar to the case without weights. PBS and similar tools can find optimal assignments for formulas including up to 50–100 weighted clauses. Optimizing over a larger number of weighted clauses is currently computationally intractable. Thus, we still check one field at a time and only optimize over constraints generated by field accesses, placing all constraints for `requires` clauses and type equality in $\bar{C}$. If $\bar{C}$ is not satisfiable, we forego the optimization step and instead generate error messages for constraints in the smallest unsatisfiable core of $\bar{C}$, which we find with Chaff [21].

4.3 Improving Precision

Rcc/Sat implements a somewhat more expressive type system than that described in Section 2 to handle the synchronization patterns of large programs more effectively. In particular:

- Unreachable code is not type checked.
- Read-shared fields do not need guarding locks. A *read-shared* field is a field that is initialized while local to its creating thread, and subsequently shared in read-only mode among multiple threads.
- A field's protecting lock need not be held for accesses occurring when only a single thread exists or when the object has not escaped its creating thread.

Programs typically relax the core lock-based synchronization discipline along these lines. The checker currently uses quite basic implementations of rapid type analysis [5], escape analysis [6], and control-flow analysis for this step. Using more precise analyses would further improve our type inference algorithm.

5 Evaluation

We applied Rcc/Sat to benchmark programs including `elevator`, a discrete event simulator [28]; `tsp`, a Traveling Salesman Problem solver [28]; `sor`, a scientific computing program [28]; the `mtrt` ray-tracing program and `jbb` business objects simulator benchmarks [23]; and the `moldyn`, `montecarlo`, and `raytracer` benchmarks [20]. We ran these experiments on a 3.06GHz Pentium 4 processor with 2GB of memory, with Rcc/Sat configured to insert one `ghost` parameter on classes, interfaces, and instance methods and two parameters on static methods.

Table 1 shows, for each benchmark, the size in lines of code, the overall time for type inference, and the average type inference time per field. It also shows the size of the constraint problem generated, in number of constraints and the number of variables and clauses in the resulting Boolean formula, after conversion to CNF. The preliminary analyses described in Section 4.3 typically consumed less than 2% of the run time on the larger benchmarks.

Table 1. Summary of test program performance.

Program	Size (LOC)	Time (s)	Time/ Field (s)	Number of Constraints	Formula Size vars	Formula Size clauses	Manual Annot.	Fields Total	read- shared	race- free	no guard
elevator	529	5.0	0.22	215	1,449	3,831	0	23	17	6	0
tsp	723	6.9	0.19	233	2,090	7,151	3	37	21	16	3
sor	687	4.5	0.15	130	562	1,205	1	29	22	7	0
raytracer	1,982	21.0	0.27	801	9,436	29,841	2	77	45	28	4
moldyn	1,408	12.6	0.12	904	4,011	10,036	3	107	57	44	6
montecarlo	3,674	20.7	0.19	1,097	9,003	25,974	1	110	68	42	0
mtrt	11,315	138.8	1.5	5,636	38,025	123,046	6	181	112	69	4
jbb	30,519	2,773.5	3.52	11,698	146,390	549,667	40	787	472	295	20

The "Manual Annotations" column reflects the number of annotations manually inserted to guide the analysis. We added these few annotations to suppress warnings only in situations where immediately identifiable local properties ensured correctness. The manual annotations were inserted, for example, to delineate single-threaded parts of the program after joining all spawned threads; to explicitly instantiate classes in two places where the scope constraint generation heuristics did not consider the appropriate locks; and to identify thread-local object references not found by our escape analysis. In jbb, we also added annotations to suppress spurious race-condition warnings on roughly 25 fields with benign races. These fields were designed to be *write-protected* [12], meaning that a lock guarded write accesses, but read accesses were not synchronized. This idiom is unsafe if misused but permits synchronization-free accessor methods.

The last four columns show the total number of fields in the program, as well as their breakdown into read-shared fields, race-free fields, and fields for which no guarding lock was inferred. The analyses described in Section 4.3 reduced the number of fields without valid guards by 20%–75%, a significant percentage.

Rcc/Sat identified three fields in the tsp benchmark on which there are intentional races. On raytracer, Rcc/Sat identified a previously known race on a checksum field and reported spurious warnings on three fields. It also identified a known race on a counter in mtrt. The remaining warnings were spurious and could be eliminated by additional annotations or, in some cases, by improving the precision of the additional analyses of Section 4.3.

Overall, these results are quite promising. Manually inserting a small number of annotations enables Rcc/Sat to verify that the vast majority (92%–100%) of fields are race-free. These results show a substantial improvement over previous type inference algorithms for race-free type systems, such as Houdini/rcc.

6   Related Work

Boyapati and Rinard have defined a race-free type system with a notion of object ownership [7]. They include special owners to indicate thread-local data, thereby allowing a single class declaration to be used for both thread-local instances and shared instances, which motivated some of our refinements in RFJ2. They present an *intra*procedural algorithm to infer ownership parameters for class instantiations within a method. This simpler intraprocedural context yields equality constraints over lock variables, which can be efficiently solved using union-find. We believe it may be possible to extend our interprocedural type inference algorithm to accommodate ownership types. Grossman has developed a race-free type system for Cyclone, a statically safe variant of C [18]. Cyclone has a number of additional features, such as existential quantification and singleton types, and it remains to be seen how our techniques would apply in this setting.

The `requires` annotations used in our type system essentially constrain the *effects* that the method may produce. Thus, we are performing a form of effect reconstruction [27, 26], but our dependent types are not amenable to traditional effect reconstruction techniques. Similarly, the constraints of our type system do not exhibit the monotonicity properties that facilitate the polynomial time solvers used in other constraint-based analyses (see, for example, Aiken's survey [2]). Cardelli [8] was among the first to explore type checking for dependent types. Our dependent types are comparatively limited in expressive power, but the resulting type checking and type inference problems are decidable.

Eraser [22] is a tool for detecting race conditions in unannotated programs dynamically (though it may fail to detect certain errors because of insufficient test coverage). Agarwal and Stoller [1] present a dynamic type inference technique for the type system of Boyapati and Rinard. Their technique extracts locking information from a program trace and then performs a static analysis involving unique pointer analysis [3] and intraprocedural ownership inference [7] to construct annotations. These dynamic analyses complement our static approach, and it may be possible to leverage their results to facilitate type inference.

A common and significant problem with many type-inference techniques is the inability to construct meaningful error messages when inference fails (see, for example, [29, 30, 19]). An interesting contribution of our approach is that we view type inference as an optimization problem over a set of constraints that attempts to produce the most reasonable error messages for a program.

7   Conclusions

This paper contributes a new type inference algorithm for race-free type systems, which is based on reduction to propositional satisfiability. Our experimental results demonstrate that this approach works well in practice on benchmarks of up to 30,000 lines of code. Extending and evaluating this approach on significantly larger benchmarks remains an issue for future work. We also demonstrate extensions to facilitate reliable error reporting. We believe the resulting annotations and race-free guarantee provided by our type inference system have a wide range of applications in the analysis, validation, and verification of multithreaded programs. In particular, they provide valuable documentation to the programmer, they facilitate checking other program properties such as atomicity, and they can help reduce state explosion in model checkers.

Acknowledgments

We thank Peter Applegate for implementing parts of Rcc/Sat.

References

1. R. Agarwal and S. D. Stoller. Type inference for parameterized race-free Java. In *Conference on Verification, Model Checking, and Abstract Interpretation*, pages 149–160. 2004.
2. A. Aiken. Introduction to set constraint-based program analysis. *Science of Computer Programming*, 35(1999):79–111, 1999.
3. J. Aldrich, V. Kostadinov, and C. Chambers. Alias annotations for program understanding. In *ACM Conference on Object-Oriented Programming, Systems, Languages and Applications*, pages 311–330, 2002.
4. F. A. Aloul, A. Ramani, I. L. Markov, and K. A. Sakallah. PBS: A backtrack-search pseudo-boolean solver and optimizer. In *Symposium on the Theory and Applications of Satisfiability Testing*, pages 346–353, 2002.
5. D. F. Bacon and P. F. Sweeney. Fast static analysis of C++ virtual function calls. In *ACM Conference on Object-Oriented Programming, Systems, Languages and Applications*, pages 324–341, 1996.
6. J. Bogda and U. Hölzle. Removing unnecessary synchronization in Java. In *ACM Conference on Object-Oriented Programming, Systems, Languages and Applications*, pages 35–46, 1999.
7. C. Boyapati and M. Rinard. A parameterized type system for race-free Java programs. In *ACM Conference on Object-Oriented Programming, Systems, Languages and Applications*, pages 56–69, 2001.
8. L. Cardelli. Typechecking dependent types and subtypes. In *Workshop on Foundations of Logic and Functional Programming*, pages 45–57, 1988.
9. M. B. Dwyer, J. Hatcliff, V. R. Prasad, and Robby. Exploiting Object Escape and Locking Information in Partial Order Reduction for Concurrent Object-Oriented Programs. *Formal Methods in System Design*, 2003.
10. C. Flanagan and S. N. Freund. Type-based race detection for Java. In *ACM Conference on Programming Language Design and Implementation*, pages 219–232, 2000.
11. C. Flanagan and S. N. Freund. Detecting Race Conditions in Large Programs. In *Workshop on Program Analysis for Software Tools and Engineering*, pages 90–96, 2001.
12. C. Flanagan and S. N. Freund. Atomizer: A dynamic atomicity checker for multi-threaded programs. In *ACM Symposium on the Principles of Programming Languages*, pages 256–267, 2004.
13. C. Flanagan and S. N. Freund. Type inference against races. Technical Note 04-06, Williams College, 2004.
14. C. Flanagan and S. Qadeer. Transactions for Software Model Checking. In *Workshop on Software Model Checking*, pages 338–349, 2003.
15. C. Flanagan and S. Qadeer. A type and effect system for atomicity. In *ACM Conference on Programming Language Design and Implementation*, pages 338–349, 2003.
16. C. Flanagan and S. Qadeer. Types for atomicity. In *ACM Workshop on Types in Language Design and Implementation*, pages 1–12, 2003.

17. M. Flatt, S. Krishnamurthi, and M. Felleisen. Classes and mixins. In *ACM Symposium on the Principles of Programming Languages*, pages 171–183, 1998.
18. D. Grossman. Type-safe multithreading in Cyclone. In *ACM Workshop on Types in Language Design and Implementation*, pages 13–25, 2003.
19. C. Haack and J. B. Wells. Type error slicing in implicitly typed higher-order languages. In *European Symposium on Programming*, pages 284–301, 2003.
20. Java Grande Forum. Java Grande benchmark suite. Available from `http://www.javagrande.org/`, 2003.
21. M. W. Moskewicz, C. F. Madigan, Y. Zhao, L. Zhang, and S. Malik. Chaff: Engineering an efficient SAT solver. In *Design Automation Conference*, pages 530–535, 2001.
22. S. Savage, M. Burrows, G. Nelson, P. Sobalvarro, and T. E. Anderson. Eraser: A dynamic data race detector for multi-threaded programs. *ACM Transactions on Computer Systems*, 15(4):391–411, 1997.
23. Standard Performance Evaluation Corporation. SPEC benchmarks. Available from `http://www.spec.org/`, 2003.
24. S. D. Stoller. Model-Checking Multi-Threaded Distributed Java Programs. *International Journal on Software Tools for Technology Transfer*, 4(1):71–91, 2002.
25. S. D. Stoller and E. Cohen. Optimistic Synchronization-Based State-Space Reduction. In International Conference on Tools and Algorithms for the Construction and Analysis of Systems, pages 489–504, 2003.
26. J.-P. Talpin and P. Jouvelot. Polymorphic type, region and effect inference. *Journal of Functional Programming*, 2(3):245–271, 1992.
27. M. Tofte and J.-P. Talpin. Implementation of the typed call-by-value lambda-calculus using a stack of regions. In *ACM Symposium on the Principles of Programming Languages*, pages 188–201, 1994.
28. C. von Praun and T. Gross. Static conflict analysis for multi-threaded object-oriented programs. In *ACM Conference on Programming Language Design and Implementation*, pages 115–128, 2003.
29. M. Wand. Finding the source of type errors. In *ACM Symposium on the Principles of Programming Languages*, pages 38–43, 1986.
30. J. Yang, G. Michaelson, P. Trinder, and J. B. Wells. Improved type error reporting. In *International Workshop on Implementation of Functional Languages*, pages 71–86, 2000.

A Type System

This appendix provides a complete definition of RFJ2. We first informally define a number of predicates. (See [17] for their precise definition.)

Predicate	Meaning
$ClassOnce(P)$	no class is declared twice in P
$FieldsOnce(P)$	no class contains two fields with the same name
$MethodsOncePerClass(P)$	no method name appears more than once per class

A typing environment is defined as:

$$E ::= \emptyset \mid E, t\, x \mid E, \text{ghost } x$$

$\boxed{P \vdash \bar{C}}$

$$\dfrac{\begin{array}{c} ClassOnce(P) \quad FieldsOnce(P) \\ MethodsOncePerClass(P) \\ P = defn_{1..n}\ e \\ P \vdash defn_i\ \&\ \bar{C}_i \quad \forall i \in 1..n \\ P; \text{ghost main\_lock}; \{\text{main\_lock}\} \vdash e : t\ \&\ \bar{C} \end{array}}{P \vdash \bar{C}_{1..n} \cup \bar{C}}$$

$\boxed{P \vdash defn\ \&\ \bar{C}}$

$$\dfrac{\begin{array}{c} garg_i = \text{ghost } x_i \quad \forall i \in 1..n \\ E = garg_{1..n}, cn\langle x_{1..n}\rangle\ \text{this} \\ P; E \vdash field_i\ \&\ \bar{C}_i \quad \forall i \in 1..j \\ P; E \vdash meth_i\ \&\ \bar{C}'_i \quad \forall i \in 1..k \\ \bar{C} = \bar{C}_{1..j} \cup \bar{C}'_{1..k} \end{array}}{\begin{array}{c} P \vdash \text{class } cn\langle \text{ghost } x_{1..n}\rangle \\ \{\, field_{1..j}\ meth_{1..k}\,\}\ \&\ \bar{C} \end{array}}$$

$\boxed{P; E \vdash wf\ \&\ \bar{C}}$

$$\dfrac{}{P; \emptyset \vdash wf\ \&\ \emptyset} \qquad \dfrac{\begin{array}{c} P; E \vdash t\ \&\ \bar{C} \\ x \notin dom(E) \end{array}}{P; E, t\, x \vdash wf\ \&\ \bar{C}} \qquad \dfrac{\begin{array}{c} P; E \vdash wf\ \&\ \bar{C} \\ x \notin dom(E) \end{array}}{P; E, \text{ghost } x \vdash wf\ \&\ \bar{C}}$$

$\boxed{P; E \vdash t\ \&\ \bar{C}}$

$$\dfrac{\begin{array}{c} P; E \vdash wf\ \&\ \bar{C} \\ \text{class } cn\langle \text{ghost } x_i{}^{i \in 1..n}\rangle\, \ldots \in P \\ \bar{C}' = \bar{C} \cup \{l_i \in dom(E)\ {}^{i \in 1..n}\} \end{array}}{P; E \vdash cn\langle l_{1..n}\rangle\ \&\ \bar{C}'}$$

$\boxed{P; E \vdash meth\ \&\ \bar{C}}$

$\boxed{P; E \vdash field\ \&\ \bar{C}}$

$$\dfrac{\begin{array}{c} P; E \vdash t\ \&\ \bar{C} \\ \bar{C}' = \bar{C} \cup \{l \in dom(E)\} \end{array}}{P; E \vdash t\ fn\ \text{guarded\_by } l\ \&\ \bar{C}'}$$

$$\dfrac{\begin{array}{c} garg_i = \text{ghost } x_i \quad \forall i \in 1..n \\ E' = E, garg_{1..n}, arg_{1..d} \\ P; E'; s \vdash e : t\ \&\ \bar{C} \\ \bar{C}' = \bar{C} \cup \{s \subseteq dom(E')\} \\ s \text{ is either } \{y_1, \ldots, y_k\} \text{ or } \beta \end{array}}{P; E \vdash t\ mn\langle \text{ghost } x_{1..n}\rangle(arg_{1..d})\ \text{requires } s\ \{\, e\,\}\ \&\ \bar{C}'}$$

$\boxed{P; E; s \vdash e : t\ \&\ \bar{C}}$

$$\dfrac{P; E \vdash c\ \&\ \bar{C}}{P; E; s \vdash \text{null} : c\ \&\ \bar{C}} \qquad \dfrac{\begin{array}{c} P; E \vdash wf\ \&\ \bar{C} \\ E = E_1, t\, x, E_2 \end{array}}{P; E; s \vdash x : t\ \&\ \bar{C}} \qquad \dfrac{\begin{array}{c} P; E; s \vdash e : cn\langle l_{1..n}\rangle\ \&\ \bar{C} \\ P; E \vdash cn\langle l'_{1..n}\rangle\ \&\ \bar{C}' \\ \bar{C}'' = \bar{C} \cup \bar{C}' \cup \{l_i = l'_i\ {}^{i \in 1..n}\} \end{array}}{P; E; s \vdash e : cn\langle l'_{1..n}\rangle\ \&\ \bar{C}''}$$

$$\dfrac{\begin{array}{c} y \text{ is fresh} \\ \theta = [x_j := l_j\ {}^{j \in 1..n}, \text{this} := y] \\ P; E, cn\langle l_{1..n}\rangle\, y; s \vdash e_i : \theta(t_i)\ \&\ \bar{C}_i \quad \forall i \in 1..k \\ \text{class } cn\langle \text{ghost } x_{1..n}\rangle\ \{\, field_{1..k}\ meth_{1..m}\,\} \in P \\ field_i = t_i\ fn_i\ \text{guarded\_by } l'_i \quad \forall i \in 1..k \\ P; E \vdash cn\langle l_{1..n}\rangle\ \&\ \bar{C}' \\ \bar{C}'' = \bar{C}_{1..k} \cup \bar{C}' \cup \{l_i \in dom(E)\ {}^{i \in 1..n}\} \end{array}}{P; E; s \vdash \text{new } cn\langle l_{1..n}\rangle(e_{1..k}) : cn\langle l_{1..n}\rangle\ \&\ \bar{C}''}$$

$$\dfrac{\begin{array}{c} P; E; s \vdash e : cn\langle l_{1..n}\rangle\ \&\ \bar{C} \\ \text{class } cn\langle \text{ghost } x_{1..n}\rangle \\ \{\ldots t\ fn\ \text{guarded\_by } l \ldots\} \in P \\ \theta = [\text{this} := e, x_j := l_j\ {}^{j \in 1..n}] \\ P; E \vdash \theta(t)\ \&\ \bar{C}' \end{array}}{P; E; s \vdash e.fn : \theta(t)\ \&\ (\bar{C} \cup \bar{C}' \cup \{\theta(l) \in s\})}$$

$$\dfrac{\begin{array}{c} P; E; s \vdash e : cn\langle l_{1..n}\rangle\ \&\ \bar{C} \\ \text{class } cn\langle \text{ghost } x_{1..n}\rangle \\ \{\ldots t\ fn\ \text{guarded\_by } l \ldots\} \in P \\ \theta = [\text{this} := e, x_j := l_j\ {}^{j \in 1..n}] \\ P; E \vdash e' : \theta(t)\ \&\ \bar{C}' \end{array}}{P; E; s \vdash e.fn = e' : \theta(t)\ \&\ (\bar{C} \cup \bar{C}' \cup \{\theta(l) \in s\})}$$

$$\dfrac{\begin{array}{c} P; E; s \vdash e_1 : t_1\ \&\ \bar{C}_1 \\ P; E, t\, x; s \vdash e_2 : t_2\ \&\ \bar{C}_2 \\ \theta = [x := e_1] \\ P; E \vdash \theta(t_2)\ \&\ \bar{C}_3 \\ C = (\bar{C}_1 \cup \bar{C}_2 \cup \bar{C}_3) \end{array}}{P; E; s \vdash \text{let } x = e_1 \text{ in } e_2 : \theta(t_2)\ \&\ C}$$

$$\dfrac{\begin{array}{c} P; E; s \vdash e : cn\langle l_{1..n}\rangle\ \&\ \bar{C} \\ \text{class } cn\langle \text{ghost } x_{1..n}\rangle\ \{\ldots t\ mn\langle \text{ghost } y_{1..k}\rangle(t_j\ z_j{}^{j \in 1..d})\ \text{requires } s'\ \{\, e'\,\} \ldots\} \in P \\ \theta = [\text{this} := e, x_i := l_i\ {}^{i \in 1..n}, y_i := l'_i\ {}^{i \in 1..k}, z_i := e_i\ {}^{i \in 1..d}] \\ P; E; s \vdash e_j : \theta(t_j)\ \&\ \bar{C}_j \quad \forall j \in 1..d \\ P; E \vdash \theta(t)\ \&\ \bar{C}' \\ \bar{C}'' = \bar{C} \cup \bar{C}_{1..d} \cup \bar{C}' \cup \{\theta(s') \subseteq s\} \end{array}}{P; E; s \vdash e.mn\langle l'_{1..k}\rangle(e_{1..d}) : \theta(t)\ \&\ \bar{C}''}$$

$$\dfrac{\begin{array}{c} P; E; s \vdash x : t'\ \&\ \bar{C} \\ P; E; s \cup \{x\} \vdash e : t\ \&\ \bar{C}' \end{array}}{P; E; s \vdash \text{synchronized } x\ e : t\ \&\ (\bar{C} \cup \bar{C}')} \qquad \dfrac{\begin{array}{c} P; E; s \vdash e : cn\langle l_{1..n}\rangle\ \&\ \bar{C} \\ \text{class } cn\langle \text{ghost } x_{1..n}\rangle\ \{\ldots meth \ldots\} \in P \\ meth = t'\ \text{run}\langle \text{ghost tl\_lock}\rangle()\ \text{requires tl\_lock}\ \{\, e'\,\} \end{array}}{P; E; s \vdash e.\text{fork} : t\ \&\ \bar{C}}$$

Pointer-Range Analysis*

Suan Hsi Yong and Susan Horwitz

Computer Sciences Department, University of Wisconsin-Madison
1210 West Dayton Street, Madison, WI 53706 USA
{suan,horwitz}@cs.wisc.edu

Abstract. Array-Range Analysis computes at compile time the range
of possible index values for each array-index expression in a program.
This information can be used to detect potential out-of-bounds array
accesses and to identify non-aliasing array accesses. In a language like C,
where arrays can be accessed indirectly via pointers, and where pointer
arithmetic is allowed, range analysis must be extended to compute the
range of possible values for each pointer dereference.

This paper describes a Pointer-Range Analysis algorithm that computes
a safe approximation of the set of memory locations that may be accessed by each pointer dereference. To properly account for non-trivial
aspects of C, including pointer arithmetic and type-casting, a range representation is described that separates the identity of a pointer's target
location from its type; this separation allows a concise representation
of pointers to multiple arrays, and precise handling of mismatched-type
pointer arithmetic.

1 Introduction

The goal of Array-Range Analysis is to compute (at compile time) the range of
possible index values for each array-index expression in a program. This information can be used for many applications, such as:

- Eliminating unnecessary or redundant bounds-checking operations, for code
  optimization [13, 26];
- Detecting potential out-of-bounds access errors, for debugging, program verification, or security [25, 17];
- Identifying non-aliasing array accesses, for program understanding, optimization, or parallelization [1, 24, 14].

The importance of Array-Range Analysis is reflected in the extensive body of
research conducted over the last three decades. However, most previous work
has focused on languages like Fortran and Java.

The C language presents new challenges for array-range analysis. First, arrays
can be accessed indirectly via pointers, so pointer arithmetic becomes an alternative way to compute the index into an array. Second, type-casts and unions

---

* This work was supported in part by the National Science Foundation under grants
  CCR-9987435 and CCR-0305387.

R. Giacobazzi (Ed.): SAS 2004, LNCS 3148, pp. 133–148, 2004.

allow an array of one type to be accessed as an array of a different type, possibly with a different size. Third, even deciding what is an "array" is difficult, especially with heap allocated storage, where the same mechanism (a call to `malloc`) is used whether one is allocating a single object or an array of objects. This also means that a pointer dereference to a single object and a pointer dereference to an array object cannot always be syntactically differentiated.

Given these features, we approach the problem of range analysis for C by treating *all* pointer dereferences as array accesses, and by treating each solitary object as an array with one element. Since an array indexing expression `a[i]` is semantically equivalent to the dereference `*(a+i)`, the analysis can be described purely in terms of pointer dereferences and pointer arithmetic, rather than array accesses and array-index computation; hence the name Pointer-Range Analysis.

This paper describes a Pointer-Range Analysis algorithm to compute, for each dereference in a program, a safe approximation of the set of memory locations that may be accessed by the dereference. An abstract representation of ranges is presented that can safely and portably handle challenging aspects of analyzing C pointers, including:

- Pointer arithmetic.
- Type mismatches, which arise due to unions or casts.
- Imprecise points-to information, where a pointer may point to one of several arrays.

The pointer-range representation has three components: target location, target type, and offset range. The separate tracking of the target's location and type allows a single location to be treated as different types, and allows precise type information to be maintained when location information is lost as a result of analysis imprecision. Maintaining types rather than numeric values of sizes preserves portability, allowing the analysis to be applied when exact sizes of types cannot be assumed. Experimental results are presented that show the potential utility of pointer-range analysis in various contexts, such as eliminating unnecessary bounds checks and identifying non-aliasing accesses.

2   Representing Ranges

We define Pointer-Range Analysis as a forward dataflow-analysis problem, where at each edge of the control-flow graph (CFG), a mapping is maintained from each location x to an abstract representation of the range of values x may hold at runtime. This abstract representation must be a safe approximation (represent a superset) of the actual range of possible values. We follow the convention in dataflow analysis of performing a meet ($\sqcap$) at control-flow merge points, so the elements of the abstract domain must be partially ordered such that $r_1 \sqsubseteq r_2$ implies r_1 is more approximate than r_2; i.e., the range represented by r_1 is a superset of the range represented by r_2.

When dealing only with numeric values, the Integer Interval Domain can be used to represent the ranges:

Integer Interval Domain $\mathcal{I} = \langle I, \sqsubseteq_i \rangle$:

- $I = \{[min, max] \mid min, max \in \mathbb{Z} \cup \{+\infty, -\infty\}, min \leq max\} \cup \{\emptyset\}$
- $[min, max]$ represents the set of integer values in the range $min \ldots max$.
- $[min_1, max_1] \sqsubseteq_i [min_2, max_2]$ iff $[min_1, max_1] \supseteq [min_2, max_2]$, that is, $min_1 \leq min_2$ and $max_1 \geq max_2$.
- Note that $\mathcal{I}$ is a lattice that satisfies our approximation requirement, with top element $\top = \emptyset$, bottom element $\bot = [-\infty, +\infty]$, and meet operator $\sqcap = \cup$.

Figure 1(a) demonstrates the analysis of a simple example using intervals, and shows how the computed range can be used to decide whether an array index is in bounds. When assigning a constant value to i, we can map i to a precise interval representation (e.g., $[6, 6]$ at line 4). When the two branches merge at line 8, we take the meet (union) of i's range along the two incoming branches to get an approximate (superset) range $[3, 6]$ of possible values for i. Since this falls within the legal range of $[0, 9]$ for indexing into array a, the array index at line 9 is guaranteed to be in-bounds.

When dealing with pointers, however, our abstract domain must be able to capture information about a pointer's target (the object to which the pointer may point). As a first step, we define the set *Loc* of abstract representatives of locations, or objects, defined in the program, to which a pointer may legally point:

Locations *Loc*:

- $Loc = \{v \mid \text{v is a variable in the program }\}$
  $\cup \{\text{MALLOC}_i \mid i \text{ is a program point where } \texttt{malloc} \text{ is called }\}$

Each location $x \in Loc$ is treated as an array object, with an associated element type τ_x and element count σ_x (for solitary objects, the element count is 1). For a heap location MALLOC_i, which represents all heap objects allocated at program point i, it may not be possible to determine a precise type and count; these values are inferred from the argument to $\texttt{malloc}$ as follows: if the argument is a constant C, we set the type to $\texttt{char}$ and count to C; if it is of the form $C * \texttt{sizeof}(\tau)$ we set the type to τ and count to C; otherwise, we set the type to $\texttt{void}$ and count to 0.

1. `int a[10];`	
2. `int i;`	
3. `if(...){`	
4. `i = 6;`	$i \mapsto [6, 6]$
5. `} else {`	
6. `i = 3;`	$i \mapsto [3, 3]$
7. `}`	
8.	$i \mapsto [3, 6]$
9. `a[i] = 0;`	(in-bounds)

(a) Arrays, with Integer Intervals

1. `int a[10];`	
2. `int * p;`	
3. `if(...){`	
4. `p = &a[6];`	$p \mapsto \langle a, [6, 6] \rangle$
5. `} else {`	
6. `p = &a[3];`	$p \mapsto \langle a, [3, 3] \rangle$
7. `}`	
8.	$p \mapsto \langle a, [3, 6] \rangle$
9. `*p = 0;`	(in-bounds)

(b) Pointers, with Location-Offset

Fig. 1. In-Bounds Access Example

	Location-Offset	Descriptor-Offset
1. `int a[10], b[8];`		
2. `int * p;`		
3. `if(...){`		
4. `    p = &a[6];`	$p \mapsto \langle a, [6,6] \rangle$	$p \mapsto \langle a : \text{int}[10], [6,6] \rangle$
5. `} else {`		
6. `    p = &b[3];`	$p \mapsto \langle b, [3,3] \rangle$	$p \mapsto \langle b : \text{int}[8], [3,3] \rangle$
7. `}`		
8.	$p \mapsto \perp$	$p \mapsto \langle \text{UNKNOWN} : \text{int}[8], [3,6] \rangle$
9. `*p = 0;`	(don't know)	(in-bounds)

Fig. 2. Multiple Target Example

We now define a Location-Offset domain whose elements represent a pointer to a location plus an offset:

Location-Offset Domain $\mathcal{LO} = \langle LO, \sqsubseteq_{lo} \rangle$:

- $LO = (Loc \cup \{\text{NULL}\}) \times I$
- The element $\langle x, [min, max] \rangle$ represents the address of location x plus an offset in the range $[min, max]$; i.e., the range $[\&x + min \cdot |\tau_x|, \&x + max \cdot |\tau_x|]$, where τ_x is the static element type of location x, and $|\tau|$ is shorthand for $\texttt{sizeof}(\tau)$, the size of τ in bytes.
- A NULL-targeted element $\langle \text{NULL}, [min, max] \rangle$ represents the integer range $[min, max]$.
- $\langle l_1, o_1 \rangle \sqsubseteq_{lo} \langle l_2, o_2 \rangle$ iff $l_1 = l_2$ and $o_1 \sqsubseteq_i o_2$.
- $\mathcal{LO}$ can be converted to a lattice $\mathcal{LO}^L$ by adding a "top" element ($\top$) and a "bottom" element ($\perp$).

Figure 1(b) shows a program that has the same behavior as the program in Figure 1(a), but which uses a pointer to indirectly access the array. At line 4, we map p to the location-offset range $\langle a, [6,6] \rangle$ which represents the constant value $\&a + 6 \cdot |\text{int}|$. At line 8, the meet operation yields the range $[\&a + 3 \cdot |\text{int}|, \&a + 6 \cdot |\text{int}|]$ of possible values for p. At line 9, when p is dereferenced, since a has 10 elements, we can verify that the range of p falls within the legal range $[\&a + 0 \cdot |\text{int}|, \&a + 9 \cdot |\text{int}|]$, thus *p will be in-bounds.

The Location-Offset representation has two weaknesses. First, it can only represent a pointer to a single target location. Consider the example in Figure 2, where p is assigned to point to two different arrays, a and b, along the two branches. Using the location-offset representation, the merge point at line 8 would map p to $\perp$, since the elements $\langle a, [6,6] \rangle$ and $\langle b, [3,3] \rangle$ from the two incoming branches are $\sqsubseteq_{lo}$-incomparable, and thus the dereference at line 9 cannot be determined to be in-bounds.

The second weakness of the Location-Offset representation is that it may lose precision when handling pointer arithmetic with mismatched types. Consider the example in Figure 3: At line 3, p is assigned to point to an array of 2 ints. However, since the static type of p is char *, the pointer arithmetic at line 4 is char-based, so it must first be translated to int-based arithmetic before being

	Location-Offset	Descriptor-Offset
1. `int a[2];`		
2. `char *p, *q;`		
3. `p = (char *)&a[0];`	$p \mapsto \langle a, [0, 0] \rangle$	$p \mapsto \langle a : \texttt{int}[2], [0, 0] \rangle$
4. `q = p + 6;`	$q \mapsto \langle a, [1, 2] \rangle$	$q \mapsto \langle a : \texttt{char}[8], [6, 6] \rangle$
5. `*q = 0;`	(not in-bounds)	(in-bounds)

Fig. 3. Mismatched Types Example, assuming $|\texttt{int}| = 4$

applied to the `int`-based range $\langle a, [0, 0] \rangle$. Assuming $|\texttt{int}| = 4$ and $|\texttt{char}| = 1$, the `char`-based addition of 6 becomes an `int`-based addition of $6 \cdot \frac{1}{4} = \frac{3}{2}$, which must be approximated as the range $[1, 2]$. With the computed fact $\langle a, [1, 2] \rangle$, the dereference at line 5 is identified as being potentially out-of-bounds, even though in fact it is in-bounds.

To address these two weaknesses of the Location-Offset domain, we track the type and element count of the pointer's target separately and explicitly. First, we define the domain of Array Descriptors, whose elements describe the identity, element type, and element count of an (array) object:

Array-Descriptor Domain $\mathcal{D} = \langle D, \sqsubseteq_d \rangle$:
- $D = Loc' \times T \times \mathbb{N}$
  - $Loc' = Loc \cup \{\text{UNKNOWN}\}$, where UNKNOWN represents "an unknown location". A flat semi-lattice $\langle Loc', \sqsubseteq_l \rangle$ is defined such that for all $x, y \in Loc$, UNKNOWN $\sqsubseteq_l x$, and $x \sqsubseteq_l y$ iff $x = y$.
  - T is the set of unqualified non-void non-array C types, with `typedefs` expanded to their underlying types, and with all pointer types treated as equivalent.
- The descriptor $\langle x, \tau, \sigma \rangle$ represents the location x treated as an array with at least σ elements each of type τ. For readability, we use the notation $x : \tau[\sigma]$ to represent the triple $\langle x, \tau, \sigma \rangle$. Multi-dimensional arrays are flattened; e.g., a 2×3 array of integers y is represented as $y : \texttt{int}[6]$.
- UNKNOWN $: \tau[\sigma]$ represents a location of unknown identity that is an array of at least σ elements of type τ.
- $(x_1 : \tau_1[\sigma_1]) \sqsubseteq_d (x_2 : \tau_2[\sigma_2])$ iff $x_1 \sqsubseteq_l x_2$ and $\tau_1 = \tau_2$ and $\sigma_1 \leq \sigma_2$.

We now define the Descriptor-Offset Domain:

Descriptor-Offset Domain $\mathcal{DO} = \langle DO, \sqsubseteq_{do} \rangle$:
- $DO = (D \cup \{\text{NULL}\}) \times I$
- The element $\langle x : \tau[\sigma], [min, max] \rangle$ represents the address of an array x with at least σ elements each of type τ, plus an offset in the range $[min \cdot |\tau|, \ max \cdot |\tau|]$.
- A NULL-targeted element $\langle \text{NULL}, [min, max] \rangle$ represents the integer range $[min, max]$.
- $\langle d_1, o_1 \rangle \sqsubseteq_{do} \langle d_2, o_2 \rangle$ iff $d_1 \sqsubseteq_d d_2$ and $o_1 \sqsubseteq_i o_2$.
  (NULL is not $\sqsubseteq_d$-comparable to any member of D).
- $\mathcal{DO}$ can be converted to a lattice $\mathcal{DO}^L$ by adding a "top" element ($\top$) and a "bottom" element ($\bot$).

Notice that $\mathcal{D}$ is partially ordered such that $d_1 \sqsubseteq_d d_2$ only if the size of the array described by d_1 is less than or equal to the size of the array described by d_2. This ensures that $\mathcal{DO}$ satisfies the safe approximation requirement, since if p points to an array of 8 elements, it is a safe approximation to say that p points to an array of 6 elements.

The rightmost columns of Figures 2 and 3 show the analysis results using Descriptor-Offset ranges. For Figure 2, the meet operation at line 8 sets the location component to UNKNOWN, but the type, count, and offset components are preserved: we are able to approximate the two incoming facts for p by taking the smaller type-count descriptor and the superset of the interval components. When dereferencing p, if p maps to an element $\langle x : \tau[\sigma], [min, max] \rangle$ such that $min \geq 0$ and $max < \sigma$, then the dereference is guaranteed to be in-bounds, even if $x = $ UNKNOWN (as is the case for the dereference on line 9 of Figure 2).

For Figure 3, at line 4 we can change the type and count components of the range, so that array a is now treated as an array of 8 chars. This allows us to recognize that the dereference at line 5 is guaranteed to be in-bounds.

3   Pointer Arithmetic

An important aspect of pointer-range analysis is the handling of pointer arithmetic. The six classes of additive operations in C for integers and pointers are listed in Figure 4, along with their semantics in terms of integer arithmetic (note that *pointer+pointer* and *int−pointer* are not allowed). Since the two pointer additions $+_{pi}^\tau$ and $+_{ip}^\tau$ are similar, and the subtractions $-_{ii}$ and $-_{pi}^\tau$ can be trivially converted to the corresponding addition with the negative of the second argument, we will only describe the handling of $+_{ii}$, $+_{pi}^\tau$, and $-_{pp}^\tau$.

3.1   Well-Typed Arithmetic

An arithmetic operation is well typed if the actual types of the arguments match the types expected by the operation. With the descriptor-offset domain, a targeted range $\langle x : \tau[\sigma], o \rangle$ represents a value of type $\tau *$, while a NULL-targeted range $\langle$NULL$, o\rangle$ represents a value of type int.

Operator : Type		Integer Semantics
$+_{ii}$:	$\text{int} \times \text{int} \rightarrow \text{int}$	$i_1 +_{ii} i_2 \equiv i_1 + i_2$
$-_{ii}$:	$\text{int} \times \text{int} \rightarrow \text{int}$	$i_1 -_{ii} i_2 \equiv i_1 - i_2$
$+_{pi}^\tau$:	$\tau* \times \text{int} \rightarrow \tau*$	$p +_{pi}^\tau i \equiv p + (i \cdot |\tau|)$
$+_{ip}^\tau$:	$\text{int} \times \tau* \rightarrow \tau*$	$i +_{ip}^\tau p \equiv (i \cdot |\tau|) + p$
$-_{pi}^\tau$:	$\tau* \times \text{int} \rightarrow \tau*$	$p -_{pi}^\tau i \equiv p - (i \cdot |\tau|)$
$-_{pp}^\tau$:	$\tau* \times \tau* \rightarrow \text{int}^\dagger$	$p_1 -_{pp}^\tau p_2 \equiv (p_1 - p_2)/|\tau|$

†The result of subtracting two pointers actually
has an implementation-defined type ptrdiff_t.

Fig. 4. C Addition and Subtraction

The addition and subtraction of two integer intervals can be safely approximated by the following equations[1]:

- $[min_1, max_1] + [min_2, max_2] = [min_1 + min_2, max_1 + max_2]$
- $[min_1, max_1] - [min_2, max_2] = [min_1 - max_2, max_1 - min_2]$

Well-typed arithmetic on descriptor-offset ranges can be evaluated by applying these equations to the interval components of the ranges:

- Integer addition $(+_{ii})$ of two NULL-targeted ranges:
  $$\langle \text{NULL}, [min_1, max_1] \rangle +_{ii} \langle \text{NULL}, [min_2, max_2] \rangle$$
  $$= \langle \text{NULL}, [min_1 + min_2, max_1 + max_2] \rangle$$
- Pointer addition $(+_{pi}^\tau)$ of a τ-based range and a NULL-targeted range:
  $$\langle x : \tau[\sigma], [min_1, max_1] \rangle +_{pi}^\tau \langle \text{NULL}, [min_2, max_2] \rangle$$
  $$= \langle x : \tau[\sigma], [min_1 + min_2, max_1 + max_2] \rangle$$
- Pointer subtraction $(-_{pp}^\tau)$ of two ranges with the same target location $x \neq$ UNKNOWN and the same element type τ:
  $$\langle x : \tau[\sigma], [min_1, max_1] \rangle -_{pp}^\tau \langle x : \tau[\sigma], [min_2, max_2] \rangle$$
  $$= \langle \text{NULL}, [min_1 - max_2, max_1 - min_2] \rangle$$

In C, subtraction of two pointers $(-_{pp}^\tau)$ is well defined only if the two pointers point to the same array. Therefore, pointer subtraction of two ranges with different or UNKNOWN target locations evaluates to $\bot$.

3.2   Mismatched-Type Arithmetic

An arithmetic operation that is not well typed can arise because C permits casting between pointers to different types, and between integers and pointers; it can also arise from the use of unions. This section addresses the handling of arithmetic operations on ranges with mismatched types. This includes integer addition $(+_{ii})$ with a pointer-typed argument, and pointer addition or subtraction where the type of the operation does not match the argument type.

How this problem is handled depends first on the requirements of the client of the analysis. Specifically, is the client interested only in well-typed accesses? If so, then the result of any pointer arithmetic operation with mismatched types should be $\bot$. However, this is usually too strong a requirement for C programs, because its weak typing discipline means any memory location could be accessed as if it were of any type. With this model of memory locations, we can weaken the definition of the array-descriptor ordering $\sqsubseteq_d$ defined on page 137 so that:

- $(x_1 : \tau_1[\sigma_1]) \sqsubseteq_d (x_2 : \tau_2[\sigma_2])$ iff $x_1 \sqsubseteq_l x_2$ and $|\tau_1[\sigma_1]| \leq |\tau_2[\sigma_2]|$.

That is, d_1 is a safe approximation of d_2 if the array described by d_1 is smaller than the array described by d_2, regardless of the element types of the descriptors.

---

[1] For brevity, we omit details concerning infinite bounds, which are handled by setting respectively the upper/lower bound to plus/minus infinity if either argument needed to compute the bound is infinite.

This means that if the size of each type is known at analysis time, we can convert a range's type from τ_a to τ_b as follows:

$$\langle x : \tau_a\,[\sigma]\,,[min, max]\rangle \implies \langle x : \tau_b\,[\,\lfloor \sigma \cdot \tfrac{|\tau_a|}{|\tau_b|} \rfloor\,]\,,\left[\left\lfloor min \cdot \tfrac{|\tau_a|}{|\tau_b|}\right\rfloor , \left\lceil max \cdot \tfrac{|\tau_a|}{|\tau_b|}\right\rceil\right]\rangle \quad (1)$$

We can also transform the base type of a pointer addition by adjusting the right-hand-side interval. A τ_b-based pointer addition $(+_{pi}^{\tau_b})$, where the right-hand-side is NULL-targeted, can be converted to a τ_a-based addition as follows:

$$r_1 +_{pi}^{\tau_b} \langle \text{NULL}, [min_2, max_2]\rangle \implies r_1 +_{pi}^{\tau_a} \langle \text{NULL}, \left[\left\lfloor min_2 \cdot \tfrac{|\tau_b|}{|\tau_a|}\right\rfloor , \left\lceil max_2 \cdot \tfrac{|\tau_b|}{|\tau_a|}\right\rceil\right]\rangle \quad (2)$$

Transformation (1) or (2) can be used to eliminate any type mismatch, to get a well-typed operation that can be evaluated by the equations in Section 3.1.

Revisiting the Figure 3 example, the addition `p + 6` at line 4 has a type mismatch, because `p` maps to an `int`-based range, while the addition is `char`-based. We can apply either transformation (1) or (2), to get the following results:

$$\langle a : \texttt{int[2]}, [0, 0]\rangle +_{pi}^{\texttt{char}} \langle \text{NULL}, [6, 6]\rangle$$
$$= (1) \Rightarrow \langle a : \texttt{char[8]}, [0, 0]\rangle +_{pi}^{\texttt{char}} \langle \text{NULL}, [6, 6]\rangle = \langle a : \texttt{char[8]}, [6, 6]\rangle$$
$$= (2) \Rightarrow \langle a : \texttt{int[2]}, [0, 0]\rangle +_{pi}^{\texttt{int}} \langle \text{NULL}, [1, 2]\rangle \quad\ = \langle a : \texttt{int[2]}, [1, 2]\rangle$$

Because of the floor and ceiling operations, there may be some loss in precision as a result of applying either transformation (1) or (2). It is therefore important to choose a transformation that minimizes loss of precision. In practice, the size of one of the types τ_a, τ_b is usually a multiple of the size of the other (making either $\tfrac{|\tau_a|}{|\tau_b|}$ or $\tfrac{|\tau_b|}{|\tau_a|}$ a round number), so that at least one of the transformations will result in no loss of precision.

Transformations (1) and (2) can only be applied if the sizes of types are known at analysis time. If an analysis is designed to be portable across all platforms, then specific sizes of types cannot be assumed. In such a case, we can still make some safe approximations to get results that are more precise than $\bot$, by making use of portable information about the sizes of types as defined or implied in the C specifications:

1. $|\texttt{char}| = 1$
2. $|\texttt{char}| \leq |\tau|$ for any non-void C type τ.
3. $|\texttt{char}| \leq |\texttt{short}| \leq |\texttt{int}| \leq |\texttt{long}| \leq |\texttt{long long}|$
4. $|\texttt{float}| \leq |\texttt{double}| \leq |\texttt{long double}|$
5. $|\tau[\sigma]| = |\tau| \cdot \sigma$
6. $|union\ \{\tau_1 \ldots \tau_n\}| \geq \max_{i=1\ldots n}(|\tau_i|)$
7. $|struct\ \{\tau_1 \ldots \tau_n\}| \geq \sum_{i=1}^{n} |\tau_i|$
8. $|struct\ \{\tau_1 \ldots \tau_n\}| \leq |struct\ \{\tau_1 \ldots \tau_n \ldots\}|$
9. $|\tau_1*| = |\tau_2*|$ for any C types τ_1, τ_2.

Item 1 implies that `char`-pointer arithmetic is equivalent to integer arithmetic $(+_{pi}^{\texttt{char}} \equiv +_{ii}, -_{pp}^{\texttt{char}} \equiv -_{ii})$. Item 6 states that a union type is at least as large as its largest member, while item 7 states that a struct type is at least as large as the sum of its constituents' sizes (it may be larger due to padding). Item 8 takes advantage of a subtype relationship between two structures that share a common initial sequence. Item 9, which states that all pointers are of the same size, is strictly speaking an unsafe assumption, but it is all but implied by the requirements that all pointers can be cast to void ∗ without loss of information, and that the return value of malloc can be safely cast to any pointer type. We therefore assume it to be true.

The first safe approximation, which arises often because of the way we normalize multi-dimensional arrays, is to convert a $\tau[\sigma]$-based pointer addition, where $\tau[\sigma]$ is an array type, to a τ-based pointer addition. This is done by applying transformation (2) with the knowledge that $\frac{|\tau[\sigma]|}{|\tau|} = \sigma$:

$$r_1 +_{pi}^{\tau[\sigma]} \langle \text{NULL}, [min_2, max_2] \rangle \implies r_1 +_{pi}^{\tau} \langle \text{NULL}, [min_2 \cdot \sigma, max_2 \cdot \sigma] \rangle$$

Next, if we only know the relative sizes of two types, we can make the following approximations for transformation (2).

If $|\tau_b| \le |\tau_a|$, $r_1 +_{pi}^{\tau_b} \langle \text{NULL}, [min_2, max_2] \rangle \implies$

$$r_1 +_{pi}^{\tau_a} \langle \text{NULL}, \left[\begin{pmatrix} min_2 & \text{if } min_2 \le 0 \\ 0 & \text{otherwise} \end{pmatrix}, \begin{pmatrix} max_2 & \text{if } max_2 \ge 0 \\ 0 & \text{otherwise} \end{pmatrix} \right] \rangle \quad (2a)$$

If $|\tau_a| \le |\tau_b|$, $r_1 +_{pi}^{\tau_b} \langle \text{NULL}, [min_2, max_2] \rangle \implies$

$$r_1 +_{pi}^{\tau_a} \langle \text{NULL}, \left[\begin{pmatrix} min_2 & \text{if } min_2 \ge 0 \\ -\infty & \text{otherwise} \end{pmatrix}, \begin{pmatrix} max_2 & \text{if } max_2 \le 0 \\ +\infty & \text{otherwise} \end{pmatrix} \right] \rangle \quad (2b)$$

For the pointer addition p + 6 at line 4 of Figure 3, since we know $|char| \le |int|$, we can apply transformation (2a) to get:

$$\langle a : \text{int}[2], [0,0] \rangle +_{pi}^{char} \langle \text{NULL}, [6,6] \rangle \implies \langle a : \text{int}[2], [0,0] \rangle +_{pi}^{int} \langle \text{NULL}, [0,6] \rangle$$
$$= \langle a : \text{int}[2], [0,6] \rangle$$

Note that the resulting range is a safe approximation (superset) of the more precise range $\langle a : \text{int}[2], [1,2] \rangle$ obtained earlier with exact size information.

A similar approximation can be made for transformation (1), but only in one direction:

If $|\tau_b| \le |\tau_a|$, let n be such that $1 \le n \le \frac{|\tau_a|}{|\tau_b|}$,
then $\langle x : \tau_a[\sigma], [min, max] \rangle \implies$

$$\langle x : \tau_b[n \cdot \sigma], \left[\begin{pmatrix} min & \text{if } min \ge 0 \\ -\infty & \text{otherwise} \end{pmatrix}, \begin{pmatrix} max & \text{if } max \le 0 \\ +\infty & \text{otherwise} \end{pmatrix} \right] \rangle \quad (1a)$$

A key here is that $|\tau_a[\sigma]| \ge |\tau_b[n \cdot \sigma]|$, which ensures that the right-hand-side of the transformation is a safe approximation of the left-hand-side. If τ_1 and τ_2 are scalar types, the exact ratio $\frac{|\tau_a|}{|\tau_b|}$ is not portably defined, so the only safe value for n is 1. But if τ_a is an aggregate type, a safe n can be obtained by counting the number of elements in τ_a that are at least as big as τ_b. For example, $\frac{|struct\{int[2], long, char\}|}{|int|} \ge 3$. It is then safe to multiply the σ component of the resultant range by n.

Thus, when evaluating the pointer addition

$$\langle x : \tau_a \left[\sigma\right], o_1 \rangle +_{pi}^{\tau_b} \langle \text{NULL}, o_2 \rangle$$

if $|\tau_a| \leq |\tau_b|$, only transformation (2b) can be applied. But if $|\tau_b| \leq |\tau_a|$, there is a choice between (1a) and (2a). As was the case for transformations (1) and (2), it is important to choose the transformation that minimizes the loss of precision. In general, transformation (1a) is more precise if the left-hand-side offset o_1 is $[0, 0]$; otherwise (2a) is more precise.

4   Experimental Results

The pointer-range analysis was implemented as a context-insensitive inter-procedural dataflow analysis (operating on a supergraph of the program). Since the interval lattice has infinite descending chains, widening [5] is used to ensure convergence, and narrowing is used to obtain more precise results. A points-to analysis [8] pass is first performed to safely account for aliasing, and also to identify targets of indirect procedure calls.

The following numbers were collected to gauge the potential utility of this analysis for various applications.

Bounded and Half-Open Ranges: We count the number of dereferences *p
  for which p maps to a range with a known location and is either
  - *bounded*: the offset component is finite, or
  - *half-open*: the offset component has at least one finite bound, e.g., $[1, +\infty]$ or $[-\infty, 3]$.
  Such ranges are potentially useful for dependence analysis, where one is interested in whether two dereferences may access the same memory location.
In-Bounds Dereferences: At each dereference *p, if $p \mapsto \langle x : \tau \left[\sigma\right], [min, max] \rangle$
  such that $min \geq 0$ and $max < \sigma$, then the dereference is guaranteed to be in-bounds. This information can be used to eliminate unnecessary bounds checks, and to detect potential out-of-bounds errors.

Figure 5 presents the results of our analysis on benchmarks from Cyclone[15], olden[4], Spec 95 and Spec 2000. Column (a) gives the number of lines of code and column (b) gives the static number of dereferences in each program.

Using the descriptor-offset (DO) representation, column (c) gives the percentage of dereferences that had bounded ranges and (d) gives the percentage that had half-bounded ranges. These may be contrasted roughly with the results of numeric range analysis given in [24], which identified about 30% bounded and 40% half-bounded ranges for non-pointer variables in some small benchmarks (100-400 statements).

Column (e) gives the percentage of dereferences found to be in-bounds. While the average percentage is quite low, there are many cases, including some larger programs, for which over 30% of dereferences were found to be in-bounds.

To contrast these numbers against how well Array-Range Analysis would fare, columns (f)-(h) give the percentages of bounded, half-bounded, and in-bounds

	LOC (a)	num derefs (b)	DO %			arrays only %			in-b diff.		kn.
			bnd (c)	half-b (d)	in-bnd (e)	bnd (f)	half-b (g)	in-bnd (h)	multi (i)	pred (j)	preds (k)
Cyclone											
aes	1,822	152	49.3	77.0	46.1	8.6	23.7	5.9	0	7	3
cacm	340	25	48.0	52.0	48.0	40.0	44.0	40.0	0	8	0
cfrac	4,218	446	2.7	4.7	3.6	0.0	0.0	0.0	6	0	1
finger	158	24	4.2	4.2	33.3	0.0	0.0	0.0	7	0	1
grobner	4,737	1,349	26.6	27.9	34.9	0.7	1.7	0.5	117	5	6
matxmult	1,377	13	30.8	30.8	30.8	0.0	0.0	0.0	0	4	0
ppm	1,421	123	5.7	7.3	5.7	0.8	1.6	0.8	0	3	0
tile	4,880	324	6.5	10.2	5.6	2.5	3.1	1.5	0	5	0
olden											
bh	3,200	219	42.5	42.5	42.5	42.5	42.5	42.5	0	60	1
bisort	690	89	10.1	10.1	10.1	0.0	0.0	0.0	0	0	0
em3d	538	51	15.7	15.7	0.0	0.0	0.0	0.0	0	0	0
health	706	84	19.0	19.0	19.0	0.0	0.0	0.0	0	1	0
mst	610	52	11.5	11.5	11.5	0.0	0.0	0.0	0	0	0
perimeter	472	44	31.8	31.8	31.8	0.0	0.0	0.0	0	0	0
power	867	190	30.5	30.5	33.2	7.4	7.4	7.4	5	22	0
treeadd	375	8	0.0	0.0	0.0	0.0	0.0	0.0	0	0	0
tsp	684	94	11.7	11.7	11.7	0.0	0.0	0.0	0	0	0
Spec95											
compress	3,900	83	19.3	32.5	18.1	12.0	14.5	10.8	0	6	0
gcc	205,106	52,108	7.9	10.6	8.6	3.0	5.2	3.0	378	412	58
go	29,629	8,893	7.1	13.0	7.5	7.0	12.7	6.9	40	369	4
ijpeg	31,215	8,718	13.9	16.2	14.5	3.0	3.3	3.0	52	36	3
li	7,630	914	1.2	2.8	5.0	0.5	0.7	0.5	35	3	1
m88ksim	19,227	2,406	25.4	28.8	38.9	21.4	23.2	21.4	326	115	4
perl	26,872	9,096	2.3	2.9	3.2	0.8	1.0	0.8	88	0	5
vortex	67,219	12,017	20.8	21.0	28.0	1.1	1.2	1.0	872	1	175
Spec2000											
ammp	13,483	5,040	9.8	14.3	10.2	7.6	9.2	7.6	22	57	4
art	1,270	258	11.6	12.8	11.6	11.6	12.8	11.6	0	8	0
bzip2	4,650	522	22.6	37.9	19.7	15.5	28.5	12.6	0	43	12
crafty	20,545	3,764	49.6	56.2	48.4	41.7	45.9	39.5	37	631	10
equake	1,513	777	31.3	34.4	32.3	12.5	14.9	12.5	8	68	0
gap	71,363	26,459	3.5	4.9	3.6	3.4	3.7	3.4	12	166	26
gzip	8,605	720	25.3	33.3	27.8	9.6	16.1	9.6	18	58	14
mcf	2,412	568	28.2	30.3	28.2	0.7	2.8	0.7	0	2	0
mesa	58,724	23,741	5.1	8.0	5.8	3.4	5.8	3.4	178	53	29
parser	11,391	2,867	3.6	9.2	3.6	1.5	6.1	1.4	0	9	3
twolf	20,461	9,573	1.0	1.5	0.9	0.8	1.3	0.8	2	9	6
vpr	17,730	2,874	14.3	14.3	16.7	3.2	3.2	3.1	74	20	1
Total		174,685							2277	2181	367
Average			17.6	20.9	18.9	7.1	9.1	6.8	61.5	58.9	9.9

Fig. 5. Results

dereferences that were *direct* array accesses, i.e., accesses of the form a[x] where a is an array object. These represent the results that could be obtained using an Array-Range Analysis approach that does not handle pointers (e.g., [5,24]). The difference is large for all three categories, confirming that handling of pointers is important when analyzing C programs.

To motivate the use of the *DO* representation rather than the simpler location-offset (*LO*) representation, we evaluated the two ways in which *DO* can give better results than *LO*:

- *multi-target: DO* can represent a pointer to multiple targets, as in the Figure 2 example.
- *transformation (1): DO* allows the application of Transformation (1) or (1a) when handling mismatched-type operations.

We found that *multi-target* made a bigger difference: column (i) gives the number of in-bounds dereferences that were not found when the *multi-target* ability was disabled – on average about 11% of the in-bounds dereferences per benchmark. Most of these come from procedure calls, where different arrays of the same size are passed as an argument to a procedure that accesses the array. As for *transformation (1)*, only 35 in-bounds dereferences were not found when this feature was disabled (one in gcc, 21 in m88ksim, and 13 in crafty). Overall, the difference between the *DO* and *LO* is significant, and shows that the type-count descriptor is an effective mechanism for handling challenging aspects of C.

To measure the price of portability, we looked at the improvement in results if exact sizes of types are assumed, i.e., if type mismatches are handled with transformations (1) and (2) rather than (1a), (2a), and (2b). Only five more in-bounds dereferences were found using exact sizes (two in gcc and three in gap), suggesting that in practice, the portable transformations produce results that are almost as good as the non-portable ones.

One aspect of range analysis that was not described in this paper is the treatment of ranges at branch nodes. For example, consider a branch node containing the predicate $v_1 < v_2$. If the before- dataflow fact mappings are:

$$v_1 \mapsto \langle x : \tau[\sigma], [min_1, max_1] \rangle$$
$$v_2 \mapsto \langle x : \tau[\sigma], [min_2, max_2] \rangle$$

then the after- fact mappings along the true branch will be:

$$v_1 \mapsto \langle x : \tau[\sigma], [min_1, \min(max_1, max_2 - 1)] \rangle$$
$$v_2 \mapsto \langle x : \tau[\sigma], [\max(min_1 + 1, min_2), max_2] \rangle$$

This is an important improvement to make for precision, as confirmed by Column (j), which gives the number of in-bounds dereferences that were missed when the range improvements at branch nodes were not applied – on average about 20% of the in-bounds dereferences per benchmark.

Precise treatment of ranges at branch nodes also lets us discover infeasible branches. For example, at the predicate $v_1 < v_2$, if v_1's range is entirely less than v_2's range, then the value of the predicate is statically known, indicating that

	LOC	time(s)		LOC	time(s)		LOC	time(s)
li	7,630	15	twolf	20,461	12	mesa	58,724	29371
parser	11,391	5	crafty	20,545	16	vortex	67,219	233
ammp	13,483	6	perl	26,872	39	gap	71,363	656
vpr	17,730	7	go	29,629	7	gcc	205,106	2640
m88ksim	19,227	21	ijpeg	31,215	487			

Fig. 6. Analysis Times

the false branch is infeasible. Column (k) gives the number of known predicates found in the programs. The large number of known predicates in vortex comes from a programming style where a series of procedure calls are each checked for success by if statements, even though some of the procedures always return the same value.

Finally, as a rough indicator of the efficiency of the algorithm, Figure 6 gives the analysis times (wallclock time, in seconds) on a 1GHz Pentium II with 500MB RAM, running Linux, listed in order of increasing size (by lines of code). The benchmarks not listed each took less than a second to analyze.

4.1 Improvements

The current implementation includes several weaknesses that can be addressed with known solutions. Among the possible improvements are adding flow-sensitivity or context-sensitivity to the points-to analysis [16, 10, 27], and adding context sensitivity to the dataflow analysis [18], but these improvements will increase the time complexity of the analysis.

Another aspect that could be improved is the handling of heap-allocated objects. Currently, only malloc calls for which the argument is a constant C or an expression $C * \texttt{sizeof}(\tau)$ are mapped to a malloc location with a non-void type and non-zero count. Such cases account for 46% of the malloc calls in the programs, so there is room for improvement. Many programs use a malloc wrapper to check for error conditions; this common practice becomes a problem for static analysis because it causes multiple conceptual allocation sites to be folded into a single malloc callsite. Limited use of inlining and constant propagation can be used to split the malloc callsite into multiple callsites, to increase the likelihood of having a MALLOC location with a meaningful type and count.

4.2 Extensions

The range analysis described in this paper only computes ranges with constant bounds. It relies on the presence of constants in the source code to derive meaningful ranges, and does not record information about the relationships between variables. Approaches that track symbolic ranges [2, 21] and constraints between variables [6, 7, 20, 3, 23] can significantly improve results in applications that are interested in bounds checking or discovering non-aliasing memory accesses. Ideas discussed in this paper could be applied to extend previous approaches to handle pointers in general.

String manipulation is another aspect of C worthy of special consideration. A string is conceptually a separate data type, with its own library to manipulate values, but its implementation on top of arrays makes it susceptible to out-of-bounds array accesses. Tracking the string length as a separate attribute from the array size, and deriving information based on the semantics of C library functions, can lead to more precise results when trying to discover potentially out-of-bounds dereferences [25, 9], which is an important concern for program security.

5   Related Work

Range analysis has been around for decades, and was the motivating example used in the seminal paper on abstract interpretation [5], which introduced the notions of widening and narrowing. Other early work on range analysis relied on the presence of structured loops to infer loop bounds information [13, 26]. Verbrugge et al describe range analysis as "generalized constant propagation" [24], and use it for dead-code elimination and array dependence testing in the Mc-CAT optimizing/parallelizing compiler. Stephenson et al [22] use range analysis to compute the number of bits needed to store a given value in hardware.

Patterson [19] uses range analysis for static branch prediction: each variable at each program point is mapped to a set of probability-weighted ranges. The weights are used at branch predicates to predict the likelihood of branching in a given direction, and is used for various code-generation optimizations. Gu et al [11] use range analysis to discover opportunities for array privatization and parallelization in loops, while Gupta et al [12] do the same for recursive divide-and-conquer procedures. They both use a Guarded Array Region representation that associates a predicate with each range. Balakrishnan and Reps [1] use range analysis to infer high-level information from binary code: with a range representation of the form $a \times [b, c] + d$, they compute value sets that are conceptually equivalent to the high-level notion of a variable, to enable high-level analyses like reaching definitions to be applied to binary code.

These four approaches all include the notion of a "stride" in their representation to capture the common access pattern of arrays. Wilson et al [27] also use a stride to improve their pointer analysis. Conceptually, the τ component in our descriptor-offset representation encodes the stride in a portable format, allowing our analysis to be used in settings where exact sizes of types cannot be assumed.

Numerous approaches compute symbolic range information, to allow tracking of constraints between variables, but few have dealt with pointers. Rugina and Rinard [21] compute symbolic ranges for variables including pointers, and use linear programming to identify non-intersecting ranges that could be used for automatic parallelization or identifying in-bounds accesses. Approaches that deal with C strings to identify potential buffer overruns [25, 9, 17] must necessarily handle pointers, but only **char** pointers; thus they do not need to address problems related to casting.

6   Conclusion

We have presented a pointer-range analysis that extends traditional array-range analysis to handle pointers as well as non-trivial aspects of C, including pointer arithmetic and type-casting. We described two possible range representations: the intuitive location-offset representation, and the descriptor-offset representation, and showed that the latter yields better results in practice. The ideas we have presented can provide useful insight into extending existing array-based range analysis to handle pointers in C-like languages.

References

1. G. Balakrishnan and T. Reps. Analyzing memory accesses in x86 executables. In *International Conference on Compiler Construction*, Barcelona, Spain, Mar. 2004.
2. W. Blume and R. Eigenmann. Demand-driven, symbolic range propagation. In *8th International workshop on Languages and Compilers for Parallel Computing*, pages 141–160, Columbus OH, Aug. 1995.
3. R. Bodik, R. Gupta, and V. Sarkar. ABCD: Eliminating array bounds checks on demand. In *ACM SIGPLAN Conference on Programming Language Design and Implementation*, pages 321–333, Vancouver, BC, June 2000.
4. M. C. Carlisle and A. Rogers. Software caching and computation migration in Olden. Technical Report TR-483-95, Princeton University, 1995.
5. P. Cousot and R. Cousot. Static determination of dynamic properties of programs. In *ACM Symposium on Principles of Programming Languages*, pages 106–130, Apr. 1976.
6. P. Cousot and N. Halbwachs. Automatic discovery of linear restraints among variables of a program. In *ACM Symposium on Principles of Programming Languages*, pages 84–96, Jan. 1978.
7. B. Creusillet and F. Irigoin. Interprocedural array region analyses. *International Journal of Parallel Programming*, 24(6):513–546, Dec. 1996.
8. M. Das. Unification-based pointer analysis with directional assignments. In *ACM SIGPLAN Conference on Programming Language Design and Implementation*, pages 35–46, Vancouver, BC, June 2000.
9. N. Dor, M. Rodeh, and M. Sagiv. Cleanness checking of string manipulations in C programs via integer analysis. In *The 8th International Static Analysis Symposium*, volume 2126 of *Lecture Notes in Computer Science*, page 194. Springer, July 2001.
10. M. Emami, R. Ghiya, and L. Hendren. Context-sensitive interprocedural points-to analysis in the presence of function pointers. In *ACM SIGPLAN Conference on Programming Language Design and Implementation*, pages 242–256, Orlando, FL, June 1994.
11. J. Gu, Z. Li, and G. Lee. Symbolic array dataflow analysis for array privatization and program parallelization. In *ACM/IEEE Conference on Supercomputing*, San Diego, CA, Dec. 1995.
12. M. Gupta, S. Mukhopadhyay, and N. Sinha. Automatic parallelization of recursive procedures. In *International Conference on Parallel Architectures and Compilation Techniques (PACT)*, pages 139–148, Newport Beach, CA, Oct. 1999. IEEE Computer Society.
13. W. H. Harrison. Compiler analysis of the value ranges for variables. In *IEEE Transactions on Software Engineering*, volume SE-3, pages 243–250, May 1977.

14. P. Havlak and K. Kennedy. An implementation of interprocedural bounded regular section analysis. *IEEE Transactions of Parallel and Distributed Computing*, 2(3):350–360, July 1991.

15. T. Jim, G. Morrisett, D. Grossman, M. Hicks, J. Cheney, and Y. Wang. Cyclone: A safe dialect of C. In *USENIX Annual Technical Conference*, Monterey, CA, June 2002.

16. W. Landi and B. G. Ryder. A safe approximate algorithm for interprocedural pointer aliasing. In *ACM SIGPLAN Conference on Programming Language Design and Implementation*, pages 235–248, San Francisco, CA, June 1992.

17. D. Larochelle and D. Evans. Statically detecting likely buffer overflow vulnerabilities. In *USENIX Security Symposium*, Washington, D.C., Aug. 2001.

18. F. Martin. Experimental comparison of *call string* and *functional* approaches to interprocedural analysis. In *6th Int. Conf. on Compiler Construction*, volume 1575 of *Lecture Notes in Computer Science*, pages 63–75. Springer, Mar. 1999.

19. J. R. C. Patterson. Accurate static branch prediction by value range propagation. In *ACM SIGPLAN Conference on Programming Language Design and Implementation*, pages 67–78, La Jolla, CA, June 1995.

20. W. Pugh and D. Wonnacott. Constraint-based array dependence analysis. *ACM Transactions on Programming Languages and Systems*, 20(3):635–678, May 1998.

21. R. Rugina and M. Rinard. Symbolic bounds analysis of pointers, array indices, and accessed memory regions. In *ACM SIGPLAN Conference on Programming Language Design and Implementation*, pages 182–195, Vancouver, BC, June 2000.

22. M. Stephenson, J. Babb, and S. Amarasinghe. Bitwidth analysis with application to silicon compilation. In *ACM SIGPLAN Conference on Programming Language Design and Implementation*, pages 108–120, Vancouver, BC, June 2000.

23. Z. Su and D. Wagner. A class of polynomially solvable range constraints for interval analysis without widenings and narrowings. In *Tools and Algorithms for the Construction and Analysis of Systems*, volume 2988 of *Lecture Notes in Computer Science*, pages 280–295, Mar. 2004.

24. C. Verbrugge, P. Co, and L. Hendren. Generalized constant propagation: A study in C. In *6th Int. Conf. on Compiler Construction*, volume 1060 of *Lecture Notes in Computer Science*, pages 74–90. Springer, Apr. 1996.

25. D. Wagner, J. Foster, E. Brewer, and A. Aiken. A first step towards automated detection of buffer overrun vulnerabilities. In *Symposium on Network and Distributed Systems Security*, pages 3–17, San Diego, CA, Feb. 2000.

26. J. Welsh. Economic range checks in Pascal. *Software–Practice and Experience*, 8:85–97, 1978.

27. R. P. Wilson and M. S. Lam. Efficient context-sensitive pointer analysis for C programs. In *ACM SIGPLAN Conference on Programming Language Design and Implementation*, pages 1–12, La Jolla, CA, June 1995.

A Scalable Nonuniform Pointer Analysis
for Embedded Programs[*]

Arnaud Venet

NASA Ames Research Center / Kestrel Technology
Moffett Field, CA 94035, USA
arnaud@email.arc.nasa.gov

Abstract. In this paper we present a scalable pointer analysis for embedded applications that is able to distinguish between instances of recursively defined data structures and elements of arrays. The main contribution consists of an efficient yet precise algorithm that can handle multithreaded programs. We first perform an inexpensive flow-sensitive analysis of each function in the program that generates semantic equations describing the effect of the function on the memory graph. These equations bear numerical constraints that describe nonuniform points-to relationships. We then iteratively solve these equations in order to obtain an abstract storage graph that describes the shape of data structures at every point of the program for all possible thread interleavings. We bring experimental evidence that this approach is tractable and precise for real-size embedded applications.

1 Introduction

The difficulty of statically computing precise points-to information is a major obstacle to the automatic verification of real programs. Recent successes in the verification of safety-critical software [3] have been enabled in part because this class of programs makes a very restricted use of pointer manipulations and dynamic memory allocation. There are numerous pointer-intensive applications that are not safety-critical yet still require a high level of dependability like unmanned spacecraft flight control, flight data visualization or on-board network management for example. These programs commonly use arrays and linked lists to store pointers to semaphores, message queues and data packets (for interprocess communication), partitions of the memory, etc. Existing scalable pointer analyses [21, 15, 12, 18] are uniform, i.e. they do not distinguish between elements of arrays or components of recursive data structures and are therefore of little help for the verification of these programs. It is the purpose of this paper to address the problem of inferring nonuniform points-to information for embedded programs.

Few nonuniform pointer analyses have been studied in the literature. The first one has been designed by Deutsch [13, 14] and applies to programs with

---

[*] This work was supported in part by the RTD project IST-1999-20527 DAEDALUS of the european IST FP5 programme.

explicit data type annotations. We first redesigned Deutsch's model in order to analyze languages like C in which the type information cannot be trusted to infer the shape of a data structure [22, 23]. However both approaches rely on a costly representation of the aliasing as an equivalence relation between access paths, which makes this kind of analysis inapplicable to programs larger than a few thousand lines. We therefore designed a new semantic model [24] that is both more compact and more expressive than the one based on access paths. The interest of the latter approch lies in the representation of dynamic memory allocation using numerical timestamps, which turns pointer analysis into the classical problem of computing the numerical invariants of an arithmetic program. In the case of a sequential program, various optimization techniques can be applied that break down the complexity of analyzing large arithmetic programs as described in [2, 3]. In the case of multithreaded arithmetic programs however, there are no proven techniques that can cope with shared data and thread interleaving efficiently and precisely. This is a major drawback knowing that most embedded applications are multithreaded.

In this paper we present a pointer analysis based on the semantic model of [24] that can infer nonuniform points-to relations for multithreaded programs. From our experience with the verification of real embedded applications we observed that collections of objects are usually manipulated in a very regular way using simple loops. Furthermore, these loops are generally controlled by local scalar variables like an array index or a pointer to the elements of a list. It is quite uncommon to find global array indices or lists that are modified across function calls. Therefore, the information flowing through this local control structure is sufficient in practice to describe exactly the layout of arrays and the shape of linked data structures. We call it the *surface structure* of a program. In the new model proposed here we first perform a flow-sensitive analysis of the surface structure that automatically discovers numerical loop invariants relating array positions and timestamps of dynamically created objects. We use these invariants to generate semantic equations that model the effect of the function on the memory. We then iteratively solve the system made of the semantic equations generated from all functions in the program. A similar approach has been applied in [26] for improving the precision of inclusion-based flow-insensitive pointer analyses. Our model can be seen as a natural extension to Andersen's algorithm [1] in which variables are indexed by integers denoting array positions and timestamps, and inclusion constraints bear numerical relations between the indices of variables. We will carry on the presentation of the analysis with this analogy in mind.

The paper is organized as follows. In Sect. 2 we define the base semantic model and the surface structure of a C program. The semantics is based on timestamps to identify instances of dynamically allocated objects. Section 3 describes the abstract interpretation of the surface structure and the inference of numerical invariants. In Sect. 4 we show how to generate nonuniform inclusion constraints from the numerical relationships obtained by the analysis of the surface structure. The iterative resolution of these constraints provides us with a global approximation of the memory graph. We describe the implementation of an analyzer for the full C language in Sect. 5 and give some experimental results from the analysis of a real device driver. We end the paper with concluding remarks and future work.

2   Base Semantic Model

In [24] we have introduced a semantic model that uniquely identifies instances of dynamically allocated objects by using timestamps of the form $\langle \lambda_1, \ldots, \lambda_n \rangle$ where the λ_i are counters associated to each loop enclosing a memory allocation command. Consider for example the following piece of code:

Example 1.

```
for(i = 0; i < 10; i++)
  for(j = 0; j < 3; j++)
    a[i][j].ptr = malloc (...);
```

In that model we would consider the couple $\langle i, j \rangle$ as a timestamp for distinguishing between calls to the `malloc` command. In this paper we use a simplified model which folds all nested loop counters into one. In the previous example, this would result into considering the timestamp $3i + j$. This amounts to having one global counter λ that is incremented whenever the execution crosses a loop and is reset to 0 whenever the execution exits an outermost loop. While both models are equivalent in uniquely identifying dynamically allocated memory, the loss of information about nested loop counters may lead to imprecisions when timestamps are represented by abstract numerical lattices [19, 11, 16, 20]. This is not an issue in embedded applications since almost all loops have constant iteration bounds and arrays are traversed in a regular way as in the example above. This type of loop invariants can be efficiently and exactly computed by using the reduced product [8] of the lattices of linear equalities [19] and intervals [6] for example.

Because C allows the programmer to change the layout of a structured block via aggressive type casts, using symbolic data selectors like in [24] for representing points-to relations is quite challenging (see [4] for a detailed discussion of type casting in C). In our case this would make the analysis overly complicated since we also have to manage numerical constraints that relate timestamps and positions within blocks. We choose a simple solution that consists of using a homogeneous byte-based representation of positions within memory blocks. This means that a field in a structure is identified by its byte offset from the beginning of the structure. As a consequence we must take architecture-dependent characteristics like alignment and padding into account. Fortunately, most C front-ends provide this information for free. In such a model an edge in the points-to graph has the form $\langle \mathbf{a}, o \rangle \triangleright \langle \mathbf{a}', o' \rangle$ where $\mathbf{a}, \mathbf{a}'$ are addresses of blocks in memory and o, o' are byte offsets within these blocks.

Our purpose is to abstract a C program into a system of points-to equations expressed by inclusion constraints similarly to Andersen's analysis [1]. Since we

$$
\begin{aligned}
Stmt ::= \mathtt{n} = c \quad & (c \in \mathbb{N}) \quad &|\; \mathtt{p} = \mathtt{*q} \\
|\; \mathtt{n} = \mathtt{m} + \mathtt{o} \quad & &|\; \mathtt{*p} = \mathtt{q} \\
|\; \mathtt{n} = \mathtt{m} * \mathtt{o} \quad & &|\; \mathtt{p} = \mathtt{malloc()} \\
|\; \mathtt{p} = \mathtt{\&x} \quad & &|\; \mathtt{while}\;(\mathtt{m} < \mathtt{n})\;\mathtt{do}\;s_1; \cdots; s_n\;\mathtt{end} \\
|\; \mathtt{p} = \mathtt{q} + \mathtt{n} \quad & &
\end{aligned}
$$

Fig. 1. Syntax of the core pointer language

want to express nonuniform aliasing relationships, we need to assign position and timestamp indices to semantic variables and relate them by using numerical constraints. For example, we would like to generate an inclusion constraint for the piece of code of Example 1 that looks like:

$$
*(\&\mathtt{a} + (i \times s + o_{\mathrm{ptr}})) \supseteq \mathbf{malloc}_t \quad \text{where} \quad i = t \wedge t \in [0, 29]
$$

where s is the size of the structure contained in the two-dimensional array, o_{ptr} is the offset of the field ptr in that structure and t is the timestamp of the memory allocation statement. In order to infer this kind of constraint we must first perform a flow-sensitive analysis over a relational numerical lattice [19, 11, 16, 20] that computes invariants relating loop counters, array indices and timestamps. The main difference from [24] comes from the fact that we generate inclusion constraints without any prior knowledge of the layout of objects in the heap. In this case it is not obvious what to do with the following piece of code:

Example 2.

```
for(i = 0; i < 10; i++) {
  p = p->next;
}
```

The rest of this section will be devoted to defining a concrete semantic model that will allow us to handle this situation simply and precisely.

We base our semantic specification on a small language that captures the core pointer arithmetic of C at the function level. The treatment of interprocedural mechanisms is postponed until Sect. 4 where we will detail the generation of inclusion constraints. We call *surface variable* a variable which has a scalar type, either integer or pointer, and which does not have its address taken. The syntax of the language is defined in Fig. 1, where we denote by $\mathtt{p}, \mathtt{q}, \mathtt{r}$ pointer-valued surface variables, by $\mathtt{m}, \mathtt{n}, \mathtt{o}$ integer-valued surface variables, and by $\mathtt{x}, \mathtt{y}, \mathtt{z}$ all other variables. We assume that the variable on the left handside of an assignment operation does not appear on the right handside. This will facilitate the design of the numerical abstract interpretation in Sect. 3. It is always possible to rewrite the program in order to satisfy this assumption. Note that in order to keep the presentation simple, we focus on fundamental arithmetic operations and loops. All other constructs can be analyzed along the same lines. We use this language to model the computations that occur locally within the body of a C function, excluding calls to other functions. A program P in this language is just a sequence of statements describing the pointer manipulations performed by a function. We provide P with a small-step operational semantics given by a transition system $(\Sigma, \rightarrow)$ defined as follows.

We first need some notations. We assume that each statement of P is assigned a unique label ℓ. If ℓ is the label of a statement, we denote by $\mathbf{next}(\ell)$ the label of the next statement of P to be executed in the natural execution order. If ℓ is the label of a loop we denote by $\mathbf{top}(\ell)$ the predicate that is true iff the statement at ℓ is an outermost loop. A state of Σ is a tuple $\langle \lambda, M, \varrho, \ell \rangle$ where λ is an integer denoting the global loop counter used for timestamping, M is a memory graph, ϱ is an environment and ℓ is the label of the next statement to execute. A memory graph is a collection of points-to edges $\langle \mathbf{a}, o \rangle \triangleright \langle \mathbf{a}', o' \rangle$ where $\mathbf{a}, \mathbf{a}'$ are addresses and o, o' are integers representing byte offsets. An address is either the location of a global variable $\&\mathbf{x}$ or a dynamically allocated block $\mathbf{blk}_\ell \langle t \rangle$, where ℓ is the location of the allocation statement and t is a timestamp. We use a special address $\mathbf{null}$ to represent the NULL pointer value in C. The mapping defined by a memory graph is functional, i.e. there is at most one outcoming edge for each memory location $\langle \mathbf{a}, o \rangle$. We denote by $M\langle \mathbf{a}, o \rangle$ the target location of the edge originating from the location $\langle \mathbf{a}, o \rangle$ if it exists or $\langle \mathbf{null}, 0 \rangle$ otherwise. We denote by $M[\langle \mathbf{a}, o \rangle \triangleright \langle \mathbf{a}', o' \rangle]$ the memory graph M which has been updated with the edge $\langle \mathbf{a}, o \rangle \triangleright \langle \mathbf{a}', o' \rangle$.

We split down each pointer variable $\mathbf{p}$ into two variables $\mathbf{p}_a$ and $\mathbf{p}_o$ that respectively denote the address of the block and the offset within this block to which $\mathbf{p}$ points. An environment ϱ maps variables $\mathbf{n}, \mathbf{p}_o$ to integers and variables $\mathbf{p}_a$ to addresses. We denote by $\varrho[u \leftarrow v]$ the environment ϱ in which the variable u has been assigned the value v. Finally, we denote by Ω a special element of Σ representing the error state. The transition relation $\rightarrow$ of the operational semantics is then defined in Fig. 2. An initial state in this operational semantics assigns arbitrary integer values to surface integer variables and the null memory location to surface pointer variables. This amounts to considering integer variables as uninitialized and pointers initialized to NULL. For consistency the initial value of λ should be 0. In our framework an initial state describes the memory configuration at the entry of the C function that is modeled by the program P.

The transition rule for loop exits requires some explanations. The global loop counter λ is incremented at the end of each loop iteration and decremented whenever the execution steps out of a nested loop. Whether the global loop counter is decremented or left unchanged at loop exit has no effect on the uniqueness of timestamps. However decrementation is required in order to preserve linear relationships between λ and byte offsets during the traversal of multidimensional arrays. Consider the two nested loops of Example 1. We keep the previous notations and we denote by O the byte offset within $\mathbf{a}$ on the lefthand side of the assignment. Then, the relation between O and the loop counters is given by $O = 3 \times s \times \mathbf{i} + s \times \mathbf{j} + o_{\mathtt{ptr}}$. If we use the decrementation rule at loop exit, the global loop counter value is given by $\lambda = 3 \times \mathbf{i} + \mathbf{j}$, hence $O = s \times \lambda + o_{\mathtt{ptr}}$. Without this rule λ would be equal to $4 \times \mathbf{i} + \mathbf{j}$ and the relationship between

$$\langle \lambda, M, \varrho, \ell : \mathtt{n} = c \rangle \rightarrow \langle \lambda, M, \varrho[\mathtt{n} \leftarrow c], \mathbf{next}(\ell) \rangle$$

$$\langle \lambda, M, \varrho, \ell : \mathtt{n} = \mathtt{m} + \mathtt{o} \rangle \rightarrow \langle \lambda, M, \varrho[\mathtt{n} \leftarrow \varrho(\mathtt{m}) + \varrho(\mathtt{o})], \mathbf{next}(\ell) \rangle$$

$$\langle \lambda, M, \varrho, \ell : \mathtt{n} = \mathtt{m} * \mathtt{o} \rangle \rightarrow \langle \lambda, M, \varrho[\mathtt{n} \leftarrow \varrho(\mathtt{m}) \times \varrho(\mathtt{o})], \mathbf{next}(\ell) \rangle$$

$$\langle \lambda, M, \varrho, \ell : \mathtt{p} = \&\mathtt{x} \rangle \rightarrow \langle \lambda, M, \varrho[\mathtt{p}_o \leftarrow 0, \mathtt{p}_a \leftarrow \&\mathtt{x}], \mathbf{next}(\ell) \rangle$$

$$\langle \lambda, M, \varrho, \ell : \mathtt{p} = \mathtt{q} + \mathtt{n} \rangle \rightarrow \langle \lambda, M, \varrho[\mathtt{p}_o \leftarrow \mathtt{q}_o + \varrho(\mathtt{n}), \mathtt{p}_a \leftarrow \varrho(\mathtt{q}_a)], \mathbf{next}(\ell) \rangle$$

$$\langle \lambda, M, \varrho, \ell : \mathtt{p} = *\mathtt{q} \rangle \rightarrow \begin{cases} \Omega & \text{if } \varrho(\mathtt{q}_a) = \mathbf{null} \\ \langle \lambda, M, \varrho[(\mathtt{p}_a, \mathtt{p}_o) \leftarrow M\langle \varrho(\mathtt{q}_a), \varrho(\mathtt{q}_o) \rangle], \mathbf{next}(\ell) \rangle & \text{otherwise} \end{cases}$$

$$\langle \lambda, M, \varrho, \ell : \mathtt{p} = \mathtt{malloc}() \rangle \rightarrow \langle \lambda, M, \varrho[\mathtt{p}_a \leftarrow \mathbf{blk}_\ell \langle \lambda \rangle, \mathtt{p}_o \leftarrow 0], \mathbf{next}(\ell) \rangle$$

$$\langle \lambda, M, \varrho, \ell : *\mathtt{p} = \mathtt{q} \rangle \rightarrow \begin{cases} \Omega & \text{if } \varrho(\mathtt{p}_a) = \mathbf{null} \\ \langle \lambda, M[\langle \varrho(\mathtt{p}_a), \varrho(\mathtt{p}_o) \rangle \triangleright \langle \varrho(\mathtt{q}_a), \varrho(\mathtt{q}_o) \rangle], \varrho, \mathbf{next}(\ell) \rangle & \text{otherwise} \end{cases}$$

$$\langle \lambda, M, \varrho, \ell : \mathtt{while}\ (\mathtt{m} < \mathtt{n})\ \mathtt{do}\ \ell^0 : s_1; \cdots \mathtt{end} \rangle \rightarrow \langle \lambda, M, \varrho, \ell^0 \rangle \quad \text{if } \varrho(\mathtt{m}) < \varrho(\mathtt{n})$$

$$\langle \lambda, M, \varrho, \ell : \mathtt{while}\ (\mathtt{m} < \mathtt{n})\ \mathtt{do}\ \ldots\ \mathtt{end} \rangle \rightarrow \begin{cases} \langle 0, M, \varrho, \mathbf{next}(\ell) \rangle & \text{if } \varrho(\mathtt{m}) \geq \varrho(\mathtt{n}) \text{ and } \mathbf{top}(\ell) \\ \langle \lambda - 1, M, \varrho, \mathbf{next}(\ell) \rangle & \text{otherwise} \end{cases}$$

$$\langle \lambda, M, \varrho, \ell : \mathtt{end} \rangle \rightarrow \langle \lambda + 1, M, \varrho, \ell^0 : \mathtt{while}\ (\ldots)\ \mathtt{do}\ \ldots\ \ell : \mathtt{end} \rangle$$

Fig. 2. Operational semantics of the core pointer language

the global loop counter and O would be lost, thereby preventing the inference of a nonuniform points-to relation.

This operational semantics is similar to the one described in [24] with a simplified timestamping. We need to instrument the semantics by adding an intermediate layer between the environment and the memory that keeps track of all memory accesses. Whenever a location is retrieved from the memory, we use a timestamp to tag it with a unique name that we call an *anchor*, and we keep the binding between this anchor and the actual memory location in a separate structure A called the *anchorage*. The local environment ϱ now maps the address component of a surface variable $\mathtt{p}_a$ either to an address that explicitly appears in the body of a C function or to an anchor. We call this refined semantics the *surface semantics*. More formally, the surface semantics $(\Sigma_s, \rightarrow_s)$ of a program P is defined as follows. A extended state of Σ_s is a tuple $\langle \lambda, A, M, \varrho, \ell \rangle$ where $\langle \lambda, M, \varrho, \ell \rangle \in \Sigma$ and A is an anchorage. An anchor $\mathbf{ref}_\ell \langle t \rangle$ denotes the value returned by the execution of a memory read command $\ell : \mathtt{p} = *\mathtt{q}$ at program point ℓ on time t. The anchorage maps an anchor $\mathbf{ref}_\ell \langle t \rangle$ to an actual memory location $\langle a, o \rangle$. If $\langle a, o \rangle$ is a location stored in the environment ρ, a may either be an address or an anchor. We define the resolution function $\mathbf{get}_A$ which maps $\langle a, o \rangle$ to the corresponding memory location as follows:

$$\mathbf{get}_A \langle a, o \rangle = \begin{cases} \langle \mathbf{null}, 0 \rangle & \text{if } a \text{ is an anchor and } A(a) = \langle \mathbf{null}, 0 \rangle \\ \langle \mathbf{a}, o + o' \rangle & \text{if } a \text{ is an anchor and } A(a) = \langle \mathbf{a}, o' \rangle \\ \langle \mathbf{a}, o \rangle & \text{if } a \text{ is an address } \mathbf{a} \end{cases}$$

If $\mathtt{p}$ is a surface pointer and ϱ is an environment, we denote by $\mathbf{get}_{A, \varrho}(\mathtt{p})$ the memory location $\mathbf{get}_A \langle \varrho(\mathtt{p}_a), \varrho(\mathtt{p}_o) \rangle$. The transition relation $\rightarrow_s$ of the surface semantics is then defined in Fig. 3. The error state in this semantics is also denoted by Ω. An initial state in the surface semantics is simply an initial state

$$\langle \lambda, A, M, \varrho, \ell : \mathsf{p} = *\mathsf{q} \rangle \to_s \begin{cases} \Omega & \text{if } \mathbf{get}_{A,\varrho}(\mathsf{q}) = \langle \mathbf{null}, o \rangle \\ \left\langle \begin{array}{l} \lambda, A[\mathbf{ref}_\ell \langle \lambda \rangle \leftarrow M(\mathbf{get}_{A,\varrho}(\mathsf{q}))], \\ M, \varrho[\mathsf{p}_a \leftarrow \mathbf{ref}_\ell \langle \lambda \rangle, \mathsf{p}_o \leftarrow 0], \mathbf{next}(\ell) \end{array} \right\rangle & \text{otherwise} \end{cases}$$

$$\langle \lambda, A, M, \varrho, \ell : *\mathsf{p} = \mathsf{q} \rangle \to_s \begin{cases} \Omega & \text{if } \mathbf{get}_{A,\varrho}(\mathsf{p}) = \langle \mathbf{null}, o \rangle \\ \left\langle \begin{array}{l} \lambda, A, M[\mathbf{get}_{A,\varrho}(\mathsf{p}) \rhd \mathbf{get}_{A,\varrho}(\mathsf{q})], \\ \varrho, \mathbf{next}(\ell) \end{array} \right\rangle & \text{otherwise} \end{cases}$$

For all other statements:

$$\frac{\langle \lambda, M, \varrho, \ell \rangle \to \langle \lambda^0, M^0, \varrho^0, \ell^0 \rangle}{\langle \lambda, A, M, \varrho, \ell \rangle \to_s \langle \lambda^0, A, M^0, \varrho^0, \ell^0 \rangle}$$

Fig. 3. Surface semantics of the core pointer language

in the base semantics with an empty anchorage. We denote by I the set of all initial states.

We are interested in the *collecting semantics* [5] of a program P, that is the set $\mathcal{C} = \{i \xrightarrow{*}_s s \mid i \in I\}$ of all states reachable from any initial state I. We define the *surface structure* $\mathcal{S}$ of P as follows:

$$\mathcal{S} = \{\langle \lambda, \varrho, \ell \rangle \mid \exists M \, \exists A : \langle \lambda, A, M, \varrho, \ell \rangle \in \mathcal{C}\}$$

An element $\langle \lambda, \varrho, \ell \rangle$ is called a *surface configuration*. The program P models the pointer manipulations performed by a single C function. Our purpose is to compute a global approximation of the memory for a whole C program by first performing an abstract interpretation of the surface structure of each function in the program. The design of this abstract interpretation is straightforward because the surface structure is independent from the data stored in the heap and does not interfere with other threads. We will then generate inclusion constraints from the results of the analysis of the surface structure that will provide us with a global approximation of the memory and the anchorage structure as well.

3   Abstract Interpretation of the Surface Structure

We describe the analysis of the surface structure within the framework of Abstract Interpretation [7, 8, 5, 9]. We define an abstract environment by a pair $\langle \nu^\sharp, \pi^\sharp \rangle$ as follows:

- The component $\nu^\sharp$ is an abstract numerical relation belonging to a given numerical lattice $\mathcal{V}^\sharp$ [19, 11, 16, 20] that we leave as a parameter of our analysis. The abstract relation $\nu^\sharp$ is a collection of numerical constraints between all integer valued variables n, p_o of the program and a special variable Λ denoting the value of the global loop counter.
- The component $\pi^\sharp$ maps every variable p_o to a set of abstract addresses.

An abstract address is either the address of a global variable $\&\mathsf{x}$, a dynamically allocated block $\mathbf{blk}_\ell^\sharp \langle \mu^\sharp \rangle$ or an anchor $\mathbf{ref}_\ell^\sharp \langle \mu^\sharp \rangle$, where $\mu^\sharp$ is an abstract numerical relation between the loop counter variable Λ and a special timestamp variable

$$[\![n = c]\!]^\sharp \langle \nu^\sharp, \pi^\sharp \rangle = \langle (\nu^\sharp \ominus \{n\}) \oplus \{n = c\}, \pi^\sharp \rangle$$
$$[\![n = m + o]\!]^\sharp \langle \nu^\sharp, \pi^\sharp \rangle = \langle (\nu^\sharp \ominus \{n\}) \oplus \{n = m + o\}, \pi^\sharp \rangle$$
$$[\![n = m * o]\!]^\sharp \langle \nu^\sharp, \pi^\sharp \rangle = \langle (\nu^\sharp \ominus \{n\}) \oplus \{n = m \times o\}, \pi^\sharp \rangle$$
$$[\![p = \&x]\!]^\sharp \langle \nu^\sharp, \pi^\sharp \rangle = \langle (\nu^\sharp \ominus \{p_o\}) \oplus \{p_o = 0\}, \pi^\sharp[p_a \leftarrow \{\&x\}] \rangle$$
$$[\![p = q + n]\!]^\sharp \langle \nu^\sharp, \pi^\sharp \rangle = \langle (\nu^\sharp \ominus \{p_o\}) \oplus \{p_o = q_o + n\}, \pi^\sharp[p_a \leftarrow \pi^\sharp(q_a)] \rangle$$
$$[\![\ell : p = *q]\!]^\sharp \langle \nu^\sharp, \pi^\sharp \rangle = \left\langle \begin{array}{l} (\nu^\sharp \ominus \{p_o\}) \oplus \{p_o = 0\}, \\ \pi^\sharp[p_a \leftarrow \{\mathbf{ref}^\sharp_\ell \langle \lfloor \nu^\sharp \oplus \{\tau = \lambda\} \rfloor_{\tau, \lambda} \rangle\}] \end{array} \right\rangle$$
$$[\![\ell : p = \mathtt{malloc}()]\!]^\sharp \langle \nu^\sharp, \pi^\sharp \rangle = \left\langle \begin{array}{l} (\nu^\sharp \ominus \{p_o\}) \oplus \{p_o = 0\}, \\ \pi^\sharp[p_a \leftarrow \{\mathbf{blk}^\sharp_\ell \langle \lfloor \nu^\sharp \oplus \{\tau = \lambda\} \rfloor_{\tau, \lambda} \rangle\}] \end{array} \right\rangle$$
$$[\![*p = q]\!]^\sharp \langle \nu^\sharp, \pi^\sharp \rangle = \langle \nu^\sharp, \pi^\sharp \rangle$$

Fig. 4. Abstract surface semantics of atomic statements

denoted by τ. We assume that for each set of abstract addresses, there is at most one abstract address $\mathbf{blk}^\sharp_\ell \langle \mu^\sharp \rangle$ or $\mathbf{ref}^\sharp_\ell \langle \mu^\sharp \rangle$ per program location ℓ. Therefore, the set $E^\sharp$ of all abstract environments is isomorphic to the product $\prod_{i \in I} \mathcal{V}^\sharp$ of the numerical lattice over a fixed family I. We provide $E^\sharp$ with the structure of a lattice by lifting all operations of $\mathcal{V}^\sharp$ to $E^\sharp$ pointwise.

The denotation $\gamma_{\mathcal{V}^\sharp}(\nu^\sharp)$ of an abstract numerical relation is a set of variable assignments ε that satisfy the numerical constraints expressed by $\nu^\sharp$. If $x_1, \dots, x_n$ are numerical variables and $v_1, \dots, v_n$ are integer values, we denote by $\nu^\sharp \langle x_1 \mapsto v_1, \dots, x_n \mapsto v_n \rangle$ the predicate that is true iff there is an assignment $\varepsilon \in \gamma_{\mathcal{V}^\sharp}(\nu^\sharp)$ such that $\varepsilon(x_i) = v_i$ for all $1 \le i \le n$. The denotation $\gamma_{E^\sharp} \langle \nu^\sharp, \pi^\sharp \rangle$ of an abstract environment is the set of all pairs $\langle \lambda, \varrho \rangle$ where $\lambda \in \mathbb{N}$ and ϱ is an environment of the surface semantics, such that:

- $\nu^\sharp \langle n \mapsto \varrho(n), \dots, p_o \mapsto \varrho(p_o), \dots, \Lambda \mapsto \lambda \rangle$ for all variables $n, \dots, p, \dots$ of the program
- $\varrho(p_a) = \&x \Rightarrow \&x \in \pi^\sharp(p_a)$
- $\varrho(p_a) = \mathbf{blk}_\ell \langle t \rangle \Rightarrow \mathbf{blk}^\sharp_\ell \langle \mu^\sharp \rangle \in \pi^\sharp(p_a) \wedge \mu^\sharp \langle \tau \mapsto t, \Lambda \mapsto \lambda \rangle$
- $\varrho(p_a) = \mathbf{ref}_\ell \langle t \rangle \Rightarrow \mathbf{ref}^\sharp_\ell \langle \mu^\sharp \rangle \in \pi^\sharp(p_a) \wedge \mu^\sharp \langle \tau \mapsto t, \Lambda \mapsto \lambda \rangle$

An abstract surface configuration of the program is a family $\langle \nu^\sharp_\ell, \pi^\sharp_\ell \rangle_{\ell \in \mathrm{Loc}(P)}$ of abstract environments, one for each location ℓ in the program P considered. We provide the set of all abstract surface configurations with a lattice structure by pointwise extension of operations from $E^\sharp$. The denotation $\gamma \langle \nu^\sharp_\ell, \pi^\sharp_\ell \rangle_{\ell \in \mathrm{Loc}(P)}$ of ans abstract configuration is the set of all surface configurations $\langle \lambda, \varrho, \ell \rangle$ such that $\langle \lambda, \varrho \rangle \in \gamma_{E^\sharp} \langle \nu^\sharp_\ell, \pi^\sharp_\ell \rangle$.

Following the methodology of Abstract Interpretation, we must now define the abstract semantics of the language. We first have to define some operations on the abstract numerical lattice $\mathcal{V}^\sharp$. If $\nu^\sharp \in \mathcal{V}^\sharp$ and V is a set of variables, we denote by $\nu^\sharp \ominus V$ the abstract numerical relation in which all information about variables in V has been lost, and by $\lfloor \nu^\sharp \rfloor_V$ the relation that only keeps information for variables in V. If S is a system of arbitrary numerical constraints, we denote by $\nu^\sharp \oplus S$ an abstract numerical relation representing all variable assignments that are in the denotation of $\nu^\sharp$ and that are also solutions of S. If v is a variable, we denote by $\nu^\sharp[v := v + c]$ the operation that consists of adding the increment c to the value of v. The implementation of these operations depends on the abstract numerical lattice considered, and we refer the reader to the corresponding papers for more details about the underlying algorithms [6, 19, 11, 16, 20]. We assign an abstract semantics $[\![s]\!]^\sharp : E^\sharp \to E^\sharp$ to each atomic statement s of the language as defined in Fig. 4.

If $\langle \nu^\sharp, \pi^\sharp \rangle$ is an abstract environment, we define the result $\langle \bar{\nu}^\sharp, \bar{\pi}^\sharp \rangle$ of the operation $\mathbf{inc}_\Lambda \langle \nu^\sharp, \pi^\sharp \rangle$ as follows:

- $\bar{\nu}^\sharp = \nu^\sharp[\Lambda := \Lambda + 1]$

- $\forall p : \bar{\pi}^\sharp(p_a) = \begin{cases} \&\mathbf{x} & \text{if } \pi^\sharp(p_a) = \&\mathbf{x} \\ \mathbf{blk}_\ell^\sharp \langle \mu^\sharp[\Lambda := \Lambda + 1] \rangle & \text{if } \pi^\sharp(p_a) = \mathbf{blk}_\ell^\sharp \langle \mu^\sharp \rangle \\ \mathbf{ref}_\ell^\sharp \langle \mu^\sharp[\Lambda := \Lambda + 1] \rangle & \text{if } \pi^\sharp(p_a) = \mathbf{ref}_\ell^\sharp \langle \mu^\sharp \rangle \end{cases}$

We define the operation $\mathbf{dec}_\Lambda \langle \nu^\sharp, \pi^\sharp \rangle$ (resp. $\mathbf{reset}_\Lambda \langle \nu^\sharp, \pi^\sharp \rangle$) similarly by substituting the operation $\Lambda := \Lambda - 1$ (resp. $\Lambda := 0$) to $\Lambda := \Lambda + 1$. The abstract semantics of a program is then given by the least solution of a recursive system of semantic equations

$$\langle \nu_\ell^\sharp, \pi_\ell^\sharp \rangle = F_\ell \left(\langle \nu_{\bar{\ell}}^\sharp, \pi_{\bar{\ell}}^\sharp \rangle_{\bar{\ell} \in \mathrm{Loc}(P)} \right)$$

where F_ℓ is defined as follows:

- If $\ell = \mathbf{next}(\ell')$ and ℓ' is the location of an atomic statement s, then

$$F_\ell \left(\langle \nu_{\bar{\ell}}^\sharp, \pi_{\bar{\ell}}^\sharp \rangle_{\bar{\ell} \in \mathrm{Loc}(P)} \right) = [\![s]\!]^\sharp \langle \nu_{\ell'}^\sharp, \pi_{\ell'}^\sharp \rangle$$

- If $\ell'' : \mathbf{while} \ (\mathbf{m} < \mathbf{n}) \ \mathbf{do} \ \ell : s; \cdots ; \ell' : \mathbf{end}$, then

$$F_\ell \left(\langle \nu_{\bar{\ell}}^\sharp, \pi_{\bar{\ell}}^\sharp \rangle_{\bar{\ell} \in \mathrm{Loc}(P)} \right) = \langle \nu_{\ell''}^\sharp \oplus \{\mathbf{m} < \mathbf{n}\}, \pi_{\ell''}^\sharp \rangle \sqcup \mathbf{inc}_\Lambda \langle \nu_{\ell'}^\sharp, \pi_{\ell'}^\sharp \rangle$$

- If $\ell = \mathbf{next}(\ell')$ and $\ell' : \mathbf{while} \ (\mathbf{m} < \mathbf{n}) \ \mathbf{do} \ \ldots \ \mathbf{end}$, then

$$F_\ell \left(\langle \nu_{\bar{\ell}}^\sharp, \pi_{\bar{\ell}}^\sharp \rangle_{\bar{\ell} \in \mathrm{Loc}(P)} \right) = \begin{cases} \mathbf{reset}_\Lambda \langle \nu_{\ell'}^\sharp \oplus \{\mathbf{m} \geq \mathbf{n}\}, \pi_{\ell'}^\sharp \rangle & \text{if } \mathbf{top}(\ell') \\ \mathbf{dec}_\Lambda \langle \nu_{\ell'}^\sharp \oplus \{\mathbf{m} \geq \mathbf{n}\}, \pi_{\ell'}^\sharp \rangle & \text{otherwise} \end{cases}$$

We apply classical fixpoint algorithms based upon iteration sequences with widening and narrowing [5, 9] in order to obtain an upper approximation $\mathcal{S}^\sharp$ of the least fixpoint of the system.

Theorem 1. $\mathcal{S}^\sharp$ *is a sound approximation of the surface semantics, i.e.* $\mathcal{S} \subseteq \gamma \left(\langle \nu_\ell^\sharp, \pi_\ell^\sharp \rangle_{\ell \in \mathrm{Loc}(P)} \right).$

For example, consider the following program in our core pointer language that fills in an array $\mathbf{a}$ of pointers with newly allocated blocks:

Example 3.

```
1:   n = 0;
2:   while (n < 10) {
3:       q = &a;
4:       p = q + n;
5:       r = malloc();
6:       *p = r;
7:       n = n + 1;
8:   }
```

If we use the lattice of convex polyhedra [11] as the numerical lattice $\mathcal{V}^\sharp$, then the abstract environment obtained after analysis of the surface structure at program point 6 is:

$$\left\langle \left\{ \begin{array}{l} 0 \leq n < 10 \\ \Lambda = n \\ q_o = r_o = 0 \\ p_o = 4 \times n \end{array} \right., \left\{ \begin{array}{l} p_a \mapsto \{\&a\} \\ q_a \mapsto \{\&a\} \\ r_a \mapsto \{\mathbf{blk}_5^\sharp \langle \tau = \Lambda, 0 \leq \Lambda < 10 \rangle\} \end{array} \right. \right\rangle$$

assuming that pointers occupy four bytes in memory.

4   Nonuniform Inclusion Constraints

We now use the analysis of the surface structure to build a global approximation of the memory graph. For this purpose we use an extension of Andersen's inclusion constraints [1] enriched with numerical indices that allow us to describe nonuniform points-to relations. The syntax of a nonuniform inclusion constraint is the following:

$$\begin{aligned} Cst ::= \ & \langle \mathcal{X}(t) \supseteq \&\mathbf{x} + o, \nu^\sharp(t,o) \rangle \\ | \ & \langle \mathcal{X}(t) \supseteq \mathbf{blk}_\ell \langle t' \rangle + o, \nu^\sharp(t,t',o) \rangle \\ | \ & \langle \mathcal{X}(t) \supseteq \mathcal{Y}(t') + o, \nu^\sharp(t,t',o) \rangle \rangle \\ | \ & \langle *\mathcal{X}(t) \supseteq \mathcal{Y}(t'), \nu^\sharp(t,t') \rangle \\ | \ & \langle \mathcal{X}(t) \supseteq *\mathcal{Y}(t'), \nu^\sharp(t,t') \rangle \end{aligned}$$

where t, t', o are special index variables denoting timestamp and offset values and $\mathcal{X}, \mathcal{Y}$ are set variables. We assume that we are provided with a countable collection of set variables. The second component $\nu^\sharp$ of a nonuniform constraint is a system of numerical relationships between the index variables appearing in the constraint.

The semantics of a system of nouniform constraints is based upon an abstract memory graph. An abstract memory graph $M^\sharp$ is a set of abstract points-to relations

$$\langle \mathbf{a}(t,o) \rhd \mathbf{a}'(t',o'), \nu^\sharp(t,t',o,o') \rangle$$

where $\mathbf{a}, \mathbf{a}'$ are addresses and t, t', o, o' are special index variables representing the timestamps and offsets associated to each address. The abstract numerical relation $\nu^\sharp$ expresses numerical constraints between these index variables. The set $\mathcal{M}^\sharp$ of abstract memory graphs can be provided with the structure of a lattice by pointwise extension of the corresponding lattice operations over $\mathcal{V}^\sharp$. The denotation $\gamma_{\mathcal{M}^\sharp}(M^\sharp)$ of an abstract memory graph is the set of memory graphs such that the offsets on the points-to edges satisfy the constraints of the corresponding abstract edges. A valuation $V^\sharp$ of set variables is a set of mappings

$$\langle \mathcal{X}(t) \mapsto \mathbf{a}(t') + o, \nu^\sharp(t, t', o)\rangle$$

where $\mathbf{a}$ is an address and t, t', o are numerical index variables. The set $Val^\sharp$ of all valuations can similarly be provided with the structure of a lattice. Note that in the case of the address of a global $\&\mathbf{x}$, the associated timestamp variable does not have any meaning and is not related by any numerical constraint. We use a uniform notation in order to keep the semantic definitions simple. A valuation can be seen as an abstraction of the anchorage structure defined in Sect. 2. The semantics $[\![C]\!]^\sharp : \mathcal{M}^\sharp \times Val^\sharp \to M^\sharp \times Val^\sharp$ of a nonuniform inclusion constraint C is defined as follows:

- $[\![\langle \mathcal{X}(t) \supseteq \&\mathbf{x} + o, \nu^\sharp\rangle]\!]^\sharp(M^\sharp, V^\sharp) = (M^\sharp, V^\sharp \sqcup \{\langle \mathcal{X}(t) \mapsto \&\mathbf{x} + o, \nu^\sharp\rangle\})$
- $[\![\langle \mathcal{X}(t) \supseteq \mathbf{blk}_\ell\langle t'\rangle + o, \nu^\sharp\rangle]\!]^\sharp(M^\sharp, V^\sharp) = (M^\sharp, V^\sharp \sqcup \{\langle \mathcal{X}(t) \mapsto \mathbf{blk}_\ell\langle t'\rangle + o, \nu^\sharp\rangle\})$
- $[\![\langle \mathcal{X}(t) \supseteq \mathcal{Y}(t') + o, \nu^\sharp\rangle\rangle]\!]^\sharp(M^\sharp, V^\sharp) = (M^\sharp, V^\sharp \sqcup \{\langle \mathcal{X}(t) \mapsto \mathbf{a}(t'') + o'',$
  $\lfloor \nu^\sharp \sqcap \mu^\sharp \oplus \{o'' = o + o'\}\rfloor_{t,t'',o''}\rangle \mid \langle \mathcal{Y}(t') \mapsto \mathbf{a}(t'') + o', \mu^\sharp\rangle \in V^\sharp\})$
- $[\![\langle *\mathcal{X}(t) \supseteq \mathcal{Y}(t'), \nu^\sharp\rangle]\!]^\sharp(M^\sharp, V^\sharp) = (M^\sharp \sqcup \{\langle \mathbf{a}(t,o) \triangleright \mathbf{a}'(t', o'), \nu^\sharp \sqcap \nu_1^\sharp \sqcap \nu_2^\sharp\rangle \mid$
  $\langle \mathcal{X}(t) \mapsto \mathbf{a}(t) + o, \nu_1^\sharp\rangle \in V^\sharp \wedge \langle \mathcal{Y}(t) \mapsto \mathbf{a}'(t') + o', \nu_2^\sharp\rangle \in V^\sharp, V^\sharp)$
- $[\![\langle \mathcal{X}(t) \supseteq *\mathcal{Y}(t'), \nu^\sharp\rangle]\!]^\sharp(M^\sharp, V^\sharp) = (M^\sharp, V^\sharp \sqcup \{\langle \mathcal{X}(t) \mapsto \mathbf{a}'(t''') + o', \mu^\sharp\rangle \mid$
  $\langle \mathcal{Y}(t') \mapsto \mathbf{a}(t'') + o, \nu_1^\sharp\rangle \in V^\sharp \wedge \langle \mathbf{a}(t'', o) \triangleright \mathbf{a}'(t''', o'), \nu_2^\sharp\rangle \in M^\sharp \wedge \mu^\sharp =$
  $\lfloor \nu^\sharp \sqcap \nu_1^\sharp \sqcap \nu_2^\sharp\rfloor_{t,t''',o'}\})$

where we have freely renamed the index variables whenever it was necessary to avoid name clashes. A solution of a system S of nonuniform set constraints is a couple $(M^\sharp, V^\sharp)$ which is invariant under the application of $[\![C]\!]^\sharp$ for any $C \in S$.

We are interested in the least solution of a system S of nonuniform set constraints. We can obtain an approximation of the least solution of S by computing the limit of the abstract iteration sequence with widening $(M_n^\sharp, V_n^\sharp)_{n \geq 0}$ defined as follows:

$$\begin{cases} (M_0^\sharp, V_0^\sharp) &= (\bot_{\mathcal{M}^\sharp}, \bot_{Val^\sharp}) \\ (M_{n+1}^\sharp, V_{n+1}^\sharp) &= (M_n^\sharp, V_n^\sharp) \nabla ([\![C]\!]^\sharp)^*_{C \in S}(M_n^\sharp, V_n^\sharp) \end{cases}$$

where $([\![C]\!]^\sharp)^*_{C \in S}$ denotes the application of all constraints of S in an arbitrary order, and ∇ is the product of the widening operators on $\mathcal{M}^\sharp$ and $Val^\sharp$. This provides us with an effective algorithm for computing an approximate solution of the system, which is similar to that defined by Andersen [1]. The main difference is the use of a widening operator to enforce convergence because some abstract numerical lattices have infinitely increasing chains of elements[6, 11, 20]. Once a post-fixpoint has been reached using this algorithm, we can further refine the result by using a decreasing iteration sequence with narrowing defined in the same way. We observed from our experiments that an iteration sequence with narrowing is always required in order to obtain precise ranges for the timestamp and offset variables.

We now have to show how to extract nonuniform inclusion constraints from the abstract interpretation of the surface semantics. Let $\mathcal{S}^\sharp$ be the abstract surface semantics of a program P obtained from the analysis described in the previous section. We assign a unique pair of set variables $(\mathcal{L}_\ell, \mathcal{R}_\ell)$ to each statement $\ell : *q = r$ or $\ell : q = *r$ of P, denoting respectively the points-to sets of the lefthand and righthand sides of the assignment. Let $\varrho^\sharp = \langle \nu^\sharp, \pi^\sharp \rangle$ be an abstract environment, p a pointer variable of P and $\mathcal{X}$ a set variable. We denote by $C_{\mathcal{X},p}\langle \varrho^\sharp \rangle$ the collection of nonuniform constraints defined as follows:

- If $\&x \in \pi^\sharp(p_a)$, then

$$\langle \mathcal{X}(t) \supseteq \&x + o, \lfloor \nu^\sharp \oplus \{t = \Lambda, o = p_o\} \rfloor_{t,o} \rangle \in C_{\mathcal{X},p}\langle \varrho^\sharp \rangle$$

- If $\mathbf{blk}_\ell^\sharp \langle \mu^\sharp \rangle \in \pi^\sharp(p_a)$, then

$$\langle \mathcal{X}(t) \supseteq \mathbf{blk}_\ell \langle t' \rangle + o, \lfloor \nu^\sharp \sqcap \mu^\sharp \oplus \{\tau = t', t = \Lambda, o = p_o\} \rfloor_{t,t',o} \rangle \in C_{\mathcal{X},p}\langle \varrho^\sharp \rangle$$

- If $\mathbf{ref}_\ell^\sharp \langle \mu^\sharp \rangle \in \pi^\sharp(p_a)$, then

$$\langle \mathcal{X}(t) \supseteq \mathcal{L}_\ell(t') + o, \lfloor \nu^\sharp \sqcap \mu^\sharp \oplus \{\tau = t', t = \Lambda, o = p_o\} \rfloor_{t,t',o} \rangle \in C_{\mathcal{X},p}\langle \varrho^\sharp \rangle$$

Now, if $\ell : *p = q$ is a memory write statement of P and $\varrho^\sharp$ is the abstract environment of $\mathcal{S}^\sharp$ at ℓ, we generate the constraints:

$$C_{\mathcal{L}_\ell,p}\langle \varrho^\sharp \rangle \cup C_{\mathcal{R}_\ell,q}\langle \varrho^\sharp \rangle \cup \{\langle *\mathcal{L}_\ell(t) \supseteq \mathcal{R}_\ell(t'), \top_{\nu^\sharp} \oplus \{t = t'\} \rangle\}$$

Similarly, for a memory read statement $\ell : *p = q$ we generate the constraints:

$$C_{\mathcal{L}_\ell,p}\langle \varrho^\sharp \rangle \cup C_{\mathcal{R}_\ell,q}\langle \varrho^\sharp \rangle \cup \{\langle \mathcal{L}_\ell(t) \supseteq *\mathcal{R}_\ell(t'), \top_{\nu^\sharp} \oplus \{t = t'\} \rangle\}$$

We denote by S_P the system of all constraints generated in this way for the program P. Let $(M_P^\sharp, V_P^\sharp)$ be an approximation of the least solution of S_P obtained by an abstract iteration sequence as described previously. The abstract memory graph $M_P^\sharp$ is a sound global approximation of the memory graph at every point of the program:

Theorem 2. *For all state $\langle \lambda, A, M, \varrho, \ell \rangle$ of the collecting semantics $\mathcal{C}$ of P, we have $M \in \gamma_{\mathcal{M}^\sharp}(M_\mathcal{S}^\sharp)$.*

The pointer analysis problem of [24] has thus been reduced to the simpler and more tractable problem of solving a system of nonuniform inclusion constraints.

We finish this formal description with a brief description of the constraint generation for function calls. We associate a special set variable $\mathcal{F}_i(f)$ to the i-th formal parameter of each function f of a C program. We denote by $\mathcal{F}_0(f)$ the variable corresponding to the return value of f. Now consider a function call $\ell : p = f(p_1, \ldots, p_n)$. Assuming that we are provided with a collection

$\mathcal{X}, \mathcal{X}_1, \ldots, \mathcal{X}_n$ of set variables describing the sets of addresses that may flow through the return value and the parameters $\mathsf{p}, \mathsf{p}_1, \ldots, \mathsf{p}_n$ of the function call, we generate the following points-to equations:

$$
\begin{cases}
\langle \mathcal{F}_1(\mathsf{f}) \supseteq \mathcal{X}_1, \top_{\mathcal{V}^{\sharp}} \rangle \\
\cdots \\
\langle \mathcal{F}_n(\mathsf{f}) \supseteq \mathcal{X}_n, \top_{\mathcal{V}^{\sharp}} \rangle \\
\langle \mathcal{X} \supseteq \mathcal{F}_0(\mathsf{f}), \top_{\mathcal{V}^{\sharp}} \rangle
\end{cases}
$$

In other words, function calls are treated *uniformly*: there are no numerical constraints on the index variables. This is not a problem in practice, since nonuniform behaviours usually take place at the function level in embedded applications. We do not detail the analysis of computed calls, which can be easily derived from the semantics of the memory read operation $\mathsf{p} = *\mathsf{q}$.

We now illustrate the generation of equations. Consider the small program of Example 3 that fills in an array of pointers. The equations generated after the surface analysis are the following:

$$
\begin{cases}
\langle *\mathcal{L}_6(t) \supseteq \mathcal{R}_6(t'), \{t = t', 0 \le t < 10\} \rangle \\
\langle \mathcal{L}_6(t) \supseteq \&\mathsf{a} + o, \{0 \le o \le 4 \times t\} \rangle \\
\langle \mathcal{R}_6(t) \supseteq \mathbf{blk}_5\langle t' \rangle + o, \{t = t', o = 0, 0 \le t < 10\} \rangle
\end{cases}
$$

After solving these constraints by using an abstract iteration sequence with widening, we obtain the following abstract memory graph:

$$
\{\langle (\&\mathsf{a}, o) \triangleright (\mathbf{blk}_5\langle t \rangle, o'), \{o = 4 \times t, o' = 0, 0 \le t < 10\} \rangle\}
$$

which describes the exact shape of the memory althrough the execution of the program.

5   Experimental Evaluation

We have implemented the static analysis described in this paper for the full C language. The analyzer itself consists of 9,000 lines of SML/NJ excluding the front-end. We have interfaced the analyzer with the ckit [17] C front-end which is also written in SML. We currently use the reduced product of the lattice of linear equalities [19] and the lattice of intervals [6] for expressing numerical constraints. The analyzer first translates the C program into an intermediate language in which all expressions and statements have been broken down using a 3-address format. We then perform a dependency analysis which is used to eliminate all arithmetic operations that are not involved in pointer manipulations. This substantially shrinks down the size of the code to analyze. Whole structure assignment has not been described in this paper and deserves some attention. There are two possible ways of handling this construct, either by expanding the assignment into a collection of individual assignments to the fields of the structure or by analyzing the assignment as an atomic operation. The former is made difficult by union types and structure-breaking type casts. We chose the latter approach, which requires a straightforward extension of nonuniform constraints in order to copy a packet of pointers at once.

We have applied the analyzer to a real piece of software: an on-board link controller. The application contains about 25,000 lines of unprocessed C code. It is a pointer intensive program with plenty of loop constructs operating on multidimensional arrays of structures. It is quite representative of an average size embedded program, which is the main target of our analysis. Very large programs like those described in [25] are quite unusual. Our analysis is quite efficient. It takes 210 seconds to parse the files, construct the abstract surface semantics and generate the nonuniform inclusion constraints on a laptop with a 900Mhz Intel Pentium and 1Gb of RAM running Linux under VmWare. The resolution of these constraints only takes 21 seconds.

The results show that the analysis does discover nonuniform points-to relations. In particular, bidimensional arrays of distinct semaphores, arrays of functions and tables of preallocated memory blocks for dedicated memory management are exactly described. Surprisingly enough, the analysis uncovered a real bug in this application. While we were reviewing the results of the analysis we noticed that for some array `array2` of dynamically allocated semaphores, there was no linear relationship between the offset and the timestamps in the points-to relations. The nonuniform points-to equations gave us instantly the location in the program where the array was initialized. The initialization code looks like:

```
for (i = 0; i < 20; i++)
  for (j = 0; j < 8; j++) {
    array1[i][j] = semCreate ();
    array2[j] = semCreate ();
  }
```

The first array is properly initialized whereas the second one is reinitialized multiple times, causing a memory leak. It should be noticed that the analysis sucessfully inferred a nonuniform points-to relation for the bidimensional array of semaphores. This bug was present from the very first version of the program and has never been detected during the 18 months the software has been undergoing testing so far. This is an interesting application of this static analysis as a sophisticated typechecker for collections of pointers.

6   Conclusion

We have presented a pointer analysis that is able to infer nonuniform points-to relationships without the cost of existing flow-sensitive analyses [14, 24]. The originality of our work is that it conciliates two approaches to pointer analysis, abstract interpretation and constraint-based analysis, which are often opposed one to each other. Although we could have expressed the whole analysis within the framework of Abstract Interpretation [10], we think that a constraint-based presentation is more compact and more intuitive for both understanding and implementing the analysis. We have shown on a representative case study that our approach is tractable and achieves the expected level of precision. Unexpectedly, this analysis has been able to detect a subtle initialization bug in a real application. It now remains to perform more extensive empirical studies and investigate the use of the analysis in a real verification tool.

References

1. L. Andersen. *Program Analysis and Specialization for the C Programming Language*. PhD thesis, DIKU, University of Copenhagen, 1994.
2. B. Blanchet, P. Cousot, R. Cousot, J. Feret, L. Mauborgne, A. Miné, D. Monniaux, and X. Rival. Design and implementation of a special-purpose static program analyzer for safety-critical real-time embedded software, invited chapter. In T. Mogensen, D.A. Schmidt, and I.H. Sudborough, editors, *The Essence of Computation: Complexity, Analysis, Transformation. Essays Dedicated to Neil D. Jones*, LNCS 2566, pages 85–108. Springer-Verlag, October 2002.
3. B. Blanchet, P. Cousot, R. Cousot, J. Feret, L. Mauborgne, A. Miné, D. Monniaux, and X. Rival. A static analyzer for large safety-critical software. In *Proceedings of the ACM SIGPLAN 2003 Conference on Programming Language Design and Implementation (PLDI'03)*, pages 196–207. ACM Press, June 7–14 2003.
4. Satish Chandra and Thomas W. Reps. Physical type checking for c. In *Workshop on Program Analysis For Software Tools and Engineering*, pages 66–75, 1999.
5. P. Cousot. Semantic foundations of program analysis. In S.S. Muchnick and N.D. Jones, editors, *Program Flow Analysis: Theory and Applications*, chapter 10, pages 303–342. Prentice-Hall, Inc., Englewood Cliffs, 1981.
6. P. Cousot and R. Cousot. Static determination of dynamic properties of programs. In *Proceedings of 2nd International Symposium on Programming*, pages 106–130, 1976.
7. P. Cousot and R. Cousot. Abstract interpretation: a unified lattice model for static analysis of programs by construction or approximation of fixpoints. In *Proceedings of the 4th Symposium on Principles of Programming Languages*, pages 238–353, 1977.
8. P. Cousot and R. Cousot. Systematic design of program analysis frameworks. In *Conference Record of the Sixth Annual ACM SIGPLAN-SIGACT Symposium on Principles of Programming Languages*, pages 269–282. ACM Press, New York, NY, 1979.
9. P. Cousot and R. Cousot. Abstract interpretation frameworks. *Journal of Logic and Computation*, 2(4):511–547, 1992.
10. P. Cousot and R. Cousot. Formal language, grammar and set-constraint-based program analysis by abstract interpretation. In *Proceedings of the Seventh ACM Conference on Functional Programming Languages and Computer Architecture*, pages 170–181. ACM Press, New York, NY, 1995.
11. P. Cousot and N. Halbwachs. Automatic discovery of linear restraints among variables of a program. In *Conference Record of the Fifth Annual ACM SIGPLAN-SIGACT Symposium on Principles of Programming Languages*, pages 84–97. ACM Press, New York, NY, 1978.
12. Manuvir Das. Unification-based pointer analysis with directional assignments. *ACM SIGPLAN Notices*, 35(5):35–46, 2000.
13. A. Deutsch. A storeless model of aliasing and its abstraction using finite representations of right-regular equivalence relations. In *Proceedings of the 1992 International Conference on Computer Languages*, pages 2–13. IEEE Computer Society Press, 1992.

14. A. Deutsch. Interprocedural may-alias analysis for pointers: beyond k-limiting. In *ACM SIGPLAN'94 Conference on Programming Language Design and Implementation*. ACM Press, 1994.

15. Manuel Fähndrich, Jeffrey S. Foster, Zhendong Su, and Alexander Aiken. Partial online cycle elimination in inclusion constraint graphs. *ACM SIGPLAN Notices*, 33(5):85–96, 1998.

16. P. Granger. Static analysis of linear congruence equalities among variables of a program. In *TAPSOFT'91*, volume 493. Lecture Notes in Computer Science, 1991.

17. Nevin Heintze, Dino Oliva, and Dave MacQueen. The ckit front-end. `ckit@research.bell-labs.com`.

18. Nevin Heintze and Olivier Tardieu. Ultra-fast aliasing analysis using CLA: A million lines of c code in a second. In *SIGPLAN Conference on Programming Language Design and Implementation*, pages 254–263, 2001.

19. M. Karr. Affine relationships among variables of a program. *Acta Informatica*, pages 133–151, 1976.

20. A. Miné. The octagon abstract domain. In *AST 2001 at WCRE 2001*, IEEE, pages 310–319. IEEE CS Press, October 2001.

21. Bjarne Steensgaard. Points-to analysis by type inference of programs with structures and unions. In *Computational Complexity*, pages 136–150, 1996.

22. A. Venet. Abstract cofibered domains: Application to the alias analysis of untyped programs. In *Proceedings of SAS'96*, volume 1145 of *Lecture Notes in Computer Science*, pages 266–382. Springer Verlag, 1996.

23. A. Venet. Automatic analysis of pointer aliasing for untyped programs. *Science of Computer Programming*, 35(2):223–248, 1999.

24. A. Venet. Nonuniform alias analysis of recursive data structures and arrays. In *Proceedings of the 9th International Symposium on Static Analysis SAS'02*, volume 2477 of *Lecture Notes in Computer Science*, pages 36–51. Springer, 2002.

25. A. Venet and G. Brat. Precise and efficient static array bound checking for large embedded C programs. In *Proceedings of the International Conference on Programming Language Design and Implementation, PLDI'04*, 2004. To appear.

26. John Whaley and Monica S. Lam. An efficient inclusion-based points-to analysis for strictly-typed languages. In *Proceedings of the 9th International Static Analysis Symposium*, pages 180–195, September 2002.

Bottom-Up and Top-Down Context-Sensitive Summary-Based Pointer Analysis

Erik M. Nystrom, Hong-Seok Kim, and Wen-mei W. Hwu

Center for Reliable and High Performance Computing
University of Illinois, Urbana-Champaign
http://www.crhc.uiuc.edu/Impact

Abstract. This paper addresses scalability and accuracy of summary-based context-sensitive pointer analysis formulated as a two-phase computation. The first phase, or *bottom-up* phase, propagates procedure summaries from callees to callers. Then, the second phase, or *top-down* phase, computes the actual pointer information. These two phases can be independently context-sensitive. Having observed the problems that procedural side effects cause, we developed a bottom-up phase that constructs concise procedure summaries in a manner that permits their subsequent removal. This transformation results in an efficient two-phase pointer analysis in the style of Andersen [1] that is simultaneously bottom-up and top-down context-sensitive. Context sensitivity becomes inherent to even a context-insensitive analysis allowing for an accurate and efficient top-down phase. The implemented context-sensitive analysis exhibits scalability comparable to that of its context-insensitive counterpart. For instance, to analyze 176.gcc, the largest C benchmark in SPEC 2000, our analysis takes 190 seconds as opposed to 44 seconds for the context-insensitive analysis. Given the common practice of treating recursive subgraphs context-insensitively, its accuracy is equivalent to an analysis which completely inlines all procedure calls.

1 Introduction

Modern programming practices encourage code reuse, which often results in programs composed of a complex network of procedure calls. For static analysis, this exacerbates the problem of unrealizable (or spurious) interprocedural data flow [24]. *Context-sensitive* analyses are often able to avoid unrealizable data flow through procedure calls thereby delivering a higher degree of accuracy than their context-insensitive counterparts.

In the literature, there have been many approaches to context-sensitive pointer analysis. Some analyses [8,16,19,25,27] mimic dynamic execution, repeating call-return sequences until the analysis reaches a global fixed point. In these analyses, a procedure must be re-analyzed whenever there is a change in its callers or callees, leading to serious scalability issues. More recent work [2,3, 12,20,21] formulates pointer analysis as a two-phase computation. This formulation has the advantage that it can be designed to analyze a procedure at most twice when given a fixed acyclic call graph.

R. Giacobazzi (Ed.): SAS 2004, LNCS 3148, pp. 165–180, 2004.
© Springer-Verlag Berlin Heidelberg 2004

In the first phase of the two-phase computation, called the *bottom-up* phase, a flow function is constructed for each procedure by propagating *procedure summaries* from callees to callers. Then, the second phase, called the *top-down* phase, computes the actual pointer information by propagating calling contexts from callers to callees.

Each phase may be independently context-sensitive or -insensitive. On one hand, from the perspective of a caller, distinct calls to the same procedure should be analyzed independently. We call this *bottom-up* context sensitivity. On the other hand, from the perspective of a callee, its calling contexts from distinct call sites should be treated independently. We call this *top-down* context sensitivity.

Previous work [2, 3, 12, 20, 21] primarily focused on the scalability of bottom-up context sensitivity and provided little discussion about scalable top-down context sensitivity. When designed to analyze each procedure at most twice, the top-down phase in previous analyses has the following limitations:

1. The merging of calling contexts from distinct call sites before analyzing a callee leads to spurious interprocedural data flow.
2. The propagation of calling context information from the outputs of callers' flow functions to the inputs of callees' flow functions involves significant copying overheads, impacting scalability.

While investigating these limitations, we realized the importance of *procedural side effects* (loosely, a callee's effects on a caller) in dealing with context sensitivity. If a program lacks procedural side effects, a context-insensitive analysis does not derive any unrealizable interprocedural data flow. Based on this finding, we have reformulated summary-based analysis as follows:

1. The bottom-up phase transforms a program into a form that lacks procedural side effects, yet, has the same overall pointer behavior. This involves the *cutting* and *pasting* of procedural side effects from callees to callers instead of the *copying* and *pasting* performed by previous work [2, 3, 12, 20, 21].
2. The top-down phase consists of a single run of the context-insensitive analysis. Since the program is free of side effects after the bottom-up phase, the context-insensitive analysis does not experience any unrealizable interprocedural data flow. Therefore, in this form, top-down context sensitivity is inherent without any need to copy calling contexts during the top-down propagation.

To demonstrate the effectiveness of the proposed scheme, we implemented a pointer analysis for C programs with the following characteristics.

1. Intraprocedurally, it is a variant of the Andersen's algorithm. In particular, we use the formulation by Heintze and Tardieu [14]. Fields are handled in an offset-based manner while array indices are ignored. For each heap allocation site, we introduce a unique global variable.
2. Procedures in a common call graph cycle are merged into a single procedure. Effectively, recursion is handled in a context-insensitive way. Indirect calls are handled optimistically and iteratively (Section 3).
3. Procedural side effects are completely specialized. Thus, given an acyclic call graph, the implemented analysis is as accurate as one that transitively inlines all procedure calls.

(a)

```
int g;

iris() {
    int a;

    jade₁(&g,1);
    jade₂(&a,3);
}

jade(int *p, int q) {
    int r;

    *p:=q;
    r:=g+5;
}
```

(b)

```
p:=&g; q:=1;
p:=&a; q:=3;
*p:=q;
r:=g+5;

         ⇓

p:=&g    *p:=q
─────────────────
g:=q     q:=3

r:=g+5   ▷ g:=3
─────────────────
     ▷ r:=8
```

(c)

```
int g;

iris() {
    int a;

    pasted for { p₁:=&g; q₁:=1;   ⇒ g:=1;
    jade₁      { *p₁:=q₁;

    pasted for { p₂:=&a; q₂:=3;   ⇒ a:=3;
    jade₂      { *p₂:=q₂;

    jade₁(&g,1);
    jade₂(&a,3);
}

jade(int *p, int q) {
    int r;

    *p:=q;
    r:=g+5;
}
```

Fig. 1. Example 1: (a) code fragment, (b) flow- and context-insensitive equivalent followed by a possible derivation where the assignments marked with ▷ are spurious due to context loss, (c) the copying and pasting of jade's summary *p:=q prevents the spurious derivation of g:=3 and a:=1.

The remainder of this paper is organized as follows. Section 2 demonstrates the limitations of previous approaches using a simple example. In Section 3, we give an overview how the proposed analysis overcomes those limitations followed by more detailed algorithmic descriptions in Section 4. Section 5 presents empirical results. In this paper, all the algorithms are presented as bottom-up logic programs [22]. In each inference rule, the information above the line compose the conditions in which the information below the line is derived. The actual algorithm only tracks pointer values, thus, ignores integer constants. However, in examples, we use integer constants as pointer surrogates for clarity.

2   Limitations with Previous Work

Through a simple example, this section illustrates the limitations of previous summary-based analyses. At the end of this section, the same example is used to demonstrate how the proposed analysis overcomes such limitations.

Example 1. The code fragment in Figure 1(a) shows typical pointer use for a C program. Within this example, the discussion focuses on the following data flow facts:

1. In iris, after the first call to jade (denoted jade₁), global variable g acquires 1. After the second call to jade (denoted jade₂), variable a acquires 3
2. In both calls to procedure jade, since global variable g always evaluates to 1, local variable r always acquires 6.

The top of Figure 1(b) shows a flow- and context-insensitive equivalent of Example 1, where the assignments from iris and jade are collected without procedural boundaries and ignoring the ordering among them. The following derivation in Figure 1(b) depicts an application of the inference rules to these assignments. When Example 1 is analyzed context-insensitively, the interaction of $p:=\&g$ from call site $jade_1$ and $q:=3$ from call site $jade_2$ produces two spurious results $g:=3$ and $r:=8$. Therefore, to capture the data flow facts in Example 1 accurately, context sensitivity is critical.

2.1   Bottom-Up Phase

In a typical summary-based analysis, the goal of the bottom-up phase is to construct a concise *flow function* for each procedure. Given a calling context as an input, this function should return the final pointer information of the procedure, incorporating all the effects of its callees.

All the flow functions are computed in a single bottom-up sweep of the call graph, propagating *procedure summaries* from callees to callers. The procedure summary is similar to the flow function except that, instead of the final pointer information for the whole procedure, it returns only the change in pointer information visible to the callers, called *procedural side effects*.

In Example 1, the only assignment in $jade$ that causes side effects is $*p:=q$. Thus, the summary of $jade$ consists of the single assignment $*p:=q$. In the bottom-up phase, as shown in Figure 1(c), a specialized version of $*p:=q$ is pasted into each call site of $jade$ (for instance, $*p_1:=q_1$ for $jade_1$) along with assignments that mimic parameter passing.

2.2   Top-Down Phase

The goal of the top-down phase is to compute the actual pointer information. Since the flow functions of each procedure are available, it can be computed in a single top-down sweep of the call graph. The top-down phase begins by analyzing procedure $iris$. As shown in 1(c), the inclusion of $jade$'s summary makes the effects of $jade_1$ and $jade_2$ exist locally. At $iris$, only the intended results $g:=1$ and $a:=3$ are derived leaving the pointer information for $iris$ accurate and complete.

To analyze the next procedure, $jade$, the calling contexts must be formed then propagated (copied) from $iris$ to $jade$. The calling contexts for the two calls to $jade$ are:

$$jade_1 \Rightarrow g:=1; \ a:=3; \ p:=\&g; \ q:=1; \quad jade_2 \Rightarrow g:=1; \ a:=3; \ p:=\&a; \ q:=3;$$

To analyze procedure $jade$ only once during the top-down phase, these calling contexts must be merged before the application of $jade$'s flow function, as shown in Figure 2(a). While bottom-up context sensitivity allowed the accurate derivation of g's and a's values in $iris$, the lack of top-down context sensitivity leads, again, to the spurious derivations $g:=3$, $a:=1$, and $r:=8$. Without intervention, at the completion of $jade$ all benefits of the context sensitive bottom-up phase have been lost.

```
int g;

iris() {
          int a;
pasted for { p₁:=&g; q₁:=1;        ⇒ g:=1;
   jade₁  { *p₁:=q₁;

pasted for { p₂:=&a; q₂:=3;        ⇒ a:=3;
   jade₂  { *p₂:=q₂;

          jade₁(&g,1);
          jade₂(&a,3);
}
```

```
jade(int *p, int q) {


calling contexts { p:=&g; q:=1;
    from iris    { p:=&a; q:=3;  g:=1; a:=3;


        int r;

        *p:=q;    ⇒ g:=3; a:=1;
        r:=g+5;   ⇒ r:=6; r:=8;
}
```

```
jade(int *p, int q) {
          int r;

          *p:=q;  ⇐ cut from jade
          r:=g+5;
}
```

(a)   (b)

Fig. 2. Example 1 continued: (a) in the top-down phase for `jade` the spurious results `g:=3` and `r:=8` are still derived, (b) after cutting out the unnecessary assignment `*p:=q` from `jade`, the top-down phase no longer derives spurious results.

In practice, despite of its negative impact on scalability, explicit copying of calling contexts during the propagation of pointer information from callers to callees contains some of the contamination. When the pointer information of `a` is needed, pointer analysis clients will look up the output of `iris`' flow function, which does not contain the spurious result `a:=1`. However, without true top-down context sensitivity, pointer analysis clients must querying `jade` for `r` and will obtain the spurious result `r:=8`.

2.3   Observation

The derivation of `r:=8` in Figure 2(a) can be avoided by removing `*p:=q` from `jade` following the construction of `jade`'s summary. After the bottom-up phase, the original assignment `*p:=q` in `jade` is irrelevant from the perspective of `iris`, since the pasting of `jade`'s summary provides local, specialized copies. Since `g`'s result is naturally available in `jade` through the calling context, the original assignment `*p:=q` in `jade` is unnecessary, and, more importantly, problematic.

This observation is reflected in Figure 2(b), where `*p:=q` has been removed from `jade`. After its removal, only the intended results are derived for both `iris` and `jade`. Moreover, since `iris` is truly unaffected by `jade` after this change, `iris`'s pointer information does not need to be set aside through explicit copying. The rest of this paper presents a generalization of the process of converting a program with procedural side effects to an equivalent one without any.

3   Overview

In C programs, indirect calls can be made using function pointers. In the presence of indirect calls, a cyclic dependency exists between call graph construction and pointer analysis. Without having a complete call graph, pointer information may be incomplete. On the other hand, without complete pointer information, the call graph may be incomplete.

The proposed analysis breaks this cyclic dependency using an iterative approach as in [3, 16]. It begins with an incomplete call graph consisting of only direct calls. Based on this incomplete call graph, pointer information is constructed. Then, using this as feedback, the call graph is updated. This process continues until there are no more changes to the call graph. Since the bottom-up phase does not terminate in the presence of recursive procedures, they are merged into a single procedure, while the recursive calls between them are converted into a set of parameter-passing assignments. Effectively, recursion is handled context-insensitively.

3.1   Impact of Side Effects

The rationale behind the proposed pointer analysis is best demonstrated by examining the impact of *procedural side effects* on the accuracy of context-insensitive analysis. Let us reconsider the example in Figure 1. By analyzing this example context-insensitively, we can derive following results.

$$\frac{[\texttt{p:=\&g}]_1 \quad \texttt{*p:=q}}{\frac{\texttt{g:=q} \qquad [\texttt{g:=1}]_1}{\texttt{g:=1}}} \qquad \frac{[\texttt{p:=\&a}]_2 \quad \texttt{*p:=q}}{\frac{\texttt{a:=q} \qquad [\texttt{q:=3}]_2}{\texttt{a:=3}}} \qquad \frac{[\texttt{p:=\&g}]_1 \quad \texttt{*p:=q}}{\frac{\texttt{g:=q} \qquad [\texttt{q:=3}]_2}{\triangleright \texttt{g:=3}}}$$

The first two derivations are from call sites 1 and 2 respectively and are both realizable in some dynamic execution of the code fragment. However, intermixing the parameter assignments from these two call sites results in the third, spurious, derivation reproduced from Figure 1(b). The key problem in this derivation stems from the fact that g:=q is valid only within the call site jade$_1$ while q:=3 only within jade$_2$. Since they are from two different call sites, the two should not be allowed to interact.

As proved in the technical report [18], no such spurious interaction can occur if a program completely lacks procedural side effects. Even though a procedure may have many input calling contexts, without procedural side effects there is no way in which the contexts can interact. For side-effect free programs, full context sensitivity is inherent even when using a context-insensitive analysis.

3.2   Specialization of Side Effects

In reality, most programs have procedural side effects. Therefore, to exploit this finding, the proposed analysis hoists *specialized* copies of the procedural side effects from callees into callers and, then, cuts the side effects from the callees. The specialization continues until the program is free of procedural side effects thereby allowing the use of a context-insensitive style analysis in the following phase while avoiding all spurious interprocedural interaction.

```
kate() {                  kate() {                        lily(int *p, int q) {
      int a,b,c;                 int a,b,c;                      int r,s;

      lily₁(&a,1);        { p₁:=&a; q₁:=1;   ⇒ a:=1;      { x₃:=&r; y₃:=q;   ⇒ r:=q;
      lily₂(&b,3);          *p₁:=q₁;                        *x₃:=y₃;
      c:=a+b;
}                         { p₂:=&b; q₂:=3;   ⇒ b:=3;      { x₄:=&s; y₄:=5;   ⇒ s:=5;
                            *p₂:=q₂;                        *x₄:=y₄;
lily(int *p, int q) {
      int r,s;                  lily₁(&a,1);                    mary₃(&r,q);
                                lily₂(&b,3);                    mary₄(&s,5);
      mary₃(&r,q);              c:=a+b;                         *p:=r;
      mary₄(&s,5);        }
      *p:=r;                                              }
}
                                              mary(int *x, int y) {
mary(int *x, int y) {                               int z,w;
      int z,w;
                                                    z:=y; *x:=z
      z:=y; *x:=z                                   w:=*x+7
      w:=*x+7                               }

      (a)                                             (b)
```

Fig. 3. Example 2: (a) code fragment, (b) demonstration of the specialization of procedural side effects.

Example 2. The code fragment in Figure 3(a) will be used to illustrate the key aspects of the specialization process in the proposed analysis.

1. In procedure mary, the assignment *x:=z is the direct cause of side effects. By specializing *x:=z into mary's call sites (pasting its copies into call sites while cutting the original one), mary is left free of side effects, as shown in Figure 3(b).
2. Procedure lily also has side effects (due to *p:=r). Note that, when procedure lily is visited, the copies of mary's summary are already present in lily. For this example, *compaction* (or simplification) is important to reduce the size of lily's summary.

The bottom-up phase of our analysis traverses the acyclic-rendered call graph in a reverse-topological order, specializing side effects along the way. First, all the potential side-effect derivations are identified based on the concept of *criticality*. Informally speaking, we say that an assignment is *critical* if it has the potential to cause a side effect. In Example 2, the assignments *x:=z in mary and *p:=r in lily fall into this category.

The role of a procedure *summary* is to promote all the necessary side effects to the caller's level where the contexts will no longer intermix. Critical assignments are used as a seed in the creation of the summary. The pasting of summaries permits *cutting* out critical assignments from procedures, leaving them free of side effects while maintaining the effect of the original assignments.

Summary size is the single most important factor governing the scalability of this pointer analysis algorithm. In an extreme case, an entire callee can be used as a summary. However, considering their transitive impact on scalability, it is necessary for summary sizes to be kept as small as possible. For instance, in mary, two assignments *x:=z and z:=y can be *compacted* into the single assignment *x:=y reducing the size of the summary. In addition, since the assignment w:=*x+7 causes only local effects, by ignoring it, one can further reduce the summary size. *Back-tracing* is used to construct compacted assignments to be added into the summary. The following describes the actual back-tracing process in `mary` and the key intermediate decisions made during the process.

1. Back-tracing is initiated from the critical assignment `*x:=z`. However, since its right-hand side `z` is not a parameter, the addition of `*x:=z` into the summary is deferred and each assignment that modifies `z` is examined.
2. The assignment `z:=y` is the only assignment modifying variable `z`. Thus, by back-substituting `z` in `*x:=z` with `y`, the data flow is compacted into `*x:=y`. Since both `x` and `y` are parameters, no further compaction is necessary. Therefore, `*x:=y` is added to `mary`'s summary.

After the summary `*x:=y` is formed, it is pasted into each call site in `lily` while the critical assignment `*x:=z` is cut from `mary`.

3.3   Coping with Aliases

For correctness, back-tracing must consider *all* data flow making it necessary to determine every location in which a variable may be modified. In reality, aliasing complicates this determination because complete data flow information is no longer explicit within the program text. The final decision on the form of the summary must be differed to higher level and will be formalized in Section 4. Consider procedure `lily` following the processing of `mary`.

1. Since the assignment `*p:=r` has the potential to modify an external variable, to construct `lily`'s summary, back-tracing is initiated from the assignment.
2. Note that no explicit data flow exists into `r`. However, since `r`'s address was taken at $x_3:=\&r$, there may be implicit data flow that modifies `r`. In this case, all the data flow of `r` can be determined through a local examination on `lily`, resulting in the derivation of the implicit data flow `r:=q` from the specialized copy of `mary`'s summary for the call site $mary_3$.
3. By continuing back-tracing, `*p:=r` and the implicit data flow `r:=q` are compacted into `*p:=q`. Since there is no other modification of `r`, the assignment `*p:=q` suffices as `lily`'s summary.

After `lily` is processed, all side effects in Example 2 can be removed while leaving the overall pointer behavior unchanged. Then, the second phase applies a single run of the context-insensitive analysis and computes all pointer information completely and accurately. Note that, during this step, all the effects of the original critical assignments, namely, `*x:=z` in `mary` and `*p:=r` in `lily`, exist at the caller's level and are propagated back into the callees via regular parameter-passing mechanisms. After specialization, `mary`'s parameter `x` still points to `r` and `s`. Thus, `*x` correctly evaluates to 1, 3, and 5 in the assignment `w:=*x+7`.

An important aspect in `lily` that simplifies summary generation is that the aliases of the address-taken variables `r` and `s` could be completely and accurately determined without knowledge of `lily`'s calling context. Unfortunately, this is not always possible.

```
nina() {                                                    oliv(int *p, int q,
        int a,b;                        nina() {                    int **r, int**s
        int *c,*d,*e;                          int a,b;             int x) {
        oliv₁(&a,1,&c,&c);                     int *c,*d,*e;
        oliv₂(&b,3,&d,&e);              ⎧ x₁:=&q;                   int y;
}                                       ⎨ *r₁:=&x₁; *p₁:=**s;        x:=q;
                                        ⎩                           *r:=&x; *p:=**s;
oliv(int *p, int q,                     ⎧ x₂:=&q;                    y:=*x+5;
        int **r, int**s) {              ⎨ *r₂:=&x₁; *p₂:=**s;
        int x,y;                        ⎩                          }
                                           oliv₁(&a,1,&c,&c);    }
        1: x:=q;
        2: *r:=&x; *p:=**s;                oliv₂(&b,3,&d,&e);
        3: y:=*x+5;                     }
}
            (a)                                           (b)
```

Fig. 4. Example 3: (a) code fragment before and (b) after side effects are specialized.

Example 3. The code fragment in Figure 4(a) depicts a situation where accurate alias relations may not be determined without the knowledge of the actual calling contexts. The following are the key aspects of the example that complicate the specialization process.

1. In `oliv`, by the assignment `*r:=&x`, the address of local variable `x` is assigned to variables nonlocal to `oliv`. Note that this is a safe use of `x` since it is used only when `oliv` is active.

2. In the first call site `oliv₁`, since `r` and `s` point to the same variable `c`, `x` is copied into `*p` at Line 2. Therefore, there is a flow from `q` through `x` into `*p`, allowing `a:=1`.

3. In the second call site `oliv₂`, since `r` and `s` point to distinct variables, `x` is not copied into `*p` at Line 2. Instead, the contents of `*e` is read. Therefore, there is no flow from `q` to `*p`, thus `b` does not acquire 3.

The last two aspects raise a dilemma. For the first call site `oliv₁`, the flow `*p:=q` must be reflected in the summary. However, for the second call site `oliv₂`, its inclusion would degrade the solution's accuracy. The problem is that the data flow in the summary depends on the calling contexts which are not available during the bottom-up phase.

There are multiple approaches to dealing with this dilemma. First, the assignment `*p:=q` can conservatively be included in the summary. Despite of accuracy degradation, this approach is sound. Second, two versions of summaries can be explicitly provided: one version for the case `*r` and `*s` are aliases and the other version for the case they are not. The summaries in [2] fall into this category.

Instead, in this paper, we take another approach. As shown in Figure 4(b), by introducing `x:=q`, `*r:=&x`, and `*p:=**s` into the summary, the alias of `x` can be resolved at the caller's level. Note that, to do so, `&x` and all potential writes to `x` have been included into the summary.

This decision has an impact on summary size. In an extreme case, where every variable behaves like `x`, the summary size will explode rapidly. However, in C programs, the lifetime of local variables is bounded by their declaring procedure

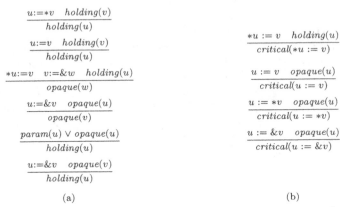

(a)   (b)

Fig. 5. Symbolic derivation of side effects: (a) symbolic simulation of the effects of calling contexts, (b) determination of criticality.

and this constraint greatly influences typical programming practice. For this reason, the address of a local variable is rarely copied into a non-local memory space (which might be safe) or returned (which would be a bug).

The promotion of variable x from the callee oliv to the caller nina has another consequence. As shown in Figure 4(b), the assignment y:=*x+5 accesses variable x, but only as a consumer. Thus, it causes only local effects and did not become a part of oliv's summary. In order to keep the overall information unchanged, especially for variable y, we merge all specialized versions of variable x (x_1 and x_2) by treating them as extra arguments at the corresponding call sites as shown in Figure 4(b), Note that, after the merging, the following run of the context-insensitive analysis computes the pointer information completely and accurately.

4   Specialization Algorithm

This section presents the specifics surrounding the identification of critical assignments and the assembly of concise summaries. The proposed analysis removes procedural side effects of a program by hoisting side effects upward in the call graph. Side effects are *specialized* until they can no longer interfere spuriously. When a procedure is about to be processed, all the side effects of its callees are already locally available in the procedure while the callees are left free of side effects. Therefore, in processing an individual procedure, we need to be concerned only with intraprocedural data flow.

4.1   Detecting Criticality

As shown in the example in Figure 3, identifying critical assignments is the key to identifying procedural side effects. The difficulty in finding critical assignments lies in the fact that, when a procedure is being processed during the bottom-up traversal, no information about its calling contexts is available.

This difficulty is resolved by capturing the effects of calling contexts through two properties *holding, opaque* : **Var** → **Bool**. Roughly speaking, a variable is said to be *holding* if it may point to an *external* variable. Provided that such information is available, critical assignments can be found by the rules in Figure 5.

Example 4. In the following code fragment, the parameter p is copied into the local variable b by the assignment *a:=p. Therefore, since b may point to an external variable, the assignment *b:=r is critical. Using the holding property described in Figure 5(a), the proposed analysis determines the criticality of *b:=r as shown in the following derivation.

```
pete(int *p, int q) {
    int *a,b;
    a:=&b; *a:=p; *b:=q;
}
```

$$\cfrac{\cfrac{\cfrac{\texttt{a:=\&b} \quad \texttt{*a:=p} \quad param(p)}{\texttt{b:=p} \qquad holding(p)}}{\texttt{*b:=q} \qquad\qquad\qquad holding(\texttt{b})}}{critical(\texttt{*b:=q})}$$

In certain cases, the address of a local variable can be copied into an external variable. In the proposed analysis, this local variable is called *opaque* in the sense that its actual data flow becomes opaque due to the lack of calling contexts. This was seen in Example 4 where variable x in oliv is opaque. For a similar reason, a variable pointed to by an opaque variable must be regarded as being opaque as well. Note that, to be conservative, an opaque variable must be regarded as holding, too.

In back-tracing, an opaque variable is problematic because its alias information is unknown making it unclear where or how it is modified. As explained in Section 3.3, we handle this ambiguity by promoting the relevant assignments into the callers thereby hoisting the alias resolution to a point where more information about the calling contexts is known. This implies that *all* potential modifications of such variables must be reflected in the summary. From this perspective, as depicted by the rules in Figure 5(b), it is convenient to treat an opaque variable as external.

4.2   Back-Tracing

Given critical assignments, including those due to opaque variables, summarization begins by initiating *back-tracing* as follows, where e and e' stand for arbitrary expressions:

$$\frac{critical(e:=e')}{traced(e:=e')}$$

Though the back-tracing rules used by our analysis (shown in Figure 6) appear complicated, the invariants behind them are straightforward: once an assignment is *traced*, all its effects must be reproduced by the summary. Actual insertion of a back-traced assignment into the summary is deferred until it becomes unavoidable and will occur due to one of the following conditions: First, back-tracing has reached an *input* to the procedure (parameter or opaque variable). Second,

$$\frac{traced(*u := v) \quad u := w \quad holding(w)}{traced(*w := v)}$$

$$\frac{traced(*u := v) \quad u := *w \quad holding(w)}{add(*u := v) \wedge traced(u := *w)}$$

(a) stuck left-hand

$$\frac{traced(*u := v) \quad v := w \quad holding(w)}{traced(*u := w)}$$

$$\frac{traced(*u := v) \quad v := \&w}{add(*u := v) \wedge traced(v := \&w)}$$

$$\frac{traced(*u := v) \quad v := *w \quad holding(w)}{add(*u := v) \wedge traced(v := *w)}$$

(b) stuck right-hand

$$\frac{traced(*u := v) \quad input(u) \quad input(v)}{add(*u := v)}$$

(c) stuck both sides

$$\frac{traced(u := v) \quad v := \&w}{traced(u := \&w)}$$

$$\frac{traced(u := v) \quad v := *w \quad holding(w)}{traced(u := *w)}$$

$$\frac{traced(u := v) \quad v := w \quad holding(w)}{traced(u := w)}$$

$$\frac{traced(u := v) \quad input(v)}{add(u := v)}$$

$$\frac{traced(u := \&v)}{add(u := \&v)}$$

(d)

$$\frac{traced(u:=*v) \quad v:=w \quad holding(w)}{traced(u:=*w)}$$

$$\frac{traced(u := *v) \quad v := *w \quad holding(w)}{add(u := *v) \wedge traced(v := *w)}$$

$$\frac{traced(u := *v) \quad input(v)}{add(u := *v)}$$

(e)

Fig. 6. Back-tracing (a)(b)(c) store, (d) plain and address, (e) and load assignments.

the net effect from two assignments cannot be represented with a single assignment in the model language (a single edge in the actual implementation). For instance, u:=**v is not allowed, thus, must be broken into u:=*t and t:=*v.

5   Empirical Results

To demonstrate the usefulness of our approach, we evaluated the presented techniques on all the C benchmarks from the SPEC 92, 95, and 2000 suites except redundant ones. This breadth of benchmarks shows a wide range of analysis characteristics. The main results are summarized in Table 7.

Since field information can greatly affect the analysis results, the analysis is implemented in a field-sensitive fashion. Our implementation tries to handle as many abuses of the C language as possible in a safe and accurate manner. For instance, our analysis is offset-based, as opposed to using field names as in [19]. Each variable is associated with *accessed offsets*, which are dynamically updated should any additional offsets be discovered during the analysis.

To reduce summary size, the bottom-up phase performs redundancy elimination [17] and cycle elimination [9]. In addition, data flow through global variables are treated context-insensitively, which allows their exclusion from procedural summaries while not impacting resultant accuracy.

Table 7 lists the percentage reduction in total points-to set size when comparing context-insensitive (CI) results to context-sensitive (CS) results. This is

Benchmark	LOC	CI	CS		R%
			BU	TD	
008.espresso	13505	1.00	0.30	0.03	89 %
023.eqntott	3393	0.02	0.02	0.01	- %
099.go	28547	0.50	0.15	0.02	- %
124.m88ksim	17251	0.70	0.40	0.04	4 %
129.compress	1426	0.01	0.01	0.01	- %
130.li	6930	8.00	2.00	0.03	- %
132.ijpeg	25897	3.50	35.00	1.00	8 %
134.perl	23969	2.50	30.00	1.50	10 %

Benchmark	LOC	CI	CS		R%
			BU	TD	
164.gzip	7759	0.02	0.01	0.01	2 %
175.vpr	16973	0.25	0.10	0.01	35 %
176.gcc	205747	45.00	190.00	2.50	2 %
181.mcf	1909	0.01	0.02	0.01	- %
186.crafty	18977	0.10	0.07	0.01	33 %
197.parser	10924	0.40	0.15	0.02	- %
253.perlbmk	57541	360.00	800.00	45.00	4 %
254.gap	59674	120.00	430.00	18.00	1 %
255.vortex	52634	6.00	10.00	1.00	- %
256.bzip2	4637	0.01	0.01	0.01	- %
300.twolf	19749	0.30	0.15	0.02	- %

Fig. 7. Analysis time in seconds for the context insensitive (CI) and context sensitive (CS) analyses. The CS time is divided into the bottom-up (BU) and top-down (TD) portions. It also shows the percentage reduction of total points-to set size in percentage (the column R%) when switching from CI to CS. Times were measured on a 2.4 GHz Pentium 4 computer and never consumed more than 300 MB of memory.

Benchmark	Proposed			Foster *et al.*		
	BU	TD	Ratio	BU	TD	Ratio
008.espresso	0.31	0.03	0.10	28.81	967.64	33.6
023.egntott	0.02	0.01	0.50	1.50	11.20	7.5
129.compress	0.01	0.01	1.00	0.41	1.42	3.5
130.li	1.96	0.03	0.02	189.49	9929.88	52.4

Fig. 8. Analysis time in seconds compared to Foster *et al.* [12]. Ratio is the ratio of TD time to BU time. There is a clear difference in ratios, with the TD phase for the proposed analysis only contributing to a small percentage of the total time.

calculated by summing the points-to set size for every location (variable offset) in the benchmark. While this may not directly correlate to beneficial accuracy improvement, we feel it provides useful comparison. There is a substantial range in benefit with some benchmarks showing little or no benefit (256.bzip and 300.twolf) while others show a fairly substantial reduction (008.espresso at 89% and 175.vpr at 35%).

Table 7 lists two sets of analysis times (in seconds) for CI and CS analysis runs. The CS run times are broken into bottom-up and top-down times. When comparing the CI and CS analysis times, there is a large span ranging from the cases where the CS times being faster (008.espresso, 130.li, 175.vpr, and 197.parser) to the other cases where the CS times being about 5-10x slower (132.ijpeg, 134.perl, and 254.gap). It is interesting to note that there is a strong correlation between the CI and CS accuracy and analysis time comparison. The more accuracy benefit the CS analysis provided, the faster the analysis performs with respect to the CI analysis.

It is also enlightening to compare the relative cost of the bottom-up and top-down phases. Aside from those benchmarks that require less than about 0.1 second, the top-down phase of the analysis contributes little to the overall analysis time. It is generally between 1% and 10% of the bottom-up time. This is expected, because, while the bottom-up phase spends time summarizing proce-

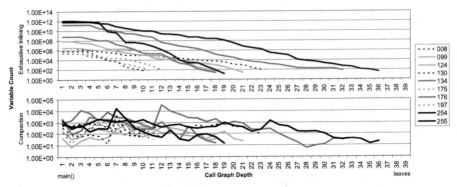

Fig. 9. Semi-log graph showing the number of variable locations versus call graph depth for both exhaustive inlining and our proposed summary-based inlining across SPEC.

dures and specializing procedural side effects, the top-down phase only needs to propagate pointer information in a context-insensitive fashion.

To provide a frame of reference concerning the efficiency of our top-down phase, Figure 8 presents top-down and bottom-up analysis times from the benchmarks in common between our work and Foster *et al.* [12]. The important comparison is the ratio of top-down to bottom-up time for each of two works. For our analysis, the top-down time is never more than the bottom-up time, even for a benchmark as small as 129.compress, and becomes increasingly insignificant as benchmark size increases (2% for 130.li). We suspect that the copying overheads are what cause the top-down phase in Foster *et al.* to generally surpass the bottom-up time, reaching a factor of 50 for 130.li.

One major concern in terms of scalability is the problem size growth caused by the inclusion of specialized summaries. Figure 9 demonstrates the effectiveness of our bottom-up phase by comparing the theoretical growth in exhaustive inlining (upper graph) against the empirical results using our summary-based analysis (lower graph). In the figure, procedure `main` is always at a depth of one while leaf procedures are at the far right of a particular line spanning depths from 11 to 39. The y-axis is a logarithmic scale of the number of variables at that level. Thus, the values in the upper graph extend to 1 trillion while the lower graph extends only to 100K.

It is apparent that the growth in our bottom-up phase is not explosive. An interesting aspect of the lower graph is that the size of summaries does not grow monotonically as it approaches `main`. Instead, it varies almost independently of the depth, increasing and decreasing according to compaction opportunities. The only spikes in the lower graph are due to the existence of large recursive cycles (100s of procedures). Even for these, summarization quickly diminishes their impact.

6   Related Work

Pointer analysis has been studied extensively in the literature. For a more complete list of previous pointer analyses, we refer readers to [15]. Context-sensitive pointer analyses have been approached from several directions. In [8, 16, 19, 25, 27], procedures are re-analyzed until a global fixed point is reached. Among these, [27] is unique in the sense that the overhead of re-analysis is reduced by memoization. On the other hand, the analyses in [2, 3, 12, 20, 21] are based on procedure summaries formulated as two-phase computation. Among those, Foster *et al.* [12] is the closest to the proposed pointer analysis. One of the analyses presented by Foster *et al.* is a context-sensitive extension of Andersen's analysis. The bottom-up phase of this algorithm is similar to ours in many aspects. The difference is that, in Foster *et al.*, the critical assignments in callees still exist after the bottom-up phase. Therefore, in addition to accuracy degradation, explicit copying seems unavoidable.

CFL reachability [24] provides an alternative approach to context sensitivity. One of its merits over other approaches is that recursion can be handled also context-sensitively. Fähndrich *et al.* [10] employed a variant of CFL reachability with unification-based modeling proposed by Steensgard [26]. Das *et al.* [7] took a similar approach using the data flow modeling proposed by Das [6] yet with one-level context sensitivity.

The philosophy behind our pointer analysis is similar to *counter-example directed refinement*, a popular scheme in model checking [5]. In this approach, refinement is driven by feedback from a less accurate abstraction. In our pointer analysis, instead, refinement is performed preemptively and exhaustively. Guyer and Lin [13] applied counter-example directed refinement to pointer analysis. When results computed by less accurate pointer analysis (both flow- and context-insensitive) turn out to be insufficient, the accuracy is refined by adding flow or context sensitivity. To add context sensitivity, a procedure call is specialized by cloning the callee's body. After being specialized, all the procedures are re-analyzed until a global fixed point is reached. From this perspective, the techniques proposed in this paper can also greatly aid the efficiency of their analysis.

Many algorithms, for instance, [11, 12], employ techniques similar to backtracing in an effort to construct a *concise* yet *observably-equivalent* summary of the analysis information. Constraint simplification in general has been thoroughly studied. For a more complete list of references and in-depth discussion, we refer readers to [23]. The concept of opacity is similar to the *escaping* of objects extensively discussed for object-oriented programs. For the list of references, we refer readers to [4].

7   Conclusion

We have proposed a fully context-sensitive yet very efficient summary-based pointer analysis. The key aspect is that the bottom-up phase transforms a program into one lacking procedural side effects by cutting side-effect causing assignments from callees after they have been summarized. This prevents all spurious interprocedural data flow in the following top-down phase while preserving the pointer behavior. Empirical results support the effectiveness of the pointer analysis both in accuracy and efficiency. We thank the IMPACT research group for their help and DARPA/MARCO-GSRC which supported this work.

References

1. L. O. Andersen. *Program analysis and specialization for the C programming language*. Ph.D thesis, DIKU, Unversity of Copenhagen, 1994.
2. R. Chatterjee, B. G. Ryder, and W. A. Landi. Relevant context inference. In *POPL*, 1999.
3. B.-C. Cheng and W. W. Hwu. Modular interprocedural pointer analysis using access paths: design, implementation, and evaluation. In *PLDI*, 2000.
4. J.-D. Choi, M. Gupta, M. J. Serrano, V. C. Sreedhar, and S. P. Midkiff. Stack allocation and synchronization optimizations for java using escape analysis. *TOPLAS*, 2003.
5. E. Clarke, O. Grunmberg, S. Jha, Y. Lu, and H. Veith. Counterexample-guided abstraction refinement for symbolic model checking. *Journal of the ACM*, 1997.
6. M. Das. Unification-based pointer analysis with directional assignments. In *PLDI*, 2000.
7. M. Das, B. Liblit, M. Fähndrich, and J. Rehof. Estimating the impact of scalable pointer analysis on optimization. In *SAS*, 2001.
8. M. Emami, R. Ghiya, and L. J. Hendren. Context-sensitive interprocedural points-to analysis in the presence of function pointers. In *PLDI*, 1994.
9. M. Fähndrich, J. S. Foster, Z. Su, and A. Aiken. Partial online cycle elimination in inclusion constraint graphs. In *PLDI*, 1998.
10. M. Fähndrich, J. Rehof, and M. Das. Scalable context-sensitive flow analysis using instantiation constraints. In *PLDI*, 2000.
11. C. Flanagan and M. Felleisen. Componential set-based analysis. In *PLDI*, 1997.
12. J. S. Foster, M. Fähndrich, and A. Aiken. Polymorphic versus monomorphic flow-insensitive points-to analysis for C. In *SAS*, 2000.
13. S. Z. Guyer and C. Lin. Client-driven pointer analysis. In *SAS*, 2003.
14. N. Heintze and O. Tardieu. Ultra-fast aliasing analysis using CLA: a million lines of C code in a second. In *PLDI*, 2001.
15. M. Hind. Pointer analysis: Haven't we solved this problem yet? In *PASTE*, 2001.
16. M. Hind, M. Burke, P. Carini, and J.-D. Choi. Interprocedural pointer alias analysis. *TOPLAS*, 21(4):848–894, 1999.
17. J. E. Hopcroft. An $n \log n$ algorithm for minimizing the states of a finite automaton. *The Theory of Machines and Computations*, pages 189–196, 1971.
18. H.-S. Kim, E. M. Nystrom, and W. W. Hwu. Bottom-up and top-down context-sensitive summary-based pointer analysis. Technical report, IMPACT research group, University of Illinois. 2004.
19. W. Landi and B. G. Ryder. A safe approximation algorithm for interprocedural pointer aliasing. In *PLDI*, 1992.
20. C. Lattner and V. Adve. Data structure analysis: a fast and scalable context-sensitive heap analysis. Technical report, CS Dept., University of Illinois. 2003.
21. D. Liang and M. J. Harrold. Efficient points-to analysis for whole-program analysis. In *FSE*, 1999.
22. D. A. McAllester. On the complexity analysis of static analysis. In *SAS*, 1999.
23. J. Rehof. Minimal typings in atomic subtyping. In *POPL*, 1997.
24. T. Reps, S. Horwitz, and M. Sagiv. Precise interprocedural dataflow analysis via graph reachability. In *POPL*, 1995.
25. E. Ruf. Context-insensitive alias analysis reconsidered. In *PLDI*, 1995.
26. B. Steensgaard. Points-to analysis in almost linear time. In *POPL*, 1996.
27. R. P. Wilson and M. S. Lam. Efficient context-sensitive pointer analysis for C programs. In *PLDI*, 1995.

Abstract Interpretation
of Combinational Asynchronous Circuits

Sarah Thompson and Alan Mycroft

Computer Laboratory, University of Cambridge
William Gates Building, JJ Thompson Avenue,
Cambridge, CB3 0FD, UK
{Sarah.Thompson,Alan.Mycroft}@cl.cam.ac.uk

Abstract. A technique, based upon abstract interpretation, is presented that allows general gate-level combinational asynchronous circuits with uncertain delay characteristics to be reasoned about. Our approach is particularly suited to the simulation and model checking of circuits where the identification of possible glitch states (static and dynamic hazards) is required.
A hierarchy of alternative abstractions linked by Galois connections is presented, each offering varying tradeoffs between accuracy and complexity. Many of these abstract domains resemble extended, multi-value logics: *transitional logics* that include extra values representing transitions as well as steady states, and *static/clean* logics that include the values S and C representing 'unknown but fixed for all time' and 'can never glitch' respectively.

1 Introduction

Most contemporary design approaches assume an underlying *synchronous* paradigm, where a single global signal drives the clock inputs of every flip flop in the circuit. As a consequence, nearly all synthesis, simulation and model checking tools assume synchronous semantics. Designs in which this rule is relaxed are generally termed *asynchronous circuits*.

In a synchronous model, glitches (also known as static and dynamic hazards) do not cause problems unless they occur on a wire used as a clock input; with purely synchronous design rules[1] this can not occur. However, such safety restrictions are *not* enforced by the semantics of either Verilog or VHDL – it is quite easy, deliberately or otherwise, to introduce unsafe logic into a clock path.

We present a technique, based upon abstract interpretation [1, 2], that allows the glitch states of asynchronous circuits to be identified and reasoned about. The approach taken involves a family of extended, multi-value *transitional* logics with an underlying dense continuous time model, and has applications in synthesis, simulation and model checking.

Our logics are extended with extra values that capture transitions as well as steady states, with an ability to distinguish *clean*, glitch-free signals from

---

[1] Exactly one global clock net driving the clock inputs of all flip flops in the circuit.

R. Giacobazzi (Ed.): SAS 2004, LNCS 3148, pp. 181–196, 2004.

dirty, potentially glitchy ones. As a motivating example, consider the circuits represented by the expressions $(a \wedge c) \vee (\neg a \wedge b) \vee (b \wedge c)$ and $(a \wedge c) \vee (\neg a \wedge b)$. With respect to steady-state values for a, b and c, both circuits would appear to be identical, with the latter representing a circuit that might result from naïve optimisation of the former. Our technique can straightforwardly illustrate differences in their dynamic behaviour, however. Consider the critical case $a = \uparrow_0$ and $b = c = \mathsf{T}_0$, representing b and c being wired to *true* for all time, and a clean transition from *false* to *true* on a (this notation is defined fully in Section 3):

$(a \wedge c) \vee (\neg a \wedge b) \vee (b \wedge c)$	$(a \wedge c) \vee (\neg a \wedge b)$
$= (\uparrow_0 \wedge \mathsf{T}_0) \vee (\neg\uparrow_0 \wedge \mathsf{T}_0) \vee (\mathsf{T}_0 \wedge \mathsf{T}_0)$	$= (\uparrow_0 \wedge \mathsf{T}_0) \vee (\neg\uparrow_0 \wedge \mathsf{T}_0)$
$= \uparrow_0 \vee \downarrow_0 \vee \mathsf{T}_0$	$= \uparrow_0 \vee \downarrow_0$
$= \mathsf{T}_0$	$= \mathsf{T}_{0..1}$

The result T_0 may be interpreted as '*true* for all time, with no glitches'. However, $\mathsf{T}_{0..1}$ represents '*true* with zero or one glitches', clearly demonstrating the poorer dynamic behaviour of the smaller circuit.

1.1   Hardware Components

In this paper we consider four[2] basic building blocks: (perfect – zero delay) AND-gates, (perfect) NOT-gates, delay elements (whose delays may depend on time, and environmental factors like temperature, and thus are non-deterministic in a formal sense), and *inertial delay* elements. The difference between an ordinary delay and an inertial delay is that in the former the number of transitions on its input and output are equal, but in the latter a short-duration pulse from high-to-low and back (or vice versa) may be removed entirely from the output.

Of course, real circuits are not so general, in particular no practically realisable circuit of non-zero size can have zero-delay. Hence real-life circuits all correspond to combinations of the above gates with some form of delay element. For the point of designing synchronous hardware all that matters is the maximum delay which can occur from a circuit, so the exact positioning of the delays is often of little importance. When circuits are used asynchronously (e.g. for designing self-timed circuits without a global clock or, more prosaically, when their output is being used to gate a clock signal locally) then their glitch behaviour is often critically important. This leads to two models (the *delay-insensitive* (DI) and *speed-independent* (SI) models) of real hardware. In the SI model logic elements may have delays, but wires do not; in the DI model both logic elements and wires have associated delay. One well-known fact about DI models is that it is impossible to have an *isochronic fork*, whereby the transitions in output from

---

[2] A perfect OR-gate can be constructed from perfect AND- and NOT-gates using de Morgan's law.

Fig. 1. The circuit $a \wedge \neg a$

a given gate will arrive delayed contemporaneously at two other gates. Reasoning in the DI model has becomine much more important recently as wire delays (e.g. due to routing) have become dominant over single-gate element delays in modern VLSI technologies [11].

Ordinary circuits may be embedded in our model as follows. In the SI model each physical logic gate at the hardware level is seen as a perfect logic gate whose *output* is then passed through a delay element. In the DI model, each physical logic gate is seen as a perfect logic gate whose *input(s)* first pass through separate delays. In essence, the SI and DI models of a circuit are translations of a physical circuit into idealised circuits composed solely of our four perfect elements.

Now consider the circuit in Fig. 1. Seen as a perfect logic element, its output is always *false* regardless of the value of its input signal. Seen as an SI circuit (i.e. delays on the output of the AND and NOT), given an input F_1 which starts at *false* then transitions to *true* and back, the circuit will be *false* at all times except (possibly) for a small period just after the rising edge of the input, when the upper AND-input will already be *true*, but before the delayed NOT-output has yet become *false*. Thus the output is $F_{0|1}$ if we assume an inertial delay and F_1 if we assume a non-inertial delay[3].

In contrast, in the DI model, the separate delays on both inputs to the AND-gate mean that the same input signal F_1 may result in small positive pulses on both the rising and falling edge of the input; thus the output is described as $F_{0|1|2}$. It is important to note that any of these three possible outputs may occur; delays may vary with time, and can also differ on whether an input signal is rising or falling.

Our abstract interpretation framework enables us to formally deduce the above behaviours of the circuit shown in Fig. 1. Our reasoning is *correct*, because of the abstract interpretation framework. In some situations our reasoning is also *complete* in that all abstractly-predicted behaviours may be made to happen by choosing suitable delay functions for the delay elements. For example, in the DI model, our abstraction of the above circuit maps abstract signal F_1 onto $F_{0|1|2}$, but the SI model cannot produce F_2 however (positive) delay intervals are chosen.

1.2 Paper Structure

In Section 2 we define a concrete domain that models signals as (possibly non-deterministic) functions from time to the Boolean values. Section 3 describes

---

[3] This argument assumes positive delays; at times later in the paper we also allow (non-physically realisable) delays by negative time.

the most accurate (though complex) of our abstract domains; Sections 5 and 6 show how this can be further abstracted. Section 4 defines the operators necessary to model circuits, Section 4.1 discusses soundness and completeness of these operators. Refinement and equivalence relations are discussed in Section 7.

2   Concrete Domain

Definition 1. Concrete time $\mathbb{R}$ *is continuous, linear and dense, having no beginning or end.*

Definition 2. *A* signal *is a total function in* $\mathbb{S} : \mathbb{R} \to \{0,1\}$ *from concrete time to the Boolean values. More precisely, we restrict* $\mathbb{S}$ *to those functions that are finitely piecewise constant[4], i.e. there exists* $\{k_1, \ldots, k_n\}$ *which uniquely determines and is determined by a signal* $s \in \mathbb{S}$ *such that*

$$
\begin{aligned}
s(k_i) &= \neg s(k_{i+1}) & \forall 1 \le i < n; \\
s(x) &= s(k_i) & \forall k_i \le x < k_{i+1}; \\
s(-\infty) &= s(x) = \neg s(k_1) & \forall x < k_1; \\
s(+\infty) &= s(x) = s(k_n) & \forall x \ge k_n.
\end{aligned}
$$

The function $\Psi s \stackrel{\text{def}}{=} \{k_1, \ldots, k_n\}$ represents the bijection which returns the set of times at which signal s has transitions; $|\Psi s|$ represents the total number, n, of transitions made by s. As a further notational convenience, we denote the values of s at the beginning and end of time respectively as $s(-\infty)$ and $s(+\infty)$.

We model nondeterministic signals as members of the set $\wp(\mathbb{S})$; e.g. delaying signal s by time δ, where $\delta_{min} \le \delta \le \delta_{max}$, gives $\{\lambda \tau . s(\tau - \delta) \mid \delta_{min} \le \delta \le \delta_{max}\}$.

3   Abstract Domain

3.1   Deterministic Traces

Definition 3. *A* deterministic trace $t \in \mathbb{T}$ *characterises a deterministic signal* $s \in \mathbb{S}$, *retaining the transitions but abstracting away the times at which they occur. Traces are denoted as finite lists of Boolean values bounded by angle brackets ('$\langle \ldots \rangle$'), and must contain at least one element – the empty trace '$\langle \rangle$' is not syntactically valid.*

A *singleton trace*, denoted $\langle 0 \rangle$ or $\langle 1 \rangle$, represents a signal that remains at 0 or 1 respectively for all time. For traces with two or more elements, e.g. $\langle a, \ldots, b \rangle$, a is the value at the beginning of time and b is the value at the end of time.

---

[4] Note that we do not consider signals that contain an infinite number of transitions, e.g. clocks that oscillate for all time. We can, however, reason about such signals by 'windowing' them within finite intervals (windows) $[p, q]$ of $\mathbb{R}$, resulting in signals that are themselves finitely piecewise constant.

Table 1. Shorthand Notation: Deterministic Traces

F_0	The trace $\langle 0 \rangle$ that is 0 for all time.
F_1	The trace $\langle 0, 1, 0 \rangle$ that has 0 at the beginning and end, containing exactly one pulse.
F_2	The trace $\langle 0, 1, 0, 1, 0 \rangle$ that begins and ends with 0, containing exactly two pulses.
F_n	The trace $\langle 0, 1_1, 0, 1_2, 0, \ldots, 0, 1_n, 0 \rangle$ that begins and ends with 0, containing exactly n positive-going pulses.
T_0	The trace $\langle 1 \rangle$ that is 1 for all time.
T_n	The trace $\langle 1, 0_1, 1, 0_2, 1, \ldots, 1, 0_n, 1 \rangle$ that begins and ends with 1, containing exactly n negative-going pulses.
$\uparrow_0$	The trace $\langle 0, 1 \rangle$ that cleanly transitions from 0 to 1.
$\uparrow_n$	The trace $\langle 0, 1_1, 0, \ldots, 0, 1_n, 0, 1 \rangle$ that transitions from 0 to 1 through exactly n intervening cycles.
$\downarrow_0$	The trace $\langle 1, 0 \rangle$ that cleanly transitions from 1 to 0.
$\downarrow_n$	The trace $\langle 1, 0_1, 1, \ldots, 1, 0_n, 1, 0 \rangle$ that transitions from 1 to 0 through exactly n intervening cycles.

The trace $\langle 0, 1, 0 \rangle$ represents a signal that at the start of time takes the value 0, then at some later time switches cleanly to 1, then back to 0 again before the end of time. The instants at which these transitions occur are undefined, although their time order must be preserved.

Values within traces may be discriminated only by their transitions. Therefore, the trace $\langle 0, 0, 0, 0, 1, 1, 1 \rangle$ is equivalent to the trace $\langle 0, 1 \rangle$. It follows from this that all traces may be reduced to a form that resembles an alternating sequence $\langle \ldots, 0, 1, 0, 1, 0, 1, \ldots \rangle$. Any such sequence can be completely characterised by its start and end values, along with the number of intervening full cycles[5]. A convenient shorthand notation that takes advantage of this is defined in Table 1.

3.2 Nondeterministic Traces

Following the approach taken in Section 2, we represent nondeterministic traces $\hat{t} \in \wp(\mathbb{T})$ as sets of deterministic traces[6].

The need for this extra structure is demonstrated by the following example. Let us attempt to specify the meaning of the expression $\langle 0, 1 \rangle \wedge \neg \langle 0, 1 \rangle$, which represents the effect of feeding a clean transition from 0 to 1 to the a input of the circuit shown in Fig. 1. The $\neg$ can be evaluated trivially, giving $\langle 0, 1 \rangle \wedge \langle 1, 0 \rangle$.

---

[5] It is of course also possible to represent traces completely in terms of their first (or last) element and their length. However, the representation chosen here turns out to be more convenient, e.g. comparing $\uparrow_0$ with $\uparrow_4$ makes it immediately obvious that both represent traces that eventually transition from 0 to 1, with $\uparrow_0$ being 'cleaner' than $\uparrow_4$. The utility of this approach will become clear later.

[6] We adopt the convention that t and $\hat{t}$ are separate variables that range over $\mathbb{T}$ and $\wp(\mathbb{T})$ respectively.

At first sight, it may appear that the resulting trace should be $\langle 0, 0 \rangle$ or just $\langle 0 \rangle$. This would be the case if certain constraints on the exact times of the transitions of the $\langle 1, 0 \rangle$ and $\langle 0, 1 \rangle$ traces were met, but it is not sufficient to cope with all possibilities. If $\langle 1, 0 \rangle$ transitions before $\langle 0, 1 \rangle$, then the result is indeed $\langle 0 \rangle$. Should the transitions occur in the opposite order, the result is $\langle 0, 1, 0 \rangle$. Formally,

$$\{\langle 0, 1 \rangle\} \wedge \neg \{\langle 0, 1 \rangle\} = \{\langle 0, 1 \rangle\} \wedge \{\langle 1, 0 \rangle\} = \{\langle 0 \rangle\} \cup \{\langle 0, 1, 0 \rangle\} = \{\langle 0 \rangle, \langle 0, 1, 0 \rangle\}$$

Definition 4. *Where $\hat{t} \in \wp(\mathbb{T})$ and $\hat{u} \in \wp(\mathbb{T})$, the* nondeterministic choice $\hat{t} \mid \hat{u}$ *is synonymous with $\hat{t} \cup \hat{u}$. For notational compactness, we alternatively allow either or both of the arguments of $\mid$ to range over $\mathbb{T}$, e.g. where $t \in \mathbb{T}$, the expression $t \mid \hat{u}$ is equivalent to $\{t\} \mid \hat{u}$.*

The '$\mid$' operator allows the above equation to be expressed more compactly as follows:

$$\langle 0, 1 \rangle \wedge \neg \langle 0, 1 \rangle = \langle 0, 1 \rangle \wedge \langle 1, 0 \rangle = \langle 0 \rangle \mid \langle 0, 1, 0 \rangle$$

Using the shorthand notation, this may equivalently be written as:

$$\downarrow_0 \wedge \neg \downarrow_0 = \downarrow_0 \wedge \uparrow_0 = \mathsf{F}_0 \mid \mathsf{F}_1$$

Definition 5. *Letting X range over $\{\mathsf{T}, \mathsf{F}, \uparrow, \downarrow\}$,*

$$X_{m..n} \overset{\text{def}}{=} \bigcup_{i=m}^{n} \{X_i\} \qquad\qquad X_{a_1 | ... | a_n} \overset{\text{def}}{=} X_{a_1} \mid ... \mid X_{a_n}$$

For example, $\mathsf{F}_0 \mid \mathsf{F}_1$ may equivalently be written as $\mathsf{F}_{0|1}$, and rather than fully enumerating a long list of alternate pulse counts of the form $\mathsf{F}_{m|m+1|...|n-1|n}$, the preferred notation $\mathsf{F}_{m..n}$ may be used instead. These notations may be combined, e.g. $\mathsf{F}_{0|3|5..7|10..12}$.

Nondeterministic choice obeys all the laws of set union, e.g.

$$a \mid a = a \qquad\qquad a \mid b = b \mid a \qquad\qquad a \mid (b \mid c) = (a \mid b) \mid c = a \mid b \mid c$$

From this, various subscript laws follow, e.g.

$$X_{a|a} = X_a \quad X_{a..a} = X_a$$

$$X_{a..b} \mid X_{c..d} = \begin{cases} X_{\min(a,c)..\max(b,d)} & \text{if } c \le b \wedge a \le d; \\ X_{a..b|c..d} & \text{otherwise.} \end{cases}$$

Definition 6. *It is convenient to name the following least upper bounds w.r.t. $\langle \wp(\mathbb{T}), \subseteq \rangle$:*

$$\mathsf{F}_\star \overset{\text{def}}{=} \bigcup_{n \in \mathbb{N}} \{\mathsf{F}_n\} \quad \mathsf{T}_\star \overset{\text{def}}{=} \bigcup_{n \in \mathbb{N}} \{\mathsf{T}_n\} \quad \uparrow_\star \overset{\text{def}}{=} \bigcup_{n \in \mathbb{N}} \{\uparrow_n\} \quad \downarrow_\star \overset{\text{def}}{=} \bigcup_{n \in \mathbb{N}} \{\downarrow_n\}$$

$$\star \overset{\text{def}}{=} \mathsf{F}_\star \cup \mathsf{T}_\star \cup \uparrow_\star \cup \downarrow_\star$$

Table 2. Boolean Functions on Traces

$\neg^\sharp$		$\wedge^\sharp$	F_0	F_n	T_0	T_n	$\uparrow_0$	$\uparrow_n$	$\downarrow_0$	$\downarrow_n$
F_0	T_0	F_m	F_0	F_0	F_0	F_0	F_0	F_0	F_0	F_0
F_n	T_n	T_m	F_0	$F_{0..m+n-1}$	F_m	$F_{0..m+n}$	$F_{0..m}$	$F_{0..m+n}$	$F_{0..m}$	$F_{0..m+n}$
T_0	F_0	T_0	F_0	F_n	T_0	T_n	$\uparrow_0$	$\uparrow_n$	$\downarrow_0$	$\downarrow_n$
T_n	F_n	T_m	F_0	$F_{0..m+n}$	T_m	$T_{1..m+n}$	$\uparrow_{0..m}$	$\uparrow_{0..m+n}$	$\downarrow_m$	$\downarrow_{0..m+n}$
$\uparrow_0$	$\downarrow_0$	$\uparrow_0$	F_0	$F_{0..n}$	$\uparrow_0$	$\uparrow_{0..n}$	$\uparrow_0$	$\uparrow_{0..n}$	$F_{0..1}$	$F_{0..n+1}$
$\uparrow_n$	$\downarrow_n$	$\uparrow_m$	F_0	$F_{0..m+n}$	$\uparrow_m$	$\uparrow_{0..m+n}$	$\uparrow_{0..m}$	$\uparrow_{0..m+n}$	$F_{0..m+1}$	$F_{0..m+n+1}$
$\downarrow_0$	$\uparrow_0$	$\downarrow_0$	F_0	$F_{0..n}$	$\downarrow_0$	$\downarrow_n$	$F_{0..1}$	$F_{0..n+1}$	$\downarrow_0$	$\downarrow_{0..n}$
$\downarrow_n$	$\uparrow_n$	$\downarrow_m$	F_0	$F_{0..m+n}$	$\downarrow_m$	$\downarrow_{0..m+n}$	$F_{0..m+1}$	$F_{0..m+n+1}$	$\downarrow_{0..m}$	$\downarrow_{0..m+n}$

where $m > 0$, $n > 0$.

3.3   Galois Connection

Definition 7. *Given a deterministic concrete signal $s \in \mathbb{S}$, the abstraction function $\beta : \mathbb{S} \to \mathbb{T}$ returns the corresponding deterministic trace:*

$$\beta s \stackrel{\text{def}}{=} \langle s(-\infty), s(k_1), \ldots, s(k_n) \rangle \qquad\qquad where\ \{k_1, \ldots, k_n\} = \Psi s$$
$$= \langle s(-\infty), \neg s(-\infty), s(-\infty), \neg s(-\infty), \ldots \rangle$$

Note that βs has exactly $1 + |\Psi s|$ elements.

Definition 8. *The abstraction function $\alpha : \wp(\mathbb{S}) \to \wp(\mathbb{T})$ and concretisation function $\gamma : \wp(\mathbb{T}) \to \wp(\mathbb{S})$ are defined as follows:*

$$\alpha \hat{s} \stackrel{\text{def}}{=} \{\beta s \mid s \in \hat{s}\} \qquad\qquad \gamma \hat{t} \stackrel{\text{def}}{=} \{s \in \mathbb{S} \mid \beta s \in \hat{t}\}$$

Definition 9. *Letting $\sim : \mathbb{S} \times \mathbb{S} \to \mathbb{B}$ represent the equivalence relation $s_1 \sim s_2 \Leftrightarrow \beta s_1 = \beta s_2$, the set $\mathbb{S}^\sharp \stackrel{\text{def}}{=} \mathbb{S}/\sim$ is the set of equivalence classes in $\mathbb{S}$ with respect to $\sim$. The set $[s] \stackrel{\text{def}}{=} \{s' \in \mathbb{S} \mid \beta s = \beta s'\}$ represents, for any $s \in \mathbb{S}$, the equivalence class containing that element.*

Note that $\mathbb{S}^\sharp$ is isomorphic with $\mathbb{T}$.

Theorem 1. *Together, the adjoint functions $\langle \alpha, \gamma \rangle$ form a Galois connection between $\wp(\mathbb{S})$ and $\wp(\mathbb{T})$. Following Cousot & Cousot [2], Theorem 5.3.0.4 and Corollary 5.3.0.5, pp. 273, it is sufficient to show that $\alpha \circ \gamma(\hat{x}) \sqsupseteq \hat{x}$ and $\gamma \circ \alpha(\hat{x}) \sqsupseteq \hat{x}$. We choose to prove instead the slightly stronger $\alpha \circ \gamma(\hat{x}) = \hat{x}$, and since the ordering relations on $\wp(\mathbb{S})$ and $\wp(\mathbb{T})$ are subset inclusion, we write $\supseteq$ rather than $\sqsupseteq$. Proof; letting $\hat{x} = \{x_1, \ldots, x_n\}$*

1. $\alpha \circ \gamma(\hat{x}) = \alpha\{s \in \mathbb{S} \mid \beta s \in \hat{x}\} = \{\beta s' \mid s' \in \{s \in \mathbb{S} \mid \beta s \in \hat{x}\}\} = \{\beta s' \mid \beta s' \in \hat{x}\} = \hat{x}$.
2. $\gamma \circ \alpha(\hat{x}) = \gamma \circ \alpha\{x_1, \ldots, x_n\} = \gamma\{\beta x_1, \ldots, \beta x_n\} = \gamma\{\beta x_1\} \cup \cdots \cup \gamma\{\beta x_n\} = \{s \in \mathbb{S} \mid \beta s = \beta\{x_1\}\} \cup \cdots \cup \{s \in \mathbb{S} \mid \beta s = \beta\{x_n\}\} = [x_1] \cup \cdots \cup [x_n] \supseteq \{x_1, \ldots, x_n\} = \hat{x}$.

4   Circuits

Definition 10. *Circuits are modeled by composing four basic operators: zero delay 'and' $\wedge$, zero delay 'not' $\neg$, transmission line delay Δ and inertial delay $\square$, which are defined on the concrete domain as follows:*

$$\wedge \overset{\text{def}}{=} \lambda(\hat{s}_1, \hat{s}_2).\{\lambda\tau.s_1(\tau) \wedge s_2(\tau) \mid s_1 \in \hat{s}_1 \wedge s_2 \in \hat{s}_2\}$$

$$\neg \overset{\text{def}}{=} \lambda\hat{s}.\{\lambda\tau.\neg s(\tau) \mid s \in \hat{s}\}$$

$$\Delta \overset{\text{def}}{=} \gamma \circ \alpha$$

$$\square \overset{\text{def}}{=} \gamma \circ \square^{\sharp} \circ \alpha$$

Their abstract counterparts are defined as follows:

$$\wedge^{\sharp} \overset{\text{def}}{=} \alpha \circ \wedge \circ \langle \gamma, \gamma \rangle$$

$$\neg^{\sharp} \overset{\text{def}}{=} \alpha \circ \neg \circ \gamma$$

$$\Delta^{\sharp} \overset{\text{def}}{=} \lambda x.x$$

$$\square^{\sharp} \overset{\text{def}}{=} \lambda\hat{t}.\{t \in \mathbb{T} \mid \exists t' \in \hat{t}. Val(t) = Val(t') \wedge Subs(t) \leq Subs(t')\}$$

where $Val : \mathbb{T} \to \{\mathsf{F}, \mathsf{T}, \uparrow, \downarrow\}$ and $Subs : \mathbb{T} \to \mathbb{N}$ are defined as follows:

$$Val(X_n) \overset{\text{def}}{=} X \qquad\qquad Subs(X_n) \overset{\text{def}}{=} n$$

And. The function $\wedge : \wp(\mathbb{S}) \times \wp(\mathbb{S}) \to \wp(\mathbb{S})$ represents a perfect zero-delay AND gate. Its abstract counterpart, $\wedge^{\sharp} : \wp(\mathbb{T}) \times \wp(\mathbb{T}) \to \wp(\mathbb{T})$, is defined in terms of $\wedge$ by composition with α and γ; note that our semantics is based upon an independent attribute model [10].

Not. The bijective function $\neg : \wp(\mathbb{S}) \to \wp(\mathbb{S})$ represents a perfect zero delay NOT gate. As with $\wedge$, we define $\neg^{\sharp} : \wp(\mathbb{T}) \to \wp(\mathbb{T})$ by composition of the concrete operator $\neg$ with α and γ. When tabulated, $\wedge^{\sharp}$ and $\neg^{\sharp}$ behave as shown in Table 2.

Transmission Line (Non-inertial) Delay. Our definition of transmission line delay is essentially a superset of all possible delay functions that preserve the underlying trace structure of the signal. The definition, $\gamma \circ \alpha$, captures this behaviour straightforwardly; the α function abstracts away all details of time, though preserves transitions and the values at the beginning and end of time, then γ concretises this, resulting in the set of all possible traces with similar structure. This definition is more permissive than more typical notions of delay in that it includes negative as well as positive time shifts as well as transformations that can stretch or compress (though not remove or reorder) pulses.

Inertial Delay. Inertial delay is broadly similar to transmission line delay, in that, as well as changing the time at which transitions may occur, one or more complete pulses (i.e. pairs of adjacent transitions) may be removed. This models a common property of some physical components, whereby very short pulses are 'soaked up' by internal capacitance and/or inductance and thereby not passed on. We model inertial delay in the abstract domain – in effect, nondeterministic traces are mapped to convex hulls of the form $F_{0..a} \mid T_{0..b} \mid \uparrow_{0..c} \mid \downarrow_{0..d}$. The concrete inertial delay operator $\square$ is defined in terms of $\square^\sharp$ by composition with γ and α, so as with transmission line delay, it encompasses all possible (correct) inertial delay functions. It can be noted that, for all $\hat{s} \in \wp(\mathbb{S})$, $\varDelta \hat{s} \subseteq \square \hat{s}$.

4.1 Soundness and Completeness

An abstract function $f^\sharp$ may be described as *sound* with respect to a concrete function f if all behaviours exhibited by f are within the set of possible behaviours predicted by $f^\sharp$. Where these sets are identical (i.e. where $f^\sharp$ predicts all possible behaviours of f), *completeness* holds [6–8, 5, 12], two forms of which are defined below.

Definition 11. *Given a concrete domain D and an abstract domain $D^\sharp$, related by adjoint functions $\langle \alpha, \gamma \rangle$ that form a Galois connection (i.e. $\alpha \circ \gamma(x) \sqsupseteq x$ and $\gamma \circ \alpha(x) \sqsupseteq x$), a pair of functions $f : D \to D$ and $f^\sharp : D^\sharp \to D^\sharp$ may be said to be* sound *iff the following (equivalent) relations hold:*

$$\alpha \circ f \sqsubseteq f^\sharp \circ \alpha \qquad\qquad f \circ \gamma \sqsubseteq \gamma \circ f^\sharp$$

Definition 12. *Let $f^\sharp_{best} \overset{\text{def}}{=} \alpha \circ f \circ \gamma$.*

Definition 13. *Where $f^\sharp = f^\sharp_{best}$ and $f \circ \gamma = \gamma \circ f^\sharp$, the property γ-completeness holds.*

Definition 14. *Where $f^\sharp = f^\sharp_{best}$ and $\alpha \circ f = f^\sharp \circ \alpha$, the property α-completeness holds.*

Note that α-completeness and γ-completeness are orthogonal properties; neither implies the other, though if either or both kinds of completeness hold, soundness must also hold.

Theorem 2. *The transmission line delay operator $(\varDelta, \varDelta^\sharp)$ is sound, α-complete and γ-complete. Proof:*

1. $\varDelta^\sharp_{best} = \alpha \circ \varDelta \circ \gamma = \alpha \circ \gamma \circ \alpha \circ \gamma = \alpha \circ \gamma = (\lambda x.x) = \varDelta^\sharp$.
2. α-completeness: $\alpha \circ \varDelta = \alpha \circ \gamma \circ \alpha = \alpha = (\lambda x.x) \circ \alpha = \varDelta^\sharp \circ \alpha$.
3. γ-completeness: $\varDelta \circ \gamma = \gamma \circ \alpha \circ \gamma = \gamma = \gamma \circ (\lambda x.x) = \gamma \circ \varDelta^\sharp$.

Theorem 3. *The inertial delay operator $(\square, \square^\sharp)$ is sound, α-complete and γ-complete. Proof:*

1. $\square_{best}^{\sharp} = \alpha \circ \square \circ \gamma = \alpha \circ \gamma \circ \square^{\sharp} \circ \alpha \circ \gamma = \square^{\sharp}$.
2. α-completeness: $\alpha \circ \square = \alpha \circ \gamma \circ \square^{\sharp} \circ \alpha = \square^{\sharp} \circ \alpha$.
3. γ-completeness: $\square \circ \gamma = \gamma \circ \square^{\sharp} \circ \alpha \circ \gamma = \gamma \circ \square^{\sharp}$.

Theorem 4. *The perfect NOT operator* $(\neg, \neg^{\sharp})$ *is sound, α-complete and γ-complete. Proof:*

1. $\neg_{best}^{\sharp} = \alpha \circ \neg \circ \gamma = \neg^{\sharp}$.
2. *Since* $\neg$ *is a bijection,* $\gamma \circ \alpha \circ \neg = \neg \circ \gamma \circ \alpha$.
3. *α-completeness:* $\alpha \circ \neg = \alpha \circ \gamma \circ \alpha \circ \neg = \alpha \circ \neg \circ \gamma \circ \alpha = \neg^{\sharp} \circ \alpha$.
4. *γ-completeness:* $\neg \circ \gamma = \neg \circ \gamma \circ \alpha \circ \gamma = \gamma \circ \alpha \circ \neg \circ \gamma = \gamma \circ \neg^{\sharp}$.

Theorem 5. *The perfect AND operator* $(\wedge, \wedge^{\sharp})$ *is sound[7]. Proof:*

1. $\wedge \circ \langle \gamma, \gamma \rangle \subseteq \gamma \circ \wedge^{\sharp} = \gamma \circ \alpha \circ \wedge \circ \langle \gamma, \gamma \rangle$.

Note that whilst perfect, zero delay AND is sound but not complete, a composite speed-insensitive AND $(\wedge_{SI} \stackrel{def}{=} \Delta \circ \wedge, \wedge_{SI}^{\sharp} \stackrel{def}{=} \Delta^{\sharp} \circ \wedge^{\sharp})$ can be straightforwardly be shown to be γ-complete, but not α-complete. Dually, delay-independent AND $(\wedge_{DI} \stackrel{def}{=} \wedge \circ \langle \Delta, \Delta \rangle, \wedge_{DI}^{\sharp} \stackrel{def}{=} \wedge^{\sharp} \circ \langle \Delta^{\sharp}, \Delta^{\sharp} \rangle)$ is α- but not γ-complete. We find, however, that $(\wedge_{complete} \stackrel{def}{=} \Delta \circ \wedge \circ \langle \Delta, \Delta \rangle, \wedge_{complete}^{\sharp} \stackrel{def}{=} \Delta^{\sharp} \circ \wedge^{\sharp} \circ \langle \Delta^{\sharp}, \Delta^{\sharp} \rangle)$ is both α- and γ-complete.

5   Finite Versions of the Abstract Domain

The abstract domain defined in Section 3 allows arbitrary asynchronous combinational circuits to be reasoned about. In this section we present a number of simplifications of this basic model which allow accuracy to be traded off against levels of abstraction. The model presented in Section 3 is useful in identifying possible glitches within circuits, though in this case generally one is interested in whether a particular signal *can* glitch, rather than the *number* of possible glitches – this requires less information than that captured by our original abstraction. It follows that further abstraction should be possible, which is indeed the case.

5.1   Collapsing Non-zero Subscripts:
The 256-Value Transitional Logic $\mathbb{T}_{256}$

Mapping all non-zero subscript traces $t \in X_{1..\infty}$ to the single abstract value X_{+}, for X ranging over $\{F, T, \uparrow, \downarrow\}$, makes it possible to define a finite abstract domain with a Galois connection to $\mathbb{T}$. This domain has the desirable property of abstracting away details of 'how glitchy' a trace may be, whilst retaining the ability to distinguish *clean* traces from *dirty* traces.

---

[7] Note that we adopt an independent attribute model when considering the dyadic nature of AND.

Table 3. Operators on $\mathbb{T}_c$

$\neg_c$		Δ_c		$\Box_c$		$\wedge_c$	F_0	F_+	T_0	T_+	$\uparrow_0$	$\uparrow_+$	$\downarrow_0$	$\downarrow_+$
F_0	T_0	F_0	F_0	F_0	F_0	F_0	F_0	F_0	F_0	F_0	F_0	F_0	F_0	F_0
F_+	T_+	F_+	F_+	F_+	$F_?$	F_+	F_0	$F_?$	F_+	$F_?$	$F_?$	$F_?$	$F_?$	$F_?$
T_0	F_0	T_0	T_0	T_0	T_0	T_0	F_0	F_+	T_0	T_+	$\uparrow_0$	$\uparrow_+$	$\downarrow_0$	$\downarrow_+$
T_+	F_+	T_+	T_+	T_+	$T_?$	T_+	F_0	$F_?$	T_+	T_+	$F_?$	$\uparrow_?$	$\downarrow_+$	$\downarrow_?$
$\uparrow_0$	$\downarrow_0$	$\uparrow_0$	$\uparrow_0$	$\uparrow_0$	$\uparrow_0$	$\uparrow_0$	F_0	$F_?$	$\uparrow_0$	$\uparrow_?$	$\uparrow_0$	$\uparrow_?$	$F_?$	$F_?$
$\uparrow_+$	$\downarrow_+$	$\uparrow_+$	$\uparrow_+$	$\uparrow_+$	$\uparrow_?$	$\uparrow_+$	F_0	$F_?$	$\uparrow_+$	$\uparrow_?$	$\uparrow_?$	$\uparrow_?$	$F_?$	$F_?$
$\downarrow_0$	$\uparrow_0$	$\downarrow_0$	$\downarrow_0$	$\downarrow_0$	$\downarrow_0$	$\downarrow_0$	F_0	$F_?$	$\downarrow_0$	$\downarrow_+$	$F_?$	$F_?$	$\downarrow_0$	$\downarrow_?$
$\downarrow_+$	$\uparrow_+$	$\downarrow_+$	$\downarrow_+$	$\downarrow_+$	$\downarrow_?$	$\downarrow_+$	F_0	$F_?$	$\downarrow_+$	$\downarrow_?$	$F_?$	$F_?$	$\downarrow_?$	$\downarrow_?$

where $F_? \stackrel{\text{def}}{=} F_0 \mid F_+$, $\quad T_? \stackrel{\text{def}}{=} T_0 \mid T_+$, $\quad \downarrow_? \stackrel{\text{def}}{=} \downarrow_0 \mid \downarrow_+$, $\quad \uparrow_? \stackrel{\text{def}}{=} \uparrow_0 \mid \uparrow_+$

Definition 15. *The abstract domain of* subscript-collapsed deterministic traces *is the set* $\mathbb{T}_c \stackrel{\text{def}}{=} \{F_0, F_+, T_0, T_+, \uparrow_0, \uparrow_+, \downarrow_0, \downarrow_+\}$. *Following the usual convention, the corresponding abstract domain of* subscript-collapsed nondeterministic traces *is the set* $\mathbb{T}_{256} \stackrel{\text{def}}{=} \wp(\mathbb{T}_c)$.

Note that unlike $\mathbb{T}$ and $\wp(\mathbb{T})$, both $\mathbb{T}_c$ and $\wp(\mathbb{T}_c)$ are finite sets, with 8 and 256 members respectively.

Definition 16. *The Galois connection* $\alpha_c : \wp(\mathbb{T}) \to \wp(\mathbb{T}_c)$, $\gamma_c : \wp(\mathbb{T}_c) \to \wp(\mathbb{T})$ *is defined as follows:*

$$\beta_c X_n \stackrel{\text{def}}{=} \begin{cases} X_0 & \textit{iff } n = 0; \\ X_+ & \textit{otherwise.} \end{cases}$$

$$\alpha_c \hat{t} \stackrel{\text{def}}{=} \{\beta_c t \mid t \in \hat{t}\} \quad \gamma_c \hat{t} \stackrel{\text{def}}{=} \{t \in \mathbb{T} \mid \beta_c t \in \hat{t}\}$$

It is possible to tabulate 256×256 truth tables that fully enumerate all members of $\mathbb{T}_{256}$ along their edges, but they are too large to reproduce here in full. For brevity, Table 3 defines the operators $\neg_c : \mathbb{T}_c \to \wp(\mathbb{T}_c)$, $\Delta_c : \mathbb{T}_c \to \wp(\mathbb{T}_c)$, $\Box_c : \mathbb{T}_c \to \wp(\mathbb{T}_c)$ and $\wedge_c : \mathbb{T}_c \times \mathbb{T}_c \to \wp(\mathbb{T}_c)$ on $\mathbb{T}_c$. Their fully nondeterministic versions, defined on $\wp(\mathbb{T}_c)$, are as follows:

$$\neg_c \hat{t} \stackrel{\text{def}}{=} \bigcup_{t \in \hat{t}} \{\neg_c t\} \quad \Delta_c \hat{t} \stackrel{\text{def}}{=} \bigcup_{t \in \hat{t}} \{\Delta_c t\} \quad \Box_c \hat{t} \stackrel{\text{def}}{=} \bigcup_{t \in \hat{t}} \{\Box_c t\} \quad \hat{t} \wedge_c \hat{u} \stackrel{\text{def}}{=} \bigcup_{\substack{t \in \hat{t} \\ u \in \hat{u}}} \{t \wedge_c u\}$$

Note that, as with $\Delta^\sharp$, the Δ_c operator is merely an identity function.

6   Further Simplification of the Abstract Domain

A fully tabulated version of the $\neg_c$, Δ_c, $\Box_c$ and $\wedge_c$ operators defined in Section 5.1 can be regarded as a 256-value *transitional logic*, where the values are the members of $\wp(\mathbb{T}_c)$. Such an approach still captures more nondeterminism than is useful in for many applications. It is possible to further reduce the abstract

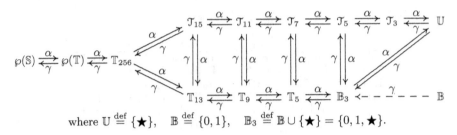

where $\mathbb{U} \overset{\text{def}}{=} \{\bigstar\}$, $\mathbb{B} \overset{\text{def}}{=} \{0, 1\}$, $\mathbb{B}_3 \overset{\text{def}}{=} \mathbb{B} \cup \{\bigstar\} = \{0, 1, \bigstar\}$.

Fig. 2. Hierarchy of Domains

domain, replacing some nondeterministic choices with appropriate least upper bound elements with respect to $\langle \wp(\mathbb{T}_c), \subseteq \rangle$. The hierarchy of domains that results is shown in Fig. 2 – the relationship to 2-value Boolean logic $\mathbb{B}$ and 3-value ternary logic $\mathbb{B}_3$ is shown[8]. Note that since $\mathbb{B}$ lacks an upper bound that corresponds with $\bigstar$, it is not possible to define $\alpha : \mathbb{B}_3 \to \mathbb{B}$ (though $\gamma : \mathbb{B} \to \mathbb{B}_3$ can be trivially defined), so a Galois connection does not exist in that particular case. Following Cousot & Cousot [1, 2], the domain $\mathbb{U}$, *useless logic*, containing only $\bigstar$, completes the lattice.

Finding the smallest lattice including $\{F_0, F_+, T_0, T_+, \uparrow_0, \uparrow_+, \downarrow_0, \downarrow_+\}$ that is closed under $\wedge_c$, and $\neg_c$ results in the 13-value transitional logic,

$$\mathbb{T}_{13} \overset{\text{def}}{=} \{F_0, F_+, F_?, T_0, T_+, T_?, \uparrow_0, \uparrow_+, \uparrow_?, \downarrow_0, \downarrow_+, \downarrow_?, \bigstar\}$$

Though much smaller than $\wp(\mathbb{T}_c)$, this logic is equivalently useful for most purposes – note that a special element needs to be explicitly included, $\bigstar$, representing the least upper bound (top element) of the lattice.

In cases where it is important to know that a trace is definitely clean, but where it is not necessary to distinguish between 'definitely dirty' and 'possibly dirty', further reducing the domain by folding F_+, T_+, $\uparrow_+$ and $\downarrow_+$ into their respective least upper bounds $F_?$, $T_?$, $\uparrow_?$ and $\downarrow_?$ results in a 9-value transitional logic, $\mathbb{T}_9 \overset{\text{def}}{=} \{F_0, F_?, T_0, T_?, \uparrow_0, \uparrow_?, \downarrow_0, \downarrow_?, \bigstar\}$. An even simpler 5-value transitional logic $\mathbb{T}_5 \overset{\text{def}}{=} \{F, T, \uparrow, \downarrow, \bigstar\}$ results from folding all remaining nondeterminism into $\bigstar$. $\mathbb{T}_{13}$ and $\mathbb{T}_9$ are well suited to logic simulation, refinement and model checking, whereas $\mathbb{T}_5$ is only recommended for glitch checking.

6.1 Static/Clean Logics

The $\mathbb{T}_{13}$, $\mathbb{T}_9$ and $\mathbb{T}_5$ logics can be usefully extended by introducing two extra upper bounds: S, the least upper bound of traces whose values are fixed for all time, and C, the least upper bound of traces that may transition, but that *never* glitch.

---

[8] As with our other logics, we assume that $F \subseteq \bigstar$ and $T \subseteq \bigstar$ – some ternary logics in the literature (notably Kleene's) lack this formal requirement.

Definition 17. *With respect to $\wp(\mathbb{T}_c)$, the* least upper bounds S, C *and* $\bigstar$ *are defined as follows:*

$$\mathsf{S} \stackrel{\text{def}}{=} \{\mathsf{F}_0, \mathsf{T}_0\} \qquad\qquad\qquad \mathsf{C} \stackrel{\text{def}}{=} \{\mathsf{F}_0, \mathsf{T}_0, \uparrow_0, \downarrow_0\}$$

$$\bigstar \stackrel{\text{def}}{=} \{\mathsf{F}_0, \mathsf{F}_+, \mathsf{T}_0, \mathsf{T}_+, \uparrow_0, \uparrow_+, \downarrow_0, \downarrow_+\}$$

The resulting *static/clean* transitional logics $\mathcal{T}_{15} \stackrel{\text{def}}{=} \mathbb{T}_{13} \cup \{\mathsf{S}, \mathsf{C}\}$, $\mathcal{T}_{11} \stackrel{\text{def}}{=} \mathbb{T}_9 \cup \{\mathsf{S}, \mathsf{C}\}$ and $\mathcal{T}_7 \stackrel{\text{def}}{=} \mathbb{T}_5 \cup \{\mathsf{S}, \mathsf{C}\}$ have applications in the design rule checking of 'impure' synchronous circuits. For example, a gated clock input represented by $\mathsf{S} \wedge \mathsf{C} = \mathsf{C}$ might be accepted by a model checker, but $\mathsf{C} \wedge \mathsf{C} = \bigstar$ would not.

Removing $\uparrow$ and $\downarrow$ from $\mathcal{T}_7$ results in a 5-value static/clean logic $\mathcal{T}_5 \stackrel{\text{def}}{=} \{\mathsf{F}, \mathsf{T}, \mathsf{S}, \mathsf{C}, \bigstar\}$ capable of reasoning about gated clock synchronous circuits; an even simpler (though less accurate) 3-value static/clean logic $\mathcal{T}_3 \stackrel{\text{def}}{=} \{\mathsf{S}, \mathsf{C}, \bigstar\}$ results from also removing F and T.

7   Refinement and Equivalence in Transitional Logics

Hardware engineers frequently concern themselves with modification and optimisation of existing circuits, so it is appropriate to support this by defining equivalence and refinement with respect to our abstract domains. Refinement relationships between circuits are analogous to concepts of refinement in process calculi, and may similarly be used to aid provably correct design. For example, the Boolean equivalence $a \wedge \neg a = \mathsf{F}$ is not a strong equivalence in our model, nor is it a weak equivalence – it actually turns out to be a (left-to-right) refinement, i.e. $a \wedge \neg a \succcurlyeq \mathsf{F}_0$, reflecting the 'engineer's intuition' that it is safe to replace $a \wedge \neg a$ with F_0, but that the converse could damage the functionality of the circuit by introducing new glitch states that were not present in the original design.

Informally, if the deterministic trace $u \in \mathbb{T}$ *refines* (i.e. retains the steady state behaviour of, but is no more glitchy than) trace $t \in \mathbb{T}$, this may be denoted $t \succcurlyeq u$.

Definition 18. *Given a pair of traces $t \in \mathbb{T}$ and $u \in \mathbb{T}$,*

$$t \succcurlyeq u \stackrel{\text{def}}{=} Val(t) = Val(u) \wedge Subs(t) \geq Subs(u)$$

For example, $\mathsf{F}_1 \succcurlyeq \mathsf{F}_0$, $\mathsf{T}_3 \succcurlyeq \mathsf{T}_2$, $\uparrow_5 \succcurlyeq \uparrow_5$, but $\downarrow_0$ and $\uparrow_1$ are incomparable. Where $t \in \mathbb{T}$ and $u \in \mathbb{T}$, if $t \succcurlyeq u$ and $u \succcurlyeq t$, it follows that $t = u$.

Refinement and equivalence for nondeterministic traces is slightly less straightforward, in that it is necessary to handle cases like $\downarrow_{1|3|5} \succcurlyeq \downarrow_{0|2|4}$. To make these comparable, we construct *convex hulls* of the form $X_{0..n}$ enclosing the nondeterministic choices, so the above case becomes equivalent to $\downarrow_{0..5} \succcurlyeq \downarrow_{0..4}$. In effect, this approach compares worst-case behaviour, disregarding finer detail; in practice, since $\wedge$, Δ, $\square$ and $\neg$ typically return results of the general form $X_{0..n}$ anyway, this tends not to cause any practical difficulties. Less permissive definitions of refinement, e.g. $\hat{t} \succcurlyeq_{strict} \hat{u} \equiv \forall t \in \hat{t} \,.\, \forall u \in \hat{u} \,.\, t \succcurlyeq u$, often disallow too many possible optimisations that in practice are quite acceptable – our model better reflects the engineer's intuition that 'less glitchy is better,' but that very detailed information about the structure of possible glitches is generally not important.

Definition 19. *Where $\hat{t} \in \wp(\mathbb{T})$ and $\hat{u} \in \wp(\mathbb{T})$,*

$$\hat{t} \succcurlyeq \hat{u} \stackrel{\text{def}}{\equiv} (\forall t \in \hat{t}, u \in \hat{u} \,.\, Val(t) = Val(u)) \wedge MaxSubs(\hat{t}) \geq MaxSubs(\hat{u})$$

where $MaxSubs(\hat{t}) \stackrel{\text{def}}{=} \max_{t \in \hat{t}} Subs(t)$ is a function returning the largest subscript of a nondeterministic trace.

Equivalence of Non-deterministic Traces. Where $\hat{t} \in \wp(\mathbb{T})$ and $\hat{u} \in \wp(\mathbb{T})$, if $\hat{t} = \hat{u}$ then the traces are *strongly equivalent*, i.e. they represent exactly the same sets of nondeterministic choices. If the convex hulls surrounding $\hat{t}$ and $\hat{u}$ are identical, as is the case when $\hat{t} \succcurlyeq \hat{u} \wedge \hat{u} \succcurlyeq \hat{t}$, the traces may be said to be *weakly equivalent*, denoted $\hat{t} \simeq \hat{u}$. Where $\hat{t} \succcurlyeq \hat{u} \vee \hat{u} \succcurlyeq \hat{t}$, the traces are *comparable*, denoted $\hat{t} \backsimeq \hat{u}$.

Finite Abstract Domains. Refinement and equivalence can also be defined for the finite abstract domain $\mathbb{T}_{256}$ and some of its simplified forms. Since $\mathbb{T}_{256}$ is implicitly nondeterministic, we do not need to consider the deterministic case.

Definition 20. *Given traces $t \in \mathbb{T}_{256}$ and $u \in \mathbb{T}_{256}$,*

$$t \succcurlyeq u \stackrel{\text{def}}{\equiv} Val(t) = Val(u) \wedge (Subs(t) = Subs(u) \vee Subs(u) = 0)$$

$$t \simeq u \stackrel{\text{def}}{\equiv} t \succcurlyeq u \wedge u \succcurlyeq t \equiv t = u$$

$$t \backsimeq u \stackrel{\text{def}}{\equiv} t \succcurlyeq u \vee u \succcurlyeq t \equiv Val(t) = Val(u)$$

8   Related Work

There seems to be relatively little work reported in the literature regarding the application of modern program analysis techniques to hardware.

Don Gaubatz [4] proposes a 4-value 'quaternary' logic that bears some resemblance to our 5-value transitional logic.

Paul Cunningham [3] extends Gaubatz's work in many respects, though his formalism is based on a conventional 2-value logic with transitions handled explicitly as events rather than as values in an extended logic.

Charles Hymans [9] uses abstract interpretation to present a safety property checking technique based upon abstract interpretation of (synchronous) behavioural VHDL specifications.

9   Conclusions

In this paper, we have presented a technique based upon the solid foundation of abstract interpretation [1, 2] that allows properties of a wide class of digital circuits to be reasoned about. We describe what is essentially a first attempt at applying abstract interpretation to asynchronous hardware – clearly more can be done, particularly in exploring completeness.

9.1   Future Work

In Section 7, we define refinement and equivalence relations on circuits. It appears to be possible to generalise this definition of refinement and equivalence to any abstract domain that is itself amenable to abstract interpretation. We have already demonstrated that our technique is potentially useful for logic simulation [13] – implementing a demonstrable simulator is a logical next step.

An experimental proof system exists for the 11-value clean/static transitional logic, and we hope to extend this to cover the more general case, $\wp(\mathbb{T})$.

Acknowledgments

This paper has greatly benefited from comments received on early drafts. In particular, we wish to thank the anonymous reviewers, Patrick and Radhia Cousot, Charles Hymans, the Semantics and Abstract Interpretation group at École Normale Supérieure, as well as the CPRG and Rainbow groups at Cambridge.

The first author wishes to thank Big Hand Ltd. and Senshutek Ltd. for financially supporting this work.

References

1. Cousot, P., and Cousot, R. Abstract interpretation: a unified lattice model for static analysis of programs by construction or approximation of fixpoints. In *Conference Record of the Fourth Annual ACM SIGPLAN-SIGACT Symposium on Principles of Programming Languages* (Los Angeles, California, 1977), ACM Press, New York, NY, pp. 238–252.
2. Cousot, P., and Cousot, R. Systematic design of program analysis frameworks. In *Conference Record of the Sixth Annual ACM SIGPLAN-SIGACT Symposium on Principles of Programming Languages* (San Antonio, Texas, 1979), ACM Press, New York, NY, pp. 269–282.
3. Cunningham, P. A. *Verification of Asynchronous Circuits*. PhD thesis, University of Cambridge, 2002.
4. Gaubatz, D. A. *Logic Programming Analysis of Asynchronous Digital Circuits*. PhD thesis, University of Cambridge, 1991.
5. Giacobazzi, R., and Mastroeni, I. Domain compression for complete abstractions. In *Fourth International Conference on Verification, Model Checking and Abstract Interpretation (VMCAI'03)* (2003), vol. 2575 of *Lecture Notes in Computer Science*, Springer-Verlag, pp. 146–160.

6. Giacobazzi, R., and Ranzato, F. Completeness in abstract interpretation: A domain perspective. In *Proc. of the 6th International Conference on Algebraic Methodology and Software Technology (AMAST'97)* (1997), M. Johnson, Ed., vol. 1349 of *Lecture Notes in Computer Science*, Springer-Verlag, Berlin, pp. 231–245.

7. Giacobazzi, R., and Ranzato, F. Refining and compressing abstract domains. In *Proc. of the 24th International Colloquium on Automata, Languages, and Programming (ICALP'97)* (1997), R. G. P. Degano and A. Marchetti-Spaccamela, Eds., vol. 1256 of *Lecture Notes in Computer Science*, Springer-Verlag, Berlin, pp. 771–781.

8. Giacobazzi, R., Ranzato, F., and Scozzari, F. Making abstract interpretations complete. *Journal of the ACM 47*, 2 (2000), 361–416.

9. Hymans, C. Checking safety properties of behavioral VHDL descriptions by abstract interpretation. In *9th International Static Analysis Symposium (SAS'02)* (2002), vol. 2477 of *Lecture Notes in Computer Science*, Springer, pp. 444–460.

10. Jones, N. D., and Muchnick, S. Complexity of flow analysis, inductive assertion synthesis, and a language due to Dijkstra. In *21st Symposium on Foundations of Computer Science* (1980), IEEE, pp. 185–190.

11. Morelli, G. Coralled: Get hold of wire delays. *Electronic Design News, September 25, 2003*, pp. 37–46.

12. Mycroft, A. Completeness and predicate-based abstract interpretation. In *Proc. ACM conf. on Partial Evaluation and Program Manipulation* (2003), pp. 179–185.

13. Thompson, S., and Mycroft, A. Sliding window logic simulation. In *15th UK Asynchronous Forum* (2004), Cambridge.

Static Analysis
of Gated Data Dependence Graphs

Charles Hymans[1] and Eben Upton[2,*]

[1] STIX, École Polytechnique, Palaiseau, France
charles.hymans@polytechnique.fr
[2] Computer Laboratory, University of Cambridge, Cambridge, UK
ecu20@cl.cam.ac.uk

Abstract. Several authors have advocated the use of the gated data dependence graph as a compiler intermediate representation. If this representation is to gain acceptance, it is important to show that we may construct static analyses which operate directly on it. In this paper we present the first example of such an analysis, developed using the methodology of abstract interpretation. The analysis is shown to be sound with respect to a concrete semantics for the representation. Experimental results are presented which indicate that the analysis performs well in comparison to conventional techniques.

1 Introduction

The classical intermediate representation for optimizing compilation is the Control Flow Graph. Static analysis techniques may be applied to a CFG to deduce properties which will hold at runtime, and this information may then be used to direct program transformations. The methodology of *abstract interpretation* [4] is often used to construct an analysis, or to demonstrate that an existing analysis is sound.

The cost of maintaining auxilliary data structures associated with the CFG, and the increasing need to extract parallelism from sequential code, has led several authors to propose alternative program respresentations, such as the Program Dependence Graph [8] and gated Data Dependence Graph [3]. If these representations are to be used in practical compilers, it is important to demonstrate that they are amenable to static analysis.

In this paper we describe the design of a static analysis for gated DDGs, using the methodology of abstract interpretation. A concrete semantics is presented, and the soundness of the analysis with respect to this semantics is shown. The analysis may be instantiated with any numerical domain which satisfies certain straightforward conditions, permitting a tradeoff between cost and the accuracy of the results.

---

* This research was supported in part by the Réseau National de recherche et d'innovation en Technologies Logicielles (RNTL).

R. Giacobazzi (Ed.): SAS 2004, LNCS 3148, pp. 197–211, 2004.

The next section describes gated DDGs, and presents an informal execution model. Section 3 presents a rule-based concrete semantics and equivalent fixpoint (collecting) semantics. Section 4 presents our abstract semantics, which is shown to be sound. Section 5 discusses the performance of our static analysis and section 6 gives conclusions and describes our ongoing work.

2 Gated Data Dependence Graphs

Gated DDGs were introduced in [3] as part of the Program Dependence Web intermediate representation. They may be generated from imperative programs using one of several techniques, including SESE-analysis and symbolic execution [10], calculation of path expressions [9] and syntax directed translation [6].

Nodes represent operations and edges represent data dependencies (i.e. they run from value consumers to value producers). Edges connect to nodes via *ports*.

Unconditional Execution. Every gated DDG has a unique *in* node, which provides an output port for each formal parameter, and a unique *out* node which provides an input port for each return value. Arithmetic nodes have either one or two input ports, and one output port. Figure 1 shows the graph for a simple function with no conditional statements. The pale grey edges represent state dependencies, described below.

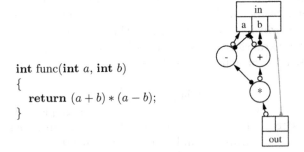

```
int func(int a, int b)
{
    return (a + b) * (a − b);
}
```

Fig. 1. Gated DDG for function with no conditional statements

Evaluation of a function involves initializing the outputs of the *in* node with the values of the parameters, and evaluating the inputs of the *out* node.

Conditional Execution. Conditional constructs are implemented using γ nodes, which have three input ports. One of two value inputs is assigned to the single output port depending on whether a predicate input is zero. Figure 2 shows the graph for the function **max**, which returns the larger of two values.

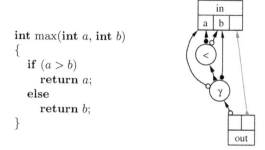

```
int max(int a, int b)
{
    if (a > b)
        return a;
    else
        return b;
}
```

Fig. 2. Gated DDG for function with conditional statement

Iteration. We use the GSA form of gated DDG [3], which represents iteration using polyadic μ loop header and η loop exit nodes. Our μ nodes have one *initial* input, one *next* input and one output for each loop variant. Our η nodes have a predicate input, and one input and one output for each loop result. Figure 3 shows the graph for an iterative factorial function.

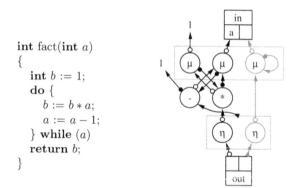

```
int fact(int a)
{
    int b := 1;
    do {
        b := b * a;
        a := a - 1;
    } while (a)
    return b;
}
```

Fig. 3. Gated DDG for function with loop statement

Evaluation of an η node involves first initializing the outputs of the corresponding μ node with values from the *initial* inputs and then repeatedly reinitializing with values from the *next* inputs until the predicate is equal to zero. The inputs of the η node may then be evaluated and assigned to their respective outputs.

Other forms of gated DDG differ in the notation used to represent iteration. The Value State Dependence Graph [6] uses θ loop nodes, and the Value Dependence Graph [10] models iteration as tail recursion. Both forms share the same execution model as GSA form however, and we anticipate that the results presented here may be readily extended to them.

State. We follow the convention of representing memory as a mapping from locations to values. Every *in* node provides an output port for the initial state, and every *out* node provides an input port for the final state. Update operations consume a state object and produce a new state object. State dependence edges (shown in light grey in the examples above), ensure necessary serialization of access to memory.

3   Concrete Semantics

In the subsequent discussion, we will restrict ourselves to functions which have a single argument, and in which only a single value varies in any given loop. This greatly simplifies our notation, as the result of evaluating a node is a single value (rather than a tuple). The reintroduction of polyadic *in*, μ and η nodes is straightforward.

Figure 4 presents the rule-based concrete semantics of gated DDGs. Judgements take the form $\rho \vdash_V x \downarrow v_x$, indicating that node x has value v_x in environment ρ, and $\rho \vdash_E (p, \mu_x(i,n)) \downarrow \rho'$, indicating that ρ' is the first environment reachable from ρ by repeated evaluation of a loop body which makes p false. An environment is a mapping from nodes to values for the *in* node and the μ nodes of all enclosing loops. The judgements $\rho \vdash_V x \downarrow false$ and $\rho \vdash_V x \downarrow true$ indicate that node x has zero and non-zero value respectively.

$$\frac{}{\rho \vdash_V const(v) \downarrow v}\text{CONST}$$

$$\frac{\rho \vdash_V x \downarrow v_x \qquad v = \mathsf{unop}(v_x)}{\rho \vdash_V unop(x) \downarrow v}\text{UNARY}$$

$$\frac{\rho \vdash_V x \downarrow v_x \qquad \rho \vdash_V y \downarrow v_y \qquad v = \mathsf{binop}(v_x, v_y)}{\rho \vdash_V binop(x,y) \downarrow v}\text{BINARY}$$

$$\frac{\rho \vdash_V p \downarrow true \qquad \rho \vdash_V t \downarrow v}{\rho \vdash_V \gamma(p,t,f) \downarrow v}\text{TRUE} \qquad \frac{\rho \vdash_V p \downarrow false \qquad \rho \vdash_V f \downarrow v}{\rho \vdash_V \gamma(p,t,f) \downarrow v}\text{FALSE}$$

$$\frac{}{\rho \vdash_V in \downarrow \rho(in)}\text{LOOKUP-IN} \qquad \frac{}{\rho \vdash_V \mu_x(i,n) \downarrow \rho(\mu_x)}\text{LOOKUP-}\mu$$

$$\frac{\rho \vdash_V i \downarrow v_i \qquad \rho[\mu_x \leftarrow v_i] \vdash_E (p, \mu_x(i,n)) \downarrow \rho' \qquad \rho' \vdash_V r \downarrow v_r}{\rho \vdash_V \eta(p, r, \mu_x(i,n)) \downarrow v_r}\text{INIT}$$

$$\frac{\rho \vdash_V p \downarrow false}{\rho \vdash_E (p, \mu_x(i,n)) \downarrow \rho}\text{END}$$

$$\frac{\rho \vdash_V p \downarrow true \qquad \rho \vdash_V n \downarrow v_n \qquad \rho[\mu_x \leftarrow v_n] \vdash_E (p, \mu_x(i,n)) \downarrow \rho'}{\rho \vdash_E (p, \mu_x(i,n)) \downarrow \rho'}\text{NEXT}$$

Fig. 4. Rule-based semantics

The first three rules correspond to the standard semantics of arithmetic expressions. The rules TRUE and FALSE give the meaning of a γ node for non-zero and zero predicate values respectively. The rules LOOKUP-IN and LOOKUP-μ retrieve the value for a particular node from the current environment.

The rule INIT gives the meaning of an η node. The environment is first extended to map the corresponding μ node to the value of its initial input. The rules NEXT and END then generate successive environments until one is found in which the predicate is false. Finally, the value of the result input is computed in this environment.

As a basis for proving that an abstract interpretation is sound, it is helpful to recast the rule-based semantics of figure 4 in fixpoint form. First, observe that substituting the rules in figure 5 for the rules INIT, NEXT and END does not alter the meaning of a μ node.

$$\frac{\rho \vdash_V i \downarrow v_i \quad \rho[\mu_x \leftarrow v_i] \vdash_E (p, \mu_x(i,n)) \downarrow \rho^{\natural} \quad \rho^{\natural} \vdash_V p \downarrow \mathit{false} \quad \rho^{\natural} \vdash_V r \downarrow v_r}{\rho \vdash_V \eta(p, r, \mu_x(i,n)) \downarrow v_r} \text{INIT}^{\natural}$$

$$\frac{}{\rho \vdash_E (p, \mu_x(i,n)) \downarrow \rho} \text{END}^{\natural}$$

$$\frac{\rho \vdash_E (p, \mu_x(i,n)) \downarrow \rho^{\natural} \quad \rho^{\natural} \vdash_V p \downarrow \mathit{true} \quad \rho^{\natural} \vdash_V n \downarrow v_n}{\rho \vdash_E (p, \mu_x(i,n)) \downarrow \rho^{\natural}[\mu_x \leftarrow v_n]} \text{NEXT}^{\natural}$$

Fig. 5. Alternative rule-based semantics for iteration

In this case, the rules NEXT$'$ and END$'$ generate all environments reachable from the initial environment by a sequence of transitions in which every intermediate environment makes the predicate true. The rule INIT$'$ selects the one environment for which the predicate is false.

By defining $[\![n]\!] \rho = \{v \mid \rho \vdash_V n \downarrow v\}$ and expressing the set of environments generated by NEXT$'$ and END$'$ as the result of a fixpoint operator, we obtain the semantics shown in figure 6.

We have $[\![n]\!] : \mathcal{E} \rightarrow \wp(\mathcal{V})$ and $(\!|p, \mu_x(i,n)|\!) : \mathcal{E} \rightarrow \wp(\mathcal{E})$, where $\mathcal{E}$ is the set of possible environments, and $\mathcal{V}$ is the set of possible values. Note that as gated DDGs are Turing powerful, the fixpoint is not effectively computable.

4   Abstract Interpretation

The goal of static analysis is to determine whether a particular assertion holds for all possible executions of a program. In the context of gated DDGs these assertions refer to the values returned by nodes. An analyzer must therefore be able to compute a conservative estimate of the set of all possible return values.

As the fixpoint in figure 6 is not effectively computable, we adopt the methodology of abstract interpretation to obtain a sound, decidable approximation of the concrete semantics.

4.1   Abstract Domains

Abstract domains $\mathcal{D}_\mathcal{E}$ and $\mathcal{D}_{\mathcal{E} \times \mathcal{V}}$ must be chosen to represent elements of $\wp(\mathcal{E})$ and $\wp(\mathcal{E} \times \mathcal{V})$. Each domain is a complete partial order $(\mathcal{D}, \sqsubseteq, \bot, \sqcup)$. The bot-

$$[\![const(v)]\!]\,\rho = \{v\}$$

$$[\![unop(x)]\!]\,\rho = \{\mathsf{unop}(v_x) \mid v_x \in [\![x]\!]\,\rho\}$$

$$[\![binop(x,y)]\!]\,\rho = \{\mathsf{binop}(v_x,v_y) \mid v_x \in [\![x]\!]\,\rho \wedge v_y \in [\![y]\!]\,\rho\}$$

$$[\![in]\!]\,\rho = \{\rho(in)\}$$

$$[\![\mu_x(i,n)]\!]\,\rho = \{\rho(\mu_x)\}$$

$$[\![\gamma(p,t,f)]\!]\,\rho = \{v \mid true \in [\![p]\!]\,\rho \wedge v \in [\![t]\!]\,\rho\} \cup$$
$$\{v \mid false \in [\![p]\!]\,\rho \wedge v \in [\![f]\!]\,\rho\}$$

$$[\![\eta(p,r,\mu_x(i,n))]\!]\,\rho = \{v_r \mid v_i \in [\![i]\!]\,\rho \wedge \rho^{\backslash} \in (\!|p,\mu_x(i,n)|\!)\,\rho[\mu_x \leftarrow v_i] \wedge$$
$$false \in [\![p]\!]\,\rho^{\backslash} \wedge v_r \in [\![r]\!]\,\rho^{\backslash}\}$$

$$(\!|p,\mu_x(i,n)|\!)\,\rho = \mathrm{lfp}_\rho\, \mathbb{F}$$

where

$$\mathbb{F}(X) = \{\rho\} \cup \{\rho^{\backslash}[\mu_x \leftarrow v_n] \mid \rho^{\backslash} \in X \wedge true \in [\![p]\!]\,\rho^{\backslash} \wedge v_n \in [\![n]\!]\,\rho^{\backslash}\}$$

Fig. 6. Fixpoint semantics

tom $\bot$ provides an abstraction of the empty set, and the join $\sqcup$ computes an upper-bound of two elements. The meanings of elements are given by monotonic concretization functions $\gamma_{\mathcal{E}} : \mathcal{D}_{\mathcal{E}} \rightarrow \wp(\mathcal{E})$ and $\gamma_{\mathcal{E} \times \mathcal{V}} : \mathcal{D}_{\mathcal{E} \times \mathcal{V}} \rightarrow \wp(\mathcal{E} \times \mathcal{V})$.

We require a number of primitives. lookup : $\mathcal{D}_{\mathcal{E}} \rightarrow \mathcal{D}_{\mathcal{E} \times \mathcal{V}}$ reads information about a loop variable, release : $\mathcal{D}_{\mathcal{E} \times \mathcal{V}} \rightarrow \mathcal{D}_{\mathcal{E} \times \mathcal{V}}$ removes information about a loop variable, assign : $\mathcal{D}_{\mathcal{E} \times \mathcal{V}} \rightarrow \mathcal{D}_{\mathcal{E}}$ writes information about a loop variable, and select : $\mathcal{D}_{\mathcal{E}} \rightarrow \mathcal{D}_{\mathcal{E}}$ asserts a boolean condition. These must obey the following soundness conditions:

$$\{(\rho,v) \mid \rho \in \gamma_{\mathcal{E}}(X) \wedge v = \rho(x)\} \subseteq \gamma_{\mathcal{E} \times \mathcal{V}}(\mathsf{lookup}_x(X))$$

$$\{(\rho',v) \mid (\rho,v) \in \gamma_{\mathcal{E} \times \mathcal{V}}(X) \wedge \forall y \neq x : \rho'(y) = \rho(y)\} \subseteq \gamma_{\mathcal{E} \times \mathcal{V}}(\mathsf{release}_x(X))$$

$$\{\rho[x \leftarrow v] \mid (\rho,v) \in \gamma_{\mathcal{E} \times \mathcal{V}}(X)\} \subseteq \gamma_{\mathcal{E}}(\mathsf{assign}_x(X))$$

$$\{\rho \mid \rho \in \gamma_{\mathcal{E}}(X) \wedge v \in [\![p]\!]\,\rho\} \subseteq \gamma_{\mathcal{E}}(\mathsf{select}_{p=v}(X)).$$

The concretization of the result of lookup must contain each environment in that of its operand, paired with the retrieved value. The concretization of the result of release must contain each environment-value pair in that of its operand, pre-serving information about all but one value. The concretization of the result of assign must contain each environment in that of its operand, updated appropri-ately. The concretization of the result of select must contain each environment in that of its operand for which the condition holds.

We also require a primitive constant : $\mathcal{D}_{\mathcal{E}} \rightarrow \mathcal{D}_{\mathcal{E} \times \mathcal{V}}$ which builds the rep-resentation of a constant, and abstract equivalents of the concrete arithmetic operators, $\mathsf{unop}^{\sharp} : \mathcal{D}_{\mathcal{E} \times \mathcal{V}} \rightarrow \mathcal{D}_{\mathcal{E} \times \mathcal{V}}$ and $\mathsf{binop}^{\sharp} : \mathcal{D}_{\mathcal{E} \times \mathcal{V}} \times \mathcal{D}_{\mathcal{E} \times \mathcal{V}} \rightarrow \mathcal{D}_{\mathcal{E} \times \mathcal{V}}$. These must obey the following soundness conditions:

$$\{(\rho, v) \mid \rho \in \gamma_{\mathcal{E}}(X)\} \subseteq \gamma_{\mathcal{E} \times \mathcal{V}}(\mathsf{constant}_v(X))$$
$$\{(\rho, \mathsf{unop}(x)) \mid (\rho, x) \in \gamma_{\mathcal{E} \times \mathcal{V}}(X)\} \subseteq \gamma_{\mathcal{E} \times \mathcal{V}}(\mathsf{unop}^\sharp(X))$$
$$\left\{ (\rho, \mathsf{binop}(x, y)) \,\middle|\, \begin{matrix} (\rho, x) \in \gamma_{\mathcal{E} \times \mathcal{V}}(X) \\ (\rho, y) \in \gamma_{\mathcal{E} \times \mathcal{V}}(Y) \end{matrix} \right\} \subseteq \gamma_{\mathcal{E} \times \mathcal{V}}(\mathsf{binop}^\sharp(X, Y)) \,.$$

The concretization of the result of constant must contain each environment in that of its operand, paired with the constant value. The concretizations of the results of $\mathsf{unop}^\sharp$ and $\mathsf{binop}^\sharp$ must contain the results of performing the corresponding concrete operations on those of their operands.

If $\mathcal{D}_{\mathcal{E}}$ possesses infinitely increasing chains, we also require a widening operator $\nabla : \mathcal{D}_{\mathcal{E}} \times \mathcal{D}_{\mathcal{E}} \to \mathcal{D}_{\mathcal{E}}$, which must obey the usual soundness conditions.

4.2 Abstract Semantics

We define the abstract semantics in terms of the primitive operations on the abstract domains, as shown in figure 7.

$$[\![const(v)]\!]^\sharp P = \mathsf{constant}_v(P)$$
$$[\![unop(x)]\!]^\sharp P = \mathsf{unop}^\sharp([\![x]\!]^\sharp P)$$
$$[\![binop(x, y)]\!]^\sharp P = \mathsf{binop}^\sharp([\![x]\!]^\sharp P, [\![y]\!]^\sharp P)$$
$$[\![in(i, n)]\!]^\sharp P = \mathsf{lookup}_{in}(P)$$
$$[\![\mu_x(i, n)]\!]^\sharp P = \mathsf{lookup}_{\mu_x}(P)$$
$$[\![\gamma(p, t, f)]\!]^\sharp P = [\![t]\!]^\sharp \mathsf{select}_{p=true}(P) \sqcup_{\mathcal{E} \times \mathcal{V}} [\![f]\!]^\sharp \mathsf{select}_{p=false}(P)$$
$$[\![\eta(p, r, \mu_x(i, n))]\!]^\sharp P = \mathsf{release}_{\mu_x}([\![r]\!]^\sharp \mathsf{select}_{p=false}((\!|p, \mu_x(i, n)|\!)^\sharp \mathsf{assign}_{\mu_x}([\![i]\!]^\sharp P)))$$
$$(\!|p, \mu(i, n)|\!)^\sharp P = \lim_0 \mathbb{F}^\sharp$$

where

$$\mathbb{F}^\sharp(X) = P \sqcup_{\mathcal{E}} \mathsf{assign}_{\mu_x}([\![n]\!]^\sharp \mathsf{select}_{p=true}(X))$$

and $\lim_0 \mathbb{F}^\sharp$ denotes the limit of the abstract iteration sequence with widening

$$\mathbb{F}^\sharp_0 = \bot^\sharp$$
$$\mathbb{F}^\sharp_{n+1} = \mathbb{F}^\sharp_n \nabla \mathbb{F}^\sharp(\mathbb{F}^\sharp_n)$$

Fig. 7. Abstract semantics

We have $[\![n]\!]^\sharp : \mathcal{D}_{\mathcal{E}} \to \mathcal{D}_{\mathcal{E} \times \mathcal{V}}$ and $(\!|p, \mu_x(i, n)|\!)^\sharp : \mathcal{D}_{\mathcal{E}} \to \mathcal{D}_{\mathcal{E}}$. If $\mathcal{D}_{\mathcal{E}}$ does not possess infinitely increasing chains, we may omit the widening operator ∇.

The rules for *const*, *unop* and *binop* nodes are straightforward. The rule for γ nodes uses select to create a pair of abstract environments in which the predicate is true and false, evaluates the nodes t and f in these environments, and combines the results using the join operator.

The rule for η nodes first uses assign to create the initial abstract environment. An approximation of the set of reachable environments is then computed as the least fixpoint of a semantic transformer, which uses select to create an abstract environment in which the loop predicate is true and assign to update it. select is used to create an abstract environment in which the loop predicate is false and r is evaluated in this environment. Finally release is used to remove unnecessary information about the loop variable.

4.3 Soundness

The concretization function $\gamma : (\mathcal{D}_{\mathcal{E}} \to \mathcal{D}_{\mathcal{E} \times \mathcal{V}}) \to (\mathcal{E} \to \wp(\mathcal{V}))$, which gives the concrete meaning of the abstract semantics, may be defined in terms of $\gamma_{\mathcal{E}}$ and $\gamma_{\mathcal{E} \times \mathcal{V}}$ as follows:

$$\gamma(\llbracket n \rrbracket^{\sharp}) = \lambda \rho. \{ v \mid \forall P : \rho \in \gamma_{\mathcal{E}}(P) \Rightarrow (\rho, v) \in \gamma_{\mathcal{E} \times \mathcal{V}}(\llbracket n \rrbracket^{\sharp} P) \} .$$

The result of γ is a function which maps an environment ρ to a set of values. A value v is in the set if applying the abstract semantics to any element of $\mathcal{D}_{\mathcal{E}}$ whose concretization contains ρ yields an element of $\mathcal{D}_{\mathcal{E} \times \mathcal{V}}$ whose concretization contains (ρ, v).

Our abstract semantics is sound, that is for all environments, the set of values computed by the concretization of the abstract semantics contains the set of values computed by the concrete semantics.

Theorem 1 (Soundness). *For any node n, we have:*

$$\forall \rho : \llbracket n \rrbracket(\rho) \subseteq \gamma(\llbracket n \rrbracket^{\sharp})(\rho) . \tag{1}$$

Proof. Using the definition of γ, we have that relation 1 is equivalent to

$$\forall \rho : \forall v : v \in \llbracket n \rrbracket(\rho) \Rightarrow (\forall P : \rho \in \gamma_{\mathcal{E}}(P) \Rightarrow (\rho, v) \in \gamma_{\mathcal{E} \times \mathcal{V}}(\llbracket n \rrbracket^{\sharp} P))$$

which is equivalent to

$$\forall P : \forall \rho : \forall v : v \in \llbracket n \rrbracket(\rho) \wedge \rho \in \gamma_{\mathcal{E}}(P) \Rightarrow (\rho, v) \in \gamma_{\mathcal{E} \times \mathcal{V}}(\llbracket n \rrbracket^{\sharp} P)$$

and to

$$\forall P : \{ (\rho, v) \mid \rho \in \gamma_{\mathcal{E}}(P) \wedge v \in \llbracket n \rrbracket(\rho) \} \subseteq \gamma_{\mathcal{E} \times \mathcal{V}}(\llbracket n \rrbracket^{\sharp} P) . \tag{2}$$

We prove 2 by induction on the depth of the graph.

- $n = const(c)$. $\{ (\rho, c) \mid \rho \in \gamma_{\mathcal{E}}(P) \} \subseteq \gamma_{\mathcal{E} \times \mathcal{V}}(\mathsf{constant}_c(P))$ follows immediately from the soundness condition on constant.
- $n = unop(x)$. This case is similar to $binop(x, y)$, below.
- $n = binop(x, y)$. By the induction hypothesis, we have

$$v_x \in \llbracket x \rrbracket \rho \wedge \rho \in \gamma_{\mathcal{E}}(P) \Rightarrow (\rho, v_x) \in \gamma_{\mathcal{E} \times \mathcal{V}}(\llbracket x \rrbracket^{\sharp} P)$$
$$v_y \in \llbracket y \rrbracket \rho \wedge \rho \in \gamma_{\mathcal{E}}(P) \Rightarrow (\rho, v_y) \in \gamma_{\mathcal{E} \times \mathcal{V}}(\llbracket y \rrbracket^{\sharp} P)$$

and therefore

$$\{ (\rho, \mathsf{binop}(v_x, v_y)) \mid \rho \in \gamma_{\mathcal{E}}(P) \wedge v_x \in \llbracket x \rrbracket \rho \wedge v_y \in \llbracket y \rrbracket \rho \}$$
$$\subseteq \{ (\rho, \mathsf{binop}(v_x, v_y)) \mid (\rho, v_x) \in \gamma_{\mathcal{E} \times \mathcal{V}}(\llbracket x \rrbracket^{\sharp} P) \wedge (\rho, v_y) \in \gamma_{\mathcal{E} \times \mathcal{V}}(\llbracket y \rrbracket^{\sharp} P) \} .$$

By the soundness condition on $\mathsf{binop}^\sharp$, this is

$$\subseteq \gamma_{\mathcal{E}\times\mathcal{V}}(\mathsf{binop}^\sharp([\![x]\!]^\sharp P, [\![y]\!]^\sharp P)) = \gamma_{\mathcal{E}\times\mathcal{V}}([\![binop(x,y)]\!]^\sharp P) .$$

- $n = in(i,n)$. This case is identical to $\mu_x(i,n)$, below.
- $n = \mu_x(i,n)$. $\{(\rho,v) \mid \rho \in \gamma_{\mathcal{E}}(P) \wedge v = \rho(\mu_x)\} \subseteq \gamma_{\mathcal{E}\times\mathcal{V}}(\mathsf{lookup}_{\mu_x}(P))$ follows immediately from the soundness condition on lookup.
- $n = \gamma(p,t,f)$. By the soundness condition on select, we have

$$\rho \in \gamma_{\mathcal{E}}(P) \wedge false \in [\![p]\!]\rho \Rightarrow \rho \in \gamma_{\mathcal{E}}(\mathsf{select}_{p=false}(P))$$

and therefore

$$\{(\rho,v) \mid \rho \in \gamma_{\mathcal{E}}(P) \wedge false \in [\![p]\!]\rho \wedge v \in [\![f]\!]\rho\}$$
$$\subseteq \{(\rho,v) \mid \rho \in \gamma_{\mathcal{E}}(\mathsf{select}_{p=false}(P)) \wedge v \in [\![f]\!]\rho\}$$

which by the induction hypothesis on f is

$$\subseteq \gamma_{\mathcal{E}\times\mathcal{V}}([\![f]\!]^\sharp \mathsf{select}_{p=false}(P)) .$$

By similar reasoning, we also have

$$\{(\rho,v) \mid \rho \in \gamma_{\mathcal{E}}(P) \wedge true \in [\![p]\!]\rho \wedge v \in [\![t]\!]\rho\} \subseteq \gamma_{\mathcal{E}\times\mathcal{V}}([\![t]\!]^\sharp \mathsf{select}_{p=true}(P))$$

and therefore

$$\{(\rho,v) \mid \rho \in \gamma_{\mathcal{E}}(P) \wedge [\![\gamma(p,t,f)]\!]\rho\}$$
$$\subseteq \gamma_{\mathcal{E}\times\mathcal{V}}([\![t]\!]^\sharp \mathsf{select}_{p=true}(P)) \cup \gamma_{\mathcal{E}\times\mathcal{V}}([\![f]\!]^\sharp \mathsf{select}_{p=false}(P)) .$$

As $\sqcup_{\mathcal{E}\times\mathcal{V}}$ is a sound approximation of the $\cup$ operator, this is

$$\subseteq \gamma_{\mathcal{E}\times\mathcal{V}}([\![t]\!]^\sharp \mathsf{select}_{p=true}(P) \sqcup_{\mathcal{E}\times\mathcal{V}} [\![f]\!]^\sharp \mathsf{select}_{p=false}(P)) = \gamma_{\mathcal{E}\times\mathcal{V}}([\![\gamma(p,t,f)]\!]^\sharp P).$$

- $n = \eta(p,r,\mu_x(i,n))$. This case is proved later by proposition 1.

To prove the soundness of the rule for η nodes, we need to establish the following subsidiary lemmas.

Lemma 1. *Given concrete and abstract domains* $(D, \subseteq, \perp, \cup)$ *and* $(D^\sharp, \sqsubseteq^\sharp, \perp^\sharp, \sqcup^\sharp)$, *concretization function* $\gamma : D^\sharp \to D$, *concrete and abstract semantic transformers* $\mathbb{F} : D \to D$ *and* $\mathbb{F}^\sharp : D^\sharp \to D^\sharp$ *and widening operator* $\nabla : D^\sharp \times D^\sharp \to D^\sharp$ *such that:*

1. γ *monotonic*
2. $\mathbb{F}$ *continuous*
3. $\forall X \in D^\sharp : \mathbb{F}(\gamma(X)) \subseteq \gamma(\mathbb{F}^\sharp(X))$
4. $\forall X, Y \in D^\sharp : X \sqsubseteq^\sharp X\nabla Y, Y \sqsubseteq^\sharp X\nabla Y$

5. *For every sequence $(x_n)_{n\in\mathbb{N}}$ of elements of $D^\sharp$, the sequence $(y_n)_{n\in\mathbb{N}}$ defined as*

$$y_0 = x_0$$
$$y_{n+1} = y_n \nabla x_{n+1}$$

is ultimately stationary,

then there exists some N after which the abstract iteration sequence with widening

$$\mathbb{F}_0^\sharp = \bot^\sharp$$
$$\mathbb{F}_{n+1}^\sharp = \mathbb{F}_n^\sharp \nabla \mathbb{F}^\sharp(\mathbb{F}_n^\sharp)$$

converges, and $\mathrm{lfp}_\bot \mathbb{F} \subseteq \gamma(\mathbb{F}_N^\sharp)$.

Proof. We prove by induction on n that $\forall n \in \mathbb{N} : \mathbb{F}_n \subseteq \gamma(\mathbb{F}_n^\sharp)$, where $\mathbb{F}_n$ is defined as:

$$\mathbb{F}_0 = \bot$$
$$\mathbb{F}_{n+1} = \mathbb{F}(\mathbb{F}_n) \, .$$

- $\mathbb{F}_0 = \bot \subseteq \gamma(\mathbb{F}_0^\sharp) = \gamma(\bot^\sharp)$
- Assuming $\mathbb{F}_n \subseteq \gamma(\mathbb{F}_n^\sharp)$, since $\mathbb{F}$ is continuous we have $\mathbb{F}_{n+1} = \mathbb{F}(\mathbb{F}_n) \subseteq \mathbb{F}(\gamma(\mathbb{F}_n^\sharp))$. From condition 3 we have $\mathbb{F}(\gamma(\mathbb{F}_n^\sharp)) \subseteq \gamma(\mathbb{F}^\sharp(\mathbb{F}_n^\sharp))$ and from condition 4 we have $\mathbb{F}^\sharp(\mathbb{F}_n^\sharp) \sqsubseteq^\sharp \mathbb{F}_n^\sharp \nabla \mathbb{F}^\sharp(\mathbb{F}_n^\sharp)$. Since γ is monotone, we have $\gamma(\mathbb{F}^\sharp(\mathbb{F}_n^\sharp)) \subseteq \gamma(\mathbb{F}_n^\sharp \nabla \mathbb{F}^\sharp(\mathbb{F}_n^\sharp))$. We have thus established that $\mathbb{F}_{n+1} \subseteq \gamma(\mathbb{F}_{n+1}^\sharp)$.

The sequence $(\mathbb{F}_n^\sharp)_{n\in\mathbb{N}}$ is increasing (condition 4), and converges (condition 5). There must therefore exist an N such that $\forall n \geq 0 : \mathbb{F}_n^\sharp \sqsubseteq^\sharp \mathbb{F}_N^\sharp$. From the above we have $\forall n \geq 0 : \mathbb{F}_n \subseteq \gamma(\mathbb{F}_N^\sharp)$, and hence $\bigcup_{n\geq 0} \mathbb{F}_n \subseteq \gamma(\mathbb{F}_N^\sharp)$. Since $\mathbb{F}$ is continuous, by Kleene's theorem [7], $\bigcup_{n\geq 0} \mathbb{F}_n$ is exactly $\mathrm{lfp}_\bot \mathbb{F}$.

Lemma 2. *Assuming that $[\![n]\!]^\sharp$ is correct, that is*

$$\forall P : \forall \rho : \forall v : \rho \in \gamma_\mathcal{E}(P) \wedge v \in [\![n]\!]\rho \Rightarrow (\rho, v) \in \gamma_{\mathcal{E}\times\mathcal{V}}([\![n]\!]^\sharp P)$$

and given the concrete and abstract semantic transformers

$$\mathbb{F}(X) = \{\rho\} \cup \{\rho'[\mu_x \leftarrow v_n] \mid \rho' \in X \wedge true \in [\![p]\!]\rho' \wedge v_n \in [\![n]\!]\rho'\}$$
$$\mathbb{F}^\sharp(X) = P \sqcup_\mathcal{E} \mathrm{assign}_{\mu_x}([\![n]\!]^\sharp \mathrm{select}_{p=true}(X))$$

and given that $\rho \in \gamma_\mathcal{E}(P)$ then the following inclusion holds:

$$\mathbb{F}(\gamma_\mathcal{E}(X)) \subseteq \gamma_\mathcal{E}(\mathbb{F}^\sharp(X)) \, .$$

Proof.

$$\mathbb{F}(\gamma_\mathcal{E}(X)) = \{\rho\} \cup \{\rho'[\mu_x \leftarrow v_n] \mid \rho' \in \gamma_\mathcal{E}(X) \wedge true \in [\![p]\!]\rho' \wedge v_n \in [\![n]\!]\rho'\} \, .$$

We know that $\rho \in \gamma_{\mathcal{E}}(P)$ by hypothesis. By the soundness condition on select we have

$$\{\rho'[\mu_x \leftarrow v_n] \mid \rho' \in \gamma_{\mathcal{E}}(X) \wedge true \in [\![p]\!]\rho' \wedge v_n \in [\![n]\!]\rho'\}$$
$$\subseteq \{\rho'[\mu_x \leftarrow v_n] \mid \rho' \in \gamma_{\mathcal{E}}(\text{select}_{p=true}(X)) \wedge v_n \in [\![n]\!]\rho'\} \,.$$

By hypothesis on $[\![n]\!]^\sharp$ this is

$$\subseteq \{\rho'[\mu_x \leftarrow v_n] \mid (\rho', v_n) \in \gamma_{\mathcal{E} \times \mathcal{V}}([\![n]\!]^\sharp \text{select}_{p=true}(X))\}$$

and by the soundness condition on assign this is

$$\subseteq \gamma_{\mathcal{E}}(\text{assign}_{\mu_x}([\![n]\!]^\sharp \text{select}_{p=true}(X))) = \gamma_{\mathcal{E}}(\mathbb{F}^\sharp(X)) \,.$$

Lemma 3. *Assuming that $[\![n]\!]^\sharp$ is correct, that is*

$$\forall P : \forall \rho : \forall v : \rho \in \gamma_{\mathcal{E}}(P) \wedge v \in [\![n]\!]\rho \Rightarrow (\rho, v) \in \gamma_{\mathcal{E} \times \mathcal{V}}([\![n]\!]^\sharp P)$$

and given that $\rho \in \gamma_{\mathcal{E}}(P)$ then the following inclusion holds:

$$(\![p, \mu_x(i, n)]\!)\rho \subseteq \gamma_{\mathcal{E}}((\![p, \mu_x(i, n)]\!)^\sharp P) \,.$$

Proof. We apply lemma 1 for

$$\mathbb{F}(X) = \{\rho\} \cup \{\rho'[\mu_x \leftarrow v_n] \mid \rho' \in X \wedge true \in [\![p]\!]\rho' \wedge v_n \in [\![n]\!]\rho'\}$$
$$\mathbb{F}^\sharp(X) = P \sqcup_{\mathcal{E}} \text{assign}_{\mu_x}([\![n]\!]^\sharp \text{select}_{p=true}(X)) \,.$$

Monotonicity of $\gamma_{\mathcal{E}}$ and contuinity of $\mathbb{F}$ are easily checked. Since $\rho' \in \gamma_{\mathcal{E}}(\text{assign}_{\mu_x}([\![i]\!]^\sharp P))$ and by induction hypothesis on $[\![n]\!]^\sharp$ we know by lemma 2 that

$$\mathbb{F}(\gamma_{\mathcal{E}}(X)) \subseteq \gamma_{\mathcal{E}}(\mathbb{F}^\sharp(X))$$

so

$$(\![p, \mu_x(i, n)]\!)\rho = \text{lfp}_\emptyset F \subseteq F^{\sharp \nabla} = \gamma_{\mathcal{E}}((\![p, \mu_x(i, n)]\!)^\sharp P) \,.$$

We may now prove the soundness of the rule for η nodes.

Proposition 1. *The rule for η nodes is sound, i.e.*

$$\forall P : \{(\rho, v) \mid \rho \in \gamma_{\mathcal{E}}(P) \wedge v \in [\![\eta(p, r, \mu_x(i, n))]\!]\rho\} \subseteq \gamma_{\mathcal{E} \times \mathcal{V}}([\![\eta(p, r, \mu_x(i, n))]\!]^\sharp(P)).$$

Proof. Using the definition of $[\![\eta(p, r, \mu_x(i, n))]\!]$ the left hand side is

$$= \{(\rho, v_r) \mid \rho \in \gamma_{\mathcal{E}}(P) \wedge v_i \in [\![i]\!]\rho \wedge \rho'' = \rho[\mu_x \leftarrow i] \wedge \rho' = (\![p, \mu_x(i, n)]\!)\rho'' \wedge$$
$$false \in [\![p]\!]\rho' \wedge v_r \in [\![r]\!]\rho'\} \,.$$

It is straightforward to verify by induction that $\forall \mu_y \neq \mu_x : \rho'(\mu_y) = \rho(\mu_y)$, as ρ'' is ρ with μ_x modified, and $(\![p, \mu_x(i, n)]\!)\rho''$ only modifies μ_x. Therefore this is

$$= \{(\rho, v_r) \mid \rho \in \gamma_{\mathcal{E}}(P) \wedge v_i \in [\![i]\!]\rho \wedge \rho'' = \rho[\mu_x \leftarrow i] \wedge \rho' = (\![p, \mu_x(i, n)]\!)\rho'' \wedge$$
$$false \in [\![p]\!]\rho' \wedge v_r \in [\![r]\!]\rho' \wedge \forall \mu_y \neq \mu_x : \rho'(\mu_y) = \rho(\mu_y)\} \,.$$

By the induction hypothesis on $[\![i]\!]^\sharp$, this is

$$\subseteq \{(\rho, v_r) \mid (\rho, v_i) \in \gamma_{\mathcal{E} \times \mathcal{V}}([\![i]\!]^\sharp P) \wedge \rho'' = \rho[\mu_x \leftarrow i] \wedge \rho' = (\!|p, \mu_x(i,n)|\!)\rho'' \wedge$$
$$\mathit{false} \in [\![p]\!]\rho' \wedge v_r \in [\![r]\!]\rho' \wedge \forall \mu_y \neq \mu_x : \rho'(\mu_y) = \rho(\mu_y)\}$$

which by the soundness condition on assign is

$$\subseteq \{(\rho, v_r) \mid \rho'' \in \gamma_{\mathcal{E}}(\mathsf{assign}_{\mu_x}([\![i]\!]^\sharp P)) \wedge \rho' = (\!|p, \mu_x(i,n)|\!)\rho'' \wedge \mathit{false} \in [\![p]\!]\rho' \wedge$$
$$v_r \in [\![r]\!]\rho' \wedge \forall \mu_y \neq \mu_x : \rho'(\mu_y) = \rho(\mu_y)\}\,.$$

By lemma 3 (correctness of $(\!|p, \mu_x(i,n)|\!)$), this is

$$\subseteq \{(\rho, v_r) \mid \rho' \in \gamma_{\mathcal{E}}((\!|p, \mu_x(i,n)|\!)^\sharp \mathsf{assign}_{\mu_x}([\![i]\!]^\sharp P)) \wedge \mathit{false} \in [\![p]\!]\rho' \wedge$$
$$v_r \in [\![r]\!]\rho' \wedge \forall \mu_y \neq \mu_x : \rho'(\mu_y) = \rho(\mu_y)\}$$

which by the soundness condition on select is

$$\subseteq \{(\rho, v_r) \mid \rho' \in \gamma_{\mathcal{E}}(\mathsf{select}_{p=\mathit{false}}(\!|p, \mu_x(i,n)|\!)^\sharp \mathsf{assign}_{\mu_x}([\![i]\!]^\sharp P)) \wedge$$
$$v_r \in [\![r]\!]\rho' \wedge \forall \mu_y \neq \mu_x : \rho'(\mu_y) = \rho(\mu_y)\}\,.$$

By the induction hypothesis on r, this is

$$\subseteq \{(\rho, v_r) \mid (\rho', v_r) \in \gamma_{\mathcal{E} \times \mathcal{V}}([\![r]\!]^\sharp \mathsf{select}_{p=\mathit{false}}(\!|p, \mu_x(i,n)|\!)^\sharp \mathsf{assign}_{\mu_x}([\![i]\!]^\sharp P)) \wedge$$
$$\forall \mu_y \neq \mu_x : \rho'(\mu_y) = \rho(\mu_y)\}\,.$$

Finally, by the soundness condition on release, this is

$$\subseteq \gamma_{\mathcal{E} \times \mathcal{V}}(\mathsf{release}_{\mu_x}([\![r]\!]^\sharp \mathsf{select}_{p=\mathit{false}}[\![p, \mu_x(i,n)]\!]^\sharp \mathsf{assign}_{\mu_x}([\![i]\!]^\sharp P)))\,.$$

5   Results

We have developed an implementation of our analysis which uses the domains of convex polyhedra of dimension N and $N+1$ (denoted by P_N and P_{N+1}) as $\mathcal{D}_{\mathcal{E}}$ and $\mathcal{D}_{\mathcal{E} \times \mathcal{V}}$ respectively. Empty polyhedra correspond to $\bot$, and the convex hull operation corresponds to $\sqcup$. As P_N possesses infinitely increasing chains, we require a widening operator.

We use the Parma Polyhedra Library [1] to provide basic operations on polyhedra. To improve the accuracy of our results, we use the improved widening operator described in [2] and widening with tokens (a form of delayed widening).

The primitives lookup, assign and select are defined as follows.

$\mathsf{lookup}_x(P)$ Add a dimension to P to produce an element of P_{N+1}. Constrain the new dimension to equal the dimension which corresponds to x.

$\mathsf{release}_x(P)$ Discard the dimension which corresponds to x, and add a new unconstrained dimension.

$\mathsf{assign}_x(P)$ Exchange the $N+1^{th}$ dimension with the dimension which corresponds to x, and discard the new $N+1^{th}$ dimension.

```
void bubblesort(int *k, int n)
{
    int b := n;
    while(b ≥ 1) {
        int j := 1, t := 0;
        while(j ≤ (b − 1)) {
            if (k[j] > k[j + 1]) {
                EXCHANGE(k, j, j + 1);
                t := j;
            }
            j := j + 1;
        }
        b := t;
    }
}
```

```
void f(int i)
{
    int j := i * i;
    if(i = 1) {
        int k := j;
        // use k
    }
}
```

Fig. 8. Bubblesort routine

Fig. 9. Routine benefitting from gated-DDG analysis

$select_{p=v}(P)$ Examine the predicate $p = v$ to determine the additional restraints which it implies, expressed as a polyhedron $Q \in P_N$. Form the intersection of P and Q.

It is straightforward to demonstrate that these primitives satisfy their respective soundness conditions.

The primitives constant, $unop^{\sharp}$ and $binop^{\sharp}$ use the PPL affine transformations for negation, addition, subtraction and multiplication by a constant, and return an unknown value for other operations.

We have applied our implementation to the graphs for a variety of programs, and have found that the results compare well with those obtained by direct abstract interpretation of the programs themselves. As an example, consider the bubblesort routine in figure 8, which is taken from [5].

Our implementation was able to deduce exactly the same set of restraints listed by the original paper. In particular, it found that the following set of restraints holds at the start of body of the inner loop.

$$b \leq n, \quad t \geq 0, \quad t + 1 \leq j, \quad j + 1 \leq b$$

The main advantage of our analysis over CFG-based analysis lies in our ability to exploit information at each use of a value, rather than at its definition. Consider the routine in figure 9.

An analysis of the CFG using convex polyhedra to represent abstract environments would be unable to deduce restraints for j, and hence for k. Our analysis can make use of information from the predicate $i = 1$ to deduce that $k = 1$. It is possible to obtain this effect in a CFG-based analysis by inlining the definition of each variable into each of its uses, but this can easily lead to an exponential increase in code size.

6   Conclusions and Further Work

We have presented a static analysis, developed using the methodology of abstract interpretation, which operates directly on gated DDGs. This is an important step in demonstrating their usefulness as a compiler intermediate representation. In terms of precision, our analysis compares very favourably with traditional CFG-based techniques.

We intend to extend our implementation to represent the relationship between values on consecutive loop iterations. This straightforward modification, which will involve allocating two dimensions to each value instead of one, will provide information useful for reasoning about loop termination.

Our eventual goal is to produce an analyzer which can form part of a DDG-based optimizing compiler. To accomplish this, we will need to improve the efficiency of our implementation. At present, we compute the return value of a node each time it is needed, which can incur a substantial performance penalty. By introducing a caching scheme and reusing previously computed values, we will be able to eliminate this problem without sacrificing accuracy.

Acknowledgements

The authors would like to thank Radhia Cousot and Alan Mycroft for their helpful comments.

References

1. R. Bagnara, P. M. Hill, E. Ricci, and E. Zaffanella. Possibly not closed convex polyhedra and the parma polyhedra library. In *Proceedings of the 9th Static Analysis Symposium*, pages 213–229, 2002.
2. R. Bagnara, P. M. Hill, E. Ricci, and E. Zaffanella. Precise widening operators for convex polyhedra. In *Proceedings of the 10th Static Analysis Symposium*, pages 337–354, 2003.
3. R. A. Ballance, A. B. Maccabe, and K. J. Ottenstein. The program dependence web: A representation supporting control-, data-, and demand-driven interpretation of imperative languages. In *Proceedings of the ACM SIGPLAN Conference on Programming Language Design and Implementation*, pages 257–271, 1990.
4. P. Cousot and R. Cousot. Abstract interpretation: a unified lattice model for static analysis of programs by construction or approximation of fixpoints. In *Conference Record of the 4th Annual ACM SIGPLAN-SIGACT Symposium on Principles of Programming Languages*, pages 238–252, 1977.
5. P. Cousot and N. Halbwachs. Automatic discovery of linear restraints among variables of a program. In *Conference Record of the 5th Annual ACM SIGPLAN-SIGACT Symposium on Principles of Programming Languages*, pages 84–97, 1978.
6. N. Johnson and A. Mycroft. Combined code motion and register allocation using the value state dependence graph. In *Proceedings of Compiler Construction*, Lecture Notes in Computer Science, 2003.
7. S. C. Kleene. *Introduction to Metamathematics*. North-Holland, 1952.

8. D. J. Kuck, R. H. Kuhn, B. Leasure, D. A. Padua, and M. Wolfe. Dependence graphs and compiler optimizations. In *Conference Record of the 8th ACM Symposium on Principles of Programming Languages*, pages 207–218, 1981.
9. P. Tu and D. A. Padua. Efficient building and placing of gating functions. In *Proceedings of the ACM SIGPLAN Conference on Programming Language Design and Implementation*, pages 47–55, 1995.
10. D. Weise, R. F. Crew, M. Ernst, and B. Steensgaard. Value dependence graphs: Representation without taxation. In *Proceedings of the 21th ACM Symposium on Principles of Programming Languages*, pages 297–310, 1994.

A Polynomial-Time Algorithm
for Global Value Numbering

Sumit Gulwani and George C. Necula

University of California, Berkeley
{gulwani,necula}@cs.berkeley.edu

Abstract. We describe a polynomial-time algorithm for global value numbering, which is the problem of discovering equivalences among program sub-expressions. We treat all conditionals as non-deterministic and all program operators as uninterpreted. We show that there are programs for which the set of all equivalences contains terms whose value graph representation requires exponential size. Our algorithm discovers all equivalences among terms of size at most s in time that grows linearly with s. For global value numbering, it suffices to choose s to be the size of the program. Earlier deterministic algorithms for the same problem are either incomplete or take exponential time.

1 Introduction

Detecting equivalence of program sub-expressions has a variety of applications. Compilers use this information to perform several important optimizations like constant and copy propagation [13], common sub-expression elimination, invariant code motion [2,11], induction variable elimination, branch elimination, branch fusion, and loop jamming [8]. Program verification tools use these equivalences to discover loop invariants, and to verify program assertions. This information is also important for discovering equivalent computations in different programs; this is useful for plagiarism detection tools and translation validation tools [10,9], which compare a program with an optimized version in order to check the correctness of the optimizer.

Checking equivalence of program expressions is an undecidable problem, even when all conditionals are treated as non-deterministic. Most tools, including compilers, attempt to only discover equivalences between expressions that are computed using the same operator applied to equivalent operands. This form of equivalence, where the operators are treated as uninterpreted functions, is also called *Herbrand equivalence* [12]. The process of discovering such restricted class of equivalences is often referred to as *value numbering*. Performing value numbering in basic blocks is an easy problem; the challenge is in doing it globally for a procedure body.

Existing deterministic algorithms for global value numbering are either too expensive or imprecise. The precise algorithms are based on an early algorithm by Kildall [7], which discovers equivalences by performing an abstract interpretation [3] over the lattice of Herbrand equivalences. Kildall's algorithm discovers all

R. Giacobazzi (Ed.): SAS 2004, LNCS 3148, pp. 212–227, 2004.

Herbrand equivalences in a function body but has exponential cost [12]. On the other extreme, there are several polynomial-time algorithms that are complete for basic blocks, but are imprecise in the presence of joins and loops in a program. The popular partition refinement algorithm proposed by Alpern, Wegman, and Zadeck (AWZ) [1] is particularly efficient, however at the price of being significantly less precise than Kildall's algorithm. The novel idea in AWZ algorithm is to represent the values of variables after a join using a fresh selection function ϕ_i, similar to the functions used in the static single assignment form [4], and to treat the ϕ_i functions as additional uninterpreted functions. The AWZ algorithm is incomplete because it treats ϕ functions as uninterpreted. In an attempt to remedy this problem, Rüthing, Knoop and Steffen have proposed a polynomial-time algorithm (RKS) [12] that alternately applies the AWZ algorithm and some rewrite rules for normalization of terms involving ϕ functions, until the congruence classes reach a fixed point. Their algorithm discovers more equivalences than the AWZ algorithm, but remains incomplete. The AWZ and the RKS algorithm both use a data structure called value graph [8], which encodes the abstract syntax of program sub-expressions, and represents equivalences by merging nodes that have been discovered to be referring to equivalent expressions. We discuss these algorithms in more detail in Section 5. Recently, Gargi has proposed a set of balanced algorithms that are efficient, but also incomplete [5].

Our algorithm is based on two novel observations. First, it is important to make a distinction between "discovering all Herbrand equivalences" vs. "discovering Herbrand equivalences among program sub-expressions". The former involves discovering Herbrand equivalences among all terms that can be constructed using program variables and uninterpreted functions in the program. The latter refers to only those terms that occur syntactically in the program. Finding all Herbrand equivalences is attractive not only to answer questions about non-program terms, but it also allows a forwards dataflow or abstract interpretation based algorithms (e.g. Kildall's algorithm) to discover all equivalences among program terms. This is because discovery of an equivalence between program terms at some program point may require detecting equivalences among non-program terms at a preceding program point. This distinction is important because we show (in Section 4) that there is a family of acyclic programs for which the set of all Herbrand equivalences requires an exponential sized (in the size of the program) value graph representation. On the other hand, we also show that Herbrand equivalences among program sub-expressions can always be represented using a linear sized value graph. This implies that no algorithm that uses value graphs to represent equivalences can discover all Herbrand equivalences and have polynomial-time complexity at the same time. This observation explains why existing polynomial-time algorithms for value numbering are incomplete, even for acyclic programs. One of the reasons why Kildall's algorithm is exponential is that it discovers all Herbrand equivalences at each program point.

The above observation not only sheds light on the incompleteness or exponential complexity of the existing algorithms, but also motivates the design of our algorithm. Our algorithm takes a parameter s and discovers all Herbrand equivalences among terms of size at most s in time that grows linearly with s. For the purpose of global value numbering, it is sufficient to set the parameter s to N, where N is the size of the program, since the size of any program expression is at most N.

The second observation is that the lattice of sets of Herbrand equivalences has finite height k, where k is the number of program variables (we prove this in Section 3.4). Therefore, an optimistic-style algorithm that performs an abstract interpretation over the lattice of Herbrand equivalences will be able to handle cyclic programs as precisely as it can handle acyclic programs, and will terminate in at most k iterations. Without this observation, one can ensure the termination of the algorithm in presence of loops by adding a degree of pessimism. This leads to incompleteness in presence of loops, as is the case with the RKS algorithm [12]. Instead, our algorithm is based on abstract interpretation, similar to Kildall's algorithm, while using a more sophisticated join operation. We continue with a description of the expression language on which the algorithm operates (in Section 2), followed by a description of the algorithm itself in Section 3.

2   Language of Program Expressions

We consider a language in which the expressions occurring in assignments belong to the following simple language of uninterpreted function terms (here x is one of the variables, and c is one of the constants):

$$e ::= x \quad | \quad c \quad | \quad F(e_1, e_2)$$

For any expression e, we use the notation $Variables(e)$ to denote the variables that occur in expression e. We use $size(e)$ to denote the number of occurrences of function symbols in expression e (when expressed as a value graph). For simplicity, we consider only one binary uninterpreted function F. Our results can be extended easily to languages with any finite number of uninterpreted functions of any constant arity. Alternatively, one can encode any finite number of uninterpreted functions of constant arity by *one* binary function symbol with only a constant factor increase in the size of the program.

3   The Global Value Numbering Algorithm

Our algorithm discovers the set of Herbrand equivalences at any program point by performing an abstract interpretation over the lattice of Herbrand equivalences. We pointed out in the introduction, and we argue further in Section 4, that we cannot hope to have a complete and polynomial-time algorithm that discovers all Herbrand equivalences implied by a program (using the standard value graph based representations) because their representation is worst-case exponential in the size of the program. Thus, our algorithm takes a parameter s (which is a positive integer) and discovers all equivalences of the form $e_1 = e_2$,

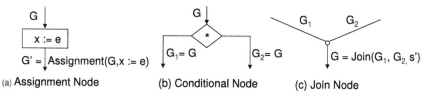

Fig. 1. Flowchart nodes

where $size(e_1) \leq s$ and $size(e_2) \leq s$. The algorithm uses a data structure called *Strong Equivalence DAG* (described in Section 3.1) to represent the set of equivalences at any program point. It updates the data structure across each flowchart node as shown in Figure 1. The `Assignment` and `Join` functions are described in Section 3.2 and Section 3.3 respectively.

3.1   Notation and Data Structure

Let T be the set of all program variables, k the total number of program variables, and N the size of the program, measured in terms of the number of occurrences of function symbol F in the program.

The algorithm represents the set of equivalences at any program point by a data structure that we call *Strong Equivalence DAG* (SED). An SED is similar to a value graph. It is a labeled directed acyclic graph whose nodes can be represented by tuples $\langle V, t \rangle$ where V is a (possibly empty) set of program variables labeling the node, and t represents the type of node. The type t is either $\perp$ or c, indicating that the node has no successors, or $F(n_1, n_2)$ indicating that the node has two ordered successors n_1 and n_2.

In any SED G, for every variable x, there is exactly one node $\langle V, t \rangle$, denoted by $Node_G(x)$, such that $x \in V$. For every type t that is not $\perp$, there is at most one node with that type. We use the notation $Node_G(c)$ to refer to the node with type c. For any SED node n, we use the notation $Vars(n)$ to denote the set of variables labeling node n, and $Type(n)$ to denote the type of node n. Every node n in an SED represents the following set of terms $Terms(n)$, which are all known to be equivalent.

$$Terms(V, \perp) = V$$
$$Terms(V, c) = V \cup \{c\}$$
$$Terms(V, F(n_1, n_2)) = V \cup \{F(e_1, e_2) \mid e_1 \in Terms(n_1), e_2 \in Terms(n_2)\}$$

We use the notation $G \models e_1 = e_2$ to denote that G implies the equivalence $e_1 = e_2$. The judgment $G \models e_1 = e_2$ is deduced as follows.

$$G \models F(e_1, e_2) = F(e'_1, e'_2) \text{ iff } G \models e_1 = e'_1 \text{ and } G \models e_2 = e'_2$$
$$G \models x = e \text{ iff } e \in Terms(Node_G(x))$$

The algorithm starts with the following initial SED at the program start, which implies only trivial equivalences.

$$G_0 = \{\langle x, \perp \rangle \mid x \in T\}$$

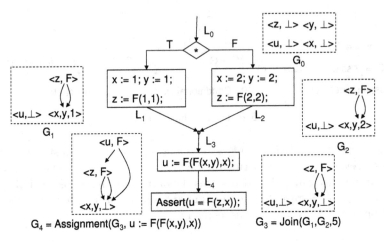

Fig. 2. This figure shows a program and the execution of our algorithm on it. G_i, shown in dotted box, represents the SED at program point L_i

In figures showing SEDs, we omit the set delimiters "{" and "}", and represent a node $\langle\{x_1,..,x_n\}, t\rangle$ as $\langle x_1,..,x_n, t\rangle$. Figure 2 shows a program and the SEDs computed by our algorithm at various points. As an example, note that $Terms(Node_{G_4}(u)) = \{u\} \cup \{F(z,\alpha) \mid \alpha \in \{x,y\}\} \cup \{F(F(\alpha_1,\alpha_2),\alpha_3) \mid \alpha_1,\alpha_2,\alpha_3 \in \{x,y\}\}$. Hence, $G_4 \models u = F(z,x)$. Note that an SED represents compactly a possibly-exponential number of equivalent terms.

3.2   The Assignment Operation

Let G be an SED that represents the Herbrand equivalences before an assignment node $x := e$. The SED that represents the Herbrand equivalences after the assignment node can be obtained by using the following algorithm. SED G_4 in Figure 2 shows an example of the **Assignment** operation.

```
1 Assignment(G, x := e) =
2    G' := G;
3    let ⟨V₁, t₁⟩ = GetNode(G', e) in
4    let ⟨V₂, t₂⟩ = Node_G'(x) in
5    if t₁ ≠ t₂ then G' := G' − {⟨V₁, t₁⟩, ⟨V₂, t₂⟩};
6                    G' := G' ∪ {⟨V₁ ∪ {x}, t₁⟩, ⟨V₂ − {x}, t₂⟩};
7    return G';
```

```
1 GetNode(G', e) =
2    match e with
3       y: return Node_G'(y);
4       c: return Node_G'(c);
5       F(e₁, e₂): let n₁ = GetNode(G', e₁) and n₂ = GetNode(G', e₂) in
6                   if ⟨V, F(n₁, n₂)⟩ ∈ G' for some V,
7                   then return ⟨V, F(n₁, n₂)⟩;
8                   else G' := G' ∪ ⟨∅, F(n₁, n₂)⟩; return ⟨∅, F(n₁, n₂)⟩;
```

GetNode(G', e) returns a node n such that $e \in Terms(n)$ (and in the process possibly extends G') in $O(size(e))$ time. Lines 5 and 6 in Assignment function move variable x to node n to reflect the new equivalence $x = e$. Hence, the following lemma holds.

Lemma 1 (Soundness and Completeness of Assignment Operation).
Let $G' = $ Assignment$(G, x := e)$. Let e_1 and e_2 be two expressions. Let $e_1' = e_1[e/x]$ and $e_2' = e_2[e/x]$. Then, $G' \models e_1 = e_2$ iff $G \models e_1' = e_2'$.

3.3   The Join Operation

Let G_1 and G_2 be two SEDs. Let s' be any positive integer. The following function Join returns an SED G that represents all equivalences $e_1 = e_2$ such that both G_1 and G_2 imply $e_1 = e_2$ and both $size(e_1)$ and $size(e_2)$ are at most s'. In order to discover all equivalences among expressions of size at most s in the program, we need to choose $s' = s + N \times k$ (for reasons explained later in Section 3.5). Figure 2 shows an example of the Join operation.

For any SED G, let $\prec_G$ denote a partial order on program variables such that $x \prec_G y$ if y depends on x, or more precisely, if $G \models y = F(e_1, e_2)$ such that $x \in Variables(F(e_1, e_2))$.

```
1  Join(G₁,G₂,s') =
2      for all nodes n₁ ∈ G₁ and n₂ ∈ G₂,  memoize[n₁,n₂] := undefined;
3      G := ∅;
4      for each variable x ∈ T in the order ≺_G₁ do
5          counter := s';
6          Intersect(Node_G₁(x),  Node_G₂(x));
7      return G;
```

```
1  Intersect(⟨V₁,t₁⟩,⟨V₂,t₂⟩) =
2      let m = memoize(⟨V₁,t₁⟩,⟨V₂,t₂⟩) in
3      if m ≠ undefined then return m;
4      let t = if counter > 0 and t₁ ≡ F(ℓ₁,r₁) and t₂ ≡ F(ℓ₂,r₂) then
5                  counter := counter − 1;
6                  let ℓ = Intersect(ℓ₁,ℓ₂) in
7                  let r = Intersect(r₁,r₂) in
8                  if (ℓ ≠ ⟨φ,⊥⟩) and (r ≠ ⟨φ,⊥⟩) then F(ℓ,r) else ⊥
9              else if t₁ = c and t₂ = c for some c, then c
10             else ⊥ in
11     let V = V₁ ∩ V₂ in
12     if V ≠ ∅ or t ≠ ⊥ then G := G ∪ {⟨V,t⟩}
13     memoize[⟨V₁,t₁⟩,⟨V₂,t₂⟩] := ⟨V,t⟩;
14     return ⟨V,t⟩
```

It is important for correctness of the algorithm that calls to the Intersect function are memoized, as done explicitly in the above pseudo code, since otherwise the counter variable will be decremented incorrectly. The use of counter variable ensures that the call to Intersect function in Join terminates in $O(s')$ time. The following proposition describes the property of Intersect function that is required to prove the correctness of the Join function (Lemma 2).

Proposition 1. *Let* $n_1 = \langle V_1, t_1 \rangle$ *and* $n_2 = \langle V_2, t_2 \rangle$ *be any nodes in SEDs* G_1 *and* G_2 *respectively. Let* $n = \langle V, t \rangle = \text{Intersect}(n_1, n_2)$. *Suppose that* $n \neq \langle \emptyset, \perp \rangle$; *hence the function* $\text{Intersect}(n_1, n_2)$ *adds the node* n *to* G. *Let* α *be the value of the counter variable when* $\text{Intersect}(n_1, n_2)$ *is first called. Then,*

P1. $Terms(n) \subseteq Terms(n_1) \cap Terms(n_2)$.
P2. $Terms(n) \supseteq \{e \mid e \in Terms(n_1), e \in Terms(n_2), size(e) \leq \alpha\}$.

The proof of Proposition 1 is by induction on sum of height of nodes n_1 and n_2 in G_1 and G_2 respectively. Claim P1 is easy since $t = F(...)$ or c only if both t_1 and t_2 are $F(...)$ or c respectively (Lines 8 and 9), and $V = V_1 \cap V_2$ (Line 11). The proof of claim P2 relies on bottom-up processing of one of the SEDs, and memoization. Let e' be one of the *smallest* expressions (in terms of *size*) such that $e' \in Terms(n_1) \cap Terms(n_2)$. If e' is not a variable, then for any variable $y \in Variables(e')$, the call $\text{Intersect}(Node_{G_1}(y), Node_{G_2}(y))$ has already finished. The crucial observation now is that if $size(e') \leq \alpha$, then the set of recursive calls to Intersect are in 1-1 correspondence with the nodes of expression e', and $e' \in Terms(n)$.

Lemma 2 (Soundness and Completeness of Join Operation). *Let* $G = \text{Join}(G_1, G_2, s)$. *If* $G \models e_1 = e_2$, *then* $G_1 \models e_1 = e_2$ *and* $G_2 \models e_1 = e_2$. *If* $G_1 \models e_1 = e_2$ *and* $G_2 \models e_1 = e_2$ *such that* $size(e_1) \leq s$ *and* $size(e_2) \leq s$, *then* $G \models e_1 = e_2$.

The proof of Lemma 2 follows from Proposition 1 and definition of $\models$.

3.4   Fixed Point Computation

The algorithm goes around loops in a program until a fixed point is reached. The following theorem implies that the algorithm needs to execute each flowchart node at most k times (assuming the standard worklist implementation [8]).

Theorem 1 (Fixed Point Theorem). *The lattice of sets of Herbrand equivalences (involving program variables) ordered by set inclusion has height at most* k *where* k *is the number of program variables.*

The proof of Theorem 1 follows easily from Lemma 3 stated and proved below. Before stating Lemma 3, we first introduce some notation. Let $\preccurlyeq$ denote any total ordering on all program variables. For notational convenience, we say that for any variable x, and any expressions e_1 and e_2, $x \preccurlyeq F(e_1, e_2)$. For any SED G, let I_G be the set of variables x such that $Type(Node_G(x)) = \perp$, and $x \preccurlyeq y$ for all $y \in Vars(Node_G(x))$. I_G is a *maximal* set of independent variables, which occur at the leaves of G. In other words, equivalences denoted by an SED G can be represented by a set of equivalences $x = e$, where $Variables(e) \subseteq I_G$ and

$x \notin I_G$. This is because for any SED G, all equivalences $e_1 = e_2$ are consequences of equivalences of the form $x = e$. For example, consider the program in Figure 2. If $u \preccurlyeq x \preccurlyeq y \preccurlyeq z$, then $I_{G_4} = \{x\}$. Note that equivalences represented by G_4 are equivalent to the set of equivalences $\{y = x, z = F(x, x), u = F(F(x, x), x)\}$.

Lemma 3. *Let G_1 and G_2 be two SEDs. If G_2 is above G_1 in the lattice (which is to say that G_1 represents a stronger set of equivalences than G_2), then $I_{G_2} \supseteq I_{G_1}$.*

Proof. We first make two useful observations. Let G be any SED. Then, (a) $G \nvDash x = e$ such that $x \in I_G$, $e \preccurlyeq x$ and $e \neq x$. (b) $G \nvDash e_1 = e_2$ such that *Variables*$(e_1) \subseteq I_G$, *Variables*$(e_2) \subseteq I_G$ and $e_1 \neq e_2$.

We first show that $I_{G_2} \supseteq I_{G_1}$. Suppose for the purpose of contradiction that $I_{G_2} \nsupseteq I_{G_1}$. Then, $G_2 \vDash x = e$ for some variable $x \in I_{G_1}$ and expression e such that $e \preccurlyeq x$ and $e \neq x$. Since G_1 represents a stronger set of equivalences, $G_1 \vDash x = e$. But this is not possible because of observation (a) above.

We now show that $I_{G_2} \supseteq I_{G_1}$. Suppose for the purpose of contradiction that $I_{G_2} = I_{G_1}$. Since G_1 is stronger than G_2, $G_1 \vDash x = e_1$ for some $x \in T - I_{G_1}$ and expression e_1 such that *Variables*$(e_1) \subseteq I_{G_1}$ and $G_2 \nvDash x = e_1$. Note that $x \in T - I_{G_2}$ since $I_{G_2} = I_{G_1}$. Hence, there exists an expression e_2 such that $G_2 \vDash x = e_2$, where *Variables*$(e_2) \subseteq I_{G_2}$. Note that $e_1 \neq e_2$ since $G_2 \nvDash x = e_1$ and $G_2 \vDash x = e_2$, Since G_1 is stronger than G_2, $G_1 \vDash x = e_2$ and hence $G_1 \vDash e_1 = e_2$. But this is not possible because of observation (b) above.

3.5   Correctness of the Algorithm

The correctness of the algorithm follows from Theorem 2 and Theorem 3.

Theorem 2 (Soundness Theorem). *Let G be the SED computed by the algorithm at some program point P after fixed point computation. If $G \vDash e_1 = e_2$, then $e_1 = e_2$ holds at program point P.*

The proof of Theorem 2 follows directly from the soundness of the assignment operation (Lemma 1 in Section 3.2) and the soundness of the join operation (Lemma 2 in Section 3.3).

Theorem 3 (Completeness Theorem). *Let $e_1 = e_2$ be an equivalence that holds at a program point P such that $size(e_1) \leq s$ and $size(e_2) \leq s$. Let G be the SED computed by the algorithm at program point P after fixed point computation. Then, $G \vDash e_1 = e_2$.*

The proof of Theorem 3 follows from an invariant maintained by the algorithm at each program point. For purpose of describing this invariant, we hypothetically extend the algorithm to maintain a set S of paths at each program point (representing the set of all paths analyzed by the algorithm), and a variable MaxSize (representing the size of the largest expression computed by the program along any path in S) besides an SED. These are updated as shown in Figure 3. The initial value of MaxSize is chosen to be 0. The initial set of paths is chosen to be the singleton set containing an empty path. The algorithm maintains the following invariant at each program point.

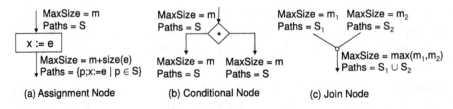

(a) Assignment Node   (b) Conditional Node   (c) Join Node

Fig. 3. Flowchart nodes

Lemma 4. *Let G be the SED, m be the value of variable MaxSize, and S be the set of paths computed by the algorithm at some program point P. Suppose $e_1 = e_2$ holds at program point P along all paths in S, $size(e_1) \leq s' - m$ and $size(e_2) \leq s' - m$. Then, $G \models e_1 = e_2$.*

Lemma 4 can be easily proved by induction on the number of operations performed by the algorithm.

Theorem 1 (the fixed point theorem) requires the algorithm to execute each node at most k times. This implies that the value of the variable MaxSize at any program point after the fixed point computation is at most $N \times k$. Hence, choosing $s' = s + N \times k$ enables the algorithm to discover equivalences among expressions of size s. The proof of Theorem 3 now follows easily from Lemma 4.

3.6   Complexity Analysis

Let j be the number of join points in the program. Let I be the maximum number of iterations of any loop performed by the algorithm. (It follows from Theorem 1 that I is upper bounded by k; however, in practice, this may be a small constant). One join operation $\texttt{Join}(G_1, G_2, s')$ takes time $O(k \times s') = O(k \times (s + N \times k))$. Hence, the total cost of all join operations is $O(k \times (s + N \times k) \times j \times I)$. The cost of all assignment operations is $O(N \times I)$. Hence, the total complexity of the algorithm is dominated by the cost of the join operations (assuming $j \geq 1$). For global value numbering, the choice of $s = N$ suffices, yielding a total complexity of $O(k^2 \times I \times N \times j) = O(k^3 \times N \times j)$ for the algorithm.

4   Programs with Exponential Sized Value Graph Representation for Sets of Herbrand Equivalences

Let m be any positive integer. In this section, we show that there is an acyclic program P_m of size $O(m^2)$ such that any value graph representation of the set of Herbrand equivalences that are true at the end of the program requires $\Theta(2^m)$ size. The program P_m is described in Section 4.2, and is shown in Figure 6. The program P_m involves some non-trivial expressions. To describe these expressions, and to prove that the set of Herbrand equivalences that are true at the end of program P_m requires $\Theta(2^m)$ size, we introduce some notation in Section 4.1.

Let n be the largest integer such that $n \leq m$ and n is a power of 2. Note that $n \geq \frac{m}{2}$.

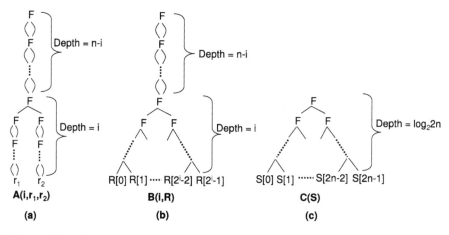

Fig. 4. The value graph representation of expressions $A(i, r_1, r_2)$, $B(i, R)$ and $C(S)$

4.1 Notation

In this section, we describe some special expressions, sets of expressions, and their properties. For any integer $i \in \{1, \ldots, n\}$ and expressions r_1 and r_2, let $A(i, r_1, r_2)$ denote the expression as shown in Figure 4(a). For any integer $i \in \{1, \ldots, n\}$ and sets of expressions $\tilde{r}_1$ and $\tilde{r}_2$, let $\tilde{A}(i, \tilde{r}_1, \tilde{r}_2)$ denote the following set of expressions:

$$\tilde{A}(i, \tilde{r}_1, \tilde{r}_2) = \{A(i, r_1, r_2) \mid r_1 \in \tilde{r}_1, r_2 \in \tilde{r}_2\}$$

For any integer $i \in \{1, \ldots, n\}$ and an array $R[0 \ldots 2^i-1]$ of expressions, let $B(i, R)$ denote the expression as shown in Figure 4(b). For any integer $i \in \{1, \ldots, n\}$ and an array $\tilde{R}[0 \ldots 2^i-1]$ of sets of expressions, let $\tilde{B}(i, \tilde{R})$ denote the following set of expressions:

$$\tilde{B}(i, \tilde{R}) = \{B(i, R) \mid \forall j \in \{0, \ldots, 2^i-1\}, R[j] \in \tilde{R}[j]\}$$

Using the definitions of $\tilde{A}(i, \tilde{r}_1, \tilde{r}_2)$ and $\tilde{B}(i, \tilde{R})$, we can show that

$$\tilde{A}(i+1, \tilde{r}_1, \tilde{r}_2) \cap \tilde{B}(i, \tilde{R}) = \tilde{B}(i+1, \tilde{R}') \tag{1}$$
$$\tilde{R}'[j] = \tilde{R}[j] \cap \tilde{r}_1, \quad 0 \leq j < 2^i$$
$$\tilde{R}'[j] = \tilde{R}[j - 2^i] \cap \tilde{r}_2, \quad 2^i \leq j < 2^{i+1}$$

Equation 1 is also illustrated diagrammatically in Figure 5. The point to note is that if $\tilde{R}[0], \ldots, \tilde{R}[2^i-1]$ are all distinct sets of expressions, then the most succinct value graph representation of $\tilde{B}(i, \tilde{R})$ is as shown in Figure 5(b). If $\tilde{r}_1$ and $\tilde{r}_2$ are such that for all $0 \leq j_1, j_2 < 2^i$, the sets $\tilde{r}_1 \cap \tilde{R}[j_1]$, $\tilde{r}_2 \cap \tilde{R}[j_2]$ both non-empty and distinct, then the most succinct value graph representation of $\tilde{B}(i, \tilde{R}) \cap \tilde{A}(i+1, \tilde{r}_1, \tilde{r}_2)$ is as shown in Figure 5(c), whose representation is almost double the size of $\tilde{B}(i, \tilde{R})$ (even though it has fewer elements!).

Note that $\tilde{A}(1, \tilde{r}_1, \tilde{r}_2) = \tilde{B}(1, \tilde{R})$ where $\tilde{R}[1] = \tilde{r}_1$ and $\tilde{R}[2] = \tilde{r}_2$. Hence, using Equation 1, we can prove by induction on i that:

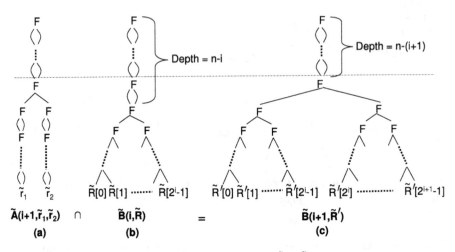

Fig. 5. Relationship between sets $\tilde{A}(i+1, \tilde{r}_1, \tilde{r}_2)$ and $\tilde{B}(i, \tilde{R})$. Nodes immediately below the horizontal dotted line are at the same depth $n - (i + 1)$ from the corresponding root nodes

Proposition 2. *For any $i \in \{1, .., n\}$, let $r_{i,1}$ and $r_{i,2}$ be some sets of expressions. For any integer j, let $j_n \ldots j_1$ be the binary representation of j. Then,*

$$\bigcap_{i=1}^{n} \tilde{A}(i, \tilde{r}_{i,1}, \tilde{r}_{i,2}) = \tilde{B}(n, \tilde{R})$$

$$\tilde{R}[j] = \bigcap_{i=1}^{n} \tilde{r}_{i,j_i+1}, \quad 0 \le j < 2^n$$

Our goal is to construct a program P_m such that it satisfies the equivalences $E_i = \{z = e \mid e \in \tilde{A}(i, \tilde{r}_{i,1}, \tilde{r}_{i,2})\}$ at the ith predecessor of some join point. Note that after the join point it will satisfy the equivalences $E = \{z = e \mid e \in \tilde{B}(n, \tilde{R})\}$, where $\tilde{B}(n, \tilde{R})$ is as defined in Proposition 2. The representation of E would require size exponential in n if the sets $\tilde{r}(i, 1)$ and $\tilde{r}(i, 2)$ are such that for each distinct choice of bits $j_1, .., j_n$, the set $\bigcap_{i=1}^{n} \tilde{r}_{i,j_i+1}$ is distinct and non-empty. This can be easily accomplished if the program has 2^n variables (by choosing sets $\tilde{r}(i, 1)$ and $\tilde{r}(i, 2)$ to contain an appropriate subset of the 2^n program variables such that $\bigcap_{i=1}^{n} \tilde{r}_{i,j_i+1}$ is a singleton set containing a distinct program variable). In the rest of this section, we show how to accomplish this using just n program variables (by choosing sets $\tilde{r}(i, 1)$ and $\tilde{r}(i, 2)$ to contain small terms constructed from just n program variables).

For any array $S[0 .. 2n-1]$ of expressions, let $C(S)$ denote the expression as shown in Figure 4(c). For any array $\tilde{S}[0 .. 2n-1]$ of sets of expressions, let $\tilde{C}(\tilde{S})$ denote the following set of expressions:

$$\tilde{C}(\tilde{S}) = \{C(S) \mid \forall i \in \{0, .., 2n - 1\}, S[i] \in \tilde{S}[i]\}$$

For any integer $i \in \{1,..,n\}$, $b \in \{1,2\}$, let $S_{i,b}[0..2n-1]$ be the following array of expressions,

$$S_{i,b}[j] = 1, \text{ if } j = 2(i-1) + b - 1$$
$$= 0, \text{ otherwise}$$

For any integer $i \in \{1,..,n\}$, $b \in \{1,2\}$, let $\tilde{S}_{i,b}[0..2n-1]$ be the following array of sets of expressions,

$$\tilde{S}_{i,b}[j] = \{x_i, 1\}, \text{ if } j = 2(i-1) + b - 1$$
$$= \{x_1,..,x_{i-1}, x_{i+1},..,x_n, 0\}, \text{ otherwise}$$

For any integer $j \in \{0,..,2^n-1\}$, let $j_n .. j_1$ be the binary representation of j. Let $T_j[0..2n-1]$ be the following array of expressions:

$$T_j[2(\ell-1) + j_\ell] = x_\ell, \quad 0 \le \ell < n$$
$$T_j[2(\ell-1) + 1 - j_\ell] = 0, \quad 0 \le \ell < n$$

Using the definitions of $\tilde{C}(\tilde{S})$, $\tilde{S}_{i,b}$ and $\tilde{T}_j)$, we can prove the following proposition.

Proposition 3. *Let $j \in \{0,..,2^n-1\}$. Let $j_n .. j_1$ be the binary representation of j. Then,*

$$\bigcap_{i=1}^{n} \tilde{C}(\tilde{S}_{i,j_i+1}) = \{C(T_j)\}$$

Note that $\tilde{C}(\tilde{S}_{i,b})$ are an appropriate choice for sets $\tilde{r}_{i,b}$. The following proposition, which follows from Proposition 2 and Proposition 3, summarizes the interesting property of these sets.

Proposition 4. *For any $i \in \{1,..,n\}$, Then,*

$$\bigcap_{i=1}^{n} \tilde{A}(i, \tilde{C}(\tilde{S}_{i,1}), \tilde{C}(\tilde{S}_{i,2})) = \{B(n,R)\}$$
$$R[j] = C(T_j), \quad 0 \le j < 2^n$$

4.2   The Program P_m

The program P_m, which contains an n-branch switch statement, is shown in Figure 6. It consists of $n+1$ local variables, $z, x_1, x_2,..,x_n$. The expressions a_i and b are defined below.

$$a_i = A(i, C(S_{i,1}), C(S_{i,2}))$$
$$b = B(n,R)$$
$$R[j] = C(T_j), \quad 0 \le j < 2^n$$

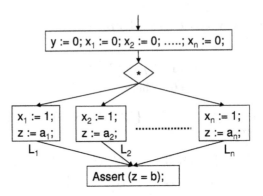

Fig. 6. The program P_m. The expressions a_i and b are defined in Section 4.2

Note that for all $i \in \{1, .., n\}$, $size(a_i) \leq 6n$. Thus, the size of program P_m is $O(n^2) = O(m^2)$. We now show that any value graph representation of the set of equivalences that hold at the end of the program P_m requires $\Theta(2^m)$ nodes. First note that it is important to maintain only equivalences of the form $x = e$ where x is a variable and e an expression. (This also follows from the fact that the SED data structure that we introduce in Section 3.1 can represent the set of equivalences at any program point). The following theorem implies that there is only one such equivalence, namely $z = b$, that holds at the end of program P_m.

Theorem 4. *Let E denote the set of all Herbrand equivalences of the form $x = e$ that are true at the end of the program P_m. Then,*

$$E = \{z = b\}$$

Proof. Let E_i denote the set of all Herbrand equivalences of the form $x = e$ that are true at point L_i in the program P_m. Then it is not difficult to see that:

$$E_i = \{z = e \mid e \in \tilde{A}(i, \tilde{C}(\tilde{S}_{i,1}), \tilde{C}(\tilde{S}_{i,2}))\} \cup \{x_i = 1\} \cup \{x_j = 0 \mid 1 \leq j \leq n, j \neq i\}$$

Using Proposition 4 we get:

$$E = \bigcap_{i=1}^{n} E_i = \{z = e \mid e \in \bigcap_{i=1}^{n} \tilde{A}(i, \tilde{C}(\tilde{S}_{i,1}), \tilde{C}(\tilde{S}_{i,2}))\}$$
$$= \{z = e \mid e \in \{b\}\} = \{z = b\}$$

Note that any value graph representation of expression b must have size $\Theta(2^n)$ since $R[j_1] \neq R[j_2]$ for $j_1 \neq j_2$. Hence, any value graph representation of the equivalence $z = b$ requires $\Theta(2^n) = \Theta(2^m)$ nodes.

5   Related Work

Kildall's Algorithm: Kildall's algorithm [7] performs an abstract interpretation over the lattice of sets of Herbrand equivalences. It represents the set of Herbrand equivalences at each program point by means of a structured partition.

The join operation for two structured partitions π_1 and π_2 is defined to be their intersection. Kildall's algorithm is complete in the sense that if it terminates, then the structured partition at any program point reflects all Herbrand equivalences that are true at that point. However, the complexity of Kildall's algorithm is exponential. The number of elements in a partition, and the size of each element in a partition can all be exponential in the number of join operations performed.

Alpern, Wegman and Zadeck's (AWZ) Algorithm: The AWZ algorithm [1] works on the value graph representation [8] of a program that has been converted to SSA form. A value graph can be represented by a collection of nodes of the form $\langle V, t \rangle$ where V is a set of variables, and the type t is either $\bot$, a constant c (indicating that the node has no successors), $F(n_1, n_2)$ or $\phi_m(n_1, n_2)$ (indicating that the node has two ordered successors n_1 and n_2). ϕ_m denotes the ϕ function associated with the mth join point in the program. Our data structure SED can be regarded as a special form of a value graph which is acyclic and has no ϕ-type nodes. The main step in the AWZ algorithm is to use congruence partitioning to merge some nodes of the value graph.

The AWZ algorithm cannot discover all equivalences among program terms. This is because it treats ϕ functions as uninterpreted. The ϕ functions are an abstraction of the if-then-else operator wherein the conditional in the if-then-else expression is abstracted away, but the two possible values of the if-then-else expression are retained. Hence, the ϕ functions satisfy the following two equations.

$$\forall e: \quad \phi_m(e, e) = e \tag{2}$$
$$\forall e_1, e_2, e_3, e_4: \quad \phi_m(F(e_1, e_2), F(e_3, e_4)) = F(\phi_m(e_1, e_3), \phi_m(e_2, e_4)) \tag{3}$$

Rüthing, Knoop and Steffen's (RKS) Algorithm: Like the AWZ algorithm, the RKS algorithm [12] also works on the value graph representation of a program that has been converted to SSA form. It tries to capture the semantics of ϕ functions by applying the following rewrite rules, which are based on equations 2 and 3, to convert program expressions into some normal form.

$$\langle V, \phi_m(n, n) \rangle \text{ and } n \;\rightarrow\; \langle V \cup Vars(n), Type(n) \rangle \tag{4}$$
$$\langle V, \phi_m(\langle V_1, F(n_1, n_2) \rangle, \langle V_2, F(n_3, n_4) \rangle) \rangle$$
$$\rightarrow\; \langle V, F(\langle \emptyset, \phi_m(n_1, n_3) \rangle, \langle \emptyset, \phi_m(n_2, n_4) \rangle) \rangle \tag{5}$$

Nodes on the left of the rewrite rules are replaced by the (new) node on the right, and incoming edges to nodes on the left are made to point to the new node. However, there is a precondition to applying the second rewriting rule.

$$P : \forall \text{ nodes } n \in succ^*(\{\langle V_1, F(n_1, n_2) \rangle, \langle V_2, F(n_3, n_4) \rangle\}), Vars(n) \neq \emptyset$$

The RKS algorithm assumes that all assignments are of the form $x := F(y, z)$ to make sure that for all original nodes n in the value graph, $Vars(n) \neq \emptyset$. This precondition is necessary in arguing termination for this system of rewrite rules, and proving the polynomial complexity bound. The RKS algorithm alternately applies the AWZ algorithm and the two rewrite rules until the value graph reaches a fixed point. Thus, the RKS algorithm discovers more equivalences than the AWZ algorithm.

The RKS algorithm cannot discover all equivalences even in acyclic programs. This is because the precondition P can prevent two equal expressions from reaching the same normal form. On the other hand lifting precondition P may result in the creation of an exponential number of new nodes, and an exponential number of applications of the rewrite rules. Such would be the case when, for example, the RKS algorithm is applied to the program P_m described in Section 4.

The RKS algorithm has another problem, which the authors have identified. It fails to discover all equivalences in cyclic programs, even if the precondition P is lifted. This is because the graph rewrite rules add a degree of pessimism to the iteration process. While congruence partitioning is optimistic, it relies on the result of the graph transformations which are pessimistic, as they are applied outside of the fixed point iteration process.

Gulwani and Necula's Randomized Algorithm: Recently, we gave a *randomized* polynomial-time algorithm that discovers all Herbrand equivalences among program terms [6]. This algorithm can also verify all Herbrand equivalences that are true at any point in a program. However, there is a small probability (over the choice of the random numbers chosen by the algorithm) that this algorithm deduces false equivalences. This algorithm is based on the idea of random interpretation, which involves performing abstract interpretation using randomized data structures and algorithms.

6   Conclusion and Future Work

We have given a polynomial-time algorithm for global value numbering. We have shown that there are programs for which the set of all equivalences contains terms whose value graph representation requires exponential size. This justifies the design of our algorithm, which discovers all equivalences among terms of size at most s in time that grows linearly with s.

An interesting theoretical question is to figure if there exist representations that may avoid the exponential lower bound for representing the set of all Herbrand equivalences.

The next step is to perform experiments to compare the different algorithms with regard to running time and number of equivalences discovered. Results of our algorithm can also be used as a benchmark to estimate the incompleteness of the existing algorithms.

An interesting direction of future work is to extend this algorithm to perform precise inter-procedural value numbering. It would also be useful to extend the algorithm to reason about some properties of program operators like commutativity, associativity or both.

Acknowledgments

This research was supported in part by the National Science Foundation Grants CCR-9875171, CCR-0085949, CCR-0081588, CCR-0234689, CCR-0326577, CCR-00225610, and gifts from Microsoft Research. The information presented here does not necessarily reflect the position or the policy of the Government and no official endorsement should be inferred.

References

1. B. Alpern, M. N. Wegman, and F. K. Zadeck. Detecting equality of variables in programs. In *15th Annual ACM Symposium on Principles of Programming Languages*, pages 1–11. ACM, 1988.
2. C. Click. Global code motion/global value numbering. In *Proccedings of the ACM SIGPLAN '95 Conference on Programming Language Design and Implementation*, pages 246–257, June 1995.
3. P. Cousot and R. Cousot. Abstract interpretation: A unified lattice model for static analysis of programs by construction or approximation of fixpoints. In *4th Annual ACM Symposium on Principles of Programming Languages*, pages 234–252, 1977.
4. R. Cytron, J. Ferrante, B. K. Rosen, M. N. Wegman, and F. K. Zadeck. Efficiently computing static single assignment form and the control dependence graph. *ACM Transactions on Programming Languages and Systems*, 13(4):451–490, Oct. 1990.
5. K. Gargi. A sparse algorithm for predicated global value numbering. In *Proceedings of the ACM SIGPLAN 2002 Conference on Programming Language Design and Implementation*, volume 37, 5, pages 45–56. ACM Press, June 17–19 2002.
6. S. Gulwani and G. C. Necula. Global value numbering using random interpretation. In *31st Annual ACM Symposium on POPL*. ACM, Jan. 2004.
7. G. A. Kildall. A unified approach to global program optimization. In *1st ACM Symposium on Principles of Programming Language*, pages 194–206, Oct. 1973.
8. S. S. Muchnick. *Advanced Compiler Design and Implementation*. Morgan Kaufmann, San Francisco, 2000.
9. G. C. Necula. Translation validation for an optimizing compiler. In *Proceedings of the ACM SIGPLAN '00 Conference on Programming Language Design and Implementation*, pages 83–94. ACM SIGPLAN, June 2000.
10. A. Pnueli, M. Siegel, and E. Singerman. Translation validation. In B. Steffen, editor, *Tools and Algorithms for Construction and Analysis of Systems, 4th International Conference*, volume LNCS 1384, pages 151–166. Springer, 1998.
11. B. K. Rosen, M. N. Wegman, and F. K. Zadeck. Global value numbers and redundant computations. In *15th Annual ACM Symposium on Principles of Programming Languages*, pages 12–27. ACM, 1988.
12. O. Rüthing, J. Knoop, and B. Steffen. Detecting equalities of variables: Combining efficiency with precision. In *Static Analysis Symposium*, volume 1694 of *Lecture Notes in Computer Science*, pages 232–247. Springer, 1999.
13. M. N. Wegman and F. K. Zadeck. Constant propagation with conditional branches. *ACM Transactions on Programming Languages and Systems*, 13(2):181–210, Apr. 1991.

Quantitative Shape Analysis

Radu Rugina

Computer Science Department, Cornell University, Ithaca, NY 14853
rugina@cs.cornell.edu

Abstract. This paper presents a static analysis that computes quantitative information for recursive heap structures in programs with destructive updates. The
algorithm targets tree structures and is able to extract quantitative information
about the height and the balancing of such structures. We formulate the algorithm as a dataflow analysis. We use a heap abstraction that captures both shape
invariants and quantities of heap structures. Then, we give a precise specification
of the transfer functions that describe how each statement updates this abstraction. The algorithm is able to verify the correctness of re-balancing operations
after AVL tree insertions.

1 Introduction

Dynamic data structures represent fundamental constructs in virtually all programming
languages. To check or enforce the correctness of programs that manipulate such structures, the compiler must automatically extract invariants that describe their *shapes*. For
programs with destructive updates, the task of identifying the invariants is significantly
more complex because such programs temporarily invalidate them. Examples include
even simple operations such as inserting or removing elements from a list. The challenge is to identify that the invariants hold after the execution of destructive operations.

In the past decades, researchers have developed a number of shape analysis algorithms that identify various properties of the heap, including aliasing, sharing, cyclicity,
or reachability [18]. Such properties allow the compiler to distinguish between trees
and arbitrary graphs, or between cyclic and acyclic lists. However, little work has been
done to characterize *quantitative information* of heap structures, such as the height, the
balancing, or the number of nodes or edges in such structures.

This paper presents a quantitative shape analysis algorithm that is able to verify invariants about the balancing of tree structures. To the best of our knowledge, none of
the existing techniques are able to check such invariants for programs with destructive
updates. The difficulty of quantitative shape analysis lies in the fact that it combines
two complex analysis problems: shape analysis, where the compiler must statically reason about unbounded numbers of heap locations; and quantitative symbolic analysis,
where the compiler must reason about numbers, symbolic quantities, and arithmetic.
This paper proposes a solution to this problem using dataflow analysis.

Our algorithm uses a heap abstraction that combines shape information and quantitative information, and computes both of them simultaneously. Computing shape is
required because quantitative properties may depend on the shape of the structure. For
example, one can talk about height or balancing only for non-cyclic structures. To provide a unified framework, our analysis captures shape information simply as another

R. Giacobazzi (Ed.): SAS 2004, LNCS 3148, pp. 228–245, 2004.

quantity: the reference count, which represents the number of incoming pointers to a given heap location.

The abstraction in our analysis consists of a points-to graph (whose nodes model heap locations), augmented with quantitative information. The analysis captures quantities in three forms. First, it keeps track of *quantitative attributes* for nodes, such as the reference count $n.c$ of a node n, its height $n.h$, and its skew $n.s$, defined as the height difference between its children. Second, it keeps track of *quantitative predicates* (or *invariants*), which describe the desired properties and are expressed in terms of the quantitative attributes. For instance, the balancing predicate is $B(n) = (-1 \leq n.s \leq 1)$ and the tree-ness (or unaliasing) predicate is $U(n) = (n.c \leq 1)$. Finally, the analysis keeps track of *auxiliary relations* that describe key pieces of information not directly captured by predicates. For our algorithm, these are relations that describe the height difference between nodes which don't necessarily have the same parents.

As in the case of other shape analyses for languages with destructive updates, the main difficulty is that the shape and the quantitative invariants (i.e., the predicates) may be temporarily broken during updating operations. To solve this problem, the analysis "zooms in" on the particular heap locations that are primarily involved in the destructive update, keeping track of numeric values for their attributes and keeping track of auxiliary relations. This information enables the analysis to determine that the invariants hold again after the update operations. This is the standard approach taken by state-of-the-art shape analyses [16, 17, 9]. Our contribution is to show how the compiler can achieve this goal when reasoning about heap quantities.

Unlike standard points-to and shape analyses, our algorithm focuses just on accurate results: when the information in the abstraction becomes somewhat imprecise, the analysis turns it into a top value. Continuing the analysis at that point would likely yield results that are too imprecise to be meaningful; in contrast, giving up and using a top value substantially simplifies parts of the algorithm. This situation happens, for instance, when the program traverses the field of a structure, but the analysis cannot determine that the resulting location is unaliased. This is also reflected in the fact that the analysis computes "must" points-to information, where each node may point to at most one other node.

The list below summarizes the key properties of our algorithm:

1. It simultaneously computes points-to information, shape and quantitative information in a unified framework. Shape is captured via the reference count quantity;
2. It subsumes shape analysis. In particular, it can successfully handle the canonical in-place list reversal example [16, 17];
3. It keeps track of numeric quantities and auxiliary relations to be able to determine that the desired quantitative invariants hold after destructive operations;
4. It it pessimistic: once the accuracy of the analysis information degrades up to a certain level, the analysis gives up and returns a top element.

The remainder of the paper is organized as follows. Section 2 presents an example. Section 3 presents the shape analysis algorithm and shows how the algorithm works for the example. Finally, Section 4 discusses related work and we present future research directions in Section 5.

```
1:   y = x.left;
2:   if (y.val == 1) {
3:       x.val = 0;
4:       y.val = 0;
5:       z = y.right;
6:       y.right = x;
7:       x.left = z;
8:   }
```

Fig. 1. Example: one of the eight possible cases for re-balancing AVL trees after insertion. Initially, the tree rooted at x has a skew of 2. The field val contains the skew value.

2   Example

Figure 1 presents an example program that our analysis is designed to handle. This is a fragment of the code that re-balances AVL trees after insertions. We use the following terms to define AVL trees. The *skew* (or *skewing factor*) of a tree is the difference between the height of its left and its right child. A tree is *balanced* if it has a skew between -1 and 1. Then, an *AVL tree* is a binary search tree such that, for each node in the tree, the subtree rooted at that node is balanced.

An insertion into an AVL tree starts by inserting the new element as a leaf in the tree. As a result, many subtrees may become no longer balanced. The insertion process walks up the tree from the leaf to the root, and re-balances internal nodes using rotations. At each point during this bottom-up traversal, it examines the current node. Depending on the skew of this node and its children, the program must examine eight possible cases; some of them require a single rotation, others require two rotations.

The code from Figure 1 presents the code for one of these eight cases. This code is written in a Java-like language. Each heap cell contains four fields: left and right are the children nodes; val is an integer field that represents the skew of the current node; and data is the data field. For the purpose of re-balancing, the data field is irrelevant and doesn't show up in this code fragment. Variable x points to the currently analyzed node; node y is the left child of x and z is the right child of y. The case being considered here is that where x is imbalanced to the left, with a skew of 2, and y is balanced, but skewed to the left with a skew of 1. In this case, the program updates the skew factors for x and y (at lines 3 and 4), and then performs a rotation to the left (lines 5, 6 and 7).

We want to prove the following property. If, before line 1, we know that:

1. the structure rooted at x is a tree; and
2. the skew of x is 2; and
3. all nodes other than x are balanced and the values in their val fields correctly describe their skews.

then, after this code fragment (after line 7), the following conditions hold:

1. the structure rooted at y is a tree; and
2. all nodes are balanced and the val fields correctly describe their skews.

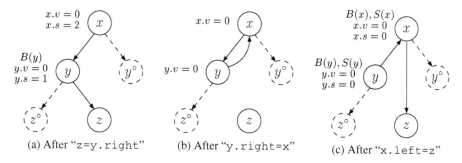

(a) After "z=y.right"   (b) After "y.right=x"   (c) After "x.left=z"

Fig. 2. Points-to and quantitative information at three program points during the rotation.

2.1 Proving the Property

The program looks very simple: it contains six assignments, one if statement, and no loops. However, checking the desired property is a non-trivial task: it requires reasoning about the skews and heights of various subtrees, and performing arithmetic on these quantities.

Figure 2 describes the key pieces of information at selected points in the program, after lines 5, 6 and 7. The graphs in these figures encode points-to information: nodes labeled x, y, and z represent the heap locations that each of these variables point to; and the edges represent points-to relations between them. The nodes and edges showed with dashed lines and circles are not being accessed by the program, but they play an important role in proving the property. These nodes, y° and z°, represent the siblings of y and z; in the rest of the paper, we refer to such nodes as the *duals* of y and z.

For each of the selected program points, Figure 2 shows the quantitative information for nodes x and y. For each node n, we show the following: the attribute $n.v$, representing the value stored in its val field; the attribute $n.s$, representing its skew; the balancing predicate $B(n)$, which shows whether or not n is balanced; and the skewing consistency predicate $S(n)$, which indicates whether or not $n.v$ and $n.s$ are the same. If an attribute or predicate is not shown for x or y, it means that its precise value cannot be determined statically. Predicates B and S hold for all of the heap locations not represented by nodes in these graphs.

Figure 2(a) shows the following information after the assignment at line 5: x has skew value 2, because of the assumption at the beginning of the program; attributes $x.v$ and $y.v$ are each 0 because of the assignments at lines 3 and 4; $B(y)$ shows that y is balanced; and y has a skew of 1, because of the test condition at line 2 and the fact that $S(y)$ was true at that point. However, several of the facts that we want to prove do not hold at this point: x is not balanced, $S(x)$ does not hold, and neither does $S(y)$.

The situation at the next program point gets even worse: Figure 2(b) shows that the assignment y.right=x makes the structure become cyclic, with a cycle between x and y. We can no longer talk about skewing or balancing for these nodes. Therefore, all of $x.s$, $y.s$, and $B(y)$ become undefined.

However, Figure 2(c) shows that we can recover all of the desired B and S predicates for x and y after the assignment x.left=z (even though none of them held at the previous program point). The key piece of information that enables us to do so is the relation between the relative heights of nodes y°, z, and z°; this information is not explicitly shown in Figure 2. Let us denote by $n.h$ the height attribute of n. We can use the following reasoning. At the program point for Figure 2(a), the skewing factors of y and x are $y.s = 1$ and $x.s = 2$, so:

$$z^\circ.h = z.h + 1 \tag{1}$$

$$y.h = y^\circ.h + 2 \tag{2}$$

Further, because y is skewed to the left, its height is 1 plus the height of its left child:

$$y.h = z^\circ.h + 1 \tag{3}$$

Now observe that the following two assignments (`y.right=x` and `x.left=z`) update x and y, but leave the structures rooted at y°, z, and z° unchanged. We therefore keep equation (1) and eliminate attribute of y from equations (2) and (3):

$$z^\circ.h = z.h + 1 \tag{4}$$

$$y^\circ.h + 2 = z^\circ.h + 1 \tag{5}$$

These facts imply that:
$$z.h = y^\circ.h \tag{6}$$

Because the structures rooted at y°, z, and z° remain unchanged, relations (4), (5), and (6) hold at all program points. Hence, we can use these equations to prove the desired invariants at the end of the program. Given the points-to relations from Figure 2(c), the skew of x is:

$$x.s = z.h - y^\circ.h = 0 \tag{7}$$

The fact that $z.h = y^\circ.h$ (from relation (6)) also implies that the height of x is equal to $z.h + 1$, since both of its children have the same height. Given the points-to relations of y after the update, its skew is:

$$y.s = z^\circ.h - x.h = z^\circ.h - (z.h + 1) = 0 \tag{8}$$

Finally, we can compare $x.s$ to $x.v$, 1, and -1, and $y.s$ to $y.v$, 1, and -1, to conclude that all of $B(x)$, $S(x)$, $B(y)$, and $S(y)$ hold again at the end of the true branch.

2.2   Shape Information

The argument above implicitly assumed that all of the nodes in the points-to graphs from Figure 2 are distinct, and that traversing edges via the assignments `y = x.next` or `z = y.right` does not create back edges from y to x, or from z to y. All of these facts hold because the original structure is a tree. Hence, shape information is critical and reasoning about quantities requires reasoning about shapes as well.

One easy way to incorporate shape information in our framework is to add one more quantitative attribute that describes shapes: the reference count. Given a node n, the reference count attribute $n.c$ represents the number of incoming pointers from other heap locations. A structure is a tree if its root has a reference count 0, and all of the nodes reachable from the root have reference counts of 1.

Similarly to the other quantitative invariants, the tree invariant is temporarily broken in our example. After the assignment y.right=x the structure becomes cyclic: at that point, reference counts of x and y are both 1, so none of them can be the root of the tree. However, the assignment x.left=z changes the count of z to 1, and that of y to zero, thus making the structure be a tree rooted at y. Hence, shape is just a particular quantitative invariant and quantitative analysis generalizes shape analysis.

Note that swapping assignments in lines 6 and 7 produces the same final result, but a different intermediate shape state: in that case there is no cycle, but node z will temporarily have a reference count of 2. That count will decrease to 1 after the last assignment.

2.3   Required Analysis Information

To be able to prove the desired property for the example discussed in this section, an analysis must keep track of the following pieces of information:

1. *Points-to information*: it must distinguish the heap locations that program variables reference and must identify points-to relations between those locations;
2. *Shape information:* it must keep track of reference counts and it must be able to precisely identify when cyclic structures and heap locations with multiple incoming references temporarily arise in the program;
3. *Quantitative information*: it must keep track of numeric values for quantities, of invariants between quantitites, and of key auxiliary relations that can enable the recovery of the invariants after destructive updates.

3   Algorithm

In this section we describe the proposed quantitative shape analysis algorithm in detail. We consider programs which manipulate recursive heap structures. Each structure has a set of field selectors. These fields include pointer fields, which hold references to other structures, and integer fields, which hold integer quantities relevant to the invariants that the analysis wants to extract. Our algorithm targets tree structures, hence there are exactly two pointer fields; also, each structure holds one integer field which models skewing. Let V_p be the set of program variables, $F_f = \{f_1, f_2\}$ the set of pointer fields (where f_1 is the left selector and f_2 is the right selector field), and $F_v = \{v\}$ the set of integer fields in our case.

We assume a program representation consisting of a control-flow graph. Each node in the graph is a statement of one of the following forms:

$$x = \text{null} \qquad x = \text{new} \qquad x = y$$
$$x = y.f \qquad x.f = y \qquad x.v = c \qquad \text{if } (x.v == c)$$

where $x, y \in V_p$ are program variables, $f \in F_f$ is a pointer field, v is the (unique) integer field, and $c \in \mathbb{Z}$ ranges over integer constants. We use a dot notation for field accesses, for instance $x.f$, $y.f$, or $x.v$ (node attributes use a similar notation, e.g., $n.s$ or $n.h$, but one can distinguish between them because we use different letters for variables and nodes). The above assignments include dynamic allocations ($x = $ new), nullification assignments ($x = $ null), copy, load, and store assignments of heap references, as well as assignments of constants to integer fields of structures. Furthermore, the analysis uses the information in conditional tests that compare integer fields against constant values: if ($x.v == c$). Without loss of generality, we assume that the variables in each load and store assignment are distinct; and that each non-null assignment $x = \ldots$ is preceded by $x = $ null, if there is a non-null definition of x that reaches the assignment.

3.1 Concrete Heaps and Properties

The concrete heap consists of a special null location and a set L of heap locations, which form a tree structure. We inductively define the quantities $height(l)$ and $skew(l)$ for the substructure rooted at location l using the standard inductive definitions:

$$\text{Height:} \quad \begin{aligned} l.height &= \max(height(l.f_1), height(l.f_2)) + 1 \quad &\text{if } l \neq \text{null} \\ l.height &= 0 &\text{if } l = \text{null} \end{aligned}$$

$$\text{Skew:} \quad \begin{aligned} l.skew &= height(l.f_1) - height(l.f_2) \quad &\text{if } l \neq \text{null} \\ l.skew &= 0 &\text{if } l = \text{null} \end{aligned}$$

If the structure rooted at l contains cycles, then these equations do not have solutions over natural numbers $\mathbb{Z}$. In that case, the height and skew have an unknown value: $height(l) = skew(l) = unk$. Hence, these quantities take values over $\mathbb{Z}_u = \mathbb{Z} \cup \{unk\}$.

If $val(l) \in \mathbb{Z}$ is the integer field of location l, and $refcount(l) \in \mathbb{N}$ is the reference count of l, the goal of the analysis is to determine that the following properties hold at the end of the program for all locations $l \in L$:

$$\begin{aligned} &\textit{Balancing}: \quad &-1 \leq skew(l) \leq 1 \\ &\textit{Consistent skews}: \quad &val(l) = skew(l) \\ &\textit{Unaliasing}: \quad &refcount(l) \leq 1 \end{aligned}$$

3.2 Abstraction

We define the heap abstraction as follows. For each variable $x \in V_p$, there is a dual variable x°. Whenever a variable x is being assigned field f_1 of some other variable y, the analysis automatically assigns x° to field f_2 of y. Similarly, when x traverses field f_2, x° traverses field f_1. Let V_p° be the set of dual variables: $V_p^\circ = \{x^\circ \mid x \in V_p\}$ and V the set of all variables: $V = V_p \cup V_p^\circ$.

The analysis uses four attributes: s is the skew of a node, v is the value stored in the integer field, c is the reference count, and h is the height of a node. These abstract attributes model the concrete quantities $skew(l)$, $val(l)$, $refcount(l)$, and $height(l)$ for locations $l \in L$. We classify the attributes into a set of *main attributes* $A_m = \{s, v, c\}$ and a set of *auxiliary attributes* $A_a = \{h\}$. The values of main attributes directly characterize the quantitative invariants; auxiliary attributes provide indirect information about the invariants, via the auxiliary relations.

The abstract information is a pair $I = (G, Q)$ consisting of an abstract heap G and an abstract quantitative information Q. The heap is a pair $G = (N, E)$, where:

- $N \subseteq \mathcal{P}(V)$ is a set of *abstract nodes*. A node $n \subseteq V$ models the heap location that is pointed to exactly by the variables in n. There is a distinguished node $n_s = \emptyset$ representing the summary node, which models all of the heap locations not pointed to by any variables. We denote by N_i the set of all individual nodes, i.e., $N_i = N - \{n_s\}$.
- $E : N \to ((N \cup \{\bot, \top\}) \times (N \cup \{\bot, \top\}))$ describes *points-to relations* between nodes. If $n, p, q \in N$ and $E(n) = (p, q)$, then p and q are the children of n. If p or q is $\bot$, then the corresponding child is null; if one of them is $\top$, then the corresponding child is not precisely known; and if p or q is a node in N, then the corresponding child is either null, or points to the location that p or q represents. Note that each field can point to at most one other node, hence this can be regarded as "must" information.

The abstract quantitative information is a triple $Q = (A, P, R)$, where:

- $A : (N_i \times A_m) \to (\mathbb{Z} \cup \{\top\})$ provides *numeric values* for the main attributes of individual nodes. A top value $\top$ indicates that a precise numeric value is not known. We write $n.a$ as an alternate notation for $A(n, a)$.
- P is a set of *predicates* (or *invariants*) for all nodes, including the summary node. For this analysis, $P : N \to \mathbb{T}^3$ (where $\mathbb{T} = \{0, 1\}$ is the two-valued logic) describes, for each node n, the truth values of the following three predicates:

$$B(n) = (-1 \le n.s \le 1)$$
$$S(n) = (n.s = n.v)$$
$$U(n) = (n.c \le 1)$$

These correspond to the balancing, consistent skewing, and unaliasing properties. A value of 1 (true) indicates that the invariant holds; a value of 0 (false) indicates that it is unknown whether or not the invariant holds. For the summary node, a value of 1 indicates that the invariant holds for all of the heap locations that the node models. We denote by $P_k(n)$, with $k = 1..3$, the projection of $P(n)$ on the k-th component (i.e, P_1 is B, P_2 is S, and P_3 is U).
- R is a set of *auxiliary relations* between the auxiliary attributes A_a of the individual nodes N_i. For our analysis, R consists of linear equations between height attributes: $n.h = n'.h + c$. We use a canonical representation of these equations in the form of a table $R : ((N_i \cup \bot) \times A_a)^2 \to (\mathbb{Z} \cup \{\top\})$. Each entry $R(n.h, n'.h) = c$ models a relation $n.h = n'.h + c$. Again, $\bot$ represents null values and $\top$ models unknown values. Despite the fact that the table may contain redundant information, we use this model to simplify the presentation of the analysis. A more compact representation can keep track only of linearly independent relations $R(n.h, n'.h) \ne \top$.

Besides the pairs (G, Q), we define a top information $\top_i$, which models imprecise information about all components. The analysis uses $\top_i$ to give up when it determines that the information has already become inaccurate and it is unlikely that it will become accurate again. Being able to do so simplifies parts of the analysis. There is also a bottom information $\bot_i$, used as initial value at all program points.

3.3 Consistency of Heap Abstraction

The key fact that enables the analysis to recover the quantitative information after destructive operations is that it maintains consistency relations between the skew of each node and the height difference of its children. More precisely, consider nodes $n \in N_i$, $p \in N_i \cup \{\bot\}$, and $q \in N_i \cup \{\bot\}$, where at least one of p and q is not null. If $E(n) = (p, q)$, the abstraction is such that:

$$n.s = c \in \mathbb{Z} \iff R(p.h, q.h) = c \in \mathbb{Z} \qquad (9)$$

In that case, the analysis guarantees that:

$$c \geq 0 \implies R(n.h, p.h) = 1 \qquad (10)$$
$$c \leq 0 \implies R(n.h, q.h) = 1 \qquad (11)$$
$$n.v = c \implies S(n) = 1 \qquad (12)$$
$$-1 \leq c \leq 1 \implies B(n) = 1 \qquad (13)$$

At load statements, the analysis uses the left-to-right implication in equation (9) to derive new auxiliary relations. After destructive updates via store assignments, the analysis uses the right-to-left implication in (9) to recover attribute values and predicates.

3.4 Notations

We use the following notations. Given a set of nodes N, we denote by $nodes(x)$ all of the nodes that contain x: $nodes(x) = \{n \mid n \in N \land x \in n\}$. Given $I = ((N, E), (A, P, R))$, a node $n \in N_i$ and another node $n' \in \mathcal{P}(V)$, we write $I[n'/n]$ for the substitution of node n with node n' into I. If $n' \notin N$, the substitution replaces n with n' in N and in the domains of E, A, P, and R. If $n' \in N$, it removes node n from N and from the domains of E, A, P, R, and merges the information of n into that of n' using the merge operation defined in Section 3.6 (if $n' = n_s$, it only merges the information of E and P).

Given a map m, then $m[x \mapsto v]$ extends the map with a new value for x, if $x \notin dom(m)$, or updates the map with a new value for x, if $x \in dom(m)$. We write $m[x_1 \mapsto v_1]..[x_k \mapsto v_k]$ to denote a sequence of updates (or extensions). If S is a set, then $m[x \mapsto v]_{x \in S}$ updates (or extends) the map for all elements in S. Finally, if b is a condition, then $m[b \Rightarrow x \mapsto v]$ conditionally updates (or extends) the map m with a new value for x, if b is true.

3.5 Analysis of Statements

This section presents in detail the transfer functions for statements in the program. Given an abstract information I before statement s, we describe the resulting information I' after the statement. Test conditions if (...) yield two outcomes: a new piece of information I' on the true branch, and unchanged information $I'' = I$ on the false branch.

If the input information is either top $I = \top_i$ or bottom $I = \bot_i$, then the resulting information is the same $I' = I$. Otherwise, if $I = ((N, E), (A, P, R))$, the analysis computes I', which is either a tuple $I' = ((N', E'), (A', P', R'))$, or is top $I' = \top_i$. The cases below show how the analysis computes I' for each statement in the program.

Case $\boxed{x = \text{null}}$ For nullification statements, the analysis nullifies both variable x and its dual x°. The resulting information is $I' = I[n'_1/n_1] \ldots [n'_k/n_k]$, where $n_1, \ldots, n_k$ represents an ordered sequence of the nodes in the set $nodes(x) \cup nodes(x^\circ)$ and $n'_i = n_i - \{x, x^\circ\}$ for all $i = 1..k$.

Case $\boxed{x = y}$ The resulting information is $I' = I[n'_1/n_1] \ldots [n'_k/n_k]$, where $n_1, \ldots, n_k$ is an ordered sequence of the set $nodes(y)$ and $n'_i = n_i \cup \{x\}$. In particular, if $nodes(y) = \emptyset$, then $I' = I$.

Case $\boxed{x = \text{new}}$ The resulting information $I' = ((N', E'), (A', P', R'))$ is:

$$N' = N \cup \{\{x\}\}$$
$$E' = E[\{x\} \mapsto (\bot, \bot)]$$
$$A' = A[(\{x\}, s) \mapsto 0, (\{x\}, v) \mapsto 0, (\{x\}, c) \mapsto 0]$$
$$P' = P[\{x\} \mapsto (1, 1, 1)]$$

In other words, the allocation produces a node with null children (E), with zero attributes (A), and with true predicates (P). For R', the analysis sets all of the relations of $\{x\}$ to $\top$, except $R(\{x\}.h, \bot.h) = 1$ and $R(\bot.h, \{x\}.h) = -1$.

Case $\boxed{x = y.f}$ Assume that f is the first field: $f = f_1$ (the other case is symmetric). For each such assignment, the algorithm manufactures an additional load for the dual, on the opposite field: $x^\circ = y.f_2$. It then analyzes the sequence of the two loads. Their analysis is similar, so we present just the processing of $x = y.f$.

Consider that $nodes(y) \neq \emptyset$ (otherwise, y is null and this assignment is guaranteed to produce a run-time error). The analysis examines the set $nodes(y)$. For each node $n_y \in nodes(y)$, the analysis traverses the field f of n_y and produces a new information I'_y. After analyzing all of the nodes that contain y, the algorithm merges all of the resulting pieces of information I'_y to derive the new information I' after the assignment.

We present how the algorithm computes each I'_y by analyzing node $n_y \in nodes(y)$. The algorithm inspects the points-to relations of n_y and considers the following cases:

- If $E(n_y) = (\bot, *)$, where "$*$" is a wildcard symbol, then $I'_y = I$ (since the field is null).
- If $E(n_y) = (\top, *)$, then $I'_y = \top_i$ (the analysis is aborted, because it is unknown where the left field of y points to).
- If $E(n_y) = (n, *)$, where $n \in N_i$, then $I'_y = I[(n \cup \{x\})/n]$.
- If $E(n_y) = (n_s, *)$ and $U(n_s) = 0$, then $I'_y = \top_i$ (the analysis is aborted, because the locations in the summary node may be aliased).

- If $E(n_y) = (n_s, *)$ and $U(n_s) = 1$, then the analysis creates a new node $n_x = \{x\}$ via materialization [15, 16]. Let $u \in N \cup \{\bot, \top\}$ such that $E(n_y) = (n_s, u)$. The resulting components of $I'_y = ((N', E'), (A', P', R'))$, except R, are:

$$N' = N \cup \{n_x\}$$
$$E' = E\,[\,n_y \mapsto (n_x, u), n_x \mapsto E(n_s)\,]$$
$$A' = A\,[\,(n_x, s) \mapsto \top, (n_x, v) \mapsto \top, (n_x, c) \mapsto 1\,]$$
$$P' = P\,[\,n_x \mapsto P(n_s)\,]$$

Note that if $u = n_s$, then the dual of x is also being materialized by the dual load statement. In other words, the analysis performs a "double materialization" in that case.

For R, the analysis enforces the consistency of the abstraction. It inspects the value of u and the skew of n_y and determines the following relations:

$$\text{if } n_y.s = c \in \mathbb{Z} \wedge u \in N_i \cup \{\bot\} \quad \text{then } R(n_x.h, u.h) = c$$
$$\text{if } n_y.s = c \geq 0 \qquad\qquad\qquad\quad \text{then } R(n_y.h, n_x.h) = 1$$

The analysis adds all of these new relations to R'. Then, it computes the closure of the resulting table R': it deduces other relations for $n_x.h$ using the relations of n_y. Finally, it sets all of the remaining relations of $n_x.h$ to $\top$.

Case $\boxed{x.f = y}$ This statement destructively updates the heap. As a result, many of the existing attributes, quantities, and relations become no longer valid. The algorithm analyzes such a statement in two steps: it first invalidates all of the quantitative information for nodes that have been affected by the update; then, it tries to derive quantitative information for the new structure, based on the available information in the auxiliary relations.

As in the case of load statements, the sets $nodes(x)$ and $nodes(y)$ may contain zero, one, or more nodes. If $nodes(x)$ is empty, that corresponds to a definite run-time error. If $nodes(y)$ is empty, then y is null and the assignment nullifies a field of x; we discuss this situation at the end of this case. Finally, if $nodes(x)$ and $nodes(y)$ each contain multiple nodes, then we analyze each pair of nodes $n_x \in nodes(x)$ and $n_y \in nodes(y)$, and combine the results. We next show the analysis of the store statement for such a pair (n_x, n_y) of nodes.

Step 1. First, the algorithm invalidates the quantitative information that no longer holds because of the destructive update, and produces a tuple $I'' = ((N, E''), (A'', P'', R''))$. To determine what pieces of information to invalidate, the analysis must compute the new points-to relations. Assume that, before the statement, the points-to information for n_x is $E(n_x) = (u_1, u_2)$, where $u_1, u_2 \in N \cup \{\bot, \top\}$. Then:

$$E'' = E\,[\,n_x \mapsto (n_y, u_2)\,]$$

Then, the analysis computes a set $K \subseteq N$ of nodes that may reach n_x; the quantitative information regarding skewing and height must be invalidated (killed) for all nodes in K. The set K is defined inductively as follows:

- if $E''(n) = (p, q)$ and $(x \in p \cup q) \vee (p = \top) \vee (q = \top)$, then $n \in K$;
- if $E''(n) = (p, q)$ and $(p \in K) \vee (q \in K)$, then $n \in K$;

The information after invalidating skews and heights, and after updating reference counts is:

$$A'' = A\,[(n,s) \mapsto \top]_{n\in K}\,[(n_y,c) \mapsto A(n_y,c)+1]\,[(u_1 \in N_i) \Rightarrow (u_1,c)$$
$$\qquad \mapsto A(u_1,c)-1]$$
$$P'' = P\,[n \mapsto (0,0,P_3(n)]_{n\in K}$$
$$R'' = R\,[(n.h,m.h) \mapsto \top]_{n\in K, m\in N\cup\{\bot\}}\,[(m.h,n.h) \mapsto \top]_{n\in K, m\in N\cup\{\bot\}}$$

Step 2. In the second step, the analysis enforces the consistency relation from Section 3.3. The algorithm looks for nodes n such that:

(C1) the skew is unknown: $n.s = \top$;
(C2) the new points-to relation is precisely known: $H''(n) = (p,q)$, with $p \neq \top$ and $q \neq \top$;
(C3) the height difference between its children is precisely known: $R''(p.h,q.h) = c \in \mathbb{Z}$.

In that case, the algorithm derives new quantitative information for n as follows:

$$A(n,s) = c$$
$$B(n) = (-1 \leq c \leq 1)$$
$$S(n) = (A(n,v) = c)$$
$$R(n.h,p.h) = 1, \quad \text{if } c \geq 0$$
$$R(n.h,q.h) = 1, \quad \text{if } c \leq 0$$

and computes the closure of the set of linear equations. The algorithm repeatedly performs this process until none of the nodes meet the above criteria. Note that deriving new information for a node may make the criteria for other nodes become true, which is why the analysis must iterate. The result of the fixed-point process is the final information I'. This completes the analysis of this step and of the statement for a pair (n_x, n_y) of nodes.

We briefly discuss the case where there is no node in N that contains y before the statement $x.f = y$. In other words y is null (so this situation is similar to handling a statement of the form $x.f = \texttt{null}$, if such a statement were in the language). The only changes occur in Step 1, in the places where n_y shows up in the formulas of E'' and A''. These formulas become:

$$E'' = E\,[n_x \mapsto (\bot, u_2)]$$
$$A'' = A\,[n.s = \top]_{n\in K}\,[(u_1 \in N_i) \Rightarrow (u_1,c) \mapsto A(u_1,c)-1]$$

Case $\boxed{x.v = c}$ This case represents assignments that update the integer fields of heap structures. The analysis updates the attribute v and the truth value of the skewing consistency predicate for all of the nodes that contain x. The resulting information is $I' = ((N,E),(A',P',R))$, where:

$$A' = A\,[(n,v) \mapsto c]_{x\in n}$$
$$P' = P\,[n \mapsto (P_1(n),(A(n,s) = c),P_3(n))]_{x\in n}$$

Case $\boxed{\text{if } (x.v == c)}$ This case tests the value of the integer field of an element of a structure. The analysis incorporates this information into the abstraction on the true branch. On the false branch, it leaves the abstraction unchanged. The resulting information on the true branch is $I' = ((N, E), (A', P, R))$, where:

$$A' = A \left[(n, v) \mapsto c\right]_{x \in n} \left[P_2(n) \Rightarrow (n, s) \mapsto c\right]_{x \in n}$$

Hence, only attributes change: the algorithm sets the value attribute of nodes of x to c, and, if the skewing consistency condition is true, it also sets the s attributes to c. Therefore, test conditions provide a way to gather information about the skewing of the constructed structure. This case completes the presentation of the analysis of statements in the program.

3.6 Merge Operation

To combine two pieces of abstract information at join points in the control-flow, the analysis uses the following merge operation. For top and bottom values, it uses the standard relations: $\top_i \sqcup I = I \sqcup \top_i = \top_i$ and $\bot_i \sqcup I = I \sqcup \bot_i = I$. Given $I_1 = (G_1, Q_1)$ and $I_2 = (G_2, Q_2)$, the merge $I = I_1 \sqcup I_2$ is a pair (G, Q) which takes the union of the nodes in I_1 and I_2 and takes the point-wise join for components in the tuple. More precisely, if $G_1 = (N_1, E_1)$ and $G_2 = (N_2, E_2)$, then $G = (N, E)$, where:

$$N = N_1 \cup N_2$$
$$E(n) = \begin{cases} E_1(n) \sqcup E_2(n) & \text{if } n \in N_1 \cap N_2 \\ E_1(n) & \text{if } n \in N_1 - N_2 \\ E_2(n) & \text{if } n \in N_2 - N_1 \end{cases}$$

and the join $\sqcup$ over elements in $N \cup \{\bot, \top\}$ is defined as follows: the join of $u, v \in N$ is u if $u = v$, and it is $\top$ otherwise; $\bot$ is the bottom element: $\bot \sqcup u = u \sqcup \bot = u$, for all $u \in N \cup \{\bot, \top\}$; and $\top$ is the top element: $\top \sqcup u = u \sqcup \top = \top$, for all u.

The merge operations for A and P similarly take the point-wise join for the functions they represent. The join of two numeric values in $\mathbb{Z} \cup \{\top\}$ is $c \in \mathbb{Z}$ if both values are equal to c, and is $\top$ otherwise. The join over $\mathbb{T}$ is the boolean "and" operation. The merge operation for R takes into account null values: the merge of relations R_1 and R_2 yields auxiliary relations R such that $R(n_1.h, n_2.h) = R_1(h_{11}, h_{21}) \sqcup R_2(h_{21}, h_{22})$, where h_{ij} is $n_i.h$ if $n_i \in N_j$, and $\bot$ otherwise, for $i, j \in \{1, 2\}$.

It can be shown that the merge operation for the abstract information is idempotent, associative, and commutative, because all of the component join operations satisfy these properties. Furthermore, the join operation for components over $\mathbb{Z} \cup \{\top\}$ corresponds to a flat ordering; and all of the other components, such as V or $\mathbb{T}$, represent finite sets. Therefore, we conclude that the resulting abstraction forms a lattice with finite height.

It can also be shown that the transfer function for statements are monotonic with respect to the partial ordering induced by the above merge operation. For store statements, starting the analysis with less precise information leads to larger sets K, so more information is being killed from the abstraction. Hence, Step 1 is monotonic. Furthermore, Step 2 is also monotonic, since every node that satisfies conditions (C1)-(C3) in a less precise abstraction will also satisfy those conditions in a more precise abstraction. For load statements, a less precise abstraction produces a less precise result, because the information in all components except R remains unchanged for all nodes except n_x; for n_x, the generated information is more precise when the analysis starts with a more precise abstraction. For auxiliary relations, the analysis generates, in a less precise abstraction, either the same relations, or no new relation, due to the flat ordering of skew values for n_y.

3.7 Example

Figure 3 shows the analysis results for the example from Section 2. Each of the following lines indicates a statement and the information after that statement. We show auxiliary relations sparsely, as sets of linearly independent relations $R(n.h, m.h) \neq \top$.

We emphasize the key aspects of the computed information. First, field load assignments, such as y=x.left and z=y.right, create new abstract nodes and generate new auxiliary relations. For instance, z=y.right creates node z and its dual z°, and generates relations $z^\circ.h = z.h + 1$ and $y.h = z^\circ.h + 1$. Second, when the analysis reaches the store assignment y.right=x, it destroys all of the information that involves the skew and the height of y and x (because x reaches y after the update). For each of them, the analysis sets the skew to top, the invariants B and S to false, and removes all auxiliary information about $y.h$ and $x.h$ (but keeps the relations between $y^\circ.h$, $z.h$, and $z^\circ.h$). The analysis also tries to infer new information, but it fails to do so because none of the nodes satisfy conditions (C1)-(C3). Finally, the algorithm analyzes the store assignment x.left=z. Again, it invalidates skew and height information, but just for x in this case. Then, it determines that x satisfies conditions (C1)-(C3), so it computes new information for it: skew value 0, true predicates B and S; it also generates relation $x.h = z.h + 1$. The key piece of information that allows the analysis to do so is the auxiliary relation between $z.h$ and $y^\circ.h$ (which validates condition (C3)). Then y also satisfies the conditions; the analysis derives similar information for y (skew value of 0 and true predicates B and S) and generates relation $y.h = z^\circ.h + 1$.

4   Related Work

We discuss existing work in the area of verification of linked data structures. We present existing techniques based on model checking, theorem proving, abstract interpretation, and dataflow analysis.

Ball et. al. propose a system [3] based on model checking and theorem proving techniques to extract invariants for arbitrary C programs, including programs that manipulate linked structures, where invariants may contain integer quantities. The system consists of: a tool C2BP [1] that relies on a theorem prover to build a boolean abstraction of the program relative to a fixed set of user-supplied predicates; a model checker BE-BOP [2] that analyzes the boolean program; and a tool NEWTON that infers additional boolean predicates when the verification fails. For the quantitative shape problems such as tree balancing, figuring out the necessary invariants is non-trivial (if possible at all): the user would have to manually prove the desired property, identify the invariants that the proof requires, and then supply those to the tool. Furthermore, the theorem prover

Statement	Points-to, Shape, and Quantitative Information			
	E	A	P	R
(initial information)	$x \mapsto (n_s, n_s)$; $n_s \mapsto (n_s, n_s)$	$x \mapsto (2, \top, 0)$	$x \mapsto (0,0,1)$; $n_s \mapsto (1,1,1)$	
y = x.left	$x \mapsto (y, y^\square)$; $y \mapsto (n_s, n_s)$; $y^\square \mapsto (n_s, n_s)$; $n_s \mapsto (n_s, n_s)$	$x \mapsto (2, \top, 0)$; $y \mapsto (\top, \top, 1)$; $y^\square \mapsto (\top, \top, 1)$	$x \mapsto (0,0,1)$; $y \mapsto (1,1,1)$; $y^\square \mapsto (1,1,1)$; $n_s \mapsto (1,1,1)$	$y.h = y^\square.h + 2$; $x.h = y.h + 1$
if (y.val == 1)	$x \mapsto (y, y^\square)$; $y \mapsto (n_s, n_s)$; $y^\square \mapsto (n_s, n_s)$; $n_s \mapsto (n_s, n_s)$	$x \mapsto (2, \top, 0)$; $y \mapsto (1,1,1)$; $y^\square \mapsto (\top, \top, 1)$	$x \mapsto (0,0,1)$; $y \mapsto (1,1,1)$; $y^\square \mapsto (1,1,1)$; $n_s \mapsto (1,1,1)$	$y.h = y^\square.h + 2$; $x.h = y.h + 1$
x.val = 0	$x \mapsto (y, y^\square)$; $y \mapsto (n_s, n_s)$; $y^\square \mapsto (n_s, n_s)$; $n_s \mapsto (n_s, n_s)$	$x \mapsto (2, 0, 0)$; $y \mapsto (1,1,1)$; $y^\square \mapsto (\top, \top, 1)$	$x \mapsto (0,0,1)$; $y \mapsto (1,1,1)$; $y^\square \mapsto (1,1,1)$; $n_s \mapsto (1,1,1)$	$y.h = y^\square.h + 2$; $x.h = y.h + 1$
y.val = 0	$x \mapsto (y, y^\square)$; $y \mapsto (n_s, n_s)$; $y^\square \mapsto (n_s, n_s)$; $n_s \mapsto (n_s, n_s)$	$x \mapsto (2, 0, 0)$; $y \mapsto (1,0,1)$; $y^\square \mapsto (\top, \top, 1)$	$x \mapsto (0,0,1)$; $y \mapsto (1,0,1)$; $y^\square \mapsto (1,1,1)$; $n_s \mapsto (1,1,1)$	$y.h = y^\square.h + 2$; $x.h = y.h + 1$
z = y.right	$x \mapsto (y, y^\square)$; $y \mapsto (z^\square, z)$; $y^\square \mapsto (n_s, n_s)$; $z \mapsto (n_s, n_s)$; $z^\square \mapsto (n_s, n_s)$; $n_s \mapsto (n_s, n_s)$	$x \mapsto (2, 0, 0)$; $y \mapsto (1,0,1)$; $y^\square \mapsto (\top, \top, 1)$; $z \mapsto (\top, \top, 1)$; $z^\square \mapsto (\top, \top, 1)$	$x \mapsto (0,0,1)$; $y \mapsto (1,0,1)$; $y^\square \mapsto (1,1,1)$; $z \mapsto (1,1,1)$; $z^\square \mapsto (1,1,1)$; $n_s \mapsto (1,1,1)$	$y.h = y^\square.h + 2$; $x.h = y.h + 1$; $z^\square.h = z.h + 1$; $y.h = z^\square.h + 1$
y.right = x	$x \mapsto (y, y^\square)$; $y \mapsto (z^\square, x)$; $y^\square \mapsto (n_s, n_s)$; $z \mapsto (n_s, n_s)$; $z^\square \mapsto (n_s, n_s)$; $n_s \mapsto (n_s, n_s)$	$x \mapsto (\top, 0, 1)$; $y \mapsto (\top, 0, 1)$; $y^\square \mapsto (\top, \top, 1)$; $z \mapsto (\top, \top, 0)$; $z^\square \mapsto (\top, \top, 1)$	$x \mapsto (0,0,1)$; $y \mapsto (0,0,1)$; $y^\square \mapsto (1,1,1)$; $z \mapsto (1,1,1)$; $z^\square \mapsto (1,1,1)$; $n_s \mapsto (1,1,1)$	$z^\square.h = z.h + 1$; $z.h = y^\square.h$
x.left = z	$x \mapsto (z, y^\square)$; $y \mapsto (z^\square, x)$; $y^\square \mapsto (n_s, n_s)$; $z \mapsto (n_s, n_s)$; $z^\square \mapsto (n_s, n_s)$; $n_s \mapsto (n_s, n_s)$	$x \mapsto (0, 0, 1)$; $y \mapsto (0, 0, 0)$; $y^\square \mapsto (\top, \top, 1)$; $z \mapsto (\top, \top, 1)$; $z^\square \mapsto (\top, \top, 1)$	$x \mapsto (1,1,1)$; $y \mapsto (1,1,1)$; $y^\square \mapsto (1,1,1)$; $z \mapsto (1,1,1)$; $z^\square \mapsto (1,1,1)$; $n_s \mapsto (1,1,1)$	$z^\square.h = z.h + 1$; $z.h = y^\square.h$; $x.h = z.h + 1$; $y.h = z^\square.h + 1$

Fig. 3. Analysis for the example. The table shows the analysis information after each instruction. We represent auxiliary relations in R sparsely, as a set of linearly independent relations.

must have knowledge about the relation between quantities (e.g., height, skew) and points-to relations. Our analysis does all this work automatically, at the expense of being specialized to solve this problem.

Yavuz-Kahveci and Bultan [19] propose a model checking technique for the verification of programs that concurrently manipulate shared list structures with counters. Their model uses shape graphs, represented using BDDs and augmented with counters for summary nodes, and numeric constraints over Presburger arithmetic. Their abstraction is not finite; to enforce termination, their system artificially bounds the number of iterations and uses widening operators. This approach is limited to structures with one selector, i.e., lists, and properties about numbers of nodes. In contrast, our technique is able to verify more complex properties for more complex structures, and it does so using a finite abstraction that automatically guarantees termination.

A large body of research has been devoted to shape analysis for programs with destructive updates, using dataflow analysis or abstract interpretation to verify various heap invariants, including aliasing, sharing, cyclicity, or reachability [18]. The techniques presented in this paper are most related to those shape analyses that distinguish between heap locations based on their points-to relationships with respect to program variables [16,9,4], and to the similar analyses which formulate the shape abstraction as 3-valued logic formulas [18,5,14,17]. Although the transfer functions in all of these analyses must be constructed by the analysis designer, recent work shows that it is also possible to derive transfer functions automatically [13]. The above techniques focus on verifying shape invariants such as sharing or cyclicity; the 3-valued logic framework has also been used to prove other invariants, such as the "is-sorted" invariant for list sorting procedures [10]. However, the 3-valued logic abstraction is based on first-order predicate logic augmented with transitive closure and, since this is a weaker theory than arithmetic, 3-valued logic is not powerful enough to verify quantitative properties such as the balancing of tree structures. Compared to all of this work, our analysis extends traditional shape analysis with quantitative heap invariants, and is able to verify such properties for programs where destructive updates may temporarily invalidate both shape and quantitative invariants.

Other approaches exclusively use theorem proving for the verification of invariants of linked structures. Møller and Schwartzbach propose the Pointer Assertion Logic Engine [11], a system that verifies non-arithmetic invariants for recursive heap structures that can be expressed using graph types [7]. The tool requires users to annotate loops and procedures with appropriate invariants; it uses Hoare logic to generate verification conditions that are checked by MONA [12], a theorem prover based on automata. In contrast, our approach does not require loop annotations and, more important, can identify arithmetic invariants. Recently, Kolpylov has proposed a type-theoretical approach to the verification of data structures using dependent intersection types [8]. This approach has been implemented in the theorem-proving system MetaPRL [6] and used to verify all properties of red-black trees, including the arithmetic manipulations. However, this work targets a functional implementation of red-black trees, and does not apply to programs with destructive updates.

5 Conclusions and Future Work

We have presented a quantitative analysis algorithm that is able to verify balancing invariants for tree structures. Our algorithm can successfully analyze programs where destructive operations temporarily invalidate both shape and quantitative invariants; thus, it generalizes techniques that compute shape information alone. We have used a heap abstraction that represents shape and quantitative information in an unified framework.

Although the proposed algorithm targets properties that refer to balancing and height of tree structures, this is a first step toward developing more general analyses that reason about quantitative invariants of heap structures. We believe that our proposed analysis framework (based on quantitative attributes, predicates, and auxiliary information) and the proposed analysis principles (of specializing and simplifying the abstraction and the analysis as much as possible to solve a particular problem) can be applied to other quantitative shape problems.

Hence, one direction of future research is to explore a range of other quantitative properties and develop analyses capable of proving such properties. A first category includes properties about the balancing and height of other tree structures, such as red-black trees, B-trees, or splay trees. For instance, proving the red-black property that every path from each node to the leaves contains the same number of black nodes requires introducing attributes to represent the node colors and attributes to record the minimum and maximum number of black nodes on all paths to the leaves. A second category of properties refers to quantities other than balancing and height; an example would be to prove that binary search invariants are being maintained. Finally, other categories include quantitative invariants for structures other than trees and invariants between quantities of multiple structures. For instance, proving that a linked list contains exactly the leaves of some other tree structure.

Since the philosophy of our proposed approach is to develop specialized analyses, proving different properties will require different abstractions and different transfer functions. Hence, another direction of future work is to develop a general specification language that succinctly describes quantitative analyses in our framework, and provide tools that automatically generate analyzers from those specifications.

Finally, since the analyses can become complex and heavyweight, it also becomes difficult to prove their correctness. Therefore, a third direction of future research is to explore the use other tools (e.g., theorem-provers) to automatically prove the correctness of the analysis, or, even better, develop tools that automatically derive correct analyses from the abstraction and the concrete semantics of the language.

Acknowledgments

The author would like to thank Stephen Chong and Brian Hackett for early work in quantitative analysis and for comments about this paper. The author also thanks the anonymous reviewers for their suggestions and comments.

References

1. T. Ball, R. Majumdar, T. Millstein, and S. Rajamani. Automatic predicate abstraction of C programs. In *Proceedings of the SIGPLAN '01 Conference on Program Language Design and Implementation*, Snowbird, UT, June 2001.
2. T. Ball and S. Rajamani. Bebop: A symbolic model checker for boolean programs. In *Proceedings of the 7th International SPIN Workshop on Model Checking of Software*, Stanford University, CA, August 2000.

3. T. Ball and S. Rajamani. The SLAM project: Debugging system software via static analysis. In *Proceedings of the 29th Annual ACM Symposium on the Principles of Programming Languages*, Portland, OR, January 2002.

4. S. Chong and R. Rugina. Static analysis of accessed regions in recursive data structures. In *Proceedings of the 10th International Static Analysis Symposium*, San Diego, CA, June 2003.

5. N. Dor, M. Rodeh, and M. Sagiv. Checking cleanness in linked lists. In *Proceedings of the 7th International Static Analysis Symposium*, Santa Barbara, CA, July 2000.

6. J. Hickey, A. Nogin, R. Constable, B. Aydemir, E. Barzilay, Y. Bryukhov, R. Eaton, A. Granicz, A. Kopylov, C. Kreitz, V. Krupski, L. Lorigo, S. Schmitt, C. Witty, and X. Yu. MetaPRL – a modular logical environment. In *Proceedings of the 16th International Conference on Theorem Proving in Higher Order Logics*, September 2003.

7. N. Klarlund and M. Schwartzbach. Graph types. In *Proceedings of the 20th Annual ACM Symposium on the Principles of Programming Languages*, Charleston, SC, January 1993.

8. Alexei Kopylov. *Type Theoretical Foundations for Data Structures, Classes, and Objects.* PhD thesis, Dept. of Computer Science, Cornell Univ., Ithaca, NY, January 2004.

9. V. Kuncak, P. Lam, and M. Rinard. Role analysis. In *Proceedings of the 29th Annual ACM Symposium on the Principles of Programming Languages*, Portland, OR, January 2002.

10. T. Lev-ami, T. Reps, M. Sagiv, and R. Wilhelm. Putting static analysis to work for verification: A case study. In *2000 International Symposium on Software Testing and Analysis*, August 2000.

11. A. Moller and M. Schwartzbach. The pointer assertion logic engine. In *Proceedings of the ACM Conference on Program Language Design and Implementation*, Snowbird, UT, June 2001.

12. Anders Møller. MONA project home page. http://www.brics.dk/MONA.

13. T. Reps, M. Sagiv, and A. Loginov. Finite differencing of logical formulas for static analysis. In *Proceedings of the 12th European Symposium on Programming*, Warsaw, Poland, April 2003.

14. N. Rinetzky and M. Sagiv. Interprocedural shape analysis for recursive programs. In *Proceedings of the 2001 International Conference on Compiler Construction*, Genova, Italy, April 2001.

15. M. Sagiv, T. Reps, and R. Wilhelm. Solving shape-analysis problems in languages with destructive updating. In *Proceedings of the 23rd Annual ACM Symposium on the Principles of Programming Languages*, St. Petersburg Beach, FL, January 1996.

16. M. Sagiv, T. Reps, and R. Wilhelm. Solving shape-analysis problems in languages with destructive updating. *ACM Transactions on Programming Languages and Systems*, 20(1):1–50, January 1998.

17. M. Sagiv, T. Reps, and R. Wilhelm. Parametric shape analysis via 3-valued logic. *ACM Transactions on Programming Languages and Systems*, 24(3), May 2002.

18. R. Wilhelm, M. Sagiv, and T. Reps. Shape analysis. In *Proceedings of the 2000 International Conference on Compiler Construction*, Berlin, Germany, April 2000.

19. T. Yavuz-Kahveci and T. Bultan. Automated verification of concurrent linked lists with counters. In *Proceedings of the 9th International Static Analysis Symposium*, Madrid, Spain, September 2002.

A Relational Approach
to Interprocedural Shape Analysis

Bertrand Jeannet[1], Alexey Loginov[2], Thomas Reps[2], and Mooly Sagiv[3]

[1] IRISA
Bertrand.Jeannet@irisa.fr
[2] Comp. Sci. Dept., University of Wisconsin
{alexey,reps}@cs.wisc.edu
[3] School of Comp. Sci., Tel Aviv University
msagiv@post.tau.ac.il

Abstract. This paper addresses the verification of properties of imperative programs with recursive procedure calls, heap-allocated storage, and destructive updating of pointer-valued fields – i.e., *interprocedural shape analysis*. It presents a way to harness some previously known approaches to interprocedural dataflow analysis – which in past work have been applied only to much less rich settings – for interprocedural shape analysis.

1 Introduction

This paper concerns techniques for static analysis of recursive programs that manipulate heap-allocated storage and perform destructive updating of pointer-valued fields. The goal is to recover shape descriptors that provide information about the characteristics of the data structures that a program's pointer variables can point to. Such information can be used to help programmers understand certain aspects of the program's behavior, to verify properties of the program, and to optimize or parallelize the program.

The work reported in the paper builds on past work by several of the authors on static analysis based on 3-valued logic [1, 2] and its implementation in the TVLA system [3]. In this setting, two related logics come into play: an ordinary 2-valued logic, as well as a related 3-valued logic. A memory configuration, or store, is modeled by what logicians call a *logical structure*, which consists of a predicate (i.e., a relation of appropriate arity) for each predicate symbol of a *vocabulary* $\mathcal{P}$. A store is modeled by a 2-valued logical structure; a set of stores is abstracted by a (finite) set of bounded-size 3-valued logical structures. An individual of a 3-valued structure's universe either models a single memory cell or, in the case of a *summary individual*, a collection of memory cells.

The constraint of working with limited-size descriptors entails a loss of information about the store. Certain properties of concrete individuals are lost due to abstraction, which groups together multiple individuals into summary individuals: a property can be true for some concrete individuals of the group but false for other individuals. It is for this reason that 3-valued logic is used; uncertainty about a property's value is captured by means of the third truth value, $1/2$.

One of the opportunities for scaling up this approach is to exploit the compositional structure of programs. In interprocedural dataflow analysis, one avenue for accomplishing this is to create a *summary transformer* for each procedure P, and use the summary

R. Giacobazzi (Ed.): SAS 2004, LNCS 3148, pp. 246–264, 2004.

transformer at each call site at which P is called. Each summary transformer must capture (an over-approximation of) the net effect of a call on P. To be able to create summary transformers, the abstract transformers for individual transitions must have a "composable representation"; that is, given the representations of two abstract transformers, it must be possible to represent their composition as an object of roughly the same size. One then carries out a fixed-point-finding procedure on a collection of equations in which each variable in the equation set has a transformer-valued value – i.e., a value drawn from the domain of transformers – rather than a dataflow value proper.

A number of approaches to interprocedural dataflow analysis based on summary transformers are known [4–9]. However, not all program-analysis problems have abstract transformers that have a composable representation.

For some problems, it is possible to address this issue by working pointwise, tabulating composed transformers as sets of pairs of input/output values [7, 8, 10]. However, for interprocedural shape analysis, this approach fails to produce useful information. The 3-valued-logic approach to shape analysis is a *storeless* one: individuals, which model memory cells, do not have fixed identities; they are identified only up to their "distinguishing characteristics", namely, their values for a specific set of unary predicates. Because these "distinguishing characteristics" can change during the course of a procedure call, there is no way to identify individuals in an input abstract structure with their corresponding individuals in the output abstract structure. In essence, a pair of input/output 3-valued structures loses track of the correlations between the input and output values of an individual's unary predicates. Consequently, an approach based on tabulating composed transformers as sets of pairs of 3-valued structures is not promising: the representation provides only a weak characterization of a procedure's net effect.

All is not lost, however: instead of "abstracting and then pairing" (as discussed above), the solution is to "pair and then abstract".

Observation 1 *By using 3-valued structures over a doubled vocabulary $\mathcal{P} \uplus \mathcal{P}'$, where $\mathcal{P}' = \{p' \mid p \in \mathcal{P}\}$ and $\uplus$ denotes disjoint union, one obtains a finite abstraction that relates the predicate values for an individual at the beginning of a transition to the predicate values for the individual at the end of the transition.*

This abstraction provides a way to create much more accurate composable representations of transformers, and hence much more accurate summary transformers, for a broad class of problems. Moreover, by extending the abstract domain of 3-valued logical structures [1] with some new operations, it is possible to perform abstract interpretation of call and return statements without losing too much precision (see §4). We have used these ideas to create a context-sensitive shape-analysis algorithm for recursive programs that manipulate heap-allocated storage and perform destructive updating.

Context-sensitive interprocedural shape analysis was also studied in [11]. A major difference is that [11] augments the store to include the runtime stack as an explicit data structure (an idea proposed in [12, 13]); the storage abstraction used in [11] is an abstraction of the store augmented in this fashion. In contrast, in our work the stack is not materialized as an explicit data structure; our approach is based on the creation of summary transformers, in the style of [4–6].

The contributions of our work include the following:

- It provides a method to create a *summary transformer* for each procedure P, which can be used at each call site at which P is called.
- Our analysis obtains more general information than that obtained in [11]:
  - In [11], the result of the analysis for the exit node e_P of a procedure P is (an approximation of) the reachable memory configurations that can arise at e_P
  - In this paper, the result for e_P is (an approximation of) the *relation* between the input memory configurations at the start node s_P of P and the configurations at e_P, restricted to the memory configurations that are reachable at s_P.

  Because of the different nature of the information obtained, our analysis is able to verify that reversing a list twice restores the original list, whereas the method of [11] would only show that it yields a list with the same head and the same set of memory cells (in some order).
- We have been able to apply our method successfully to a richer set of programs. In particular, [11] only studied how to perform interprocedural analysis for recursive *list*-manipulation programs. The method described in this paper is capable of handling certain programs that manipulate *binary trees*. (While list-manipulation programs can often be implemented in tail-recursive fashion – and hence can be converted easily into loop programs – tree-manipulation programs are much less easily converted to non-recursive form.)

The remainder of the paper is organized as follows: §2 describes the features of the language to which our analysis applies. §3 reviews the abstract domain of 3-valued logical structures [1]. §4 describes how abstractions of logical structures over a doubled vocabulary are used to create summary transformers and perform interprocedural analysis. §5 discusses experimental results. §6 discusses related work.

2   Programs and Memory Configurations

The analysis applies to programs written in an imperative programming language in which (i) it is forbidden to take the address of a local variable, global variable, or parameter; and (ii) parameters are passed by value. These two features prevent direct aliasing among variables; thus, only heap-allocated structures can be aliased. (Both JAVA and ML follow these conventions.) The running example used in the paper is the list-reversal program of Fig. 1.

```
typedef struct node{
    struct node *n;
    int data;
} *List;

List res;
void main(List l) {
    res = rev(l);
}
```

```
List rev(List x) {
    List y, z;
    z = x->n;
    x->n = NULL;
    if (z != NULL) {
        y = rev(z);
        z->n = x;
    }
    else y = x;
    return y;
}
```

Fig. 1. Recursive list-reversal program.

2.1   Program Syntax

A *program* is defined by a set of procedures P_i, $0 \le i \le K$. Each procedure has a set of local variables, and has a number of formal *input parameters* and *output parameters*. To simplify our notation, we will assume that each procedure has only *one* input (resp. output) parameter and *one* local variable; the generalization to multiple parameters and local variables is straightforward. We also assume that an input parameter is not modified during the execution of the procedure. (This assumption is made solely for convenience, and involves no loss of generality because it is always possible to copy input parameters to additional local variables.) Thus, a *procedure* $P_i = \langle \mathsf{fpi}_i, \mathsf{fpo}_i, \mathsf{loc}_i, G_i \rangle$ is defined by its in-

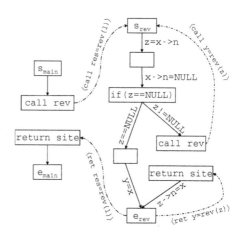

Fig. 2. Interprocedural CFG of the list-reversal program.

put parameter fpi_i, its output parameter fpo_i, its local variable loc_i, and G_i, its intraprocedural control flow graph (CFG).

A program is represented by a directed graph $G^* = (N^*, E^*)$ called an *interprocedural CFG*. G^* consists of a collection of intraprocedural CFGs $G_1, G_2, \dots, G_K$, one of which, G_{main}, represents the program's main procedure. Each CFG G_i contains exactly one *start* node s_i and exactly one *exit* node e_i. The other nodes of a CFG represent individual statements and branches of a procedure in the usual way[1], except that a procedure call is represented by two nodes, a *call* node and a *return-site* node. For $n \in N^*$, $proc(n)$ denotes the (index of the) procedure that contains n. In addition to the ordinary intraprocedural edges that connect the nodes of the individual flowgraphs in G^*, each procedure call, represented by call-node c and return-site node r, has two edges: (i) a *call-to-start* edge from c to the start node of the called procedure, and (ii) an *exit-to-return-site* edge from the exit node of the called procedure to r. The functions *call* and *ret* record matching call and return-site nodes: $call(r) = c$ and $ret(c) = r$. We assume that a start node has no incoming edges except call-to-start edges.

2.2   Representing Memory Configurations with Logical Structures

As in the static-analysis framework defined in [1], concrete memory configurations – or *stores* – are modeled by logical structures. A logical structure is associated with a vocabulary of predicate symbols (with given arities): $\mathcal{P} = \{eq, p_1, \dots, p_n\}$ is a finite set of predicate symbols, where $\mathcal{P}_k$ denotes the set of predicate symbols of arity k (and $eq \in \mathcal{P}_2$). A logical structure supplies a predicate for each of the vocabulary's predicate symbols. A concrete store is modeled by a 2-valued logical structure for a fixed

---

[1] Alternatively, nodes can represent basic blocks.

Table 1. Core predicates used for representing the stores manipulated by programs that use type List. (We write predicate names in *italics* and code in typewriter font.)

Predicate	Intended Meaning
$eq(v_1, v_2)$	Do v_1 and v_2 denote the same memory cell?
$q(v)$	Does pointer variable q point to memory cell v?
$n(v_1, v_2)$	Does the n-field of v_1 point to v_2?
$dle(v_1, v_2)$	Is the data-field of $v_1 \leq$ the data-field of v_2?

vocabulary of *core predicates*, C. Core predicates are part of the underlying semantics of the language to be analyzed; they record atomic properties of stores. For instance, Tab. 1 lists the predicates that would be used to represent the stores manipulated by programs that use type List from Fig. 1, such as the store shown in Fig. 3. 2-valued logical structures then represent memory configurations: the individuals are the set of memory cells; a nullary predicate represents a Boolean variable of the program; a unary predicate represents either a pointer variable or a Boolean-valued field of a record; and a binary predicate represents a pointer field of a record[2].

The 2-valued structure S, shown in the left-hand side of Fig. 4, encodes the store of Fig. 3. S's four individuals, u_1, u_2, u_3, and u_4, represent the four list cells.

The following graphical notation is used for depicting 2-valued structures:

Fig. 3. A possible store, consisting of a four-node linked list pointed to by x and y.

- An individual is represented by a circle with its name inside.
- A unary predicate p is represented by having a solid arrow from p to each individual u for which $p(u) = 1$, and by the absence of a p-arrow to each individual u' for which $p(u') = 0$. (If predicate p is 0 for all individuals, p is not shown.)
- A binary predicate q is represented by a solid arrow labeled q between each pair of individuals u_i and u_j for which $q(u_i, u_j) = 1$, and by the absence of a q-arrow between pairs u'_i and u'_j for which $q(u'_i, u'_j) = 0$.

Thus, in structure S, pointer variables x and y point to individual u_1, whose n-field points to individual u_2; pointer variable z does not point to any individual.

Often we only want to use a restricted class of logical structures to encode stores. To exclude structures that do not represent admissible stores, integrity constraints can be imposed. For instance, the predicate $x(v)$ of Fig. 4 captures whether pointer variable x points to memory cell v; x would be given the attribute "unique", which imposes the integrity constraint that $x(v)$ can hold for at most one individual in any structure.

---

[2] To simplify matters, our examples do not involve modeling numeric-valued variables and numeric-valued fields (such as data). It is possible to do this by introducing other predicates, such as the binary predicate *dle* (which stands for "data-less-than-or-equal-to") listed in Tab. 1; *dle* captures the relative order of two nodes' data values. Alternatively, numeric-valued entities can be handled by combining abstractions of logical structures with previously known techniques for creating numeric abstractions [14].

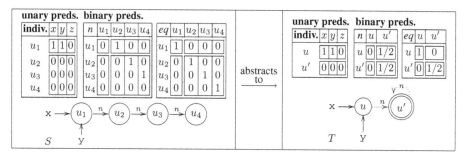

Fig. 4. The abstraction of 2-valued structure S to 3-valued structure T when we use $\{x, y, z\}$-abstraction.

The concrete operational semantics of a programming language is defined by specifying a structure transformer for each kind of edge e that can appear in a control-flow graph. Formally, the structure transformer τ_e for edge e is defined using a collection of *predicate-update formulas*, $c(v_1, \ldots, v_k) = \tau_{c,e}(v_1, \ldots, v_k)$, one for each core predicate c (e.g., see [1]). These formulas define how the core predicates of a logical structure S that arises at the source of e are transformed by e to create a logical structure S' at the target of e; they define the value of predicate c in S' as a function of c's value in S. Edge e may optionally have a *precondition formula*, which filters out structures that should not follow the transition along e. (In Fig. 2, edges are labeled with statements and conditions of the programming language, rather than with such collections of predicate-update formulas.)

The set of all 2-valued structures over vocabulary $\mathcal{P}$ is denoted by $\mathcal{S}_2[\mathcal{P}]$.

3   The Abstract Domain of 3-Valued Logical Structures

To create abstractions of 2-valued logical structures (and hence of the stores that they encode), we use the related class of 3-valued logical structures over the same vocabulary. In 3-valued logical structures, a third truth value, denoted by $1/2$, is introduced to denote uncertainty: in a 3-valued logical structure, the value $p(u)$ of predicate p on a tuple of individuals u is allowed to be $1/2$. The set of all 3-valued structures over vocabulary $\mathcal{P}$ is denoted by $\mathcal{S}_3[\mathcal{P}]$. (We drop "$[\mathcal{P}]$" when $\mathcal{P}$ is clear from the context.)

Definition 1. The truth values 0 and 1 are *definite values*; $1/2$ is an *indefinite value*. For $l_1, l_2 \in \{0, 1/2, 1\}$, the *information order* is defined as follows: $l_1 \sqsubseteq l_2$ iff $l_1 = l_2$ or $l_2 = 1/2$. The symbol $\sqcup$ denotes the least-upper-bound operation with respect to $\sqsubseteq$.

The abstract stores used for program analysis are 3-valued logical structures that, by the construction discussed below, are *a priori* of bounded size. In general, each 3-valued logical structure corresponds to a (possibly infinite) set of 2-valued logical structures. Members of these two families of structures are related by *canonical abstraction*.

The principle behind canonical abstraction is illustrated in Fig. 4, which shows how 2-valued structure S is abstracted to 3-valued structure T. The abstraction function is determined by a subset $\mathcal{A}$ of the unary predicates. The predicates in $\mathcal{A}$ are called the *abstraction predicates*. Given $\mathcal{A}$, the act of applying the corresponding abstraction function is called $\mathcal{A}$-*abstraction*. The canonical abstraction illustrated in Fig. 4 is $\{x, y, z\}$-abstraction.

Abstraction is driven by the values of the "vector" of abstraction predicates for each individual w – i.e., for S, by the values $x(w)$, $y(w)$, and $z(w)$, for $w \in \{u_1, u_2, u_3, u_4\}$ – and, in particular, by the equivalence classes formed from the individuals that have the same vector of values for their abstraction predicates. In S, there are two such equivalence classes: (i) $\{u_1\}$, for which x, y, and z are 1, 1, and 0, respectively, and (ii) $\{u_2, u_3, u_4\}$, for which x, y, and z are all 0. (The boxes in the table of unary predicates for S show how individuals of S are grouped into two equivalence classes.) All of the members of each equivalence class are mapped to the same individual of the 3-valued structure. Thus, all members of $\{u_2, u_3, u_4\}$ from S are mapped to the same individual in T, called u' [3]; similarly, all members of $\{u_1\}$ from S are mapped to same individual in T, called u.

For each non-abstraction predicate p^S of 2-valued structure S, the corresponding predicate p^T in 3-valued structure T is formed by a "truth-blurring quotient". The value for a tuple $\boldsymbol{u}_0$ in p^T is the join ($\sqcup$) of all p^S tuples that the equivalence relation on individuals maps to $\boldsymbol{u}_0$. For instance,

- In S, $n^S(u_1, u_1)$ equals 0. Therefore, the value of $n^T(u, u)$ is 0.
- In S, $n^S(u_2, u_1)$, $n^S(u_3, u_1)$, and $n^S(u_4, u_1)$ all equal 0. Therefore, the value of $n^T(u', u)$ is 0.
- In S, $n^S(u_1, u_3)$ and $n^S(u_1, u_4)$ both equal 0, whereas $n^S(u_1, u_2)$ equals 1; therefore, the value of $n^T(u, u')$ is $1/2 \, (= 0 \sqcup 1)$.
- In S, $n^S(u_2, u_3)$ and $n^S(u_3, u_4)$ both equal 1, whereas $n^S(u_2, u_2)$, $n^S(u_2, u_4)$, $n^S(u_3, u_2)$, $n^S(u_3, u_3)$, $n^S(u_4, u_2)$, $n^S(u_4, u_3)$, and $n^S(u_4, u_4)$ all equal 0; therefore, the value of $n^T(u', u')$ is $1/2 \, (= 0 \sqcup 1)$.

In Fig. 4, the boxes in the tables for predicates n and eq indicate these four groupings.

In a 2-valued structure, the eq predicate represents the equality relation on individuals. In general, under canonical abstraction some individuals "lose their identity" because of uncertainty that arises in the eq predicate. For instance, $eq^T(u, u) = 1$ because u in T represents a single individual of S. On the other hand, u' represents three individuals of S and the quotient operation causes $eq^T(u', u')$ to have the value $1/2$. An individual like u' is called a *summary individual*.

A 3-valued logical structure T is used as an abstract descriptor of a set of 2-valued logical structures. In general, a summary individual models a *set* of individuals in each of the 2-valued logical structures that T represents. The graphical notation for 3-valued logical structures (cf. structure T of Fig. 4) is derived from the one for 2-valued structures, with the following additions:

- Individuals are represented by circles containing their names. (In Fig. 5, discussed in §5, we also place non-0-valued unary predicates that do not correspond to pointer-valued program variables inside the circles.)

---

[3] The names of individuals are completely arbitrary: what distinguishes u^0 is the value of its vector of abstraction predicates.

- A summary individual is represented by a double circle.
- Unary and binary predicates with value $1/2$ are represented by dotted arrows.

Thus, in every concrete structure $\tilde{S}$ that is represented by abstract structure T of Fig. 4, pointer variables x and y definitely point to the concrete node of $\tilde{S}$ that u represents. The n-field of that node may point to one of the concrete nodes that u' represents; u' is a summary individual, i.e., it may represent more than one concrete node in $\tilde{S}$. Possibly there is an n-field in one or more of these concrete nodes that points to another of the concrete nodes that u' represents, but there cannot be an n-field in any of these concrete nodes that points to the concrete node that u represents.

Note that 3-valued structure T also represents

- the acyclic lists of length 3 or more that are pointed to by x and y.
- the cyclic lists of length 3 or more that are pointed to by x and y, such that the backpointer is not to the head of the list, but to the second, third, or later element.
- some additional memory configurations with a cyclic or acyclic list pointed to by x and y that also contain some garbage cells that are not reachable from x and y.

That is, T is a finite representation of an infinite set of (possibly cyclic) concrete lists, each of which may also be accompanied by some unreachable cells. Later in this section, we discuss options for fine-tuning an abstraction. For instance, it is possible to use canonical abstraction to define abstractions in which the acyclic lists and the cyclic lists are mapped to different 3-valued structures (and in which the presence or absence of unreachable cells is readily apparent).

Canonical abstraction ensures that each 3-valued structure has an *a priori* bounded size, which guarantees that a fixed-point will always be reached by an iterative static-analysis algorithm. Another advantage of using 2- and 3-valued logic as the basis for static analysis is that the language used for extracting information from the concrete world and the abstract world is identical: *every* syntactic expression – i.e., every logical formula – can be interpreted either in the 2-valued world or the 3-valued world[4].

The consistency of the 2-valued and 3-valued viewpoints is ensured by a basic theorem that relates the two logics, which eliminates the need for the user to write the usual proofs required with abstract interpretation – i.e., to demonstrate that the abstract descriptors that the analyzer manipulates correctly model the actual heap-allocated data structures that the program manipulates. Thanks to a single meta-theorem (the Embedding Theorem [1, Theorem 4.9]), which shows that information extracted from a 3-valued structure T by evaluating a formula φ is sound with respect to the value of φ in each of the 2-valued structures that T represents, an abstract semantics falls out automatically from a specification of the concrete semantics (which has to be provided in any case whenever abstract interpretation is employed). In particular, the formulas that define the concrete semantics when interpreted in 2-valued logic define a sound abstract semantics when interpreted in 3-valued logic. Soundness of *all* instantiations of the analysis framework is ensured by the Embedding Theorem.

---

[4] Formulas are first-order formulas with transitive closure: a *formula* over the vocabulary $\mathcal{P} = \{eq, p_1, \ldots, p_n\}$ is defined as follows (where $p^0(v_1, v_2)$ stands for the reflexive transitive closure of $p(v_1, v_2)$):

$p \in \mathcal{P}, \varphi \in \textit{Formulas},$
$v \in \textit{Variables}$

$\varphi ::= \mathbf{0} \mid \mathbf{1} \mid p(v_1, \ldots, v_k) \mid (\neg\varphi_1) \mid (\varphi_1 \wedge \varphi_2) \mid (\varphi_1 \vee \varphi_2)$
$\mid (\exists v \colon \varphi_1) \mid (\forall v \colon \varphi_1) \mid p^0(v_1, v_2)$

Instrumentation Predicates. Unfortunately, unless some care is taken in the design of an analysis, there is a danger that as abstract interpretation proceeds, the indefinite value $1/2$ will become pervasive. This can destroy the ability to recover interesting information from the 3-valued structures collected (although soundness is maintained). A key role in combating indefiniteness is played by *instrumentation predicates*, which record auxiliary information in a logical structure. They provide a mechanism for the user to fine-tune an abstraction: an instrumentation predicate p of arity k, which is defined by a logical formula $\psi_p(v_1, \ldots, v_k)$ over the core predicate symbols, captures a property that each k-tuple of nodes may or may not possess. In general, adding additional instrumentation predicates refines the abstraction, defining a more precise analysis that is prepared to track finer distinctions among stores. This allows more properties of the program's stores to be identified during analysis.

Table 2. Defining formulas of some commonly used instrumentation predicates. Typically, there is a separate predicate symbol $r[n, q]$ for every pointer-valued variable q.

p	IntendedMeaning	ψ_p
$t[n](v_1, v_2)$	Is v_2 reachable from v_1 along n-fields?	$n^{*}(v_1, v_2)$
$r[n, q](v)$	Is v reachable from pointer variable q along n-fields?	$\exists v_1 : q(v_1) \wedge t[n](v_1, v)$
$c[n](v)$	Is v on a directed cycle of n-fields?	$\exists v_1 : n(v, v_1) \wedge t[n](v_1, v)$

The introduction of unary instrumentation predicates that are then used as abstraction predicates provides a way to control which concrete individuals are merged together into summary nodes, and thereby to control the amount of information lost by abstraction. Instrumentation predicates that involve reachability properties, which can be defined using transitive closure, often play a crucial role in the definitions of abstractions. For instance, in program-analysis applications, reachability properties from specific pointer variables have the effect of keeping disjoint sublists or subtrees summarized separately. This is particularly important when analyzing a program in which two pointers are advanced along disjoint sublists. Tab. 2 lists some instrumentation predicates that are important for the analysis of programs that use type List.

From the standpoint of the concrete semantics, instrumentation predicates represent cached information that could always be recomputed by reevaluating the instrumentation predicate's defining formula in the current store. From the standpoint of the abstract semantics, however, reevaluating a formula in the current (3-valued) store can lead to a drastic loss of precision. To gain maximum benefit from instrumentation predicates, an abstract-interpretation algorithm must obtain their values in some other way. This problem, the *instrumentation-predicate-maintenance problem*, is solved by incremental computation; the new value that instrumentation predicate p should have after a transition via abstract state transformer τ from state σ to σ' is computed incrementally from the known value of p in σ. An algorithm that uses τ and p's defining formula $\psi_p(v_1, \ldots, v_k)$ to generate an appropriate incremental predicate-maintenance formula for p is presented in [2].

The problem of automatically identifying appropriate instrumentation predicates, using a process of abstraction refinement, is addressed in [15]. In that paper, the input required to specify a program analysis consists of (i) a program, (ii) a characterization of the inputs, and (iii) a query (i.e., a formula that characterizes the intended output). That work, along with [2], provides a framework for eliminating previously required user inputs for which TVLA has been criticized in the past. Although the abstraction-refinement mechanism was not available for the experiments reported on in the present paper, we believe that it will work equally well when applied to the analysis of programs with recursive procedure calls. In particular, we have observed that the abstraction-refinement mechanism is capable of generating instrumentation predicates that record in/out relationships: most of the experiments described in [15] involved 2-vocabulary structures similar to those used in the present paper, and several of the instrumentation predicates identified relate pairs of predicates $p[in]/p[out]$.

Other Operations on Logical Structures. Thanks to the fact that the Embedding Theorem applies to any pair of structures for which one can be embedded into the other, most operations on 3-valued structures need not be constrained to manipulate 3-valued structures that are images of canonical abstraction. Thus, it is not necessary to perform canonical abstraction after the application of each abstract structure transformer. To ensure that abstract interpretation terminates, it is only necessary that canonical abstraction be applied as a widening operator somewhere in each loop, e.g., at the target of each backedge in the CFG.

Several additional operations on logical structures help prevent an analysis from losing precision:

- Focus is an operation that can be invoked to elaborate a 3-valued structure – allowing it to be replaced by a set of more precise structures (not necessarily images of canonical abstraction) that represent the same set of concrete stores.
- Coerce is a clean-up operation that may "sharpen" a 3-valued logical structure by setting an indefinite value $(1/2)$ to a definite value (0 or 1), or discard a structure entirely if the structure exhibits some fundamental inconsistency (e.g., it cannot represent any possible concrete store).

4   The Use of Logical Structures for Interprocedural Analysis

Given an abstract value A_0 that represents a set of initial stores, the goal is to compute – for each control point of each procedure – an overapproximation to the set of values for the local variables and the heap that can arise at that point. More precisely, the goal is to compute the "join-over-valid-paths" value for each node n:

$$\text{JOVP}(n) = \bigsqcup_{q \in \text{ValidPaths}(s_{main}, n)} \text{pf}_q(A_0)$$

where $\text{ValidPaths}(s_{main}, n)$ denotes the set of paths from s_{main} to n in which the call-to-start and exit-to-return-site edges in path q form a string in which each exit-to-return-site edge is balanced by a preceding call-to-start edge, and pf_q is the composition, in order, of the dataflow transformers for the edges of q.

Let $Id|_D$ denote the identity transformer restricted to inputs in D. For dataflow transformers that distribute over $\sqcup$, the JOVP solution can be obtained by finding the least solution to the following set of equations:

$$\phi(s_{main}) = Id|_{A_0} \quad A_0 \text{ describes the set of initial stores at } s_{main} \tag{1}$$

$$\phi(s_p) = Id|_D \quad s_p \in \text{StartNodes}, p \neq main, \text{ and } D = \bigsqcup_{(c,s_p)\in \text{ CallToStartEdges}} \text{range}(\phi(c)) \tag{2}$$

$$\phi(n) = \bigsqcup_{(m,n)\in E^*} \tau_{m,n} \circ \phi(m) \qquad \text{for } n \in N^{\square}, n \notin (\text{ReturnSites} \cup \text{StartNodes}) \tag{3}$$

$$\phi(n) = \phi(e_q) \circ \phi(call(n)) \qquad \text{for } n \in \text{ReturnSites, and } call(n) \text{ calls } q \tag{4}$$

Eqns. (1)–(4) can be understood as a variant of the "functional approach" of Sharir and Pnueli [5]; in [5], this is expressed with two fixed-point-finding phases: the first phase propagates transformer-valued values; the second phase propagates dataflow values proper. Eqns. (1)–(4) combine these into a single phase that propagates transformer-valued values only. Each summary transformer $\phi(n)$ is a partial function: the domain of $\phi(n)$ overapproximates the set of reachable states at $s_{proc(n)}$ from which it is possible to reach n; the range of $\phi(n)$ equals $\text{JOVP}(n)$, which overapproximates the set of reachable states at n. (A two-phase approach à la Sharir and Pnueli [5] could also be used[5].)

To simplify the presentation, in §4.1 we will assume that the language does not support either local variables or parameter passing. In §4.2, we extend the approach to handle local variables and parameters.

4.1 A Simplified Setting: No Local Variables or Parameters

To use Eqns. (1)–(4) for interprocedural shape analysis, we follow Observation 1 and represent each $\phi(n)$ transformer as a set of 2-vocabulary 3-valued structures. As described below, suitable operations on 3-valued structures provide a way to compose such transformers.

The composition operation $\phi(e_q) \circ \phi(call(n))$ in Eqn. (4), which represents an interprocedural-propagation step, involves transformers represented by two sets of 2-vocabulary 3-valued structures. Intuitively, this involves collecting up a set of structures, where each structure is the "natural join" of two structures – one from each argument set. Below, we define the operation $T_2 \circ T_1$ for a single pair, T_2 and T_1.

In fact, to do this really requires three vocabularies: for each original predicate p, we use three predicates $p[in]$, $p[out]$, and $p[tmp]$. A 2-vocabulary 3-valued structure uses only $p[in]$ and $p[out]$ – or rather, the values of the $p[tmp]$ predicates are "irrelevant". (When a predicate p is irrelevant, then $p(u)$ evaluates to $1/2$ for every tuple of individuals u.) Another obstacle is to reconcile the values of the predicates in the different 2-vocabulary 3-valued structures. The solution has several parts:

---

[5] In the two-phase approach, the first phase is defined by Eqns. (1)–(4), except that the right-hand sides of Eqns. (1) and (2) are both replaced by Id. This permits summary transformers to be computed in a more modular fashion – i.e., bottom-up over the call graph's strongly-connected components. However, it also causes the analysis to consider more input possibilities for each procedure, which is an important consideration in our context. Eqns. (1)–(4) (as written) lead to a less modular analysis that requires a fixed-point iteration over the entire program.

- We need an operation to move predicates in one vocabulary to predicates in another vocabulary. The notation $T[tmp \leftarrow out; out \leftarrow 1/2]$ denotes the (simultaneous) transformation on structure T in which the $p[out]$ predicates are moved to $p[tmp]$, and the $p[out]$ predicates are all set to $1/2$. For instance, to perform the composition $T_2 \circ T_1$, we use $T_1[tmp \leftarrow out; out \leftarrow 1/2]$ and $T_2[tmp \leftarrow in; in \leftarrow 1/2]$.
- We need structures that have the same sets of individuals. Because the individuals in 3-valued structures are identified by the values they have for the (unary) abstraction predicates, we use the operation $canonical: S_3 \rightarrow \wp(S_3)$, which refines a 3-valued structure T into a set of structures – each member of which is in the image of canonical abstraction – such that the set describes the same set of concrete structures as T [16].
- We define the meet of two 3-valued structures that have the same set of individuals. Let $S_1 = (U, \iota_1)$ and $S_2 = (U, \iota_2)$ be two logical structures with the same universe U and vocabulary $\mathcal{P}$. The interpretations ι_1, ι_2 map each relation symbol $p \in \mathcal{P}_k$ to a k-ary truth-valued function: $\iota_i(p): U^k \rightarrow \{0, 1/2, 1\}$. For convenience, we implicitly add a bottom element $\bot$ to the lattice $(\{0, 1, 1/2\}, \sqsubseteq)$ of Def. 1. The meet operator $S_1 \sqcap S_2$ is defined as

$$S_1 \sqcap S_2 \stackrel{\text{def}}{=} \begin{cases} (U, \iota_1 \sqcap \iota_2) & \text{if } \iota_1 \sqcap \iota_2 \neq \bot \\ \bot & \text{otherwise} \end{cases}$$

where

$$\iota_1 \sqcap \iota_2 \stackrel{\text{def}}{=} \begin{cases} \bot & \text{if } \iota_1(p)(\boldsymbol{u}) \sqcap \iota_2(p)(\boldsymbol{u}) = \bot \\ & \text{for some } p \in \mathcal{P}_k \text{ and } \boldsymbol{u} \in U^k \\ \lambda p \in \mathcal{P}_k . \lambda \boldsymbol{u} \in U^k . \iota_1(p)(\boldsymbol{u}) \sqcap \iota_2(p)(\boldsymbol{u}) & \text{otherwise} \end{cases}$$

If a predicate is irrelevant in S_1, its value in $S_1 \sqcap S_2$ is its value in S_2.
- We extend the previous definition to any pair of 3-valued structures by

$$S_1 \sqcap S_2 = \{S_1^\natural \sqcap S_2^\natural \mid S_1^\natural \in canonical(S_1) \wedge S_2^\natural \in canonical(S_2) \wedge U^{S_1'} = U^{S_2'}\} - \{\bot\} \tag{5}$$

With this notation, the composition of transformers $T_2 \circ T_1$, where T_1 and T_2 are 2-vocabulary 3-valued structures (which are really 3-vocabulary 3-valued structures) is expressed as follows:

$$T_2 \circ T_1 \stackrel{\text{def}}{=} \left(T_1[tmp \leftarrow out; out \leftarrow 1/2] \sqcap T_2[tmp \leftarrow in; in \leftarrow 1/2] \right) [tmp \leftarrow 1/2] \tag{6}$$

The effect is to perform a natural join on the $p[tmp]$ predicates to create structures that have T_1's $p[in]$ predicates, T_2's $p[out]$ predicates, and common $p[tmp]$ predicates. The $p[tmp]$ predicates are then eliminated by setting them to $1/2$ [6].

The composition operation is extended to sets of structures in the usual way:

$$SS_2 \circ SS_1 = \bigcup \{S_2 \circ S_1 \mid S_2 \in SS_2 \wedge S_1 \in SS_1\}.$$

---

[6] A different view of this step is that making the $p[tmp]$ predicates irrelevant corresponds to existentially quantifying them out. If expressed by means of a formula, the operation of making $p[tmp]$ irrelevant would involve second-order quantification over $p[tmp]$; however, the operation is performed directly on a logical structure, and hence it is not a problem for us that the operation cannot be expressed by means of a first-order formula.

In contrast, the composition operation $\tau_{m,n} \circ \phi(m)$ in Eqn. (3), which represents an intraprocedural-propagation step, is heterogeneous: $\tau_{m,n}$ is defined using a collection of *predicate-update formulas*, $c(v_1, \ldots, v_k) = \tau_{c,(m,n)}(v_1, \ldots, v_k)$, whereas $\phi(m)$ is a set of 2-vocabulary 3-valued structures. Thus, the composition operation in Eqn. (3) can be implemented merely by performing the standard TVLA intraprocedural-propagation step for $\tau_{m,n}$ on the *out* predicates (only) for each of the structures in $\phi(m)$. (Note that the $\sqcup$ operation in Eqn. (3) is union of sets of 3-valued structures. Each $\tau_{m,n}$ operates elementwise on a set of 3-valued structures, and hence distributes over $\sqcup$.)

In practice, Eqns. (1)–(4) are solved by propagating *changes* in values, rather than full values. Such a differential algorithm is presented in [17].

4.2 Local Variables and Parameters

Until now, we have assumed that a state of a program is defined by a memory configuration, and that relations between states are represented using structures over doubled vocabularies. Things are actually a bit more complicated: a state also includes the values of local variables, formal input parameters, and formal output parameters. The summary transformer $\phi(n)$ must thus also relate the values of formal input parameters at node $s_{proc(n)}$ to the state of the heap and the values of local variables at n.

To incorporate local variables and parameters, we merely have to expand the vocabulary to $\mathcal{P}_{loc} \uplus \mathcal{P}_g[in] \uplus \mathcal{P}_g[out] \uplus \mathcal{P}_g[tmp]$, where the vocabulary $\mathcal{P}_{loc}$ captures Boolean-valued and pointer-valued local variables and parameters, and $\mathcal{P}_g$ is the tripled vocabulary from §4.1. The assumption that formal input parameters are not modified in the body of a procedure makes it unnecessary to duplicate/triplicate the predicate symbols for parameters in $\mathcal{P}_{loc}$. Eqn. (2) then becomes:

$$\phi(s_q) = Id|_D \quad s_p \in \text{StartNodes}, p \neq main, \text{ and}$$
$$D = \bigsqcup_{\substack{(c,s_p) \in \text{ CallToStartEdges} \\ \text{and the call is } y := p(x)}} \text{range}(\tau_{\mathrm{fpi}_p := x} \circ \phi(c))[loc \setminus \{\mathrm{fpi}_p\} \leftarrow 1/2] \quad (7)$$

where $\tau_{.:=.}$ denotes the transformer generated by update formulas that correspond to the assignment in the subscript. Eqn. (7) reflects the binding of the actual parameter x at node c to the formal input parameter fpi_p at node s_p. All relations corresponding to the other local variables and parameters are set to irrelevant at this node.

For a call statement of the form $y := q(x)$, where $T_2 = \phi(e_q)$ and $T_1 = \phi(call(n))$, the transformer-composition operation $T_2 \circ T_1$ used in Eqn. (4) to implement the abstract procedure-return operation can be expressed as

$$T_2 \circ T_1 \stackrel{def}{=} \left(\tau_{y := \mathrm{fpo}} \circ \left(\begin{matrix} (\tau_{\mathrm{fpi} := x} \circ T_1)[tmp \leftarrow out; out \leftarrow 1/2] \\ \sqcap \\ (\tau_{\mathrm{fpi} := \mathrm{fpi}_q;} \circ T_2) \\ {}_{\mathrm{fpo} := \mathrm{fpo}_q} \end{matrix} \right) \left[\begin{matrix} tmp \leftarrow in; in \leftarrow 1/2; \\ loc \leftarrow 1/2 \end{matrix} \right] \right) \left[\begin{matrix} tmp \leftarrow 1/2; \\ \{\mathrm{fpi}, \mathrm{fpo}\} \leftarrow 1/2 \end{matrix} \right]$$
$$(8)$$

where fpi and fpo are fresh unary core predicates (not in $\mathcal{P}_{loc}$ or $\mathcal{P}_g$) that are used to impose parameter-passing constraints as follows: fpi is bound to the value of the actual input parameter x of T_1; fpi is also bound to the value of formal input parameter fpi_q of

T_2; and fpo is bound to the value of formal output parameter fpo_q of T_2. In particular, the fpi relation and all of the *tmp* relations are common in the meet operation performed in Eqn. (8). Then, because the local variables in T_2 are set to be irrelevant, the values for the local variables in the structures of the answer set are the values from T_1, with the exception of the actual output parameter y, which is assigned the value of $\text{fpo} = \text{fpo}_q$.

4.3   An Efficient Implementation of the Meet Operation

There are two sources of combinatorial explosion in Eqns. (4), (5), (6), and (8):

1. The number of pairs $(S_1, S_2) \in \phi(e_q) \times \phi(call(n))$ (quadratic explosion);
2. The cardinality of the sets $canonical(S_1)$ and $canonical(S_2)$ in Eqn. (5) defining the meet operator $\sqcap$ (exponential explosion).

Point 1 is inherited from the nature of our abstract lattice, which is a *powerset* domain, and the fact that we apply a binary operation (composition) to values in the domain. We do not address this problem here.

Point 2 is specific to our abstract lattice and concerns only the meet operation, especially when it is used to implement relational composition. Consider a pair of 3-valued structures T_1 and T_2 for which a composition is performed in Eqn. (4). In T_1, the core predicates that represent variables of the called procedure q are irrelevant, so they have the value $1/2$. This means that the operation *canonical* will enumerate all possible *definite* interpretations for these predicates; the number of these interpretations is exponential in the number of such predicates. A similar situation holds for T_2.

More generally, consider a structure $S = \langle U^S, \iota^S \rangle$ with n irrelevant unary core predicates; the cost of *canonical* is $\mathcal{O}((2^{|U^S|})^n)$. Even if the unary predicates represent only pointer-valued variables, which means that such predicates may evaluate to 1 on at most one individual, there are still $\mathcal{O}(|U|^n)$ possible interpretations.

In our case, this combinatorial explosion is all the more frustrating because it is only temporary: the meet $S_1 \sqcap S_2$ will reject (by evaluating to $\bot$) most of the structures obtained by enumerating definite interpretations of irrelevant predicates in S_1 (resp. S_2). Indeed, predicates that are irrelevant in one structure and relevant in the other usually have definite interpretations in the latter.

A Better Implementation of $\sqcap$. The approach that we actually followed in our extended version of TVLA was to implement an approximation to the meet operation using systems of 3-valued constraints [1], which were already supported by the base TVLA system. In TVLA, there is a global set of constraints C_0 that is used to express integrity constraints on the set of 2-valued structures that a 3-valued structure represents. For instance, some of the constraints in C_0 express the fact that a unary predicate that represents a pointer-valued variable can evaluate to 1 on at most one individual. For convenience, we will associate a constraint set C^S with each structure, so that a 3-valued structure S is now a triple: $\langle U^S, \iota^S, C^S \rangle$. ($C^S$ is generally C_0.)

A set of constraints C represents the set of concrete structures that satisfy C:

$$\gamma_c(C) \overset{\text{def}}{=} \{S \in \mathcal{S}_2 \mid S \models C\} \tag{9}$$

in the same way that a 3-valued structure S represents the set of concrete structures $\gamma(\{S\})$ that can be embedded into S via canonical abstraction [1].

Assume now that we have an operation $cons : \mathcal{S}_3 \rightarrow \wp(\mathcal{C})$ that associates to a given structure a set of constraints such that for any S, $\gamma(\{S\}) \subseteq \gamma_c(cons(S))$. In other words, constraint set $cons(S)$ overapproximates S. For any logical structures $S_1 = \langle U^{S_1}, \iota^{S_1}, C^{S_1} \rangle$ and $S_2 = \langle U^{S_2}, \iota^{S_2}, C^{S_2} \rangle$, we now define the operation $\sqcap^c$:

$$S_1 \sqcap^c S_2 \stackrel{\text{def}}{=} \langle U^{S_1}, \iota^{S_1}, C^{S_1} \cup cons(S_2) \rangle.$$

This operator has the following property: $\gamma(\{S_1 \sqcap^c S_2\}) \supseteq \gamma(\{S_1\}) \cap \gamma(\{S_2\})$, with equality if the $cons$ operation is exact.

To summarize, the approximate meet operator consists of adding $cons(S_2)$ to S_1 temporarily, then performing Focus and Coerce operations to transfer the information that is initially contained in the additional constraints to the universe U^{S_1} and the interpretation ι^{S_1}. Afterwards, the additional constraints are removed.

For instance, when we use the meet operation in Eqns. (6) and (8), we replace $S_1' \sqcap S_2'$ in Eqn. (5) by $Coerce(Focus(S_1' \sqcap^c S_2', \{\text{fpo}(v)\}))$. This forces fpo to be given a definite interpretation that is constrained by the set $cons(S_2)$, which represents the summary transformer of the callee.

Converting a 3-Valued Structure to a Set of Constraints. To achieve this, we adapted a result from [18], which shows how to characterize a 3-valued logical structure that is in the image of canonical abstraction by means of a formula in first-order logic with transitive closure. The resulting formula can easily be converted to a set of constraints that satisfy the restricted syntax given in [1]. However, one of the constraints that would be generated according to [18] would be too expensive to check from an algorithmic point of view, so this constraint is dropped, which induces a safe overapproximation. (Roughly, this constraint captures the fact that any *concrete* structure represented by the abstract structure should contain a number of individuals greater than or equal to the number of individuals in the abstract structure.)

5   Implementation and Experiments

To perform interprocedural shape analysis by the method that is described in §4, we created a modified version of TVLA [3], an existing shape-analysis system, to allow it to support the following features:

- We replaced the built-in notion of an intraprocedural CFG by the more general notion of *equation system*.
- We designed a more general language in which to specify equation systems.
- We implemented an approximation to the meet operation on 3-valued structures (and hence to the composition operation), as described in §4.3.

Fig. 5 shows how the summary information we obtain captures the behavior of the recursive list-reversal procedure of Figs. 1 and 2. The descriptor of the initial summary transformer at start node s_{main} was the 3-valued structure S_0, shown in Fig. 5(a), which

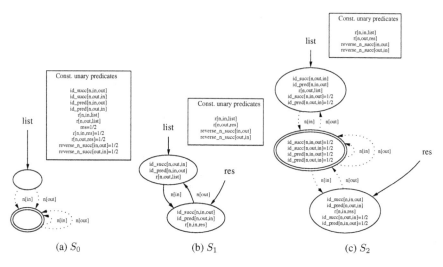

Fig. 5. List-reversal example. (In each structure, unary predicates that have the same non-0 value for all individuals are displayed in the box labeled "Const. unary predicates". The values of the "irrelevant" predicates of the vocabulary are not shown.)

represents (the identity transformation on) all linked lists of length at least two that are pointed to by program-variable `list`. The head of the answer list is pointed to by program-variable `res`. At the program's exit node e_{main}, the summary transformers were the structures S_1 and S_2 of Fig. 5(b)–(c), which represent the transformations that reverse lists of length two, and all lists of length greater than two, respectively.

As discussed in §3, to prevent the loss of essential information, several families of instrumentation predicates were introduced:

- The unary predicates $id\_succ[n, m_1, m_2]$ and $id\_pred[n, m_1, m_2]$, where $m_1, m_2 \in \{in, out\}$ and $m_1 \neq m_2$, record information about the values of different modes of predicate n, in particular, whether the value of predicate $n[m_1]$ implies $n[m_2]$. These are defined by

$$id\_succ[n, m_1, m_2](v) = \forall v_1 : (n[m_1](v, v_1) \Rightarrow n[m_2](v, v_1))$$
$$id\_pred[n, m_1, m_2](v) = \forall v_1 : (n[m_1](v_1, v) \Rightarrow n[m_2](v_1, v)).$$

  The fact that $id\_succ[n, in, out](v) \wedge id\_succ[n, out, in](v) \wedge id\_pred[n, in, out](v) \wedge id\_pred[n, out, in](v)$ holds globally in S_0 (cf. Fig. 5(a)) captures the condition that the $n[in]$ and $n[out]$ predicates are identical at the entry node of the procedure. The $n[in]$ predicates serve as an indelible record of the state of the n-links at the entry node.

- The unary predicates $reverse\_n\_succ[m_1, m_2]$, again with $m_1, m_2 \in \{in, out\}$ and $m_1 \neq m_2$, record whether $n[m_2]$ is an inverse of $n[m_1]$. These are defined by

$$reverse\_n\_succ[m_1, m_2](v) = \forall v_1 : (n[m_1](v, v_1) \Rightarrow n[m_2](v_1, v)).$$

The values for these predicates in S_1 and S_2 show that for each n-link $n[in](v_1, v_2)$ at the entry node s_{main}, we have an n-link $n[out](v_2, v_1)$ at the exit node e_{main}. In other words, the procedure has reversed all the n-links.

In addition, during the composition operation, some additional constraint rules were needed for the system to be able to deduce a relationship between $n[in]$ and $n[out]$. These are defined by

$$id\_succ[n, in, tmp](v) \land reverse\_n\_succ[tmp, out](v) \Rightarrow reverse\_n\_succ[in, out](v)$$
$$reverse\_n\_succ[in, tmp](v) \land id\_pred[tmp, out](v) \Rightarrow reverse\_n\_succ[in, out](v)$$

Notice that only the $reverse\_n\_succ[m_1, m_2]$ predicates and the related constraint rules are particular to the list-reversal example. The other predicates that appear in Fig. 5 were already used in previous papers on shape analysis of list-manipulation programs (see [1]): for instance, $r[n, out, list](v)$ holds the value 1 for individuals that are reachable from variable list through a chain of $n[out]$ links. From the above definitions of the instrumentation predicates, it should be clear that the set of 3-valued structures $\{S_1, S_2\}$ accurately captures the fact that the output list is the reversal of the input list, and that the result is a list of length at least two.

Our second experiment involved comparing our results with [11] on the following examples: (i) list reversal (as discussed above), and (ii) non-deterministic insertion and deletion of a cell in a list. Results are shown in Fig. 6. Our method performs better than that of [11] for the list-reversal program, but worse for the latter two programs. For those, we considered programs where the cell to be inserted is passed as an input parameter (in the insert example), and the deleted cell is received back as an output parameter (in the delete example); this provides information about where the cell has been inserted (resp. deleted).

Program	Our method			Method of [11]		
	# of structs.	Time (sec)	Space (Mb)	# of structs.	Time (sec)	Space (Mb)
reverse	7/3	11	26	·/3	37	17
insert	23/9	188	43	·/9	70	18
delete	32/13	222	43	·/7	47	17
tree exch.	22/10	92	33	—		

The experiments were performed on a PC equipped with a 2 GHz Pentium 4 processor and 768 Mb of memory. *Time* and *Space* information were obtained with the time and top commands. The two numbers in each entry of the columns labeled *# of structs.* give the number of structures for the summary transformer of the recursive procedure and the number of structures at the end of the main procedure, respectively.

Fig. 6. Experimental results.

For the versions of the programs analyzed by the method of [11], we added a global variable cell, which plays a similar role.

Concerning the slower computation times, we think they are mainly due to the higher number of predicates to be manipulated (because of the different modes) and the cost of the meet operation. However, it is important to keep in mind that our method computes a *summary transformer* for each procedure, which [11] does not. The summary transformer $\phi(e_q)$ at an exit node e_q is a partial function: the domain of $\phi(e_q)$ overapproximates the set of reachable states at $s_{proc(e_q)}$ from which it is possible to reach e_q; the range of $\phi(e_q)$ overapproximates the set of reachable states at e_q. This has an impact on the results: for the delete example, the method of [11] is not able to keep track of the original position in the list of the deleted cell, unlike our method. (For the insert example, however, the two methods are similar w.r.t. this kind of information.)

Our third experiment was to analyze a procedure that recursively exchanges the right and left subtrees of a binary tree. This example is interesting because it would be difficult to implement this operation as a non-recursive procedure. The analysis was able to establish that after the procedure finishes, the subtrees of all cells reachable from the root have been exchanged, whereas the other cells have not been modified.

Statistics are given in Fig. 6. More information about the experiments is available at http://www.irisa.fr/prive/bjeannet/interproctvla/interproctvla.html.

6   Related Work

The analysis described in this paper uses 3-valued structures over a doubled vocabulary. A similar approach is standard when concrete transition relations are expressed by means of formulas. For instance, the semantics of a statement x := y+1 can be expressed as $(x' = y + 1) \land (y' = y)$. Statements such as x := y+1 can be transformed into composable abstract transformers for programs that manipulate numeric data, using several numeric lattices (e.g., polyhedra [19], octagons [20], etc.). In contrast, Observation 1 provides a way to create composable abstract transformers for the analysis of programs that support both dynamically-allocated storage and destructive updating of pointer-valued fields of structures. A key feature of the approach is that instrumentation predicates can refer to both the $\mathcal{P}[in]$ and $\mathcal{P}[out]$ vocabularies. For instance, the family of unary predicates $reverse\_n\_succ[m_1, m_2]$ discussd in §5 (with $m_1, m_2 \in \{in, out\}$ and $m_1 \neq m_2$) records whether $n[m_2]$ is an inverse of $n[m_1]$.

As discussed in the introduction, interprocedural shape analysis was also studied in [11]. The approach used in the present paper was inspired by the functional approaches of [4–6]. In contrast, the approach used in [11] is more reminiscent of the "call-strings" approach of [5].

A method for performing interprocedural shape analysis using procedure specifications and assume-guarantee reasoning is presented in [16]. There it is assumed that a specification for each procedure – a pre- and post-condition – is already known; the technique presented in [16] can be used to interpret a procedure's pre- and post-condition in the most precise way (for a given abstraction). For every procedure invocation, one checks if the current abstract value potentially violates the precondition; if it does, a warning is produced. At the point immediately after the call, one can assume that the post-condition holds. Similarly, when a procedure is analyzed, the pre-condition is assumed to hold on entry, and at end of the procedure the post-condition is checked. The work described in the present paper is *complementary* to [16]: the work described here – particularly in the modified form sketched in footnote 5 – provides a way to identify procedure specifications (in the form of sets of 2-vocabulary 3-valued structures) that can be used with the method from [16].

A second connection is that [16] provides a method to compute the most-precise overapproximation of the meet of two abstract values, which is the operation needed for composing transformers that are expressed as sets of 2-vocabulary 3-valued structures (see Eqns. (6) and (8)). Consequently, [16] provides a more precise alternative to the approximate meet operation described in §4.3. (At present, implementations of the methods from [16] are based on theorem provers, and are much slower than the method from §4.3, which does not involve a theorem prover.)

Acknowledgments

We thank Viktor Kuncak for several helpful discussions about the approach taken in this paper.

References

1. Sagiv, M., Reps, T., Wilhelm, R.: Parametric shape analysis via 3-valued logic. Trans. on Prog. Lang. and Syst. **24** (2002) 217–298
2. Reps, T., Sagiv, M., Loginov, A.: Finite differencing of logical formulas for static analysis. In: European Symp. on Programming. (2003) 380–398
3. Lev-Ami, T., Sagiv, M.: TVLA: A system for implementing static analyses. In: Static Analysis Symp. (2000) 280–301
4. Cousot, P., Cousot, R.: Static determination of dynamic properties of recursive procedures. In Neuhold, E., ed.: Formal Descriptions of Programming Concepts, (IFIP WG 2.2, St. Andrews, Canada, August 1977). North-Holland (1978) 237–277
5. Sharir, M., Pnueli, A.: Two approaches to interprocedural data flow analysis. In Muchnick, S., Jones, N., eds.: Program Flow Analysis: Theory and Applications. Prentice-Hall, Englewood Cliffs, NJ (1981) 189–234
6. Knoop, J., Steffen, B.: The interprocedural coincidence theorem. In: Comp. Construct. (1992) 125–140
7. Reps, T., Horwitz, S., Sagiv, M.: Precise interprocedural dataflow analysis via graph reachability. In: Princ. of Prog. Lang., New York, NY, ACM Press (1995) 49–61
8. Sagiv, M., Reps, T., Horwitz, S.: Precise interprocedural dataflow analysis with applications to constant propagation. Theor. Comp. Sci. **167** (1996) 131–170
9. Reps, T., Schwoon, S., Jha, S.: Weighted pushdown systems and their application to interprocedural dataflow analysis. In: Static Analysis Symp. (2003) 189–213
10. Ball, T., Rajamani, S.: Bebop: A path-sensitive interprocedural dataflow engine. In: Prog. Analysis for Softw. Tools and Eng. (2001) 97–103
11. Rinetzky, N., Sagiv, M.: Interprocedural shape analysis for recursive programs. In: Comp. Construct. Volume 2027 of Lec. Notes in Comp. Sci. (2001) 133–149
12. Jones, N., Muchnick, S.: A flexible approach to interprocedural data flow analysis and programs with recursive data structures. In: Princ. of Prog. Lang. (1982) 66–74
13. Deutsch, A.: On determining lifetime and aliasing of dynamically allocated data in higher-order functional specifications. In: Princ. of Prog. Lang. (1990) 157–168
14. Gopan, D., DiMaio, F., N.Dor, Reps, T., Sagiv, M.: Numeric domains with summarized dimensions. In: Tools and Algs. for the Construct. and Anal. of Syst. (2004) 512–529
15. Loginov, A., Reps, T., Sagiv, M.: Abstraction refinement for 3-valued-logic analysis. Tech. Rep. 1504, Comp. Sci. Dept., Univ. of Wisconsin (2004)
16. Yorsh, G., Reps, T., Sagiv, M.: Symbolically computing most-precise abstract operations for shape analysis. In: Tools and Algs. for the Construct. and Anal. of Syst. (2004) 530–545
17. Jeannet, B., Loginov, A., Reps, T., Sagiv, M.: A relational approach to interprocedural shape analysis. Tech. Rep. 1505, Comp. Sci. Dept., Univ. of Wisconsin (2004)
18. Yorsh, G.: Logical characterizations of heap abstractions. Master's thesis, School of Computer Science, Tel Aviv University, Israel (2003)
19. Cousot, P., Halbwachs, N.: Automatic discovery of linear constraints among variables of a program. In: Princ. of Prog. Lang. (1978) 84–96
20. Miné, A.: The octagon abstract domain. In: 8th Working Conf. on Rev. Eng. (2001) 310–322

Partially Disjunctive Heap Abstraction

Roman Manevich[1], Mooly Sagiv[1], Ganesan Ramalingam[2], and John Field[2]

[1] Tel Aviv University
{rumster,msagiv}@tau.ac.il
[2] IBM T.J. Watson Research Center
{rama,jfield}@watson.ibm.com

Abstract. One of the continuing challenges in abstract interpretation is the creation of abstractions that yield analyses that are both *tractable* and *precise enough* to prove interesting properties about real-world programs. One source of difficulty is the need to handle programs with different behaviors along different execution paths. Disjunctive (powerset) abstractions capture such distinctions in a natural way. However, in general, powerset abstractions increase space and time costs by an exponential factor. Thus, powerset abstractions are generally perceived as very costly.

In this paper, we partially address this challenge by presenting and empirically evaluating a new heap abstraction. The new heap abstraction works by merging shape descriptors according to a partial isomorphism similarity criteria, resulting in a partially disjunctive abstraction.

We implemented this abstraction in TVLA – a generic system for implementing program analyses. We conducted an empirical evaluation of the new abstraction and compared it with the powerset heap abstraction. The experiments show that analyses based on the partially disjunctive heap abstraction are as precise as the ones based on the powerset heap abstraction. In terms of performance, analyses based on the partially disjunctive heap abstraction are often superior to analyses based on the powerset heap abstraction. The empirical results show considerable speedups, up to 2 orders of magnitude, enabling previously non-terminating analyses, such as verification of the Deutsch-Schorr-Waite scanning algorithm, to terminate with no negative effect on the overall precision. Indeed, experience indicates that the partially disjunctive shape abstraction improves performance across all TVLA analyses uniformly, and in many cases is essential for making precise shape analysis feasible.

1 Introduction

One of the continuing challenges in abstract interpretation [3] is the creation of abstractions that yield analyses that are both *tractable* and *precise enough* to prove interesting properties about real-world programs. In this paper we partially address this challenge by presenting and empirically evaluating a new heap abstraction, i.e., an abstraction for the (potentially unbounded) dynamically allocated storage manipulated by programs (e.g., see [7, 9, 2, 8, 16, 14, 15]). Heap abstractions are of fundamental importance to static analysis and verification of programs written in modern languages. Heap abstractions have been used, for instance, in the context of shape analysis (e.g., for proving that

R. Giacobazzi (Ed.): SAS 2004, LNCS 3148, pp. 265–279, 2004.
© Springer-Verlag Berlin Heidelberg 2004

a program fragment preserves certain tree structure invariants), as well as in verifying that a client program satisfies certain conformance constraints for the correct usage of a library.

We present our abstraction in the context of the parametric abstract interpretation framework of [15], which is based on the idea of representing program states using 3-valued logical structures. While it is very natural to view the abstraction we present as a heap abstraction, it can be used for abstracting other domains as well.

The TVLA framework presented in [15] uses a disjunctive (powerset) heap abstraction: the abstract value at every program point is a *set* of shape descriptors (of bounded size) and set union is used as the join operation. In particular, this abstraction does not attempt to combine (or merge) different shape descriptors into one and relies on the fact that there are only finitely many shape descriptors (as they are of bounded size). This leads to powerful and sophisticated analyses for proving interesting program properties but is usually too expensive to be applied to real-world programs. (The number of distinct shape descriptors is doubly exponential in the size of the program in the worst case.)

The heap abstractions most commonly used in practice, especially when scalability is important, tend to be *single-shape* heap abstractions, which use a single shape descriptor to describe all possible program states at a program point [9, 2, 14]. The current TVLA implementation provides options to utilize such single-shape heap abstractions. However, our experience has been that for the kind of applications that we have used TVLA for (mostly verification problems), the single-shape abstraction tends to be imprecise and causes a number of "false alarms" (i.e., verification fails for correct programs). Hence, this abstraction is not widely used by TVLA users. (A detailed discussion of the single-shape abstractions is beyond the scope of this paper, because of the complexity of formalizing the single-shape abstractions within the framework of 3-valued-logic.)

This paper presents a *partially disjunctive* heap abstraction which, in our experience, is significantly more efficient than the powerset heap abstraction, but has turned out to be precise enough for all the applications we have experimented with. Indeed, this abstraction has turned out to be the abstraction of choice for all TVLA users. The main idea behind this abstraction is to reduce the set of shape descriptors arising at a program point by merging "similar" shape descriptors but keeping "dissimilar" shape descriptors apart.

1.1 Running Example

Figure 1 shows a method implementing the mark phase of a mark-and-sweep garbage collector. The challenge here is to show that this procedure is partially correct, i.e., to establish that "upon termination, an element is marked if and only if it is reachable from the root." This simple program serves as a running example in this paper. The partial correctness of this program was established using abstract interpretation in [13]. This abstract interpretation was created using TVLA – a generic system for implementing program analyses [10]. The default implementation of TVLA uses the powerset heap abstraction. Verification of the above property using the powerset heap abstraction took 584 cpu seconds and generated 189,772 different shape descriptors – definitely too

```
// @Ensures marked == REACH(root)
void mark(Node root, NodeSet marked) {
    Node x;
    if (root != null) {
        NodeSet pending = new NodeSet();
        pending.add(root);
        marked.clear();
        while (!pending.isEmpty()) {
            x = pending.selectAndRemove();
            marked.add(x);
            if (x.left != null)
                if (!marked.contains(x.left))
                    pending.add(x.left);
            if (x.right != null)
                if (!marked.contains(x.right))
                    pending.add(x.right);
        }
    }
}
```

Fig. 1. A simple Java-like implementation of the mark phase of a mark-and-sweep garbage collector

many for such a simple program and simple property. The situation is worse for verifying a similar property for an implementation of the Deutsch-Schorr-Waite scanning procedure [11]. This verification took 4 hours when the powerset heap abstraction was used.

Powerset heap abstractions are costly since they may distinguish between too many shape descriptors, which may not be necessary in order to verify program properties. In this paper, we define a partially disjunctive heap abstraction, which is coarser than the powerset heap abstraction. The main idea is to reduce the set of shape descriptors arising at a program point by merging "similar" shape descriptors. In the mark example, verification using the partially disjunctive heap abstraction took 3 cpu seconds and generated 1, 133 shape descriptors – a two orders of magnitude improvement over verification using the powerset heap abstraction – with the same precision. Similarly, the verification of an implementation of the Deutsch-Schorr-Waite scanning procedure terminated successfully in 158 cpu seconds using the partially disjunctive heap abstraction.

1.2   Main Results

A New Abstraction. We define a new heap abstraction, which we refer to as the *partial-isomorphism* heap abstraction. The new abstraction is coarser than the powerset heap abstraction and yet keeps certain shape descriptors apart. Our abstraction is parametric. It allows the user to specify which heap properties are of importance for a given analysis, and this guides the abstraction in determining which shape descriptors are merged together.

Robust Implementation. We implemented our abstraction in TVLA. This abstraction has turned out to be the abstraction of choice for all TVLA users (e.g., see [19]). We

believe that it is simple enough to be implemented in other systems besides TVLA
(e.g., [17]).

Empirical Evaluation. We empirically evaluated our abstraction by comparing it with
the powerset heap abstraction. In the largest benchmark, SQLExecuter, powerset
heap abstraction did not terminate within $20,000$ cpu seconds. In contrast, the new
abstraction took $9,673$ cpu seconds and proved correct usage of JDBC objects and
absence of null-dereferences.

1.3   Outline

In Section 2, we give an overview of 3-valued-logic based program analysis. In Section 3, we describe the partial-isomorphism heap abstraction. In Section 4, we provide
an empirical evaluation of the partial-isomorphism heap abstraction and powerset heap
abstraction. In Section 5, we outline several other heap abstractions that we are investigating as ongoing work. In Section 6, we discuss related work.

2   3-Valued Shape Analysis Primer

We now present an overview of *first order transition systems* (FOTS), the formalism
underlying the parametric analysis framework of [15]. FOTS may be thought of as an
imperative language built around an expression sub-language based on first-order logic
with transitive closure.

Concrete Program Configurations

In FOTS, program states are represented using 2-valued logical structures.

Definition 1. *A* 2-*valued logical structure over a set of predicates P is a pair $C^\natural = \langle U^\natural, I^\natural \rangle$ where:*

- *$U^\natural$ is the universe of the 2-valued structure.*
- *$I^\natural$ is the interpretation function mapping predicates to their truth-value in the structure: for every predicate $p \in P$ of arity k, $I^\natural(p) : U^{\natural^k} \to \{0, 1\}$.*

In the context of shape analysis, a logical structure is used as a shape descriptor, with
each individual corresponding to a heap-allocated object and predicates of the structure
corresponding to properties of heap-allocated objects.

In the following, we use $p^{C^\natural}(v)$ as alternative notation for $I^\natural(p)(v)$, omitting the
superscript $C^\natural$, when no confusion is likely. We denote the set of all 2-valued logical
structures over a set of predicates P by 2-STRUCT$_P$. We will mostly assume that the
set of predicates P is fixed and abbreviate 2-STRUCT$_P$ to 2-STRUCT.

Table 1 shows the predicates used to record properties of individuals for the analysis
of our running example. A unary predicate $ref(v)$ holds when the reference (or pointer)
variable ref points to the object v; in our example ref $\in \{x, root\}$. Similarly, a binary

Table 1. Predicates used to verify the running example

Predicates	Intended Meaning
$x(v)$	Does reference variable x point to object v?
$root(v)$	Does reference variable $root$ point to object v?
$\texttt{left}(v_1, v_2)$	Does field $\texttt{left}$ of object v_1 point to object v_2?
$\texttt{right}(v_1, v_2)$	Does field $\texttt{right}$ of object v_1 point to object v_2?
$r[root](v)$	Is object v heap-reachable from reference variable $root$?
$set[marked](v)$	Is object v a member of the $marked$ set?
$set[pending](v)$	Is object v a member of the $pending$ set?

predicate $fld(v_1, v_2)$ records the value of a reference (or pointer-valued) field $\texttt{fld}$; in our example $\texttt{fld} \in \{\texttt{left}, \texttt{right}\}$. A unary predicate $set[s](v)$ holds when the object v belongs to the set s; in our example $s \in \{marked, pending\}$.

In this paper, program configurations (i.e., 2-valued logical structures) are depicted as directed graphs. Each individual of the universe is drawn as a node. A unary predicate $p(u)$, which holds for a node u, is drawn inside the node u. If a unary predicate represents a reference variables it is shown by having an arrow drawn from its name to the node pointed by the variable. A binary predicate $p(u_1, u_2)$ which evaluates to 1 is drawn as directed edge from u_1 to u_2 labelled with p.

Figure 2(a) shows a concrete configuration arising at the exit label of the mark procedure, where all the individuals that are reachable from $root$ are marked, as indicated by the value of the $set[marked]$ predicate. The individuals represented by the empty nodes correspond to garbage objects.

Operational Semantics

In FOTS, program statements are modelled by *actions* that specify how statements transform an incoming logical structure into an outgoing logical structure. This is done primarily by defining the values of the predicates in the outgoing structure using first-order logical formulae with transitive closure over the incoming structure [15].

Abstract Program Configurations

We now describe the abstractions used to create a finite (bounded) representation of a potentially unbounded set of 2-valued structures (representing heaps) of potentially unbounded size. The abstractions we use are based on 3-valued logic [15], which extends boolean logic by introducing a third value $1/2$, denoting values that may be 0 or 1. In particular, we utilize the partially ordered set $\{0, 1, 1/2\}$ with the join operation $\sqcup$, defined by $x \sqcup y = x$ if $x = y$ and $1/2$ otherwise.

Definition 2. *A 3-valued logical structure over a set of predicates P is a pair $C = \langle U, I \rangle$ where:*

- *U is the universe of the 3-valued structure.*
- *I is the interpretation function mapping predicates to their truth-value in the structure: for every predicate $p \in P$ of arity k, $I(p) : U^k \to \{0, 1, 1/2\}$.*

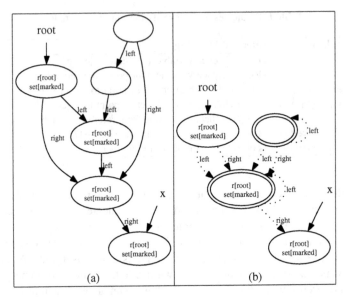

Fig. 2. (a) A concrete program configuration arising at the exit label of the mark procedure, where all non-garbage nodes have been marked; (b) An abstract program configuration that approximates the concrete configuration in (a)

A 3-valued logical structure can be used as an abstraction of a larger 2-valued logical structure. This is achieved by letting an abstract configuration (i.e., a 3-valued logical structure) include *summary individuals*, i.e., an individual which corresponds to one or more individuals in a concrete configuration represented by that abstract configuration. In the rest of the paper, we assume that the set of predicates P includes a distinguished unary predicate *sm* to indicate if an individual is a summary individual.

In this paper, 3-valued logical structures are also depicted as directed graphs, where binary predicates with $1/2$ values are shown as dotted edges and summary individuals are shown as double-circled nodes.

We denote the set of all 3-valued logical structures over a set of predicates P by 3-STRUCT$_P$, usually abbreviating it to 3-STRUCT. We define a preorder on structures, denoted by $\sqsubseteq$, based on the concept of *embedding*.

Definition 3. *Let S and S' be two structures and let $f\colon U^S \to U^{S'}$ be surjective. We say that f **embeds** S in S' (denoted by $S \sqsubseteq^f S'$) if (i) for every predicate p (including sm) of arity k, and every $k-tuple$ of individuals $u_1, \dots, u_k \in U^S$,*

$$p^S(u_1, \dots, u_k) \sqsubseteq p^{S'}(f(u_1), \dots, f(u_k)) \tag{1}$$

and (ii) for all $u' \in U^{S'}$

$$(|\{u \mid f(u) = u'\}| > 1) \sqsubseteq sm^{S'}(u') \tag{2}$$

We say that S **can be embedded** in S' (denoted by $S \sqsubseteq S'$) if there exists a function f such that $S \sqsubseteq^f S'$.

Bounded Program Configurations

Note that the size of a 3-valued structure is potentially unbounded and that 3-STRUCT is infinite. The abstractions studied in this paper rely on a fundamental abstraction function for converting a potentially unbounded structure (either 2-valued or 3-valued) into a bounded 3-valued structure, which we define now. This abstraction function $\alpha_{blur[A]}$ is parameterized by a special set of unary predicates A referred to as the *abstraction predicates*.

Let A be a set of unary predicates. An individual u_1 in a structure S_1 is said to be A-compatible to an individual u_2 in a structure S_2 iff for every predicate $p \in A$, $p^{S_1}(u_1) \sqsubseteq p^{S_2}(u_2)$ or $p^{S_2}(u_2) \sqsubseteq p^{S_1}(u_1)$. (Recall that the partial order $\sqsubseteq$ on $\{0, 1, 1/2\}$ is defined by $x \sqsubseteq y$ iff $x = y$ or $y = 1/2$.)

A 3-valued structure is said to be A-bounded if no two different individuals in its universe are A-compatible. A structure that is A-bounded can have at most $2^{|A|}$ individuals. We denote the set of all 3-valued A-bounded structures over a set of predicates by B-STRUCT$_{P,A}$, and, as usual, omit the subscripts when no confusion is likely.

The abstraction function β_{blur} : 3-STRUCT $\rightarrow$ B-STRUCT, which converts a (potentially unbounded) 3-valued structure into a bounded 3-valued structure, is defined as follows: we obtain an A-bounded structure from a given structure by merging all pairs of A-compatible individuals. $\beta_{blur}(\langle U_1, I \rangle) = \langle U_2, J \rangle$, where U_2 is the set of A-compatible equivalence classes of U_1, and the interpretation J is defined by:

$$\begin{aligned} p^J(c_1, \dots, c_k) &= \bigsqcup_{u_1 \in c_1, \dots, u_k \in c_k} p^I(u_1, \dots, u_k) &&\text{for } p \neq sm \\ sm^J(c) &= 1/2 &&\text{if } |c| > 1 \\ sm^J(c) &= sm^I(u) &&\text{if } c = \{u\}. \end{aligned}$$

Figure 2(b) shows an A-bounded structure obtained from the structure in Figure 2(a) with $A = \{x, root, r[root], set[marked], set[pending]\}$.

The abstraction function β_{blur} serves as the basis for abstract interpretation in TVLA. In particular, it serves as the basis for defining various different abstractions for the (potentially unbounded) *set of 2-valued logical structures* that arise at a program point.

2.1 Powerset Heap Abstraction

This abstraction is based on the fact that there can only be a finite number of bounded structures that are not *isomorphic* to one another. (Two structures are isomorphic when there is a bijection between their universes that preserves all predicate values.) The powerset abstraction function operates by bounding 2-valued structures with respect to a subset of the unary predicates, and removing duplicates (isomorphic structures).

For the sake of simplicity we will work with *canonic* bounded structures. Note that the individuals of an A-bounded structure are uniquely identified by the set of values of the predicates in A; we refer to such a set of predicate values as the individual's *canonical name*. For example, the individual pointed by $root$ in Figure 2(b) has the canonical name $u_{\{x=0,root=1,r[root]=1,set[marked]=1,set[pending]=0\}}$. A canonic bounded structure is a bounded structure in which the individuals are identified by their canonical names. We refer to the set of all canonic bounded structures by CB-STRUCT$_{P,A}$. Note that for a given P and A, CB-STRUCT$_{P,A}$ is finite. The *canonic* abstraction function $\beta_{canonic}$: 2-STRUCT $\rightarrow$ CB-STRUCT is defined as follows: $\beta_{canonic}(S)$ is obtained by renaming the individuals of $\beta_{blur}(S)$, giving them canonic names.

The powerset heap abstraction function α_{pow} : $2^{\text{2-STRUCT}} \rightarrow 2^{\text{CB-STRUCT}}$ is defined by

$$\alpha_{pow}(XS) = \{\beta_{canonic}(S) \mid S \in XS\} .$$

3   The Partial-Isomorphism Heap Abstraction

The idea behind partial-isomorphism heap abstraction is fairly simple. The powerset heap abstraction keeps all the canonic bounded structures that arise at a program point separate. Single-shape heap abstraction merges all canonic bounded structures arising at a program point into one structure. The partial-isomorphism heap abstraction, in contrast, merges canonic bounded structures into one structure only when they have the same universe.

We say that a pair of canonic bounded structures are *universe congruent* iff the two structures have the same universe. Universe congruence induces an equivalence relation over sets of canonic bounded structures. This equivalence relation lets us define an abstraction function α_{pi} : $2^{\text{2-STRUCT}} \rightarrow 2^{\text{CB-STRUCT}}$ that merges all universe congruent structures. Given a set of canonic bounded structures XS with the same universe U, we define the merged structure $\bigsqcup XS = \langle U, I \rangle$ that has the same universe as all structures in XS and the following interpretation of predicates. For every predicate p of arity k and tuple of individuals $\langle u_1, \dots , u_k \rangle \in U^k$:

$$p^{\bigsqcup XS}(u_1, \dots , u_k) = \bigsqcup_{S \in XS} p^S(u_1, \dots , u_k) .$$

We are now ready to define the partial-isomorphism heap abstraction function α_{pi}:

$$\alpha_{pi}(XS) = \left\{ \bigsqcup C \mid C \subseteq \alpha_{pow}(XS) \text{ is a universe congruence equivalence class} \right\} .$$

Thus, partial-isomorphism heap abstraction is less precise than the powerset heap abstraction[1]. As the empirical results presented later show, the partial-isomorphism heap abstraction seems to work as well as (i.e., is as precise as) the powerset heap abstraction, *in practice*. The following propositions may help explain why.

Proposition 1. *If a pair of bounded structures S_1 and S_2 are universe congruent, then the merged structure $S_1 \bigsqcup S_2$ is the least bounded structure that approximates (embeds) both S_1 and S_2.*

When partial-isomorphism abstraction is applied to a pair of structures S_1 and S_2, there are two possibilities:

---

[1] Here, precision is used in the sense of a Galois Connection between a pair of abstract domains.

- Structures S_1 and S_2 are not universe congruent. In this case, the result of the abstraction is $\alpha_{pi}(\{S_1, S_2\}) = \{S_1, S_2\}$, which is the least upper-bound of the powerset abstraction – the most precise approximation of both structures.
- Structures S_1 and S_2 are universe congruent. In this case, the result of the abstraction is $\alpha_{pi}(\{S_1, S_2\}) = S_1 \bigsqcup S_2$, which is the most precise upper bound among all (singleton sets of) bounded structures.

Proposition 2. *Partial-isomorphism heap abstraction preserves the values of abstraction predicates.*

In other words, partial-isomorphism heap abstraction only loses the same kind of distinctions that can also be lost by β_{blur} – values of non-abstraction predicates.

In terms of worst-case complexity, partial-isomorphism heap abstraction has the same complexity as powerset heap abstraction – doubly-exponential in the number of abstraction predicates. This is due to the number of sets of canonical names, which is the dominant factor in the worst-case complexity. However, partial-isomorphism heap abstraction can save an exponential factor due to binary predicates, which is the dominant factor in many cases, in practice.

3.1   Illustrating Example

To illustrate the operation of partial-isomorphism heap abstraction, consider the abstract program configuration shown in Figure 2(b) and the abstract program configuration shown in Figure 3(a). Both configurations represent cases where all of the non-garbage nodes have been marked and non-garbage nodes have not been marked, i.e., the program property we want to verify holds for those configurations. The difference between the configurations is in the position of the node pointed by x in the part of the heap that has been marked. In this case, the partial-isomorphism heap abstraction results in the structure shown in Figure 3(b), which ignores the precise position of the node pointed by x inside the part of the heap that was marked.

The mark program non-deterministically selects an object and removes it from the pending set. This non-determinism allows many different ways of traversing the set of objects reachable from root, which results in many different abstract program configurations that sustain the program property we want to verify and only differ by values of binary predicates. Partial-isomorphism heap abstraction ignores the values of the binary predicates, but keeps precise the overall property for an abstract configuration of having sets of nodes with the same garbage/non-garbage and mark/unmarked properties. This allows the analysis to merge many similar structures without losing the information needed to prove the partial correctness of the mark program.

4   Implementation and Empirical Evaluation

We implemented the partial-isomorphism abstraction described in the previous section in TVLA, and the implementation is publicly available [10]. We applied it to verify various specification for the Java programs described in Table 2. To translate Java programs and their specifications to TVP (TVLA's input language), we used a front-end

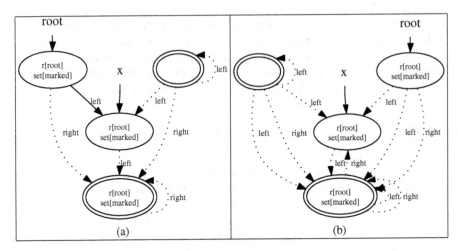

Fig. 3. (a) An abstract program configuration arising at the exit label of the mark procedure, where all non-garbage nodes have been marked and x points to a node adjacent to root; (b) The result of merging the structure in (a) and the structure in Figure 2(b)

Table 2. Benchmarks and properties used for comparing the analysis based on powerset heap abstraction with the analysis based on partial-isomorphism heap abstraction. Treeness means preservation of tree structure invariants

Benchmark	Description	Property
GC.mark	Figure 1	Partial correctness
DSW	Deutsch-Schorr-Waite	Partial correctness of tree scanning + Treeness
ISPath	Input streams	Correct usage of Java IOStreams
InputStream5	Input stream holders	Correct usage of Java IOStreams
InputStream5b	Input stream holders with error	Correct usage of Java IOStreams
InputStream6	Input stream holders	Correct usage of Java IOStreams
SQLExecutor	A JDBC framework	Correct usage of JDBC objects
KernelBench.1	CMP benchmark [12]	Absence of concurrent modification exceptions
InsertSorted	Insertion into sorted trees	Tree sortedness + Treeness
DeleteSorted	Deletion from sorted trees	Tree sortedness

for Java, which is based on the Soot framework [18]. For all benchmarks, we checked the absence of null dereferences in addition to the properties described in Table 2. Our specifications include correct usage of JDBC objects, correct usage of Java I/O streams, correct usage of Java collections and iterators, and additional small but interesting specifications.

The experiments were conducted using TVLA version 2, running with SUN's JRE 1.4, on a 1 GHZ Intel Pentium Processor machine with 1.5 GB RAM. We optimized for precision and simplicity by using TVLA's Focus and Coerce operations in all benchmarks. We compared partial isomorphism to the full powerset abstraction in terms of time and space performance and precision.

The results of the analyses are shown in Table 3. In all the benchmarks the analysis based on the partial-isomorphism heap abstraction achieved the same precision as the

Table 3. Time, space and number of errors measurements. Rep. Err. is the number of errors reported by the analysis, and Act. Err. is the number of errors that indicate real problems. Time and space measurements for non-terminating benchmarks are prefixed with > to indicate the measurements taken when the analysis timed out. The number of reported errors is the same for both the analysis based on the powerset heap abstraction and the analysis based on partial-isomorphism heap abstraction on all (terminating) benchmarks. For benchmarks that did not terminate with the powerset heap abstraction, the numbers are taken from the analysis based on partial-isomorphism heap abstraction

Benchmark	Time in seconds		Space in Mb.		Rep. Err. / Act. Err.
	Powerset	Partial iso.	Powerset	Partial iso.	
GC.mark	584	3	56	1.4	0/0
DSW	14,364	157	116.3	5.6	0/0
ISPath	79	79	2.8	2.9	0/0
InputStream5	4,530	1,706	14.0	11.9	1/0
InputStream5b	3,492	1,394	9.8	9.1	1/0
InputStream6	15,558	3,929	23.6	15.9	1/0
SQLExecutor	>20,000	9,673	>109.3	104.8	0/0
KernelBench.1	7,393	5,355	13.3	10.8	1/1
InsertSorted	264	37	4.5	2.4	0/0
DeleteSorted	>20,000	3,271	>62.6	21.8	0/0

analysis based on the powerset heap abstraction, and other TVLA users reported the same phenomenon. In all but one example, the analysis based on partial-isomorphism heap abstraction achieved significant performance improvements.

4.1   Implementation Independent Results

Although the results shown in Table 3 measure the time and space consumption of analyses using different abstractions, they are also influenced by the various implementation details of the abstractions.

In Table 4, we supply implementation independent measurements. We measured the total number of abstract configurations generated by the analysis and the maximal number of abstract configurations that exist in the transition system at any given time during the analysis. The total number of abstract configurations and the maximal number of abstract configurations are always the same with the powerset heap abstraction, since structures are only accumulated in the transition system. For the partial-isomorphism heap abstraction, the maximal number of abstract configurations is often lower than the total number of abstract configurations, indicating that structures discovered in different iterations were merged together.

The results show a consistency between the improvements in time and space performance of the partial-isomorphism heap abstraction, relative to the powerset heap abstraction, and the reduced number of abstract configurations.

5   Extensions and Future Work

The partial-isomorphism heap abstraction has so far performed quite satisfactorily in our experience with TVLA. However, we cannot assume that this will always be ad-

Table 4. Implementation independent measurements. Total #structs is the total number of abstract configurations that arose during the analysis, and Max #structs is the maximal number of abstract configurations that existed in the transition system at any time during the analysis. The results of non-terminating benchmarks are prefixed with $>$ to indicate the measurements taken when the analysis timed out

Benchmark	Total #structs		Max #structs	
	Powerset	Partial iso.	Powerset	Partial iso.
GC.mark	189,772	1,133	189,772	748
DSW	320,387	6,480	320,387	2,986
ISPath	2,168	2,168	2,168	2,168
InputStream5	8,164	3,366	8,164	2,204
InputStream5b	5,973	2,598	5,973	1,729
InputStream6	24,461	6,678	24,461	4,411
SQLExecutor	>8,824	4,107	>8,824	2,164
KernelBench.1	12,594	9,296	12,594	5,748
InsertSorted	7,487	1,318	7,487	905
DeleteSorted	>158,780	30,386	>158,780	25,673

equate. Analysis and verification of larger programs may require more aggressive abstractions, while in some cases we may require more precise abstractions. In this section we describe various other abstractions that may be of value. We are currently in the process of evaluating the effectiveness of some of the abstractions described below.

Parametric Partial Isomorphism

We now present a parametric abstraction that includes both the powerset heap abstraction and the partial-isomorphism heap abstraction as special cases.

Definition 4. *We say that a pair of bounded structures* $S_1 = \langle U_1, I_1 \rangle$ *and* $S_2 = \langle U_2, I_2 \rangle$ *are **partially isomorphic** with respect to a set of predicates* R, *denoted by* $S_1 \equiv_R S_2$, *iff there exists a bijection* $f^{pi} : U_1 \rightarrow U_2$, *such that, for every predicate* $p \in R$ *of arity* k *and tuple of nodes* $\langle u_1, \ldots, u_k \rangle \in U_1^k$, *the following holds:*

$$p^{S_1}(u_1, \ldots, u_k) = p^{S_2}(f^{pi}(u_1), \ldots, f^{pi}(u_k)) \ .$$

Note that $\equiv_R$ is an equivalence relation among 3-valued structures. Given any set of predicates R that includes the set of all abstraction predicates A, we define an abstraction function $\alpha_{pi[R]} : 2^{\text{2-STRUCT}} \rightarrow 2^{\text{CB-STRUCT}}$ as follows:

$$\alpha_{pi[R]}(XS) = \left\{ \bigsqcup C \mid C \subseteq \alpha_{pow}(XS) \text{ is a } \equiv_R \text{ equivalence class} \right\} \ .$$

This function defines a whole family of abstractions. Further, $\alpha_{pow} = \alpha_{pi[P]}$ (where P is the set of all predicates) is the most precise among this family of abstractions, and $\alpha_{pi} = \alpha_{pi[A]}$ is the least precise among this family of abstractions.

The reason we restrict ourselves to sets R that contain the set of all abstraction predicates A is the following. If R includes A, then for any two $\equiv_R$-equivalent bounded structures, the bijection between the universes of the two structures that preserves the values of predicates in R is uniquely determined, and this bijection is used to determine which individuals should be "merged" together.

This parametric definition allows users to choose abstractions in a more fine-grained fashion, by specifying the set of predicates R. The parametric abstraction could also be used by an appropriate iterative refinement technique, which starts with $R = A$ and iteratively adds predicates to R, until a sufficiently precise abstraction is obtained or $R = P$.

Deflating Reductions

Deflating reductions can potentially yield performance improvements without a loss of precision. A very simple deflating reduction is the following: consider a set of 3-valued structures X containing structures S_1 and S_2, such that $S_1 \sqsubseteq S_2$. Clearly, the set $X' = X - \{S_1\}$ is semantically equivalent to X, and removing S_1 involves no loss of precision (even when the abstract transformer that is used is not the best). This reduction is referred to as "non-redundancy" in [1]. Making this reduction feasible requires testing for the partial order relation over 3-valued structures, which can be done in polynomial time for bounded 3-valued structures. The key question with this reduction is whether the subsequent (performance) benefits of doing the reduction outweigh extra cost of performing the reduction. Our initial experience shows that this reduction is worth using. This reduction transforms TVLA's preorder over sets of 3-valued structures into a proper (Hoare powerdomain) partial ordering.

6   Related Work

A substantial body of literature exists on abstractions for various different domains and for creating new abstractions from existing abstractions. The distinguishing aspect of our work is its focus on heap abstractions and its focus on an empirical evaluation of the effectiveness of the proposed heap abstraction.

Function Space Domain Construction. Function space domain construction is one way of creating abstractions that are "partly disjunctive". Examples of previous work using such a domain construction include [5], where the abstraction is composed of two components – a lattice of symbolic access paths and a parametric numerical lattice. In this abstraction, abstract elements with the same symbolic access path component are merged by joining the numerical lattice component. The ESP system [4] also utilizes a similar function space domain construction, but not for heap abstractions.

Least Disjunctive Basis. In [6], a technique is defined for obtaining the "least disjunctive basis", which is the most abstract domain inducing the same disjunctive completion as another domain. Unfortunately, this may result in larger sets of abstract elements, as abstract elements are substituted by sets of other abstract elements, causing inflation.

Deflating Operators and Widening Operators. In [1], different widening operators and congruence relations are considered for the powerset polyhedra domain, and in more general settings.

Acknowledgements

The authors wish to thank Alexey Loginov for supplying us the tree benchmarks and the DSW benchmark, and Eran Yahav for supplying us the IOStream benchmarks, the KernelBench.1 benchmark and the SQLExecutor benchmark. The authors also wish to thank Noam Rinetzky and Greta Yorsh for supplying helpful comments on earlier drafts of this paper.

References

1. R. Bagnara, P. M. Hill, and E. Zaffanella. Widening operators for powerset domains. In B. Steffen and G. Levi, editors, *Proceedings of the Fifth International Conference on Verification, Model Checking and Abstract Interpretation (VMCAI 2004)*, volume 2937 of *Lecture Notes in Computer Science*, pages 135–148, Venice, Italy, 2003. Springer-Verlag, Berlin.
2. D. Chase, M. Wegman, and F. Zadeck. Analysis of pointers and structures. In *Proc. ACM SIGPLAN Conf. on Programming Language Design and Implementation*, pages 296–310, New York, NY, 1990. ACM Press.
3. P. Cousot and R. Cousot. Abstract interpretation: A unified lattice model for static analysis of programs by construction of approximation of fixed points. In *Proc. ACM Symp. on Principles of Programming Languages*, pages 238–252, New York, NY, 1977. ACM Press.
4. M. Das, S. Lerner, and M. Seigle. Esp: Path-sensitive program verification in polynomial time. In *Proc. ACM SIGPLAN Conf. on Programming Language Design and Implementation*, Jan. 2002.
5. A. Deutsch. Interprocedural may-alias analysis for pointers: Beyond k-limiting. In *Proc. ACM SIGPLAN Conf. on Programming Language Design and Implementation*, pages 230–241, New York, NY, 1994. ACM Press.
6. R. Giacobazzi and F. Ranzato. Optimal domains for disjunctive abstract interpretation. *Science of Computer Programming*, 32(1-3):177–210, 1998.
7. N. Jones and S. Muchnick. Flow analysis and optimization of Lisp-like structures. In S. Muchnick and N. Jones, editors, *Program Flow Analysis: Theory and Applications*, chapter 4, pages 102–131. Prentice-Hall, Englewood Cliffs, NJ, 1981.
8. J. Larus. *Restructuring Symbolic Programs for Concurrent Execution on Multiprocessors*. PhD thesis, Univ. of Calif., Berkeley, CA, May 1989.
9. J. Larus and P. Hilfinger. Detecting conflicts between structure accesses. In *Proc. ACM SIGPLAN Conf. on Programming Language Design and Implementation*, pages 21–34, New York, NY, 1988. ACM Press.
10. T. Lev-Ami and M. Sagiv. TVLA: A framework for implementing static analyses. In J. Palsberg, editor, *Proc. Static Analysis Symp.*, volume 1824 of *Lecture Notes in Computer Science*, pages 280–301. Springer-Verlag, 2000. Available from http://www.cs.tau.ac.il/~tvla/.
11. G. Lindstrom. Scanning list structures without stacks or tag bits. *Inf. Process. Lett.*, 2(2):47–51, June 1973.
12. G. Ramalingam, A. Warshavsky, J. Field, D. Goyal, and M. Sagiv. Deriving specialized program analyses for certifying component-client conformance. In *Proc. ACM SIGPLAN Conf. on Programming Language Design and Implementation*, pages 83–94. ACM Press, June 2002.

13. T. Reps, M. Sagiv, and R. Wilhelm. Automatic verification of a simple mark and sweep garbabge collector. Presented in the 2001 University of Washington and Microsoft Research Summer Institute, Specifying and Checking Properties of Software, http://research.microsoft.com/specncheck/, 2001.

14. M. Sagiv, T. Reps, and R. Wilhelm. Solving shape-analysis problems in languages with destructive updating. *ACM Trans. Prog. Lang. Syst.*, 20(1):1–50, Jan. 1998.

15. M. Sagiv, T. Reps, and R. Wilhelm. Parametric shape analysis via 3-valued logic. *ACM Transactions on Programming Languages and Systems*, 24(3):217–298, 2002.

16. J. Stransky. A lattice for abstract interpretation of dynamic (lisp-like) structures. *Information and Computation*, 101(1):70–102, Nov. 1992.

17. T.Yavuz-Kahveci and T. Bultan. Automated verification of concurrent linked lists with counters. In *Static Analysis Symposium*, pages 69–84, 2002.

18. R. Vallée-Rai, L. Hendren, V. Sundaresan, P. Lam, E. Gagnon, and P. Co. Soot - a java optimization framework. In *Proceedings of CASCON 1999*, pages 125–135, 1999.

19. E. Yahav and G. Ramalingam. Verifying safety properties using separation and heterogeneous abstraction. In *Proc. ACM SIGPLAN Conf. on Programming Language Design and Implementation*, New York, NY, 2004. ACM Press. To Appear.

An Abstract Interpretation Approach for Automatic Generation of Polynomial Invariants*

Enric Rodríguez-Carbonell[1] and Deepak Kapur[2]

[1] Technical University of Catalonia, Barcelona
www.lsi.upc.es/~erodri
[2] University of New Mexico, Albuquerque
www.cs.unm.edu/~kapur

Abstract. A method for generating polynomial invariants of imperative programs is presented using the abstract interpretation framework.
It is shown that for programs with polynomial assignments, an invariant
consisting of a conjunction of polynomial equalities can be automatically
generated for each program point. The proposed approach takes into account tests in conditional statements as well as in loops, insofar as they
can be abstracted to be polynomial equalities and disequalities. The semantics of each statement is given as a transformation on polynomial
ideals. Merging of paths in a program is defined as the intersection of
the polynomial ideals associated with each path. For a loop junction, a
widening operator based on selecting polynomials up to a certain degree
is proposed. The algorithm for finding invariants using this widening
operator is shown to terminate in finitely many steps. The proposed approach has been implemented and successfully tried on many programs.
A table providing details about the programs is given.

1 Introduction

There has recently been a surge of interest in research on automatic generation
of loop invariants of imperative programs. This is perhaps due to the successful
development of powerful automated reasoning tools including BDD packages,
SAT solvers, model checkers, decision procedures for common data structures
in applications (such as numbers, lists, arrays, ...), as well as theorem provers
for first-order logic, higher-order logic and induction. These tools have been
successfully used in application domains such as hardware circuits and designs,
software and protocol analysis.

A method for generating polynomial invariants for imperative programs is
developed in this paper. It is analogous to the approach proposed in [6] for finding linear inequalities as invariants based on the abstract interpretation framework [5]. The proposed method, in contrast, generates polynomial equations as

* This research was partially supported by an NSF ITR award CCR-0113611, the
Prince of Asturias Endowed Chair in Information Science and Technology at the
University of New Mexico, an FPU grant from the Spanish Secretaría de Estado
de Educación y Universidades, ref. AP2002-3693, and the Spanish project MCYT
TIC2001-2476-C03-01.

R. Giacobazzi (Ed.): SAS 2004, LNCS 3148, pp. 280–295, 2004.

invariants by interpreting the semantics of programming language constructs in terms of ideal-theoretic operations, which we consider by itself as an exciting novel contribution of this paper. The semantics of each statement is given as a transformation on polynomial ideals. It is shown that for programs with polynomial assignments, an invariant consisting of a conjunction of polynomial equalities can be automatically generated for each program point.

The proposed approach is able to handle nested loops[1] and also takes into account tests in conditional statements and loops, insofar as they can be abstracted to be polynomial equalities and disequalities. Merging of paths in a program is defined as the intersection of the polynomial ideals associated to each path. For ensuring the termination of the invariant generation procedure, a *widening operator* is proposed. This widening operator is based on retaining only the polynomials of degree $\leq d$ in the intersection; this is achieved by computing a Gröbner basis [7] with a graded term ordering and keeping only those polynomials in the basis with degree $\leq d$. The procedure for finding invariants using this widening operator is shown to terminate in finitely many steps.

The proposed algorithm has been implemented using Macaulay2 [12], an algebraic geometry tool that supports operations on polynomial ideals such as the computation of Gröbner bases. Using this implementation, loop invariants for several numerical programs have been successfully generated automatically.

The method, as well as the implementation, do not need pre/postconditions for deriving loop invariants. Further, under conditions on the semantics of programs, it finds all polynomial invariants of degree $\leq d$, where d is the degree bound in the widening. In that sense, the method is sound and complete.

The rest of the paper is organized as follows. In the next subsection, related work is briefly reviewed. Section 2 gives background information on polynomial ideals, operations on them and special bases of polynomial ideals called Gröbner bases. Section 3 introduces a simple programming language used in the paper for presenting the method. Section 4 discusses abstraction and concretization functions from variable values to ideals and viceversa, so that the framework of abstract interpretation is applicable. Section 5 gives the semantics of programming constructs using ideal-theoretic operations. For each kind of statement, it is shown how the output polynomial ideal can be constructed from the input polynomial ideals. Most importantly, Subsection 5.5 discusses the semantics of loop junction nodes using a widening operator. Section 6 shows that, under specific conditions of the semantics, the proposed method is sound and complete in the sense that, for every program point, our algorithm indeed finds all the invariants of degree $\leq d$, where d is the parameter used in the widening operator. Section 7 illustrates the application of the method on some examples; this is followed by a table giving details of programs successfully tried for which our implementation discovers loop invariants. Section 8 concludes and discusses ideas for extending this research.

---

[1] The method also works for unnested loops with spaghetti control flow, using Bourdoncle's algorithm [1] to find adequate widening points in the control-flow graph.

1.1 Related Work

As stated above, the proposed approach is a complement of the method proposed by Cousot and Halbwachs [6], who applied the framework of abstract interpretation [5] for finding invariant linear inequalities. That work extended Karr's algorithm in [16] for finding invariant linear equalities at any program point.

Recently, there has been a renewed surge of interest in automatically deriving invariants of imperative programs. In [4] Colón et al. have used non-linear constraint solving based on Farkas' lemma to attack the problem of finding invariant linear inequalities. Extending Karr's work, for programs with affine assignments Müller-Olm and Seidl [18] proposed an interprocedural method for computing polynomial equations of bounded degree as invariants. In [21], we developed an abstract framework for generating invariants of loops. This framework was instantiated to generate conjunctions of polynomial equations as invariants for loop programs. The method used the Gröbner basis algorithm for computing such invariants, and was shown to be sound and complete. However, that method cannot handle nested loops; furthermore, tests in conditional statements and loops are abstracted to be *true*. In [22], a method is proposed for generating nonlinear polynomials as invariants, which starts with a template polynomial with undetermined coefficients and attempts to find values for the coefficients so that the template is invariant using the Gröbner basis algorithm.

In contrast, not only can the method proposed in this paper generate invariants of programs with nested loops, but also it is not necessary to know a priori the structure of the polynomials appearing as invariants. However, the widening operator does need as input the degree of the polynomial invariants of interest to the user. Furthermore, unlike the methods of [22], the proposed method has been implemented and tried on many examples with considerable success. We believe that the technique discussed in [6] for linear inequalities can be easily integrated with our method since they share the framework, thus resulting in a powerful effective method for automatically generating loop invariants expressible using linear inequalities and polynomial equalities.

2   Preliminaries

Given a field $\mathbb{K}$, let $\mathbb{K}[\bar{x}] = \mathbb{K}[x_1, ..., x_n]$ denote the ring of polynomials in the variables $x_1, ..., x_n$ with coefficients from $\mathbb{K}$. An *ideal* is a set $I \subseteq \mathbb{K}[\bar{x}]$ which contains 0, is closed under addition and such that if $p \in \mathbb{K}[\bar{x}]$ and $q \in I$, then $pq \in I$. Given a set of polynomials $S \subseteq \mathbb{K}[\bar{x}]$, the *ideal spanned by* S is $\{f \in \mathbb{K}[\bar{x}] \mid \exists k \geq 1 \; f = \sum_{j=1}^{k} p_j q_j \text{ with } p_j \in \mathbb{K}[\bar{x}], q_j \in S\}$. This is the minimal ideal containing S and we denote it by $\langle S \rangle_{\mathbb{K}[\bar{x}]}$ or simply by $\langle S \rangle$. For an ideal $I \subseteq \mathbb{K}[\bar{x}]$, a set $S \subseteq \mathbb{K}[\bar{x}]$ such that $I = \langle S \rangle$, is called a *basis* of I and we say that S *generates* I.

Given two ideals $I, J \subseteq \mathbb{K}[\bar{x}]$, their *intersection* $I \cap J$ is an ideal. However, the union of ideals is, in general, not an ideal. The *sum* of I and J, $I + J = \{p + q \mid p \in I, q \in J\}$, is the minimal ideal that contains $I \cup J$. The quotient of I into J is the ideal $I : J = \{p \mid \forall q \in J, pq \in I\}$.

For any set S of polynomials in $\mathbb{K}[\bar{x}]$, the *variety* of S over $\mathbb{K}^n$ is defined as its set of zeroes, $\mathbf{V}(S) = \{\bar{\omega} \in \mathbb{K}^n \mid p(\bar{\omega}) = 0 \; \forall p \in S\}$. When taking varieties we can assume S to be an ideal, since $\mathbf{V}(\langle S \rangle) = \mathbf{V}(S)$. On the other hand, if $A \subseteq \mathbb{K}^n$ the ideal $\mathbf{I}(A) = \{p \in \mathbb{K}[\bar{x}] \mid p(\bar{\omega}) = 0 \; \forall \bar{\omega} \in A\}$ is called the *ideal of A*. We write $\mathbf{IV}(S)$ instead of $\mathbf{I}(\mathbf{V}(S))$ and $\mathbf{VI}(A)$ instead of $\mathbf{V}(\mathbf{I}(A))$.

Ideals and varieties are dual concepts, in the sense that given ideals I, J, $\mathbf{V}(I \cap J) = \mathbf{V}(I) \cup \mathbf{V}(J)$ and $\mathbf{V}(I + J) = \mathbf{V}(I) \cap \mathbf{V}(J)$. Moreover, if $I \subseteq J$ then $\mathbf{V}(I) \supseteq \mathbf{V}(J)$. Analogously, if $A, B \subseteq \mathbb{K}^n$ (in particular, if A, B are varieties), then $\mathbf{I}(A \cup B) = \mathbf{I}(A) \cap \mathbf{I}(B)$ and $A \subseteq B$ implies $\mathbf{I}(A) \supseteq \mathbf{I}(B)$. However, in general for any two varieties V, W the inclusion $\mathbf{I}(V \cap W) \supseteq \mathbf{I}(V) + \mathbf{I}(W)$ holds and may be strict; but $\mathbf{I}(V \cap W) = \mathbf{IV}(\mathbf{I}(V) + \mathbf{I}(W))$ is always true.

For any ideal the inclusion $I \subseteq \mathbf{IV}(I)$ holds; $\mathbf{IV}(I)$ represents the largest set of polynomials with the same set of zeroes as I. Since any I satisfying $I = \mathbf{IV}(I)$ is the ideal of the variety $\mathbf{V}(I)$, we say that any such I is an *ideal of variety*. For any $A \subseteq \mathbb{K}^n$, it can be seen that the ideal $\mathbf{I}(A)$ is an ideal of variety. Moreover, if I is an ideal of variety, then $\mathbf{I}(\mathbf{V}(I) - \mathbf{V}(J)) = I : J$, where $-$ denotes difference of sets. For further detail on these concepts, see [8, 7].

A *term* in a set $\bar{x} = (x_1, ..., x_n)$ of variables is an expression of the form $\bar{x}^{\bar{\alpha}} = x_1^{\alpha_1} x_2^{\alpha_2} \cdots x_n^{\alpha_n}$, where $\bar{\alpha} = (\alpha_1, ..., \alpha_n) \in \mathbb{N}^n$. The set of terms is denoted by $\mathcal{T}$. A *monomial* is an expression of the form $c \cdot p$, with $c \in \mathbb{K}$ and $p \in \mathcal{T}$. The *degree* of a monomial $c \cdot \bar{x}^{\bar{\alpha}}$ with $c \neq 0$ is $\deg(c \cdot \bar{x}^{\bar{\alpha}}) = \alpha_1 + \cdots + \alpha_n$. The degree of a non-null polynomial is the maximum of the degrees of its monomials. We denote the set of all polynomials of $\mathbb{K}[\bar{x}]$ of degree $\leq d$ by $\mathbb{K}_d[\bar{x}]$.

An *admissible term ordering* $\succ$ is a relation over $\mathcal{T}$ such that:

1. $\succ$ is a total ordering over $\mathcal{T}$.
2. If $\bar{\alpha}, \bar{\beta}, \bar{\gamma} \in \mathbb{N}^n$ and $\bar{x}^{\bar{\alpha}} \succ \bar{x}^{\bar{\beta}}$, then $\bar{x}^{\bar{\alpha}+\bar{\gamma}} \succ \bar{x}^{\bar{\beta}+\bar{\gamma}}$.
3. $\forall \bar{\alpha} \in \mathbb{N}^n, \; \bar{x}^{\bar{\alpha}} \succeq 1 = \bar{x}^{\bar{0}}$.

Moreover, $\succ$ is called a *graded term ordering* if $\forall \bar{\alpha}, \bar{\beta} \in \mathbb{N}^n$, $\deg(\bar{x}^{\bar{\alpha}}) > \deg(\bar{x}^{\bar{\beta}})$ implies $\bar{x}^{\bar{\alpha}} \succ \bar{x}^{\bar{\beta}}$.

Term orderings extend to monomials by ignoring the coefficients and comparing the corresponding terms. The most common term orderings are defined as follows, assuming that $x_1 \succ x_2 \succ \cdots \succ x_n$:

- **Lexicographical Ordering (lex).** If $\bar{\alpha}, \bar{\beta} \in \mathbb{N}^n$, then $\bar{x}^{\bar{\alpha}} \succ_{lex} \bar{x}^{\bar{\beta}}$ iff the leftmost nonzero entry in $\bar{\alpha} - \bar{\beta}$ is positive.
- **Graded Lexicographical Ordering (grlex).** If $\bar{\alpha}, \bar{\beta} \in \mathbb{N}^n$, then $\bar{x}^{\bar{\alpha}} \succ_{grlex} \bar{x}^{\bar{\beta}}$ iff $\deg(\bar{x}^{\bar{\alpha}}) > \deg(\bar{x}^{\bar{\beta}})$, or $\deg(\bar{x}^{\bar{\alpha}}) = \deg(\bar{x}^{\bar{\beta}})$ and $\bar{x}^{\bar{\alpha}} \succ_{lex} \bar{x}^{\bar{\beta}}$.
- **Graded Reverse Lexicographical Ordering (grevlex).** If $\bar{\alpha}, \bar{\beta} \in \mathbb{N}^n$, then $\bar{x}^{\bar{\alpha}} \succ_{grevlex} \bar{x}^{\bar{\beta}}$ iff $\deg(\bar{x}^{\bar{\alpha}}) > \deg(\bar{x}^{\bar{\beta}})$, or $\deg(\bar{x}^{\bar{\alpha}}) = \deg(\bar{x}^{\bar{\beta}})$ and the rightmost nonzero entry in $\bar{\alpha} - \bar{\beta}$ is negative.

Each of these orderings is a total ordering on terms. The orderings **grlex** and **grevlex** are examples of graded term orderings.

Given a term ordering $\succ$, for any polynomial $f \in \mathbb{K}[\bar{x}]$, $\mathrm{lm}(f)$ stands for the leading monomial of f with respect to $\succ$. Given an ideal I different from $\{0\}$, a *Gröbner basis* for I is a finite set of polynomials $G = \{g_1, ..., g_k\}$ satisfying $\langle \{\mathrm{lm}(p) \mid p \in I\} \rangle = \langle \mathrm{lm}(g_1), ..., \mathrm{lm}(g_k) \rangle$. For such a set G, $I = \langle G \rangle$ holds (and so G is indeed a basis for I).

3   Programming Model

To simplify presentation, a program is represented as a finite connected flowchart with one entry node, assignment, test, junction and exit nodes, as in [6]. We also assume that the evaluation of arithmetic and boolean expressions has no side effects and so does not affect the values of program variables, which are denoted by $x_1, ..., x_n$.

Formally, nodes for flowcharts are taken from a set **Nodes**, which is partitioned into the following subsets (we show between parentheses the respective symbol for pictures):

1. **Entry** ($\triangleright\!\!\rightarrow$). There is just one entry node, which has no predecessors and one successor. It means where the flow of the program begins.
2. **Assignments** ($\square$). Assignment nodes have one predecessor and one successor. Every assignment node is labelled with an identifier x_i and an expression $f(\bar{x})$, thus representing the assignment $x_i := f(\bar{x})$.
3. **Tests** ($\bigcirc$). A test node has a predecessor and two successors, corresponding to the *true* and *false* paths. It is labelled with a boolean expression $C(\bar{x})$, which is evaluated when the flow reaches the node.
4. **Junctions** ($\bigcirc$). Junction nodes have one successor and more than one predecessor. They involve no computation and only represent the merging of execution paths (in conditional and loop statements).
5. **Exits** ($\rightarrow\!\!\triangleleft$). Exit nodes have just one predecessor and no successors. They represent where the flow of the program halts.

For example, the program below incrementally computes the sequence of squares for the first x_3 natural numbers, stored in the variable x_1.

4   Ideals of Varieties as Abstract Values

The state of the computation at any given node in a program is the set of values each program variable can take. This is represented as a subset of $\mathbb{K}^n$. Program constructs change the state. A state can be abstracted to the ideal consisting of

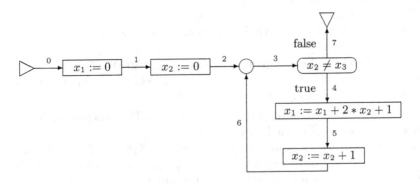

Fig. 1. Example of program

all polynomials that vanish in that state. This is how the abstraction function is intuitively defined.

At the abstract level, we work with polynomial ideals (more specifically, with ideals of variety, i.e. with ideals I such that $I = \mathbf{IV}(I)$). To each arc a of the flowchart, we attach an assertion P_a of the form $P_a = \{\bigwedge_{j=1}^{k} p_{aj}(\bar{x}) = 0\}$, or equivalently the ideal $I_a = \langle p_{a1}(\bar{x}), ..., p_{ak}(\bar{x})\rangle$, where the $p_{aj} \in \mathbb{K}[\bar{x}]$ are polynomials. The abstraction function,

$$\alpha = \mathbf{I} : 2^{\mathbb{K}^n} \to \mathcal{I},$$

is the ideal operator, which yields the ideal of the polynomials that vanish at the points in the given subset of $\mathbb{K}^n$; and the concretization function,

$$\gamma = \mathbf{V} : \mathcal{I} \to 2^{\mathbb{K}^n},$$

is the variety operator (where $2^{\mathbb{K}^n}$ denotes the powerset of $\mathbb{K}^n$ and $\mathcal{I}$ is the set of ideals of variety in $\mathbb{K}[\bar{x}]$). Both $(2^{\mathbb{K}^n}, \subseteq, \cup, \emptyset, \mathbb{K}^n)$ and $(\mathcal{I}, \supseteq, \cap, \langle 1\rangle, \langle 0\rangle)$ are semi-lattices, and the functions defined above are morphisms between these semi-lattices. These operators form a Galois connection, as $\forall A \subseteq \mathbb{K}^n \; \forall I \in \mathcal{I}$, $\mathbf{I}(A) \supseteq I \Leftrightarrow A \subseteq \mathbf{V}(I)$. The semantics of program constructs for abstract values is given later on as transformations on polynomial ideals.

The algorithm for computing the invariant ideal of variety for each program point works as follows. The output ideal of the entry node represents the precondition, i.e. what is known about the variables at the start of the execution of the program. Assuming at first that variables are undefined on any arc (i.e. $I_a = \langle 1\rangle$, the bottom of $\mathcal{I}$), we propagate the precondition ideal around the flowchart by application of the semantics until stabilization. In order to guarantee termination, we assume that each cycle in the graph contains a special junction node, called loop junction node, for which the respective assertion is approximated using a *widening operator* ∇. Intuitively, loop junction nodes correspond to loops, whereas simple junction nodes are associated to conditional statements.

5   Transformation of Ideals of Variety by Language Constructs

This section develops a semantics of programs for ideals of variety, i.e., for each kind of program node, we show how the output ideal of variety can be obtained in terms of the input ideals of variety and the relevant information attached to the node.

5.1   Program Entry Node

If we are given a precondition for the procedure to be analyzed, the $\mathbf{IV}(\cdot)$ of the polynomial equations in it can be used as the output ideal of variety for the program entry node. Otherwise, if the variables are assumed not to be initialized, they do not satisfy any constraints and the vector of their values may be any point in $\mathbb{K}^n$. This is represented by the zero ideal $\langle 0\rangle = \mathbf{I}(\mathbb{K}^n)$, whose corresponding assertion is the tautology $0 = 0$.

5.2   Assignments

Let $I = \langle p_1, ..., p_k \rangle$ be the input ideal of variety of the assignment node, x_i be the variable that is assigned and $f(\bar{x})$ be the right-hand side of the assignment.

The strongest postcondition of the assertion $\{\bigwedge_{j=1}^{k} p_j(\bar{x}) = 0\}$ after the assignment $x_i := f(\bar{x})$ is

$$\{\exists x_i'(x_i = f(x_i \leftarrow x_i') \wedge (\wedge_{j=1}^{k} p_j(x_i \leftarrow x_i') = 0))\},$$

where intuitively x_i' stands for the value of the assigned variable previous to the assignment and $\leftarrow$ denotes substitution of variables. Our goal now is to translate this formula in terms of ideals of variety.

Let us assume $f(\bar{x}) \in \mathbb{K}[\bar{x}]$. We translate the equality $x_i = f(x_i \leftarrow x_i')$ into the polynomial $x_i - f(x_i \leftarrow x_i')$ and consider the ideal

$$I' = \langle x_i - f(x_i \leftarrow x_i'), p_1(x_i \leftarrow x_i'), ..., p_k(x_i \leftarrow x_i') \rangle_{\mathbb{K}[x_i', \bar{x}]}.$$

This ideal I' captures the effect of the assignment, with the drawback that a new variable x_i' has been introduced. We have to eliminate this variable x_i' from I' and then compute the corresponding ideal of variety; in other words, we need to compute all those polynomials in I' that depend only on the $\bar{x}$ variables, i.e. $I' \cap \mathbb{K}[\bar{x}]$, and then take $\mathbf{IV}(I' \cap \mathbb{K}[\bar{x}])$. As it can be proved that $\mathbf{IV}(I' \cap \mathbb{K}[\bar{x}]) = I' \cap \mathbb{K}[\bar{x}]$, the final output is $I' \cap \mathbb{K}[\bar{x}]$.

In our running example, assume that $I_0 = \langle 0 \rangle$ and that we want to compute the output ideal I_1 of the assignment $x_1 := 0$. Applying the ideas above, we take $\langle x_1 \rangle \cap \mathbb{K}[\bar{x}] = \langle x_1 \rangle$. This means that if we know nothing about the variables and apply the assignment $x_1 := 0$, then $x_1 = 0$ after the assignment.

Invertible Assignments. A common particular case is the following: $f(\bar{x}) = c \cdot x_i + f'(x_1, ..., x_{i-1}, x_{i+1}, ..., x_n)$, where $c \in \mathbb{K}$, $c \neq 0$ and f' does not depend on x_i. Then the assignment is invertible, and we can express the previous value of the variable x_i in terms of its new value. It is easy to see that in this case

$$I' = \langle x_i' - \frac{1}{c}(x_i - f'(x_1, ..., x_{i-1}, x_{i+1}, ..., x_n)), p_1(x_i \leftarrow x_i'), ..., p_k(x_i \leftarrow x_i') \rangle.$$

To eliminate x_i' from I', we substitute x_i' by $\frac{1}{c} \cdot (x_i - f'(x_1, ..., x_{i-1}, x_{i+1}, ..., x_n))$ in the p_j. The output is $\langle \cup_{j=1}^{k} \{p_j(x_i \leftarrow \frac{1}{c} \cdot (x_i - f'(x_1, ..., x_{i-1}, x_{i+1}, ..., x_n)))\} \rangle$.

For instance, assume that $I_4 = \langle x_1, x_2 \rangle$ (i.e. $x_1 = x_2 = 0$) and that we want to compute the output ideal I_5 of the assignment $x_1 := x_1 + 2 * x_2 + 1$. As the right-hand side of the assignment has the required form, we take $I_5 = I_4(x_1 \leftarrow x_1 - 2x_2 - 1) = \langle x_1 - 2x_2 - 1, x_2 \rangle$. Then, at program point 5, the variables satisfy $x_1 = 2x_2 + 1$ and $x_2 = 0$, which is consistent with the result of applying $x_1 := x_1 + 2 * x_2 + 1$ to $(x_1, x_2) = (0, 0)$.

5.3   Test Nodes

Let $C = C(\bar{x})$ be the boolean condition attached to a test node with the input ideal $I = \langle p_1, ..., p_k \rangle$. Then the strongest postconditions for the *true* and *false* paths are respectively

$$\{C(\bar{x}) \land (\land_{j=1}^{k} p_j(\bar{x}) = 0)\}, \qquad \{\neg C(\bar{x}) \land (\land_{j=1}^{k} p_j(\bar{x}) = 0)\}.$$

For simplicity, below we just show how to express the assertion for the *true* path in terms of ideals when C is an atomic formula. More complex boolean expressions can be handled easily [14].

Polynomial Equalities. If C is a polynomial equality, i.e., it is of the form $q = 0$ with $q \in \mathbb{K}[\bar{x}]$, then the states of the *true* path are $\mathbf{V}(q) \cap \mathbf{V}(I)$; in this case we take as output

$$\mathbf{IV}(\langle q \rangle + I) = \mathbf{IV}(\langle q, p_1, ..., p_k \rangle),$$

since $\mathbf{V}(\langle q \rangle + I) = \mathbf{V}(q) \cap \mathbf{V}(I)$.

For instance, assume that in our example, $I_3 = \langle x_1 - x_2^2 \rangle$ and we want to compute the output ideal I_7 of the *false* path. Now $C(\bar{x}) = (x_2 \neq x_3)$, and so $\neg C(\bar{x}) = (x_2 = x_3)$. According to our discussion above, then $I_7 = \mathbf{IV}(x_2 - x_3, x_1 - x_2^2) = \langle x_2 - x_3, x_1 - x_2^2 \rangle$, which means that at program point 7, $x_2 = x_3$ and $x_1 = x_2^2$.

Polynomial Disequalities. If C is a polynomial disequality, i.e. it is of the form $q \neq 0$ with $q \in \mathbb{K}[\bar{x}]$, then the states of the *true* path are the points that belong to $\mathbf{V}(I)$ but not to $\mathbf{V}(q)$, in other words $\mathbf{V}(I) - \mathbf{V}(q)$. So the output should be the ideal of the polynomials vanishing in this difference of sets, $\mathbf{I}(\mathbf{V}(I) - \mathbf{V}(q))$. As it can be proved that $\mathbf{I}(\mathbf{V}(I) - \mathbf{V}(q)) = I : \langle q \rangle$, we take $I : \langle q \rangle$ as output.

For example, if the input ideal of the test node with condition $C(\bar{x}) = (x_1 \neq 0)$ is $I = \langle x_1 x_2 \rangle$ (either $x_1 = 0$ or $x_2 = 0$), the output for the *true* path is $\langle x_1 x_2 \rangle : \langle x_1 \rangle = \langle x_2 \rangle$, which means that, after the test, we have that $x_2 = 0$ on the *true* path.

Polynomial Inequalities. Over $\mathbb{K} = \mathbb{R}, \mathbb{Q}$, a polynomial inequality $q > 0$ (or $q < 0$) cannot be made equivalent to a boolean combination of polynomial equalities. In this case we have to perform an approximation of C to polynomial dis/equalities. For both $q > 0$ or $q < 0$, we approximate it by $q \neq 0$.

5.4 Simple Junction Nodes

Typically, simple junction nodes correspond to the merging of the execution paths of conditional statements. In general, if the input ideals of variety $I_1, ..., I_l$ are such that for $1 \leq i \leq l$, we have $I_i = \langle p_{i1}, ..., p_{ik} \rangle$, then the strongest postcondition after the execution of the simple junction node is

$$\{\lor_{i=1}^{l} (\land_{j=1}^{k} p_{ij}(\bar{x}) = 0)\}.$$

Then the output ideal of variety has to be $\mathbf{I}(\cup_{i=1}^{l} \mathbf{V}(I_i)) = \cap_{i=1}^{l} \mathbf{IV}(I_i) = \cap_{i=1}^{l} I_i$, since the I_i are ideals of variety and so satisfy $I_i = \mathbf{IV}(I_i)$.

5.5 Loop Junction Nodes

Intuitively, a loop junction node represents the merging of the execution paths of a `while` statement. As the following example illustrates, if we treat loop junctions as simple junctions, the forward propagation procedure may not terminate. That implies that we need to approximate.

For instance consider the loop junction in the running example, with input arcs 2,6 and output arc 3. Assume that $I_2 = \langle x_1, x_2 \rangle$ (so $x_1 = x_2 = 0$), $I_3 = \langle x_1 - x_2^2, x_2(x_2 - 1) \rangle$ (either $x_1 = x_2 = 0$ or $x_1 = x_2 = 1$) and $I_6 = \langle x_1 - x_2^2, (x_2 - 1)(x_2 - 2) \rangle$ (either $(x_1, x_2) = (1, 1)$ or $(x_1, x_2) = (4, 2)$). The new value for I_3 should be

$$I_3 \cap I_2 \cap I_6 =$$

$$= \langle x_1 - x_2^2, x_2(x_2 - 1) \rangle \cap \langle x_1, x_2 \rangle \cap \langle x_1 - x_2^2, (x_2 - 1)(x_2 - 2) \rangle =$$

$$= \langle x_1 - x_2^2, x_2(x_2 - 1)(x_2 - 2) \rangle.$$

Notice that the solutions for the polynomials above are such that $x_1 = x_2^2$ and either $x_2 = 0$ or $x_2 = 1$ or $x_2 = 2$, which is consistent with the behaviour of the loop, since the semantics captures the effect after the loop body has been executed ≤ 2 times.

At the next step of the forward propagation procedure, $I_2 = \langle x_1, x_2 \rangle$, $I_3 = \langle x_1 - x_2^2, x_2(x_2 - 1)(x_2 - 2) \rangle$ and $I_6 = \langle x_1 - x_2^2, (x_2 - 1)(x_2 - 2)(x_2 - 3) \rangle$. Then the next value for I_3 should be

$$I_3 \cap I_2 \cap I_6 = \langle x_1 - x_2^2, x_2(x_2 - 1)(x_2 - 2)(x_2 - 3) \rangle.$$

After t iterations of the forward propagation procedure, thus,

$$I_3 = \langle x_1 - x_2^2, \prod_{s=0}^{t+1} (x_2 - s) \rangle.$$

It is clear that only the first polynomial $x_1 - x_2^2$ yields an invariant for the loop, as it persists to be in I_3 after arbitrarily many executions of the loop.

In [20], we gave an algebraic geometry-based approach to capture the effect of arbitrarily many iterations. Ideal-theoretic manipulations were employed to consider the effect of executing a path arbitrarily many times using new parameters standing for the number of times a path is executed and then eliminating those parameters using quantifier-elimination and projection.

An approximate method is proposed below using a *widening operator*, similar to the approach for linear inequalities based on abstract interpretation [5, 6]

Widening Operator. Let I be the output ideal of variety associated with a loop junction node, I_{ant} be its previous value and $J_1, ..., J_l$ be the input ideals going into the loop junction node. An upper approximation of the set of states $\mathbf{V}(I_{ant}) \cup (\cup_{i=1}^{l} \mathbf{V}(J_i))$, or by duality a lower approximation of $I_{ant} \cap (\cap_{i=1}^{l} J_i)$, needs to be computed; the polynomials in the intersection should be picked so that:

    i) the result is still sound, i.e., all values of variables possible at the junction node are accounted for,

    ii) the procedure for computing invariants terminates; and

    iii) the method is powerful enough to generate useful invariants.

Formally, we introduce a widening operator ∇ so that $I_{ant}\nabla(\cap_{i=1}^{l} J_i)$ replaces $I_{ant} \cap (\cap_{i=1}^{l} J_i)$. In this context:

Definition 1. *A widening ∇ is an operator between ideals of variety such that:*

1. *Given two ideals of variety I and J, then $I\nabla J \subseteq I \cap J$ (so that $\mathbf{V}(I\nabla J) \supseteq \mathbf{V}(I \cap J)$ as we do not wish to miss any states).*
2. *For any decreasing chain of ideals of variety $J_0 \supseteq J_1 \supseteq ... \supseteq J_j \supseteq ...$, the chain defined as $I_0 = J_0$, $I_{j+1} = I_j\nabla J_{j+1}$ is not an infinite decreasing chain.*

These two properties take care of the conditions i) and ii) mentioned earlier. As regards iii), in Sections 6 and 7, we will give evidence that our choice of the widening operator is quite powerful.

Definition 2. *Given two ideals of variety $I, J \subseteq \mathbb{K}[\bar{x}]$, $d \in \mathbb{N}$ and a graded term ordering $\succ$ (such as **grlex**, **grevlex**), we define $I\nabla_d J$ as*

$$I\nabla_d J = \mathbf{IV}(\{p \in GB(I \cap J, \succ) \mid \deg(p) \leq d\}) = \mathbf{IV}(GB(I \cap J, \succ) \cap \mathbb{K}_d[\bar{x}]),$$

where $GB(I, \succ)$ stands for a Gröbner basis of an ideal I with respect to the term ordering $\succ$.

Theorem 1. *The operator ∇_d is a widening.*

Proof. It is easy to see from the following relation that given two ideals of variety $I, J \subseteq \mathbb{K}[\bar{x}]$, then $I\nabla_d J \subseteq I \cap J$:

$$I\nabla_d J = \mathbf{IV}(GB(I \cap J, \succ) \cap \mathbb{K}_d[\bar{x}]) \subseteq \mathbf{IV}(GB(I \cap J, \succ)) =$$
$$= \mathbf{IV}(I \cap J) = \mathbf{IV}(I) \cap \mathbf{IV}(J) = I \cap J.$$

Now let us prove that for any decreasing chain of ideals $J_0 \supseteq J_1 \supseteq ... \supseteq J_j \supseteq ...$, the chain defined as $I_0 = J_0$, $I_{j+1} = I_j\nabla_d J_{j+1}$ is not an infinite decreasing chain. Since $I_0 \supseteq I_1 \supseteq ... \supseteq I_j \supseteq ...$, we also have the decreasing chain

$$I_0 \cap \mathbb{K}_d[\bar{x}] \supseteq I_1 \cap \mathbb{K}_d[\bar{x}] \supseteq ... \supseteq I_j \cap \mathbb{K}_d[\bar{x}] \supseteq ....$$

But each $I_j \cap \mathbb{K}_d[\bar{x}]$ is a $\mathbb{K}$-vector space: if $p, q \in I_j \cap \mathbb{K}_d[\bar{x}]$, then $p+q \in I_j \cap \mathbb{K}_d[\bar{x}]$, as I_j is an ideal and $\mathbb{K}_d[\bar{x}]$ is closed under addition; and if $p \in I_j \cap \mathbb{K}_d[\bar{x}]$ and $\lambda \in \mathbb{K}$, we can consider $\lambda \in \mathbb{K}[\bar{x}]$ and since I_j is an ideal, $\lambda \cdot p \in I_j \cap \mathbb{K}_d[\bar{x}]$. So taking dimensions (as vector spaces) we have that

$$\dim(I_0 \cap \mathbb{K}_d[\bar{x}]) \geq \dim(I_1 \cap \mathbb{K}_d[\bar{x}]) \geq ... \geq \dim(I_j \cap \mathbb{K}_d[\bar{x}]) \geq ....$$

But this chain of natural numbers cannot decrease indefinitely, as it is bounded from below by 0. Therefore there exists $i \in \mathbb{N}$ such that $\forall j > i \ \dim(I_i \cap \mathbb{K}_d[\bar{x}]) = \dim(I_j \cap \mathbb{K}_d[\bar{x}])$. We can assume that $i \geq 1$ without loss of generality. As $I_i \cap \mathbb{K}_d[\bar{x}] \supseteq I_j \cap \mathbb{K}_d[\bar{x}]$ and the two vector spaces have the same dimension, we get the equality $I_i \cap \mathbb{K}_d[\bar{x}] = I_j \cap \mathbb{K}_d[\bar{x}]$. Since $i \geq 1$ there exists $S \subseteq \mathbb{K}_d[\bar{x}]$ such that $I_i = \mathbf{IV}(S)$ (namely, $S = GB(I_{i-1} \cap J_i, \succ) \cap \mathbb{K}_d[\bar{x}])$. Then

$$I_i = \mathbf{IV}(S) \subseteq \mathbf{IV}(I_i \cap \mathbb{K}_d[\bar{x}]) = \mathbf{IV}(I_j \cap \mathbb{K}_d[\bar{x}]) \subseteq \mathbf{IV}(I_j) = I_j,$$

as I_j is an ideal of variety. But by construction, we already know that $I_i \supseteq I_j$; so $I_i = I_j$, which implies that the chain must stabilize in a finite number of steps.
$\square$

Applying the Widening. Let us apply the widening to our running example for $d = 2$. Assume that $I_2 = \langle x_1, x_2 \rangle$, $I_3 = \langle x_1 - x_2^2, x_1^2 - 6x_2x_1 + 11x_1 - 6x_2 \rangle$ and $I_6 = \langle x_1 - x_2^2, x_1^2 - 10x_1x_2 + 35x_1 - 50x_2 + 24 \rangle$. Taking the graded term ordering $\succ = \mathbf{grevlex}(x_1 > x_2)$,

$$I_3 \nabla_2 (I_2 \cap I_6) = \mathbf{IV}(GB(I_3 \cap I_2 \cap I_6, \succ) \cap \mathbb{K}_2[\bar{x}]) =$$

$$= \mathbf{IV}(\{x_1 - x_2^2, x_1^2 x_2 - 10x_1^2 + 35x_1x_2 - 50x_1 + 24x_2,$$

$$x_1^3 - 65x_1^2 + 300x_1x_2 - 476x_1 + 240x_2\} \cap \mathbb{K}_2[\bar{x}]) = \mathbf{IV}(x_1 - x_2^2) = \langle x_1 - x_2^2 \rangle .$$

Example 1. Here we give the first iteration of the forward propagation algorithm on our running example for $d = 2$. Due to lack of space, we cannot provide the full trace; for more details about the algorithm as well as the trace of the algorithm, please consult [19].

The calculations are done using $\succ = \mathbf{grevlex}(x_1 > x_2)$. By definition, $\forall j : 0 \le j \le 7$, $I_j^{(0)} = \langle 1 \rangle$. Assuming nothing about the values of variables at the entry point, $I_0^{(1)} = \langle 0 \rangle$. After the assignments $x_1 := 0$ and $x_2 := 0$ (which are not invertible), respectively

$$I_1^{(1)} = (\langle x_1 \rangle + \langle 0 \rangle) \cap \mathbb{K}[\bar{x}] = \langle x_1 \rangle,$$
$$I_2^{(1)} = (\langle x_2 \rangle + \langle x_1 \rangle) \cap \mathbb{K}[\bar{x}] = \langle x_1, x_2 \rangle.$$

When dealing with the loop header, since $I_3^{(0)} = I_6^{(0)} = \langle 1 \rangle$,

$$I_3^{(1)} = I_3^{(0)} \nabla_2 (I_2^{(1)} \cap I_6^{(0)}) = I_2^{(1)} = \langle x_1, x_2 \rangle.$$

When taking the *true* output path,

$$I_4^{(1)} = I_3^{(1)} : \langle x_2 - x_3 \rangle = \langle x_1, x_2 \rangle.$$

The assignments $x_1 := x_1 + 2 * x_2 + 1$ and $x_2 := x_2 + 1$ are invertible, and so:

$$I_5^{(1)} = I_4^{(1)}(x_1 \leftarrow x_1 - 2x_2 - 1) = \langle x_1 - 2x_2 - 1, x_2 \rangle,$$
$$I_6^{(1)} = I_5^{(1)}(x_2 \leftarrow x_2 - 1) = \langle x_1 - 2x_2 + 1, x_2 - 1 \rangle.$$

Finally, taking the *false* output path of the loop test we add the condition $x_2 - x_3$:

$$I_7^{(1)} = \mathbf{IV}(\langle x_2 - x_3 \rangle + I_3^{(1)}) = \mathbf{IV}(x_1, x_2, x_2 - x_3) = \langle x_1, x_2, x_3 \rangle.$$

Of the subsequent iterations, we just show the computation of $I_3^{(5)}$, which corresponds to the above example illustrating the application of the widening operator:

$$I_3^{(5)} = I_3^{(4)} \nabla_2 (I_2^{(5)} \cap I_6^{(4)}) = \mathbf{IV}(\{x_1 - x_2^2, x_1^2 x_2 - 10x_1^2 + 35x_1x_2 - 50x_1 + 24x_2,$$

$$x_1^3 - 65x_1^2 + 300x_1x_2 - 476x_1 + 240x_2\} \cap \mathbb{K}_2[\bar{x}]) = \mathbf{IV}(x_1 - x_2^2) = \langle x_1 - x_2^2 \rangle .$$

Then, $\forall i : 0 \le i \le 7$, $I_i^{(6)} = I_i^{(5)}$. In this case, the widening operator accomplishes its function and the algorithm stabilizes in 6 iterations, yielding the loop invariant $\{x_1 = x_2^2\}$.

6   Completeness

We show in this section that, under certain assumptions on the semantics of program constructs, the method is complete for finding polynomial invariants up to the degree d, where d is the parameter in the widening. We simplify the semantics as given in Section 5 as follows: firstly, conditions in test nodes are considered to be $true$[2]; further, all assignments are assumed to be linear (i.e., of the form $x_i := p(\bar{x})$, with p a polynomial of degree 1).

   The ideal-theoretic semantics of program constructs is used to associate a system of equations $\bar{I} = F(\bar{I})$ to a program, where the unknowns are the invariant ideals and F is an expression using sum, intersection and quotient of ideals and elimination of variables. The least of the solutions to this fix point equation with respect to $\supseteq$ can be shown to yield the optimal invariants; but, in general, it cannot be computed in a finite number of steps by applying forward propagation. The above proposed widening approximates the intersection of ideals when handling loop junction nodes with a loss of completeness of the method. The following theorem, however, shows that the widening is fine enough so as to keep all those polynomials of degree $\leq d$ of any fix point (for a proof, see [19]).

Theorem 2. *Let $\bar{I}^*$ be a fix point of the application F given by the semantics of a program (without widening). Let $\bar{I}^{(i)}$ be the approximation obtained at the i-th iteration of the forward propagation procedure using ∇_d instead of intersection at loop junction nodes. Then $\forall i \in \mathbb{N}$ and $\forall a$ program point, $I_a^* \cap \mathbb{K}_d[\bar{x}] \subseteq I_a^{(i)}$.*

   In particular, $\bar{I}^*$ may be the least fix point of F with respect to $\supseteq$. Therefore, on termination of the approximate forward propagation with widening, the theorem guarantees that we have computed all the invariant polynomials of degree $\leq d$. The proof is by induction over i. The inductive step is proved by considering all possible cases of program points and checking that all polynomials of degree $\leq d$ of the fix point are retained. For that we use the key property of the widening: the approximation includes all polynomials of degree $\leq d$ of the intersection; in other words, given I, J ideals, $I \cap J \cap \mathbb{K}_d[\bar{x}] \subseteq I \nabla_d J$.

7   Examples

We have implemented a modified version of the above method on Macaulay2 ([12]), an algebraic geometry tool that supports the ideal-theoretic operations needed in the method. In the implementation, the semantics of programs as given in Section 5 has been simplified: i) in order to speed up the algorithm, the **IV**($\cdot$) computations are not performed (although in practice for all our examples, some of which are shown in this section, we found the expected invariants without losing any information), ii) coefficients of terms in polynomials are considered over a finite field (with a large prime) for Gröbner basis computations, iii) the only boolean conditions considered are polynomial equalities, and iv) various paths in conditional statements are incrementally selected.

---

[2] As stated earlier, the method can deal with polynomial dis/equalities in test nodes.

Since we are interested in determining nonlinear invariants, we start with the value of d to be 2. If that does not work, then we increment the value.

Example 2. In order to compare the techniques, the first example has been extracted from [22]. It is a program that, given two natural numbers a and b, computes simultaneously the *gcd* and the *lcm*, which on termination, are x and $u + v$ respectively. Notice that the program has nested loops.

```
var a, b, x, y, u, v: integer end var
(x, y, u, v):=(a, b, b, 0);
while x ≠ y do
      while x > y do (x, v):=(x − y, u + v); end while
      while x < y do (y, u):=(y − x, u + v); end while
end while
```

Our implementation gives the same invariant for the three loops, $\{xu + yv = ab\}$, computed in 1.96 sec. (using $d = 2$). On termination of the outer loop, for which the invariant $\{gcd(x, y) = gcd(a, b)\}$ can be found by other methods, we have $x = y \wedge gcd(x, y) = gcd(a, b) \wedge xu + yv = ab$, which implies $u + v = lcm(a, b)$.

Example 3. The next example is an implementation of extended Euclid's algorithm to compute Bezout's coefficients (p, r) of two natural numbers x, y (see [17]), using a division program extracted from [3]. Notice that it has several levels of nested loops and non-linear polynomial assignments.

```
var x, y, a, b, p, q, r, s: integer end var
(a, b, p, q, r, s):=(x, y, 1, 0, 0, 1);
while b ≠ 0 do
      var c, k: integer end var
      (c, k):=(a, 0);
      while c ≥ b do
            var d, D: integer end var
            (d, D):=(1, b);
            while c ≥ 2D do  (d, D):=(2d, 2D); end while
            (c, k):=(c − D, k + d);
      end while
      (a, b, p, q, r, s):=(b, c, q, p − qk, s, r − sk);
end while
```

We get the following invariants in 9.34 sec. using $d = 2$:

1. Outermost loop: $\{px + ry = a \wedge qx + sy = b\}$.
2. Middle loop: $\{px + ry = a \wedge qx + sy = b \wedge kb + c = a\}$.
3. Innermost loop: $\{px + ry = a \wedge qx + sy = b \wedge kb + c = a \wedge db = D \wedge Dk + dc = da\}$.

The invariant of the outermost loop $\{px + ry = a \wedge qx + sy = b\}$ ensures that (p, r) is a pair of Bezout's coefficients for x, y on termination of the program.

Example 4. The following example is a version of a program in [17] that tries to find a divisor d of a natural number N using a parameter D:

```
var N, D, d, r, t, q: integer end var
```
$(d, r, t, q) := (D, N \bmod D, N \bmod (D - 2), 4(N \text{ div } (D - 2) - N \text{ div } D));$
```
while
```
$d \leq \lfloor \sqrt{N} \rfloor \wedge r \neq 0$
```
do
    if
```
$2r - t + q < 0$
```
then
```
$(d, r, t, q) := (d + 2, 2r - t + q + d + 2, r, q + 4);$
```
    else if
```
$0 \leq 2r - t + q < d + 2$
```
then
```
$(d, r, t) := (d + 2, 2r - t + q, r);$
```
    else if
```
$d + 2 \leq 2r - t + q < 2d + 4$
```
then
```
$(d, r, t, q) := (d + 2, 2r - t + q - d - 2, r, q - 4);$
```
    else
```
$(d, r, t, q) := (d + 2, 2r - t + q - 2d - 4, r, q - 8);$
```
    end if
end while
```

This is the most nontrivial program we have attempted. With $d = 2$, after 7.86 sec. we do not get any invariant; with $d = 3$, the invariant $\{d(dq - 4r + 4t - 2q) + 8r = 8N\}$ is generated in 48.82 sec. Even though we abstract the tests to be *true*, this is a strong enough polynomial invariant; together with other non-polynomial invariants, it can be used to prove that on termination, if $r = 0$ then d is a divisor of N.

Other Examples. The table below summarizes the results obtained using our implementation on other examples[3]. The execution times above as well as in the table are for a Pentium 4 2.5 GHz. processor with 512 MB of memory. There is a row for each program; the columns provide the following information:

1. 1st column is the name of the program; 2nd column states what the program does; 3rd column gives the source where the program was picked from (the entry $(*)$ is for the examples developed up by the authors).
2. 4th column is the bound d for the widening operator.
3. 5th column gives the number of variables in the program; 6th column gives the number of conditionals; 7th column is the number of loops; 8th column is the maximum depth of nested loops.
4. 9th column is the number of polynomials in the loop invariant for each loop.
5. 10th column gives the time taken by the implementation (in seconds).

8   Conclusions

We have presented an approach based on abstract interpretation for generating polynomial invariants of imperative programs. The techniques have been implemented using the algebraic geometry tool Macaulay2 [12]. The implementation has successfully computed invariants for many nontrivial programs. Its performance is very good as evident from the above table.

In the proposed method, the semantics of statements is given using ideal-theoretic operations; this is a novel idea in contrast to the axiomatic semantics or denotational semantics typically given for program constructs. Obviously, only

---

[3] These examples are available at www.lsi.upc.es/~erodri

Table 1. Table of examples

PROGRAM	COMPUTING	SOURCE	d	VAR	IF	LOOP	DEPTH	INV	TIME
cohencu	cube	[3]	3	5	0	1	1	4	2.45
dershowitz	real division	[9]	2	7	1	1	1	3	1.71
divbin	integer division	[13]	2	5	1	2	1	2-1	1.91
euclidex1	Bezout's coefs	[17]	2	10	0	2	2	3-4	7.15
euclidex2	Bezout's coefs	(*)	2	8	1	1	1	5	3.69
fermat	divisor	[2]	2	5	0	3	2	1-1-1	1.55
prod4br	product	(*)	3	6	3	1	1	1	8.49
freire1	integer sqrt	[11]	2	3	0	1	1	1	0.75
hard	integer division	[22]	2	6	1	2	1	3-3	2.19
lcm2	lcm	[10]	2	6	1	1	1	1	2.03
readers	simulation	[22]	2	6	3	1	1	2	4.15

certain kinds of statements can be considered this way; in particular, restrictions on tests in conditionals and loops, as well as on assignments, must be imposed. However, using the approach discussed in [15], where an ideal-theoretic interpretation of first-order predicate calculus is presented, it might be possible to give an algebraic semantics of arbitrary programming constructs using ideal-theoretic operations. This needs further investigation.

Another issue for further research is the widening operator for the semantics of loop junctions. The widening here presented, which retains polynomials of degree less than or equal to a certain a priori bound, works very well. But we will miss out invariants if the guess made for the upper bound on the degree of the invariants is incorrect. In that sense, the proposed method is complementary to our earlier work in [20], in which no a priori bound on the degree of polynomial invariants needs to be assumed.

Also, since the method here introduced is based on abstract interpretation, it will be easy to integrate it with the techniques for generating invariant linear inequalities discussed in [6]. Such an integration will result in an effective powerful method for generating loop invariants expressed as a combination of linear inequalities and polynomial equations, thus handling a large class of programs. In contrast, we do not see how this is feasible with the recent approaches presented in [22]. The use of the abstract interpretation framework is also likely to open doors for extending our approach to consider programs manipulating complex data structures including arrays, records and recursive data structures.

Acknowledgements

The authors would like to thank R. Clarisó, R. Nieuwenhuis, A. Oliveras and the anonymous referees for their help and advice.

References

1. François Bourdoncle. Efficient Chaotic Iteration Strategies with Widenings. In *Proceedings of the International Conference on Formal Methods in Programming and their Applications*, volume 735 of *Lecture Notes in Computer Science*, pages 128–141. Springer-Verlag, 1993.

2. David M. Bressoud. *Factorization and Primality Testing.* Springer-Verlag, 1989.
3. Edward Cohen. *Programming in the 1990s.* Springer-Verlag, 1990.
4. M. A. Colón, S. Sankaranarayanan, and H.B. Sipma. Linear Invariant Generation Using Non-Linear Constraint Solving. In *Computer-Aided Verification (CAV 2003)*, volume 2725 of *Lecture Notes in Computer Science*, pages 420–432. Springer-Verlag, 2003.
5. P. Cousot and R. Cousot. Abstract Interpretation: a Unified Lattice Model for Static Analysis of Programs by Construction or Approximation of Fixpoints. In *Conference Record of the Fourth Annual ACM SIGPLAN-SIGACT Symposium on Principles of Programming Languages*, pages 238–252, 1977.
6. P. Cousot and N. Halbwachs. Automatic Discovery of Linear Restraints among Variables of a Program. In *Conference Record of the Fifth Annual ACM SIGPLAN-SIGACT Symposium on Principles of Programming Languages*, pages 84–97, 1978.
7. D. Cox, J. Little, and D. O'Shea. *Ideals, Varieties and Algorithms. An Introduction to Computational Algebraic Geometry and Commutative Algebra.* Springer-Verlag, 1998.
8. J.H. Davenport, Y.Siret, and E.Tournier. *Computer Algebra: Systems and Algorithms for Algebraic Computation.* Academic Press, 1988.
9. N. Dershowitz and Z. Manna. Inference rules for program annotation. In *Proceedings of the 3rd International Conference on Software Engineering*, pages 158–167, 1978.
10. E. Dijkstra. *A Discipline of Programming.* Prentice Hall, 1976.
11. Pedro Freire. `www.pedrofreire.com/crea2_en.htm?`
12. Daniel R. Grayson and Michael E. Stillman. Macaulay 2, a Software System for Research in Algebraic Geometry. Available at `http://www.math.uiuc.edu/Macaulay2/`.
13. A. Kaldewaij. *Programming. The Derivation of Algorithms.* Prentice-Hall, 1990.
14. D. Kapur. A Refutational Approach to Geometry Theorem Proving. *Artificial Intelligence*, 37:61–93, 1988.
15. D. Kapur and P. Narendran. An equational approach to theorem proving in first-order predicate calculus. In *Proceedings of the Ninth International Joint Conference on Artificial Intelligence (IJCAI-85)*, pages 1146–1153, August 1985.
16. M. Karr. Affine Relationships Among Variables of a Program. *Acta Informatica*, 6:133–151, 1976.
17. D. E. Knuth. *The Art of Computer Programming. Volume 2, Seminumerical Algorithms.* Addison-Wesley, 1969.
18. M. Müller-Olm and H. Seidl. Computing Interprocedurally Valid Relations in Affine Programs. In *ACM SIGPLAN Principles of Programming Languages (POPL 2004)*, pages 330–341, 2004.
19. E. Rodríguez-Carbonell and D. Kapur. An Abstract Interpretation Approach for Automatic Generation of Polynomial Invariants. (extended version) `www.lsi.upc.es/~erodri`.
20. E. Rodríguez-Carbonell and D. Kapur. Automatic Generation of Polynomial Loop Invariants: Algebraic Foundations. `www.lsi.upc.es/~erodri`. To appear in *International Symposium on Symbolic and Algebraic Computation 2004 (ISSAC04)*.
21. E. Rodríguez-Carbonell and D. Kapur. Program Verification Using Automatic Generation of Polynomial Invariants. `www.lsi.upc.es/~erodri`.
22. S. Sankaranarayanan, H. B. Sipma, and Z. Manna. Non-linear Loop Invariant Generation Using Gröbner Bases. In *ACM SIGPLAN Principles of Programming Languages (POPL 2004)*, pages 318–329, 2004.

Approximating the Algebraic Relational Semantics of Imperative Programs

Michael A. Colón*

Center for High Assurance Computer Systems
Naval Research Laboratory
Washington, D.C.
colon@itd.nrl.navy.mil

Abstract. We present a novel static analysis for approximating the algebraic relational semantics of imperative programs. Our method is based on abstract interpretation in the lattice of *polynomial pseudo ideals* of bounded degree – finite-dimensional vector spaces of polynomials of bounded degree which are closed under bounded degree products. For a fixed bound, the space complexity of our approach and the iterations required to converge on fixed points are bounded by a polynomial in the number of program variables. Nevertheless, for several programs taken from the literature on non-linear polynomial invariant generation, our analysis produces results that are as precise as those produced by more heavy-weight Gröbner basis methods.

1 Introduction

The relational semantics of a program characterize its input-output behavior as a relation on states [22, 21]. A pair of states is included in the relation if the program, when started in the first state, can halt in the second. The algebraic relational semantics approximate the relational semantics by a system of polynomial equalities in the variables V, denoting the values of program variables in the initial state, and V', denoting the values in the final state. The expressiveness provided by non-linear polynomial equations allows for more precise approximations of program behavior than is possible with linear equalities [15]. In the presence of loops, even programs with purely linear assignments and guards can have input-output relations that cannot be adequately approximated linearly.

Consider the program presented in Fig. 1(a), which contains only linear assignments. Assuming the variable x is initially non-negative, the program halts with the final value of z equal to the square of the initial value of x. When x is initially negative, the program never terminates. More formally, the program's relational semantics are given by

$$[\![x' = x \ \wedge \ y' = x \ \wedge z' = x^2]\!],$$

where x', y', and z' represent the values of the variables in the final state. There are several uses for this relation: A program verification system might view it

---

* This research was supported by the Office of Naval Research.

R. Giacobazzi (Ed.): SAS 2004, LNCS 3148, pp. 296–311, 2004.
© Springer-Verlag Berlin Heidelberg 2004

var x, y, z : integer;   var x, y, z : integer;

$\ell_1 : \langle y, z \rangle := \langle 0, 0 \rangle;$ $\ell_1 : \langle y, z \rangle := \langle x, x^2 \rangle;$

ℓ_2 : while $y \neq x$ do ℓ_2 : halt

$\quad \ell_3 : \langle y, z \rangle := \langle y + 1, z + 2y + 1 \rangle;$

ℓ_4 : halt

(a)   (b)

Fig. 1. Computing the square

as an abstraction of the program suitable for compositional reasoning. A re-engineering system might annotate the program with the relation to document the program's behavior. A compiler, noting that the relation defines a function, might produce the more efficient and terminating version shown in Fig. 1(b).

The algebraic relational semantics can be approximated directly by abstract interpretation [4, 3]. Alternatively, traditional invariant generation methods [12, 27, 16, 5] can be applied by first augmenting the program with auxiliary variables which preserve the initial values of program variables, and then approximating the set of reachable states. This reduction, however, may cause some analyses to become infeasible, *i.e.*, those with high complexity in the number of program variables. For example, the extreme points and rays of a polyhedron may exceed the available memory while computing convex hulls in linear relation analysis [7, 14]. When approximating the relational semantics of a program, we must be attentive to the complexity of our methods in terms of the number of variables, since there are twice as many – representing the initial and final values.

Related Work. Recently, a number of proposals have been advanced for generating non-linear invariants of imperative programs: Sankaranarayanan *et al.* propose a constraint solving approach for generating non-linear invariants of bounded degree [25]. They first construct Gröbner bases of the polynomial systems expressing the initial states of the program and its transition relation, and extract from these bases a system of constraints characterizing the inductive polynomial equalities of a given degree. They then generate invariants by solving these constraints. The principal advantage of their method is that it eliminates the need for heuristic widening. The disadvantages are that the resulting constraints are not easily solved and that it is necessary to guess the number of equations when generating mutually inductive invariants.

Rodríguez Carbonell and Kapur propose another non-linear invariant generation method based on Gröbner bases [24]. While not presented as such, their approach is essentially an abstract interpretation in the lattice of polynomial ideals, with the proviso that all assignments appearing in the program be invertible and satisfy a certain condition which permits quantifier elimination by substitution. They do not provide a widening, but rather present conditions under which their method is guaranteed to converge on the strongest invariant. It is unclear whether the method terminates with an invariant for programs not meeting these conditions.

Müller-Olm and Seidl generate invariant polynomial equalities of bounded degree by backward propagation [23]. Their approach is limited to programs with linear assignments and ignores all guards. However, their analysis is based on methods from linear algebra and can be performed in both space and time that is polynomial in the number of program variables. The approaches based on Gröbner bases, on the other hand, have space and time complexity that is potentially exponential in the number of variables [28].

Contribution. We present a method which approximates the algebraic relational semantics by abstract interpretation in the lattice of bounded degree *polynomial pseudo ideals* – vector spaces of polynomials of degree no greater than some bound d which are closed under monomial products of degree no greater than d. For a fixed bound, the space required to represent pseudo ideals and the number of iterations required to converge on fixed points are both bounded by a polynomial in the number of program variables.

Our method builds upon the work of Karr on generating invariant linear equalities [15], and can be seen as a hybrid of the Gröbner basis methods and the method of Müller-Olm and Seidl. Like the Gröbner methods, our method achieves increased precision due to its firm grounding in the theory of polynomial ideals. Like the method of Müller-Olm and Seidl, our method gains space and time efficiency by using representations and algorithms from linear algebra. We have implemented our method and have applied it to a number of programs taken from the literature on non-linear polynomial invariant generation. For these programs, our method produces results as precise as those produced by other methods.

2   Preliminaries

Let $V = \{x_1, \ldots, x_n\}$ be a finite set of *variables*. A *state* $\sigma : V \to \mathbb{Q}$ maps each variable to a rational, and Σ denotes the set of all states. A *state formula* φ is a first-order expression whose free variables belong to V. A state σ *satisfies* φ, denoted $\sigma \models \varphi$, precisely when φ holds in σ. The set of all states satisfying φ is denoted $[\![\varphi]\!]$.

A *(binary) relation* ρ on Σ is a subset of $\Sigma \times \Sigma$. Each pair $\langle \sigma, \sigma' \rangle \in \rho$ consists of a *prestate* σ and a *poststate* σ'. The *composition* $\rho_1 \circ \rho_2$ of two relations is the set of pairs $\langle \sigma, \sigma' \rangle$ such that $\langle \sigma, \bar\sigma \rangle \in \rho_1$ and $\langle \bar\sigma, \sigma' \rangle \in \rho_2$ for some *intermediate state* $\bar\sigma$. The set of all relations on Σ is $\mathcal{R}$. A *relation formula* ψ is a first-order expression whose free variables belong to $V \cup V'$, where the variables in V denote the values in the prestate, and those in $V' = \{x'_1, \ldots, x'_n\}$ denote values in the poststate. A pair $\langle \sigma, \sigma' \rangle$ *satisfies* ψ ($\langle \sigma, \sigma' \rangle \models \psi$) if ψ holds in the model which interprets V as in the prestate and V' as in the poststate. A relation ρ *satisfies* ψ if $\langle \sigma, \sigma' \rangle \models \psi$ for every $\langle \sigma, \sigma' \rangle \in \rho$, and $[\![\psi]\!]$ denotes the largest relation satisfying ψ.

A *program* $\mathcal{P} = \langle L, \mathcal{T}, L_i, L_f \rangle$ consists of a finite set of *locations* L; a finite set of *transitions* $\mathcal{T}$, where each $\tau \in \mathcal{T}$ is a tuple $\langle \ell, \ell', \rho \rangle$ consisting of a *pre-location* ℓ, a *postlocation* ℓ', and a relation ρ, called the *transition relation*; a subset $L_i \subseteq L$ of *initial locations*; and a subset $L_f \subseteq L$ of *final locations*. A *path* $\pi = \ell_0 \overset{\tau_0}{\to} \ell_1 \ldots \ell_{n-1} \overset{\tau_{n-1}}{\to} \ell_n \overset{\tau_n}{\to} \ldots$ of a program is a potentially infinite sequence of interleaved locations and transitions such that, for each $i \geq 0$, ℓ_i is the prelocation of τ_i and ℓ_{i+1} is its postlocation. A finite path $\ell_0 \overset{\tau_0}{\to} \ldots \overset{\tau_{n-1}}{\to} \ell_n$ is *proper* iff $\ell_0 \in L_i$ and $\ell_n \in L_f$. The *path relation* $[\![\pi]\!]$ of a finite path π is the composition of the transition relations along π.

Definition 1 (Relational Semantics) *The* program relation $[\![\mathcal{P}]\!]$ *is the union of the path relations of the proper paths of* $\mathcal{P}$. *The program relation is also known as the* input-output relation.

A *cycle* is a finite path $\ell_0 \overset{\tau_0}{\to} \ldots \overset{\tau_{n-1}}{\to} \ell_0$ which begins and ends at the same location. Since acyclic programs contain only finitely many paths, the difficulty of program analysis lies in programs containing cycles. Let $\mathcal{P}$ be a program with cycles, and suppose that $\mathcal{P}$ contains a single *cut point* c, *i.e.*, a location contained in every cycle of $\mathcal{P}$ [1]. Call a path π *simple* if c appears only as the initial or final location, and *complex* otherwise. Then the proper paths of $\mathcal{P}$ can be partitioned into a set Π_s of simple paths and a set of complex paths. Let Π_i be the set of simple paths from an initial location to c, Π_c be the set of simple cycles from c, and Π_f be the set of simple paths from c to a final location. Then,

$$[\![\mathcal{P}]\!] = [\![\Pi_s]\!] \cup (\rho_\infty \circ [\![\Pi_f]\!]),$$

where ρ_∞ is the least fixed point of the following function on relations:

$$f(\rho) = [\![\Pi_i]\!] \cup (\rho \circ [\![\Pi_c]\!]).$$

Thus, the problem of computing the relational semantics of a program with cycles reduces to that of computing least fixed points in $\mathcal{R}$.

Abstract Interpretation. A *lattice* $\langle L, \sqsubseteq, \sqcap, \sqcup \rangle$ is a nonempty partially ordered set in which every pair of *points* $p_1, p_2 \in L$ has a *greatest lower bound* $p_1 \sqcap p_2$ (*meet*) and a *least upper bound* $p_1 \sqcup p_2$ (*join*). A lattice is *complete* if every subset of L has a greatest lower and a least upper bound in L. Every finite lattice is complete, and every complete lattice possesses a *least element* $\bot$ and a *greatest element* $\top$. The *dual* of $\langle L, \sqsubseteq, \sqcap, \sqcup \rangle$ is the lattice $\langle L, \sqsupseteq, \sqcup, \sqcap \rangle$ [9].

An *ascending chain* $p_1 \sqsubseteq p_2 \sqsubseteq \ldots \sqsubseteq p_n \sqsubseteq \ldots$ and a *descending chain* $p_1 \sqsupseteq p_2 \sqsupseteq \ldots \sqsupseteq p_n \sqsupseteq \ldots$ are potentially infinite sequences of ordered points. A chain *eventually stabilizes* iff there is an i such that $p_j = p_i$ for all $j \geq i$. A lattice satisfies the *ascending (descending) chain condition* if every infinite ascending (descending) chain eventually stabilizes. Every lattice satisfying both chain conditions is complete. A function $f : L \to L$ on a lattice is *monotone* if

---

[1] The approach extends to sets of cut points.

$p_1 \sqsubseteq p_2$ implies $f(p_1) \sqsubseteq f(p_2)$, and a point p with $p = f(p)$ is a *fixed point* of f. In a lattice satisfying both chain conditions, the *least fixed point* $\mathrm{lfp}(f)$ and the *greatest fixed point* $\mathrm{gfp}(f)$ can be computed iteratively:

$$\mathrm{lfp}(f) = \bigsqcup_{i \geq 0} f^i(\bot) \qquad \mathrm{gfp}(f) = \bigsqcap_{i \geq 0} f^i(\top)$$

When the lattice L does not satisfy the chain conditions, there are essentially two approaches to approximating fixed points: The first involves devising a *widening* to extrapolate the limits of unstable chains, while the second entails constructing another lattice M, along with a *Galois connection* $\langle \alpha, \gamma \rangle$ from L to M, *i.e.*, a pair of monotone functions $\alpha : L \to M$, $\gamma : M \to L$ satisfying $l \sqsubseteq \gamma(\alpha(l))$ for all $l \in L$ and $\alpha(\gamma(m)) \sqsubseteq m$ for all $m \in M$. The Galois connection ensures that fixed points in L can be approximated by corresponding fixed points in M [4, 6].

Polynomial Ideals. A *monomial* in variables $x_1, \ldots, x_n$ is a product of powers $\boldsymbol{x}^{\boldsymbol{e}} = x_1^{d_1} \cdots x_n^{d_n}$. A *polynomial* p is a linear combination $c_1 \boldsymbol{x}^{\boldsymbol{e}_1} + \cdots + c_m \boldsymbol{x}^{\boldsymbol{e}_m}$ of monomials with rational coefficients. The *polynomial ring* $\mathbb{Q}[V, V']$ is the set of all polynomials in V and V'. The *degree* $\deg(x_1^{d_1} \cdots x_n^{d_n})$ of a monomial is the sum $d_1 + \cdots + d_n$. The degree $\deg(p)$ of a polynomial p is the maximal degree of its monomials with non-zero coefficients. A polynomial is *linear* if its degree is one, *quadratic* if two, and *cubic* if three. A set of polynomials P is said to be *of degree* d if $\deg(p) \leq d$ for every $p \in P$.

The largest relation ρ on Σ for which $\rho \models p = 0$ for all p in a set P of polynomials is denoted $\llbracket P \rrbracket$. A relation ρ is *algebraic* iff $\rho = \llbracket P \rrbracket$ for some set of polynomials P. Given a relation ρ, the *theory* $Th(\rho)$ of ρ is the set of polynomials that vanish on ρ, *i.e.*, $\{p \mid \rho \models p = 0\}$. All theories are polynomial ideals.

Definition 2 (Polynomial Ideal) *A set I of polynomials from $\mathbb{Q}[V, V']$ is an ideal iff i) $p_1 + p_2 \in I$ for all $p_1, p_2 \in I$ and ii) $qp \in I$ for all $p \in I$ and $q \in \mathbb{Q}[V, V']$. The generated ideal $\mathcal{I}d(P)$ of a subset P of $\mathbb{Q}[V, V']$ is the set of linear combinations $q_1 p_1 + \cdots + q_m p_m$, with $p_1, \ldots, p_m \in P$ and $q_1, \ldots, q_m \in \mathbb{Q}[V, V']$. A set P is a basis of an ideal I iff $I = \mathcal{I}d(P)$.*

The least ideal is $\{0\}$, and the greatest is $\mathbb{Q}[V, V']$. Ideals are closed under intersection, but not union. The sum $I_1 + I_2$ of two ideals is the least ideal which contains them. The set $\mathcal{I}$ of all ideals of $\mathbb{Q}[V, V']$ forms a complete lattice $\langle \mathcal{I}, \subseteq, \cap, + \rangle$, and $\langle Th, \llbracket \cdot \rrbracket \rangle$ forms a Galois connection from $\mathcal{R}$ to the dual of $\mathcal{I}$.

By the Hilbert basis theorem, every polynomial ideal has a finite basis [8]. A special family of bases, known as *reduced Gröbner bases*, provides canonical representations of polynomial ideals, can be constructed using Buchberger's algorithm, and is suitable for implementing lattice operations [1, 11]. However, the size of a Gröbner basis can be exponential in the number of variables [28].

Vector Spaces. A *vector* $v : X \to \mathbb{Q}$ maps elements of a finite *index set* X to rationals. A *vector space* is a set of vectors closed under addition and multiplication by scalars. The *generated space* $Sp(V)$ of a set of vectors is the set of linear combinations $q_1 v_1 + \cdots + q_m v_m$, where $v_1, \ldots, v_m \in V$ and $q_1, \ldots, q_m \in \mathbb{Q}$. Let $\mathcal{S}$ be the set of spaces of vectors indexed by X. Then $\langle \mathcal{S}, \subseteq, \cap, + \rangle$ forms a lattice satisfying both chain conditions. A *basis* of a space S is a minimal set of vectors V with $S = Sp(V)$, and canonical bases of vector spaces can be found in polynomial time using Gauss-Jordan reduction [26]. All bases of a vector space S are of the same size – the *dimension* $\dim(S)$ of the space. The dimension of a space of vectors indexed by X never exceeds $|X|$, and all chains of such spaces contain no more than $|X| + 1$ distinct points [17].

3   Approximating the Algebraic Relational Semantics

Our method approximates the relational semantics of *algebraic programs*, *i.e.*, programs all of whose transition relations are algebraic. Algebraic programs can model imperative programs over rational variables constructed using assignment, alternation and iteration, provided assignments are polynomials in the program variables and the conditions of *if* and *while* statements are conjunctions of polynomial equalities. Programs with integer variables can be modeled by treating those variables as rational, but programs with integer division must be afforded special treatment to ensure the soundness of the analysis: For example, the assignment $x := x$ div 2 can be modeled by the relation $[\![x' = \frac{1}{2}x]\!]$ only if x is known to be even. This property can often be established using other static analyses, *e.g.*, congruence analysis [13]. Programs not meeting these conditions can be analyzed by first constructing algebraic abstractions, *e.g.*, treating non-polynomial assignments as non-deterministic and modeling non-algebraic conditions by the identity relation.

One approach to approximating the algebraic relational semantics, suggested by the Galois connection $\langle Th, [\![\cdot]\!] \rangle$ from $\mathcal{R}$ to the dual of $\mathcal{I}$, is abstract interpretation in the lattice of polynomial ideals. However, in addition to the high complexity of operations on ideals, the iterative method of computing fixed points is hampered by the presence of unstable descending chains. For example, an analysis of the program presented in Fig. 2 would visit the chain

$$\mathcal{I}d\left(\{x' - 1\}\right) \supset \mathcal{I}d\left(\{(x' - 1)(x' - 2)\}\right) \supset \ldots \supset \mathcal{I}d\left(\left\{\prod_{i=1}^{n}(x' - i)\right\}\right) \supset \ldots,$$

where multiplication is used to express disjunction. The method we present performs abstract interpretation in the lattice of polynomial pseudo ideals of bounded degree, a lattice satisfying both chain conditions.

Polynomial Pseudo Ideals. Given a relation ρ and a non-negative integer d, let the *theory* $Th_d(\rho)$ *of degree* d be the set of polynomials p in $Th(\rho)$ such that $\deg(p) \leq d$. If we treat polynomials as vectors indexed by monomials, then $Th_d(\rho)$ is a vector space. A *polynomial space of degree* d is a vector space indexed by the set of monomials of degree no greater than d. For a fixed degree d, the

```
var x : integer;
ℓ₁ : x := 1;
ℓ₂ : while true do
    ℓ₃ : x := x + 1;
ℓ₄ : halt
```

Fig. 2. Descending a chain of ideals

sizes of bases of polynomial spaces and the number of distinct points in chains are bounded by a polynomial function in the number of variables n: The number of monomials in $V \cup V'$ of degree d or less is $\left(\!\binom{2n+1}{d}\!\right)$ – the number of multisets of size d chosen from $2n + 1$ elements, where the additional element, *i.e.*, 1, allows for monomials of degree less than d. Now, $\left(\!\binom{2n+1}{d}\!\right) = \binom{2n+d}{d} = O\left((2n + d)^d\right)$, which is polynomial in n for a fixed d. Thus, iterative computation of fixed points in the lattice of polynomial spaces of degree d is feasible – provided d is small, *e.g.*, two or three.

This lattice, however, contains extraneous points which can impede precise analysis. Consider the relation $[\![x + y = 0 \ \wedge \ x' = x^2 + xy \ \wedge \ y' = y]\!]$. This relation satisfies $x' = 0$, but the polynomial x' is not in the space generated by $P = \{x + y, x' - x^2 - xy, y' - y\}$. To improve the accuracy of the analysis, linear combinations with polynomial coefficients must be considered: $x' = x(x + y) + (x' - x^2 - xy)$. However, allowing the use of arbitrary polynomial coefficients would lead, once again, to the lattice of polynomial ideals. Instead, we limit the polynomial coefficients which can appear in a linear combination by bounding the degree of the terms appearing in that combination.

Definition 3 (Polynomial Pseudo Ideal) *A polynomial space J of degree d is a polynomial pseudo ideal of degree d iff $qp \in J$ for all $p \in J$, $q \in \mathbb{Q}[V, V']$ with $\deg(qp) \leq d$. The generated pseudo ideal $\mathcal{P}s_d(P)$ of a set of polynomials of degree d is the least pseudo ideal of degree d containing P.*

While pseudo ideals of degree d are closed under intersection, they are not closed under sum. Thus we define the join $J_1 \uplus_d J_2$ as $\mathcal{P}s_d(J_1 \cup J_2)$. The set $\mathcal{J}_d$ of pseudo ideals of degree d forms a lattice $\langle \mathcal{J}_d, \subseteq, \cap, \uplus_d \rangle$. While not a sublattice of the lattice of polynomial spaces, all chains in this lattice are chains of spaces, and thus this lattice satisfies both chain conditions. For any relation ρ, $\mathcal{T}h_d(\rho)$ is a pseudo ideal of degree d: If p_1, p_2 vanish on ρ and are of degree no greater than d, then $p_1 + p_2$ vanishes on ρ and $\deg(p_1 + p_2) \leq d$. If p vanishes on ρ and $\deg(p) \leq d$, then for any q with $\deg(qp) \leq d$, qp also vanishes on ρ. Furthermore, $\mathcal{T}h_d([\![P]\!]) \supseteq \mathcal{P}s_d(P)$ for any set P of polynomials of degree no greater than d. In other words, moving to the generated pseudo ideal is always sound, but not necessarily complete. Based on these observations, the following result can be established:

Lemma 1 *For any $d \geq 0$, $\langle \mathcal{T}h_d, [\![\cdot]\!] \rangle$ forms a Galois connection from $\mathcal{R}$ to the dual of $\mathcal{J}_d$.*

Polynomial pseudo ideals are not merely the restrictions of ideals to polynomials of bounded degree. Due to the possibility of canceling high-degree monomials while taking linear combinations of polynomials, the ideal I generated by a set P of polynomials of degree d generally contains more polynomials than the pseudo ideal J generated by P, even if we consider only polynomials of degree no greater than d. There can exist a polynomial p with $\deg(p) \le d$ for which the only linear combinations $q_1 p_1 + \cdots + q_m p_m$ of P generating p, have $\deg(q_i p_i) > d$ for some $i \in \{1, \ldots, m\}$. In such a case, $p \in I$, but $p \in J$ need not hold.

In the worst case, the linear combinations establishing membership of the polynomial p in the ideal $\mathcal{I}d(P)$ can all have terms whose degrees are doubly exponential in the number of variables, even when the degrees of p and the basis P are fixed [28]. As a result, the membership problem for polynomial ideals requires exponential space [20]. In contrast, membership in the pseudo ideal generated by P can be decided in polynomial time. Pseudo ideals provide tractable approximations to polynomial ideals, and the precision of the approximation can be improved by increasing the degree bound.

For the remainder of this section, we assume a fixed degree bound d.

Representing Pseudo Ideals. We represent pseudo ideals by their basis *as polynomial spaces*. A pseudo ideal J is represented by a set of polynomials P such that $J = \mathcal{S}p(P)$. Such a set P always exists, since pseudo ideals are spaces. Although often containing redundancy, this representation allows us to apply well known methods from linear algebra to solve problems on pseudo ideals.

Essential to our representation of pseudo ideals is an algorithm to compute the *pseudo ideal hull*: Given a set of polynomials P of degree d, find a set Q such that the polynomial space generated by Q is the pseudo ideal generated by P. Before presenting our algorithm, we state, without proof, the following result:

Lemma 2 *A space S of degree d is a pseudo ideal iff $xp \in S$ for every variable $x \in V \cup V'$ and every polynomial $p \in S$ with $\deg(p) \le d - 1$.*

Based on this lemma, it is easy to decide whether a given space S is a pseudo ideal. We first compute a basis $P = \{p_1, \ldots, p_m\}$ of the subset S_{d-1} of polynomials in S of degree no greater than $d-1$ by eliminating all monomials of degree d using Gauss-Jordan reduction. Then we verify that xp is in S for every $p \in P$ and $x \in V \cup V'$. Since any polynomial $p \in S_{d-1}$ is a linear combination $q_1 p_1 + \cdots + q_m p_m$ of P, this condition is both necessary and sufficient for xp to be a member of S for an arbitrary $p \in S_{d-1}$. Should we discover that S is not a pseudo ideal, its pseudo ideal hull can be computed iteratively as the least fixed point of the following monotone function on polynomial spaces:

$$f(T) = S \cup \{xp \mid p \in T_{d-1}, x \in V \cup V'\}$$

Computing Lattice Operators. Membership of a polynomial p in the pseudo ideal $J = \mathcal{S}p(P)$ can be decided using Gauss-Jordan reduction: $p \in J$ iff the canonical form of P is identical to that of $P \cup \{p\}$. Similarly, the pseudo ideal

$J_1 = \mathcal{S}p(P_1)$ is contained in $J_2 = \mathcal{S}p(P_2)$ iff the canonical form of $P_1 \cup P_2$ is identical to that of P_2. The intersection of pseudo ideals can be computed using Karr's algorithm [15], and the union of pseudo ideals $J_1 = \mathcal{S}p(P_1)$ and $J_2 = \mathcal{S}p(P_2)$ can be computed by taking the hull of $P_1 \cup P_2$.

To approximate the composition $[\![J_1]\!] \circ [\![J_2]\!]$, we introduce a new operator on pseudo ideals, $J_1 \bullet_d J_2$, computed using the following algorithm: Suppose $J_1 = \mathcal{S}p(P_1)$ and $J_2 = \mathcal{S}p(P_2)$. We switch temporarily to the polynomial ring $\mathbb{Q}[V, \bar{V}, V']$, where $\bar{V}$ denotes the variable values in intermediate states. In this ring, we compute the pseudo ideal hull of $Q = P_1[V' \to \bar{V}] \cup P_2[V \to \bar{V}]$, where $P_i[U \to W]$ denotes substitution of the variables in U by the corresponding variables in W. We then apply Gauss-Jordan reduction to eliminate all monomials in which a variable of $\bar{V}$ appears. The resulting set P of polynomials forms the basis of $J_1 \bullet_d J_2$. By construction, any tuple $\langle \sigma, \bar{\sigma}, \sigma' \rangle$ satisfying $\langle \sigma, \bar{\sigma} \rangle \in [\![P_1]\!]$ and $\langle \bar{\sigma}, \sigma' \rangle \in [\![P_2]\!]$ causes every polynomial in Q to vanish, where the variables $\bar{V}$ are interpreted as in $\bar{\sigma}$. Since P consists of linear combinations of polynomials of Q in which the variables of $\bar{V}$ do not appear, $\langle \sigma, \sigma' \rangle \in [\![P]\!]$. Therefore, $J_1 \bullet_d J_2$ soundly approximates the composition, i.e., $Th_d([\![J_1]\!] \circ [\![J_2]\!]) \supseteq J_1 \bullet_d J_2$.

Example. We now illustrate our method by applying it to the program of Fig 1(a), using quadratic pseudo ideals. The first step is to approximate the relational semantics to the cut point ℓ_2. The precise relational semantics are given by the least fixed point of the following function:

$$f(\rho) = \rho_1 \cup (\rho \circ \rho_2),$$

where $\rho_1 = [\![x' = x \wedge y' = 0 \wedge z' = 0]\!]$ is the relation from ℓ_1 to ℓ_2, and $\rho_2 = [\![x' = x \wedge y' = y+1 \wedge z' = z + 2y + 1]\!]$ is the relation of the cycle from ℓ_2 back to ℓ_2. To approximate $\mathrm{lfp}(f)$, we apply the Galois connection $\langle Th_2, [\![\cdot]\!] \rangle$ from $\mathcal{R}$ to the dual of $\mathcal{J}_2$ and compute the greatest fixed point of g,

$$g(J) = J_1 \cap (J \bullet_2 J_2),$$

where $J_1 = \mathcal{P}s_2(\{x' - x, y', z'\})$ approximates the relation ρ_1, while the relation ρ_2 is approximated by $J_2 = \mathcal{P}s_2(\{x' - x, y' - y - 1, z' - z - 2y - 1\})$. The soundness of the analysis follows from the fact that $Th_2(f([\![J]\!])) \supseteq g(J)$ for any quadratic pseudo ideal J. Iterating from $\top$ converges on $\mathrm{gfp}(g)$:

$$J_\infty = \mathcal{S}p\left(\left\{ \begin{array}{c} x^2 - (x')^2,\ xy - yx',\ xz - zx',\ xx' - (x')^2, \\ xy' - x'y',\ xz' - x'z',\ (y')^2 - z',\ x - x' \end{array} \right\} \right)$$

The second step of the analysis computes the approximation J of the input-output relation as the composition of J_∞ and the quadratic pseudo ideal approximating the path relation from ℓ_2 to ℓ_4.

var x, y, z : **integer**;

$\ell_1 : z := 0$

ℓ_2 : **while** $y \neq 0$ **do**

    ℓ_3 : **if** $y \bmod 2 = 1$ **then**

        $\ell_4 : \langle x, y, z \rangle := \langle 2x, (y-1) \text{ div } 2, x+z \rangle$

    else

        $\ell_5 : \langle x, y, z \rangle := \langle 2x, y \text{ div } 2, z \rangle;$

  ℓ_6 : **halt**

Fig. 3. Product by Binary Decomposition

var a, b, p, q : **integer**;

$\ell_1 : \langle p, q \rangle := \langle 1, 0 \rangle;$

ℓ_2 : **while** $a \neq 0 \wedge b \neq 0$ **do**

$$
\left[
\begin{array}{l}
\ell_3 : \textbf{if } a \bmod 2 = 0 \wedge b \bmod 2 = 0 \textbf{ then} \\
\quad \ell_4 : \langle a, b, p, q \rangle := \langle a \text{ div } 2, b \text{ div } 2, 4p, q \rangle \\
\textbf{else if } a \bmod 2 = 1 \wedge b \bmod 2 = 0 \textbf{ then} \\
\quad \ell_5 : \langle a, b, p, q \rangle := \langle a - 1, b, p, q + bp \rangle \\
\textbf{else if } a \bmod 2 = 0 \wedge b \bmod 2 = 1 \textbf{ then} \\
\quad \ell_6 : \langle a, b, p, q \rangle := \langle a, b - 1, p, q + ap \rangle \\
\textbf{else} \\
\quad \ell_7 : \langle a, b, p, q \rangle := \langle a - 1, b - 1, p, q + (a + b - 1)p \rangle
\end{array}
\right]
$$

ℓ_8 : **halt**

Fig. 4. Alternate Product

$$
J = \mathcal{S}p\left(\left\{
\begin{array}{l}
x^2 - z',\ xy - yy',\ xz - zy',\ xx' - z',\ xy' - z',\ xz' - y'z', \\
yx' - yy',\ zx' - zy',\ (x')^2 - z',\ x'y' - z',\ x'z' - y'z', \\
(y')^2 - z',\ x - y',\ x' - y'
\end{array}
\right\}\right)
$$

The representation of a pseudo ideal by its basis as a polynomial space is convenient, but frequently redundant. Simplifying to a pseudo ideal basis of J gives a more perspicuous description of the relational semantics:

$$
[\![x' = x \wedge y' = x \wedge z' = x^2]\!].
$$

4   Applications

To demonstrate the utility of our approach, we have implemented the method in Java and applied it to several programs taken from the literature on non-linear invariant generation. For each of the programs we have examined, our analysis produces results as precise as those produced by other methods [25, 24].

var x_1, x_2, y_1, y_2 : **integer**;

$\ell_1 : \langle y_1, y_2 \rangle := \langle 0, x_1 \rangle;$

$\ell_2 :$ **while** $y_2 \geq x_2$ **do**

$\qquad \ell_3 : \langle y_1, y_2 \rangle := \langle y_1 + 1, y_2 - x_2 \rangle;$

$\ell_4 :$ **halt**

Fig. 5. Division by Subtraction

Lacking the ability to express inequalities between variables, algebraic relations are frequently incapable of adequately capturing the input-output behavior of the programs we consider. This limitation, however, can often be overcome by combining our analysis with linear relation analysis [7, 14].

Product by Binary Decomposition. Our first example, taken from Rodríguez Carbonell and Kapur [24], is shown in Fig. 3. It is a variant of a program for exponentiation by binary decomposition studied by Manna [18]. Our method computes the relational semantics as

$$[\![y' = 0 \ \wedge \ z' = xy]\!].$$

The analysis takes 90ms to complete[2]. The soundness of the analysis depends on the fact that $y - 1$ is even at ℓ_4 and y is even at ℓ_5. These properties can be established automatically by Granger's congruence analysis [13].

Alternate Product. Our second example, also from Rodríguez Carbonell and Kapur and shown in Fig. 4, demonstrates the need to work with pseudo ideals of degree greater than two. Conducting the analysis in the lattice of cubic pseudo ideals, our method approximates the relational semantics to cut point ℓ_2 as

$$[\![q' = ab - a'b'p']\!],$$

and the semantics of the program as

$$[\![a'b' = 0 \ \wedge \ q' = ab]\!].$$

Note that the fixed point at ℓ_2 is a cubic relation, while the input-output relation of the program is quadratic. Had we approximated the semantics using quadratic pseudo ideals, the result of the analysis would not have been as precise. By working with cubic rather than quadratic pseudo ideals, we increase the accuracy of our analysis, along with the space used and the time taken (2.2s).

---

[2] Reported times are for a 1.4GHz Pentium with 512MB running NetBeans 3.5.1.

var $x_1, x_2, y_1, y_2, y_3, y_4$: **integer**;

ℓ_1 : $\langle y_1, y_2, y_3, y_4 \rangle := \langle x_1, x_2, 1, 0 \rangle$;

ℓ_2 : **while** $y_1 \geq y_2$ **do**

$\qquad \ell_3$: $\langle y_2, y_3 \rangle := \langle 2y_2, 2y_3 \rangle$;

ℓ_4 : **while** true **do**

$$\begin{bmatrix} \ell_5 : \textbf{if } y_1 \geq y_2 \textbf{ then} \\ \qquad \ell_6 : \langle y_1, y_4 \rangle := \langle y_1 - y_2, y_4 + y_3 \rangle; \\ \ell_7 : \textbf{if } y_3 = 1 \textbf{ then} \\ \qquad \ell_8 : \textbf{halt}; \\ \ell_9 : \langle y_2, y_3 \rangle := \langle y_2 \text{ div } 2, y_3 \text{ div } 2 \rangle \end{bmatrix}$$

Fig. 6. Hardware Integer Division

Division by Subtraction. The program in Fig. 5 also appears in Sankaranarayanan *et al.* [25]. Returning to quadratic pseudo ideals, our method computes the following relation in 190ms:

$$[\![x_1' = x_1 \wedge x_2' = x_2 \wedge x_1 = y_1' x_2 + y_2']\!]$$

Assuming that x_1 is initially non-negative and x_2 is positive, linear relation analysis [7, 14] can discover the invariant $0 \leq y_2' < x_2'$ at ℓ_4. Thus, upon termination, y_1 holds the quotient of x_1 and x_2, while y_2 holds the remainder.

Hardware Integer Division. Our next example, also from Manna and appearing in Sankaranarayanan *et al.*, is shown in Fig. 6. This program computes the quotient and remainder of x_1 and x_2 by binary search. The fact that y_3 is a positive power of 2 at ℓ_9, which appears to be derivable by numerical power analysis [19], combined with the invariant $y_2 = x_2 y_3$, generated by our method, guarantees that both y_2 and y_3 are even at ℓ_9.

Our analysis approximates the relational semantics in 700ms, producing

$$[\![x_1' = x_1 \wedge x_2' = x_2 \wedge y_2' = x_2 \wedge y_3' = 1 \wedge x_1 = x_2 y_4' + y_1']\!].$$

To guarantee correctness of the program, *i.e.*, guarantee that it produces the quotient and remainder, the additional property $0 \leq y_1' < x_2$ is required.

Dijkstra's Square Root. Fig. 7 shows a program, due to Dijkstra [10], for computing the integer square root of a non-negative integer n. The fact that q holds a positive power of 4 at ℓ_5 and the loop invariant $p^2 = qn - qr$ ensure the soundness of treating these variables as rational.

In 230ms, our analysis approximates the relational semantics as

$$[\![n' = n \wedge n = (p')^2 + r' \wedge q' = 1]\!].$$

Applying linear relation analysis again, it is possible to infer that $0 \leq r' < 2p' + 1$ at location ℓ_9. Thus, the program halts with $(p')^2 \leq n < (p' + 1)^2$.

var n, p, q, r, h : **integer**;

$\ell_1 : \langle p, q, r \rangle := \langle 0, 1, n \rangle;$

$\ell_2 :$ **while** $q \le n$ **do**

$\quad \ell_3 : q := 4q;$

$\ell_4 :$ **while** $q \ne 1$ **do**

$$\left[\begin{array}{l} \ell_5 : q := q \text{ div } 4; \\ \ell_6 : \langle h, p \rangle := \langle p + q, p \text{ div } 2 \rangle \\ \ell_7 : \textbf{if } r \ge h \textbf{ then} \\ \qquad \ell_8 : \langle p, r \rangle := \langle p + q, r - h \rangle \end{array} \right]$$

$\ell_9 :$ **halt**

Fig. 7. Dijkstra's Square Root

var x, y_1, y_2, y_3 : **integer**;

$\ell_1 : \langle y_1, y_2, y_3 \rangle := \langle 0, 1, 1 \rangle;$

$\ell_2 :$ **while** $y_2 \le x$ **do**

$\quad \ell_3 : \langle y_1, y_2, y_3 \rangle := \langle y_1 + 1, y_2 + y_3 + 2, y_3 + 2 \rangle;$

$\ell_4 :$ **halt**

Fig. 8. Integer Square Root

Integer Square Root. The program in Fig. 8, taken from Manna, computes the integer square root of a non-negative integer x. Our analysis yields the following relation in 240ms:

$$[\![x' = x \ \wedge \ y_2' = (y_1')^2 + 2y_1' + 1 = (y_1' + 1)^2 \ \wedge \ y_3' = 2y_1' + 1]\!]$$

Linear relation analysis can be used to infer $y_2' = (y_1' + 1)^2 > x$ at ℓ_4. Thus, while the final value of y_1 cannot be too small, it might be too large.

A more refined analysis results from splitting the proper paths into those in which the loop does not execute and those for which it iterates at least once. In the former case, the input-output relation is

$$[\![1 > x \ \wedge \ x' = x \ \wedge \ y_1' = 0 \ \wedge \ y_2' = 1 \ \wedge \ y_2' = 1]\!].$$

Since x is non-negative, $x = 0$ and $y_1' = x^2$. In the latter case, the loop condition must hold for the penultimate iteration of the loop, *i.e.*, $y_2' - y_3' \le x$, giving

$$[\![(y_1')^2 \le x < (y_1' + 1)^2 \ \wedge \ x' = x \ \wedge \ y_2' = (y_1' + 1)^2 \ \wedge \ y_3' = 2y_1' + 1]\!].$$

In either case, y_1' is the integer square root of x.

5   Conclusion

We have presented a static analysis which approximates the algebraic relational semantics of imperative programs by abstract interpretation in the lattice of

$$\textbf{var } x : \textbf{integer};$$
$$\ell_1 : \textbf{if } x^2 \neq 0 \textbf{ then}$$
$$\ell_2 : x := 0;$$
$$\ell_3 : \textbf{halt}$$

Fig. 9. Incompleteness of ideals

polynomial pseudo ideals of a given degree. For a fixed degree, the space required to represent points in this lattice and the number of iterations needed to converge on fixed points are both bounded by a polynomial in the number of program variables. Our work continues the tradition of using linear reasoning to infer consequences of non-linear constraints [2], and our method is incomplete relative to an abstract interpretation in the lattice of polynomial ideals. However, our method is tractable, while the complexity of abstract interpretation using polynomial ideals can be exponential in the worst case [20, 28]. Furthermore, for a number of programs drawn from the literature on non-linear polynomial invariant generation, our method produces results as precise as those produced by Gröbner basis methods.

In any event, while abstract interpretation using polynomial ideals provides a reasonable measure of relative completeness, it too is incomplete. All algebraic theories are radical, but the lattice of polynomial ideals contains non-radical points[3]. As a result, an analysis in the lattice of ideals will fail to deduce that the program of Fig. 9 halts with x equal to zero. The analysis of this program should be conducted using radical ideals, and the example suggests that the precision of our method would be improved by closing pseudo ideals under radicals.

Our decision to approximate the relational semantics in a lattice of polynomial pseudo ideals rather than devise a widening for the lattice of ideals was a pragmatic one, driven by the computational complexity of operations on ideals. For some applications, however, the increased precision afforded by abstract interpretation in the lattice of ideals justifies the cost. In these cases, the family of lattices of polynomial pseudo ideals can serve as the basis of a widening for the lattice of ideals [6]. For example, we can iterate for a finite number of steps using polynomial ideals, then move to pseudo ideals of degree d, where d is the maximal degree of a polynomial appearing in a Gröbner basis. Alternatively, we can use the monomials appearing in a Gröbner basis along with their factors to construct the index set of a polynomial space and move to the corresponding lattice of pseudo ideals. In other words, we can base the choice of lattice on the particular monomials which are observed, and not simply their degrees.

Acknowledgments

Many thanks are due to Ramesh Bharadwaj, Constance Heitmeyer, Ralph Jeffords, Elizabeth Leonard, and the anonymous reviewers for their helpful suggestions.

---

[3] An ideal I is *radical* if $p^d \in I$ implies $p \in I$.

References

1. T. Becker and V. Weispfenning. *Gröbner Bases: A Computational Approach to Commutative Algebra.* Springer-Verlag, New York, 1993.
2. A. Colmerauer. Naive solving of non-linear constraints. In F. Benhamou and A. Colmerauer, editors, *Constraint Logic Programming: Selected Research*, pages 89–112. MIT Press, 1993.
3. P. Cousot. Constructive design of a hierarchy of semantics of a transition system by abstract interpretation. *Electronic Notes in Theoretical Computer Science*, 6, 1997. http://www.elsevier.nl/locate/entcs/volume6.html.
4. P. Cousot and R. Cousot. Abstract Interpretation: A unified lattice model for static analysis of programs by construction or approximation of fixpoints. In *Conference Record of the 4th ACM Symposium on Principles of Programming Languages*, pages 238–252, 1977.
5. P. Cousot and R. Cousot. Automatic synthesis of optimal invariant assertions: Mathematical foundations. In *Proceedings of the ACM Symposium on Artificial Intelligence and Programming Languages*, pages 1–12, 1977.
6. P. Cousot and R. Cousot. Comparing the Galois connection and widening/narrowing approaches to Abstract Interpretation. In M. Bruynooghe and M. Wirsing, editors, *Proceedings of the 4th International Symposium on Programming Language Implementation and Logic Programming*, pages 269–295. Springer-Verlag, 1992.
7. P. Cousot and N. Halbwachs. Automatic discovery of linear restraints among variables of a program. In *Conference Record of the 5th ACM Symposium on Principles of Programming Languages*, pages 84–96, 1978.
8. D. Cox, J. Little, and D. O'Shea. *Ideals, Varieties, and Algorithms. An Introduction to Computational Algebraic Geometry and Commutative Algebra.* Springer-Verlag, New York, 1992.
9. B. A. Davey and H. A. Priestley. *Introduction to Lattices and Order.* Cambridge University Press, Cambridge, 1990.
10. E. W. Dijkstra. *A Discipline of Programming.* Prentice-Hall, Inc., Englewood Cliffs, New Jersey, 1976.
11. R. Fröberg. *An Introduction to Gröbner Bases.* John Wiley & Sons, Chichester, 1997.
12. S. M. German and B. Wegbreit. A synthesizer of inductive assertions. *IEEE Transactions on Software Engineering*, SE-1(1):68–75, March 1975.
13. P. Granger. Static analysis of linear congruence equalities among variables of a program. In S. Abramsky and T. S. E. Maibaum, editors, *Proceedings of the International Joint Conference on Theory and Practice of Software Development*, pages 169–192. Springer-Verlag, 1991.
14. N. Halbwachs, Y-E. Proy, and P. Roumanoff. Verification of real-time systems using linear relation analysis. *Formal Methods in System Design*, 11(2):157–185, August 1997.
15. M. Karr. Affine relationships among variables of a program. *Acta Informatica*, 6:133–151, 1976.
16. S. Katz and Z. Manna. Logical analysis of programs. *Communications of the ACM*, 19(4):188–206, April 1976.
17. R. W. Kaye and R. Wilson. *Linear Algebra.* Oxford University Press, 1998.
18. Z. Manna. *Mathematical Theory of Computation.* McGraw-Hill, New York, 1974.

19. I. Mastroeni. Numerical power analysis. In *Proceedings of the 2nd Symposium on Programs as Data Objects*, pages 117–137. Springer-Verlag, 2001.
20. E. W. Mayr and A. R. Meyer. The complexity of the word problems for commutative semigroups and polynomial ideals. *Adv. Math.*, 46:305–329, 1982.
21. A. Mili. A relational approach to the design of deterministic programs. *Acta Informatica*, 20:315–328, 1983.
22. H. Mills. The new math of computer programming. *Communications of the ACM*, 18(1):43–48, January 1975.
23. M. Müller-Olm and H. Seidl. Precise interprocedural analysis through linear algebra. In N. D. Jones and X. Leroy, editors, *31st ACM Symposium on Principles of Programming Languages*, pages 330–341, 2004.
24. E. Rodríguez-Carbonell and D. Kapur. Automatic generation of polynomial loop invariants for imperative programs. Technical Report TR-CS-2003-39, University of New Mexico, 2003.
25. S. Sankaranarayanan, H. B. Sipma, and Z. Manna. Non-linear loop invariant generation using Gröbner bases. In N. D. Jones and X. Leroy, editors, *31st ACM Symposium on Principles of Programming Languages*, pages 318–329, 2004.
26. G. Strang. *Linear Algebra and Its Applications*. Harcourt Brace Jovanovich, San Diego, 1988.
27. B. Wegbreit. Property extraction in well-founded property sets. *IEEE Transactions on Software Engineering*, SE-1(3):270–285, September 1975.
28. C. K. Yap. A new lower bound construction for the word problem for commutative Thue systems. *Journal of Symbolic Computation*, 12(1):1–28, 1991.

The Octahedron Abstract Domain

Robert Clarisó and Jordi Cortadella

Universitat Politècnica de Catalunya
Barcelona, Spain

Abstract. An interesting area in static analysis is the study of numeric properties. Complex properties can be analyzed using *abstract interpretation*, provided that an adequate abstract domain is defined. Each domain can represent and manipulate a family of properties, providing a different trade-off between the precision and complexity of the analysis. The contribution of this paper is a new numeric abstract domain called *octahedron* that represents constraints of the form $(\pm x_j \pm \ldots \pm x_k \geq c)$, where x_i are numerical variables such that $x_i \geq 0$. The implementation of octahedra is based on a new kind of decision diagrams called *Octahedron Decision Diagrams* (OhDD).

1 Introduction

Abstract interpretation [5] defines a generic framework for the static analysis of dynamic properties of a system. This framework can be used, for instance, to analyze termination or to discover invariants in programs automatically. However, each analysis requires the framework to be parametrized for the relevant domain of properties being studied, e.g. numerical properties.

There is a wide selection of numeric abstract domains that can be used to represent and manipulate properties. Some examples are intervals, octagons and convex polyhedra. Each domain provides a different trade-off between the precision of the properties that can be represented and the efficiency of the manipulation. An interesting problem in abstract interpretation is the study of new abstract domains that are sufficiently expressive to analyze relevant problems and allow an efficient implementation.

In this paper, a new numerical abstract domain called *octahedron* is described. This abstract domain can represent conjunctions of restricted linear inequalities of the form $(\pm x_j \pm \ldots \pm x_k \geq c)$, where x_i are numerical variables such that $x_i \geq 0$. A new kind of decision diagram called *Octahedron Decision Diagram* (OhDD) has been specifically designed to represent and manipulate this family of constraints efficiently. Several analysis problems can be solved using these constraints, such as the analysis of timed systems [1, 12], the analysis of string length in C programs [8] and the discovery of bounds on the size of asynchronous communication channels.

The remaining sections of the paper are organized as follows. Section 2 explains related work in the definition of numeric domains for abstract interpretation, and previous decision diagram techniques used to represent numerical constraints. Section 3 defines the numeric domain of octahedra, and section 4 describes the data structure and its operations. In section 5, some possible applications of the octahedron abstract domain are discussed, and some experimental results are provided. Finally, section 6 draws some conclusions and suggests some future work.

R. Giacobazzi (Ed.): SAS 2004, LNCS 3148, pp. 312–327, 2004.

Table 1. A comparison of numeric abstract domains based on inequality properties.

Abstraction	Cite	Properties	Example
Intervals	[5]	$k_1 \leq x \leq k_2$	$2 \leq x \leq 5$
Difference Bound Matrices (DBMs)	[7, 15]	$k_1 \leq x \leq k_2$ $x - y \leq k$	$1 \leq x \leq 3$ $x - y \leq 5$
Octagons	[16]	$\pm x \pm y \leq k$	$2 \leq x + y \leq 6$
Two variables per inequality	[22]	$c_1 \cdot x_1 + c_2 \cdot x_2 \geq k$	$2 \leq 3x - 2y \leq 5$
Octahedra	This paper	$\pm x_i \pm \ldots \pm x_k \geq k$	$x - y + z \geq 5$
Convex polyhedra	[6, 11]	$c_1 \cdot x_1 + \ldots + c_n \cdot x_n \geq k$	$x + 3y - 2z \geq 6$

2 Related Work

2.1 Numeric Abstract Domains

Abstract domain is a concept used to denote a computer representation for a family of constraints, together with the algorithms to perform the abstract operators such as union, intersection, widening or the transfer function. Several abstract domains have been defined for interesting families of numeric properties, such as *inequality* or *modulo* properties. The octahedron abstract domain belongs to the former category. Other abstract domains based on inequalities are *intervals*, *difference bound matrices*, *octagons*, *two-variables-per-inequality*, and *convex polyhedra*. An example of these abstract domains and their relation to octahedra can be seen in Table 1.

Intervals are a representation for constraints on the upper or lower bound of a single variable, e.g. ($k_1 \leq x \leq k_2$). Interval analysis is very popular due to its simplicity and efficiency: an interval abstraction for n variables requires $O(n)$ space, and all operations require $O(n)$ time in the worst case. *Octagons* are an efficient representation for a system of inequalities on the sum or difference of variable pairs, e.g. ($\pm x \pm y \leq k$) and ($x \leq k$). The implementation of octagons is a based on *difference bound matrices* (DBM), a data structure used to represent constraints on differences of variables, as in ($x - y \leq k$) and ($x \leq k$). Efficiency is an advantage of this representation: the spatial cost for representing constraints on n variables is $O(n^2)$, while the temporal cost is between $O(n^2)$ and $O(n^3)$, depending on the operation. *Convex polyhedra* are an efficient representation for conjunctions of linear inequality constraints. This abstraction is very popular due to its ability to express precise constraints. However, this precision comes with a very high complexity overhead. This complexity has motivated the definition of abstract domains such as *two-variables per inequality*, which try to retain the expressiveness of linear inequalities with a lower complexity.

The abstract domain presented in this paper, *octahedra*, also attempts to keep some of the flexibility of convex polyhedra with a lower complexity. Instead of limiting the number of variables per inequality, the coefficients of the variables are restricted to $\{-1, 0, +1\}$. From this point of view, octahedra provide a precision that is between octagons and convex polyhedra.

2.2 Decision Diagrams

The implementation of octahedra is based on decision diagrams. Decision diagram techniques have been applied successfully to several problems in different application domains. Binary Decision Diagrams (BDD) [3] provide an efficient mechanism to represent boolean functions. Zero Suppressed BDDs (ZDD) [14] are specially tuned to represent sparse functions more efficiently. Multi-Terminal Decision Diagrams (MTBDD) [10] represent functions from boolean variables to reals, $f : \mathbb{B}^n \to \mathbb{R}$

The paradigm of decision diagrams has also been applied to the analysis of numerical constraints. Most of this approaches compare the value of numeric variables with constants or intervals, or compare the value of pairs of variables. Some examples of these representations are *Difference Decision Diagrams* (DDD) [17], *Numeric Decision Diagrams* (NDD) [9], and *Clock Difference Diagrams* (CDD) [2]. These data structures encode contraints on *a maximum of two* variables at a time. In other representations, each node encodes one complex constraint like a linear inequality. Some examples of these representations are *Decision Diagrams with Constraints* (DDC) [13] and *Hybrid-Restriction Diagrams* (HRD) [24]. The Octahedron Decision Diagrams described in this paper use an innovative approach to encode linear inequalities. This approach is presented in Section 4.

3   Octahedra

3.1   Definitions

The octahedron abstract domain is now introduced. In the same way as convex polyhedra, an octahedron abstracts a set of vectors in $\mathbb{Q}^n$ as a system of linear inequalities satisfied by all these vectors. The difference between convex polyhedra and octahedra is the family of constraints that are supported.

Definition 1 (Unit linear inequality). *A linear inequality is a constraint of the form* $(c_1 \cdot x_1 + \ldots + c_n \cdot x_n \geq k)$ *where the constant term k and the coefficients c_i are in* $\mathbb{Q} \cup \{-\infty\}$, *e.g.* $(3x + 2y - z \geq -7)$. *A linear inequality will be called* unit *if all coefficients are in* $\{-1, 0, +1\}$, *such as* $(x + y - z \geq -7)$.

Definition 2 (Octahedron). *An octahedron O over $\mathbb{Q}^n$ is the set of solutions to the system of m unit inequalities* $O = \{X \mid AX \geq B \wedge X \geq 0^n\}$, *where $B \in (\mathbb{Q} \cup \{-\infty\})^m$ and $A \in \{-1, 0, +1\}^{m \times n}$. Octahedra satisfy the following properties:*

1. Convexity: *An octahedron is a convex set.*
2. Closed for intersection: *The intersection of two octahedra is also an octahedron.*
3. Non-closed for union: *The union of two octahedra might not be an octahedron.*

Figure 1(a) shows some examples of octahedra in two-dimensional space. In Fig. 1(b) there are several regions of space which are not octahedra, either because they contain a region with negative values (1), they are not convex (2), they cannot be represented by a finite system of linear inequalities (3), or because they can be represented as system of linear inequalities, but not unit linear inequalities (4). Notice that in two-dimensional space all octahedra are octagons; octahedra can only show a better precision than octagons in higher-dimensional spaces.

During the remaining of this paper, we will use C to denote a vector in $\{-1, 0, +1\}^n$ where n is the number of variables. Therefore, $(C^T X \geq k)$ denotes the unit linear inequality $(c_1 \cdot x_1 + \ldots + c_n \cdot x_n \geq k)$.

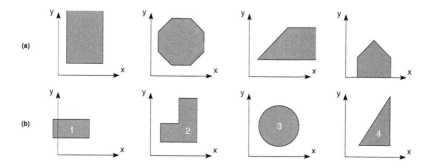

Fig. 1. Some examples of (a) octahedra and (b) non-octahedra in two-dimensional space.

Lemma 1. *An octahedron over n variables can be represented by at most 3^n non-redundant inequalities.*

Proof. Each variable can have at most three different coefficients in a unit linear inequality. These means that if an octahedron has more than 3^n unit inequalities, some of them will only differ in the constant term, e.g. $(C^T X \geq k_1)$ and $(C^T X \geq k_2)$. Only one of these inequalities is non-redundant, the one with the tightest bound (the largest constant), i.e. $(C^T X \geq \max(k_1, k_2))$. □

A problem when dealing with convex polyhedra and octahedra is the lack of canonicity of the systems of linear inequalities: the same polyhedron/octahedron can be represented with different inequalities. For example, both $(x = 3) \wedge (y \geq 5)$ and $(x = 3) \wedge (x + y \geq 8)$ define the same octahedron with different inequalities. Given a convex polyhedron, there are algorithms to minimize the number of constraints in a system of inequalities, i.e. removing all constraints that can be derived as linear combinations. However, in the previous example both representations are minimal and even then, they are different. Given that the number of possible linear inequalities in a convex polyhedron is infinite, the definition of a canonical form for convex polyhedra seems a difficult problem. However, a canonical form for octahedra can be defined using the result of lemma 1. Even though the number of inequalities of this canonical form makes an explicit representation impractical, symbolic representations based on decision diagrams can manipulate sets of unit inequalities efficiently.

Definition 3 (Canonical form of octahedra). *The canonical form of an octahedron $O \subseteq \mathbb{Q}^n$ is either (i) the empty octahedron or (ii) a system of 3^n unit linear inequalities, where in each inequality $(C^T X \geq k)$, k is the tightest bound satisfied by O.*

Theorem 1. *Two octahedra O_1 and O_2 represent the same subset of $\mathbb{Q}^n$ if and only if they both have the same canonical form.*

Proof. ($\rightarrow$) Given a constraint $(C^T X \geq k)$, there is a single tightest bound to that constraint. So if two octahedra are equal, they will have the same bound for each possible linear constraint, and therefore, the same canonical form. □

($\leftarrow$): From its definition, an octahedron is completely characterized by its system of inequalities. If two octahedra O_1 and O_2 have the same canonical form, then they satisfy exactly the same system of inequalities and therefore are equal. □

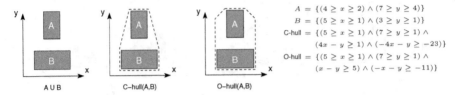

$$A = \{(4 \geq x \geq 2) \wedge (7 \geq y \geq 4)\}$$
$$B = \{(5 \geq x \geq 1) \wedge (3 \geq y \geq 1)\}$$
$$\text{C-hull} = \{(5 \geq x \geq 1) \wedge (7 \geq y \geq 1) \wedge$$
$$(4x - y \geq 1) \wedge (-4x - y \geq -23)\}$$
$$\text{O-hull} = \{(5 \geq x \geq 1) \wedge (7 \geq y \geq 1) \wedge$$
$$(x - y \geq 5) \wedge (-x - y \geq -11)\}$$

Fig. 2. Two upper approximations of the union: convex hull (C-hull) and octahedral hull (O-hull).

Theorem 2. *Let A and B be two non-empty octahedra represented by systems of inequalities of the form $(C^T X \geq k_a)$ and $(C^T X \geq k_b)$ for all $C \in \{-1, 0, +1\}^n$. The intersection $A \cap B$ is defined by the system of inequalities $(C^T X \geq \max(k_a, k_b))$, which might be in non-canonical form even if the input systems were canonical.*

Proof. Any point $P \in \mathbb{Q}^n$ that satisfies $(C^T P \geq \max(k_a, k_b))$ will also satisfy $(C^T P \geq k_a)$ and $(C^T P \geq k_b)$. Therefore, any point P satisfying the new system of inequalities will also appear in both A and B. □

Lemma 2. *An octahedron B is an upper approximation of an octahedron A, noted $A \subseteq B$, iff (i) A is empty or (ii) for any constraint $(C^T X \geq k_a)$ in the canonical form of A, the equivalent constraint $(C^T X \geq k_b)$ in the canonical form of B has a constant term k_b such that $(k_a \geq k_b)$.*

Proof. By definition, $A \subseteq B$ iff $A = A \cap B$. This lemma is a direct consequence of this property and Theorem 2. □

Definition 4 (Convex and octahedral hull). *The* convex hull (C-hull) *of two convex polyhedra A and B is the intersection of all convex polyhedra that include both A and B. The* octahedral hull (O-hull) *of two octahedra A and B is the intersection of all octahedra that include both A and B.*

Figure 2 shows an example of the convex and octahedral hulls of two octahedra A and B. Notice that the convex hull is always an upper approximation of the union, and the octahedral hull is always an upper approximation of the convex hull, i.e. $A \cup B \subseteq$ C-hull$(A, B) \subseteq$ O-hull(A, B).

Theorem 3. *Let A and B be two non-empty octahedra whose canonical form are respectively $(C^T X \geq k_a)$ and $(C^T X \geq k_b)$ for all $C \in \{-1, 0, +1\}^n$. Then, the octahedral hull O-hull(A, B) is defined by the system of inequalities $(C^T X \geq \min(k_a, k_b))$*

Proof. Given a bound k for one inequality $(C^T X \geq k)$ of O-hull(A, B), the proof can be split into two parts: proving that $k \leq \min(k_a, k_b)$ and proving that $k \geq \min(k_a, k_b)$.

As the octahedral hull includes A and B, all points $P \in A$ and $P \in B$ should also be in O-hull(A, B). Therefore, any point in A or B should satisfy the constraints of O-hull(A, B). Given a constraint $(C^T X \geq k)$, it is known that points in A satisfy $(C^T X \geq k_a)$ and points in B satisfy $(C^T X \geq k_b)$. If both sets of points must satisfy the constraint in O-hull(A, B), then k must satisfy $k \leq \min(k_a, k_b)$.

On the other side, the octahedral hull is the least octahedron that includes A and B. Therefore, the bounds of each constraint should be as tight as possible, i.e. as large as possible. If we know that $k \leq \min(k_a, k_b)$ should hold for a given unit inequality, the tightest bound for that inequality is precisely $k = \min(k_a, k_b)$. As a **corollary**, the octahedral hull computed in this way is in canonical form.

$\square$

3.2 Abstractions of Octahedra

As it was shown in the previous section, the canonical form of an octahedron provides a useful mechanism to define operations such as the test for inclusion, the intersection or the octahedral hull. However, finding an *efficient* algorithm that can compute the canonical form of an octahedron from a non-canonical system of inequalities is an open problem at the time of writing this paper.

On the other hand, octahedra are defined in the context of abstract interpretation of numeric properties. In this context, the problem is the abstraction of a set of values in $\mathbb{Q}^n$, and the main concern is ensuring that our abstraction is an *upper approximation* of the concrete set of values. Thus, as long as an upper approximation can be guaranteed, an exact representation of octahedra is not required, as octahedra are already abstractions of more complex sets. Keeping this fact in mind, efficient algorithms that operate with upper approximations of the canonical form can be designed.

The first step is the definition of a relaxed version of the canonical form, which is called *saturated* form. While the canonical form has the tightest bound in each of its inequalities, the bounds in the saturated form may be more relaxed. A system of unit inequalities is in saturated form as long as the bounds imposed by the sum of any pair of constraints appear explicitly. For example, a saturated form of the octahedron $(a \geq 3) \wedge (b \geq 0) \wedge (c \geq 0) \wedge (b - c \geq 7) \wedge (a + b \geq 8) \wedge (a + c \geq 6)$ can be defined by the following system of inequalities:

$$(a \geq 3) \wedge (b \geq 7) \wedge (c \geq 0) \wedge (a + b \geq 10) \wedge (a + c \geq 6) \wedge (b + c \geq 7)$$
$$\wedge (b - c \geq 7) \wedge (a + b - c \geq 10) \wedge (a + b + c \geq 13)$$

where the constraints with a bound of $-\infty$ have been removed for brevity. In this example, saturation has exposed explicitly that $(a + b \geq 10)$. This inequality is the linear combination of $(a \geq 3)$, $(b - c \geq 7)$ and $(c \geq 0)$.

A saturated form O^* of an octahedron $O = \{X \mid AX \geq B \wedge X \geq 0^n\}$ can be computed using the following *saturation* procedure:

1. Initialize the system of 3^n unit inequalities for all possible values of the coefficients $C \in \{-1, 0, +1\}^n$. The bound k of a given inequality $(C^T X \geq k)$ is chosen as:

$$k = \begin{cases} \max(0, b) & \text{if } C^T X \geq b \text{ appears in } AX \geq B \text{ and } C \geq 0^n \\ b & \text{if } C^T X \geq b \text{ appears in } AX \geq B \text{ and } C \not\geq 0^n. \\ 0 & \text{if } C^T X \geq b \text{ does not appear in } AX \geq B \text{ but } C \geq 0^n \\ -\infty & \text{otherwise} \end{cases}$$

2. Select two inequalities $C_1^T X \geq k_1$ and $C_2^T X \geq k_2$ such that $k_1 > -\infty$ and $k_2 > -\infty$. Let us define $C_* = C_1 + C_2$ and $k_* = k_1 + k_2$.
3. If $C_* \notin \{-1, 0, +1\}^n$ return to step 2.
4. If $C_*^T X \geq k$ appears in the system of inequalities with $k \geq k_*$, return to step 2.

5. Replace the inequality $C_*^T X \geq k$ by $C_*^T X \geq k_*$.
6. Repeat steps 2-5 until:
   - A fixpoint is reached *or*
   - An inequality $C_*^T X \geq k$ with $C = 0^n$ and $k > 0$ is found. In this case, the octahedron is empty.

Theorem 4. *Let* $O = \{X \mid AX \geq B \wedge X \geq 0^n\}$ *be a non-empty octahedron. The* saturation *algorithm applied to* O *terminates.*

Proof. Each step of the saturation algorithm defines a tighter bound for an inequality of the octahedron. The new inequality $(C_3^T X \geq k_3')$ is obtained from two previously known inequalities $(C_1^T X \geq k_1)$ and $(C_2^T X \geq k_2)$, so that $C_3 = C_1 + C_2$ and $k_3' = k_1 + k_2$, and $k_3' > k_3$, where k_3 is the previously known bound for the inequality. If inequalities 1 and 2 were computed in previous rounds of the saturation algorithm, this dependency chain can be expanded, e.g. if inequality 2 comes from inequalities 4 and 5, then $C_3 = C_1 + C_4 + C_5$ and $k_3' = k_1 + k_4 + k_5$. Non-termination of the saturation algorithm implies that there will be infinitely many sums of pairs of inequalities. Ignoring the bound k, there are only finitely many inequalities over n variables. Therefore, it is always possible to find a step that computes a bound k_j' that depends on a previously known bound k_j, i.e. $C_j = C_j + \sum C_l$ and $k_j' = k_j + \sum k_l$. As $C_j - C_j = \sum C_l = 0^n$ and $k_j' - k_j = \sum k_l > 0$, the linear combination $((\sum C_l)^T X \geq (\sum k_l))$ is equivalent to $(0 > 0)$, which implies that O is empty. $\qquad\square$

At each step, the saturation algorithm computes a new linear combination between two unit inequalities. If this linear combination has a tighter bound than the one already known, the bound is updated, and so on until a fixpoint is reached. Notice that this fixpoint *may not be reached* if the octahedron is empty. For example, the octahedron in Fig. 3(a) is empty because the sum of the last four inequalities is $(0 > 4)$. The saturation algorithm applied to this octahedron does not terminate. Adding the constraints in bottom-down order allows the saturation algorithm to produce $(x_2 - x_4 \geq 5)$, which can again be used to produce $(x_2 - x_4 \geq 9)$ and so on. Even then, the saturation algorithm is used to perform the emptiness test because of two reasons. First, there are special kinds of octahedra where termination is guaranteed. For instance, if all inequalities describe constraints between symbols (all constant term is zero), saturation is guaranteeed to terminate. Second, the conditions required to build an octahedron for which the saturation algorithm does not terminate are complex and artificial, and therefore they will rarely occur.

Even if the saturation algorithm terminates, in some cases it might fail to discover the tightest bound for an inequality. For example, in the octahedron in Fig. 3(b), saturation will fail to discover the constraint $(x_1 - x_2 + x_3 + x_4 + x_5 + x_6 \geq 6)$, as any sum of two inequalities will yield a non-unit linear inequality. Therefore, given a constraint $(C^T X \geq k_s)$ in the saturated form, the bound k_c for the same inequality in the canonical form may be different, $k_c \not\leq k_s$. But $k_c \geq k_s$ always holds, as k_c is the tightest bound for that inequality. Using this property, operations like the union or intersection that have been defined for the canonical form can also be used for the saturated form. The result will always be an upper approximation of the exact canonical result, as $k_c \geq k_s$ is the exact definition for upper approximation of octahedra (Lemma 2).

$$
\begin{array}{rcl}
+ x_2 \quad\quad - x_4 & \geq & 1 \\
-x_1 - x_2 + x_3 + x_4 + x_5 - x_6 & \geq & 1 \\
+x_1 - x_2 - x_3 + x_4 - x_5 + x_6 & \geq & 1 \\
+x_1 + x_2 + x_3 - x_4 - x_5 - x_6 & \geq & 1 \\
-x_1 + x_2 - x_3 - x_4 + x_5 + x_6 & \geq & 1
\end{array}
$$

$$
\begin{array}{rcl}
+x_1 - x_2 - x_3 + x_4 & \geq & 1 \\
-x_1 - x_2 + x_3 + x_5 & \geq & 2 \\
+x_1 + x_2 + x_3 + x_6 & \geq & 3
\end{array}
$$

(a)   (b)

Fig. 3. (a) Empty octahedron where the saturation algorithm does not terminate and (b) Non-empty octahedron where the saturated form is different from the canonical form.

3.3 Abstract Semantics of the Operators

In order to characterize the octahedron abstract domain, the abstract semantics of the abstract interpretation operators must be defined. Intuitively, this abstract semantics is defined as simple manipulations of the saturated form of octahedra. All operations are guaranteed to produce upper approximations of the exact result, as it was justified in section 3.2. Some operations like the intersection can deal with non-saturated forms without any loss of precision, while others like the union can only do so at the cost of additional over-approximation.

In the definition of the semantics, A and B will denote octahedra, whose saturated forms contain inequalities of the form $(C^T X \geq k_a)$ and $(C^T X \geq k_b)$, respectively.

- **Intersection** $A \cap B$ is represented by system of inequalities $(C^T X \geq \max(k_a, k_b))$, which might be in non-saturated form.
- **Union** $A \cup B$ is approximated by the saturated form $(C^T X \geq \min(k_a, k_b))$.
- **Inclusion** Let A and B be two octahedra. If $k_a \geq k_b$ for all inequalities in their saturated form, then $A \subseteq B$. Notice that the implication does not work in the other direction, i.e. if $k_a \not\geq k_b$ then we don't know whether $A \subseteq B$ or $A \not\subseteq B$.
- **Widening** $A \nabla B$ is defined as the octahedron with inequalities $(C^T X \geq k)$ such that k:

$$
k = \begin{cases} -\infty & \text{if } k_a > k_b \\ k_a & \text{otherwise} \end{cases}
$$

  As established in [16], the result should *not* be saturated in order to guarantee convergence in a finite number of steps.
- **Extension** An octahedron O can be extended with a new variable $y \geq 0$ by modifying the constraints of its saturated form O^*. Let $(c_1 \cdot x_1 + \ldots + c_n \cdot x_n \geq k)$ be a constraint of O^*, the inequalities that will appear in the saturated form of the extension are:
  - $c_1 \cdot x_1 + \ldots + c_n \cdot x_n - 1 \cdot y \geq -\infty$
  - $c_1 \cdot x_1 + \ldots + c_n \cdot x_n + 0 \cdot y \geq k$
  - $c_1 \cdot x_1 + \ldots + c_n \cdot x_n + 1 \cdot y \geq k$
- **Projection** A projection of an octahedron O removing a dimension x_i can be performed by removing from its saturated form O^* all inequalities where x_i has a coefficient that is not zero.
- **Unit linear assignment** A unit linear assignment $[x_i := \sum_{j=1}^{m} c_j \cdot x_j]$ with coefficients $c_i \in \{-1, 0, +1\}$ can be defined using the following steps:

- Extend the octahedron with a new variable t.
- Intersect the octahedron with the octahedron $(t = \sum_{j=1}^{m} c_j \cdot x_j)$
- Project the variable x_i.
- Rename t as x_i.

Impact of the conservative inclusion test on abstract interpretation: Using these operations, upper approximations of the concrete values will be computed in abstract interpretation. A special mention is the case of test of inclusion, where the result is only definite if the answer is true. Intuitively, this lack of accuracy appears from the impossiblity to discover the tightest bound with saturation. In abstract interpretation, the analysis is performed until a fixpoint is reached, and the fixpoint is detected using the test for inclusion. The inaccurate test of inclusion might lead to additional iterations in the abstract interpretation loop. Each iteration will add new constraints to our octahedra that were not being discovered by saturation, until the test for inclusion is able to detect the fixpoint. However, in practical examples, this theoretical scenario does not seem to arise, as constraints tend to be generated in a structured way that allows saturation to obtain good approximations of the exact canonical form.

4   Octahedra Decision Diagrams

4.1   Overview

The constraints of an octahedron can be represented compactly using a specially devised decision diagram representation. This representation is called *Octahedron Decision Diagram* (OhDD). Intuitively, it can be described as a Multi-Terminal Zero-Suppressed Ternary Decision Diagram:

- *Ternary*: Each non-terminal node represents a variable x_i and has three output arcs, labelled as $\{-1, 0, +1\}$. Each arc represents a coefficient of x_i in a linear constraint.
- *Multi-Terminal* [10]: Terminal nodes can be constants in $\mathbb{R} \cup \{-\infty\}$. The semantics of a path σ from the root to a terminal node k is the linear constraint $(c_1 \cdot x_1 + c_2 \cdot x_2 + \ldots + c_n \cdot x_n \geq k)$, where c_i is the coefficient of the arc taken from the variable x_i in the path σ.
- *Zero-Suppressed* [14]: If a variable does not appear in any linear constraint, it also does not appear in the OhDD. This is achieved by using special reduction rules as it is done in Zero-Suppressed Decision Diagrams.

Figure 4 shows an example of a OhDD and the octahedron it represents on the right. The shadowed path highlights one constraint of the octahedron, $(x + y - z \geq 2)$. All constraints that end in a terminal node with $-\infty$ represent constraints with an unknown bound, such as $(x - y \geq -\infty)$. As the OhDD represents the saturated form of the octahedron, some redundant constraints such as $(x + y + z \geq 3)$ appear explicitly.

This representation based on decision diagrams provides three main advantages. First, decision diagrams provide many opportunities for reuse. For example, nodes in a OhDD can be shared. Furthermore, different OhDD can share internal nodes, leading to a greater reduction in the memory usage. Second, the reduction rules avoid representing the zero coefficients of the linear inequalities. Finally, symbolic algorithms on OhDD can deal with sets of inequalities instead of one inequality at a time. All these factors combined improve the efficiency of operations with octahedra.

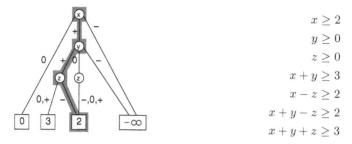

$$x \geq 2$$
$$y \geq 0$$
$$z \geq 0$$
$$x + y \geq 3$$
$$x - z \geq 2$$
$$x + y - z \geq 2$$
$$x + y + z \geq 3$$

Fig. 4. An example of a OhDD. On the right, the constraints of the octahedron.

4.2 Definitions

Definition 5 (Octahedron Decision Diagram - OhDD). *An Octahedron Decision Diagram is a tuple* (V, G) *where* V *is a finite set of positive real-valued variables, and* $G = (N \cup K, E)$ *is a labeled single rooted directed acyclic graph with the following properties. Each node in* K, *the set of* terminal *nodes, is labeled with a constant in* $\mathbb{R} \cup \{-\infty\}$, *and has an outdegree of zero. Each node* $n \in N$ *is labeled with a variable* $v(n) \in V$, *and it has three outgoing arcs, labeled* $-$, 0 *and* $+$.

By establishing an order among the variables of the OhDD, the notion of *ordered* OhDD can be defined. The intuitive meaning of ordered is the same as in BDDs, that is, in every path from the root to the terminal nodes, the variables of the decision diagram always appear in the same order. For example, the OhDD in Fig. 4 is an ordered OhDD.

Definition 6 (Ordered OhDD). *Let* $\succ$ *be a total order on the variables* V *of a OhDD. The OhDD is ordered if, for any node* $n \in N$, *all of its descendants* $d \in N$ *satisfy* $v(d) \succ v(n)$.

In the same way, the notion of a *reduced* OhDD can be introduced. However, the reduction rules will be different in order to take advantage of the structure of the constraints. In an octahedron, most variables will not appear in all the constraints. Avoiding the representation of these variables with a zero coefficient would improve the efficiency of OhDD. This can be achieved as in ZDDs by using a special reduction rule: whenever the target of the $-$ arc of a node n is $-\infty$, and the 0 and $+$ arcs have the same target m, n is reduced as m. The rationale behind this rule is the following: if a constraint $(c_1 \cdot x_1 + \ldots + c_i \cdot x_i + \ldots + c_n \cdot x_n \geq k)$ holds for $c_i = 0$, it will also hold for $c_i = +1$ as $x_i \geq 0$. However, it is not known if it will hold for $c_i = -1$. This means that in the OhDD, if a variable has coefficient zero in a constraint, it is very likely that it will end up creating a node where the 0 and $+$ arcs have the same target, and the target of the $-$ arc is $-\infty$. By reducing these nodes, the zero coefficient is not represented in the OhDD. Remarkably, using this reduction rule, the set of constraints stating that "any sum of variables is greater or equal to zero" is represented only as the terminal node 0.

Figure 5 shows an example of the two reduction rules. Notice that contrary to BDDs, nodes where all arcs have the same target will not be reduced.

Definition 7 (Reduced OhDD). *A reduced OhDD is an ordered OhDD where none of the following rules can be applied:*

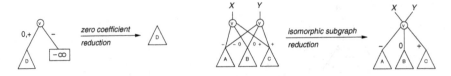

Fig. 5. Reduction rules for OhDD.

- Reduction of zero coefficients: *Let* $n \in N$ *be a node with the* $-$ *arc going to the terminal* $-\infty$, *and with the arcs* 0 *and* $+$ *point to a node* m. *Replace* n *by* m.
- Reduction of isomorphic subgraphs: *Let* D_1 *and* D_2 *be two isomorphic subgraphs of the* OhDD. *Merge* D_1 *and* D_2.

4.3 Implementation of the Operations

The octahedra abstract domain and its operations have been implemented as OhDD on top of the CUDD decision diagram package [23]. Each operation on octahedra performs simple manipulations such as computing the maximum or the minimum between two systems of inequalities, where each inequality is encoded as a path in a OhDD. These operations can be implemented as recursive procedures on the decision diagram. The algorithm may take as arguments one or more decision diagrams, depending of the operation. All these recursive algorithms share the same overall structure:

1. Check if the call is a base case, e.g. all arguments are constant decision diagrams. In that case, the result can be computed directly.
2. Look up the cache to see if the result of this call was computed previously and is available. In that case, return the precomputed result.
3. Select the top variable t in all the arguments according to the ordering. The algorithm will only consider this variable during this call, leaving the rest of the variables to be handled by the subsequent recursive calls.
4. Obtain the cofactors of t in each of the arguments of the call. In our case, each cofactor represents the set of inequalities for each coefficient of the top variable.
5. Perform recursive calls on the cofactors of t.
6. Combine the results of the different calls into the new top node for variable t.
7. Store the result of this recursive call in the cache.
8. Return the result to the caller.

The saturation algorithm is a special case: all sums of pairs of constraints are computed by a single traversal; but if new inequalities have been discovered, the traversal must be repeated. The process continues until a fixpoint is reached. Even though this fixpoint might not be reached, as seen in Fig. 3, the number of iterations required to saturate an octahedron tends to be very low (1-4 iterations) if it is derived from saturated octahedra, e.g. the intersection of two saturated octahedra.

These traversals might have to visit 3^n inequalities/paths in the OhDD in the worst case. However, as OhDD are directed graphs, many paths share nodes so many recursive calls will have been computed previously, and the results will be reused without the need to recompute. The efficiency of the operations on decision diagrams depends upon on two very important factors. The first one is the *order of the variables* in the decision diagram. Intuitively, each call should perform as much work as possible. Therefore, the variables that appear early in the decision diagram should discriminate the result as much as possible. Currently there is no *dynamic reordering* [21] in our implementation of OhDD, but we plan to add it in the near future. A second factor in the performance of these algorithms is the *effectivity of the cache* to reuse previously computed results.

5   Applications of the Octahedron Abstract Domain

5.1   Motivating Application

Asynchronous circuits are a kind of circuits where there is no global clock to synchronize its different components. Asynchronous circuits replace the global clock by a local hand-shake between components, gaining several advantages such as lower power usage. However, the absence of a clock makes the verification of asynchronous circuits more complex. The lack of clock makes the circuit more dependent on *timing constraints* that ensure the correctness of the synchronization within the circuit. This means that the correctness of the circuit depends on the delays of its gates and wires.

In many asynchronous circuits implementing control logic, the timing constraints that arise are unit inequalities. Intuitively, they correspond to constraints of the type

$$\underbrace{(\delta_1 + \cdots + \delta_i)}_{\text{delay(path}_1)} - \underbrace{(\delta_{i+1} + \cdots + \delta_n)}_{\text{delay(path}_2)} \geq k$$

hinting that certain paths in the circuit must be longer than other paths. In very rare occasions, coefficients different from ± 1 are necessary. A typical counterexample would be a circuit where one path must be c times longer than another one, e.g. a fast counter.

Example. Figure 6(a) depicts a D flip-flop [20]. Briefly stated, a D flip-flop is a 1-bit register. It stores the data value in signal D whenever there is a rising edge in the clock signal CK. The output Q of the circuit is the value which was stored in the last clock rising edge. We would like to characterize the behavior of this circuit in terms of the internal gate delays. The flip-flop has to be characterized with respect to three parameters (see Figure 6(b)):

- *Setup time*, noted as T_{setup}, is the amount of time that D should remain stable before a clock rising edge.
- *Hold time*, noted as T_{hold}, is the amount of time that D should remain stable after a clock rising edge.
- *Delay* or *clock-to-output time*, noted as $T_{CK \rightarrow Q}$, is the amount of time required by the latch to propagate a change in the input D to the output Q.

The timing analysis algorithm is capable of deriving a set of sufficient linear constraints that guarantee the correctness of the circuit's behavior. This behavior will be correct if the output Q matches the value of D in the last clock rising edge. Any behavior not fulfilling this property is considered to be a failure. Fig. 6(c) reports the set of sufficient timing constraints derived by the algorithm. Each gate g_i has a symbolic delay in the interval $[d_i, D_i]$. Notice that the timing constraints are unit inequalities.

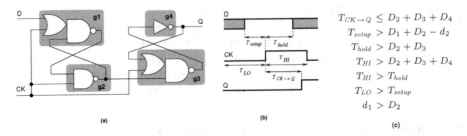

$$T_{CK \to Q} \leq D_2 + D_3 + D_4$$
$$T_{setup} > D_1 + D_2 - d_2$$
$$T_{hold} > D_2 + D_3$$
$$T_{HI} > D_2 + D_3 + D_4$$
$$T_{HI} > T_{hold}$$
$$T_{LO} > T_{setup}$$
$$d_1 > D_2$$

(a)   (b)   (c)

Fig. 6. (a) Implementation of a D flip-flop [20], (b) description of variables that characterize any D flip-flop and (c) sufficient constraints for correctness for any delay of the gates.

Table 2. Experimental results using convex polyhedra and octahedra.

Example	States	Variables	Time - Poly (sec)	Time - Oct (sec)
nowick	60	30	0.5	0.1
sbuf-read-ctl	74	31	1.2	1.4
rcv-setup	72	27	2.1	8.3
alloc-outbound	82	39	1.3	0.2
ebergen	83	27	1.3	1.7
mp-forward-pkt	194	29	1.9	3.8
chu133	288	26	1.3	1.0

Experimental Results. Timing verification has been performed on several asynchronous circuits from the literature. This verification can be seen as the analysis of a set of clock variables, and the underlying timing behavior can be modeled as assignments and guards on these variables [4]. The analysis of clock variables has been performed using two different numeric abstractions: convex polyhedra and octahedra. The implementation of polyhedra uses the New Polka polyhedra library [19], while the library of OhDD is implemented on top of the CUDD package [23]. Table 2 shows a comparison of the experimental results for some examples. All these examples were verified successfully using both octahedra and polyhedra, as all relevant constraints were unit linear inequalities. For all these cases, the execution time of convex polyhedra and octahedra is comparable, while the memory usage for octahedra is lower. For each example, we provide the number of different states (configurations) of the circuit, the number of clock and delay variables of the abstractions and the execution time required by the analysis with each abstraction.

The difference in memory usage is quantified in the next example, an asynchronous pipeline with different number of stages and an environment running at a fixed frequency. The processing time required by each stage i has a processing time bounded by an interval, with unknown upper and lower bound $[d_i, D_i]$. Whenever a stage finishes its computation, it sends the result to the next stage if it is empty. The safety property being verified in this case was *"the environment will never have to wait before sending new data to the pipeline"*, i.e. whenever the environment sends new data to the pipeline, the first stage is empty. Fig.7 shows the pipeline, with an example of a correct and incorrect behavior. The tool discovers that correct behavior can be ensured if the following holds:

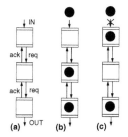

# of stages	# of States	# of variables	Polyhedra		OhDD	
			CPU Time	Memory	CPU Time	Memory
2	36	20	0.6s	64Mb	1s	5Mb
3	108	24	2s	67Mb	17s	8Mb
4	324	28	13.5s	79Mb	249s	39Mb
5	972	32	259.2s	147Mb	3974s	57Mb
6	2916	36	–	–	143058s	83Mb

Fig. 7. (a) Asynchronous pipeline with N=3 stages, (b) correct behavior of the pipeline and (c) incorrect behavior. Dots represent data elements. On the right, the CPU time and memory required to verify pipelines with different number of stages.

$$d_{IN} > D_1 \wedge \ldots \wedge d_{IN} > D_N \wedge d_{IN} > D_{OUT}$$

where D_i is the delay of stage i, and d_{IN} and D_{OUT} refer to environment delays. This property is equivalent to:

$$d_{IN} > max(D_1, \ldots, D_N, D_{OUT})$$

Therefore, the pipeline is correct if the environment is slower than the slowest stage of the pipeline. Both the polyhedra and octahedra abstract domain are able to discover this property. This example is interesting because it exhibits a very high degree of concurrency. The verification times and memory usage for different lengths of the pipeline can be found in Fig.7. Notice that the memory consumption of OhDD is lower than that of convex polyhedra. This reduction in memory usage is sufficient to verify larger pipelines (n = 6 stages) not verifiable with our convex polyhedra implementation. However, this memory reduction comes at the expense of an increase in the execution time.

5.2   Other Applications

In general, the octahedron abstract domain may be interesting in any analysis problem where convex polyhedra can be used. Many times, the precision obtained with convex polyhedra is very good, but the efficiency of the analysis limits the applicability. In these scenarios, using octahedra might be adequate as long as the variables involved in the analysis are positive and unit linear inequalities provide sufficient information for the specific problem. Some examples of areas of applications are the following:

– *Analysis of program invariants involving unsigned variables.*
– *Static discovery of bounds in the size of asynchronous communication channels*:
   Many systems communicate using a non-blocking semantics, where the sender does not wait until the receiver is ready to read the message. In these systems, each channel requires a buffer to store the pending messages. Allocating these buffers statically would improve performance but it is not possible, as the amount of pending messages during execution is not known in advance. Analysis with octahedra could discover these bounds statically. This problem is related to the problem of structural boundedness of a Petri Net [18], where an upper bound on the number of tokens that can be in each place of the Petri Net must be found.

- *Analysis of timed systems*: Clocks and delays are restricted to positive values in many types of models. Octahedra can be used to analyze these values and discover complex properties such as timing constraints or worst-case execution time(WCET).
- *Analysis of string length in C programs* [8]: Checking the absence of buffer overflows is important in many scenarios, specially in the applications where security is critical, e.g an operating system. C programs are prone to errors related to the manipulation of strings. Several useful constraints on the length of strings can be represented with octahedra. For instance, a constraint on the concatenation of two strings can be $\texttt{strlen}(\texttt{strcat}(s_1, s_2)) = \texttt{strlen}(s_1) + \texttt{strlen}(s_2)$.

6   Conclusions and Future Work

A new numeric abstract domain called octahedron has been presented. This domain can represent and manipulate constraints on the sum or difference of an arbitrary number of variables. In terms of precision, this abstraction is between octagons and convex polyhedra. Regarding complexity, the worst case complexity of octahedra operations over n variables is $O(3^n)$ in memory, and $O(3^n)$ in execution time in addition to the cost of saturation. However, worst-case performance is misleading due to the use of a decision diagram approach. For instance, BDDs have a worst-case complexity of $O(2^n)$, but they have a very good behavior in many real examples. Performance in this case depends on factors such as the ordering of the variables in the decision diagram and the effectiveness of the cache. In the experimental results of OhDD, memory consumption was shown to be smaller than that of our convex polyhedra implementation. Running time was comparable to that of convex polyhedra in small and medium-sized examples, while in more complex examples the execution time was worse. This shows that OhDD trade speed for a reduction in memory usage.

Future work in this area will try to improve the execution time of octahedra operations. For example, dynamic reordering [21] would improve efficiency if proper heuristics to find good variable orders can be developed. Another area where there is room for improvement is the current bottleneck of the representation, the saturation procedure.

Acknowledgements

This work has been partially funded by CICYT TIC2001-2476 and the FPU grant AP2002-3862 from the Spanish Ministry of Education, Culture and Sports. The authors would like to thank the referees for their valuable comments.

References

1. R. Alur and D. L. Dill. A theory of timed automata. *Theoretical Computer Science*, 126(2):183–235, 1994.
2. G. Behrmann, K. G. Larsen, J. Pearson, C. Weise, and W. Yi. Efficient timed reachability analysis using clock difference diagrams. In *Computer Aided Verification*, pages 341–353, 1999.

3. R. E. Bryant. Graph-based algorithms for Boolean function manipulation. *IEEE Transactions on Computers*, C-35(8):677–691, 1986.
4. R. Clarisó and J. Cortadella. Verification of timed circuits with symbolic delays. In *Proc. of Asia and South Pacific Design Automation Conference*, pages 628–633, 2004.
5. P. Cousot and R. Cousot. Abstract interpretation: a unified lattice model for static analysis of programs by construction or approximation of fixpoints. In *Proc. of the ACM Symposium on Principles of Programming Languages*, pages 238–252. ACM Press, 1977.
6. P. Cousot and N. Halbwachs. Automatic discovery of linear restraints among variables of a program. In *Proc. of the ACM Symposium on Principles of Programming Languages*, pages 84–97. ACM Press, New York, 1978.
7. D. L. Dill. Timing assumptions and verification of finite-state concurrent systems. In *Automatic Verification Methods for Finite State Systems*, LNCS 407, pages 197–212. Springer-Verlag, 1989.
8. N. Dor, M. Rodeh, and M. Sagiv. CSSV: towards a realistic tool for statically detecting all buffer overflows in C. In *Proceedings of the ACM SIGPLAN 2003 conference on Programming lan guage design and implementation*, pages 155–167. ACM Press, 2003.
9. E. Asarin, M. Bozga, A. Kerbrat, O. Maler, M. Pnueli, and A. Rasse. Data structures for the verification of timed automata. In O. Maler, editor, *Hybrid and Real-Time Systems*, pages 346–360, Grenoble, France, 1997. Springer Verlag, LNCS 1201.
10. M. Fujita, P. C. McGeer, and J. C.-Y. Yang. Multi-terminal binary decision diagrams: An efficient data structure for matrix representation. *Formal Methods in System Design*, 10(2/3):149–169, 1997.
11. N. Halbwachs, Y.-E. Proy, and P. Roumanoff. Verification of real-time systems using linear relation analysis. *Formal Methods in System Design*, 11(2):157–185, 1997.
12. T. A. Henzinger. *The Temporal Specification and Verification of Real-Time Systems*. PhD thesis, Stanford University, Aug. 1991.
13. C. Mauras. Symbolic simulation of interpreted automata. In *3rd Workshop on Synchronous Programming*, Dec. 1996.
14. S. Minato. Zero-supressed BDDs for set manipulation in combinatorial problems. In *Proc. ACM/IEEE Design Automation Conference*, pages 272–277, 1993.
15. A. Miné. A new numerical abstract domain based on difference-bound matrices. In *Programs as Data Objects II*, volume 2053 of *LNCS*, pages 155–172. Springer-Verlag, May 2001.
16. A. Miné. The octagon abstract domain. In *Analysis, Slicing and Tranformation (in Working Conference on Reverse Engineering)*, IEEE, pages 310–319. IEEE CS Press, Oct. 2001.
17. J. Møller, J. Lichtenberg, H. R. Andersen, and H. Hulgaard. Difference decision diagrams. In *Computer Science Logic*, The IT University of Copenhagen, Denmark, 1999.
18. T. Murata. State equation, controllability and maximal matchings of Petri nets. *IEEE Transactions on Automatic Control*, AC-22(3):412–416, 1977.
19. New Polka: Convex Polyhedra Library. http://www.irisa.fr/prive/bjeannet/newpolka.html.
20. C. Piguet et al. Memory element of the Master-Slave latch type, constructed by CMOS technology. US Patent 5,748,522, 1998.
21. R. Rudell. Dynamic variable ordering for ordered binary decision diagrams. In *Proc. International Conf. Computer-Aided Design (ICCAD)*, pages 42–47, 1993.
22. A. Simon, A. King, and J. M. Howe. Two Variables per Linear Inequality as an Abstract Domain. In M. Leuschel, editor, *Proceedings of Logic Based Program Development and Transformation*, LNCS 2664, pages 71–89. Springer-Verlag, 2002.
23. F. Somenzi. CUDD: Colorado university decision diagram package. Available online at http://vlsi.colorado.edu/~fabio/CUDD.
24. F. Wang. Symbolic parametric safety analysis of linear hybrid systems with BDD-like datastructures. In *Proceedings of Computer Aided Verification*. Springer-Verlag, July 2004.

Path-Sensitive Analysis for Linear Arithmetic and Uninterpreted Functions[*]

Sumit Gulwani and George C. Necula

University of California, Berkeley
{gulwani,necula}@cs.berkeley.edu

Abstract. We describe data structures and algorithms for performing a path-sensitive program analysis to discover equivalences of expressions involving linear arithmetic or uninterpreted functions. We assume that conditionals are abstracted as boolean variables, which may be repeated to reflect equivalent conditionals. We introduce *free conditional expression diagrams* (FCEDs), which extend binary decision diagrams (BDDs) with internal nodes corresponding to linear arithmetic operators or uninterpreted functions. FCEDs can represent values of expressions in a program involving conditionals and linear arithmetic (or uninterpreted functions). We show how to construct them easily from a program, and give a randomized linear time algorithm (or quadratic time for uninterpreted functions) for comparing FCEDs for equality. FCEDs are compact due to maximal representation sharing for portions of the program with independent conditionals. They inherit from BDDs the precise reasoning about boolean expressions needed to handle dependent conditionals.

1 Introduction

Data structures and algorithms for manipulating boolean expressions (e.g., binary decision diagrams) have played a crucial role in the success of model checking for hardware and software systems. Software programs are often transformed using boolean abstraction [4] to boolean programs: arithmetic operations and other operators are modeled conservatively by their effect on a number of boolean variables that encode predicates on program state. In this paper, we show that we can reason efficiently and precisely about programs that contain not only boolean expressions but also linear arithmetic and uninterpreted functions. Such algorithms are useful when the desired level of precision cannot be achieved with boolean abstraction of linear arithmetic expressions in a program.

Consider the program fragment shown in Figure 1. The atomic boolean expressions in the conditionals (e.g. $x < y$, $y == z$) have been abstracted as boolean variables c_1 and c_2. We assume that the conditional abstraction procedure can

---

[*] This research was supported in part by the National Science Foundation Grant CCR-0081588, and gifts from Microsoft Research. The information presented here does not necessarily reflect the position or the policy of the Government and no official endorsement should be inferred.

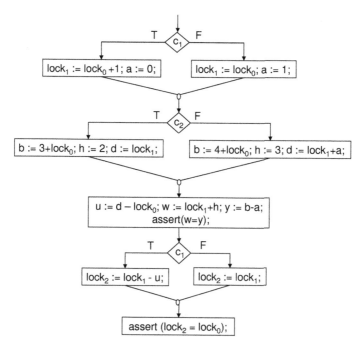

Fig. 1. An example program fragment.

sometimes detect equivalences of atomic boolean expressions (e.g. $x < y$ and $y > x$ are equivalent), as is the case for the first and last conditionals in the program. Suppose our goal is to determine the validity of the two assertions in the program. The first assertion holds because it is established on all four paths that can reach it. The second assertion holds only because the first and last conditionals use identical guards. A good algorithm for verifying these assertions should be able to handle such dependent conditionals (Two conditionals are dependent if truth-value of one depends on the other), or in other words perform a path-sensitive analysis, without individually examining an exponential number of paths that arise for portions of the program with independent conditionals.

Since there is no obvious boolean abstraction for this example, we need to reason about the linear arithmetic directly. There are two kinds of algorithms known to solve this problem. On one extreme, there are abstract/random interpretation based polynomial-time algorithms, which perform a path-insensitive analysis. Karr described a deterministic algorithm [22] based on abstract interpretation [11]. Recently, we gave a faster randomized algorithm [18] based on random interpretation. These algorithms are able to decide the first assertion in the program since the first two conditionals preceding it are independent of each other. However, these algorithms cannot verify that the second assertion holds, because they would attempt to do so over all the eight paths through the program, including four infeasible ones.

On the other extreme, there are multi-terminal binary decision diagram (MTBDD) [15] based algorithms that consider all feasible paths in a program

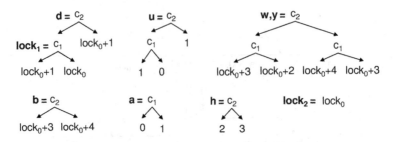

Fig. 2. The MTBDD representation for symbolic values of variables of the program in Figure 1. The internal nodes are conditionals whose left child corresponds to the conditional being true. The leaves are canonicalized linear arithmetic expressions.

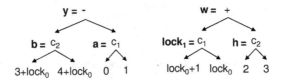

Fig. 3. The VDG/FCED representations for symbolic values of variables of the program in Figure 1. The internal nodes also involve arithmetic operations. This leads to succinct representations, and allows sharing.

explicitly, and hence are able to decide both assertions in our example. However, these algorithms run in exponential time even when most of the conditionals in a program are independent of each other, which is quite often the case. MTBDDs are binary decision diagrams whose leaves are not boolean values but canonicalized linear expressions. For the example program, the MTBDDs corresponding to final values of the various variables are shown in Figure 2. These MTBDDs use the same ordering of boolean variables and the same canonicalization for leaves. With MTBDDs we can verify both assertions; however note that checking equality between w and y essentially involves performing the check individually on each of the four paths from the beginning of the program to the first assertion. Also note that there is little opportunity for sharing subexpressions in a MTBDD due to the need to push computations down to the leaves and to canonicalize the leaves. This algorithm is exponential in the number of boolean variables in the program. Its weak point is the handling of sequences of independent conditionals and its strong point is that it can naturally handle dependent conditionals, just like a BDD does for a boolean program.

In this paper, we describe data structures and algorithms that combine the efficiency of the path-insensitive polynomial-time algorithms with the precision of the MTBDD-based algorithms. Consider representing the values of w and y using value dependency graph (VDG) [28], as shown in Figure 3. Such a representation can be easily obtained by symbolic evaluation of the program. Note that this representation is exponentially more succinct than MTBDDs. For example, note that $|VDG(y)| = |VDG(b)| + |VDG(a)|$ while

$|MTBDD(y)| = |MTBDD(b)| \times |MTBDD(a)|$ (here $|VDG(y)|$ denotes the size of VDG representation for y). This is because VDGs do not need to maintain a normal form for expressions unlike MTBDDs, which even require a normal form for their leaves. For example, w and y, which are equivalent expressions, have distinct VDG representations as shown in Figure 3. A VDG for any expression can share nodes with the VDGs for its subexpressions. For example, note that $VDG(y)$ shares nodes with $VDG(b)$ and $VDG(a)$. On the other hand, an MTBDD typically cannot exploit any sharing that is induced by the order in which a program computes expressions.

The challenge now is to check equivalence of two VDGs. We do not know of any efficient deterministic algorithm to solve this problem. We show in this paper a randomized algorithm that can check equivalence of two *free* VDGs in linear time. A VDG is said to be *free* if every boolean variable occurs at most once on any path from the root node to a leaf. Note that if all conditionals in a program are independent of each other, then the VDG for any expression in the program is free. For example, the VDGs shown in Figure 3 are free.

In this paper, we propose *Free Conditional Expression Diagrams* (FCEDs), which are a generalization of free VDGs. We describe a transformation that generates an FCED for any expression in a loop-free program, and a randomized algorithm that checks equivalence of two FCEDs in linear time. This, in turn, gives an algorithm for checking the validity of assertions $e_1 = e_2$ in programs that contain linear arithmetic and conditionals. This algorithm is more efficient than the MTBDD-based algorithm. In particular, if all conditionals in a program are independent of each other, then this algorithm is as fast as the random interpretation based algorithm, which runs in polynomial time, as opposed to the MTBDD-based algorithm, which has exponential cost. However, the new algorithm still has the same worst-case complexity as the MTBDD-based algorithm (This happens when all conditionals in the program are arbitrary boolean expressions involving the same set of boolean variables). This is not surprising since the problem of checking equality assertions in a program with dependent conditionals is NP-hard and it is generally believed that even randomized algorithms cannot solve such problems in polynomial time.

In Section 2, we describe the FCED construction and the randomized equivalence testing algorithm for conditional linear arithmetic expressions. In Section 3, we describe the FCED construction and the randomized equivalence testing algorithm for conditional uninterpreted function terms.

2   Analysis for Linear Arithmetic

2.1   Problem Definition

Let $\mathcal{L}_a$ be the following conditional arithmetic expression language over rational constants q, rational variables x, boolean variables c, and boolean expressions b.

$$e ::= q \quad | \quad x \quad | \quad e_1 + e_2 \quad | \quad e_1 - e_2 \quad | \quad q \times e \quad | \quad \textit{if } b \textit{ then } e_1 \textit{ else } e_2$$
$$b ::= c \quad | \quad b_1 \wedge b_2 \quad | \quad b_1 \vee b_2$$

We want a data structure FCED to succinctly represent the expressions in language $\mathcal{L}_a$ and support efficient algorithms for the following two problems:

P1. Given the FCEDs for the sub-expressions of an expression $e \in \mathcal{L}_a$, construct the FCED for the expression e.

P2. Given the FCED representations for two expressions $e_1, e_2 \in \mathcal{L}_a$, decide whether $e_1 = e_2$.

Note that the symbolic value of any expression in our example program belongs to the language $\mathcal{L}_a$. For example, the value of $lock_1$ is " *if c_1 then $lock_0 + 1$ else $lock_0$*". Hence, algorithms for problems P1 and P2 can be used to check equivalence of two expressions in a loop-free program. In general, if a program has loops, then since the lattice of linear equality facts has finite height k (where k is the number of variables in the program), one can analyze a suitable unrolling of the loops in the program to verify the assertions [22, 18].

Note that we assume that there is an abstraction procedure for conditionals that maps atomic conditionals to boolean variables such that only equivalent conditionals are mapped to the same boolean variable. Equivalent conditionals can be detected by using standard value numbering heuristics [25, 1] (e_1 *relop* $e_2 \equiv e_1'$ *relop* e_2' if $e_1 = e_1'$ and $e_2 = e_2'$ and *relop = relop'*) or other sophisticated heuristics [24] (e.g. e_1 *relop* $e_2 \equiv e_1'$ *relop'* e_2' if $e_1 - e_2 = e_1' - e_2'$ and *relop = relop'*). Here *relop* stands for a relational operator, e.g. $=, <$ or $>$. Note that detecting equivalence of conditionals involves detecting equivalence of expressions, which in turn can be done by using a simple technique like value numbering. We can even use the result of our analysis to detect those equivalences on the fly.

2.2   FCED Construction

An FCED for linear arithmetic is a DAG generated by the following language over rational constants q, rational variables x and boolean expressions g, which we call guards.

$$f ::= x \mid q \mid Plus(f_1, f_2) \mid Minus(f_1, f_2)$$
$$\mid Times(q, f) \mid Choose(f_1, f_2) \mid Guard_g(f)$$

The *Choose* and *Guard* node types are inspired by Dijkstra's guarded command language [14]. Given a boolean assignment ρ, the meaning of $Guard_g(f)$ is either the meaning of f (if g is true in ρ) or undefined (otherwise). The meaning of a *Choose* node is the meaning of its child that is defined. The *Choose* operator here is deterministic in the sense that at most one of its children is defined given any boolean assignment.

The guards g are represented using Reduced Ordered Binary Decision Diagrams (ROBDDs). Let $\preccurlyeq$ be the total ordering on program variables used in these ROBDD representations. For any sets of boolean variables B_1 and B_2, we use the notation $B_1 \prec B_2$ to denote that $B_1 \cap B_2 = \emptyset$ and $c_1 \preccurlyeq c_2$ for all variables

$c_1 \in B_1$ and $c_2 \in B_2$. The guards g can be described by the following language over boolean variables c.

$$g ::= true \quad | \quad false \quad | \quad c \quad | \quad If(c, g_1, g_2)$$

We assume that we can compute conjunction ($\wedge$) of two guards and negation ($\neg$) of a guard. For any boolean guard g, let $BV(g)$ denote the set of boolean variables that occur in g. Similarly, for any FCED node f, let $BV(f)$ denote the set of boolean variables that occur below node f. An FCED f must satisfy the following invariant:

Invariant 1 *For any guard node $Guard_{g_1}(f_1)$ in FCED f, $BV(g_1) \prec BV(f_1)$.*

Invariant 1 is similar to the ROBDDs' requirement that boolean variables on any path from the root node to a leaf must be ordered. As we shall see, it plays an important role in the randomized equivalence testing algorithm that we propose.

The FCED representation of any expression e is denoted by $FCED(e)$ and is computed inductively as follows:

$$FCED(x) = x$$
$$FCED(q) = q$$
$$FCED(e_1 + e_2) = Plus(FCED(e_1), FCED(e_2))$$
$$FCED(e_1 - e_2) = Minus(FCED(e_1), FCED(e_2))$$
$$FCED(q \times e) = Times(q, FCED(e))$$
$$FCED(if\ b\ then\ e_1\ else\ e_2) = Choose(||g_b, FCED(e_1)||, ||\neg g_b, FCED(e_2)||),$$

where g_b is the ROBDD representation of the boolean expression b as a guard. The normalization operator $||g, f||$ takes as input a boolean guard g and an FCED f and returns another FCED whose meaning is equivalent to $Guard_g(f)$, except that Invariant 1 is satisfied:

$$||g, f|| = Guard_g(f), \quad if\ BV(g) \prec BV(f)$$
$$||g, f|| = Guard_g(f[g]), \quad if\ g\ is\ a\ conjunction\ of\ literals$$
$$||g, Plus(f_1, f_2)|| = Plus(||g, f_1||, ||g, f_2||)$$
$$||g, Minus(f_1, f_2)|| = Minus(||g, f_1||, ||g, f_2||)$$
$$||g, Times(q, f')|| = Times(q, ||g, f'||)$$
$$||g, Choose(f_1, f_2)|| = Choose(||g, f_1||, ||g, f_2||)$$
$$||g, Guard_{g'}(f')|| = Guard_{g'}(||g, f'||), \quad if\ BV(g') \prec BV(g)$$
$$= ||g \wedge g', f'|| \quad otherwise$$

where $f[g]$ denotes the FCED obtained from f by replacing any boolean variable c by true or false, if it occurs in g in non-negated or negated form respectively. The purpose of the normalization $||g, f||$ is to simplify f or to push the guard g down into f until a point when the boolean variables in g and f are disjoint, thus ensuring that Invariant 1 is maintained. Figure 4 shows the FCED for variable

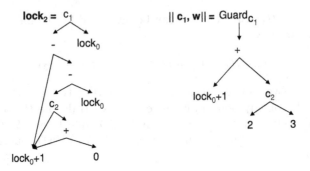

Fig. 4. An example of FCED and normalization operator.

$lock_2$ in our example program. Figure 4 also shows the FCED for $||c_1, w||$, where the FCED for w has been shown in Figure 3. We use the notation $c(f_1, f_2)$ as a syntactic sugar for the FCED $Choose(Guard_c(f_1), Guard_{\neg c}(f_2))$. We also simplify an FCED $Choose(Guard_g(f_1), Guard_{false}(f_2))$ to $Guard_g(f_1)$.

2.3   Randomized Equivalence Testing

In this section, we describe an algorithm that decides equivalence of two FCEDs. The algorithm assigns a hash value $V(n)$ to each node n in an FCED, computed in a bottom-up manner from the hash values of its immediate children. The hash value of an FCED is defined to be the hash value assigned to its root. Two FCEDs are declared equivalent iff they have same hash values. This algorithm has a one-sided error probability. If two FCEDs have different hash values, then they are guaranteed to be non-equivalent. However, if two FCEDs are not equivalent, then there is a very small probability (over the random choices made by the algorithm) that they will be assigned same hash values. The error probability can be made arbitrarily small by setting the parameters of the algorithm appropriately.

For the purpose of assigning a hash value to an FCED representation of any expression in $\mathcal{L}_a$, we choose a random value for each of the boolean and rational variables. The random values for both kind of variables are chosen independently of each other and uniformly at random from some finite set of rationals. (Note that we choose a rational random value even for boolean variables). For any variable y, let r_y denote the random value chosen for y. The hash value $V(n)$ is assigned inductively to any node n in an FCED as follows:

$$V(q) = q$$
$$V(x) = r_x$$
$$V(Plus(f_1, f_2)) = V(f_1) + V(f_2)$$
$$V(Minus(f_1, f_2)) = V(f_1) - V(f_2)$$
$$V(Times(q, f)) = q \times V(f)$$
$$V(Choose(f_1, f_2)) = V(f_1) + V(f_2)$$
$$V(Guard_g(f)) = H(g) \times V(f)$$

where the hash function H for a boolean guard g is as defined below.

$$H(true) = 1$$
$$H(false) = 0$$
$$H(c) = r_c$$
$$H(If(c, g_1, g_2)) = r_c \times H(g_1) + (1 - r_c) \times H(g_2)$$

For example, note that $w = (if\ c_1\ then\ lock_0 + 1\ else\ lock_0) + (if\ c_2\ then\ 2\ else\ 3)$ and $y = (if\ c_2\ then\ 3 + lock_0\ else\ 4 + lock_0) - (if\ c_1\ then\ 0\ else\ 1)$ in our example program. If we choose $r_{lock_0} = 3, r_{c_1} = 5, r_{c_2} = -3$, then $V(w) = V(y) = 14$, thereby validating the assertion $w = y$. If we choose random boolean values for boolean variables while computing hash values, then we would essentially be hashing the symbolic values of expressions on one random path (corresponding to the random boolean choice). However, it is essential to check for the equivalence of expressions on *all* paths. Choosing non-boolean random values for boolean variables help us to do that by essentially computing a random weighted combination of the hash values of expressions on all paths. In the next section, we explain more formally why, with high probability, this hashing scheme assigns equal values only to equivalent expressions.

2.4   Completeness and Probabilistic Soundness of the Algorithm

Let e be any expression in language $\mathcal{L}_a$. Let $P(FCED(e))$ denote the polynomial obtained by using variables x and c instead of random values r_x and r_c, while computing $V(FCED(e))$. The following properties hold.

T1. $V(FCED(e))$ is the result of evaluating the polynomial $P(FCED(e))$ at random values r_y chosen for each variable y that occurs in $P(FCED(e))$.
T2. For any FCED f, $P(f)$ is a multi-linear polynomial, i.e. the degree of any variable is at most 1. This is due to the freeness property of an FCED (ensured by Invariant 1).
T3. $e_1 = e_2$ iff $P(FCED(e_1))$ and $P(FCED(e_2))$ are equivalent polynomials.

Property T1 is trivial to prove. The proof of property T2 is based on the observation that $H(g)$ is multi-linear for any guard g (this is because every boolean variable occurs at most once on any path from the root node to a leaf in an ROBDD), and for any $Guard_g(f)$ node in an FCED, $BV(g) \cap BV(f) = \emptyset$. The proof of property T3 is given in the full version of the paper [20].

These properties imply that the equivalence testing algorithm is complete, i.e., it assigns same hash values to equal expressions. Suppose e_1 and e_2 are equal expressions. It follows from T3 that $P(FCED(e_1)) = P(FCED(e_2))$. Since $P(FCED(e_1))$ and $P(FCED(e_2))$ are multi-linear (implied by T2), they are equivalent even when the boolean variables are treated as rational variables. This is a standard fact and is the basis of several algorithms [5, 17, 13, 12]. Therefore, it follows from T1 that $V(FCED(e_1)) = V(FCED(e_2))$.

Properties T1 and T3 imply that the algorithm is probabilistically sound, i.e., it assigns different hash values to non-equivalent expressions with high

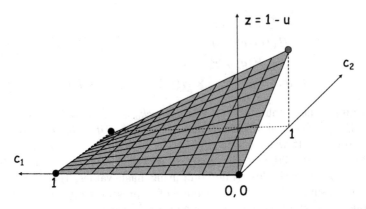

Fig. 5. The surface shows values of expression $1 - u$ for different values of c_1 and c_2.

probability over the random choices that it makes. Suppose $e_1 \neq e_2$. It follows from T3 that $P(FCED(e_1)) \neq P(FCED(e_2))$. Trivially, $P(FCED(e_1)) \neq P(FCED(e_2))$ even when boolean variables are treated as rational variables. It then follows from the classic Schwartz's theorem [27] (on testing equivalence of two polynomials) that the probability that $P(FCED(e_1))$ and $P(FCED(e_2))$ evaluate to the same value on random assignment is bounded above by $\frac{d}{s}$, where d is the maximum of the degrees of the polynomials $P(FCED(e_1))$ and $P(FCED(e_2))$ (these are bounded above by the size of the expressions e_1 and e_2 respectively), and s is the size of the set from which random values are chosen. Therefore, it follows from T1 that $Pr[V(FCED(e_1)) \neq V(FCED(e_2))] \geq 1 - \frac{d}{s}$. (Here $Pr[V(FCED(e_1)) \neq V(FCED(e_2))]$ denotes the probability of the event $V(FCED(e_1) \neq V(FCED(e_2))$ over the choice of the random values r_y for all variables y.)

Note that the error probability can be made arbitrarily small by choosing random values from a large enough set. For boolean variables, this set cannot contain more than 2 elements. It is precisely for this reason that we require property T2, so as to be able to treat boolean variables as rational variables without affecting equivalences of polynomials. Note that multi-linearity is a necessary requirement. For example, consider the two equivalent polynomials $c_2 c_3 + c_1^2$ and $c_1 + c_3 c_2$ over the boolean variables c_1 and c_2. These polynomials are not equivalent when the variables c_1 and c_2 are interpreted as rational variables since the first polynomial is not multi-linear in c_1.

This randomized algorithm for equivalence checking can be explained informally using a geometric argument. For example, consider the validity of the statement $u = 1$ at the place of the first assertion in Figure 1. This statement is false since it holds on only three of the four paths that reach it. It is false when c_1 is false and c_2 is true. Figure 5 shows a surface in a 3-dimensional space whose z coordinate reflects the value of expression $1 - u$ as a function of (rational) assignment for c_1 and c_2. Since there is at least one boolean assignment for c_1 and c_2 where $1 - u$ is not zero, and since the degree of the surface is small (2 in this case), it follows that the surface intersects the c_1-c_2 plane in a "small"

$e =$	$e_1 \pm e_2$	if b then e_1 else e_2	$q \times e_1$	$F(e_1, e_2)$
$T(e)$ for FCED $=$	$Constant$	$S(g_b) \times (S(e_1) + S(e_2))$	$Constant$	$Constant$
$T(e)$ for MTBDD $=$	$S(e_1) \times S(e_2)$	$S(g_b) \times (S(e_1) + S(e_2))$	$S(e_1)$	$S(e_1) \times S(e_2)$

Fig. 6. A table comparing the time and space complexity $T(e)$ for constructing FCEDs and MTBDDs of an expression from the representation of its subexpressions.

number of points. This allows the quick discovery, with high probability, of this false assertion by random sampling of the surface (this corresponds to choosing random rational values for boolean variables). If, on the other hand, the surface corresponds to a true assertion, then it is included in the c_1-c_2 plane and any sampling would verify that.

2.5   Time and Space Complexity

The time required to compute the hash value of an FCED is clearly linear in the size of the FCED. However, this is under the assumption that all basic arithmetic operations (like addition, multiplication) to compute the hash value can be performed in unit time. This assumption is not necessarily true since the size of the numbers involved may increase with each arithmetic operation. The standard technique to deal with this problem is to do the arithmetic operations modulo a randomly chosen prime p [23]. This makes sure that at each stage, the numbers can be represented within a constant number of bits and hence each arithmetic operation can be performed in constant time. The modular arithmetic adds an additional small probability of error in our algorithm.

The time and extra space $T(e)$ required to construct the FCED of an expression e from the FCEDs of the subexpressions of e depends on the structure of e. If e is of the form q, x, $e_1 \pm e_2$, or $q \times e$, then it is easy to see that $T(e)$ is constant. If e is of the form *if b then e_1 else e_2*, then an amortized cost analysis would show that $T(e) = O(S(g_b) \times (S(e_1) + S(e_2)))$, where $g_b = ROBDD(b)$ and $S(g_b)$ denotes the size of the ROBDD g_b. $S(e_1)$ denotes the size of the FCED of expression e_1 (when represented as a tree; however, the boolean guards in e_1 may be represented as DAGs). The upper bound on time complexity for this case relies on Invariant 1 and assumes some sharing of common portions of ROBDDs that arise while construction of $FCED(e)$.

If all conditionals in a program are independent of each other, then, it is easy to see that $FCED(e)$ is linear in size of e, as opposed to the possibly exponential size implied by the above-mentioned bounds on $T(e)$. Figure 6 compares $T(e)$ for FCED and MTBDD representations. The last column in the table refers to the next section.

3   Analysis for Uninterpreted Functions

Reasoning precisely about program operators other than linear arithmetic operators is in general undecidable. A commonly used abstraction is to model any n-

ary non-linear program operator as an uninterpreted function under the theory of equality, which has only one axiom, namely, $F(x_1, .., x_n) = F'(x_1, .., x'_n) \iff F = F'$ and $x_i = x'_i$ for all $1 \le i \le n$. The process of detecting this form of equivalence, where the operators are treated as uninterpreted functions, is also referred to as value numbering. In this section, we describe how to construct FCEDs for uninterpreted functions.

3.1   Problem Definition

Let $\mathcal{L}_u$ be the following language over boolean expressions b, variables x and an uninterpreted function symbol F of arity two.

$$e ::= x \quad | \quad F(e_1, e_2) \quad | \quad \text{if } b \text{ then } e_1 \text{ else } e_2$$

For simplicity, we consider only one binary uninterpreted function F. Our results can be extended easily to languages with any finite number of uninterpreted functions of any finite arity. However, note that this language does not contain any linear arithmetic operators.

We want a data structure to succinctly represent the expressions in language $\mathcal{L}_u$ and support efficient algorithms for the problems similar to those mentioned in Section 2.1. This would be useful to check equivalence of two expressions in any loop-free program. As before, it turns out the lattice of sets of equivalences among uninterpreted function terms has finite height k (where k is the number of variables in the program). Hence, if a program has loops, then one can analyze a suitable unrolling of loops in the program to verify assertions [19, 21].

3.2   FCED Construction

An FCED in this case is a DAG generated by the following language over variables x and boolean guards g represented using ROBDDs.

$$f ::= x \quad | \quad F(f_1, f_2) \quad | \quad Choose(f_1, f_2) \quad | \quad Guard_g(f)$$
$$g ::= true \quad | \quad false \quad | \quad c \quad | \quad If(c, g_1, g_2)$$

Here c denotes a boolean variable. As before, an FCED satisfies Invariant 1. The FCED representation of any expression e is computed inductively as follows:

$$FCED(x) = x$$
$$FCED(F(e_1, e_2)) = F(FCED(e_1), FCED(e_2))$$
$$FCED(\text{if } b \text{ then } e_1 \text{ else } e_2) = Choose(||g_b, FCED(e_1)||, ||\neg g_b, FCED(e_2)||)$$

where $g_b = ROBDD(b)$. The normalization operator $||g, f||$ takes as input a boolean guard g and an FCED f and returns another FCED as follows:

$$||g, f|| = Guard_g(f), \quad if\ BV(g) \prec BV(f)$$
$$||g, f|| = Guard_g(f[g]), \quad if\ g\ is\ a\ conjunction\ of\ literals$$
$$||g, F(f_1, f_2)|| = F(||g, f_1||, ||g, f_2||)$$
$$||g, Choose(f_1, f_2)|| = Choose(||g, f_1||, ||g, f_2||)$$
$$||g, Guard_{g'}(f')|| = Guard_{g'}(||g, f'||), \quad if\ BV(g') \prec BV(g)$$
$$= ||g \wedge g', f'|| \quad otherwise$$

where $f[g]$, $BV(g)$ and $BV(f)$ are as defined before in Section 2.2.

3.3 Randomized Equivalence Testing

The hash values assigned to nodes of FCEDs of expressions in the language $\mathcal{L}_u$ are vectors of k rationals, where k is the largest depth of any expression that arises. For the purpose of assigning hash values, we choose a random value r_y for each variable y and two random $k \times k$ matrices M and N. The following entries of the matrices M and N are chosen independently of each other and uniformly at random from some set of rationals: $M_{1,1}, N_{1,1}$, and $M_{i-1,i}, M_{i,i}, N_{i-1,i}, N_{i,i}$ for all $2 \leq i \leq k$. The rest of the entries are chosen to be 0. The hash value $V(n)$ is assigned inductively to any node n in an FCED as follows:

$$V(x) = [r_x, .., r_x]$$
$$V(F(f_1, f_2)) = V(f_1) \times M + V(f_2) \times N$$
$$V(Choose(f_1, f_2)) = V(f_1) + V(f_2)$$
$$V(Guard_g(f)) = H(g) \times V(f)$$

where $H(g)$ is as defined before in Section 2.3. Note that $H(g) \times V(f)$ denotes multiplication of vector $V(f)$ by the scalar $H(g)$, while $V(f_1) \times M$ denotes multiplication of vector $V(f_1)$ by the matrix M.

The proof of property T3 (given in the full version of the paper [20]) explains the reason behind this fancy hashing scheme. Here is some informal intuition. To maintain multi-linearity, it is important to choose a random linear interpretation for the uninterpreted function F. However, if we let $k = 1$, the hashing scheme cannot always distinguish between non-equivalent expressions. For example, consider $e_1 = F(F(x_1, x_2), F(x_3, x_4))$ and $e_2 = F(F(x_1, x_3), F(x_2, x_4))$. Note that $e_1 \neq e_2$ but $V(FCED(e_1)) = V(FCED(e_2)) = r_{x_1}m^2 + r_{x_2}mn + r_{x_3}nm + r_{x_4}n^2$, where m and n are some random rationals. This happens because scalar multiplication is commutative. This problem is avoided if we work with vectors and matrices because matrix multiplication is not commutative.

3.4 Completeness and Probabilistic Soundness of the Algorithm

Let e be any expression in language $\mathcal{L}_u$. Let $P(FCED(e))$ denote the kth polynomial in the symbolic vector obtained by using variable names x and c instead of random values r_x and r_c, and by using variable names $M_{i,j}$ and $N_{i,j}$ instead of random values for the matrix entries, while computing $V(FCED(e))$. The properties T1,T2,T3 stated in Section 2.4 hold here also. Properties T1 and T2 are easy to prove as before. However, the proof of property T3 is non-trivial, and is given in the full version of the paper [20]. These properties imply that the randomized equivalence testing algorithm is complete and probabilistically sound as before. The error probability is bounded above by $\frac{d}{s}$, where d and s are as mentioned in Section 2.4.

3.5   Time and Space Complexity

The time required to compute the hash value for an FCED f is $O(n \times k)$ where n is the size of f and k is the size of the largest FCED in the context. The time and extra space $T(e)$ required to construct FCED of an expression e in language $\mathcal{L}_u$ from the FCED of its sub-expressions can be estimated similarly as in Section 2.5, and is shown in Figure 6.

4   Comparison with Related Work

Path-insensitive version of the analyses that we have described in this paper have been well studied. Karr described a polynomial-time abstract interpretation based algorithm [22] to reason precisely about linear equalities in a program with non-deterministic conditionals. Recently, we described a more efficient algorithm based on the idea of random interpretation [18]. Several polynomial-time algorithms have been described in literature for value numbering, which is the problem of discovering equivalences among program expressions when program operators are treated as uninterpreted [1, 26]. All these algorithms are complete for basic blocks, but are imprecise in the presence of joins and loops in a program. Recently, we described algorithms for global value numbering that discover all equivalences among expressions under the assumption that all conditionals are non-deterministic and program operators are uninterpreted [19, 21].

Karthik Gargi described a path-sensitive global value numbering algorithm [16] that first discovers equivalent conditionals, and then uses that information to do a simple predicated global value numbering. However, this algorithm is not complete and cannot handle conditionals as precisely as our algorithm. Our algorithm is complete with respect to the abstraction of conditionals to boolean variables. Gargi's algorithm treats all operators as uninterpreted and hence does not handle linear arithmetic.

The model checking community has been more concerned with path-sensitivity, in an attempt to do whole state-space exploration. The success of ROBDDs has inspired efforts to improve their efficiency and to expand their range of applicability [7]. Several generalizations of ROBDDs have been proposed for efficient boolean manipulation [2, 17]. There have been some efforts to extend the concept to represent functions over boolean variables that have non-boolean ranges, such as integers or real numbers (e.g.Multi Terminal Binary Decision Diagrams (MTBDDs) [3, 9], Edge-Valued Binary Decision Diagrams (EVBDDs), Binary

	Handles Dependent Conditionals	Handles Arithmetic	Handles Independent Conditionals	Randomized or Deterministic
ROBDD	good	no	good	deterministic
MTBDD	good	poor	poor	deterministic
FBG	no	no	good	randomized
RI	no	good	good	randomized
FCED	good	good	good	randomized

Fig. 7. A table comparing different data structures for software model-checking.

Moment Diagrams (BMDs) [6] and Hybrid Decision Diagrams (HDDs) [8]). Multiway Decision Graphs (MDGs) have been proposed to represent quantifier-free formulas over terms involving function symbols [10]. None of the above mentioned extensions and generalizations of ROBDDs seem well-suited for software model checking since they do not directly and efficiently support manipulation of conditional expressions, i.e. expressions that are built from boolean expressions and expressions from some other theory like that of arithmetic or uninterpreted functions. This is because most of these techniques rely on having a canonical representation for expressions. Figure 2 illustrates the problems that arise with canonicalization. However, our proposed representation, FCED, can efficiently represent and manipulate such expressions since it does not require a canonical representation.

The idea behind hashing boolean guards g in our randomized equivalence testing algorithm is similar to that used for checking equivalence of Free Boolean Graphs (FBG) [5], FBDDs [17] and d-DNNFs [13, 12] all of which represent boolean expressions. We have extended this line of work with checking equivalence of conditional arithmetic expressions or conditional expressions built from uninterpreted function terms. Similar ideas have also been used in the random interpretation (RI) technique for linear arithmetic [18] and for uninterpreted function terms [19] for detecting equivalence of conditional expressions that involve independent conditionals. Figure 7 compares these related techniques.

5   Conclusion and Future Work

We describe in this paper a compact representation of expressions involving conditionals and linear arithmetic (or uninterpreted functions) such that they can be compared for equality in an efficient way. In the absence of linear arithmetic and uninterpreted functions, our technique behaves like ROBDDs. In fact, FCEDs inherit from ROBDDs the precise handling of dependent conditionals necessary for discriminating the feasible paths in a program with dependent conditionals. However, the main strength of FCEDs is the handling of the portions of the program with independent conditionals. In those situations, the size of FCEDs and the time to compare two FCEDs is linear (quadratic for uninterpreted functions) in the size of the program.

The simpler problem involving only independent conditionals can be solved in polynomial time by deterministic [22, 21] and randomized algorithms [18, 19].

In this special case, randomization brings a lower computational complexity and the simplicity of an interpreter, without having to manipulate symbolic data structures. Once we allow dependent conditionals, the problem becomes NP-hard and we should not expect randomization alone to solve it in polynomial time. We show in this paper that randomization can still help even for NP-hard problems, if we combine it with a symbolic algorithm. We expect that there are other NP-hard program analysis problems that can benefit from integrating the symbolic techniques with randomization.

The next step is to implement our algorithms and compare them with the existing algorithms with regard to running time and number of equivalences discovered. The results of our algorithm can also be used as a benchmark to measure the number of equivalences that are missed by path-insensitive algorithms.

We have presented randomized algorithms for checking equivalence of two FCEDs for the languages $\mathcal{L}_u$ and $\mathcal{L}_a$. It is an open problem to extend these results to the combined language, i.e. the language that involves both conditional arithmetic expressions as well as conditional uninterpreted function terms. It would also be useful to extend these results to other languages/theories apart from linear arithmetic and uninterpreted functions, for example, the theory of lists, the theory of uninterpreted functions modulo commutativity, associativity, or both. Such theories can be used to model program operators more precisely.

References

1. B. Alpern, M. N. Wegman, and F. K. Zadeck. Detecting equality of variables in programs. In *15th Annual ACM Symposium on POPL*, pages 1–11. ACM, 1988.
2. H. Andersen and H. Hulgaard. Boolean expression diagrams. In *12th Annual IEEE Symposium on Logic in Computer Science*, pages 88–98. IEEE, June 1997.
3. R. Bahar, E. Frohm, C. Gaona, G. Hachtel, E. Macii, A. Pardo, and F. Somenzi. Algebraic Decision Diagrams and Their Applications. In *IEEE /ACM International Conference on CAD*, pages 188–191. ACM/IEEE, Nov. 1993.
4. T. Ball, R. Majumdar, T. Millstein, and S. K. Rajamani. Automatic predicate abstraction of C programs. In *Proceedings of the ACM SIGPLAN '00 Conference on PLDI*. ACM, May 2001.
5. M. Blum, A. Chandra, and M. Wegman. Equivalence of free boolean graphs can be decided probabilistically in polynomial time. *Information Processing Letters*, 10:80–82, 1980.
6. R. Bryant and Y. Chen. Verification of Arithmetic Circuits with Binary Moment Diagrams. In *32nd ACM/IEEE Design Automation Conference*, June 1995.
7. R. E. Bryant. Binary decision diagrams and beyond: Enabling technologies for formal verification. In *International Conference on Computer Aided Design*, pages 236–245. IEEE Computer Society Press, Nov. 1995.
8. E. M. Clarke, M. Fujita, and X. Zhao. Hybrid decision diagrams overcoming the limitations of MTBDDs and BMDs. In *International Conference on Computer Aided Design*, pages 159–163. IEEE Computer Society Press, Nov. 1995.
9. E. M. Clarke, K. L. McMillan, X. Znao, M. Fujiia, and J. Yang. Spectral transforms for large boolean functions with applications to technology mapping. In *Proceedings of the 30th ACM/IEEE Design Automation Conference*, pages 54–60, June 1993.

10. F. Corella, Z. Zhou, X. Song, M. Langevin, and E. Cerny. Multiway decision graphs for automated hardware verification. *Formal Methods in System Design: An International Journal*, 10(1):7–46, Feb. 1997.

11. P. Cousot and R. Cousot. Abstract interpretation: A unified lattice model for static analysis of programs by construction or approximation of fixpoints. In *4th Annual ACM Symposium on Principles of Programming Languages*, pages 234–252, 1977.

12. A. Darwiche. A compiler for deterministic decomposable negation normal form. In *Proceedings of the Fourteenth Conference on Innovative Applications of Artificial Intelligence*, pages 627–634. AAAI Press, July 2002.

13. A. Darwiche and J. Huang. Testing equivalence probabilistically. Technical Report D-23, Computer Science Department, UCLA, June 2002.

14. E. W. Dijkstra. Guarded commands, nondeterminacy and formal derivation of programs. *Communications of the ACM*, 18(8):453–457, Aug. 1975.

15. M. Fujita and P. C. McGeer. Introduction to the special issue on multi-terminal binary decision diagrams. *Formal Methods in System Design*, 10(2/3), Apr. 1997.

16. K. Gargi. A sparse algorithm for predicated global value numbering. In *Proceedings of the ACM SIGPLAN 2002 Conference on Programming Language Design and Implementation*, volume 37, 5, pages 45–56. ACM Press, June 17–19 2002.

17. J. Gergov and C. Meinel. Efficient boolean manipulation with OBDDs can be extended to FBDDs. *IEEE Trans. on Computers*, 43(10):1197–1209, Oct. 1994.

18. S. Gulwani and G. C. Necula. Discovering affine equalities using random interpretation. In *30th Annual ACM Symposium on POPL*. ACM, Jan. 2003.

19. S. Gulwani and G. C. Necula. Global value numbering using random interpretation. In *31st Annual ACM Symposium on POPL*. ACM, Jan. 2004.

20. S. Gulwani and G. C. Necula. Path-sensitive analysis for linear arithmetic and uninterpreted functions. Technical Report UCB//CSD-04-1325, UC-Berkeley, 2004.

21. S. Gulwani and G. C. Necula. A polynomial-time algorithm for global value numbering. In *Static Analysis Symposium*, LNCS. Springer, 2004.

22. M. Karr. Affine relationships among variables of a program. In *Acta Informatica*, pages 133–151. Springer, 1976.

23. R. Motwani and P. Raghavan. *Randomized Algorithms*. Cambridge University Press, 1995.

24. G. C. Necula. Translation validation for an optimizing compiler. In *Proceedings of the ACM SIGPLAN '00 Conference on PLDI*, pages 83–94. ACM, jun 2000.

25. B. K. Rosen, M. N. Wegman, and F. K. Zadeck. Global value numbers and redundant computations. In *15th Annual ACM Symposium on Principles of Programming Languages*, pages 12–27. ACM, 1988.

26. O. Rüthing, J. Knoop, and B. Steffen. Detecting equalities of variables: Combining efficiency with precision. In *Static Analysis Symposium*, volume 1694 of *LNCS*, pages 232–247. Springer, 1999.

27. J. T. Schwartz. Fast probabilistic algorithms for verification of polynomial identities. *JACM*, 27(4):701–717, Oct. 1980.

28. D. Weise, R. F. Crew, M. Ernst, and B. Steensgaard. Value dependence graphs: representation without taxation. In *21st Annual ACM Symposium on POPL*. ACM, Jan. 1994.

On Logics of Aliasing

Marius Bozga, Radu Iosif, and Yassine Lakhnech

VERIMAG
2 Avenue de Vignate
38610 Gières, France
{bozga,iosif,lakhnech}@imag.fr

Abstract. In this paper we investigate the existence of a deductive verification method based on a logic that describes pointer aliasing. The main idea of such a method is that the user has to annotate the program with loop invariants, pre- and post-conditions. The annotations are then automatically checked for validity by propagating weakest preconditions and verifying a number of induced implications. Such a method requires an underlying logic which is decidable and has a sound and complete weakest precondition calculus. We start by presenting a powerful logic (**wAL**) which can describe the shapes of most recursively defined data structures (lists, trees, etc.) has a complete weakest precondition calculus but is undecidable. Next, we identify a decidable subset (**pAL**) for which we show closure under the weakest precondition operators. In the latter logic one loses the ability of describing unbounded heap structures, yet bounded structures can be characterized up to isomorphism. For this logic two sound and complete proof systems are given, one based on natural deduction, and another based on the effective method of analytic tableaux. The two logics presented in this paper can be seen as extreme values in a framework which attempts to reconcile the naturally oposite goals of expressiveness and decidability.

1 Introduction

The problem of pointer *aliasing* plays an important role in the fields of static analysis and software model checking. In general, static analyses used in optimizing compilers check basic properties such as data sharing and circularities in the heap of a program, while model checking deals with the evolution of heap structures, in both shape and contents, over time. An early result [21] shows that precise may-alias analysis in the presence of loops is undecidable. As a consequence, the approach adopted by the static analysis community, is the abstraction-based *shape analysis* [23]. This method is effective in the presence of loops, since the domain of the analysis is bounded, but often imprecise. In this paper we present an orthogonal solution to the aliasing problem, in that precision is the primary goal. To ensure termination, we use Floyd's method [10] of annotating the program with pre-, post-conditions and loop invariants. The annotations are subsequently verified by a push-button procedure, that computes weakest preconditions expressed using an effectively decidable logic.

R. Giacobazzi (Ed.): SAS 2004, LNCS 3148, pp. 344–360, 2004.
© Springer-Verlag Berlin Heidelberg 2004

The key is to find a logic that can altogether (i) express aliasing and shape properties of the program heap, (ii) is effectively decidable, and moreover, (iii) has a sound and complete weakest precondition calculus with respect to the atomic statements. While the second and third requirements are clear, the first one is still ambiguous: what kind of specifications can we express in a decidable heap logic with weakest preconditions? The contribution of this paper is the definition of a formal framework in which we prove that such logics *can* be found. Our focus is on imperative programs with destructive updating, in which heaps are viewed as shape graphs with labels only on edges i.e., we ignore from the start the internal states of the objects.

As a starting point, we present a general logic Weak Alias Logic (**wAL**) that is expressive enough to describe the recursive data structures of interest (lists, trees, dags etc.) as infinite classes of finite graphs. This logic has also a sound and complete weakest precondition calculus with respect to atomic statements such as new object creation and assignment of pointers. The satisfiability problem of the **wAL** logic is found to be undecidable but recursively enumerable, which motivates further searches for semi-decision procedures and non-trivial decidable subsets.

In the rest of the paper, we define a decidable subset of **wAL**, called Propositional Alias Logic (**pAL**) for describing pointer aliasing that is, moreover, able to characterize arbitrary finite structures and finite classes of structures. The tradeoff in defining **pAL** is losing the ability to describe a number of interesting shape properties such as listness, (non)circularity, etc. For this logic, we give a proof-theoretic system based on natural deduction, and an effective tableau decision method. Both systems are shown to be sound and complete. Moreover, the satisfiability problem for **pAL** is shown to be NP-complete. The last point concerns the definition, in **pAL**, of weakest preconditions for imperative programs with destructive updating. At this point, we use the **wAL** weakest precondition calculus, previously developped in [2]. Our weakest precondition calculus for **pAL** is sound and complete, as a consequence of the soundness and completness of the definitions for **wAL** weakest preconditions.

Related Work. To describe properties of dynamic program stores, various formalisms have been proposed in the literature e.g., L_r [1], BI (Bunched Implications) [13], Separation Logic [22] and PAL (Pointer Assertion Language) [17]. As a common point with our work, L_r [1] uses regular expressions to describe reachability between two points in the heap and is shown to be decidable, yet the weakest precondition calculus is not developed. On the other hand, BI [13] and Separation Logic [22] produce remarkably simple preconditions and have quite clean proof-theoretic models [18]. Another feature of these formalisms is that they allow for compositional reasoning [19]. As a downside, the quantifier fragment, essential to express weakest preconditions, is undecidable [5], while the ground (propositional) fragment is decidable, a tableau procedure being proposed in [11]. In a later publication [6], a specialization of the ground fragment of BI to tree models is used as a type system for a language, based on λ-calculus,

that handles trees. An effectively decidable formalism is PAL [17], an extension
of second-order monadic logic on trees that allows to describe a restricted class
of graphs, known as "graph types" [16], as opposed to our approach that deals
with unrestricted graphs. Programs that manipulate such graphs are restricted
to updating only the underlying tree (backbone). The resulting actions can thus
be described in monadic second-order logic, and the validity of Hoare triples
expressed in PAL can be automatically decided [15].

The decision procedures for both L_r and PAL use Rabin's result on the
monadic second order theory of n successors (SnS) [20]. The decision procedure
for the satisfiability of SnS is however non-elementary. We show that the decision
problem for the **pAL** logic is NP-complete, thus drastically improving the complexity bounds. Also, to the best of our knowledge, no previously published work
on the verification of heap properties has the ability to deal with *unrestricted* (destructively updated) data structures, developing a sound and complete weakest
precondition calculus on top of a decidable logic for graphs.

2   Weak Alias Logic

In this section we introduce Weak Alias Logic (**wAL**), a logic that is expressive
enough for defining recursive data structures (lists, trees, etc) as infinite classes of
finite graphs, as well as for defining a weakest precondition calculus of imperative
programming languages with destructive updating [2]. This section defines the
logic, and Section 5 briefly recalls the weakest precondition calculus that has
been developed on top of it.

Before giving the syntax of **wAL**, let us introduce the notion of *heap*, which
is central in defining interpretations of **wAL** formulas. Intuitively, a heap is represented by a graph where the nodes model objects and the edges model pointers
between objects. The heap edges are labeled with symbols from a given alphabet Σ, which stands for the set of all program pointers, including all program
variables and record fields (selectors). It is furthermore required that the graph
be deterministic, as a program pointer can only point to one object at a time.

In this paper we adopt the *storeless representation* [2], [12], [14], [8] of a graph,
in which each node is associated the language recognized by the automaton whose
set of states is given by the set of graph nodes, the transition relation by the
set of edges, the initial state is a designated entry point in the heap, and the
unique final state, the node itself. The interested reader is referred to [2] for a
detailed discussion on the advantages of the storeless representation of heaps,
such as compatibility with garbage collection and isomorphic transformations.

Definition 1 (Heap). *A heap $\mathcal{M} \subseteq \mathcal{P}(\Sigma^+)$ is either the empty set or a finite
set $\{X_1, X_2, \ldots, X_n\}$ satisfying the following conditions, for all $1 \leq i, j \leq n$:*

(C1) non-emptiness: $X_i \neq \emptyset$,
(C2) determinism: $i \neq j \Rightarrow X_i \cap X_j = \emptyset$,
(C3) prefix closure and right regularity:

$$\forall x \in X_i \ [\forall y, z \in \Sigma^+ [x = yz \Rightarrow \exists\, 1 \leq k \leq n \ [y \in X_k \wedge X_k z \subseteq X_i]]]$$

One can also think of a heap element as the set of all incoming paths leading to it, paths that start with a program variable. The (C1),(C2) and (C3)
restrictions must be imposed on the elements of a heap in order to maintain the
correspondence (up to isomorphism) with the graph model [2]. An equivalent
approach, taken in [14], [8], is to consider the languages in the heap as equivalence classes of a right-regular relation on $\Sigma^* \times \Sigma^*$. The set of all heaps over an
alphabet Σ is denoted in the following by $\mathcal{H}(\Sigma)$.

Figure 1 introduces the abstract syntax (upper part) and semantics (lower
part) of the **wAL** logic. The terms of a **wAL** formula are regular expressions ρ
over the alphabet Σ with free variables from a set Var. We allow the classical
composition operations on regular expressions, together with the left derivate,
denoted by $\rho_1^{-1}\rho_2 \overset{\Delta}{=} \{\sigma \in \Sigma^* \mid \rho_1\sigma \cap \rho_2 \neq \emptyset\}$ [1]. Formulas are built from
the atomic propositions $\rho_1 = \rho_2$ (language equivalence) and $\langle X \rangle \rho_1$ (modality)
connected with the classical first-order operators $\wedge$, $\neg$ and $\exists$. A less usual requirement is imposed on the syntax of the existential quantifier: the quantified
variable need to occur at least once within the angled brackets of a modality
in the scope of the quantifier, which is formally captured by the $\varphi\langle X \rangle$. Notice
also that only free variables can occur inside the modality brackets. A formula
φ is said to be *closed* if no variables occur free i.e., $FV(\varphi) = \emptyset$, where FV is
defined recursively on the syntax, as usual. We define $\forall X . \varphi \overset{\Delta}{=} \neg\exists X . \neg\varphi$,
$\varphi_1 \vee \varphi_2 \overset{\Delta}{=} \neg(\neg\varphi_1 \wedge \neg\varphi_2)$, and $\varphi_1 \rightarrow \varphi_2 \overset{\Delta}{=} \neg\varphi_1 \vee \varphi_2$. The set of all **wAL** formulas
over the alphabet Σ is formally denoted by **wAL**$[\Sigma]$.

$$\rho ::= v \in \Sigma \mid X \in Var \mid \Sigma \mid \rho_1 \cdot \rho_2 \mid \rho^\partial \mid \rho_1 \cup \rho_2 \mid \rho_1 \cap \rho_2 \mid \bar{\rho} \mid \rho_1^{-1}\rho_2$$
$$\varphi ::= \rho_1 = \rho_2 \mid \langle X \rangle \rho_1 \mid \varphi_1 \wedge \varphi_2 \mid \neg\varphi \mid \exists X . \varphi\langle X \rangle$$

$$\mathcal{M} \in \mathcal{H}(\Sigma), \ \nu : Var \rightarrow \mathcal{P}(\Sigma^\partial)$$
$$[\![\rho]\!]_\nu \overset{\Delta}{=} \rho[\nu(FV(\rho))/FV(\rho)]$$
$$[\![\rho_1 = \rho_2]\!]_{\mathrm{M},\nu} = 1 \iff [\![\rho_1]\!]_\nu = [\![\rho_2]\!]_\nu$$
$$[\![\langle X \rangle \rho_1]\!]_{\mathrm{M},\nu} = 1 \iff \nu(X) \in \mathcal{M} \text{ and } \nu(X) \cap [\![\rho_1]\!]_\nu \neq \emptyset$$
$$[\![\exists X [\varphi]]\!]_{\mathrm{M},\nu} = 1 \iff \exists \rho \in \mathcal{P}(\Sigma^\partial) . [\![\varphi]\!]_{\mathrm{M},[X\partial \rho]\nu} = 1$$

Fig. 1. Weak Alias Logic

A **wAL** formula is interpreted with respect to a heap $\mathcal{M}$ and a valuation
ν assigning free variables to languages. The only non-standard operator is the
modality $\langle X \rangle \rho_1$, where X is bound to denote a heap entity which intersects (the
interpretation of) ρ_1. As a consequence of the syntactic restriction imposed on
the existential quantifier, all variables in a closed formula are bound to heap

---

[1] Intuitivelly, we need the left derivate to describe paths between two objects in the
   heap. If X and Y are two objects in a heap, then $X^{-1}Y$ is the language of all paths
   between X and Y.

entities[2]. A heap $\mathcal{M}$ is said to be a *model* for a closed **wAL** formula φ if and only if $[\![\varphi]\!]_{\mathcal{M},\lambda X.\bot} = 1$. In case where φ has at least one model, it is said to be *satisfiable*.

At this point, the reader can notice an embedding of **wAL** into the Monadic Second Order Logic on graphs. Indeed, a **wAL** formula is composed of equivalences of regular expressions ($\rho_1 = \rho_2$) related using first order connectives. Such equivalences can be described by finite automata which, in turn, can be specified in MSOL. However, we found using regular expressions, instead of MSOL, more intuitive for the specification of heap properties, as it is shown in the following.

Path properties	
$reach(X,Y)$	$\langle Y \rangle X \Sigma^+$
$next(X,Y)$	$\langle Y \rangle X \Sigma \wedge \forall Y^\natural . \langle Y^\natural \rangle X \Sigma \to Y = Y^\natural$
$linear(X,Y)$	$reach(X,Y) \wedge \forall Z . \neg Z = Y \wedge (X = Z \vee reach(X,Z)) \wedge$ $reach(Z,Y) \to \exists Z^\natural . \neg Z^\natural = Z \wedge next(Z,Z^\natural)$
$cycle(X,Y)$	$reach(X,Y) \wedge reach(Y,X)$
$share(X,Y)$	$\exists Z . reach(X,Z) \wedge reach(Y,Z)$
Recursive data structures	
$nclist(head)$	$\forall X . \langle X \rangle head \to \exists Y . \langle Y \rangle X next^\natural \wedge linear(X,Y) \wedge \neg cycle(Y,Y)$
$dlist(head,next,prev)$	$\forall X, Y \exists Z . (\langle X \rangle head \Rightarrow \neg \langle Y \rangle X prev) \wedge$ $(\langle Z \rangle X next \Rightarrow X \neq Z \wedge \langle X \rangle Z prev)$
$tree(root)$	$\forall X . \langle X \rangle root \to \forall Y, Z . (reach(X,Y) \wedge reach(X,Z)) \to \neg share(Y,Z))$
$dag(root)$	$\exists X . \langle X \rangle root \to \forall Y, Z . reach(X,Y) \wedge reach(X,Z) \to \neg cycle(Y,Z)$

Fig. 2. Expressing properties of heaps

The properties in Figure 2 describe various paths in the structure. We consider the predicate $reach(X,Y)$ stating that node Y is reachable from node X by some non-empty path. A node Y is said to be *next* to a node X if Y is the only neighbor of X. A path from X to Y is *linear* if there is no branching i.e., if all the nodes on the path have only one successor. The existence of a cycle containing both X and Y is given by the $cycle(X,Y)$ predicate.

The **wAL** logic can also describe the shapes of most typical recursive data structures used in programming languages with dynamic memory allocation: lists, trees, dags, etc. For instance, non-cyclic simply-linked lists pointed to by the *head* variable and using the *next* field as forward selector, are being described by the *nclist* predicate. Doubly-linked lists pointed to by the *head* variable and using the *next* and *prev* field pointers as forward and backward selectors, respectively, can be captured by the *dlist* predicate. Some data structures, such as trees, require the absence of sharing. A sharing predicate expressing that X and Y belong to two structures that share some node can be given by $share(X,Y)$. A tree structure pointed to by a variable *root* is described by the *tree* formula. A

---

[2] This syntactic restriction on the quantification domain was mainly suggested by the fact that, allowing quantification over $\mathcal{P}(\Sigma^\natural)$ makes the logic undecidable even when modalities are not used at all in formulas. A formal proof will be included in an extended version of this paper.

dag structure in which every node is reachable from a *root* variable is given by the *dag* formula.

2.1 Undecidability of wAL

The result of this section comes with no surprise, in the light of similar undecidability results for logics able to express graph properties such as e.g, the logic of Bunched Implications (BI) [5], and Monadic Second-Order Logic of graphs [7]. Given along the same lines as the undecidability proof for BI [5], our proof for **wAL** relies on a classical result in finite model theory [9], namely that the first order logic interpreted over finite structures is undecidable.

Given a vocabulary $\mathcal{V}$ of relation symbols, let FO[$\mathcal{V}$] be the set of first-order formulas with symbols from $\mathcal{V}$. For each relation symbol $R \in \mathcal{V}$, let $\#(R)$ denote its *arity* i.e., its number of arguments. Let $\mathcal{V} = \{R_1, \ldots, R_n\}$ for the rest of this section. We interpret first-order formulas over structures $\mathcal{A} = \langle A, R_1^{\mathcal{A}}, \ldots, R_n^{\mathcal{A}} \rangle$, where A is the *universe* and $R_i^{\mathcal{A}} \subseteq A^{\#(R_i)}$, $1 \leq i \leq n$ are the *interpretations* of the relation symbols from $\mathcal{V}$ over A. A structure is said to be *finite* if and only if its universe is finite. Given a valuation $v : FV(\varphi) \to A$ of the free variables in a formula $\varphi \in$ FO[$\mathcal{V}$], we denote by $[\![\varphi]\!]_{\mathcal{A}, v}$ the interpretation of φ in $\mathcal{A}$. We say that $\mathcal{A}$ is a *model* of a closed first-order formula φ if and only if $[\![\varphi]\!]_{\mathcal{A}, \lambda X. \perp} = 1$. It is known that the problem of finding a finite model for a closed FO[$\mathcal{V}$] formula is undecidable [9]:

Theorem 1 (Trahtenbrot's Theorem). *Let $\mathcal{V}$ be a vocabulary with at least one symbol of arity two or more. Then the set $Sat[\mathcal{V}] \triangleq \{\varphi \in FO[\mathcal{V}] \mid FV(\varphi) = \emptyset,\ \varphi \text{ has a finite model } \}$ is not decidable.*

Given an arbitrary first order formula, we shall translate it into a **wAL** formula such that satisfiability is strongly preserved by the translation. Considering that $\mathcal{V} = \{R_1, \ldots, R_n\}$, we define $\Sigma_{\mathcal{V}} = \{\alpha_{i1}, \ldots, \alpha_{i\#(R_i)}, \beta_i \mid 1 \leq i \leq n\} \cup \{\gamma\}$. That is, for each relation symbol of arity k we consider k different α-symbols and a β-symbol in $\Sigma_{\mathcal{V}}$. The translation is given by the recursive function Θ : FO[$\mathcal{V}$] $\to$ **wAL**[$\Sigma_{\mathcal{V}}$], defined as:

$$\Theta(R_k(X_1, \ldots, X_{\#(R_k)})) \triangleq \exists X \,.\, \langle X \rangle \Sigma^{\lhd} \wedge \bigwedge_{i=1}^{\#(R_k)} \langle X_i \rangle X \alpha_{ki}$$
$$\Theta(X = Y) \triangleq X = Y \qquad \Theta(\varphi_1 \wedge \varphi_2) \triangleq \Theta(\varphi_1) \wedge \Theta(\varphi_2)$$
$$\Theta(\neg\varphi) \triangleq \neg\Theta(\varphi) \qquad \Theta(\exists X \,.\, \varphi) \triangleq \exists X \,.\, \langle X \rangle \Sigma^{\lhd} \wedge \Theta(\varphi)$$

Note that the translation of a closed first-order formula respects the syntactic constraints of **wAL**, that each quantified variable must occur inside the brackets of a modality, and that only a variable can occur on this position. Moreover, a closed first-order formula translates into a closed **wAL** formula. Now it remains to be shown that the translation strongly preserves satisfiability. We remind that satisfiability for **wAL** is implicitly defined on finite models (Definition 1). Due to space constraints, all proofs are deferred to [3].

Lemma 1. *A closed first-order formula φ is finitely satisfiable if and only if $\Theta(\varphi)$ is satisfiable.*

Considering for the moment that the alphabet Σ is sufficiently large to code the vocabulary $\mathcal{V}$ of a given first order logic, Theorem 1 and Lemma 1 lead immediately to the following result.

Theorem 2. *For a sufficiently large alphabet Σ, the set $Sat[\Sigma] \stackrel{\Delta}{=} \{\varphi \in \mathbf{wAL}[\Sigma] \mid FV(\varphi) = \emptyset, \varphi \text{ has a model } \}$ is not recursive.*

Since Theorem 1 holds for vocabularies containing at least one relation symbol of arity two, by the definition of $\Sigma_{\mathcal{V}}$ it follows that Theorem 2 holds for generic heaps over alphabets of size at least four. Here, a more refined heap model could provide us with more intuition in identifying classes of heaps over which the satisfiability problem becomes decidable. For instance, considering $\Sigma = \Pi \cup \Omega$, $\Pi \cap \Omega = \emptyset$, $\|\Omega\| = 1$ and all heaps of the form $\mathcal{M} \subseteq \mathcal{P}(\Pi \times \Omega^*)$ i.e., heaps consisting only of (possibly circular) singly linked lists. In this simple case, we propose to revisit the decidability of the satisfiability problem for **wAL**.

In order to show that the satisfiability problem for **wAL** is recursively enumerable, let us first consider the *model checking* problem. The model checking problem asks whether a given heap $\mathcal{M}$ is a model for a formula ψ. This problem is decidable, by the fact that any heap model is finite. The interested reader is referred to [4] for an algorithm. But the set $\mathcal{H}(\Sigma)$ of all heaps over a finite alphabet is enumerable. Hence, if a given formula ψ is satisfiable, an algorithm that enumerates all models $\mathcal{M}_1, \mathcal{M}_2, \ldots$, testing whether each $\mathcal{M}_i$ is a model of ψ, will eventually stop.

Lemma 2. *For every finite Σ, the set $Sat[\Sigma]$ is recursively enumerable.*

An interesting open problem is then how to find useful semi-decision procedures for **wAL**.

3   Propositional Alias Logic

The negative result from the previous section motivates the search for decidable subsets of **wAL** that are able to express meaningful properties of heaps. One basic property encountered in many applications is *data sharing*. In this section we define a simpler logic based directly on the notion of *aliasing* of finite heap access paths (Propositional Alias Logic, or **pAL** for short). The rest of this paper is concerned with the study of **pAL** from three perspectives: proof theory, automated reasoning and program logic. The ability of **pAL** to express other heap properties besides aliasing, is also investigated.

Figure 3 defines the abstract syntax (upper part) and the semantics (lower part) of **pAL**. The terms are finite words over an alphabet Σ, with $w_1^{-1} w_2$ being the suffix of w_2 that, concatenated with w_1, yields w_2, if such suffix exists, or the empty word ϵ, otherwise. The atomic propositions are the *prefix test* $(w_1 \leq w_2)$ and the *alias proposition* $(w_1 \diamond w_2)$. Formulas are built from atomic propositions connected with the propositional operators $\wedge$ and $\neg$. In the syntax definition, $\perp$

$$w := v \in \Sigma \mid w_1 \cdot w_2 \mid w_1^{-1} w_2$$

$$\varphi := w_1 \leq w_2 \mid w_1 \Diamond w_2 \mid \varphi_1 \wedge \varphi_2 \mid \neg \varphi \mid \bot$$

$$[\![w_1 \Diamond w_2]\!]_{\mathbf{M}} = 1 \iff \exists X \in \mathcal{M} . w_1, w_2 \in X$$

Fig. 3. Propositional Alias Logic

denotes the *false* literal[3]. The set of all **pAL** formulas over the alphabet Σ is formally denoted by **pAL**$[\Sigma]$.

The semantics of **pAL** is defined with respect to a heap $\mathcal{M}$. An alias proposition $w_1 \Diamond w_2$ is true if and only if there exists an element of $\mathcal{M}$ such that both terms w_1, w_2 belong to it. Note that, since $\mathcal{M} \subseteq \mathcal{P}(\Sigma^+)$, if either one of the terms is ϵ, the alias proposition is false. The intended meaning of $w \Diamond w$ for some $w \in \Sigma^+$, is to say that w is a well-defined path in the heap. The following semantic equivalence is a trivial check: $w_1 \Diamond w_2 \iff \exists X . \langle X \rangle w_1 \wedge \langle X \rangle w_2$. The prefix relation $w_1 \leq w_2$ can be encoded in **wAL** as $w_1^{-1} w_2 \neq \emptyset^*$, where $\epsilon \overset{\Delta}{=} \emptyset^*$ is a possible definition of the empty word in **wAL**. These considerations justify the fact that **pAL** is a subset of **wAL**. The embedding is proper (**pAL**$[\Sigma] \subset$ **wAL**$[\Sigma]$), since e.g. reachability and linearity are not expressible in **pAL**.

3.1   Natural Deduction System

This section introduces a natural deduction system [25] for **pAL** that proves to be a useful tool in reasoning about aliases. Although later in this paper we adopt the automated reasoning view, as opposed to the proof theoretic, a number of results from this sections are used in the rest of the paper. The system (Figure 4) is that of propositional calculus à la Gentzen (rules $\wedge$E, $\wedge$I, $\neg$E, $\neg$I, $\bot$E, $\bot$I) to which we add three rules concerning only alias propositions (sufE, sufI and sym). For these rules we take $\Gamma \subseteq$ **pAL**$[\Sigma]$, $x, y, z \in \Sigma^+$ and $t \in \Sigma^*$.

$$\frac{xt \Diamond y}{x \Diamond x} \text{ (sufE)} \qquad \frac{x \Diamond y \quad yt \Diamond z}{xt \Diamond z} \text{ (sufI)} \qquad \frac{x \Diamond y}{y \Diamond x} \text{ (sym)}$$

$$\frac{\varphi \wedge \psi}{\varphi} \text{ (}\wedge E\text{)} \qquad \frac{\varphi \quad \psi}{\varphi \wedge \psi} \text{ (}\wedge I\text{)} \qquad \frac{\bot}{\varphi} \text{ (}\bot E\text{)} \qquad \frac{\varphi \quad \neg \varphi}{\bot} \text{ (}\bot I\text{)}$$

$$\frac{\Gamma, \neg \varphi \vdash \bot}{\Gamma \vdash \varphi} \text{ (}\neg E\text{)} \qquad \frac{\Gamma, \varphi \vdash \bot}{\Gamma \vdash \neg \varphi} \text{ (}\neg I\text{)}$$

Fig. 4. Natural Deduction System for **pAL**

The natural deduction system presented in Figure 4 exhibits a number of interesting properties: it is sound, complete and, all proofs of alias propositions can be given in a normal form. To formalize these notions, we need further

---

[3] False could have been defined as $\varphi \wedge \neg \varphi$ for an arbitrary formula φ. However an explicit definition is preferred for the purposes of the proof theoretic system of Section 3.1.

notation. If p is an alias proposition, we say that $\Gamma \vdash_{PA} p$ if and only if there exists a derivation of p with premises in Γ that uses *only* the (sufI), (sufE) and (sym) rules. Otherwise, if ψ is any formula, we say that $\Gamma \vdash \psi$ if and only if there exists a derivation of ψ with premises in Γ. By $Th(\Gamma)$ we denote the *theory* of Γ i.e., the set of all formulas that can be deduced from it i.e., $Th(\Gamma) \overset{\Delta}{=} \{\varphi \mid \Gamma \vdash \varphi\}$.

Given a finite set of alias propositions, there exists a heap that is a model for the entire set.

Lemma 3. *Let Γ be a set of formulas containing a finite number of alias propositions, $\approx_\Gamma \subseteq \Sigma^+ \times \Sigma^+$ be a relation on finite sequences, defined as $x \approx_\Gamma y$ if and only if $\Gamma \vdash_{PA} x \Diamond y$, and H_Γ be the set $\{x \mid x \approx_\Gamma x\}$. Then $\approx_\Gamma$ is a total equivalence relation on H_Γ, and the quotient $H_{\Gamma/\approx_\Gamma}$ is a heap. Moreover, $\|H_{\Gamma/\approx_\Gamma}\| \le k \cdot \|\Gamma\|$, where $k \in \mathbb{N}$ is a constant.*

Note that, for arbitrary sets of formulas, the existence of a model occurs as a consequence of the downward closure property[4].

3.2   Expressiveness of pAL

In this section we investigate the expressiveness of the **pAL** language. We show that any finite heap structure over a finite alphabet can be uniquely characterized by a **pAL** formula. As a consequence, any finite class of heap structures can be defined in **pAL**[5]. This extends our previous result in [2], that **pAL** has the power to distinguish between any two non-isomorphic heap configurations[6]. However, the far more interesting question, of whether and how could **pAL** be extended to describe recursive data structures and still preserve decidability, is subject to ongoing and future work.

For the rest of this section, let $\mathcal{M} = \{X_1, \ldots, X_n\}$ be a given heap. We shall define a formula $\phi_\mathcal{M}$ such that $[\![\phi_\mathcal{M}]\!]_\mathcal{M} = 1$ and, for any other heap $\mathcal{M}'$ such that $[\![\phi_\mathcal{M}]\!]_{\mathcal{M}'} = 1$, we have $\mathcal{M} = \mathcal{M}'$. For a finite word $w \in \Sigma^+$, we denote by $Pref(w)$ the set of all its prefixes, including w. For a set $X \in \mathcal{M}$, a word $w \in X$ is *elementary* if and only if it has at most two prefixes in X and at most one prefix in any other set $Y \in \mathcal{M}$, $Y \neq X$. Formally, we have $Elem_\mathcal{M}(X) \overset{\Delta}{=} \{w \in X \mid \|Pref(w) \cap X\| \le 2 \text{ and } \forall Y \neq X . \|Pref(w) \cap Y\| \le 1\}$. An important property of the sets of elementary words is finiteness. This results as a consequence of the fact that both $\mathcal{M}$ and Σ are finite, since the length of any $w \in Elem_\mathcal{M}(X)$ is $|w| \le \|\mathcal{M}\| + 1$, thus $\|Elem_\mathcal{M}(X)\| \le \|\Sigma\|^{\|\mathcal{M}\|+1}$. A *dangling* word is a minimal undefined path in $\mathcal{M}$. Formally, we define $Dang_\mathcal{M}(X) = \{wa \mid w \in Elem_\mathcal{M}(X), a \in \Sigma, wa \notin \bigcup \mathcal{M}\}$. Since $Elem_\mathcal{M}$ and Σ are finite, so is $Dang_\mathcal{M}(X)$. With this notation, we define:

---

[4] Definition 2 in Section 4.

[5] Even if a **pAL** formula, e.g $x \Diamond y$, is in general satisfied by an infinite number of heaps.

[6] There we proved ony that two structures are isomorphic if and only if they are models of the same **pAL** formulas.

$$\Gamma_{\mathcal{M}} \triangleq \bigcup_{X \in \mathcal{M}} \{w \diamond w' \mid w, w' \in Elem_{\mathcal{M}}(X)\} \cup \tag{1}$$

$$\bigcup_{X,Y \in \mathcal{M}, X \neq Y} \{\neg(w \diamond w') \mid w \in Elem_{\mathcal{M}}(X), w' \in Elem_{\mathcal{M}}(Y)\} \cup \tag{2}$$

$$\bigcup_{X \in \mathcal{M}} \{\neg(w \diamond w) \mid w \in Dang_{\mathcal{M}}(X)\} \cup \{\neg(a \diamond a) \mid a \in \Sigma \setminus \bigcup \mathcal{M}\} \tag{3}$$

This set is constructed as follows: the first component (1) describes each object as a set of alias propositions composed of elementary sequences, the second component (2) distinguishes between objects using negated alias propositions and the third and fourth components (3) describe the dangling sequences. Notice that $\Gamma_{\mathcal{M}}$ is not minimal, since for instance in (2) it is sufficient to choose only one $w \in Elem_{\mathcal{M}}(X)$ and one $w' \in Elem_{\mathcal{M}}(Y)$. However, it is finite, according to our previous considerations. Intuitively, $\Gamma_{\mathcal{M}}$ contains all the necessary information to characterize $\mathcal{M}$, thus we shall take $\phi_{\mathcal{M}} \triangleq \bigwedge \Gamma_{\mathcal{M}}$. To show that $\mathcal{M}$ is a model of $\phi_{\mathcal{M}}$ is a trivial but tedious check. That it is indeed the only model, will be shown in the rest of this section.

Lemma 4. *Let $\mathcal{M}$ be a heap with $X \in \mathcal{M}$, and $\Gamma_{\mathcal{M}}$ be the characteristic set defined in the previous. Then the following hold:*

1. *for each $w \in X$ there exists $w_0 \in Elem_{\mathcal{M}}(X)$ such that $\Gamma_{\mathcal{M}} \vdash w \diamond w_0$.*
2. *for all $w \notin \bigcup \mathcal{M}$ we have $\Gamma_{\mathcal{M}} \vdash \neg(w \diamond w)$.*
3. *for any $x, y \in \Sigma^+$ we have $[\![x \diamond y]\!]_{\mathcal{M}} = 1 \Rightarrow \Gamma_{\mathcal{M}} \vdash x \diamond y$ and $[\![x \diamond y]\!]_{\mathcal{M}} = 0 \Rightarrow \Gamma_{\mathcal{M}} \vdash \neg(x \diamond y)$.*

Notice that, from the third point of Lemma 4, and since $\Gamma_{\mathcal{M}}$ is satisfiable, hence consistent, we obtain that $[\![\varphi]\!]_{\mathcal{M}} = 1$ if and only if $\Gamma_{\mathcal{M}} \vdash \varphi$. Thus, the set of formulas that are satisfied by $\mathcal{M}$ is finitely axiomatisable since $Th(\Gamma_{\mathcal{M}}) = \{\varphi \mid [\![\varphi]\!]_{\mathcal{M}} = 1\}$, and $\Gamma_{\mathcal{M}}$ is finite by definition.

Theorem 3. *Let $\mathcal{M}$ be a heap and $\phi_{\mathcal{M}}$ be the formula $\bigwedge \Gamma_{\mathcal{M}}$. If $[\![\phi_{\mathcal{M}}]\!]_{\mathcal{M}'} = 1$, then $\mathcal{M} = \mathcal{M}'$.*

Example. Given $\Sigma = \{a, b, c\}$, the heap $\mathcal{M} = \{ab^*\}$ composed of one element pointed to by a with a b self loop is characterized by the formula $a \diamond ab \wedge \neg c \diamond c \wedge \neg ac \diamond ac$.

4   Tableau Decision Procedure for pAL

A proof that uses natural deduction is mainly based on manually adding assumptions in order to reach contradictions (and deleting them afterwards). This makes, in general, natural deduction unsuitable for automated reasoning and motivates our preference for the method of *analytic tableaux* [24], an elegant and efficient proof procedure for propositional logic, which we subsequently extend to **pAL**. Traditionally, a tableau for a propositional formula φ is a tree having φ

as the root node and subformulas of φ or negations of subformulas of φ as nodes. A tableau branch is said to be *closed* if it contains a formula together with its negation, and *open* otherwise. A tableau is said to be closed if and only if all its branches are closed. To check whether a formula φ is a tautology one builds the tableau for $\neg\varphi$, and infers that φ is a tautology if and only if the tableau eventually closes. In case at least one branch remains open, a counterexample for φ can be extracted.

$$\frac{\neg(xt\Diamond z)\ldots yt\Diamond z}{\neg(x\Diamond y)} \ (T_1) \qquad \frac{xt\Diamond y}{x\Diamond x} \ (T_2) \qquad \frac{x\Diamond y}{y\Diamond x} \ (T_3) \qquad \frac{\neg(x\Diamond y)}{\neg(y\Diamond x)} \ (T_4)$$

$$\frac{\varphi_1 \wedge \varphi_2}{\varphi_1; \varphi_2} \ (T_5) \qquad \frac{\neg(\varphi_1 \wedge \varphi_2)}{\neg\varphi_1 \mid \neg\varphi_2} \ (T_6) \qquad \frac{\neg\neg\varphi}{\varphi} \ (T_7) \qquad \frac{\varphi \ldots \neg\varphi}{\bot} \ (T_8)$$

Fig. 5. Tableau Expansion Rules

Figure 5 shows the tableau expansion rules for **pAL**. We consider that $x, y, z \in \Sigma^+$ and $t \in \Sigma^*$ that is, we can apply the rules also for an empty suffix ($t = \epsilon$). The tableau is constructed top-down. A rule whose hypothesis are of the form $\varphi \ldots \psi$ (namely T_1 and T_8) can be applied at a node, as soon as both φ and ψ are on the path from the root to the current node, order independent. Rule (T_5) expands by putting both φ_1 and φ_2 on the same branch of the tableau, while rule (T_6) creates two new branches, one containing φ_1 and the other one containing φ_2. All other rules expand by appending their conclusion to the current branch. We use rule (T_8) to close a branch, since $\bot$ does not expand any further. Each rule can only be applied provided that its conclusion does not already appear on the current branch, otherwise the procedure runs the risk of looping forever (for instance, applying one of rules $T_{3,4}$), without introducing any new formulas[7].

Example. Figure 6 presents a sample run of the tableau procedure whose goal is to prove that, for some *given* $k \in \mathbb{N}$, $\phi_k \stackrel{\triangle}{=} a\Diamond ab \rightarrow a\Diamond ab^k$ is a tautology. First, we eliminate the implication: $\phi_k = \neg(a\Diamond ab \wedge \neg(a\Diamond ab^k))$ and start the tableau procedure with $\neg\phi_k$ as the root node. To the right of each node occurs the number of the node(s) used in the hypothesis, followed by the name of the rule applied in order to obtain that node. In this example, the tableau closes after $k + 6$ steps. Branching lacks in this tableau because the rule (T_6) is never applied. $\square$

The tableau expansion rules can be easily understood with the natural deduction rules in mind. For instance, rule (T_1) can be derived using (sufI), ($\bot$I) and ($\neg$I). Rules (T_2) and (T_3) are (sufE) and (sufI), respectively, while (T_4) is easily derived using (sym) and ($\neg I$). The rest of the rules correspond to the purely propositional part of the natural deduction system and are an easy check. This (and the fact that the natural system is sound and complete) ensures that

---

[7] The definition of a finer notion of redundancy is planned in the full version.

$$[1] \quad \neg\neg(a\Diamond ab \wedge \neg(a\Diamond ab^k))$$

$$[2] \quad a\Diamond ab \wedge \neg(a\Diamond ab^k)) \quad (1, T_7)$$

$$[3] \quad a\Diamond ab \quad (2, T_5)$$

$$[4] \quad \neg(a\Diamond ab^k)) \quad (2, T_5)$$

$$[5] \quad ab\Diamond a \quad (3, T_3)$$

$$[6] \quad \neg(ab^k\Diamond a) \quad (4, T_4)$$

$$[7] \quad \neg(ab^{k-1}\Diamond a) \ (5, 6, T_1)$$

$$\vdots$$

$$[k+5] \quad \neg(ab\Diamond a) \quad (5, k+4, T_1)$$

$$[k+6] \quad \bot \quad (5, k+5, T_8)$$

Fig. 6. Tableau Example

the tableau rules are sound i.e., if a tableau started with $\neg\varphi$ closes, then φ is a tautology. The dual implication, if φ is a tautology then every tableau started with $\neg\varphi$ will eventually close, will be dealt with in the following.

Note that the rules in Figure 5 do not cover the entire **pAL** syntax from Figure 3: the atomic propositions of the form $x \leq y$ are not considered. The reason is that such propositions trivially evaluate to either true or false and could be eliminated from a formula a priori. For completeness, rules for the prefix test are given in [3].

The rest of this section is concerned with proving that the tableau method is both complete and effective. To handle the tableau rules in an uniform way, we use the unified notation of [24]: let an α-rule be one of the rules $(T_{1...5})$ and β-rule be the rule (T_6). We denote the premises of a R-rule by $R_1 \ldots R_n$ and its conclusions by $\widetilde{R}_1, \ldots \widetilde{R}_m$, where $R = \alpha, \beta$.

Definition 2. *A set of formulas Γ is said to be* downward closed *if and only if it respects the following conditions:*

- *for no $x, y \in \Sigma^+$, we have $x\Diamond y, \neg(x\Diamond y) \in \Gamma$,*
- *for any α-rule, if $\alpha_1, \ldots, \alpha_n \in \Gamma$, then $\widetilde{\alpha}_1, \ldots \widetilde{\alpha}_m \in \Gamma$,*
- *for any β-rule, if $\beta_1, \ldots, \beta_n \in \Gamma$, then either $\widetilde{\beta}_1 \in S$ or $\ldots$ or $\widetilde{\beta}_m \in \Gamma$.*

A tableau branch is said to be *complete* if no more rules can be applied to expand it. A tableau is said to be complete if and only if each of its branches is complete. It is manifest that an open complete tableau branch is a downward closed set. The following technical lemma is key to showing satisfiability of downward closed sets. We recall here the definition of the $\approx_\Gamma$ relation from Lemma 3. The following theorem is the main result of this section.

Lemma 5. *For any downward closed set of formulas Γ, $\neg(x\Diamond y) \in \Gamma$ implies $x \not\approx_\Gamma y$.*

Theorem 4. *Any downward closed set of formulas containing a finite number of alias propositions is satisfiable.*

The proof of the above theorem uses the model construction technique from Lemma 3. The same method can be moreover used to derive a counterexample of a non-valid formula, starting from an open tableau branch. Before stating our completeness result for the tableau method, let us show that the method is effective. That is, each tableau procedure started with a finite formula as the root node, using the rules from Figure 5, eventually terminates.

Lemma 6. *The tableau of a finite formula is finite.*

Besides showing termination of the tableau procedure, the above lemma, together with Theorem 4 ensure that the tableau approach is complete.

Corollary 1. *If a formula φ is a tautology then every complete tableau starting with $\neg\varphi$ eventually closes.*

In the light of the decidability result concerning **pAL**, we are next investigating the time complexity of the above satisfiability problem, and find that it is NP-complete. The proof uses Lemma 3 to show that satisfiability is in NP, and a reduction from the satisfiability problem for a set of boolean clauses with three literals (3-SAT) to show NP-hardness.

Theorem 5. *The satisfiability problem for* **pAL** *is NP-complete.*

5   An Effective Program Logic

In this section we demonstrate the possibility of using **pAL** as a weakest precondition calculus for imperative programs with destructive updating. Otherwise stated, we show that **pAL** is closed under applications of the weakest preconditions predicate transformers. Intuitivelly, this is a consequence of the fact that **pAL** formulas refer to finite portions of the heap, and also that straight-line statements affect bounded regions of the heap. Our proof of closure is constructive i.e., we define weakest preconditions in terms as predicate transformers directly on **pAL**. This is achieved by means of the sound and complete program logic defined on top of **wAL** [2]. Moreover, soundness and completness of the **pAL** weakest precondition axioms are consequences of soundness and completness in the case of **wAL**.

We consider a simple imperative language consisting of the following three atomics statements. Note that the statements of most object-oriented languages can be precompiled in this form, possibly by introducing fresh temporary variables:

$$Stmnt := uv = \text{null} \mid uv = \text{new} \mid uv = w \quad (\text{where } uv \not\preceq w)$$

Here $v, w \in \Sigma$ denote pointer variables, and $u \in \Sigma^*$ is a (possibly empty) dereferencing path. The first statement resets the v field of the object pointed to by u, if $u \neq \epsilon$, or the v top-level variable, otherwise. This may cause the builtin garbage collector recall all non-reachable objects. The second statement allocates a fresh object for further uses, and the third statement assigns its left-hand side the object pointed to by the right-hand side variable. The syntactic constraint that comes with the last statement is due to the following technical problem. The semantics of the assignment is given as the composition of two primitive operations: first one removes the v arc from the node pointed to by u, and then it assigns it to w. If $uv \leq w$ and there are no other paths to the cell pointed to by w, the garbage collection caused by the first operation removes the unreachable cell before the assignment is finished. The requirement $uv \not\leq w$ is however sufficient to ensure that, in practice, this situation never occurs.

The axiomatic semantics of this language has been introduced in [2], by defining a weakest precondition operator $\widetilde{pre}$ on **wAL** formulas, and is briefly recalled here. For any transition relation over a sequence of statements $\omega \in Stmnt^+$, $\widetilde{pre}$ distributes over conjunction and universal quantification i.e., $\widetilde{pre}(\omega, \varphi_1 \wedge \varphi_2) = \widetilde{pre}(\omega, \varphi_1) \wedge \widetilde{pre}(\omega, \varphi_2)$ and $\widetilde{pre}(\omega, \forall X . \varphi) = \forall X . \widetilde{pre}(\omega, \varphi)$. For total transition relations we have $\widetilde{pre}(\omega, \varphi) \Rightarrow \neg\widetilde{pre}(\omega, \neg\varphi)$. If, moreover, the transition relation is total and deterministic, we have that $\widetilde{pre}$ is its own dual i.e., $\widetilde{pre}(\omega, \varphi) \Leftrightarrow \neg\widetilde{pre}(\omega, \neg\varphi)$. In the latter case, $\widetilde{pre}$ distributes over disjunction and existential quantification too. These properties of $\widetilde{pre}$ for total, deterministic programs allow us to define general inference rules for the precondition inductively on the structure of the postcondition. In particular, it is sufficient to define preconditions only for modalities, the rest of the atomic propositions in **wAL** being pure i.e., having model-independent denotations. Figure 7 (upper part) gives the precondition of primitive storeless operations *add*, *rem* and *new* for arbitrary modalities. This is generalized to the statements defined in the previous (lower part).

$$\{\exists X. X \setminus Sv\Sigma^{\emptyset} = T \wedge \langle X \rangle (\sigma \setminus Sv\Sigma^{\emptyset})\} \ \mathbf{rem(S,v)} \ \{\langle T \rangle \sigma\}$$
$$\{\exists X. \chi^v(S, T, X) = U \wedge \bigvee\nolimits_{i=1,2} \psi_i^{\sigma,\sigma}(X, X)\} \ \mathbf{add(S,v,T)} \ \{\langle U \rangle \sigma\}$$

$$\text{where } \chi^v(S, T, X) \triangleq X \cup Sv((T^{-1}S)v)^{\emptyset} (T^{-1}X)$$
$$\psi_1^{x,y}(X, Y) \triangleq Sv((T^{-1}S)v)^{\emptyset} (T^{-1}X) \cap x = \emptyset \wedge \langle Y \rangle y$$
$$\psi_2^{x,y}(X, Y) \triangleq Sv((T^{-1}S)v)^{\emptyset} (T^{-1}X) \cap x \neq \emptyset \wedge \langle Y \rangle \Sigma^{\emptyset} \qquad (3)$$

$$\{(T = Sv \wedge \sigma \cap Sv \neq \emptyset) \vee \langle T \rangle \sigma\} \ \mathbf{new(S,v)} \ \{\langle T \rangle \sigma\}$$

$$\{\exists S. \langle S \rangle u \wedge \widetilde{pre}(rem(S, v), \varphi)\} \ \mathbf{uv = null} \ \{\varphi\}$$
$$\{\exists S. \langle S \rangle u \wedge \widetilde{pre}(rem(S, v), \widetilde{pre}(new(S, v), \varphi))\} \ \mathbf{uv = new} \ \{\varphi\}$$
$$\{\exists S \exists T. \langle S \rangle u \wedge \langle T \rangle w \wedge \widetilde{pre}(rem(S, v), \widetilde{pre}(add(S, v, T), \varphi))\} \ \mathbf{uv = w} \ \{\varphi\}$$

Fig. 7. wAL Weakest Preconditions

For the rest of this section, let $\sigma, \tau, \theta, u, v, w$ denote constant words, and x, y, z denote variables ranging over words. We introduce the following notation: $\exists x \leq \sigma . \varphi(x) \triangleq \bigvee_{\tau \in Pref(\sigma)} \varphi(\tau)$. Since σ is a finite word, so is the formula on the right. Figure 8 introduces a number of syntactic shorthands, providing context-dependent translations from **wAL** to **pAL** for them. That is, we do not translate the shorthands individually, but rather in an existentially closed context.

Definition	wAL	pAL
$\alpha_\sigma \; : \; \sigma \in Sv\Sigma^\partial$	$\exists S \; . \; \langle S\rangle u \wedge \alpha_\sigma$	$\exists x \leq \sigma \; . \; x\Diamond u \wedge xv \leq \sigma$
	$\exists S \; . \; \langle S\rangle u \wedge \neg\alpha_\sigma$	$u\Diamond u \wedge \neg(\exists x \leq \sigma \; . \; x\Diamond u \wedge xv \leq \sigma)$
$\beta_\sigma \; : \; \sigma \in Sv(T^{-1}X)$	$\exists S \exists T \exists X \; . \; \langle S\rangle u \wedge \langle T\rangle w \wedge$ $\langle X\rangle\theta \wedge \beta_\sigma$	$\exists x \leq \sigma \; . \; x\Diamond u \wedge xv \leq \sigma \wedge$ $w((xv)^{-1}\sigma)\Diamond\theta$
	$\exists S \exists T \exists X \; . \; \langle S\rangle u \wedge \langle T\rangle w \wedge$ $\langle X\rangle\theta \wedge \neg\beta_\sigma$	$u\Diamond u \wedge w\Diamond w \wedge \theta\Diamond\theta \wedge$ $\neg(\exists x \leq \sigma \; . \; x\Diamond u \wedge xv \leq \sigma \wedge$ $w((xv)^{-1}\sigma)\Diamond\theta)$
$\gamma_\sigma \; : \; \sigma \in Sv(T^{-1}S)v\Sigma^\partial$	$\exists S \exists T \; . \; \langle S\rangle u \wedge \langle T\rangle w \wedge \gamma_\sigma$	$\exists x \leq \sigma \; \exists y \leq (xv)^{-1}\sigma \; . \; x\Diamond u \wedge$ $xv \leq \sigma \wedge wy\Diamond u \wedge yv \leq (xv)^{-1}\sigma$
	$\exists S \exists T \; . \; \langle S\rangle u \wedge \langle T\rangle w \wedge \neg\gamma_\sigma$	$u\Diamond u \wedge w\Diamond w \wedge$ $\neg(\exists x \leq \sigma \; \exists y \leq (xv)^{-1}\sigma \; . \; x\Diamond u \wedge$ $xv \leq \sigma \wedge wy\Diamond u \wedge yv \leq (xv)^{-1}\sigma)$

Fig. 8. wAL to pAL translation shorthands

We assert that all translations defined in Figure 8 preserve logical equivalence. To convince ourselves of this fact, let us perform the step-by-step derivation for the positive form of α_σ. The rest of the formulas are translated along the same lines.

$$\exists S \; . \; \langle S\rangle u \wedge \alpha_\sigma \equiv \exists S \; . \; \langle S\rangle u \wedge \sigma \in Sv\Sigma^* \iff$$
$$\exists S \; . \; \exists x \leq \sigma \; . \; \langle S\rangle u \wedge \langle S\rangle x \wedge xv \leq \sigma \iff \exists x \leq \sigma \; . \; x\Diamond u \wedge xv \leq \sigma$$

The goal of this section is to prove that the logic **pAL** is expressive enough to characterize the destructive updating program statements considered in the previous. The following theorem captures the result.

Theorem 6. *For any sequence of statements $\omega \in Stmnt^*$ and any formula $\varphi \in \mathbf{pAL}[\Sigma]$, we have $\widetilde{pre}(\omega, \varphi) \in \mathbf{pAL}[\Sigma]$.*

The proof proceeds by deriving the weakest precondition for an arbitrary alias proposition $\sigma\Diamond\tau$ (equivalently written in **wAL** using the embedding rule) i.e., applying the rules in Figure 7. The result is then translated back from **wAL** to **pAL** using the shorthands from Figure 8. Then we can extend the result to arbitrary post-conditions using the distributivity properties for $\widetilde{pre}$, and to arbitrary sequences of statements by induction on the length of the sequence.

It is important to notice that the translations from **pAL** to **wAL** and back are logical equivalences. Since the $\widetilde{pre}$ operators defined on **wAL** formulas are sound and complete, according to the development in [2], we can infer the existence of a sound and complete weakest precondition calculus also for **pAL**.

6   Conclusions and Future Work

This paper concerns a deductive verification method for aliasing properties in imperative programming languages with destructive updating. Starting from previous work on storeless semantics and alias logic with a weakest precondition calculus **wAL**, we show that the satisfiability problem is undecidable but recursively enumerable. Next, we focus on a decidable subset **pAL** that allows to express sound and complete weakest preconditions. The kind of properties expressible in this logic are related to pointer aliasing, but also arbitrary finite heaps can be defined. We give two sound and complete proof systems for **pAL**, one based on natural deduction, and another based on analytic tableaux. The satisfiability problem for **pAL** is shown to be NP-complete. A tool based on the **pAL** framework is planned in the near future.

The main question related to the existence of a decidable program logic that can express non-trivial shape properties of heap is not fully answered. Although undecidable, the **wAL** logic offers a reach framework in which one can define decidable fragments having complete weakest precondition calculi. One such example is **pAL**. A still open question is the existence of a fragment of **wAL** that encompasses **pAL**, in which one can express properties such as reachability, circularity, etc. One such extension, called **kAL**, is currently under investigation. This logic is obtained from **pAL**, by considering words (over the heap alphabet) with integer counters (parameters indicating the repetition of a finite subword) and first order quantification over the counters. In this way we can express for instance the existence of an unbounded *next*-path between two pointers *head* and *tail*: $\exists k . head.\{next\}^k \diamond tail$, a property that is not expressible in **pAL**. We plan an extensive study of this logic, in order to cover both aspects of satisfiability and expressiveness.

References

1. Benedikt, M., Reps, T., and Sagiv, M.: A decidable logic for describing linked data structures. European Symposium on Programming, (1999) LNCS, Vol. 1576, 2–19.
2. M. Bozga, R. Iosif and Y. Lakhnech: Storeless Semantics and Alias Logic. Proc. ACM SIGPLAN 2003 Workshop on Partial Evaluation and Semantics Based Program Manipulation, 55 – 65.
3. M. Bozga, R. Iosif and Y. Lakhnech: On Logics of Aliasing. Technical Report TR-2004-4, VERIMAG http://www-verimag.imag.fr/~iosif/TR-2004-4.ps
4. M. Bozga, R. Iosif: On Model Checking Generic Topologies. Technical Report TR-2004-10, VERIMAG http://www-verimag.imag.fr/~iosif/TR-2004-10.ps
5. C. Calcagno, H. Yang and P.W. O'Hearn: Computability and Complexity Results for a Spatial Assertion Language for Data Structures. In Foundations of Software Technology and Theoretical Computer Science, LNCS, Volume 2245 (2001), 108–119
6. C. Calcagno, L. Cardelli, and A. Gordon: Deciding Validity in a Spatial Logic of Trees. In ACM Workshop on Types in Language Design and Implementation (2003) 62–73
7. B. Courcelle: The expression of graph properties and graph transformations in monadic second-order logic, Chapter 5 of the "Handbook of graph grammars and computing by graph transformations, Vol. 1 : Foundations" (1997) 313–400
8. A. Deutsch: A storeless model of aliasing and its abstractions using finite representations of right-regular equivalence relations. In Proceedings of the IEEE 1992 Conference on Computer Languages (1992) 2–13

9. H.D Ebbinghaus and J. Flum: Finite Model Theory. Springer-Verlag (1999)
10. R.W. Floyd: Assigning meaning to programs, Proc. Symposium on Applied Mathematics, American Mathematical Society, 1967, Vol. 1, 19–32.
11. D. Galmiche and D. Mery: Semantic Labelled Tableaux for propositional BI (without bottom). Journal of Logic and Computation, vol. 13, n. 5 (2003)
12. C.A.R Hoare and He Jifeng: A Trace Model for Pointers and Objects. In Proc. ECOOP'99, LNCS, Vol. 1628 (1999) 1–18
13. S. Ishtiaq and P. O'Hearn: BI as an Assertion Language for Mutable Data Structures. Proc. of 28th ACM-SIGPLAN Symposium on Principles of Programming Languages (2001)
14. H. B. M. Jonkers. Abstract Storage Structures. Algorithmic Languages, North-Holland (1981) 321–343
15. N. Klarlund and M. I. Schwartzbach: Graphs and Decidable Transductions Based on Edge Constraints, In Proc. 19th Colloquium on Trees and Algebra in Programming, LNCS, Volume 787 (1994) 187–201
16. N. Klarlund and M. I. Schwartzbach: Graph Types. In Proc. 20th Annual Symposium on Principles of Programming Languages (1993) 196–205
17. A. Moeller and M. I. Schwartzbach: The Pointer Assertion Logic Engine. In Proc. ACM SIGPLAN Conference on Programming Languages Design and Implementation, (2001).
18. P.W. O'Hearn and D.J. Pym: The Logic of Bunched Implications. Bulletin of Symbolic Logic, 5(2) (1999) 215–244
19. P.W. O'Hearn, J.C. Reynolds and H. Yang: Local reasoning about programs that alter data structures. Computer Science Logic, LNCS, Volume 2142 (2001) 1–19
20. M. O. Rabin: Decidability of second order theories and automata on infinite trees, Trans. Amer. Math. Soc. vol 141 (1969)
21. G. Ramalingam: The Undecidability of Aliasing. ACM Transactions on Programming Languages and Systems, Vol 16, No 5 (1994) 1467–1471.
22. John C. Reynolds. Separation Logic: A Logic for Shared Mutable Data Structures. Proc 17th IEEE Symposium on Logic in Computer Science (2002)
23. M. Sagiv, M., T. Reps and R. Wilhelm: Parametric Shape Analysis via 3-Valued Logic. ACM Transactions on Programming Languages and Systems, Vol 24, No 3 (2002), 217–298
24. R. M. Smullyan: First-Order Logic. Dover Publications (1993)
25. D. van Dalen: Logic and Structure. Springer-Verlag (1997)

Generalized Records and Spatial Conjunction in Role Logic*

Viktor Kuncak and Martin Rinard

MIT Computer Science and Artificial Intelligence Laboratory
{vkuncak,rinard}@csail.mit.edu

Abstract. Role logic is a notation for describing properties of relational structures in shape analysis, databases and knowledge bases. A natural fragment of role logic corresponds to two-variable logic with counting and is therefore decidable.

In this paper, we show how to use role logic to describe open and closed records, as well as the dual of records, inverse records. We observe that the spatial conjunction operation of separation logic naturally models record concatenation. Moreover, we show how to eliminate the spatial conjunction of formulas of quantifier depth one in first-order logic with counting. As a result, allowing spatial conjunction of formulas of quantifier depth one preserves the decidability of two-variable logic with counting. This result applies to the two-variable role logic fragment as well.

The resulting logic smoothly integrates type system and predicate calculus notation and can be viewed as a natural generalization of the notation for constraints arising in role analysis and similar shape analysis approaches.

Keywords: Records, Shape Analysis, Static Analysis, Program Verification, Two-Variable Logic with Counting, Description Logic, Types

1 Introduction

In [22] we introduced *role logic*, a notation for describing properties of relational structures that arise in shape analysis, databases and knowledge bases. The role logic notation aims to combine the simplicity of role declarations [19] and the well-established first-order logic. The use of implicit arguments and syntactic sugar of role logic supports easy and concise expression of common idioms for describing data structures with mutable references and makes role logic attractive as a generalization of type systems in imperative languages, without sacrificing the expressiveness of a specification language based on first-order logic.

The decidability properties of role logic make it appropriate for communicating information to static analysis tools that go beyond simple type checkers. In [22, Section 4] we establish the decidability of the fragment RL^2 of role logic by exhibiting a correspondence with two-variable logic with counting C^2, which was

---

* This research was supported in part by DARPA Contract F33615-00-C-1692, NSF Grant CCR00-86154, NSF Grant CCR00-63513, and the Singapore-MIT Alliance.

R. Giacobazzi (Ed.): SAS 2004, LNCS 3148, pp. 361–376, 2004.

shown decidable in [12]. The fragment RL^2 is closed under all boolean operations, generalizes boolean shape analysis constraints [23] of shape analysis [34, 38] and generalizes the non-transitive constraints of role analysis [19].

Generalized Records in Role Logic. In this paper we give a systematic account of the field and slot declarations of role analysis [19] by introducing a set of role logic shorthands that allows concise description of records. Our basic idea is to generalize types to unary predicates on objects. Some of the aspects of our notion of records that indicate its generality are: **1)** We allow building new records by taking the conjunction, disjunction, or negation of records. **2)** In our notation, a record indicates a property of an object at a particular program point; objects can satisfy different record specifications at different program points. As a result, our records can express typestate changes such as object initialization [10, 35] and more general changes in relationships between objects such as movements of objects between data structures [19, 34]. **3)** We allow *inverse records* as a dual of records that specify incoming edges of an object in the graph of objects representing program heap. Inverse records allow the specification of aliasing properties of objects, generalizing unique pointers. Inverse records enable the convenient specification of movements of objects that participate in multiple data structures. **4)** We allow the specification of both open and closed records. Closed records specify a complete set of outgoing and incoming edges of an object. Open records leave certain edges unspecified, which allows orthogonal data structures to be specified independently and then combined using logical conjunction. **5)** We allow the concatenation of generalized records using a form of spatial conjunction of separation logic, while remaining within the decidable fragment of two-variable role logic.

Separation Logic. Separation logic [16, 33] is a promising approach for specifying properties of programs in the presence of mutable data structures. One of the main uses of separation logic in previous approaches is dealing with frame conditions [5, 16]. In contrast, our paper identifies another use of spatial logic: expressing record concatenation. Although our approach is based on essentially same logical operation of spatial conjunction, our use of spatial conjunction for records is more local, because it applies to the descriptions of the neighborhood of an object.

To remain within the decidable fragment of role logic, we give in Section 7 a construction that eliminates spatial conjunction when it connects formulas of quantifier depth one. This construction also illustrates that spatial conjunction is useful for reasoning about counting stars [12] of the two-variable logic with counting C^2. To our knowledge, this is the first result that combines two-variable logic with counting and a form of spatial conjunction.

Using the Resulting Logic. We can use specifications written in our notation to describe properties of objects and relations between objects in programs with dynamically allocated data structures. These specifications can act as assertions, preconditions, postconditions, loop invariants or data structure invariants [19, 22, 26]. By selecting a finite-height lattice of properties for a given program fragment, abstract interpretation [9] can be used to synthesize proper-

ties of objects at intermediate program points [2,3,14,19,34,37,39]. Decidability
and closure properties of our notation are essential for the completeness and
predictability of the resulting static analysis [24].

Outline and Contributions. Section 2 reviews the syntax and the semantics
of role logic [22]. Section 3 defines spatial conjunction in role logic and identifies its novel use: describing record concatenation. Sections 4 and 5 show how
to use spatial conjunction in role logic to describe a generalization of records.
These generalizations are useful for expressing properties of objects and memory cells in imperative programs. Section 6 demonstrates that our notation is a
generalization of local constraints arising in role analysis [19] by giving a natural
embedding of role constraints into our notation. Section 7 shows how to eliminate the spatial conjunction connective ⊛ from a spatial conjunction $F_1 ⊛ F_2$ of
two formulas F_1 and F_2 when F_1 and F_2 have no nested counting quantifiers;
this is the core technical result of this paper. As a result, we obtain a decidable
notation for generalized records that supports record concatenation.

2   A Decidable Two-Variable Role Logic RL^2

Figure 1 presents the two-variable role logic RL^2 [22]. We proved in [22] that RL^2
has the same expressive power as the two-variable logic with counting C^2. The
logic C^2 is a first-order logic 1) extended with counting quantifiers $\exists^{\geq k} x.F(x)$,
saying that there are at least k elements x satisfying formula $F(x)$ for some
constant k, and 2) restricted to allow only two variable names x, y in formulas.
An example formula in two-variable logic with counting is

$$\forall x.A(x) \Rightarrow (\forall y.f(x,y) \Rightarrow \exists^{=1} x.\, g(x,y)) \tag{1}$$

The formula (1) means that all nodes that satisfy $A(x)$ point along the field f
to nodes that have exactly one incoming g edge. Note that the variables x and y
may be reused via quantifier nesting, and that formulas of the form $\exists^{=k} x.\, F(x)$
and $\exists^{\leq k} x.\, F(x)$ are expressible as boolean combinations of formulas of the form
$\exists^{\geq k} x.\, F(x)$. The logic C^2 was shown decidable in [12] and the complexity for
the C_1^2 fragment of C^2 (with counting up to one) was established in [30]. We can
view role logic as a variable-free version of C^2. Variable-free logical notations are
attractive as generalizations of type systems because traditional type systems
are often variable-free. The formula (1) can be written in role logic as $[A \Rightarrow$
$[f \Rightarrow \mathsf{card}^{\geq 1}{\sim}g]]$ where the construct $[F]$ is a shorthand for $\neg\mathsf{card}^{\geq 1}\neg F$ and
corresponds to the universal quantifier. The expression ${\sim}g$ denotes the inverse
of relation g.

In [22] we show how to perform static analysis with RL^2 by observing that
straight-line code with procedure invocations can be encoded in RL^2. When
loop invariants and procedure specifications are expressed in RL^2, the resulting
verification conditions belong to RL^2 and can be discharged using a decision procedure. The analysis of sequences of non-deterministic actions, such as partially
specified procedure calls, is possible because RL^2 has a decision procedure that
is parametric with respect to the vocabulary of sets and relations, which means

$$F ::= A \mid f \mid \mathsf{EQ} \mid F_1 \wedge F_2 \mid \neg F \mid F^0 \mid \sim F \mid \mathsf{card}^{\geq k} F$$

$d \in D$ — domain of first-order structure (set of all objects)

$A \in \mathcal{A}$ — unary predicates (sets)

$f \in \mathcal{F}$ — binary predicates (relations)

$e :: (\{1,2\} \to D) \cup (\mathcal{A} \to D \to \mathsf{bool}) \cup (\mathcal{F} \to D^2 \to \mathsf{bool})$

$$[\![A]\!]e = e\,A(e\,1) \qquad\qquad [\![f]\!]e = e\,f(e\,2, e\,1)$$

$$[\![\mathsf{EQ}]\!]e = (e\,2) = (e\,1)$$

$$[\![F_1 \wedge F_2]\!]e = ([\![F_1]\!]e) \wedge ([\![F_2]\!]e) \qquad [\![\neg F]\!]e = \neg([\![F]\!]e)$$

$$[\![F^0]\!]e = [\![F]\!](e[1 \mapsto (e\,2)]) \qquad [\![\sim F]\!]e = [\![F]\!](e[1 \mapsto (e\,2), 2 \mapsto (e\,1)])$$

$$[\![\mathsf{card}^{\geq k} F]\!]e = |\{d \in D \mid [\![F]\!](e[1 \mapsto d, 2 \mapsto (e\,1)])\}| \geq k$$

$$F_1 \vee F_2 \equiv \neg(\neg F_1 \wedge \neg F_2) \qquad F_1 \Rightarrow F_2 \equiv \neg F_1 \vee F_2$$

Fig. 1. The Syntax and the Semantics of RL^2

that the intermediate program states can be modelled by introducing a fresh copy of the state vocabulary for each program point. Moreover, given a family of abstraction predicates [34] expressible in RL^2, the techniques of [24, 39] can be used to synthesize loop invariants.

In this paper, we focus on the use of role logic to describe generalized records. The results of this paper further demonstrate the expressive power of RL^2, and the appropriateness of RL^2 as the foundation of both the constraints supplied by the developer, and the constraints synthesized by a static analysis.

3   Spatial Conjunction

This section introduces our notion of spatial conjunction $\circledast$. To motivate our use of spatial conjunction, we first illustrate how role logic supports the description of simple properties of objects in a concise way.

Example 1. The formula $[f \Rightarrow A]$ is true for an object whose every f-field points to an A object, the formula $[g \Rightarrow B]$ means that every g-field points to a B object, so $[f \Rightarrow A] \wedge [g \Rightarrow B]$ denotes the objects that have both f pointing to an A object and g pointing to a B object. Such specification is as concise as the following Java class declaration class C { A f; B g; }.

Example 1 illustrates how the presence of conjunction $\wedge$ in role logic enables the combination of orthogonal properties such as constraints on distinct fields. However, not all properties naturally compose using conjunction.

Example 2. Consider a program that contains three fields, modelled as binary relations f, g, h. The formula $P_f \equiv (\mathsf{card}^{=1} f) \wedge (\mathsf{card}^{=0}(g \vee h))$ means that the object has only one outgoing f-edge and no other edges. The formula $P_g \equiv$

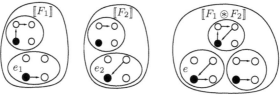

$\llbracket F_1 \circledast F_2 \rrbracket e = \exists e_1, e_2. \text{ split } e\,[e_1\,e_2] \ \wedge \ \llbracket F_1 \rrbracket e_1 \wedge \llbracket F_2 \rrbracket e_2$
$\text{split } e\,[e_1\,e_2] =$

$\quad \forall A \in \mathcal{A}. \ \forall d \in D. \ (e\,A)\,d \iff (e_1\,A)\,d \vee (e_2\,A)\,d \ \wedge \ \neg((e_1\,A)\,d \wedge (e_2\,A)\,d) \ \wedge$

$\quad \forall f \in \mathcal{F}. \ \forall d_1, d_2 \in D.$

$\quad\quad e\,f\,(d_1, d_2) \iff (e_1\,f\,(d_1, d_2) \vee e_2\,f\,(d_1, d_2)) \ \wedge \ \neg(e_1\,f\,(d_1, d_2) \wedge e_2\,f\,(d_1, d_2))$

$\text{emp} \ \equiv \ [\![\,\bigwedge_{A \Downarrow A} \neg A \ \wedge \ \bigwedge_{f \Downarrow F} \neg f\,]\!]$

priority: $\wedge$ binds strongest, then $\circledast$, then $\vee$; $\quad F \approx G$ means $\forall e. \llbracket F \rrbracket e = \llbracket G \rrbracket e$

$(F_1 \circledast F_2) \circledast F_3 \ \approx \ F_1 \circledast (F_2 \circledast F_3) \quad\quad\quad F \circledast \text{emp} \ \approx \ \text{emp} \circledast F \ \approx \ F$

$F_1 \circledast F_2 \ \approx \ F_2 \circledast F_1 \quad\quad\quad\quad\quad\quad\quad F_1 \circledast (F_2 \vee F_3) \ \approx \ F_1 \circledast F_2 \ \vee \ F_1 \circledast F_3$

Fig. 2. Semantics and Properties of Spatial Conjunction $\circledast$

$(\text{card}^{=1} g) \wedge (\text{card}^{=0}(f \vee h))$ means that the object has only one outgoing g-edge and no other edges. If we "physically join" the two records, each of which has one field, we obtain a record that has two fields, and is described by the formula $P_{fg} \ \equiv \ (\text{card}^{=1} f) \wedge (\text{card}^{=1} g) \wedge (\text{card}^{=0} h)$. Note that it is *not* the case that $P_{fg} \approx P_f \wedge P_g$. In fact, no boolean combination of P_f and P_g yields P_{fg}.

Example 2 prompts the question: is there an operation that allows joining specifications that will allow us to combine P_f and P_g into P_{fg}? Moreover, can we define such an operation on records viewed as arbitrary formulas in role logic?

It turns out that there is a natural way to describe the set of models of formula P_{fg} in Example 2 as the result of "physically merging" the edges (relations) of the models of P_f and the models of P_g. The merging of disjoint models of formulas is the idea behind the definition of spatial conjunction $\circledast$ in Figure 2. The predicate $(\text{split } e\,[e_1\,e_2])$ is true iff the relations of the model (environment) e can be split into e_1 and e_2. The idea of splitting is that each unary relation $(e\,A)$ is a disjoint union of relations $(e_1\,A)$ and $(e_2\,A)$, and similarly each binary relation $(e\,f)$ is a disjoint union of relations $(e_1\,f)$ and $(e_2\,f)$. For $\text{split } e\,[e_1\,e_2]$ we also require that the domain D of objects is the same in all of e_1, e_2, and e. If we consider models e as graphs, then our notion of spatial conjunction keeps a fixed set of nodes, and splits the edges of the graph[1], as illustrated in Figure 2. The notion of splitting generalizes to splitting into any number of environments. Having introduced spatial conjunction $\circledast$, we observe that for P_f, P_g, and P_{fg} of Example 2, we simply have $P_{fg} = P_f \circledast P_g$.

---

[1] See [22, Page 6] for a comparison of our notion of spatial conjunction with [16].

4   Field Complement

As a step towards a record calculus in role logic, this section introduces the notion of a *field complement*, which makes it easier to describe records in role logic.

Example 3. Consider the formula $P_f \equiv (\mathsf{card}^{=1} f) \wedge (\mathsf{card}^{=0}(g \vee h))$ from Example 2, stating the property that an object has only one outgoing f-edge and *no other edges*. Property P_f has little to do with g or h, yet g and h explicitly occur in P_f. Moreover, we need to know the entire set of relations in the language to write P_f; if the language contains an additional field i, the property P_f would become $P_f \equiv (\mathsf{card}^{=1} f) \wedge (\mathsf{card}^{=0}(g \vee h \vee i))$. Note also that $\neg f$ is *not* the same as $g \vee h \vee i$, because $\neg f$ computes the complement of the value of the relation f with respect to the universal relation D^2, whereas $g \vee h \vee i$ is the union of all relations other than f.

To address the notational problem illustrated in Example 3, we introduce the symbol edges, which denotes the union of all binary relations, formally $\mathsf{edges} \equiv \bigvee_g g$, and the notation $-f$ (*field complement* of f), which denotes the union of all relations other than f, formally $-f \equiv \bigvee_{g \neq f} g$. This additional notation allows us to avoid explicitly listing all fields in the language when stating properties like P_f. Formula P_f from Example 3 can be written as $P_f \equiv (\mathsf{card}^{=1} f) \wedge (\mathsf{card}^{=0} - f)$, which mentions only f. Even when the language is extended with additional relations, P_f still denotes the intended property. Similarly, to denote the property of an object that has outgoing fields given by P_f and has no incoming fields, we use the predicate $P_f \wedge \mathsf{card}^{=0} \sim\!\mathsf{edges}$.

5   Records and Inverse Records

In this section we use role logic with spatial conjunction and field complement from Section 4 to introduce a notation for records and inverse records.

$$\text{multifield: } f \xrightarrow{0} A \equiv \mathsf{card}^{=0}(-f \vee (f \wedge \neg A))$$

$$\text{field: } f \xrightarrow{s} A \equiv \mathsf{card}^s(A \wedge f) \wedge f \xrightarrow{0} A$$
$$s \text{ of the form } =k, \leq k, \text{ or } \geq k, \text{ for } k \in \{0, 1, 2, \ldots\}$$

$$\text{multislot: } A \xleftarrow{0} f \equiv \mathsf{card}^{=0}(\sim\!-f \vee (\sim\!f \wedge \neg A))$$

$$\text{slot: } A \xleftarrow{s} f \equiv \mathsf{card}^s(A \wedge \sim\!f) \wedge A \xleftarrow{0} f$$
$$s \text{ of the form } =k, \leq k, \text{ or } \geq k, \text{ for } k \in \{0, 1, 2, \ldots\}$$

Fig. 3. Record Notation

The notation for records and inverse records is presented in Figure 3. A *multifield* predicate $f \xrightarrow{*} A$ is true iff the object has any number of outgoing f-edges terminating at A, and no other edges. Dually, a *multislot* predicate $A \xleftarrow{*} f$ is true iff the object has any number of incoming f-edges originating from A, and no other edges. We also allow notation $f \xrightarrow{s} A$ where s is an expression of the form $=k$, $\leq k$, or $\geq k$. This notation gives a bound on the number of outgoing edges, and implies that there are no other outgoing edges. We similarly introduce $A \xleftarrow{s} f$. A *closed record* is a spatial conjunction of fields and multifields. An *open record* is a spatial conjunction of a closed record with True. While a closed record allows only the listed fields, an open record allows any number of additional fields. Inverse records are dual to records, and we similarly distinguish open and closed inverse records. We abbreviate $f \xrightarrow{=1} A$ by $f \to A$ and $A \xleftarrow{=1} f$ by $A \leftarrow f$.

Example 4. To describe a closed record whose only fields are f and g where f-fields point to objects in the set A and g-fields point to objects in the set B, we use the predicate $P_1 \equiv f \to A \circledast g \to B$. The definition of P_1 lists all fields of the object. To specify an open record which certainly has fields f and g but may or may not have other fields, we write $P_2 \equiv f \to A \circledast g \to B \circledast \mathsf{True}$. Neither P_1 nor P_2 restrict incoming references of an object. To specify that the only incoming references of an object are from the field h, we conjoin P_2 with the closed inverse record consisting of a single multislot $\mathsf{True} \xleftarrow{*} h$, yielding the predicate $P_3 \equiv P_2 \wedge \mathsf{True} \xleftarrow{*} h$. To specify that an object has exactly one incoming reference, and that the incoming reference is from the h field and originates from an object belonging to the set C, we use $P_4 \equiv P_2 \wedge C \leftarrow h$. Note that specifications P_3 and P_4 go beyond most standard type systems in their ability to specify the incoming (in addition to the outgoing) references of objects.

6 Role Constraints

Role constraints were introduced in [18, 19]. In this section we show that role logic is a natural generalization of role constraints by giving a translation from role constraints to role logic. A logical view of role constraints is also suggested in [20, 21]. A role is a set of objects that satisfy a conjunction of the following four kinds of constraints: field constraints, slot constraints, identities, acyclicities. In this paper we show that role logic naturally models field constraints, slot constraints, and identities[2].

Roles Describing Complete Sets of Fields and Slots. Figure 4 shows the translation of role constraints [19, Section 3] into role logic formulas. The simplicity of the translation is a consequence of the notation for records that we have developed in this paper.

Simultaneous Roles. In object-oriented programs, objects may participate in multiple data structures. The idea of simultaneous roles [19, Section 7.2] is to associate one role for the participation of an object in one data structure. When the object participates in multiple data structures, the object plays multiple

---

[2] Acyclicities go beyond first-order logic because they involve non-local transitive closure properties.

roles. Role logic naturally models simultaneous roles: each role is a unary predicate, and if an object satisfies multiple roles, then it satisfies the conjunction of predicates. Figure 5 presents the translation of field and slot constraints of simultaneous roles into role logic. Whereas the roles of [19, Section 3] translate to closed records and closed inverse records, the simultaneous roles of [19, Section 7.2] translate specifications that are closer to open records and open inverse records.

$$\mathcal{C}[\![\text{fields } F; \text{ slots } S; \text{ identities } I]\!] = \mathcal{C}[\![\text{fields } F]\!] \wedge \mathcal{C}[\![\text{slots } S]\!] \wedge$$
$$[\![\text{identities } I]\!]$$

$$\mathcal{C}[\![\text{fields } f_1 : S_1, \ldots, f_n : S_n]\!] = f_1 \to S_1 \circledast \ldots \circledast f_n \to S_n$$
$$\mathcal{C}[\![\text{slots } S_1.f_1, \ldots, S_n.f_n]\!] = S_1 \leftarrow f_1 \circledast \ldots \circledast S_n \leftarrow f_n$$
$$[\![\text{identities } f_1.g_1, \ldots, f_n.g_n]\!] = \bigwedge_{i=1}^{n} [f_i \Rightarrow \sim g_i]$$

Fig. 4. Translation of Role Constraints [19] into Role Logic Formulas

$$\mathcal{O}[\![\text{fields } F; \text{ slots } S; \text{ identities } I]\!] = \mathcal{O}[\![\text{fields } F]\!] \wedge \mathcal{O}[\![\text{slots } S]\!] \wedge$$
$$[\![\text{identities } I]\!]$$

$$\mathcal{O}[\![\text{fields } f_1 : S_1, \ldots, f_n : S_n]\!] = \mathcal{C}[\![\text{fields } f_1 : S_1, \ldots, f_n : S_n]\!] \circledast \text{card}^{=0}(\bigvee_{i=1}^{n} f_i)$$
$$\mathcal{O}[\![g_1, \ldots, g_m \text{ slots } S_1.f_1, \ldots, S_n.f_n]\!] = \mathcal{C}[\![\text{slots } S_1.f_1, \ldots, S_n.f_n]\!] \circledast \text{card}^{=0}(\bigvee_{i=1}^{m} \sim g_i)$$

Fig. 5. Translation of Simultaneous Role Constraints [19, Section 7.2] into Role Logic Formulas

7   Eliminating Spatial Conjunction in $\mathbf{RL}^2$

Preserving the Decidability. Previous sections have demonstrated the usefulness of adding record concatenation in the form of spatial conjunction to our notation for generalized records. However, a key question remains: is the resulting extended notation decidable? In this section we give an affirmative answer to this question by showing how to compute the spatial conjunction for a large class of record specifications using the remaining logical operations.

Approach. Consider two formulas F_1 and F_2 in first-order logic with counting, where both F_1 and F_2 have quantifier depth one. An equivalent way of stating the condition on F_1 and F_2 is that there are no nested occurrences of quantifiers. (Note that we count one application of $\exists^{\geq k}x. P$ as one quantifier, regardless of the value k.) We show that, under these conditions, the spatial conjunction $F_1 \circledast F_2$ can be written as an equivalent formula F_3 where F_3 does not contain the spatial conjunction operation $\circledast$. The proof proceeds by writing formulas F_1, F_2 in a normal form, as a disjunction of counting stars [12], and showing that the spatial conjunction of counting stars is equivalent to a disjunction of counting stars. It follows that adding $\circledast$ to (full first-order or two-variable) logic with counting does not change the expressive power of that logic, provided that the operands of ⊛ have quantifier depth at most one. Here we allow F_1 and F_2 themselves to contain spatial conjunction, because we may eliminate spatial conjunction in F_1 and F_2 recursively. Applying these results to two-variable logic with counting C^2, we conclude that introducing into C^2 the spatial conjunction of formulas of quantifier depth one preserves the decidability of C^2. Furthermore, thanks to the translations between C^2 and RL^2 in [22], if we allow the spatial conjunction of RL^2 formulas with no nested card occurrences, we preserve the decidability of the logic RL^2. The formulas of the resulting logic are given by

$$F ::= A \mid f \mid \mathsf{EQ} \mid F_1 \wedge F_2 \mid \neg F \mid F^{\emptyset} \mid \sim F \mid \mathsf{card}^{\geq k} F$$
$$\mid F_1 \circledast F_2, \text{ if } F_1 \text{ and } F_2 \text{ have no nested card occurrences}$$

Note that record specifications in Figure 3 contain no nested card occurrences, so joining them using ⊛ yields formulas in the decidable fragment. Hence, in addition to quantifiers and boolean operations, the resulting logic supports a generalization of record concatenation, and is still decidable; this decidability property is what we show in the sequel. We present the sketch of the proof, see [25] for proof details and additional remarks.

7.1   Atomic Type Formulas

In this section we introduce classes of formulas that correspond to the model-theoretic notion of atomic type [29, Page 20]. We then introduce formulas that describe the notion of counting stars [12, 30]. We conclude this section with Proposition 9, which gives the normal form for formulas of quantifier depth one.

If $\mathcal{C} = C_1, \ldots, C_m$ is a finite set of formulas, then a *cube over* $\mathcal{C}$ is a conjunction of the form $C_1^{\alpha_1} \wedge \ldots C_m^{\alpha_m}$ where $\alpha_i \in \{0, 1\}$, $C^1 = C$ and $C^0 = \neg C$. For simplicity, fix a finite language $L = \mathcal{A} \cup \mathcal{F}$ with $\mathcal{A}$ a finite set of unary predicate symbols and $\mathcal{F}$ a finite set of binary predicate symbols. We work in predicate calculus with equality, and assume that the equality "=", where $= \notin \mathcal{F}$, is present as a binary relation symbol, unless explicitly stated otherwise. We use D to denote a finite domain of interpretation and e to denote a model with variable assignment; e maps $\mathcal{A}$ to 2^D, maps $\mathcal{F}$ to $2^{D \times D}$ and maps variables to elements of D. Let $x_1, \ldots, x_n$ be a finite list of distinct variables. Let $\mathcal{C}$ be the set of all atomic formulas F such that $\mathsf{FV}(F) \subseteq \{x_1, \ldots, x_n\}$. The set $\mathcal{C}$ is finite (in our case it has $|\mathcal{A}|n + (|\mathcal{F}| + 1)n^2$ elements). We call a cube over $\mathcal{C}$ a *complete atomic type (CAT) formula*. From the disjunctive normal form theorem for propositional logic, we obtain the following Proposition 5.

Proposition 5. *Every quantifier-free formula F such that $\mathsf{FV}(F) \subseteq \{x_1, \ldots, x_n\}$ is equivalent to a disjunction of CAT formulas C such that $\mathsf{FV}(C) = \{x_1, \ldots, x_n\}$.*

A CAT formula may be contradictory if, for example, it contains the literal $x_i \neq x_i$ as a conjunct. We next define classes of CAT formulas that are satisfiable in the presence of equality. A *general-case CAT (GCCAT)* formula describes the case where all variables denote distinct values: a GCCAT formula is a CAT formula F such that the following two conditions hold: 1) $\mathsf{FV}(F) = \{x_1, \ldots, x_n\}$;

2) for all $1 \leq i, j \leq n$, the conjunct $x_i = x_j$ is in F iff $i \equiv j$. An *equality CAT (EQCAT)* formula is a formula of the form $\bigwedge_{j=1}^{m} y_j = x_{i_j} \wedge F$, where $1 \leq i_1, \ldots, i_m \leq n$ and F is a GCCAT formula such that $\mathsf{FV}(F) = \{x_1, \ldots, x_n\}$.

Lemma 6. *Every CAT formula F is either contradictory, or is equivalent to an EQCAT formula F' such that $\mathsf{FV}(F') = \mathsf{FV}(F)$.*

From Proposition 5 and Lemma 6, we obtain the following Proposition 7.

Proposition 7. *Every quantifier-free formula F such that $\mathsf{FV}(F) \subseteq \{x_1, \ldots, x_n\}$ can be written as a disjunction of EQCAT formulas C such that $\mathsf{FV}(C) = \{x_1, \ldots, x_n\}$.*

We next introduce the notion of an extension of a GCCAT formula. Let $x, x_1, \ldots, x_n$ be distinct variables and F be a GCCAT formula such that $\mathsf{FV}(F) = \{x_1, \ldots, x_n\}$. We say that F' is an *x-extension* of F, and write $F' \in \mathsf{exts}(F, x)$ iff all of the following conditions hold: 1) $F \wedge F'$ is a GCCAT formula; 2) $\mathsf{FV}(F \wedge F') = \{x, x_1, \ldots, x_n\}$; 3) F and F' have no common atomic formulas. Note that if $\mathsf{FV}(F_1) = \mathsf{FV}(F_2)$, then $\mathsf{exts}(F_1, x) = \mathsf{exts}(F_2, x)$ i.e. the set of extensions of a GCCAT formula depends only on the free variables of the formula; we introduce additional notation $\mathsf{exts}(x_1, \ldots, x_n, x)$ to denote $\mathsf{exts}(F, x)$ for $\mathsf{FV}(F) = \{x_1, \ldots, x_n\}$.

To define a normal form for formulas of quantifier depth one, we introduce the notion of k-counting star. If $p \geq 2$ is an integer, let p^+ be a new symbol representing the co-finite set of integers $\{p, p+1, \ldots\}$. Let $C_p = \{0, 1, \ldots, p-1, p^+\}$. If $c \in C_p$, by $\exists^c x. P$ we mean $\exists^{=c} x. P$ if c is an integer, and $\exists^{\geq p} x. P$ if $c = p^+$. We say that a formula F has a *counting degree* of at most p iff the only counting quantifiers in F are of the form $\exists^c x. G$ for some $c \in C_{p+1}$. A counting star formula describes the neighborhood of an object by specifying an approximation of the number of objects x that realize each extension.

Definition 8 (Counting Star Formula). *Let x, $x_1, \ldots, x_n$, and $y_1, \ldots, y_m$ be distinct variables, $k \geq 1$ a positive integer, and F a GCCAT formula such that $\mathsf{FV}(F) = \{x_1, \ldots, x_n\}$. A k-counting star function for F is a function $\gamma : \mathsf{exts}(F, x) \to C_{k+1}$. A k-counting-star formula for γ is a formula of the form $\bigwedge_{j=1}^{m} y_j = x_{i_j} \wedge F \wedge \bigwedge_{F' \in \mathsf{exts}(F, x)} \exists^{\gamma(F')} x. F'$, where $1 \leq i_1, \ldots, i_m \leq n$.*

Note that in Definition 8, formula $\bigwedge_{j=1}^{m} y_j = x_{i_j} \wedge F$ is an EQCAT formula, and formula $\bigwedge_{j=1}^{m} y_j = x_{i_j} \wedge F \wedge F'$ is an EQCAT formula for each $F' \in \mathsf{exts}(F, x)$.

Proposition 9 (Depth-One Normal Form). *Let F be a formula such that F has quantifier depth at most one, F has counting degree at most k, and $\mathsf{FV}(F) \subseteq \{x_1, \ldots, x_n\}$. Then F is equivalent to a disjunction of k-counting-star formulas F_C where $\mathsf{FV}(F_C) = \{x_1, \ldots, x_n\}$.*

7.2   Spatial Conjunction of Stars

Sketch of the Construction. Let F_1 and F_2 be two formulas of quantifier depth at most one, and not containing the logical operation $\circledast$. By Proposition 9, let F_1 be equivalent to the disjunction of counting star formulas

$\bigvee_{i=1}^{n_1} C_{1,i}$ and let F_2 be equivalent to the disjunction of counting star formulas $\bigvee_{j=1}^{n_2} C_{2,j}$. By distributivity of $\circledast$ with respect to $\vee$, we have $F_1 \circledast F_2 \approx (\bigvee_{i=1}^{n_1} C_{1,i}) \circledast (\bigvee_{j=1}^{n_2} C_{2,j}) \approx \bigvee_{i=1}^{n_1} \bigvee_{j=1}^{n_2} C_{1,i} \circledast C_{2,j}$. In the sequel we show that a spatial conjunction of counting-star formulas is either contradictory or is equivalent to a disjunction of counting star formulas. This suffices to eliminate spatial conjunction of formulas of quantifier depth at most one. Moreover, if F is any formula of quantifier depth at most one, possibly containing $\circledast$, by repeated elimination of the innermost $\circledast$ we obtain a formula without $\circledast$.

To compute the spatial conjunction of counting stars we establish an alternative syntactic form for counting star formulas. The idea of this alternative form is roughly to replace a counting quantifier such as $\exists^{=k} x. F'$ with a spatial conjunction of k formulas each of which has the meaning similar to $\exists^{=1} x. F'$, and then combine a formula $\exists^{=1} x. F'_1$ resulting from one counting star with a formula $\exists^{=1} x. F'_2$ resulting from another counting star into the formula $\exists^{=1} x. (F'_1 \odot F'_2)$ where $\odot$ denotes merging of GCCAT formulas by taking the union of their positive literals. We next develop this idea in greater detail.

Notation for Spatial Representation of Stars. Let $G_E(x_1, \ldots, x_n)$ be the unique GCCAT formula F with $\mathsf{FV}(F) = \{x_1, \ldots, x_n\}$ such that the only positive literals in F are literals $x_i = x_i$ for $1 \leq i \leq n$. Similarly, there is a unique formula $F' \in \mathsf{exts}(x_1, \ldots, x_n, x)$ such that every atomic formula in F' distinct from $x = x$ occurs in a negated literal. Call F' an *empty extension* and denote it $\mathsf{empEx}(x_1, \ldots, x_n, x)$.

To compute a spatial conjunction of counting star formulas C_1 and C_2 in the language L, we temporarily consider formulas in an extended language $L' = L \cup \{B_1, B_2\}$ where B_1 and B_2 are two new unary predicates used to mark formulas. We use B_1 to mark formulas derived from C_1, and use B_2 to mark formulas derived from C_2. For $m \in \{\emptyset, \{1\}, \{2\}, \{1, 2\}\}$, define

$$\mathsf{Mark}_\emptyset(x) = \neg B_1(x) \wedge \neg B_2(x) \quad \mathsf{Mark}_1(x) = B_1(x) \wedge \neg B_2(x)$$
$$\mathsf{Mark}_2(x) = \neg B_1(x) \wedge B_2(x) \quad \mathsf{Mark}_{1,2}(x) = B_1(x) \wedge B_2(x)$$

Let $F' \in \mathsf{exts}(x_1, \ldots, x_n, x)$. Define

$$\mathsf{empEx}_\emptyset(x_1, \ldots, x_n, x) \equiv \mathsf{empEx}(x_1, \ldots, x_n, x) \wedge \mathsf{Mark}_\emptyset(x)$$

$$\mathsf{empe}(x_1, \ldots, x_n) \equiv G_E(x_1, \ldots, x_n) \wedge \forall x. (\textstyle\bigwedge_{i=1}^n x \neq x_i) \Rightarrow \mathsf{empEx}_\emptyset(x_1, \ldots, x_n, x)$$

We write $\mathsf{empEx}_\emptyset(F, x)$ for $\mathsf{empEx}_\emptyset(x_1, \ldots, x_n, x)$ if $\mathsf{FV}(F) = \{x_1, \ldots, x_n\}$, and similarly for $\mathsf{empe}(F, x)$. We write simply empe if F and x are understood.

We next introduce formulas $(\!|F'|\!)^*_m$ and $(\!|F'|\!)_m$, which are the building blocks for representing counting star formulas. Formula $(\!|F'|\!)^*_m$ means that F' marked with m and $\mathsf{empEx}_\emptyset(F, x)$ are the only extensions of F that hold in the neighborhood of $x_1, \ldots, x_n$ (F' may hold for *any number* of neighbors). Formula $(\!|F'|\!)_m$ means that F' holds for *exactly one* element in the neighborhood of $x_1, \ldots, x_n$, and all other neighbors have empty extensions. More precisely, let $F' \in \mathsf{exts}(x_1, \ldots, x_n, x)$. Define

$$(\!|F'|\!)^*_m \equiv G_E(x_1, \ldots, x_n) \wedge \forall x. (\textstyle\bigwedge_{i=1}^n x \neq x_i) \Rightarrow (F' \wedge \mathsf{Mark}_m(x)) \vee \mathsf{empEx}_\emptyset(F, x)$$

$$(\!|F'|\!)_m \equiv (\!|F'|\!)^*_m \wedge \exists^{=1} x. \textstyle\bigwedge_{i=1}^n x \neq x_i \wedge F' \wedge \mathsf{Mark}_m(x)$$

$E \wedge F$ – EQCAT formula, F – GCCAT formula

$$\mathcal{S}_m[E \wedge F \wedge \exists^{s_1} x.F_1^{\mathfrak{q}} \wedge \ldots \wedge \exists^{s_k} x.F_k^{\mathfrak{q}}] =$$
$$= E \wedge \mathcal{K}[F] \circledast \mathcal{X}_m[\exists^{s_1} x.F_1^{\mathfrak{q}}] \circledast \ldots \circledast \mathcal{X}_m[\exists^{s_k} x.F_k^{\mathfrak{q}}]$$

$$\mathcal{K}[F] = F \wedge (\forall x.(\textstyle\bigwedge_{i=1}^{n} x \neq x_i) \Rightarrow \mathsf{empEx}_{\mathfrak{q}}(F, x))$$

$$\mathcal{X}_m[\exists^0 x. F^{\mathfrak{q}}] = \mathsf{empe} \qquad \mathcal{X}_m[\exists^{i+1} x. F^{\mathfrak{q}}] = (F^{\mathfrak{q}})_m \circledast \mathcal{X}_m[\exists^i x. F^{\mathfrak{q}}]$$

$$\mathcal{X}_m[\exists^{i^+} x. F^{\mathfrak{q}}] = \mathcal{X}_m[\exists^i x. F^{\mathfrak{q}}] \circledast (F^{\mathfrak{q}})_m^{\mathfrak{q}}$$

Fig. 6. Translation of Counting Stars to Spatial Notation

(1) $(T_1)_1 \circledast (T_2)_2 \rightsquigarrow (T_1 \odot T_2)_{1,2}$
(2) $(T_1)_1 \circledast (T_2)_2^{\mathfrak{q}} \rightsquigarrow (T_1 \odot T_2)_{1,2} \circledast (T_2)_2^{\mathfrak{q}}$
(3) $(T_1)_1^{\mathfrak{q}} \circledast (T_2)_2 \rightsquigarrow (T_1)_1^{\mathfrak{q}} \circledast (T_1 \odot T_2)_{1,2}$
(4) $(T_1)_1^{\mathfrak{q}} \circledast (T_2)_2^{\mathfrak{q}} \rightsquigarrow (T_1)_1^{\mathfrak{q}} \circledast (T_2)_2^{\mathfrak{q}} \circledast (T_1 \odot T_2)_{1,2}^{\mathfrak{q}}$
(5) $(T)_1^{\mathfrak{q}} \rightsquigarrow \mathsf{empe}$
(6) $(T)_2^{\mathfrak{q}} \rightsquigarrow \mathsf{empe}$

Fig. 7. Transformation Rules for Combining Spatial Conjuncts

where $m \in \{\emptyset, \{1\}, \{2\}, \{1, 2\}\}$. Observe that $G \circledast \mathsf{empe} \approx G$ if $G \equiv (F')_m^*$ or $G \equiv (F')_m$ for some F' and m. Also note that $(F')_m^* \circledast (F')_m^* \sim (F')_m^*$.

Translation of Counting Stars. Figure 6 presents the translation of counting stars to spatial notation. The idea of the translation is to replace $\exists^{=k} x. F'$ with the spatial conjunction of k formulas $(F')_m \circledast \ldots \circledast (F')_m$ where $m \in \{\{1\}, \{2\}\}$. The purpose of the marker m is to ensure that each of the k witnesses for x that are guaranteed to exist by $(F')_m \circledast \ldots \circledast (F')_m$ are distinct. The reason that the witnesses are distinct for $m \neq \emptyset$ is that no two of them can satisfy $B_i(x)$ at the same time for $i \in m$.

To show the correctness of the translation in Figure 6, define e^m to be the L'-environment obtained by extending the L-environment e according to marking m, and $\overline{e_1}$ to be the restriction of the L'-environment e_1 to the language L. More precisely, if e is an L-environment, for $m \in \{\emptyset, \{1\}, \{2\}, \{1, 2\}\}$, define the L'-environment e^m by 1) $e^m r = er$ for $r \in L$ and 2) for $q \in \{1, 2\}$, let $(e B_q) d = \mathsf{True} \iff q \in m \wedge d \notin \{e x_1, \ldots, e x_n\}$. Conversely, if e_1 is an L'-environment, define the L-environment $\overline{e_1}$ by $\overline{e_1} r = e_1 r$ for all $r \in L$. Lemma 10 below gives the correctness criterion for the translation in Figure 6.

Lemma 10. *If e is an L-environment, C a counting star formula in L, and $m \in \{\{1\}, \{2\}, \{1, 2\}\}$, then $[C]e = \mathcal{S}_m[C]e^m$.*

Combining Quantifier-Free Formulas. Let $C_1 \circledast C_2$ be a spatial conjunction of two counting-star formulas

$$C_1 \equiv E \wedge F_1 \wedge \exists^{s_{1,1}} x.F_{1,1}^{\mathfrak{q}} \wedge \ldots \wedge \exists^{s_{1,k}} x.F_{1,k}^{\mathfrak{q}}$$
$$C_2 \equiv E \wedge F_2 \wedge \exists^{s_{2,1}} x.F_{2,1}^{\mathfrak{q}} \wedge \ldots \wedge \exists^{s_{2,l}} x.F_{2,l}^{\mathfrak{q}}$$

where F_1 and F_2 are GCCAT formulas with $\mathsf{FV}(F_1) = \mathsf{FV}(F_2) = \{x_1, \ldots, x_n\}$, $E \wedge F_1$ and $E \wedge F_2$ are EQCAT formulas, and $E \equiv \bigwedge_{j=1}^{m} y_j = x_{i_j}$. To show how to transform the formula $S_1[\![C_1]\!] \circledast S_2[\![C_2]\!]$ into a disjunction of formulas of the form $S_{1,2}[\![C_3]\!]$, we introduce the following notation. If T is a formula, let $S(T)$ denote the set of positive literals in T that do not contain equality. Let $T_1 \in \mathsf{exts}(F_1, x)$ and $T_2 \in \mathsf{exts}(F_2, x)$. (Note that $\mathsf{exts}(F_1, x) = \mathsf{exts}(F_2, x)$.) We define the partial operation $T_1 \odot T_2$ as follows. The result of $T_1 \odot T_2$ is defined iff $S(T_1) \cap S(T_2) = \emptyset$. If $S(T_1) \cap S(T_2) = \emptyset$, then $T_1 \odot T_2 = T$ where T is the unique element of $\mathsf{exts}(F_1, x)$ such that $S(T) = S(T_1) \cup S(T_2)$. Similarly to $\odot$, we define the partial operation $F_1 \oplus F_2$ for F_1 and F_2 GCCAT formulas with $\mathsf{FV}(F_1) = \mathsf{FV}(F_2) = \{x_1, \ldots, x_n\}$. The result of $F_1 \oplus F_2$ is defined iff $S(F_1) \cap S(F_2) = \emptyset$. If $S(F_1) \cap S(F_2) = \emptyset$, then $F_1 \oplus F_2$ is the unique GCCAT formula F such that $\mathsf{FV}(F) = \{x_1, \ldots, x_n\}$ and $S(F) = S(F_1) \cup S(F_2)$. The following Lemma 11 notes that $\odot$ and $\oplus$ are sound rules for computing spatial conjunction of certain quantifier-free formulas.

Lemma 11. *If* $T_1, T_2 \in \mathsf{exts}(x_1, \ldots, x_n, x)$ *then* $T_1 \circledast T_2 \approx T_1 \odot T_2$. *If* F_1 *and* F_2 *are GCCAT formulas with* $\mathsf{FV}(F_1) = \mathsf{FV}(F_2) = \{x_1, \ldots, x_n\}$, *then* $F_1 \circledast F_2 \approx F_1 \oplus F_2$.

Rules for Transforming Spatial Conjuncts. We transform the formula $S_1[\![C_1]\!] \circledast S_2[\![C_2]\!]$ into a disjunction of formulas of the form $S_{1,2}[\![C_3]\!]$ as follows.

The first step in transforming $C_1 \circledast C_2$ is to replace $\mathcal{K}[\![F_1]\!] \circledast \mathcal{K}[\![F_2]\!]$ with $\mathcal{K}[\![F_1 \oplus F_2]\!]$ if $F_1 \oplus F_2$ is defined, or False if $F_1 \oplus F_2$ is not defined.

The second step is summarized in Figure 7, which presents rules for combining conjuncts resulting from $\mathcal{X}_1[\![\exists^{s_1}.F_1]\!]$ and $\mathcal{X}_2[\![\exists^{s_2} x.F_2]\!]$ into conjuncts of the form $\mathcal{X}_{1,2}[\![\exists^s x.F]\!]$. The intuition is that $(\!|T|\!)_m^*$ and $(\!|T|\!)_m$ represent a finite abstraction of all possible neighborhoods of $x_1, \ldots, x_n$, and the rules in Figure 7 represent the ways in which different portions of the neighborhoods combine using spatial conjunction. We apply the rules in Figure 7 modulo commutativity and associativity of $\circledast$, the fact that emp is a unit for $\circledast$, and the idempotence of $(\!|T|\!)_m^*$. Rules (1)–(4) are applicable only when the occurrence of $T_1 \odot T_2$ on the right-hand side of the rule is defined. We apply rules (1)–(4) as long as possible, and then apply rules (5), (6). Moreover, we only allow the sequences of rule applications that eliminate all occurrences of $(\!|T|\!)_1, (\!|T|\!)_1^*, (\!|T|\!)_2, (\!|T|\!)_2^*$, leaving only $(\!|T|\!)_{1,2}$ and $(\!|T|\!)_{1,2}^*$. The following Lemma 12 gives the partial correctness of the rules in Figure 7.

Lemma 12. *If* $G_1 \rightsquigarrow G_2$, *then* $G_2 \Rightarrow G_1$ *is valid.*

Define $G_1 \overset{C}{\Longrightarrow} G_2$ to hold iff both of the following two conditions hold: **1)** G_2 results from G_1 by replacing $\mathcal{K}[\![F_1]\!] \circledast \mathcal{K}[\![F_2]\!]$ with $\mathcal{K}[\![F_1 \oplus F_2]\!]$ if $F_1 \oplus F_2$ is defined, or False if $F_1 \oplus F_2$ is not defined, and then applying some sequence of rules in Figure 7 such that rules (5), (6) are applied only when rules (1)–(4) are not applicable; **2)** G_2 contains only spatial conjuncts of the form $(\!|T|\!)_{1,2}$ and $(\!|T|\!)_{1,2}^*$. From Lemma 12 and Lemma 11 we immediately obtain Lemma 13.

Lemma 13. *If* $G_1 \overset{C}{\Longrightarrow} G_2$, *then* $G_2 \Rightarrow G_1$ *is valid.*

The rule for computing the spatial conjunction of counting star formulas is the following. If C_1, C_2, and C_3 are counting star formulas, define $\mathcal{R}(C_1, C_2, C_3)$ to hold iff $\mathcal{S}_1[\![C_1]\!] \circledast \mathcal{S}_2[\![C_2]\!] \overset{C}{\Longrightarrow} \mathcal{S}_{1,2}[\![C_3]\!]$. We compute spatial conjunction by replacing $C_1 \circledast C_2$ with $\bigvee_{\mathcal{R}(C_1,C_2,C_3)} C_3$. Our goal is therefore to show the equivalence

$$C_1 \circledast C_2 \approx \bigvee_{\text{R} (C_1,C_2,C_3)} C_3 \qquad (2)$$

The validity of $\bigvee_{\mathcal{R}(C_1,C_2,C_3)} C_3 \Rightarrow (C_1 \circledast C_2)$ follows from Lemma 13 and Lemma 10.

Lemma 14. $(\bigvee_{\mathcal{R}(C_1,C_2,C_3)} C_3) \Rightarrow (C_1 \circledast C_2)$ *is a valid formula for every pair of counting star formulas C_1 and C_2.*

We next consider the converse claim. If $[\![C_1 \circledast C_2]\!]e$, then there are e_1 and e_2 such that split $e\, e_1\, e_2$, $[\![C_1]\!]e_1$, and $[\![C_2]\!]e_2$. By considering the atomic types induced in e, e_1 and e_2 by elements in $D \setminus \{e\, x_1, \ldots, e\, x_n\}$, we can construct a sequence of $\rightsquigarrow$ transformations in Figure 7 that convert $\mathcal{S}_1[\![C_1]\!] \circledast \mathcal{S}_2[\![C_2]\!]$ into a formula $\mathcal{S}_{1,2}[\![C_3]\!]$ such that $[\![C_3]\!]e = \mathsf{True}$.

Lemma 15. $C_1 \circledast C_2 \Rightarrow \bigvee_{\mathcal{R}(C_1,C_2,C_3)} C_3$ *is a valid formula for every pair of counting star formulas C_1 and C_2.*

Theorem 16. *The equivalence (2) holds for every pair of counting star formulas C_1 and C_2.*

8   Further Related Work

Records have been studied in the context of functional and object-oriented programming languages [7, 13, 17, 31, 32, 36]. The main difference between existing record notations and our system is that the interpretation of a record in our system is a predicate on an object, where an object is linked to other objects forming a graph, as opposed to being a type that denotes a value (with values typically representable as trees). Our view is appropriate for programming languages such as Java and ML that can manipulate structures using destructive updates. Our generalizations allow the developers to express both incoming and outgoing references of objects, and to allow the developers to express typestate changes.

We have developed role logic to provide a foundation for role analysis [19]. We have subsequently studied a simplification of role analysis constraints and characterized such constraints using formulas [20, 21]. Multifields and multislots are present already in [18, Section 6.1]. In this paper we have shown that role logic provides a unifying framework for all these constraints and goes beyond them in 1) being closed under boolean operations, and 2) being closed under spatial conjunction for an interesting class of formulas. The view of roles as predicates is equivalent to the view of roles as sets and works well in the presence of data abstraction [27].

The parametric analysis based on three-valued logic is presented in [34]. Other approaches to verifying shape invariants include [8, 11, 15, 28]. A decidable logic for expressing connectivity properties of the heap was presented in [4]. We use spatial conjunction from separation logic that has been used for reasoning about the heap [6, 16, 33]. Description logics [1] share many of the properties of role logic and have been traditionally applied to knowledge bases.

9   Conclusions

We have shown how to add notation for records to two-variable role logic while preserving its decidability. The resulting notation supports a generalization of traditional records with record specifications that are closed under all boolean operations as well as record concatenation, allow the description of typestate properties, support inverse records, and capture the distinction between open and closed records. We believe that such an expressive and decidable notation is useful as an annotation language used with program analyses and type systems.

Acknowledgements

We thank the participants of the Dagstuhl Seminar 03101 "Reasoning about Shape" for useful discussions on separation logic and shape analysis.

References

1. F. Baader, D. Calvanese, D. McGuinness, D. Nardi, and P. Patel-Schneider, editors. *The Description Logic Handbook: Theory, Implementation and Applications.* Cambridge University Press, 2003.
2. T. Ball, R. Majumdar, T. Millstein, and S. K. Rajamani. Automatic predicate abstraction of C programs. In *Proc. ACM PLDI*, 2001.
3. T. Ball, A. Podelski, and S. K. Rajamani. Relative completeness of abstraction refinement for software model checking. In *TACAS'02*, volume 2280 of *LNCS*, page 158, 2002.
4. M. Benedikt, T. Reps, and M. Sagiv. A decidable logic for linked data structures. In *Proc. 8th ESOP*, 1999.
5. L. Birkedal, N. Torp-Smith, and J. C. Reynolds. Local reasoning about a copying garbage collector. In *31st ACM POPL*, pages 220–231. ACM Press, 2004.
6. C. Calcagno, L. Cardelli, and A. D. Gordon. Deciding validity in a spatial logic for trees. In *ACM TLDI'02*, 2002.
7. L. Cardelli and J. C. Mitchell. Operations on records. In *Theoretical Aspects of Object-Oriented Programming*. The MIT Press, Cambridge, Mass., 1994.
8. D. R. Chase, M. Wegman, and F. K. Zadeck. Analysis of pointers and structures. In *Proc. ACM PLDI*, 1990.
9. P. Cousot and R. Cousot. Abstract interpretation: a unified lattice model for static analysis of programs by construction or approximation of fixpoints. In *Proc. 4th POPL*, 1977.
10. M. Fähndrich and K. R. M. Leino. Declaring and checking non-null types in an object-oriented language. In *OOPSLA'03*, 2003.
11. P. Fradet and D. L. Métayer. Shape types. In *Proc. 24th ACM POPL*, 1997.
12. E. Grädel, M. Otto, and E. Rosen. Two-variable logic with counting is decidable. In *Proceedings of 12th IEEE Symposium on Logic in Computer Science LICS '97, Warschau*, 1997.
13. R. Harper and B. Pierce. A record calculus based on symmetric concatenation. In *18th ACM POPL*, pages 131–142, Orlando, Florida, 1991.
14. T. A. Henzinger, R. Jhala, R. Majumdar, and K. L. McMillan. Abstractions from proofs. In *31st POPL*, 2004.

15. J. Hummel, L. J. Hendren, and A. Nicolau. A general data dependence test for dynamic, pointer-based data structures. In *Proc. ACM PLDI*, 1994.
16. S. Ishtiaq and P. W. O'Hearn. BI as an assertion language for mutable data structures. In *Proc. 28th ACM POPL*, 2001.
17. M. Jones and S. P. Jones. Lightweight extensible records for Haskell. In *Haskell Workshop*, 1999.
18. V. Kuncak. Designing an algorithm for role analysis. Master's thesis, MIT Laboratory for Computer Science, 2001.
19. V. Kuncak, P. Lam, and M. Rinard. Role analysis. In *Proc. 29th POPL*, 2002.
20. V. Kuncak and M. Rinard. Typestate checking and regular graph constraints. Technical Report 863, MIT Laboratory for Computer Science, 2002.
21. V. Kuncak and M. Rinard. Existential heap abstraction entailment is undecidable. In *10th Annual International Static Analysis Symposium (SAS 2003)*, San Diego, California, June 11-13 2003.
22. V. Kuncak and M. Rinard. On role logic. Technical Report 925, MIT CSAIL, 2003.
23. V. Kuncak and M. Rinard. On the boolean algebra of shape analysis constraints. Technical report, MIT CSAIL, August 2003.
24. V. Kuncak and M. Rinard. Boolean algebra of shape analysis constraints. In *Proc. 5th International Conference on Verification, Model Checking and Abstract Interpretation*, 2004.
25. V. Kuncak and M. Rinard. On generalized records and spatial conjunction in role logic. Technical Report 942, MIT CSAIL, April 2004.
26. P. Lam, V. Kuncak, and M. Rinard. On modular pluggable analyses using set interfaces. Technical Report 933, MIT CSAIL, December 2003.
27. P. Lam, V. Kuncak, and M. Rinard. Generalized typestate checking using set interfaces and pluggable analyses. *SIGPLAN Notices*, 39:46–55, March 2004.
28. A. Møller and M. I. Schwartzbach. The Pointer Assertion Logic Engine. In *Proc. ACM PLDI*, 2001.
29. M. Otto. *Bounded Variable Logics and Counting: A Study in Finite Models*. Lecture Notes in Logic 9. Springer, 1997.
30. L. Pacholski, W. Szwast, and L. Tendera. Complexity results for first-order two-variable logic with counting. *SIAM J. on Computing*, 29(4):1083–1117, 2000.
31. F. Pottier. A constraint-based presentation and generalization of rows. In *18th IEEE LICS*, June 2003.
32. D. Remy. Typing record concatenation for free. In *POPL*, pages 166–176, 1992.
33. J. C. Reynolds. Separation logic: a logic for shared mutable data structures. In *17th LICS*, pages 55–74, 2002.
34. M. Sagiv, T. Reps, and R. Wilhelm. Parametric shape analysis via 3-valued logic. *ACM TOPLAS*, 24(3):217–298, 2002.
35. R. E. Strom and S. Yemini. Typestate: A programming language concept for enhancing software reliability. *IEEE TSE*, January 1986.
36. M. Wand. Type inference for record concatenation and multiple inheritance. *Information and Computation*, 93(1):1–15, 1991.
37. E. Yahav and G. Ramalingam. Verifying safety properties using separation and heterogeneous abstractions. In *PLDI*, 2004.
38. G. Yorsh. Logical characterizations of heap abstractions. Master's thesis, Tel-Aviv University, March 2003.
39. G. Yorsh, T. Reps, and M. Sagiv. Symbolically computing most-precise abstract operations for shape analysis. In *10th TACAS*, 2004.

Non-termination Inference
for Constraint Logic Programs

Etienne Payet and Fred Mesnard

IREMIA - Université de La Réunion, France
{epayet,fred}@univ-reunion.fr

Abstract. Termination has been a subject of intensive research in the logic programming community for the last two decades. Most works deal with proving universal left termination of a given class of queries, *i.e.* finiteness of all the possible derivations produced by a Prolog engine from any query in that class. In contrast, the study of the *dual* problem: non-termination w.r.t. the left selection rule *i.e* the existence of one query in a given class of queries which admits an infinite left derivation, has given rise to only a few papers. In this article, we study non-termination in the more general constraint logic programming framework. We rephrase our previous logic programming approach into this more abstract setting, which leads to a criterion expressed in a logical way and simpler proofs, as expected. Also, by reconsidering our previous work, we now prove that in some sense, we already had the best syntactic criterion for logic programming. Last but not least, we offer a set of correct algorithms for inferring non-termination for CLP.

1 Introduction

Termination has been a subject of intensive research in the logic programming community for the last two decades, see the survey [4]. A more recent look on the topic, and its extension to the constraint logic programming paradigm [8, 9] is given in [14]. Most works deal with proving universal left termination of a given class of queries, *i.e.* finiteness of all the possible derivations produced by a Prolog engine from any query in that class. Some of these works, *e.g.* [11,7,12] consider the *reverse* problem of inferring classes of queries for which universal left termination is ensured.

In contrast, the study of the *dual* problem: non-termination w.r.t. the left selection rule *i.e* the existence of one query in a given class of queries which admits an infinite left derivation, has given rise to only a few papers, *e.g.* [3, 5]. Recently we have also investigated this problem in the logic programming setting [13], where we proposed an analysis to infer non-termination.

In this paper, we study non-termination in the more general constraint logic programming framework. We rephrase our approach into this more abstract setting, which leads to a necessary and sufficient criterion expressed in a logical way and simpler proofs, as expected. Also, by reconsidering our previous work, we now prove that in some sense, we already had the best syntactic criterion for

R. Giacobazzi (Ed.): SAS 2004, LNCS 3148, pp. 377–392, 2004.
© Springer-Verlag Berlin Heidelberg 2004

logic programming. Last but not least, we offer a set of correct algorithms for inferring non-termination for CLP. The analysis is fully implemented[1].

We organize the paper as follows. After the preliminaries presented in Section 2, some basic properties related to non-termination for CLP is given in Section 3. The technical machinery behind our approach is described in Section 4 and Section 5. Section 6 concludes.

2 Preliminaries

We recall some basic definitions on CLP, see [9] for more details.

2.1 Constraint Domains

In this paper, we consider a constraint logic programming language $\mathrm{CLP}(\mathcal{C})$ based on the constraint domain $\mathcal{C} := \langle \Sigma_\mathcal{C}, \mathcal{L}_\mathcal{C}, \mathcal{D}_\mathcal{C}, \mathcal{T}_\mathcal{C}, solv_\mathcal{C} \rangle$.

$\Sigma_\mathcal{C}$ is the constraint domain *signature*, which is a pair $\langle F_\mathcal{C}, \Pi_\mathcal{C} \rangle$ where $F_\mathcal{C}$ is a set of function symbols and $\Pi_\mathcal{C}$ is a set of predicate symbols. The class of constraints $\mathcal{L}_\mathcal{C}$ is a set of first-order $\Sigma_\mathcal{C}$-formulas. The *domain of computation* $\mathcal{D}_\mathcal{C}$ is a $\Sigma_\mathcal{C}$-structure that is the intented interpretation of the constraints and $D_\mathcal{C}$ is the *domain* of $\mathcal{D}_\mathcal{C}$. The *constraint theory* $\mathcal{T}_\mathcal{C}$ is a $\Sigma_\mathcal{C}$-theory describing the logical semantics of the constraints. We suppose that $\mathcal{C}$ is *ideal i.e.* the *constraint solver, $solv_\mathcal{C}$*, is a computable function which maps each formula in $\mathcal{L}_\mathcal{C}$ to one of true or false indicating whether the formula is satisfiable or unsatisfiable.

We assume that the predicate symbol = is in $\Sigma_\mathcal{C}$ and that it is interpreted as identity in $\mathcal{D}_\mathcal{C}$. A *primitive constraint* is either the always satisfiable constraint *true* or the unsatisfiable constraint *false* or has the form $p(\tilde{t})$ where $p \in \Pi_\mathcal{C}$ and $\tilde{t}$ is a finite sequence of terms in $\Sigma_\mathcal{C}$. We suppose that $\mathcal{L}_\mathcal{C}$ contains all the primitive constraints and that it is closed under variable renaming, existential quantification and conjunction.

We suppose that $\mathcal{D}_\mathcal{C}$ and $\mathcal{T}_\mathcal{C}$ *correspond* on $\mathcal{L}_\mathcal{C}$ *i.e.*

- $\mathcal{D}_\mathcal{C}$ is a model of $\mathcal{T}_\mathcal{C}$ and
- for every constraint $c \in \mathcal{L}_\mathcal{C}$, $\mathcal{D}_\mathcal{C} \models \exists c$ if and only if $\mathcal{T}_\mathcal{C} \models \exists c$.

Moreover, we suppose that $\mathcal{T}_\mathcal{C}$ is *satisfaction complete* w.r.t. $\mathcal{L}_\mathcal{C}$ *i.e.* for every constraint $c \in \mathcal{L}_\mathcal{C}$, either $\mathcal{T}_\mathcal{C} \models \exists c$ or $\mathcal{T}_\mathcal{C} \models \neg \exists c$. We also assume that the theory and the solver *agree* in the sense that for every $c \in \mathcal{L}_\mathcal{C}$, $solv_\mathcal{C}(c) = \mathtt{true}$ if and only if $\mathcal{T}_\mathcal{C} \models \exists c$. Consequently, as $\mathcal{D}_\mathcal{C}$ and $\mathcal{T}_\mathcal{C}$ correspond on $\mathcal{L}_\mathcal{C}$, we have, for every $c \in \mathcal{L}_\mathcal{C}$, $solv_\mathcal{C}(c) = \mathtt{true}$ if and only if $\mathcal{D}_\mathcal{C} \models \exists c$.

A *valuation* is a function that maps all variables into $D_\mathcal{C}$. We write $O\sigma$ (instead of $\sigma(O)$) to denote the result of applying a valuation σ to an object O. If c is a constraint, we write $\mathcal{D}_\mathcal{C} \models c$ if for every valuation σ, $c\sigma$ is true in $\mathcal{D}_\mathcal{C}$ *i.e.* $\mathcal{D}_\mathcal{C} \models_\sigma c$. Hence, $\mathcal{D}_\mathcal{C} \models c$ is the same as $\mathcal{D}_\mathcal{C} \models \forall c$. Valuations are denoted by $\sigma, \eta, \theta, \ldots$ in the sequel of this paper.

---

[1] http://www.univ-reunion.fr/~gcc/

Example 1 ($\mathcal{R}_{lin}$). The constraint domain $\mathcal{R}_{lin}$ has $<$, $\leq$, $=$, $\geq$ and $>$ as predicate symbols, $+$, $-$, $*$, $/$ as function symbols and sequences of digits (possibly with a decimal point) as constant symbols. Only linear constraints are admitted. The domain of computation is the structure with reals as domain and where the predicate symbols and the function symbols are interpreted as the usual relations and functions over reals. The theory $\mathcal{T}_{\mathcal{R}_{lin}}$ is the theory of real closed fields [16]. A constraint solver for $\mathcal{R}_{lin}$ always returning either **true** or **false** is described in [15]. □

Example 2 (Logic Programming). The constraint domain *Term* has $=$ as predicate symbol and strings of alphanumeric characters as function symbols. The domain of computation of *Term* is the set of *finite trees* (or, equivalently, of finite terms), *Tree*, while the theory $\mathcal{T}_{Term}$ is Clark's equality theory [1]. The interpretation of a constant is a tree with a single node labeled with the constant. The interpretation of an n-ary function symbol f is the function $f_{Tree} : Tree^n \rightarrow Tree$ mapping the trees $T_1, \ldots, T_n$ to a new tree with root labeled with f and with $T_1, \ldots, T_n$ as child nodes. A constraint solver always returning either **true** or **false** is provided by the *unification* algorithm. CLP(*Term*) coincides then with logic programming. □

2.2   Operational Semantics

The signature in which all programs and queries under consideration are included is $\Sigma_L := \langle F_L, \Pi_L \rangle$ with $F_L := F_{\mathcal{C}}$ and $\Pi_L := \Pi_{\mathcal{C}} \cup \Pi'_L$ where Π'_L, the set of predicate symbols that can be defined in programs, is disjoint from $\Pi_{\mathcal{C}}$. We assume that each predicate symbol p in Π_L has a unique arity denoted by $arity(p)$.

An *atom* has the form $p(\tilde{t})$ where $p \in \Pi'_L$, $arity(p) = n$ and $\tilde{t}$ is a sequence of n terms in Σ_L. A CLP($\mathcal{C}$) *program* is a finite set of rules. A *rule* has the form $p(\tilde{x}) \leftarrow c \diamond q_1(\tilde{y}_1), \ldots, q_n(\tilde{y}_n)$ where $p, q_1, \ldots, q_n$ are predicate symbols in Π'_L, c is a finite conjunction of primitive constraints and $\tilde{x}, \tilde{y}_1, \ldots, \tilde{y}_n$ are disjoint sequences of distinct variables. Hence, c is the conjunction of all constraints, including unifications. A *query* has the form $\langle Q \,|\, d \rangle$ where Q is a finite sequence of atoms and d is a finite conjunction of primitive constraints. When Q contains exactly one atom, the query is said to be *atomic*. The empty sequence of atoms is denoted by □. The set of variables occurring in a syntactic object O is denoted $Var(O)$.

The examples of this paper make use of the language CLP($\mathcal{R}_{lin}$) and the language CLP(*Term*). Program and query examples are presented in **teletype** font. Program and query variables begin with an upper-case letter, [*Head*|*Tail*] denotes a list with head *Head* and tail *Tail*, and [] denotes an empty list.

We consider the following operational semantics given in terms of *left derivations* from queries to queries. Let $\langle p(\tilde{t}), Q \,|\, d \rangle$ be a query and r be a rule. Let $r' := p(\tilde{x}) \leftarrow c \diamond \mathbf{B}$ be a variant of r variable disjoint with $\langle p(\tilde{t}), Q \,|\, d \rangle$ such that $solv_{\mathcal{C}}(\tilde{x} = \tilde{t} \wedge c \wedge d) = $ **true** (where $\tilde{x} = \tilde{t}$ denotes the constraint $x_1 = t_1 \wedge \cdots \wedge x_n = t_n$ with $\tilde{x} := x_1, \ldots, x_n$ and $\tilde{t} := t_1, \ldots, t_n$). Then,

$\langle p(\tilde{t}), Q \mid d \rangle \underset{r}{\Longrightarrow} \langle \mathbf{B}, Q \mid \tilde{x} = \tilde{t} \wedge c \wedge d \rangle$ is a *left derivation step* with r' as its *input rule*. We write $S \underset{P}{\overset{+}{\Longrightarrow}} S'$ to summarize a finite number (> 0) of left derivation steps from S to S' where each input rule is a variant of a rule of P. Let S_0 be a query. A maximal sequence $S_0 \underset{r_1}{\Longrightarrow} S_1 \underset{r_2}{\Longrightarrow} \cdots$ of left derivation steps is called a *left derivation* of $P \cup \{S_0\}$ if r_1, r_2, ... are rules from P and if the *standard-ization apart* condition holds, *i.e.* each input rule used is variable disjoint from the initial query S_0 and from the input rules used at earlier steps. A finite left derivation ends up either with a query of the form $\langle \square \mid d \rangle$ with $\mathcal{T}_\mathcal{C} \models \exists d$ (then it is a *successful* left derivation) or with a query of the form $\langle Q \mid d \rangle$ with $Q \neq \square$ or $\mathcal{T}_\mathcal{C} \models \neg \exists d$ (then it is a *failed* left derivation). We say S_0 *left loops* with respect to P if there exists an infinite left derivation of $P \cup \{S_0\}$.

2.3   The Binary Unfoldings of a CLP($\mathcal{C}$) Program

We say that $H \leftarrow c \diamond \mathbf{B}$ is a *binary rule* if $\mathbf{B}$ contains at most one atom. A *binary program* is a finite set of binary rules.

Now we present the main ideas about the *binary unfoldings* [6] of a program, borrowed from [2]. This technique transforms a program P into a possibly infinite set of binary rules. Intuitively, each generated binary rule $H \leftarrow c \diamond \mathbf{B}$ specifies that, with respect to the original program P, a call to $\langle H \mid d \rangle$ (or any of its instances) necessarily leads to a call to $\langle \mathbf{B} \mid c \wedge d \rangle$ (or its corresponding instance) if $c \wedge d$ is satisfiable.

More precisely, let S be an atomic query. Then, the atomic query $\langle A \mid d \rangle$ is a *call* in a left derivation of $P \cup \{S\}$ if $S \overset{+}{\underset{P}{\Longrightarrow}} \langle A, Q \mid d \rangle$. We denote by $calls_P(S)$ the set of calls which occur in the left derivations of $P \cup \{S\}$. The specialization of the goal independent semantics for call patterns for the left-to-right selection rule is given as the fixpoint of an operator T_P^β over the domain of binary rules, viewed modulo renaming. In the definition below, id denotes the set of all binary rules of the form $p(\tilde{x}) \leftarrow \tilde{x} = \tilde{y} \diamond p(\tilde{y})$ for any $p \in \Pi'_L$ and $\exists_V c$ denotes the projection of a constraint c onto the set of variables V. Moreover, for atoms $A := p(\tilde{t})$ and $A' := p(\tilde{t}')$ we write $A = A'$ as an abbreviation for the constraint $\tilde{t} = \tilde{t}'$.

$$T_P^\beta(X) = \left\{ H \leftarrow c \diamond \mathbf{B} \mid H \leftarrow c \diamond \mathbf{B} \in P, \mathcal{D}_\mathcal{C} \models \exists c, \mathbf{B} = \square \right\} \bigcup$$

$$\left\{ H \leftarrow c \diamond \mathbf{B} \left| \begin{array}{l} r := H \leftarrow c_0 \diamond B_1, \ldots, B_m \in P, \ i \in [1, m] \\ \langle H_j \leftarrow c_j \diamond \square \rangle_{j=1}^{i-1} \in X \text{ renamed apart from } r \\ H_i \leftarrow c_i \diamond \mathbf{B} \in X \cup id \text{ renamed apart from } r \\ i < m \Rightarrow \mathbf{B} \neq \square \\ c = \exists_{Var(H,\mathbf{B})} \left[c_0 \wedge \overset{i}{\underset{j=1}{\bigwedge}} (c_j \wedge \{B_j = H_j\}) \right] \\ \mathcal{D}_\mathcal{C} \models \exists c \end{array} \right. \right\}$$

We define its powers as usual. It can be shown that the least fixpoint of this monotonic operator always exists and we set

$$bin\_unf(P) := lfp(T_P^\beta).$$

Then, the calls that occur in the left derivations of $P \cup \{S\}$, with $S := \langle p(\tilde{t}) \mid d \rangle$, can be characterized as follows:

$$calls_P(S) = \left\{ \langle \mathbf{B} \mid \tilde{t} = \tilde{t}' \wedge c \wedge d \rangle \,\middle|\, \begin{array}{l} p(\tilde{t}') \leftarrow c \diamond \mathbf{B} \in bin\_unf(P) \\ \mathcal{D}_{\mathcal{C}} \models \exists (\tilde{t} = \tilde{t}' \wedge c \wedge d) \end{array} \right\}$$

Similarly, $bin\_unf(P)$ gives a goal independent representation of the success patterns of P. But we can extract more information from the binary unfoldings of a program P: universal left termination of an atomic query S with respect to P is identical to universal termination of S with respect to $bin\_unf(P)$. Note that the selection rule is irrelevant for a binary program and an atomic query, as each subsequent query has at most one atom. The following result lies at the heart of Codish's approach to termination [2]:

Theorem 1 (Observing Termination). *Let P be a* CLP($\mathcal{C}$) *program and S be an atomic query. Then, S left loops w.r.t. P if and only if S loops w.r.t. $bin\_unf(P)$.*

Notice that $bin\_unf(P)$ is a possibly infinite set of binary rules. For this reason, in the algorithms of Section 5, we compute only the first max iterations of T_P^β where max is a parameter of the analysis. As an immediate consequence of Theorem 1 frequently used in our proofs, assume that we detect that S loops with respect to a subset of the binary rules of $T_P^\beta \uparrow i$, with $i \in N$. Then S loops with respect to $bin\_unf(P)$ hence S left loops with respect to P.

Example 3. Consider the CLP(*Term*) program P (see [10], p. 56–58):

$$r_1 := \mathsf{q}(\mathsf{X}_1, \mathsf{X}_2) \leftarrow \mathsf{X}_1 = \mathsf{a} \wedge \mathsf{X}_2 = \mathsf{b} \diamond \square$$
$$r_2 := \mathsf{p}(\mathsf{X}_1, \mathsf{X}_2) \leftarrow \mathsf{X}_1 = \mathsf{X}_2 \diamond \square$$
$$r_3 := \mathsf{p}(\mathsf{X}_1, \mathsf{X}_2) \leftarrow \mathsf{Y}_1 = \mathsf{Z}_2 \wedge \mathsf{Y}_2 = \mathsf{X}_2 \wedge \mathsf{Z}_1 = \mathsf{X}_1 \diamond \mathsf{p}(\mathsf{Y}_1, \mathsf{Y}_2), \mathsf{q}(\mathsf{Z}_1, \mathsf{Z}_2)$$

Let c_1, c_2 and c_3 be the constraints in r_1, r_2 and r_3, respectively. The binary unfoldings of P are:

$$T_P^\beta \uparrow 0 = \varnothing$$
$$T_P^\beta \uparrow 1 = \{r_1, r_2, p(x_1, x_2) \leftarrow c_3 \diamond p(y_1, y_2)\} \cup T_P^\beta \uparrow 0$$
$$T_P^\beta \uparrow 2 = \{p(x_1, x_2) \leftarrow x_1 = a \wedge x_2 = b \diamond \square,$$
$$\qquad\qquad p(x_1, x_2) \leftarrow x_1 = z_1 \wedge x_2 = z_2 \diamond q(z_1, z_2)\} \cup T_P^\beta \uparrow 1$$
$$T_P^\beta \uparrow 3 = \{p(x_1, x_2) \leftarrow x_1 = z_1 \wedge x_2 = b \wedge z_2 = a \diamond q(z_1, z_2),$$
$$\qquad\qquad p(x_1, x_2) \leftarrow x_2 = z_2 \diamond q(z_1, z_2)\} \cup T_P^\beta \uparrow 2$$
$$T_P^\beta \uparrow 4 = \{p(x_1, x_2) \leftarrow x_2 = b \wedge z_2 = a \diamond q(z_1, z_2)\} \cup T_P^\beta \uparrow 3$$
$$T_P^\beta \uparrow 5 = T_P^\beta \uparrow 4 = bin\_unf(P)$$

2.4 Terminology

In this paper, we design an algorithm that infers a finite set of left looping atomic queries from the text of any CLP($\mathcal{C}$) program P. First, the algorithm computes a finite subset of $bin\_unf(P)$ and then it proceeds with this subset only. For this reason, and to simplify the exposition, the theoretical results we describe below only deal with atomic queries and binary rules but can be easily extended to any form of queries or rules. Consequently, in the sequel of this paper up to Section 5, by a *query* we mean an *atomic query*, by a *rule*, we mean a *binary rule* and by a *program* we mean a *binary program*. Moreover, as mentioned above, the selection rule is irrelevant for a binary program and an atomic query, so we merely speak of *derivation step*, of *derivation* and of *loops*.

3   Loop Inference with Constraints

In the logic programming framework, the subsumption test provides a simple way to infer looping queries: if, in a logic program P, there is a rule $p(\tilde{t}) \leftarrow p(\tilde{t}')$ such that $p(\tilde{t}')$ is more general than $p(\tilde{t})$, then the query $p(\tilde{t})$ loops with respect to P. In this section, we extend this result to the constraint logic programming framework. First, we generalize the relation "is more general than":

Definition 1 (More General Than). *Let* $S := \langle p(\tilde{t}) \,|\, d\rangle$ *and* $S' := \langle p(\tilde{t}') \,|\, d'\rangle$ *be two queries. We say that* S' *is more general than* S *if* $\{p(\tilde{t})\eta \mid \mathcal{D}_\mathcal{C} \models_\eta d\} \subseteq \{p(\tilde{t}')\eta \mid \mathcal{D}_\mathcal{C} \models_\eta d'\}$.

Example 4. Suppose that $\mathcal{C} = Term$. Let $S := \langle p(X) \,|\, X = f(f(Y))\rangle$ and $S' := \langle p(X) \,|\, X = f(Y)\rangle$. Then, as $\{p(X)\eta \mid \mathcal{D}_\mathcal{C} \models_\eta (X = f(f(Y)))\} \subseteq \{p(X)\eta \mid \mathcal{D}_\mathcal{C} \models_\eta (X = f(Y))\}$, S' is more general than S.   □

This definition allows us to state a lifting result:

Theorem 2 (Lifting). *Consider a derivation step* $S \underset{r}{\Longrightarrow} S_1$, *a query* S' *that is more general than* S *and a variant* r' *of* r *variable disjoint with* S'. *Then, there exists a query* S_1' *that is both more general than* S_1 *and such that* $S' \underset{r}{\Longrightarrow} S_1'$ *with input rule* r'.

From this theorem, we derive two corollaries that can be used to infer looping queries just from the text of a CLP($\mathcal{C}$) program:

Corollary 1. *Let* $r := p(\tilde{x}) \leftarrow c \diamond p(\tilde{y})$ *be a rule such that* $\mathcal{D}_\mathcal{C} \models \exists c$. *If* $\langle p(\tilde{y}) \,|\, c\rangle$ *is more general than* $\langle p(\tilde{x}) \,|\, c\rangle$ *then* $\langle p(\tilde{x}) \,|\, c\rangle$ *loops w.r.t.* $\{r\}$.

Corollary 2. *Let* $r := p(\tilde{x}) \leftarrow c \diamond q(\tilde{y})$ *be a rule from a program* P. *If* $\langle q(\tilde{y}) \,|\, c\rangle$ *loops w.r.t.* P *then* $\langle p(\tilde{x}) \,|\, c\rangle$ *loops w.r.t.* P.

Example 5. Consider the CLP(*Term*) program APPEND:

$$r_1 := \text{append}(X_1, X_2, X_3) \leftarrow X_1 = [\,] \wedge X_2 = X_3 \diamond \square$$
$$r_2 := \text{append}(X_1, X_2, X_3) \leftarrow X_1 = [A|Y_1] \wedge X_2 = Y_2 \wedge X_3 = [A|Y_3] \diamond$$
$$\text{append}(Y_1, Y_2, Y_3)$$

Let c_2 be the constraint in the rule r_2. Then, $\mathcal{D}_{Term} \models \exists c_2$. Moreover, we note that $\langle \text{append}(Y_1, Y_2, Y_3) \,|\, c_2\rangle$ is more general than $\langle \text{append}(X_1, X_2, X_3) \,|\, c_2\rangle$.

So, by Corollary 1, $\langle append(X_1, X_2, X_3) \mid c_2 \rangle$ loops w.r.t. $\{r_2\}$, hence w.r.t. APPEND. Hence, there exists an infinite derivation ξ of APPEND$\cup \{\langle append(X_1, X_2, X_3) \mid c_2 \rangle\}$. Then, if S is a query that is more general than $\langle append(X_1, X_2, X_3) \mid c_2 \rangle$, by successively applying the Lifting Theorem 2 to each step of ξ, one can construct an infinite derivation of APPEND $\cup \{S\}$. So, S also loops w.r.t. APPEND.   □

An extended version of Corollary 1, presented in the next section, together with the above Corollary 2 will be used to design the algorithms of Section 5 which infer classes of looping queries from the text of a program.

4   Loop Inference Using Sets of Positions

A basic idea in our work lies in identifying arguments in rules which can be disregarded when unfolding a query. Such arguments are said to be *neutral*. The point is that in many cases, considering this kind of arguments allows to infer more looping queries.

Example 6 (Example 5 continued). The second argument of the predicate symbol *append* is neutral for derivation with the rule r_2: if we hold a derivation ξ of a query $\langle append(t_1, t_2, t_3) \mid c \rangle$ w.r.t. $\{r_2\}$, then for any term t there exists a derivation of $\{r_2\} \cup \{\langle append(t_1, t, t_3) \mid c \rangle\}$ whose length is the same as that of ξ. This means that we still get a looping query if we replace, in every looping query inferred in Example 5, the second argument of *append* by *any* term.   □

In this section, we present a framework to describe specific arguments inside a program. Using this framework, we then give an operational definition of neutral arguments leading to a result extending Corollary 1 above. Finally, we relate the operational definition to an equivalent logical characterization and to a non-equivalent syntactic criterion. Hence, the results of this section extend those we presented in [13] where we defined, in the scope of logic programming, neutral arguments in a very syntactical way.

4.1   Sets of Positions

Definition 2 (Set of Positions). *A set of positions, denoted by τ, is a function that maps each predicate symbol $p \in \Pi'_L$ to a subset of $[1, arity(p)]$.*

Example 7. If we want to disregard the second argument of the predicate symbol *append* defined in Example 5, we set $\tau := \langle append \mapsto \{2\} \rangle$.   □

Using a set of positions τ, one can *restrict* any atom by "erasing" the arguments whose position is distinguished by τ:

Definition 3 (Restriction). *Let τ be a set of positions.*

- *Let $p \in \Pi'_L$ be a predicate symbol of arity n. The restriction of p w.r.t. τ is the predicate symbol p_τ. Its arity equals the number of elements of $[1, n] \setminus \tau(p)$.*

- Let $A := p(t_1, \ldots, t_n)$ be an atom. The restriction of A w.r.t. τ, denoted by A_τ, is the atom $p_\tau(t_{i_1}, \ldots, t_{i_m})$ where $\{i_1, \ldots, i_m\} = [1, n] \setminus \tau(p)$ and $i_1 \leq \cdots \leq i_m$.
- Let $S := \langle A \mid d \rangle$ be a query. The restriction of S w.r.t. τ, denoted by S_τ, is the query $\langle A_\tau \mid d \rangle$.

Example 8 (Example 7 continued). The restriction of the query

$$\langle \mathtt{append}(\mathsf{X}, \mathsf{Y}, \mathsf{Z}) \mid \mathsf{X} = [\mathsf{A}|\mathsf{B}] \wedge \mathsf{Y} = \mathsf{a} \wedge \mathsf{Z} = [\mathsf{A}|\mathsf{C}] \rangle$$

w.r.t. τ is the query $\langle \mathtt{append}_\tau(\mathsf{X}, \mathsf{Z}) \mid \mathsf{X} = [\mathsf{A}|\mathsf{B}] \wedge \mathsf{Y} = \mathsf{a} \wedge \mathsf{Z} = [\mathsf{A}|\mathsf{C}] \rangle$.   □

Sets of positions, together with the restriction they induce, lead to a generalization of the relation "is more general than":

Definition 4 (τ-More General). *Let τ be a set of positions and S and S' be two queries. Then, S' is τ-more general than S if S'_τ is more general than S_τ.*

Example 9 (Example 7 continued). Since $\tau = \langle append \mapsto \{2\} \rangle$, we do not care what happens to the second argument of *append*. So $\langle \mathtt{append}(\mathsf{X}, \mathsf{a}, \mathsf{Z}) \mid \mathbf{true} \rangle$ is τ-more general than $\langle \mathtt{append}(\mathsf{X}, \mathsf{Y}, \mathsf{Z}) \mid \mathbf{true} \rangle$ because $\{ append_\tau(X, Z)\eta \mid \mathcal{D}_C \models_\eta \mathbf{true} \} \subseteq \{ append_\tau(X, Z)\eta \mid \mathcal{D}_C \models_\eta \mathbf{true} \}$.   □

4.2   Derivation Neutral Sets of Positions

Now we give a precise operational definition of the kind of arguments we are interested in. The name "derivation neutral" stems from the fact that τ-arguments do not play any rôle in the derivation process.

Definition 5 (Derivation Neutral). *Let r be a rule and τ be a set of positions. We say that τ is DN for r if for each derivation step $S \underset{r}{\Longrightarrow} S_1$, for each query S' that is τ-more general than S and for each variant r' of r variable disjoint with S', there exists a query S'_1 that is τ-more general than S_1 and such that $S' \underset{r}{\Longrightarrow} S'_1$ with input rule r'. This definition is extended to programs: τ is DN for P if it is DN for each rule of P.*

Therefore, while lifting a derivation, we can safely ignore derivation neutral arguments which can be instantiated to any term. As a consequence, we get the following extended version of Corollary 1:

Proposition 1. *Let $r := p(\tilde{x}) \leftarrow c \diamond p(\tilde{y})$ be a rule such that $\mathcal{D}_C \models \exists c$. Let τ be a set of positions that is DN for r. If $\langle p(\tilde{y}) \mid c \rangle$ is τ-more general than $\langle p(\tilde{x}) \mid c \rangle$ then $\langle p(\tilde{x}) \mid c \rangle$ loops w.r.t. $\{r\}$.*

Finding out neutral arguments from the text of a program is not an easy task if we use the definition above. The next subsections present a logical and a syntactic characterization that can be used (see Section 5.2) to compute neutral arguments that appear inside a given program.

– Let $r_2 := p_2(X_1, X_2) \leftarrow X_1 = A \wedge X_2 = 0 \wedge Y_2 = A - A \diamond p_2(Y_1, Y_2)$. The set of positions $\tau_2 := \langle p_2 \mapsto \{1\} \rangle$ is DNlog for r_2, so τ_2 is DN for r_2. But τ_2 is not DNsyn for r_2 because, as the terms A and $A - A$ share the variable A, **(C3)** does not hold. □

In the special case of logic programming, we have an equivalence:

Theorem 4 (Logic Programming). *Suppose that $\mathcal{C} = Term$. Let r be a flat rule and τ be a set of positions. Then, τ is DNsyn for r if and only if τ is DN for r.*

Every rule $p(\tilde{s}) \leftarrow q(\tilde{t})$ in logic programming can be easily translated to a rule $p(\tilde{x}) \leftarrow (\tilde{x} = \tilde{s} \wedge \tilde{y} = \tilde{t}) \diamond q(\tilde{y})$ in flat form. As the only universal terms in Σ_{Term} are the variables, Definition 10 is equivalent to that we gave in [13] for Derivation Neutral. Therefore, Theorem 4 states that in the case of logic programming, we have a form of completeness because we cannot get a better syntactic criterion than that of [13] (by "better", we mean a criterion allowing to distinguish at least the same positions).

5 Algorithms

In this section, we describe a set of correct algorithms that allow to infer classes of left looping atomic queries from the text of a (non necessary binary) given program P. Using the operator T_P^β, our technique first computes a finite subset of $bin\_unf(P)$ which is then analysed using DN sets of positions and a data structure called *loop dictionary*.

5.1 Loop Dictionaries

Definition 11 (Looping Pair, Loop Dictionary). *A looping pair has the form $(BinSeq, \tau)$ where $BinSeq$ is a finite ordered sequence of binary rules, τ is a set of positions that is DN for $BinSeq$ and*

- *either $BinSeq = [p(\tilde{x}) \leftarrow c \diamond p(\tilde{y})]$ where $\mathcal{D}_\mathcal{C} \models \exists c$ and $\langle p(\tilde{y}) \,|\, c \rangle$ is τ-more general than $\langle p(\tilde{x}) \,|\, c \rangle$*
- *or $BinSeq = [p(\tilde{x}) \leftarrow c \diamond q(\tilde{y}), p_1(\tilde{x}_1) \leftarrow c_1 \diamond q_1(\tilde{y}_1) | BinSeq']$ and there exists a set of positions τ' which is such that $([p_1(\tilde{x}_1) \leftarrow c_1 \diamond q_1(\tilde{y}_1) | BinSeq'], \tau')$ is a looping pair and $\langle q(\tilde{y}) \,|\, c \rangle$ is τ'-more general than $\langle p_1(\tilde{x}_1) \,|\, c_1 \rangle$.*

A loop dictionary is a finite set of looping pairs.

Example 16. In the constraint domain $\mathcal{R}_{lin}$, the pair $(BinSeq, \tau)$ where $BinSeq := [p(X) \leftarrow X > 0 \wedge X = Y \diamond q(Y), q(X) \leftarrow Y = 2 * X \diamond q(Y)]$ and τ is the set of positions $\langle p \mapsto \varnothing, q \mapsto \{1\} \rangle$, is a looping one because:

- as τ is DNlog for $BinSeq$, by Theorem 3 it is DN for $BinSeq$,
- $([q(X) \leftarrow Y = 2 * X \diamond q(Y)], \tau')$, where $\tau' := \langle q \mapsto \{1\} \rangle$, is a looping pair because τ' is DN for $[q(X) \leftarrow Y = 2 * X \diamond q(Y)]$ (because it is DNlog for that program), $\mathcal{D}_{\mathcal{R}_{lin}} \models \exists (Y = 2 * X)$ and $\langle q(Y) \,|\, Y = 2 * X \rangle$ is τ'-more general than $\langle q(X) \,|\, Y = 2 * X \rangle$,
- $\langle q(Y) \,|\, X > 0 \wedge X = Y \rangle$ is τ'-more general than $\langle q(X) \,|\, Y = 2 * X \rangle$. □

One motivation for introducing this definition is that a looping pair immediately provides a looping atomic query:

Proposition 3. *Let* $([p(\tilde{x}) \leftarrow c \diamond q(\tilde{y}) | BinSeq], \tau)$ *be a looping pair. Then,* $\langle p(\tilde{x}) | c \rangle$ *loops w.r.t.* $[p(\tilde{x}) \leftarrow c \diamond q(\tilde{y}) | BinSeq]$.

Proof. By induction on the length of *BinSeq*, using Proposition 1 and Corollary 2. □

A second motivation for using loop dictionaries is that they can be built incrementally by simple algorithms as those described below.

5.2   Getting a Loop Dictionary from a Binary Program

The most simple form of a looping pair is $([p(\tilde{x}) \leftarrow c \diamond p(\tilde{y})], \tau)$ where τ is a set of positions that is DN for $[p(\tilde{x}) \leftarrow c \diamond p(\tilde{y})]$, where $\mathcal{D}_C \models \exists c$ and $\langle p(\tilde{y}) | c \rangle$ is τ-more general than $\langle p(\tilde{x}) | c \rangle$. So, given a binary rule $p(\tilde{x}) \leftarrow c \diamond p(\tilde{y})$ such that $\mathcal{D}_C \models \exists c$, if we hold a set of positions τ that is DN for $p(\tilde{x}) \leftarrow c \diamond p(\tilde{y})$, it suffices to test if $\langle p(\tilde{y}) | c \rangle$ is τ-more general than $\langle p(\tilde{x}) | c \rangle$. If so, we have a looping pair $([p(\tilde{x}) \leftarrow c \diamond p(\tilde{y})], \tau)$. This is how the following function works.

$\texttt{unit\_loop}(p(\tilde{x}) \leftarrow c \diamond p(\tilde{y}), Dict)$:

in: $p(\tilde{x}) \leftarrow c \diamond p(\tilde{y})$: a binary rule
          $Dict$: a loop dictionary
out: $Dict'$: a loop dictionary

1:   $Dict' := Dict$
2:   **if** $\mathcal{D}_C \models \exists c$ **then**
3:       $\tau :=$ a DN set of positions for $p(\tilde{x}) \leftarrow c \diamond p(\tilde{y})$
4:       **if** $\langle p(\tilde{y}) | c \rangle$ is τ-more general than $\langle p(\tilde{x}) | c \rangle$ **then**
5:           $Dict' := Dict' \cup \{([p(\tilde{x}) \leftarrow c \diamond p(\tilde{y})], \tau)\}$
6:   **return** $Dict'$

Termination of $\texttt{unit\_loop}$ is straightforward, provided that at line 3 we use a terminating algorithm to compute τ. Partial correctness is deduced from the following theorem.

Theorem 5 (Partial Correctness of $\texttt{unit\_loop}$). *If* $p(\tilde{x}) \leftarrow c \diamond p(\tilde{y})$ *is a binary rule and Dict a loop dictionary, then* $\texttt{unit\_loop}(p(\tilde{x}) \leftarrow c \diamond p(\tilde{y}), Dict)$ *is a loop dictionary, every element* $(BinSeq, \tau)$ *of which is such that* $(BinSeq, \tau) \in Dict$ *or* $BinSeq = [p(\tilde{x}) \leftarrow c \diamond p(\tilde{y})]$.

Now suppose we hold a loop dictionary *Dict* and a rule $p(\tilde{x}) \leftarrow c \diamond q(\tilde{y})$. Then we may get some more looping pairs: it suffices to take the elements $([p_1(\tilde{x}_1) \leftarrow c_1 \diamond q_1(\tilde{y}_1) | BinSeq'], \tau')$ of *Dict* such that $\langle q(\tilde{y}) | c \rangle$ is τ'-more general than $\langle p_1(\tilde{x}_1) | c_1 \rangle$ and to compute a set of positions τ that is DN for $[p(\tilde{x}) \leftarrow c \diamond q(\tilde{y}), p_1(\tilde{x}_1) \leftarrow c_1 \diamond q_1(\tilde{y}_1) | BinSeq']$. Then $([p(\tilde{x}) \leftarrow c \diamond q(\tilde{y}), p_1(\tilde{x}_1) \leftarrow c_1 \diamond q_1(\tilde{y}_1) | BinSeq'], \tau)$ is a looping pair. The following function works this way.

---

loops_from_dict($p(\tilde{x}) \leftarrow c \diamond q(\tilde{y})$, $Dict$):

   in: $p(\tilde{x}) \leftarrow c \diamond q(\tilde{y})$: a binary rule
          $Dict$: a loop dictionary
out: $Dict'$: a loop dictionary

  1: $Dict' := Dict$
  2: **for each** $\big([p_1(\tilde{x}_1) \leftarrow c_1 \diamond q_1(\tilde{y}_1)|BinSeq'], \tau'\big) \in Dict$ **do**
  3:    **if** $\langle q(\tilde{y}) \,|\, c \rangle$ is τ'-more general than $\langle p_1(\tilde{x}_1) \,|\, c_1 \rangle$ **then**
  4:      $BinSeq := [p(\tilde{x}) \leftarrow c \diamond q(\tilde{y}), p_1(\tilde{x}_1) \leftarrow c_1 \diamond q_1(\tilde{y}_1)|BinSeq']$
  5:      $\tau :=$ a DN set of positions for $BinSeq$
  6:      $Dict' := Dict' \cup \{(BinSeq, \tau)\}$
  7: **return** $Dict'$

Termination of loops_from_dict follows from finiteness of $Dict$ (because $Dict$ is a loop dictionary), provided that we use a terminating algorithm to compute τ at line 5. Partial correctness follows from the result below.

Theorem 6 (Partial Correctness of loops_from_dict). *Suppose that $p(\tilde{x}) \leftarrow c \diamond q(\tilde{y})$ is a binary rule and $Dict$ is a loop dictionary. Then, loops_from_dict($p(\tilde{x}) \leftarrow c \diamond q(\tilde{y})$, $Dict$) is a loop dictionary, every element $(BinSeq, \tau)$ of which is such that $(BinSeq, \tau) \in Dict$ or $BinSeq = [p(\tilde{x}) \leftarrow c \diamond q(\tilde{y})|BinSeq']$ for some $(BinSeq', \tau')$ in $Dict$.*

Finally, here is the top-level function for inferring loop dictionaries from a finite set of binary rules.

---

infer_loop_dict($BinProg$):

   in: $BinProg$: a finite set of binary rules
out: a loop dictionary

  1: $Dict := \varnothing$
  2: **for each** $p(\tilde{x}) \leftarrow c \diamond q(\tilde{y}) \in BinProg$ **do**
  3:    **if** $q = p$ **then**
  4:      $Dict := $ unit_loop($p(\tilde{x}) \leftarrow c \diamond q(\tilde{y})$, $Dict$)
  5:      $Dict := $ loops_from_dict($p(\tilde{x}) \leftarrow c \diamond q(\tilde{y})$, $Dict$)
  6: **return** $Dict$

Theorem 7 (Correctness of infer_loop_dict). *Let $BinProg$ be a finite set of binary rules. Then, infer_loop_dict($BinProg$) terminates and returns a loop dictionary, every element $(BinSeq, \tau)$ of which is such that $BinSeq \subseteq BinProg$.*

Proof. By Theorem 5 and Theorem 6. □

5.3   Inferring Looping Conditions

Finally, we present an algorithm which infers classes of left looping atomic queries from the text of a given program. The classes we consider are defined by a pair (S, τ) which finitely denotes the possibly infinite set $[S]^\tau$:

Definition 12. *Let S be an atomic query and τ be a set of positions. Then $[S]^\tau$ denotes the class of atomic queries defined as:*

$$[S]^\tau \overset{def}{=} \{S' : \text{ an atomic query} \mid S' \text{ is } \tau\text{-more general than } S\} \,.$$

Once each element of $[S]^\tau$ left loops w.r.t. a $CLP(\mathcal{C})$ program, we get a *looping condition* for that program:

Definition 13 (Looping Condition). *Let P be a $CLP(\mathcal{C})$ program. A looping condition for P is a pair (S, τ) such that each element of $[S]^\tau$ left loops w.r.t. P.*

Looping conditions can be easily infered from a loop dictionary. It suffices to consider the property of looping pairs stated by Proposition 3. The following function computes a finite set of looping conditions for any given $CLP(\mathcal{C})$ program.

---

infer_loop_cond(P, *max*):

   in: P: a $CLP(\mathcal{C})$ program

          max: a non-negative integer

  out: a finite set of looping conditions for P

   1: $L := \varnothing$

   2: $Dict := $ infer_loop_dict($T_P^\beta \uparrow max$)

   3: **for each** $([p(\tilde{x}) \leftarrow c \diamond q(\tilde{y}) \mid BinSeq], \tau) \in Dict$ **do**

   4:      $L := L \cup \{(\langle p(\tilde{x}) \mid c \rangle, \tau)\}$

   5: **return** L

A call to infer_loop_cond(P, *max*) terminates for any program P and any non-negative integer *max* because, as $T_P^\beta \uparrow max$ is finite, at line 2 the call to infer_loop_dict terminates and the loop at line 3 has a finite number of iterations (because, by correctness of infer_loop_dict, $Dict$ is finite.) From some preliminary experiments we made over 50 logic programs, we find that the maximum value for *max* is 4. Partial correctness of infer_loop_cond follows from the next theorem.

Theorem 8 (Partial Correctness of infer_loop_cond). *If P is a program and max a non-negative integer, then* infer_loop_cond(P, max) *is a finite set of looping conditions for P.*

Proof. By Proposition 3, Theorem 7 and the Observing Termination Theorem 1. ∎

We point out that correctness of infer_loop_cond is independent of whether the predicate symbols are analysed according to a topological sort of the strongly connected components of the call graph of P. However, inference of looping classes is much more efficient if predicate symbols are processed bottom-up. Precision issues could be dealt with by comparing non-termination analysis with termination analysis, as in [13].

Example 17. Consider the CLP($\mathcal{R}_{lin}$) program SUM:

$\text{sum}(X_1, X_2) \leftarrow X_1 > 0 \land Y_1 = X_1 \land Y_2 = 1 \land Z_1 = X_1 - 1 \land X_2 = Y_3 + Z_2 \diamond$
$\qquad \text{pow2}(Y_1, Y_2, Y_3), \text{sum}(Z_1, Z_2)$

$\text{pow2}(X_1, X_2, X_3) \leftarrow X_1 \leq 0 \land X_2 = X_3 \diamond \square$
$\text{pow2}(X_1, X_2, X_3) \leftarrow X_1 > 0 \land Y_1 = X_1 - 1 \land Y_2 = 2 * X_2 \land Y_3 = X_3 \diamond$
$\qquad \text{pow2}(Y_1, Y_2, Y_3)$

The set $T^{\beta}_{\text{SUM}} \uparrow 1$ includes:

$br_1 := \text{sum}(X_1, X_2) \leftarrow X_1 > 0 \land Y_1 = X_1 \land Y_2 = 1 \land Z_1 = X_1 - 1 \land$
$\qquad X_2 = Y_3 + Z_2 \diamond \text{pow2}(Y_1, Y_2, Y_3)$

$br_2 := \text{pow2}(X_1, X_2, X_3) \leftarrow X_1 > 0 \land Y_1 = X_1 - 1 \land Y_2 = 2 * X_2 \land Y_3 = X_3 \diamond$
$\qquad \text{pow2}(Y_1, Y_2, Y_3)$

A call to unit_loop($br_2, \varnothing$) returns $Dict_1 := \{([br_2], \tau_2)\}$ where $\tau_2 = \langle pow2 \mapsto \{2, 3\}\rangle$. A call to loops_from_dict($br_1, Dict_1$) returns $Dict_1 \cup \{([br_1, br_2], \tau_1)\}$ where $\tau_1 = \langle sum \mapsto \{2\}, pow2 \mapsto \{2, 3\}\rangle$. Hence, a call to infer_loop_cond(SUM, 1) returns the looping conditions $(\langle \text{sum}(X_1, X_2) \,|\, c_1\rangle, \tau_1)$ and $(\langle \text{pow2}(X_1, X_2, X_3) \,|\, c_2\rangle, \tau_2)$ where c_1 and c_2 are the constraints of br_1 and br_2 respectively.   □

6   Conclusion

We have proposed a self contained framework for non-termination analysis of constraint logic programs. As usual [9], we were able to give simpler definitions and proofs than in the logic programming setting. Also, starting from an operational definition of *derivation neutrality*, we have given a new *equivalent* logical definition. Then, by reexamining the syntactic criterion of derivation neutrality that we proposed in [13], we have proved that this syntactic criterion can be considered as a correct and complete implementation of derivation neutrality.

Acknowledgements

We thank Mike Codish for some useful comments on a previous version of this paper.

References

1. K. L. Clark. Negation as failure. In H. Gallaire and J. Minker, editors, *Logic and Databases*, pages 293–322. Plenum Press, New York, 1978.
2. M. Codish and C. Taboch. A semantic basis for the termination analysis of logic programs. *Journal of Logic Programming*, 41(1):103–123, 1999.
3. D. De Schreye, M. Bruynooghe, and K. Verschaetse. On the existence of non-terminating queries for a restricted class of Prolog-clauses. *Artificial Intelligence*, 41:237–248, 1989.

4. D. De Schreye and S. Decorte. Termination of logic programs : the never-ending story. *Journal of Logic Programming*, 19-20:199–260, 1994.

5. D. De Schreye, K. Verschaetse, and M. Bruynooghe. A practical technique for detecting non-terminating queries for a restricted class of Horn clauses, using directed, weighted graphs. In *Proc. of ICLP'90*, pages 649–663. The MIT Press, 1990.

6. M. Gabbrielli and R. Giacobazzi. Goal independency and call patterns in the analysis of logic programs. In *Proceedings of the ACM Symposium on applied computing*, pages 394–399. ACM Press, 1994.

7. S. Genaim and M. Codish. Inferring termination condition for logic programs using backwards analysis. In *Proceedings of Logic for Programming, Artificial intelligence and Reasoning*, Lecture Notes in Computer Science. Springer-Verlag, Berlin, 2001.

8. J. Jaffar and J. L. Lassez. Constraint logic programming. In *Proc. of the ACM Symposium on Principles of Programming Languages*, pages 111–119. ACM Press, 1987.

9. J. Jaffar, M. J. Maher, K. Marriott, and P. J. Stuckey. The semantics of constraint logic programs. *Journal of Logic Programming*, 37(1-3):1–46, 1998.

10. J. W. Lloyd. *Foundations of Logic Programming*. Springer-Verlag, 1987.

11. F. Mesnard. Inferring left-terminating classes of queries for constraint logic programs by means of approximations. In M. J. Maher, editor, *Proc. of the 1996 Joint Intl. Conf. and Symp. on Logic Programming*, pages 7–21. MIT Press, 1996.

12. F. Mesnard and U. Neumerkel. Applying static analysis techniques for inferring termination conditions of logic programs. In P. Cousot, editor, *Static Analysis Symposium*, volume 2126 of *Lecture Notes in Computer Science*, pages 93–110. Springer-Verlag, Berlin, 2001.

13. F. Mesnard, E. Payet, and U. Neumerkel. Detecting optimal termination conditions of logic programs. In M. Hermenegildo and G. Puebla, editors, *Proc. of the 9th International Symposium on Static Analysis*, volume 2477 of *Lecture Notes in Computer Science*, pages 509–525. Springer-Verlag, Berlin, 2002.

14. F. Mesnard and S. Ruggieri. On proving left termination of constraint logic programs. *ACM Transactions on Computational Logic*, pages 207–259, 2003.

15. P. Refalo and P. Van Hentenryck. CLP ($\mathcal{R}_{lin}$) revised. In M. Maher, editor, *Proc. of the Joint International Conf. and Symposium on Logic Programming*, pages 22–36. The MIT Press, 1996.

16. J. Shoenfield. *Mathematical Logic*. Addison Wesley, Reading, 1967.

Author Index